Classroom Companion: Business

Classroom Companion: Business

The Classroom Companion series in Business features foundational and introductory books aimed at students to learn the core concepts, fundamental methods, theories and tools of the subject. The books offer a firm foundation for students preparing to move towards advanced learning. Each book follows a clear didactic structure and presents easy adoption opportunities for lecturers.

More information about this series at http://www.springer.com/series/16374

Sergey K. Aityan

Business Research Methodology

Research Process and Methods

Springer

Sergey K. Aityan
Lincoln University - California
Oakland, CA, USA

ISSN 2662-2866 ISSN 2662-2874 (electronic)
Classroom Companion: Business
ISBN 978-3-030-76856-0 ISBN 978-3-030-76857-7 (eBook)
https://doi.org/10.1007/978-3-030-76857-7

This Springer imprint is published by the registered company Springer Nature Switzerland AG
The registered company address is: Gewerbestrasse 11, 6330 Cham, Switzerland

Preface

Business research is an important part of any business. This is a core subject in the curriculum of many business and economic schools. I have been teaching the graduate course in business research methodology for many years at Lincoln University in California, which celebrated its centenary in 2019. The challenging goal of this course is to teach students sufficient theoretical knowledge and practical skills to conduct at least a simple research, from the initiation through completion and delivery of results, after taking the course. The course teaches students the entire research project process, which is divided into three major phases: preparation for research, conducting the research, and delivery of the results. Also, the course introduces the students to the major research methods used in business research, such as probabilities, statistical analysis, surveys, and comparative analysis.

The objectives of the book are:

- To present equally the research process and the major research methods used in business research
- To develop solid knowledge and practical skills sufficient for conducting a research project from its initiation, through completion, and delivery.
- To explain major methods in a way business students would understand, without redirection to other sources, and practically apply them
- To help the learning process by providing multiple examples as well as questions and problems for self-evaluation
- To fit the course in the one-semester time frame

The structure and logic of this book is based on the course, which I have taught for many years. The book is structured in four parts, logically bringing the reader from the beginning of the research through the entire research process including delivery of results. The parts are:

- Part 1: The Journey to the Land of Unknown
- Part 2: Preparation for Research
- Part 3: Research Methods
- Part 4: Conducting Research
- Part 5: Delivering the Results

Part 1 is dedicated to the general information about research, research types, approaches, and challenges, including the philosophical frameworks and logical foundations.

Parts 2, 4, and 5 are dedicated to the research process, which is divided into three phases: preparation for research, conducting the research, and delivery of the research results. All three phases of research are very important and are described in the appropriated chapters.

Part 3 is dedicated to the most popular research methods used in business research. Those methods are described and explained with multiple examples for better understanding and earning. No single book is sufficient to describe and discuss all methods used in business research, so this book is limited to the most frequently used methods.

I hope this book will be helpful for those who want to know what business research is and how to come up with sound and credible results. Have a good journey to the exciting land of research, to the land of unknown.

I would like to express great appreciation to my colleagues and friends who helped me in the preparation of this book. Special thanks to my lovely wife Valentina, who fully supported me in the challenge of writing this book.

Sergey K. Aityan, PhD, DSc
Oakland, CA, USA

Contents

I The Journey to the Land of Unknown

1 **The Nature of Research** 3
1.1 **What Is Research?** 5
1.1.1 Research and the World 5
1.1.2 Defining Research 6
1.1.3 Research Starts with Questions and Ends with Answers 7
1.2 **Continuity of Knowledge and Research** 9
1.3 **Fundamental and Applied Research** 10
1.3.1 Definition of Fundamental and Applied Research 10
1.3.2 Examples of Fundamental and Applied Research 10
1.3.3 Link Between Fundamental and Applied Research 11
1.4 **Major Research Approaches** 12
1.4.1 Exploratory Research 13
1.4.2 Descriptive Research 14
1.4.3 Theoretical Research 15
1.4.4 Experimental Research 16
1.4.5 Simulation Research 16
1.4.6 Analytical Research 17
1.4.7 Creative Research 18
1.4.8 Relationship Between Different Research Approaches 18
1.5 **Research Versus Reporting** 18
1.6 **Credible Research** 19
1.7 **Business Research** 21
1.7.1 Specifics of Business Research 21
1.7.2 Business Research Methods 23

2 **Scientific Method** 25
2.1 **Methodology** 27
2.2 **The Scientific Method** 27
2.3 **The Framework for the Scientific Method** 28
2.3.1 The Epistemological Cornerstone of the Scientific Method 28
2.3.2 The Methodological Cornerstone of the Scientific Method 29
2.3.3 The Empirical Cornerstone of the Scientific Method 31
2.3.4 The Cornerstones of the Scientific Method 32
2.4 **Are There Alternatives to the Scientific Method?** 32
2.5 **Hypotheses** 33
2.5.1 Logical Negation 35
2.5.2 Alternative Hypotheses 36
2.6 **Hypothesis Evaluation** 39
2.7 **Hypothesis Verification** 39
2.7.1 Hypothesis Truth Status 39

2.7.2 Hypothesis Verification Process 39
2.7.3 Logical Hypotheses 40
2.7.4 Statistical Hypotheses 42
2.7.5 Deterministic Hypothesis Verification 42
2.7.6 Does Every Research Need a Hypothesis? 42
2.8 **Occam's Razor** 43
2.9 **Reasoning and Logic** 44
2.9.1 Modus Ponens 44
2.9.2 Inductive and Deductive Logic 46
2.9.3 Deductive Logic 46
2.9.4 Inductive Logic 47

3 **The Research Process** 51
3.1 **Logical Phases of Research** 53
3.2 **Phase I: Preparation for Research** 53
3.2.1 Select a Research Field Related to Your Interest and Expertise 54
3.2.2 Formulate the Research Problem 55
3.2.3 Formulate the Research Purpose 57
3.2.4 Conduct a Review of the Literature 57
3.2.5 Define the Major Terms Used in the Research 58
3.2.6 Formulate Key Hypotheses and Models if Needed 59
3.2.7 Develop the Research Design 59
3.2.8 Define the Research Objectives and the Expected Results 61
3.2.9 Write and Submit the Research Proposal for Approval 61
3.2.10 Discussion, Negotiation, and Approval of the Research Proposal 62
3.3 **Phase II: Conducting Research** 62
3.3.1 Finalize the Models and Hypotheses for the Research if Needed 62
3.3.2 Finalize the Data Collection Plan and Collect Data 63
3.3.3 Organize and Process the Data, Using the Models if Appropriate 63
3.3.4 Analyze and Interpret the Data and Verify the Hypotheses If Any 63
3.3.5 Summarize the Research Findings and Interpret the Results 64
3.3.6 Derive Conclusions 64
3.3.7 Make Recommendations and Predictions if Appropriate 65
3.4 **Phase III: Delivery of the Results** 65
3.4.1 Write the Research Report 65
3.4.2 Develop and Make Presentations 66
3.4.3 Defending the Project 66
3.5 **Summary of the Research Process** 67
3.6 **Major Reasons for Possible Research Failures** 68
3.6.1 Ambiguous or Unclear Problem Statement 68
3.6.2 Unclear Scope and Limitations 68
3.6.3 Unclearly Formulated Hypotheses 68
3.6.4 Controversial and Conflicting Terms Used in the Research 68
3.6.5 Wrong Methods and Procedures Used in the Research 69
3.6.6 Inaccurate or Unreliable Data 69
3.6.7 Unclear or Inconsistent Conclusions 69

II Preparation for Research

4	**Formulating a Research Problem**	73
4.1	**Research Starts with a Question**	75
4.2	**Research Purpose**	75
4.3	**First Ask a Question to Start Formulating a Research Problem**	75
4.4	**Correctly Ask Research Questions**	77
4.4.1	Try to Avoid Questions That Allow for Just "Yes" or "No" Answer	77
4.4.2	Phrase Questions to Deal with Cause-and-Effect Relationship	77
4.4.3	Avoid Phrasing Value Judgment Types of Questions	78
4.5	**Factoring the Research Problem**	79
4.5.1	Subproblems	79
4.5.2	Scope and Limitations	80
4.6	**Evaluating the Research Problem**	81
4.6.1	Scholarly Acceptability	81
4.6.2	Depth and Complexity	82
4.6.3	Researchability	82
4.6.4	Researcher Accountability	83
4.7	**Difficulties in Selecting a Research Problem**	83
4.7.1	Difficulties	83
4.7.2	Major Advices	83
5	**Review of Literature**	85
5.1	**Continuity of Knowledge**	86
5.2	**Value of Literature Review**	86
5.3	**Sources of Information**	87
5.3.1	Primary and Secondary Sources	87
5.3.2	Evaluating the Quality of Secondary Sources	87
5.4	**How to Review Literature**	88
5.4.1	The Sense of Review of Literature	88
5.4.2	How to Write a Review of Literature	88
5.5	**Basic Terminology**	89
5.5.1	Bibliography vs. Index	89
5.5.2	Outline vs. Table of Contents vs. Presentation Time Table	90
5.5.3	Journal vs. Magazine	91
5.6	**List of Bibliography**	91
5.7	**References, Citations, and Quotations**	92
5.7.1	Citations	92
5.7.2	Quotations	94
5.8	**Footnotes and Endnotes**	94
5.8.1	Footnotes	94
5.8.2	Endnotes	95
6	**Research Design**	97
6.1	**A Good Research Deserves a Good Design**	99

6.2 **Major Factors in Research Design** 100
6.3 **Determining the Research Approach** 100
6.4 **Construct the Models** 101
6.5 **Formulate the Hypotheses if Needed** 102
6.6 **Decide on Data Sources and Data Collection Methods** 102
6.7 **Experiment Planning** 103
6.8 **Selecting Research Methods and Procedures** 104
6.9 **Skills, Expertise, and Equipment Needed for Research** 104
6.10 **Size of the Research Team** 104
6.11 **Budget and Timelines** 105
6.12 **Pilot Study** 105
6.13 **Research Plan Implementation** 105
6.13.1 The Ideal Case 105
6.13.2 Quite Possible Case 106
6.13.3 Most Likely Case 106
6.14 **The Reasons of Biggest Errors in Research** 106

7 **Research Proposal** 109
7.1 **What Is the Research Proposal?** 111
7.2 **Suggested Content of the Research Proposal** 111
7.3 **Tentative Title of the Research** 112
7.4 **Purpose of the Proposal** 112
7.5 **Summary** 112
7.6 **Writing Introduction** 113
7.7 **Purpose of the Research** 114
7.8 **Definition of Terms** 114
7.9 **Review of Literature** 115
7.10 **Problem Statement** 115
7.11 **Research Objectives** 115
7.12 **Research Design** 116
7.12.1 Hypotheses if Applicable 116
7.12.2 Data Sources and Data Collection Plan 116
7.12.3 Data Collection Methods Including Experiment Planning (if Applicable) 116
7.12.4 Data Processing and Data Analysis Techniques, Methods, and Procedures 117
7.12.5 Required Knowledge, Skill Set, and Expertise 117
7.12.6 Researcher or Research Staff Qualifications and the Team Size 117
7.12.7 Project Timelines and Project Budget (if Applicable) 118
7.13 **Overview of Expected Outcome and the Project Acceptance Criteria** 118
7.14 **Bibliography** 118
7.15 **Appendices** 119
7.16 **Formatting the Research Proposal** 119
7.17 **Submission and Approval** 121

III Research Methods

8 **Foundations of Probability** 125
8.1 **Uncertainty and Risk** 127
8.2 **Fundamentals of Probability** 127
8.2.1 The Universal Sample Space 129
8.2.2 Probability 129
8.3 **Major Properties of Probability** 132
8.3.1 Probability Is a Number Between Zero and One 132
8.3.2 Operations on the Universal Sample Space 133
8.3.3 The Sum of All Probabilities Equals One 134
8.4 **Operations with Probabilities** 135
8.4.1 Probability of a Negation 135
8.4.2 Operation "AND" of Independent Events 136
8.4.3 Operation "OR" of Independent Events 138
8.5 **Interpretations of Probability** 140
8.5.1 Classical Interpretation 140
8.5.2 Frequential Interpretation 140
8.5.3 Subjective Interpretation 140
8.6 **Calculating Probabilities Using Classical Interpretation** 141
8.6.1 Calculating Probability From Symmetry 141
8.6.2 Calculating Probabilities From Content Percentage 143
8.7 **Estimating Probabilities Using Frequential Interpretation** 143
8.7.1 Estimating Probabilities From Sampling Experiments 143
8.7.2 Estimating Probabilities From Historical Data 144
8.8 **Subjective Determination of Probabilities** 144
8.8.1 New Product Marketing 144
8.8.2 Business Strategy 144
8.9 **Problems for Practicing** 145
8.9.1 Flipping a Coin 145
8.9.2 Rolling the Dice 146
8.9.3 Electronic Devices 147
8.10 **What More to Lean About Probabilities** 150

9 **Distribution, Expectation, and Risk** 153
9.1 **Random Variables** 154
9.2 **Probability Distribution** 155
9.2.1 Notation Convention for Random Variables 155
9.2.2 Probability Distribution for a Discrete Random Variable 155
9.2.3 Probability Distribution for a Continuous Random Variable 156
9.3 **Expectation and Risk** 159
9.3.1 What to Expect From a Random Draw 159
9.3.2 Expected Value 160
9.3.3 Standard Deviation and Risk 162
9.3.4 Coefficient of Variation 166

9.3.5 Risk-Reward Analysis ... 166
9.4 **Case 1: Beach Café** ... 167
9.5 **Case 2: Investment Risk and Decision-Making** ... 168
9.6 **A Decision Tree** ... 169

10 **Bayesian Probability** ... 175
10.1 **Conditional Probability** ... 176
10.2 **Bayes' Theorem** ... 177
10.2.1 Conditional, Marginal, and Joint Probabilities ... 177
10.2.2 Analysis of the Inverse Conditional Probabilities ... 180
10.3 **Bayesian Probability and Information** ... 181
10.4 **The Monty Hall Problem** ... 181
10.4.1 Bayesian Solution to the Monty Hall Problem ... 183
10.4.2 Decision Tree Solution to the Monty Hall Problem ... 184
10.5 **Analysis of Posterior Probabilities** ... 185
10.6 **General Form of Bayes' Theorem** ... 187
10.7 **Further Probability Revisions** ... 188

11 **Major Distributions** ... 191
11.1 **Probability Density Versus Probability Distribution** ... 193
11.2 **Normal Distribution** ... 196
11.3 **Cumulative Normal Probability** ... 198
11.4 **The Normal Distribution and the Real World** ... 199
11.5 **The Standard Normal Distribution** ... 200
11.6 **Calculating Standard Normal Cumulative Probabilities Using Tables** ... 201
11.6.1 Cumulative Standard Normal Probabilities Tables ... 202
11.6.2 Centered Cumulative Standard Normal Probabilities Table ... 202
11.7 **Transformation to the Standard Normal Distribution** ... 204
11.8 **The Importance and Utility of the Standard Normal Distribution** ... 204
11.9 **Calculating Normal Distribution with Computers** ... 205
11.9.1 NORMDIST: Normal Distribution Density and Cumulative Probability ... 206
11.9.2 NORM.INV: Inverse Calculation of Cumulative Normal Probabilities ... 207
11.9.3 NORM.S.DIST: Cumulative Standard Normal Probabilities ... 208
11.9.4 NORMSINV: Inverse Cumulative Standard Normal Probabilities ... 209
11.9.5 STANDARDIZE: Transformation From Normal Distribution to Standard Normal Distribution ... 210
11.10 **Binomial Distribution** ... 211
11.11 **Calculating Binomial Distribution with Computers** ... 214
11.12 **Relationship Between Normal and Binomial Distributions** ... 214

12 **Introduction to Statistics** ... 217
12.1 **The Sense of Statistics** ... 218
12.2 **Sample Versus Population** ... 218
12.3 **Types of Statistics** ... 221
12.4 **Statistical Nature of Samples** ... 222

12.5 **Major Parameters on Population** 223
12.6 **Population Parameters Versus Sample Statistic** 226
12.7 **Sample Statistic: Measuring Car Mileage** 228
12.7.1 The Range, Median, Mode, Mean Variance, and Standard Deviation 228
12.7.2 Covariance and Coefficient of Correlation 229
12.8 **Calculations with the Microsoft Excel and OpenOffice Calc** 231

13 **Confidence Intervals** 233
13.1 **Simple Random Sampling** 236
13.1.1 A Simple Random Sample 236
13.1.2 The Mean on a Sample Versus the Mean on a Population 237
13.2 **A Sample as an Estimator for the Population** 239
13.2.1 Central Limit Theorem 240
13.3 **Confidence Level, Margin of Error, and Confidence Interval** 243
13.3.1 Meaning of Confidence Level 245
13.3.2 Margin of Error and Confidence Interval 246
13.4 *Critical Value* **for Confidence Interval** 247
13.5 **Student's *t*-Distribution** 252
13.6 ***T*-Distribution Versus *Z*-Distribution for Large Samples** 254
13.7 **Confidence Intervals for Two Unpaired Samples** 257
13.7.1 The Confidence Interval for Two Unpaired Large Samples 258
13.7.2 The Confidence Interval When at Least One Sample Is Small 259
13.7.3 Both Samples Have the Same Standard Deviation 260
13.7.4 Both Samples of the Same Size 260
13.8 **Confidence Interval for Paired Samples** 261
13.8.1 Confidence Interval for a Large Paired Sample 262
13.8.2 Confidence Interval for a Small Paired Sample 262
13.9 **Confidence Interval for Binomial Distribution** 264
13.9.1 Large Sample 265
13.9.2 Small Sample 266
13.10 **Confidence Interval for Probability or Percentage Difference from Two Independent Samples** 267
13.10.1 Large Samples 268
13.10.2 Small Samples 268
13.11 **Most Popular Confidence Levels and Respective *Z*-Scores** 269
13.11.1 1-Sigma, 2-Sigma, and 3-Sigma Rule for Confidence Intervals 269
13.12 **Interpretation of Confidence Intervals** 270
13.13 **One-Sided and Two-Sided Tests** 271
13.14 **Summary of Confidence Intervals** 272
13.14.1 Confidence Interval for the Mean on One Sample 272
13.14.2 Confidence Interval for the Difference of Means of Two Unpaired Samples 273
13.14.3 Confidence Interval for the Difference of Means on Two Paired Samples 273
13.14.4 Confidence Interval for the Binomial Distribution 274
13.14.5 Confidence Interval for Probability or Percentage Difference on Two Samples 275

14 **Statistical Hypothesis Testing** 279
14.1 **The Philosophy of Statistical Hypothesis Testing** 282
14.1.1 Hypothesis Formulation and Acceptance/Rejection Framework 284
14.1.2 Hypothesis Testing Method 284
14.2 **The Null and Alternative Hypotheses** 288
14.2.1 Examples: The Null and Alternative Hypotheses 288
14.3 **Significance Level and *p*-Value** 288
14.3.1 Significance Level 288
14.3.2 *p*-Value 289
14.4 **The Null Hypothesis Acceptance/Rejection Rule** 290
14.4.1 Examples: Acceptance or Rejection of the Null Hypothesis 290
14.5 **Two-Tailed and One-Tailed Tests** 292
14.6 **Unpaired and Paired Tests** 293
14.6.1 The Null Hypothesis Is the Focus of the Test 293
14.7 **Critical Value** 294
14.7.1 Calculating Critical Values Using Distribution Tables 295
14.7.2 Calculating Critical Values Using Software Algorithms 295
14.8 **Conducting the *z*-Test** 295
14.8.1 Calculating *p*-Values Using the Standard Normal Distribution Table 296
14.8.2 Calculating *p*-Values Using Software Algorithms 297
14.9 **The Student's *t*-Test** 300
14.9.1 *t*-Distribution and *t*-Test 300
14.9.2 Unpaired and Paired Two-Sample *t*-Tests 301
14.10 ***t*-Test Technique and Degrees of Freedom** 301
14.10.1 One-Sample *t*-Test 302
14.10.2 Independent (Unpaired) Two-Sample *t*-Test 302
14.10.3 Dependent Two-Sample *t*-Test (Paired) 304
14.10.4 Calculating *p*-Value for the Student's *t*-Test 304
14.11 **The Statistical Hypothesis Testing Process** 306
14.11.1 First Comes Research Question 307
14.11.2 Formulate the Null Hypothesis (H_0) and the Alternative Hypothesis (H_1) 308
14.11.3 Choose the Significance Level 309
14.11.4 Decide About Two-Tailed or One-Tailed Test 309
14.11.5 Select a Random Sample and Collect Data 310
14.11.6 Decide About the Test Type 310
14.11.7 Conduct the Test and Calculate *p*-Value for H_0 311
14.11.8 Reject or Accept H_0 by Comparing the *p*-Value Against the Significance Level 311
14.12 **Type I and Type II Errors** 312
14.12.1 False Positive and False Negative Judgments 312
14.12.2 Type I Error 313
14.12.3 Type II Error 314
14.12.4 Relationship Between the Type I and Type II Errors 315
14.13 **Statistical Power vs. Significance of a Hypothesis Test** 317
14.13.1 Significance vs. Power 317
14.13.2 Calculating the Statistical Power 318
14.13.3 The Reasons to Analyze the Test Power 318

15	**Sampling Experiments**	321
15.1	**Analysis of Samples**	323
15.1.1	Defining the Population of Concern	323
15.1.2	Choosing the Appropriate Significance (or Confidence) Level	325
15.1.3	Specifying a Sampling Method to Form a Sample or Samples	326
15.1.4	Determining the Minimum Sample Size to Meet the Objectives	326
15.1.5	Forming a Sample or Samples, Collecting Data, and Calculating Relevant Statistic	326
15.1.6	Making Conclusions About the Population	327
15.2	**Sampling Methods**	327
15.2.1	Random Sampling	327
15.2.2	Systematic Sampling	328
15.2.3	Stratified Sampling	329
15.2.4	Cluster Sampling	330
15.2.5	Convenience Sampling	331
15.3	**Standard Error, Margin of Error, and Confidence Level**	332
15.4	**Margin of Error and Sample Size**	333
15.5	**Minimum Required Sample Size**	334
15.5.1	Standard Deviation on the Population Is Known	334
15.5.2	Standard Deviation on the Population Is Unknown	334
15.5.3	One Sample for Binomial Distribution	337
15.5.4	Two Unpaired Samples	339
15.5.5	Two Paired Samples	339
15.6	**Summary of the Sampling Experiment Process**	340
16	**Survey Method**	343
16.1	**The Purpose of a Survey**	345
16.2	**Statistical Nature of Surveys**	345
16.3	**Phases of the Survey Method**	346
16.3.1	Preparation for Survey	346
16.3.2	Conducting the Survey and Collecting Data	346
16.3.3	Data Processing	347
16.3.4	Deriving Conclusions and Making Recommendations	347
16.4	**Closed-Ended and Open-Ended Questions**	347
16.4.1	Closed-Ended Questions	347
16.4.2	Open-Ended Questions	350
16.5	**Constructing a Questionnaire**	350
16.5.1	A Survey Questionnaire as a Story With Variables for Data Acquisition	350
16.5.2	General Structure of a Questionnaire	351
16.5.3	The Form, Size, and Format	351
16.5.4	Anonymity and Confidentiality	353
16.6	**Media for Survey**	353
16.6.1	Verbal Surveys	353
16.6.2	Printed Paper Surveys	353
16.6.3	Online Surveys	354
16.7	**Testing the Survey Before Running It**	354
16.7.1	General	354

16.7.2 Form 355
16.7.3 Cover and Follow-Up Letters 355
16.8 **Selecting a Sample: Whom to Ask?** 356
16.9 **The Sample Size: How Many People to Ask?** 356

17 **Linear Regression** 359
17.1 **The Purpose of Regression Analysis** 360
17.2 **The Principles of Linear Regression** 360
17.3 **Definition of the Best-Fit Line** 361
17.4 **Finding the Best-Fit Line** 363
17.5 **Interpretation of the Regression Line** 366
17.5.1 Variance and Correlation Analysis 366
17.6 **Coefficient of Determination** 367
17.7 **Technical Forecasting** 370
17.8 **Finding a Relationship Between Variables** 373
17.9 **Finding a Trend** 377
17.10 **Calculating a Trend Line Using MS Excel or OO Calc Functions** 385
17.11 **Confidence Interval for Regression Parameters** 386
17.12 **Multiple Regression** 392

18 **Comparative Analysis** 395
18.1 **Purpose and Specifics of Comparative Analysis** 396
18.2 **The Process of a Comparative Analysis** 398
18.3 **Data Organization and Information Structure for Comparative Analysis** 399
18.4 **Qualitative Comparative Analysis and Harvey Balls** 401
18.5 **Models for Industry and Business Analysis** 403
18.5.1 SWOT Model 403
18.5.2 PEST Model 405
18.5.3 Porter's Five Forces Model 408

IV **Conducting Research**

19 **Theories, Experiments, Data Collection, and Analysis** 415
19.1 **Developing Theories** 417
19.2 **Business Experiment** 418
19.3 **Computer Simulation** 418
19.4 **Data Collection** 419
19.5 **Cyber Intelligence** 419
19.6 **Measurements** 420
19.6.1 Sense of Data 420
19.6.2 Accuracy of Measurements 420
19.6.3 Number Rounding Rules 421
19.6.4 Significant Figures and Decimal Places 422
19.6.5 Scientific Notation for Numbers 424

19.6.6 Operations with Numbers of Specific Accuracy 425
19.7 **Accuracy and Rounded Numbers** 427
19.8 **Units of Measurement** 429
19.8.1 Time 429
19.8.2 Metric System 430
19.8.3 English System 434
19.8.4 Conversion Between the Metric and English Systems 436
19.9 **Qualitative Data Collection and Analysis** 438

20 **Deriving Conclusions** 441
20.1 **The Role of Conclusions in Research** 442
20.2 **Research Result Evaluation** 442
20.2.1 Research Problem and Subproblem Assessment 442
20.2.2 Research Design Assessment 443
20.2.3 Data Quality Assessment 443
20.3 **Research Result Interpretation** 444
20.4 **First Answer Subquestions and Then the Main Question** 445
20.5 **Cause and Effect Rather Than Value Judgment** 446
20.6 **Make Recommendations and Predictions if Applicable** 446
20.7 **New Questions Arise From Research Conclusions** 447

21 **Ethical and Legal Issues of Research** 449
21.1 **Difference Between Law and Ethics** 450
21.2 **Ethical Aspects of Research** 450
21.3 **Ethics in Business Research** 451
21.4 **Data Collection Ethics** 451
21.5 **Ethics of Research Topic** 451
21.6 **Information Privacy** 453
21.7 **Plagiarism** 453
21.7.1 Can Words and Ideas Really Be Stolen? 454
21.7.2 Forms of Plagiarism 454
21.7.3 Preventing Plagiarism 455
21.8 **Legal Aspect of Research** 456
21.9 **A Research Ethics Board** 456

V **Delivering the Results**

22 **Writing Research Report** 461
22.1 **Delivery of Research Results** 463
22.2 **Developing Report Outline** 463
22.3 **Typographical Gradations** 464
22.4 **Types of Outline Numbering Systems** 465
22.5 **Suggested Generic Structure of the Research Report** 467
22.6 **The Report Title Page** 468

22.7 **Providing Chapter Transition** 468
22.8 **Formatting the Research Report** 469
22.9 **Writing the Introduction Part** 471
22.9.1 The Introduction Part of the Report 471
22.9.2 The Purpose of the Research 471
22.9.3 Definition of Terms 471
22.10 **Review of Literature** 472
22.11 **Problem Statement** 472
22.12 **Research Objectives** 473
22.13 **Research Methods, Tools, Techniques, and Procedures** 473
22.14 **Data Collection and Analysis** 473
22.14.1 Data Collection 473
22.14.2 Data Analysis 474
22.14.3 The Interpretation Process 474
22.15 **Research Findings and Analysis** 476
22.16 **Conclusions, Recommendations, and Predictions** 476
22.17 **Bibliography and Citation** 477
22.18 **Appendices** 477
22.19 **Structuring the Summary Section** 478
22.20 **Acknowledgment** 478

23 **Making Presentations** 481
23.1 **Specifics of Presentations** 482
23.2 **Developing Presentation Outline and Timeline** 483
23.3 **Developing Presentation Slides** 484
23.4 **Slide Design and Animation** 485
23.5 **Get Prepared for the Presentation and Questions** 486
23.6 **Making Presentations** 487
23.7 **Answering Questions** 490

Supplementary Information
Appendix A: The Standard Normal Distribution Tables 494
Appendix B: Student's t-Distribution Tables 501
Appendix C: Business Research Case Studies 504

The Journey to the Land of Unknown

Contents

Chapter 1 The Nature of Research – 3

Chapter 2 Scientific Method – 25

Chapter 3 The Research Process – 51

The Nature of Research

Contents

1.1 What Is Research? – 5
1.1.1 Research and the World – 5
1.1.2 Defining Research – 6
1.1.3 Research Starts with Questions and Ends with Answers – 7

1.2 Continuity of Knowledge and Research – 9

1.3 Fundamental and Applied Research – 10
1.3.1 Definition of Fundamental and Applied Research – 10
1.3.2 Examples of Fundamental and Applied Research – 10
1.3.3 Link Between Fundamental and Applied Research – 11

1.4 Major Research Approaches – 12
1.4.1 Exploratory Research – 13
1.4.2 Descriptive Research – 14
1.4.3 Theoretical Research – 15
1.4.4 Experimental Research – 16
1.4.5 Simulation Research – 16
1.4.6 Analytical Research – 17
1.4.7 Creative Research – 18
1.4.8 Relationship Between Different Research Approaches – 18

1.5 Research Versus Reporting – 18

1.6 Credible Research – 19

S. K. Aityan, *Business Research Methodology*, Classroom Companion: Business,
https://doi.org/10.1007/978-3-030-76857-7_1

1.7 Business Research – 21
1.7.1 Specifics of Business Research – 21
1.7.2 Business Research Methods – 23

1.1 What Is Research?

1.1.1 Research and the World

Humans have been acquiring and accumulating knowledge as long as mankind has existed. We want to understand phenomena, events, and processes in the world where we live. Some of us do it just for curiosity but some for the purpose of making our lives better. What makes day turn into night and then day come back? Why does lightning strike? Why is my business not as profitable as the business of my competitor? People ask such questions all the time. Finding the answers to them requires research.

We have made extraordinary progress in understanding the world. For example, we figured out that the Earth is a spherical planet (actually, an oblate spheroid) revolving around the Sun, rather than a flat land resting on three whales or three elephants, as once people believed.

Many modern scientific disciplines, even abstract ones like mathematics, trace their origin to practical needs. The study of numbers began from the need to count objects, and geometry started from the need to measure land, dwellings, and other objects.

Albert Schweitzer (Source: Bundesarchiv, Bild 145 Bild-0014770/CC-BY-SA)
1875–1965

Knowledge about our world has been acquired step-by-step by accumulating and building up on the previous knowledge and previous experience. Some ancient civilizations possessed extraordinary knowledge that was more advanced than the research tools they had at their disposal. For instance, ancient Mayans, as early as the sixth century BC, had a very precise calendar and knew more about the planets and stars than some later civilizations did. The Mayans had no telescopes, and the source of their knowledge is not yet completely understood.

Day after day, people learn more and more about the world. However, our knowledge is limited. Every new piece of knowledge reveals new horizons of things we don't yet know. This brings up a legitimate question; how much can humans learn about the world? An old saying gives an answer to this question: "The more we learn, the better we realize how little we know." Albert Schweitzer, German-French theologian, musician, philosopher, and physician, made a similar point: "As we acquire more knowledge, things do not become more comprehensible, but more mysterious."

1.1.2 Defining Research

Research can be defined as intellectual activity in the investigation of matter, life, society, and even abstract entities in all their aspects. The term *matter* refers to the substance of which our universe and all bodies in it are made, including traditional material objects, life, society, and even abstract entities. *Life* comprises living creatures, including humans and their functions, psychology, and health. *Society* includes human relationships, economics, business, sociology, and politics. *Physical science* is the study of the world excluding life. The four main branches of physical science are astronomy, physics, chemistry, and the Earth sciences, which include meteorology and geology. By *abstract sciences*, we mean mathematics, information, and all derivatives from them.

Research is a systematic inquiry to discover new knowledge, to find new truths, and to go beyond the status quo. Research should be an orderly, exhaustive investigation to find new principles, knowledge, or conclusions or to revise accepted ones. Procedurally, it must be a diligent, objective examination to find new truths and revise accepted principles or conclusions.

Research includes formulation of a problem, collection and processing of data, interpretation and analysis of the results, deriving conclusions, and making predictions and recommendations. Collecting facts or data is just one step in research. Research must turn the facts and data into knowledge; this includes finding relationships between new and existing facts and data, explanations, verifications, and logical conclusions.

Every research project must be objective, logical, comprehensive, unbiased, and based on reliable data. A good researcher must be very critical about his or her own research and be open to facts and logical constructs that not only support the research results but also may contradict them. You must keep asking yourself questions that lead you into your research even if they might contradict your hypotheses or beliefs regardless of how much you like them.

To keep their research objective, ancient philosophers used the rhetorical method of dialogues; they asked provocative questions in order to analyze the problem from all sides and explain the meaning of terms and words used in their discussion. This is called the Socratic method after Socrates (*c*. 469–399 BC), who is renowned as one of the founders of modern Western philosophy, even though he is known only through the accounts of his students referring to his teaching and analysis. Today, the principle of objectivity is still a cornerstone of research methodology.

Research involves such activities as inquiry, investigation, logical inference, experimentation, examination, simulation, and creation. Merriam-Webster defines *inquiry* as an examination into facts or principles.

All research activities and efforts must be objective, systematic, studious, logical, critical, diligent, exhaustive, and orderly. *Objective* means that research must be independent of the researcher's personal opinion or the opinion of any group of people and instead reflect reality.

Thus, research is an activity characterized by intellectual curiosity, using systematic planning to collect facts, performing objective analysis through logical thinking, and ending with a new truth or verification of an existing one.

1.1.3 Research Starts with Questions and Ends with Answers

Research Starts with a Question

A very important element of research is curiosity. To be a researcher, one has to have an attitude of inquisitiveness and keep asking questions:
- I wonder how … ?
- I wonder why … ?
- I wonder what … ?
- I wonder where … ?
- I wonder … ?

The researcher seeks reasons and causes behind events, phenomena, and behavior.

Every research project starts with a question, one that does not have a known answer. If the answer to the question is known, such a question does not lead to research. One just needs to find the answer in literature, on the Internet, or in other sources. However, if no answer to the question is known, this could be a good reason to start researching to find the answer. The answers found by research must be previously unknown, nontrivial, and original.

For instance, the simple question "What does make the Sun rise in the morning and go down at night?" has a very good and clear answer today and hence is not a subject for research. However, thousand years ago, this question did not have a proven answer and therefore constituted a legitimate subject for comprehensive research. The most advanced researchers of those times did not believe in a flat Earth resting on three whales and tried to find a real answer. Some of them paid a high price for their quest for truth. The Italian philosopher Giordano Bruno (1548–1600) was burned at the stake as a heretic for his support of heliocentrism, and the Italian astronomer and physicist Galileo Galilei (1564–1642) barely escaped the same fate.

Research Ends with the Answer

Any research stats with a question and answers to that question conclude it. The answers should address the research question and must be given in the form of a detailed explanation of the research findings, the causes of and reasons for the facts, phenomena, and relationships discovered along with thorough conclusions logically derived from the findings. If the research has practical purpose and the results support it, it is good to provide practical recommendations that came up in the course of the research. Without such explanations and conclusions, a research project cannot be considered complete.

Sometimes, research ends up with negative results that prove the impossibility of answering the questions asked or revising existing knowledge or understanding of things. However, such research has value if it was conducted correctly and the negative results were proven.

- Research starts with a question and ends up with the answer.
- The research question should be original and nontrivial, and the answer should be unknown.

- Collecting data is just one step in research.
- Research must turn the data into knowledge and answer the research question.

Difference Between Search and Research

Both search and research start with a question and consist of the activities to find the answer.

Search is the activity to find an answer to the question if we believe that the answer is already known and somewhere available and just should be found. Research is the activity to find an answer to the question if we believe that the answer is not yet known. Both search and research are completed, when the answer is found.

The difference between search and research is schematically shown in ◘ Fig. 1.1.

Thus, it is very important to run a search before starting a research project to make sure that the answer is not yet known.

1.2 Continuity of Knowledge and Research

The knowledge that humanity currently possesses has been accumulated over thousands of years, piece by piece adding to the "pyramid of knowledge" as illustrated in ◘ Fig. 1.2. Every discovery and every big and small research result add a piece of new knowledge to the top of the pyramid of existing knowledge.

It would be unwise to ignore accumulated knowledge and conduct research "from a blank sheet of paper." All research is based on previously existing knowledge, even knowledge that is incomplete or erroneous, and represents continuity of the knowledge accumulation process. Without anchoring themselves

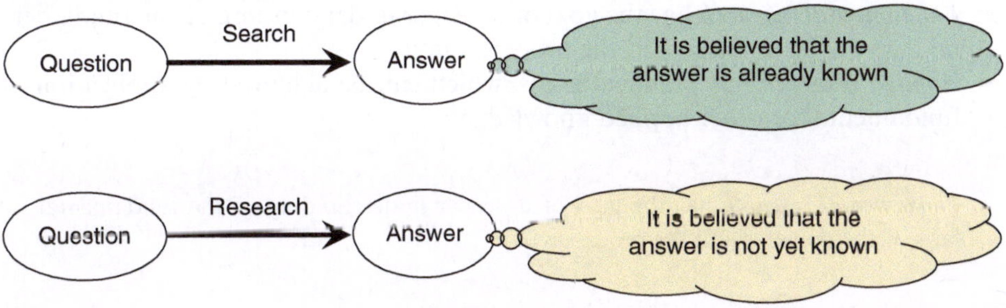

◘ **Fig. 1.1** The commonality and difference between search and research

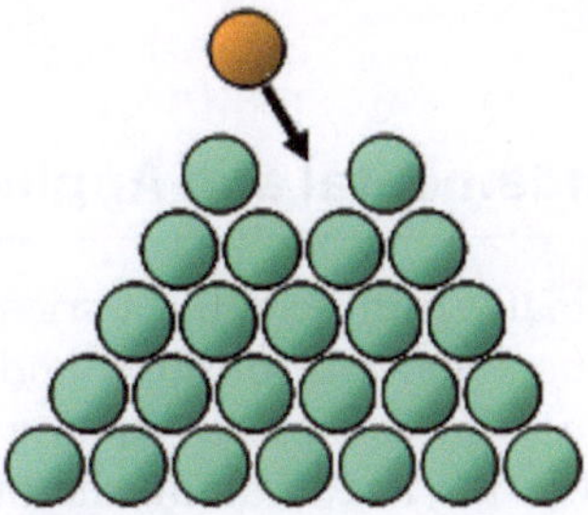

◘ **Fig. 1.2** The pyramid of knowledge

on the pyramid of knowledge, researchers would face the unbearable problem of duplicating the existing knowledge and repeating mistakes already made in the past.

Thus, it is very important to be aware of previous research conducted in your area of interest, to continue logically building up the pyramid of knowledge and do good and valuable research. Even if your research results are negative, they will still add to the pyramid of knowledge, at least as a warning of what not to do or how not to approach the problem.

1.3 Fundamental and Applied Research

1.3.1 Definition of Fundamental and Applied Research

There is a variety of research types, and they can be classified in a number of ways. Such classification can be done by the goal, purpose, methods, activity, scale, subject, or some other features depending on the point of view and the reason for classification. A very convenient and useful classification is according to the utilization of the research results. With such an approach, research can be classified in two categories: fundamental and applied research:

- ***Fundamental research*** has the goal of a deeper understanding of the fundamental laws of the universe and the processes in it.
- ***Applied research*** has practical goals, which can be achieved by application of fundamental or other applied knowledge.

Fundamental research has the goal of a deeper understanding of the fundamental laws of the universe and the processes in it.

Applied research has practical goals, which can be achieved by application of fundamental or other applied knowledge for practical purpose.

1.3.2 Examples of Fundamental and Applied Research

Fundamental research originates from scientific curiosity about our world and the desire to explain facts, phenomena, relationships, and processes in it for the purpose of understanding them without explicitly aiming at any practical application of the knowledge acquired in the research. On the other hand, applied research starts with the clear practical goal of applying the research results. Some examples of fundamental and applied research are listed in ◘ Table 1.1.

Table 1.1 Examples of fundamental and applied research

Fundamental research	Applied research
Nuclear physics	Application of nuclear physics to the production of energy
Stem cells in biology	Uses of stem cells in healthcare
Cosmology	Impact of cosmic radiation on telecommunication
Theory of finite element analysis	Stress analysis in automotive design
Optimization methods in mathematics	Competitive analysis and production optimization
Probability theory	Probabilistic studies of device failure
Biochemistry	Application of biochemical processes in medicine
Laser physics	Application of lasers in electronic devices

Physics of elementary particles, for instance, belongs to fundamental research because it studies general properties of matter without any specific goal of applying the acquired knowledge for practical purposes. On the other hand, research on the stability of chain reactions in nuclear reactors can be applied in the design of nuclear power stations; for this reason, it would be classified as applied research because it has a very specific practical goal.

Another example of fundamental research is study of the human brain and human psychology without any immediate or specific practical application of the results. However, such research may become applied research for practical application of cognitive abilities of humans. In business, psychological studies for the purpose of improving business efficiency definitely belong to applied research.

1.3.3 Link Between Fundamental and Applied Research

Sometimes, it is not easy to draw a distinct demarcation line between fundamental and applied research. Often, initial curiosity ends up with fundamental discoveries which sooner or later find practical applications.

By ***general knowledge***, we mean a collection of results of both fundamental and applied research; however, we may differentiate between fundamental and applied knowledge. Fundamental knowledge over time finds practical application; it becomes applied knowledge. For example, fundamental research in electromagnetism turned into applied research in radio and television. On the other hand, some

1

Table 1.2 Relationship between fundamental and applied research

Fundamental research		Applied research
Math, statistics	⟺	Sampling research in marketing
Cellular biology	⟺	Research in treating HIV
Nuclear physics	⟺	Nuclear power plants
Nuclear physics	⟺	3D tomography and MRI
Geophysics	⟺	Research on earthquake prediction

fundamental research has originated from applied research. For example, applied research on earthquake prediction facilitated a number of directions in fundamental geophysical research about tectonic plates.

Some research may belong to both categories, fundamental and applied research, at the same time. For example, research in advanced lasers could lead to new discoveries in physics and to the development of new technologies for industrial needs.

Thus, there is a close relationship between fundamental and applied research. Fundamental research can evolve into applied research and vice versa. Nowadays, most fundamental and applied research projects contribute to and facilitate each other. Examples of related fundamental and applied research are illustrated in Table 1.2.

1.4 Major Research Approaches

Another helpful way of research classification is by used methods, regardless of whether the research is fundamental or applied. Such classification includes, but is not limited to, the following categories:

- Exploratory research
- Descriptive research
- Theoretical research
- Experimental research
- Simulation research
- Analytical research
- Creative research

Any research project may use a single approach or a combination of methods.

1.4.1 Exploratory Research

Exploratory research helps researchers understand and define a problem which was not previously clearly understood or defined. For example, the stunning failure of Coca-Cola's "New Coke" led to exploratory research to figure out what had happened. Why did consumers, who preferred the new Coca-Cola to the old one during testing, refuse to buy it when it was released in the market on April 23, 1985? "New Coke" had been unanimously supported by consumers in blind testing against traditional Coke prior to the new product launch. However, when the Coca-Cola Company introduced "New Coke" in the market, public reaction was extremely poor. It was one of history's major marketing failures, and the Coca-Cola Company had to reintroduce the traditional Coke. To assure consumers that the Coke in stores was really the traditional one rather than the new one, it was relabeled "Coca-Cola Classic" on July 10, 1985 (◘ Fig. 1.3). Such labeling was in place for a long time till the early 2000s.

> ***Exploratory research*** helps researchers understand and define a problem which was not previously clearly understood or defined.

The research conducted to understand the problem that arose with the New Coca-Cola was a typical exploratory research. Its initial goal was to find the reasons for the mismatch between consumer behavior and decision-making in testing and in the real-life market and to formulate the problem for further study.

◘ Fig. 1.3 Coca-Cola Classic and New Coke. (Source: ©Mike Licht)

1.4.2 Descriptive Research

Descriptive research or, as it is also known, statistical research can be characterized as the collecting of factual data (statistic) to describe objects, subjects, situations, behaviors, relationships, events, and phenomena that exist in the real world. This data is used to identify categories, calculate averages and frequencies of occurrence, verify hypotheses, and make forecasts and for some other purposes. Typically, such data is collected from a limited sample to derive conclusions about a population. The term *population* in descriptive research comes from statistics and means a complete set of objects of interest. The term *sample* means a limited subset of the population.

Descriptive research or, as it is also known, statistical research can be characterized as the collecting of factual data (statistics) to describe objects, subjects, situations, behaviors, relationships, events, and phenomena that exist in the real world.

For example, in order to learn whether the 2020 Chevrolet Malibu or Ford Fusion consumes less gas, we might take measurements on 50 Malibu and 50 Fusion and use them to calculate the average gas consumption of each model. In this case, all Malibu produced in 2020 constitute the population of Chevrolet Malibu of the 2020 model year, and all Fusion produced in 2020 constitute the population of Ford Fusion of the 2020 model year. The 50 Chevrolet Malibu selected for the gas consumption measurements make a sample of Malibu, and the 50 Fusion make a sample of Ford Fusion. The average gas consumption measured from the samples gives an estimate for gas consumption by the entire population of the respective car models. The major problem in statistics is to identify how close the measurements on the samples are to the similar parameters on the respective populations. We will discuss statistical analysis of this problem later in this book in a greater detail.

Descriptive research is a very popular method in business research, particularly in market research. For example, a retail firm wants to find out what fashions and colors of clothing to order from its supplier for the next quarter. To find the answer to the question, the firm might conduct descriptive research by asking a certain number of customers (a sample of customers) about their preferences in clothing fashions and colors. When the collected information is statistically processed, the results can be used for placing orders to the firm's suppliers for the next quarter. For another example of descriptive research, let's consider healthcare. Hospitals want to know how many days patients typically stay in the hospital after open-heart surgery. Though every patient recovers differently, hospitals need information about the averages in order to plan for the number of beds they will need for a given number of surgeries. This research can be conducted by collecting information about the length of stay in the hospital from a sample of previous patients, processing the information, and making a forecast for the future by extending the results to all prospective patients, that is, to the population of patients.

1.4.3 Theoretical Research

Theoretical research can be characterized as the development of models to explain certain facts, phenomena, or processes and to make appropriate predictions about them. A *model* can be defined as an abstract construct which includes major parameters and their relationships and dependencies of the related objects of interest for the purpose of the analysis. The last comment is quite essential because different parameters and different relationships may be chosen for the model subject for the purpose of the analysis.

For example, a university keeps the record of its students. A student is a human with a very complex physical and psychological structure. To keep the record of students, the major parameters were chosen for the purpose of academic recording. Such parameters are the student name, courses, grades, and others. A medical doctor, when treats the same student, also keeps the patient's record. The major parameters in that records are quite different from the parameters in the university record. The medical record includes the patient name, height, weight, blood pressure, and other medical information.

As the model is developed and the appropriate conclusions are derived, it becomes a theory. A ***theory*** can be defined as a set of statements or principles which are put together to explain certain facts, events, or phenomena and can be used for making predictions about those facts, events, or phenomena.

A ***model*** can be defined as an abstract construct which includes major parameters and their relationships and dependencies of the related objects of interest for the purpose of the analysis.

A ***theory*** can be defined as a set of statements or principles which are put together to explain certain facts and can be used for making predictions about those facts.

Typically, theoretical research is based on mathematical, logical, or numerical methods. Often, theoretical research based on numerical methods has significant overlap with simulation research, which is described below.

Theoretical research can be characterized as the development of models to explain certain facts, phenomena, or processes and to make appropriate predictions about them.

Theoretical research is very popular in mathematics, physics, and other fundamental sciences associated with fundamental research. However, economics, supply chains, sociology, computer science, and many other areas of applied research, including business research, use theoretical research too. As an example, theoretical research based on modeling the global economy could describe and predict global crises and provide recommendations to help prevent them. Theoretical research about principles of optimization in the supply chain is another vivid example of theoretical research in business.

1.4.4 Experimental Research

Experimental research can be characterized as intentionally reproducing certain phenomena, events, or processes with the purpose of learning about them, including major relationships and dependencies. The experimental approach is actively used in both fundamental and applied research.

> ***Experimental research*** can be characterized as intentionally reproducing certain phenomena, events, or processes with the purpose of learning about them, including major relationships and dependencies.

For example, experiments in nuclear physics can help us understand the universe and hence belong to fundamental research. On the other hand, experiments in the thermal conductivity of different materials help us build more comfortable homes and reduce energy consumption to heat and cool them; such experiments with practical purpose belong to the category of applied research. Experimenting with different layouts of shelves and goods on them can help a retail company improve sales and customer satisfaction.

Experiments can be conducted in *natural* or in *laboratory* conditions. Experiments in natural conditions include observation and measurement of facts, phenomena, events, or processes as they occur in real life. On the other hand, laboratory experiments are conducted in artificially controlled conditions that the researcher sets up for the experiment. For example, measuring mechanical stress on a construction frame during an actual earthquake is an experiment conducted in natural conditions. Reproducing "shaky" conditions in the lab and measuring the stress imposed on construction frames are a laboratory experiment.

Experiments in life sciences can be conducted in vivo or in vitro. For in vivo experiments, researchers use living organisms; in vitro experiments are conducted in a controlled environment such as a test tube, Petri dish, or other laboratory equipment. For example, if the researcher studies biological cells in a living organism, such research is considered in vivo, but if the cells are taken out of the living organism and studied separately, such research is in vitro.

1.4.5 Simulation Research

Sometimes, real experiments would be too costly or even impossible, so researchers use computers to simulate the appropriate phenomena, events, or processes using the appropriate models. Such experiments are known as computer experiments or computer simulations, and nowadays, they constitute a distinct approach in research referred to as simulation research.

Simulation research, also referred to as ***computer simulation*** or ***computer experiments***, can be characterized as running models on computers to simulate the phenomena, events, or processes under study. Such simulation emulates a real-world experiment within the constraints imposed by the model. The better the model describes the appropriate real-world phenomenon, event, or process, the closer the result of the simulation can be to the real-world situation. Simulation research became possible with the advances in computers over the last 50 years. The simulation approach has been getting more popular as computers have become more powerful, with greater calculation speed and capacity.

Computer simulation of molecular structures, referred to as molecular dynamics, is a good example of simulation research. It allows researchers to learn more about various chemical and physical substances, particularly when direct real-world experiments would be too expensive or even impossible. Simulation research is widely used in both fundamental and applied research.

A very vivid example of computer simulation in applied research is the simulation of a nuclear power station's operational and critical modes to learn more about them in order to predict and prevent nuclear disasters. Definitely, it would be irresponsible and practically impossible to run such critical modes on a real nuclear power station or in real-world conditions without risking a real disaster.

For another example, suppose a city wants to minimize traffic jams at an intersection by building a new overpass. It would be a huge and costly disappointment if the new overpass is built but the traffic did not ease up. To avoid such an outcome, a computer simulation can be conducted to simulate different designs of overpasses and different traffic scenarios to find the best solution.

> ***Simulation research***, also referred to as ***computer simulation*** or ***computer experiments***, can be characterized as running models on computers to simulate the phenomena, events, or processes under study.

In business, computer simulation is becoming more popular. Simulation of various supply chain modes, stock market behavior, financial flows, and other business processes is hard to overestimate.

1.4.6 Analytical Research

Analytical research can be characterized as the use of logical inference to analyze certain situations, make appropriate assessments, predict possible consequences and outcomes, and develop appropriate strategies. Analytical research is mostly used when mathematical modeling is too hard or impossible, but logical inference can provide a productive way of answering the research question.

Analytical research can be characterized as research conducted by logical inference to analyze certain situations, make the appropriate assessments, predict possible consequences and outcomes, and develop the appropriate strategies.

Philosophy is a good example of the analytical approach used for fundamental research. Examples of applied analytical research are political research and competitive marketing research. Suppose a company wants to assess its competitive position and make the appropriate decisions for its improvement. It is not always easy and sometimes impossible to define and develop a numerical metrics for such analysis, but the analytical approach could help the researchers or managers in such an endeavor.

1.4.7 Creative Research

Creative research can be characterized as research about new forms, shapes, colors, and other features that cannot be formalized by any other research approaches. For example, the development of new car body styles, the best colors for clothing, and new forms in architecture belongs to creative research.

Suppose a car manufacturer is developing a new car model. The car's body must meet technical specifications, but at the same time, it has to have an attractive shape and color. There is neither a recipe nor a mathematical formula for solving such problems. Creative research is the right way to go.

Creative research can be characterized as research about new forms, shapes, colors, and other features that cannot be formalized by any other research approaches.

1.4.8 Relationship Between Different Research Approaches

All the research approaches described in this chapter can coexist or work complementary to each other. For example, the results of experimental research are frequently used to lay the foundation for theoretical models and to verify the results in theoretical research. Computer simulation often goes along with theoretical and experimental research. A variety of combinations of research approaches can be used for many problems to find the most comprehensive and complete solution.

1.5 Research Versus Reporting

Confusing research and reporting are very common, particularly among young researchers and students. Sometimes, they believe that their research is complete because they have collected the data and organized, processed, and analyzed it.

This is not correct. The major outcome of research is the answers to the questions posed in the research problem statement. This is the key and the meaning of research. When a research project is completed, it must be delivered in some form, such as a report, presentation, research publication, or book. A report is just a form of delivery of research results.

A report is a document that presents information about an inquiry or investigation to an audience. The purpose of reports is usually to inform.

Quite often, young researchers and students start working on their research project by writing the research report. This is a completely wrong way to proceed with research. A research report is a document that informs other people about a completed research project. Thus, do not write your research report until your research is not done and the conclusion is derived.

A report is just one form of delivery of research results.

In contrast to a report, research aims to answer the questions asked in the research problem. A research project is completed when such answers are obtained in the form of conclusions, possibly predictions, and, in case of applied research, practical recommendations.

Research should provide answers to the questions posed in the research problem statement.

1.6 Credible Research

Credible research must have a meaningful problem and a clearly defined and needed purpose, employ appropriate methods and procedures, and have properly derived and supported conclusions that result from logical analysis and provide answers to the questions in the problem statement. It also must be presented in a proper form and be based upon the scientific method.

Credible research must have a meaningful problem and a clearly defined and needed purpose, employ appropriate methods and procedures, and have properly derived and supported conclusions that result from logical analysis and provide answers to the questions in the problem statement. It also must be presented in a proper form and be based upon the scientific method.

For the research community to regard a research project as credible, all the research steps must meet the required and expected quality standards. There are seven basic characteristics of credible research:

1. The research problem must be meaningful, reasonably limited, and clearly defined.
2. The research purpose must be clearly stated.
3. The related literature must be reviewed and analyzed.
4. All methods used in the research must be clearly described and accurately followed.
5. Data must be properly collected from reliable sources or otherwise acquired by using accurate and reliable methods and then properly processed and analyzed.
6. The research conclusions must be meaningful, original, and nontrivial; clearly answer the questions posed in the problem statement; and be logically derived from the research results.
7. The research results must be properly delivered with a complete, logical, and structurally solid report, presentation, or research publication.

There are several mistakes inexperienced researchers may typically make in their research:

- The problem statement is unclear.
- The literature is not reviewed, and existing knowledge is ignored.
- The purpose of the research is not clear. A clear purpose is particularly important for applied research.
- The research project ends with the collection of data.
- Conclusions are trivial or unoriginal.
- Conclusions are not related to the problem statement.
- The research report and presentation do not clearly and completely deliver the research results.

Please note that just a collection of data, data comparison, or data processing do not constitute a complete research. Research is the analysis of the collected data followed by conclusions and recommendations that are derived from the data and data analysis and that answer the questions posed in the problem statement about the purpose of the research.

> There are seven basic characteristics of credible research:
> 1. The research problem must be meaningful, reasonably limited, and clearly defined.
> 2. The research purpose must be clearly stated.
> 3. The related literature must be reviewed and analyzed.
> 4. All methods used in the research must be clearly described and accurately followed.
> 5. Data must be properly collected from reliable sources or otherwise acquired by using accurate and reliable methods and then properly processed and analyzed.

6. The research conclusions must be meaningful, original, and nontrivial; clearly answer the questions posed in the problem statement; and be logically derived from the research results.
7. The research results must be properly delivered with a complete, logical, and structurally solid report, presentation, or research publication.

1.7 Business Research

1.7.1 Specifics of Business Research

Definitely, business research belongs to the category of applied research because every business research project must have a very clear practical purpose. Business research is needed for a variety of practical purposes including the following:

- To make decisions about business strategy and operations
- To analyze markets
- To understand and predict demand and supply
- To improve competitive power
- To improve markcting and sales efforts
- To introduce new products and services

Business research is normally applied research with a focused practical purpose and a clearly defined practical problem. The outcome of business research must be practical, answering the practical questions formulated in the research problem. It is quite common that the conclusions of business research lead to practical recommendations on specific actions to be taken to improve the business.

- The outcome of business research must be practical and constructive, with clearly formulated conclusions.
- A good business research project provides practical recommendations within the scope of the problem to be solved.

The variety of business research is quite diverse in terms of types, goals, and methods. We will illustrate this variety with several examples for a better understanding of what business research is. Certainly, these examples do not cover the entire variety of research in business, but at least, they will provide a clear sense of what business research is.

Business Research 1: Research on Prospective Service Volume

A car manufacturing company, ABC, initiates sales of its cars in country X and plans to sell a certain number of cars annually. Before it can start selling its cars, the company needs to establish a service infrastructure in that country. The question is what size of service infrastructure should be developed in country X?

To answer this business question, the company conducts research to assess the number of ABC cars expected for service annually in order to establish the appropriate service infrastructure to meet the expected volume of service requests as well as the expected growth dynamics. The research is based on the analysis of local specifics and the ABC car's quality. Local specifics include the service frequency for similar cars from other manufacturers in country X (let's call them *reference cars*) and local conditions in country X, such as climate, the quality of local roads, local traffic flow and driving habits, frequency of accidents, and other parameters related to country X. In addition, the company collects information on the frequency of service requests for ABC cars and the reference cars in the countries where ABC cars are already available. By comparing the frequencies of these service requests for ABC and reference cars, the adjustment factor is derived to find the potential frequency of service requests for ABC cars in country X.

Business Research 2: Customer Satisfaction Survey

Company XYZ sets a goal of providing a higher quality of services. To decide what improvements are needed for the currently rendered services, company XYZ needs to know how satisfied its customers are with its current services. Such information will provide clear grounds for planning and implementing the appropriate improvements.

To obtain information on customer satisfaction, XYZ conducts research in the form of a questionnaire distributed to its customers. If the number of XYZ's customers is big, the questionnaire is distributed to a randomly selected group of customers, called a *sample group*. As the information from the sample group's responses arrive and are processed, the company receives a clear picture of how its services should be improved for higher customer satisfaction.

However, before making any decisions based on the responses from the sample groups, the company must estimate how closely the responses from the sample group represent the opinion of all the company's customers. XYZ uses statistical techniques to make an estimate about the responses from the sample group.

Business Research 3: Comparative Product Analysis

A software development company would like to improve the competitive power of its product. To do so, the company needs to know the strengths and weaknesses of its product in comparison with similar products from the competitors.

To conduct such research, the company develops a comparative metric for analysis feature by feature for the company product versus the competitive products. The metric may also include customer convenience and satisfaction. Then, information about the appropriate features of all the products is collected and analyzed. The results of such comparative research provide a clear picture for appropriate improvements of the company's product.

Business Research 4: Forecast and Planning Research

A food-producing company, FBC, experiences a growing demand for its products and plans to increase its production for the next year. To meet the growing demand, the company may need to hire and train some new employees, increase its supply level, and invest in new equipment. To make decision about these issues, FBC needs to make a reasonable forecast about the demand in the next year.

To make the forecast, FBC conducts research that includes assessment of demand growth in the past along with trends in general economic conditions. Based on the demand forecast, FBC decides whether to expand its production power.

Business Research 5: Strategic Planning Research

A company, SBT, plans to expand its business by reinvesting the company-retained profit. There are several opportunities in the market for expansion, but SBT wants to select the most promising one.

To solve this problem, SBT conducts research by developing different scenarios for expansion and estimating the potential outcomes and risks from each scenario. Based on the results of this research, the company selects the best scenario for its expansion.

1.7.2 Business Research Methods

Each type of business research requires the appropriate method or methods. Those methods may significantly vary for different research types. Some of the most commonly used methods in business research are presented and discussed in Part III of this book. The methods presented in this book by no means cover all possible methods used in business research, but they will provide a good foundation for conducting the most frequently needed kinds of research in business.

Questions for Self-Review for Chap. 1

1. How would you define the term research?
2. Is just collection of data research?
3. What is the goal of research?
4. What activities, including their types and purposes, are involved in research?
5. How does research start?
6. What should conclude the research?
7. How do you understand the term continuity of knowledge?
8. How would you define fundamental research?
9. How would you define applied research?
10. What is the difference between fundamental and applied research?
11. Provide examples of fundamental and applied research and explain the difference.
12. What is the relationship between fundamental and applied research?
13. What are the major research approaches?
14. What is the difference between theoretical research and simulation research?
15. When is simulation research the most productive?
16. Provide examples of descriptive, theoretical, experimental, simulation, analytical, and creative research.
17. What is the difference between research and reporting?

18. How would you describe credible research?
19. Why is business research needed?
20. What does the term research conclusions mean?
21. How are research conclusions different from recommendations?
22. Provide an example of business research.

Scientific Method

Contents

2.1 Methodology – 27

2.2 The Scientific Method – 27

2.3 The Framework for the Scientific Method – 28
2.3.1 The Epistemological Cornerstone of the Scientific Method – 28
2.3.2 The Methodological Cornerstone of the Scientific Method – 29
2.3.3 The Empirical Cornerstone of the Scientific Method – 31
2.3.4 The Cornerstones of the Scientific Method – 32

2.4 Are There Alternatives to the Scientific Method? – 32

2.5 Hypotheses – 33
2.5.1 Logical Negation – 35
2.5.2 Alternative Hypotheses – 36

2.6 Hypothesis Evaluation – 39

2.7 Hypothesis Verification – 39
2.7.1 Hypothesis Truth Status – 39
2.7.2 Hypothesis Verification Process – 39
2.7.3 Logical Hypotheses – 40
2.7.4 Statistical Hypotheses – 42
2.7.5 Deterministic Hypothesis Verification – 42
2.7.6 Does Every Research Need a Hypothesis? – 42

S. K. Aityan, *Business Research Methodology*, Classroom Companion: Business,
https://doi.org/10.1007/978-3-030-76857-7_2

2.8 Occam's Razor – 43

2.9 Reasoning and Logic – 44
2.9.1 Modus Ponens – 44
2.9.2 Inductive and Deductive Logic – 46
2.9.3 Deductive Logic – 46
2.9.4 Inductive Logic – 47

2.1 Methodology

The term ***methodology*** is defined by Merriam-Webster dictionary[1] as follows:

- A body of methods, rules, and postulates employed by a discipline
- A particular procedure or set of procedures
- The analysis of the principles or procedures of inquiry in a particular field

Research methodology defines the methods, activities, and processes engaged in a research; the way to proceed with research; and how to make research successful. Research methodology evolves over time as new concepts are introduced and new foundations are developed. Different research schools and different generations of researchers may use different research methodologies. However, a core methodology of research has been established and is commonly accepted by the modern research community. This core methodology represents the cornerstone of all methodologies used in all areas of research today.

2.2 The Scientific Method

The philosophical, methodological, and procedural frameworks of the ways that researchers conduct research and present evidence and proofs are not the same now as they were in the past. Different cultures have also had different research frameworks throughout their history.

Francis Bacon. (Source: Wellcome Library no. 671i)

The modern philosophical, methodological, and procedural framework for research is known as the ***scientific method***. It takes its origin from the English philosopher Francis Bacon (1561–1626), who developed a blueprint for acquisition of "scientific knowledge." Actually, the term "scientific method" is a misnomer because it provides a framework rather than a research method. The scientific method belongs to the branch of philosophy called ***epistemology***, which takes its name from the Greek words *episteme* ("knowledge") and *logos* ("theory") and could be translated as "theory of knowledge."

1 Merriam-Webster, methodology, ► https://www.merriam-webster.com/dictionary/methodology

2.3 The Framework for the Scientific Method

2.3.1 The Epistemological Cornerstone of the Scientific Method

Francis Bacon suggested the epistemological cornerstone for the scientific method by following a fourfold rule of work in research:
- Observe
- Measure
- Explain
- Verify

which by now constitutes the guideline for knowledge-acquisition rule in the modern sciences.

Observe
If you want to investigate something, you have to be able first to observe it. If there is no observation, there is no subject for investigation, and investigation turns into speculation.

Observation can be direct or indirect. You can directly observe a building, but you are able to observe molecules only with the help of a microscope or some other device. An electromagnetic field can be observed with the help of devices that transform it into phenomena that human senses can feel. Generally speaking, the human eye is also a device that transmits information from the external world to human senses.

For example, how can we learn about the structure of extraterrestrial life if we have never observed it? If there is no way to observe it directly or indirectly, we can only speculate on this issue until we manage to observe a form of extraterrestrial life.

Measure
Just observing things is not enough to make any conclusions. Different people may see things differently and may interpret things subjectively. Measurement is a comparison with a commonly accepted system of units and provides a more objective view about the object of investigation. For example, we can keep debating which river is longer until we measure their lengths and make an objective conclusion. Thus in research, properties of the studied phenomenon, event, or process have to be measured, which means compared with similar properties of known and commonly accepted objects, for an objective approach.

Explain
Even when we are able to observe something and measure it, we still need to explain it; otherwise, it might be a hoax or a just an erroneous observation. For example, you can clearly observe the geometric body shown in ◘ Fig. 2.1; you can even measure it, but our perception of its light and dark areas suggests that it is a three-dimensional object. A more detailed analysis of the object shows that such a three-dimensional object cannot exist in the reality. Thus, our attempt to explain what we saw and measured leads us to the conclusion that our initial understanding was wrong.

Fig. 2.1 Magic triangle

The optical illusion in Fig. 2.1 is a vivid illustration of the need for explanation as a step in research.

Explanation of an unexplained fact or phenomenon can be done by a hypothesis.

Verify

Any observation or measurement can occur under specific conditions which make the observation and measurement unique. Such unique conditions may lead to a wrong explanation that turns the research toward a misleading direction. For example, we might have observed that all objects dropped in the room fell not directly down but at some angle. We measured the angle and tried to explain this fact as an anomaly of the gravitational field at that location. However, we did not know that there was a strong horizontal magnetic field at that location, and all the objects with which we were experimenting were made of magnetic material. An attempt to verify this experiment by duplicating it with some nonmagnetic objects would prove the explanation was wrong.

The step of verification is very important in research to make sure that the research does not go in a wrong direction due to misleading circumstances.

Researchers must always maintain a reasonable doubt to make sure that they do not fall into the trap of their beliefs, predispositions, and biases. As Francis Bacon said in *The Advancement of Learning*, "If a man will begin with certainties, he shall end in doubts; but if he will be content to begin with doubts, he shall end in certainties."

A hypothesis can be verified by matching it with the observed facts.

2.3.2 The Methodological Cornerstone of the Scientific Method

Research typically presents problems to solve. The solutions to the problems are not obvious. The question then is how to find the solutions. Problem-solving in most disciplines consists of the following five approaches:

- Trial and error
- Logic and inference
- Speculation and argumentation (philosophizing)
- Developing and testing hypothesis
- Continuity of knowledge

Trial and Error

There is no recipe for problem-solving, and solutions can be found in unexpected directions. For this reason, the methodology of ***trial and error*** is common in research. Definitely, trials should be done with random samples, and they must be selected for serious and justifiable reasons.

For example, in research to develop new drugs, researchers keep trying different molecular structures to get the desired properties. However, such trials are based on a deep knowledge of biochemistry, genetics, and other disciplines rather than on haphazard actions. Negative results should not be discouraging for researchers because they show what way not to go in a trial and error path.

Logic and Inference

New knowledge cannot be found in its complete and final form. Typically, new knowledge is generated by following logical inference. To do so, the researcher must be familiar with the accepted logical rules and rule of inference.

For example, if it is rainy, then clouds must be in the sky. However, if there are clouds in the sky, it is not necessarily rainy.

Speculation and Argumentation (Philosophizing)

In the attempt to solve complex problems or provide an explanation about the observed phenomenon, researchers may speculate by generating hypotheses or apply logical constructs to lay out logical grounds for the explanation.

For example, many years ago, people believed that the Earth is flat, but that concept left the daily sunrise and sunset quite unexplained. A speculative hypothesis was generated that the Earth is a body of spherical shape, called a globe, and the heavens rotate around the globe. This speculative hypothesis helped to explain many things and was proven correct for that time. However, some astronomical phenomena could not be explained by the new theory, such as the relative location of the Sun, the planets, and the stars. To solve this problem, another speculative hypothesis was made, stating that all planets rotate around the Sun. Further experimental observations have validated that hypothesis.

Developing and Testing Hypotheses

The necessity of explaining what you observed and measured is an important step in the empirical framework of the scientific method. An explanation of a new phenomenon may not be clear from first glance. We come up with a possible explanation that we call a hypothesis, and we test this explanation using either formal logic or real-world data.

For example, the fact that consumers chose the new Coca-Cola in the blind testing but did not want to buy it in store preferring the old Coca-Cola appeared a very unpleasant surprise for the Coca-Cola Company. Multiple research projects were initiated to explain the phenomenon. The hypothesis was generated that explained this phenomenon by consumer inertia. The hypothesis was tested to verify it.

Continuity of Knowledge

Knowledge has been accumulated throughout a long time for thousands of years, piece by piece, adding up on the top of "pyramid of knowledge." Each new research is based on the accumulated knowledge that provides the continuity of knowledge.

For example, behavioral economics as a branch of economics appeared as a new piece of knowledge based on the advanced knowledge in human psychology and traditional economics. A corporate research on consumer preferences adds a new piece of knowledge to the existing knowledge related to consumer behavior.

2.3.3 The Empirical Cornerstone of the Scientific Method

The scientific method is based upon the assumption that events in nature have a cause and a natural explanation and are reproducible under similar conditions. These two concepts constitute the empirical cornerstone of the scientific method:

- Causality
- Reproducibility

Causality

A fundamental paradigm of philosophy and the sciences states that every effect has a cause. We should not apply this paradigm mechanically, however, because cause-effect relationships in the real world are sometimes probabilistic or have some other kind of nondeterministic nature.

Reproducibility

The cause-effect philosophical paradigm leads to the conclusion that we would expect to get similar results under the similar conditions (similar causes). It means that a result should be reproducible under similar conditions. Reproducibility of research results is one of the ultimate requirements for recognition of any new phenomena, events, or processes discovered in research.

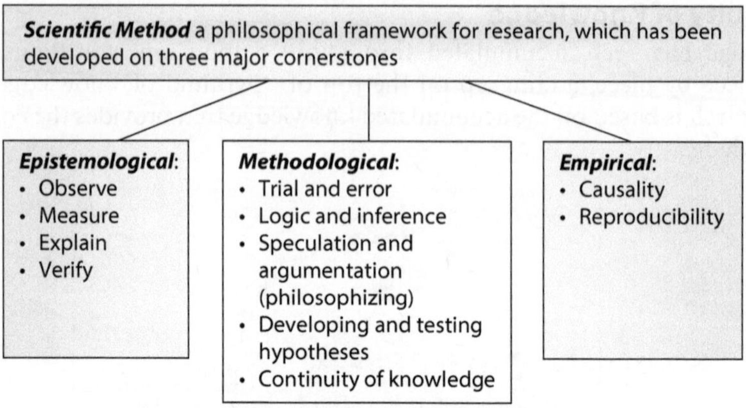

Fig. 2.2 The framework of the scientific method

2.3.4 The Cornerstones of the Scientific Method

Thus, as summarized in Fig. 2.2, the scientific method relates to procedural, empirical, and philosophical approaches used in research. In fact, the scientific method can be viewed as an attitude or a philosophy that provides guidance for researchers. All three cornerstones of the scientific method – the procedural, the empirical, and the philosophical – form a solid framework used in modern research and accepted by the research community.

2.4 Are There Alternatives to the Scientific Method?

As stated above, the scientific method provides a solid framework for research which is commonly accepted and used by modern research community. However, for the complete picture, it is worth mentioning that other frameworks, based on other paradigms, may exist. For example, the theological paradigm is based on the belief in the existence of God. The theological paradigm does not require observation of God in order to accept God's existence. Alternative knowledge-acquisition paradigms have also been proposed by Hinduism, Buddhism, and other philosophies that do not link knowledge directly with observation and measurement. It would be quite interesting to compare the scientific method with other knowledge-acquisition paradigms. These alternative approaches may have certain merits, but they lie outside the scope of the modern scientific paradigm and for this reason outside the scope of this book. However, the bottom line is if you want to do research whose results and proofs are accepted by the modern research community, you should stay within the framework of the scientific method.

2.5 Hypotheses

Research frequently aims to explain a phenomenon, a relationship, an event, or a process whose causes are unknown or obscure. In such situations, researchers normally suggest a possible explanation or a solution to the problem based on the existing knowledge, experience, or sometimes on pure speculation. Definitely, the suggested solution must be proven or verified to become accepted as correct. Such suggested solutions are referred to as ***hypotheses***.

A ***hypothesis*** is a suggested solution to a research problem.

The term ***hypothesis*** originates from Greek word *ὑπόθεσις* (iˈpoθesis), which means "to put under" or "to suppose."

Merriam-Webster dictionary[2] defines hypothesis as "an idea that is the starting point for making a case or conducting an investigation." Wikipedia[3] defines *hypothesis* as "A hypothesis (plural hypotheses) is a proposed explanation for a phenomenon." A *hypothesis* could be also defined as a statement that tentatively explains facts about the subject of investigation. Our first definition of *hypothesis* fits the research framework well because any research starts from a question that constitutes the research problem.

To generalize the definition of *hypothesis*, one can say that a ***hypothesis*** is a statement that is not yet accepted or rejected. Such a definition is more general because some hypotheses, that is, as-yet-unproven statements, may be unaccepted for reasons much broader than just solving research problems.

A ***hypothesis*** is a statement that is not yet accepted or rejected.

A hypothesis can be generated from available information and the researcher's knowledge, experience, and scientific intuition. To become accepted as correct, the hypothesis must be validated with empirical data or logical inference by using rules, statistics, and other appropriate methods. Please be careful with the wording about acceptance of hypotheses. Logical hypotheses can be proven correct by logical inference. However, statistical hypothesis cannot be proven correct or incorrect. The right thing to say when rejecting a statistical hypothesis is "there were enough evidences to reject the hypothesis with the given significance level and therefore the hypothesis was rejected." On the other hand, the right thing to say when accepting

2 Merriam-Webster, hypothesis, ► https://www.merriam-webster.com/thesaurus/hypothesis
3 Wikipedia, hypothesis, ► https://en.wikipedia.org/wiki/Hypothesis

a statistical hypothesis is "there were not enough evidences to reject the hypothesis with the given significance level and therefore it was accepted." We will discuss statistical hypotheses in a greater detail in ▶ Chap. 14 of this book.

Hypothesis generation and its validation are the heart of every research project when the research uses a hypothesis. Data used for hypothesis validation must be real-world data (also referred to as ***empirical data***)

A hypothesis should be formulated in the form of a statement, clearly and explicitly. Formulating a hypothesis in the form of a question is wrong and should be avoided. An explicitly and clearly formulated hypothesis helps guide the research in the right direction. On the other hand, an unclearly and ambiguously formulated hypothesis could obscure the research path and lead to a wrong direction in the research.

A well-formulated hypothesis helps in the research process by:

- Establishing research boundaries and narrowing the research
- Helping researchers to organize their thinking and problem-solving efforts
- Bringing a clear structure to the research by making it a consistently goal-oriented process rather than a random search for "a black cat in a dark room."

Let's discuss some examples of hypotheses.

▶ Example 1

- The *problem question*: What is the shortest way by air between two cities located on the same latitude?
- A *hypothesis*: The shortest way by air between two points on the same latitude lies along the latitude line. (Note that this hypothesis is not true.) ◀

▶ Example 2

- The *problem question*: What is the relationship between catheti and hypotenuse in a right triangle?
- A *hypothesis*: The square of the hypotenuse is equal to the sum of squares of both catheti. (This is known as Pythagoras theorem.) ◀

▶ Example 3

- The *problem question*: Do children like ice cream?
- A *hypothesis*: All children like ice cream. ◀

▶ Example 4

- The *problem question*: Are male and female workers paid equally for the same work in the USA?
- A *hypothesis*: Male and female workers are paid equally for the same work in the USA. ◀

▶ Example 5

- The *problem question*: Does gravitation force always work?
- A *hypothesis*: Gravitation force always works. ◀

The examples above present hypotheses as statements that need to be accepted or rejected.

If a hypothesis happens to be rejected, it may be replaced by some other hypothesis, referred to as an alternative hypothesis, that answers the research question.

2.5.1 Logical Negation

Sometimes, we want to make a statement that is opposite to an original statement; in other words, we want to negate the original statement.

Simple Negation

If the original statement consists of a single fact, for example, "It is raining," the negation to that statement is "It is not raining," which is quite easy to understand. We just need to add *not* to the statement to negate it. If the original statement already contains the negation, for example, "The color of the car is not red," then the negation to that statement is "The color of the car is red." We just removed *not* from the statement. We could instead add *not* to the statement: "The color of the car is *not not* red." A double negation, *not not*, eliminates the negation and results in the statement that means "The color of the car is red."

Complex Negation

To make a negation to a statement is a logical operation that sometimes is not as easy as it looks at first glance. For example, if the original statement is "There are clouds in the sky, and it is raining," what is the statement that negates it?

Original Statement There are clouds in the sky, and it is raining.

Let's think of possible options for negation:

- *Option 1*: There are no clouds in the sky, and it is raining.
- *Option 2*: There are clouds in the sky, but it is not raining.
- *Option 3*: There are no clouds in the sky, and it is not raining.
- *Option 4*: Either there are no clouds in the sky or it is not raining.

Which one of the options is a negation to the original statement? Let's analyze. First of all, we should clearly understand what the original statement means for us, whether the original statement is a conditional or an unconditional statement. Syntactically, the original statement could be either conditional or unconditional depending on the semantics of the statement.

An unconditional statement is a statement that contains no conditions, explicitly or implicitly. The original statement "There are clouds in the sky, and it is raining" has two parts: "there are clouds in the sky" and "it is raining." To be true, both parts of the statement must be true. If the statement is an unconditional statement, then we have four logical choices as shown above (◘ Table 2.1).

Table 2.1 Logical negation for an unconditional statement

		Clouds in the sky	
		True	**False**
Rain	**True**	Original statement	Negation
	False	Negation	Negation

For the entire statement to be false, at least one part of the statement should be false. All three "negation" choices in Table 2.1 other than the original statement as shown above constitute a negation to at least one part of the original statement. Thus, if the original statement is an unconditional statement, Option 4 is its negation.

Negation Either there are no clouds in the sky or it is not raining.

Negation in Classical and Nonclassical Logic

Typically, negation is based on truth values (true, false) in classical mathematics and logic. Classical truth values often are associated with Boolean logic. However, some modern theories deviate from the classical approach and may have more diverse truth values. For example:

- True, false, and unknown
- Partially true and partially false

In this book, we will follow classical truth values, which fit the most typical kinds of research in business. However, some modern approaches with nonclassical truth values, like fuzzy logic, have begun to be used in business research in the last decade.

2.5.2 Alternative Hypotheses

An ***alternative hypothesis*** is another hypothesis that makes sense to propose if the ***primary hypothesis*** fails. Various alternative hypotheses could be proposed in case of failure (rejection) of the primary hypothesis. An alternative hypothesis is not a complete negation of the primary hypothesis but, instead, covers only some of the other options that are of major interest for the research. Sometimes, we can technically formulate many different alternative hypotheses to the same primary hypothesis, but we have to choose one that makes semantic sense for our research. An alternative hypothesis is one that is semantically related to the sense of the problem rather than to the formal meaning of the problem statement and is selected according to the sense of the problem question. Let's show an alternative hypothesis for the six examples provided above.

▶ Example 1

- The *problem question*: What is the shortest way by air between two cities located on the same latitude?
- A *hypothesis*: The shortest way by air between two points on the same latitude lies along the latitude line. (Note that this hypothesis is not true.)
- An *alternative hypothesis*: The shortest way by air between two points on the same latitude lies on the geodesic curve between these points. (A geodesic curve is an intersection of the surface of the Earth with a plane including three points, two on the surface of the Earth and one at the center of the Earth.) ◀

Definitely, one can generate many alternative hypotheses in case of failure of the primary hypothesis. For this example, it could be the alternative hypothesis just stated, the counterhypothesis stated in the previous section, or still another hypothesis, such as "The shortest way by air between two points on the same latitude goes through North Pole." We might have heard about the properties of geodesic curves, which are the shortest distance between two points on a sphere, and want to try that as an alternative hypothesis if the primary hypothesis fails.

▶ Example 2

- The *problem question*: What is the major difference between the US and European automotive markets?
- A *hypothesis*: The European automotive market is mostly focused on gas/mileage optimization while the US market on the car performance.
- An *alternative hypothesis*: The European automotive market *is similar to* the US market in its focus on gas/mileage minimization. ◀

As with the previous example, one can generate many alternative hypotheses in case of failure of the primary hypothesis. For this example, it could be the alternative hypothesis just stated, the counterhypothesis stated in the previous section, or "The European automotive market *is less* focused on gas/mileage minimization than the US market."

It is clear that "is not more," "is similar to," and "is less" are different statements, and the first one, which is a negation of the primary hypothesis "is more," includes both "is less" and "is similar to." However, all of us are aware of the inclination of Americans to drive big muscle cars, and therefore, we select the "is similar to" hypothesis to be an alternative hypotheses because we are interested in learning whether the European automotive market is different from the American one; we already know for sure that Europeans do not prefer bigger cars than Americans do.

► Example 3

- The *problem question*: Do children like ice cream?
- A *hypothesis*: All children like ice cream.
- An *alternative hypothesis*: Children do not like ice cream. ◄

An alternative hypothesis to the primary hypothesis can be "Not all children do not like ice cream" or "Children do not like ice cream" subject to the objectives of the analysis.

There are many candidates for the role of an alternative hypothesis in this case if the primary hypothesis fails. Among them are the alternative hypothesis ("the majority of children"), the counterhypothesis from the previous section ("not all children"), and "*No children* like ice cream" and "*Few children* like ice cream."

Based on our life experience, we know that children like ice cream, but we are not sure whether all children or just a majority of children like ice cream. In this case, we would select as an alternative hypothesis "The majority of children like ice cream."

► Example 5

- The *problem question*: How many hours per week do Americans work on average?

► Example 4

- The *problem question*: Are male and female workers paid equally for the same work in the USA?
- A *hypothesis*: Male and female workers are paid equally for the same work in the USA.
- An *alternative hypothesis*: Female workers are paid less for the same work in the USA. ◄

- A *hypothesis*: On average, Americans work 42 hour per week.
- An *alternative hypothesis*: The average number of work hours among the working population of the USA *is more than 42 hours per week*. ◄

Again, we can generate several hypotheses to suggest if the primary hypothesis fails in this case. Among them are the alternative hypothesis above ("more than

42 hours"), the counterhypothesis from the previous section ("not 42 hours"), and "The average number of work hours among the working population of the United States *is less than 42 hours per week*."

If our experience suggests that Americans work hard, we would select "more than 42 hours" as our alternative hypothesis. However, if we believe that Americans do not work hard, we might select "less than 42 hours." Selecting "is not 42 hours" as an alternative hypothesis would make no sense because there would be no point in disproving the number 42.

2.6 Hypothesis Evaluation

When a hypothesis is generated, it is necessary to evaluate the hypothesis to make sure that it is internally consistent and does not contain any logical inconsistencies or problems. The step of hypothesis evaluation is quite important. When the evaluation is conducted correctly, it may save quite a bit of time and effort. It can help the researcher to formulate a hypothesis that makes sense and is worth the time and effort for the further verification and work.

2.7 Hypothesis Verification

2.7.1 Hypothesis Truth Status

Any hypothesis, as formulated, is in one of the three truth statuses shown in ◘ Table 2.2.

2.7.2 Hypothesis Verification Process

As a hypothesis is generated and evaluated, it must be verified in order to be accepted or rejected. Researchers may employ various approaches for hypothesis verification depending on the nature of the facts, events, processes, and relation-

◘ **Table 2.2** Hypothesis truth statuses

Status	Description
Unknown	The hypothesis has not yet been tested enough to make any conclusions about whether it is true or false
Accepted	The hypothesis has been accepted as true
Rejected	The hypothesis has been rejected as false

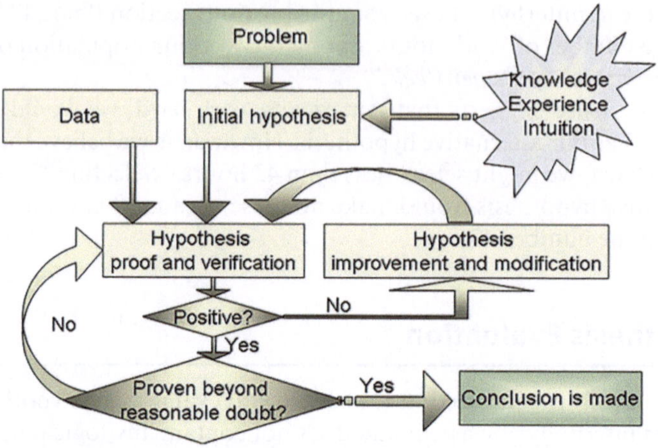

◘ **Fig. 2.3** Hypothesis verification process

ships included in the hypothesis. However, regardless of the nature of its contents, the hypothesis must be verified beyond reasonable doubt to be accepted as true or rejected as false. A generic schema for hypothesis verification is shown in ◘ Fig. 2.3. Each specific case may require some variations to this generic schema. However, the fundamental approach is the same for verifying all hypotheses.

Subject to the nature of the hypothesis, the following are the major methodologies for hypothesis verification:

- *Logical hypothesis verification*, which proves a hypothesis to be true or false by using rules of formal logic or other formal inference rules more appropriate for the case
- *Statistical hypothesis verification*, which tests a hypothesis by using statistical methods based on empirical data
- *Deterministic hypothesis verification*, which tests a hypothesis based on the presumption that the hypothesis must be always correct to be accepted. A single fact that opposes the hypothesis leads to its rejection.

The processes and approaches for logical, deterministic, and statistical hypothesis verification may differ significantly. Researchers should choose the best approach for hypothesis verification depending on the nature of the phenomenon described by the hypothesis.

Accordingly, hypotheses can be classified as follows:

- Logical
- Statistical
- Deterministic

2.7.3 Logical Hypotheses

Logical hypothesis verification is based on formal rules of classical or nonclassical logic or any other formal rules accepted and applicable for the case. The

Table 2.3 Hypotheses as candidates for logical, statistical, and deterministic verification

No.	Hypothesis	Logical verification	Statistical verification	Deterministic verification
1	The shortest way by air between two points on the same latitude lies along the latitude line	This hypothesis can be easily proven wrong (false) by using rules of geometry		
2	The square of the hypotenuse is equal to the sum of squares of both catheti	This hypothesis was logically (mathematically) proven by Pythagoras		
3	All children like ice cream		This hypothesis can be tested using statistical methods	
4	Male and female workers are paid equally for the same work in the USA		This hypothesis can be tested using statistical methods	
5	Gravitation force always works			A single negative case will disprove the theory

logical approach can be used only for those hypotheses for which such rules exist and can be applied. Not all hypotheses can be verified by using the logical approach.

The hypotheses in Examples 1 and 2 above are good candidates for logical verification (Table 2.3). The hypothesis in Example 1 about the shortest way by air between two points on the same latitude could be rejected by finding a shorter way using rules of geometry.

The hypothesis in Example 2 about the relationship of the catheti and the hypotenuse in a right triangle was known for many years in ancient Egypt before Pythagoras from actual measuring different triangles. However, it was not clear if all right triangles would obey the relationship. Pythagoras has proven mathematically that this relationship takes place for any right triangle. This relationship is known as the Pythagoras theorem. As soon as the Pythagoras theorem is proven logically, there is no need to verify it by collecting statistical information and applying statistical methods.

No empirical data may be needed for hypothesis verification with the logical approach because the hypothesis can be proven for all instances in general.

2.7.4 Statistical Hypotheses

Most hypotheses have a statistical nature, which means that the hypothesis statement is true for a significant part of cases rather than for all cases without exception. For example, if hypothesis "All children like ice cream" in Example 3 is true, it means that most children like ice cream, but it does not mean that we could not find a single kid who does not like ice cream. Hypothesis "The European automotive market is more focused on gas/mileage minimization than American market" means that proportion of fuel-efficient cars sold in Europe is higher than in the USA. However, the hypothesis does not mean that no fuel-efficient cars are sold in the USA or that no "muscle cars" are sold in Europe. Hypothesis in Example 4 "Male and female workers are paid equally for the same work in the USA" means that the difference in pay for male and female workers for the same work in the USA is not statistically significant.

Statistical hypotheses should be tested and verified beyond reasonable doubt to be accepted and referred to as the significance level. We will discuss statistical methods for hypotheses testing in a greater detail in ► Chap. 14 of this book.

◘ Table 2.3 shows the hypotheses from our examples along with the applicability of the statistical approach for their verification.

In statistics, the term ***hypothesis testing*** is commonly used as a synonym of *hypothesis verification*, and a *primary hypothesis* is normally called a ***null hypothesis***.

2.7.5 Deterministic Hypothesis Verification

A deterministic hypothesis can be defined as one that is based on the presumption that to be accepted as true, the statement in the hypothesis must always be correct. A single piece of evidence contradicting the hypothesis is false leads to the rejection of the hypothesis. For example, the gravitation theory is based on the hypothesis that all masses are attracted to each other, if no other forces are applied to them. This hypothesis has been tested for centuries and always found working. If a single piece of evidence ever appears that shows a different effect, the hypothesis will be rejected.

Deterministic hypotheses can be considered an extreme case of statistical hypothesis verification with zero level of allowed error.

2.7.6 Does Every Research Need a Hypothesis?

Not every research needs a hypothesis. Those research projects that aim at explaining certain facts or phenomena need a hypothesis or a number of hypotheses to find the explanation. For example, if a research project aims at an explanation of consumer behavior under certain circumstances, we need to formulate and verify a hypothesis that explains that behavior.

- A ***logical hypothesis*** is a hypothesis that can be accepted or rejected based on the rule of classical or nontraditional logic accepted in the subject area.
- A ***statistical hypothesis*** is a hypothesis that can be verified by using statistical methods based on empirical data.
- A ***deterministic hypothesis*** is a hypothesis that can be rejected based on a single evidence contradicting the hypothesis.

On the other hand, if a research project aims at finding the car gas mileage, the research needs no hypotheses but direct measurement and statistical analysis. If a research project objective is to identify the expected future demand on cars, the research needs no hypotheses neither, if it is based on the numerical analysis of the previous sales patterns. However, if there are some other issues involved like change of consumer habits or patterns that need an explanation, then a hypothesis would be needed.

2.8 Occam's Razor

Occam's razor is a fundamental methodological principle which states that among all possible explanations (hypotheses) of a fact or a phenomenon, the least complex explanation should be considered first. Though the authorship of this principle is not certain, the fourteenth-century Franciscan friar William of Ockham (*c.* 1288–1348) was credited as the principle's author. The word *razor* is used here in the sense of "cutting off all that is unnecessary."

The principle applies common sense to the choice of possible explanations of a fact or a phenomenon. The point is that we should not develop more complex explanations if a simpler one explains things under the same conditions.

Occam's razor

Among all competitive explanations (hypotheses), the simplest explanation (hypothesis) should be selected first.

▶ Example 1

There could be many possible explanations for a student failing an exam:
(a) The student was not prepared for the exam.
(b) Aliens remotely locked the student's mind during the exam.
(c) It was a conspiracy to fail the student.

However, if we have no additional knowledge about reasons for the student's failure, the most reasonable explanation probably is the simplest one, (a), that is, the student was not prepared. ◀

2

► Example 2

Suppose we would like to explain why our competitor's products are in greater demand than similar products of our company. We could suggest a number of hypotheses:

(a) The competitor spreads rumors about how bad our products are.
(b) The competitor's products are just better than our products.
(c) The competitor pays $100 to every customer for buying their products instead of our products. ◄

If we have no specific information to support explanations (a) and (c), we should choose explanation (b) as the most likely because it is the simplest one.

Occam's razor should be applied to all scientific explanations. The only reason for increasing the complexity of an explanation should be the inability of the simplest explanation to handle all the evidence.

2.9 Reasoning and Logic

Research is associated with reasoning because researchers have to analyze facts and phenomena, make statements, and derive logical conclusions. The term *reasoning* can be defined as "the cognitive process of looking for reasons for beliefs and conclusions."[4] The need for reasoning and logic goes back to the beginnings of philosophy. The ancient Greek philosophers Socrates (about 470–399 BC), Plato (427–347 BC), and Aristotle (384–322 BC) addressed this issue with fundamental accuracy and precision. Aristotle, one of the world's greatest philosophers, said, "We must first state what our inquiry is about and what its object is."[5] Correct reasoning and valid arguments are the fundamental cornerstones of logical analyses.

2.9.1 Modus Ponens

Modus ponens is a common rule of logical inference. In Latin, *modus ponendo ponens* means "mode that affirms by affirming"; the term is usually abbreviated as *modus ponens*. It consists of two statements: antecedent (A) and consequent (C) that can be true or false. The modus ponens rule takes the following form:

$$\begin{aligned}&\text{if } A \text{ then } C.\\&A.\\&\text{Therefore } C.\end{aligned} \tag{2.1}$$

4 Kirwin, Christopher. 1995. 'Reasoning'. In Ted Honderich (ed.), The Oxford Companion to Philosophy. Oxford: Oxford University Press: p. 748
5 Aristotle. 1989. Prior Analytics (Robin Smith, Editor). Hackett Publishing, page 1

Table 2.4 Modus ponens logical construct

Statement	Role	Truth value
If A, then C	The rule	True
A	Antecedent	True
Therefore C	Consequent	True

Table 2.5 Truth values for logical implications

A	C	$A \rightarrow C$
True	True	True
True	False	False
False	True	True
False	False	True

The logical construct for modus ponens is shown in Eq. (2.1) and means that if the rule "if A then C" is true and A is true, then C is true (Table 2.4).

Modus ponens can be written in the notation of formal logic as follows:

$$\frac{A \rightarrow C, A}{C} \tag{2.2}$$

The truth values for logical implications in classical logic (true, false)[6] are shown in Table 2.5. These values show that if A is true and C is true, then the implication $A \rightarrow C$ is true (row 1 in the table). If A is true but C is false, then the implication $A \rightarrow C$ is false (row 2 in the table). However, if A is false, then the implication $A \rightarrow C$ is always true regardless of whether C is true or false.

Let's go through an example using the statements A = "it is rain" and B = "take an umbrella." The implication is $A \rightarrow C$ = "if it is raining, then take an umbrella." If A is true, it means that "it is raining," and if B is true, it means that you "take an umbrella." Thus, the implication $A \rightarrow C$ "if it is raining, then take an umbrella" is true. If A = "it is raining" is true but B = "take an umbrella" is false (i.e., it is raining, but you do not take an umbrella), then the implication $A \rightarrow C$ = "if it is raining, then take an umbrella" is false. Now, if it is not raining, that means A is false, but the implication $A \rightarrow C$ = "if it is raining, then take an umbrella" is true regardless of whether you take an umbrella or not.

Modus ponens is commonly used for formal logical inference. With this principle, all statements are considered either true or false without any compromises in

6 Quine, W.V. (1982), Methods of Logic, 4th edition, Harvard University Press, Cambridge, MA

between. Some other systems of logic have been developed, particularly in recent years, such as fuzzy logic, that consider compromises between true and false. For those who are curious about nonclassical approaches in logic, refer to the sources provided in the bibliography at the end of this chapter. In this book, however, we will be using mostly classical logic for the sake of simplicity.

2.9.2 Inductive and Deductive Logic

Inductive and deductive reasoning are two methods of reasoning and logic. Both methods are used for making conclusions based on statements assumed to be true. Inductive reasoning starts with a specific statement and makes generalizations, or inferences, about it. In contrast, deductive reasoning uses generalizations to make a specific conclusion.

2.9.3 Deductive Logic

Deductive reasoning, which is frequently called ***deductive logic***, starts with a general statement and through other statements deduces a conclusion about a specific instance. The statements used in deductive logic are called ***premises***. Here are three examples.

▶ Example 1

Premise 1: All Greeks are human.
Premise 2: Aristotle is Greek.
Conclusion: Aristotle is human.

◀

▶ Example 2

Premise 1: All corporations are supposed to make profit.
Premise 2: Pacific Electronics is a corporation.
Conclusion: Pacific Electronics is supposed to make profit.

◀

▶ Example 3

Premise 1: Safety is key for all transportation companies
Premise 2: Airlines are transportation companies.
Premise 3: Star Airways is an airline.
Conclusion: Safety is key for Star Airways.

◀

Deductive logic is used for deriving conclusions about specific things if general features and general relationships are known.

> ***Deductive reasoning***, which is frequently called ***deductive logic***, starts with a general statement and through other statements deduces a conclusion about a specific instance.

2.9.4 Inductive Logic

Inductive reasoning or ***inductive logic*** starts with the property of a specific instance or instances and ends with a general conclusion about the objects of study based on recurring patterns. Typical inductive reasoning begins with one or more specific observations. Then, a general pattern for that class of objects is identified (this is key for induction). Finally, a general conclusion is derived from the propositions (observations) and the identified patterns.

▶ Example 1

Proposition: The bankers I met are greedy.

Pattern: All bankers must be similar.

Conclusion: All bankers are greedy.

◀

▶ Example 2

Proposition: My friends like Toyota cars.

Pattern: We have no reason to think that other people are different.

Conclusion: All people like Toyota cars.

◀

▶ Example 3

Proposition: Increasing oil prices lessen the profit of my company.

Pattern: The profit structure of all companies resembles the one for my company.

Conclusion: Increasing oil prices lessen the profit of all companies.

◀

Now is the time to make two important points about inductive logic:
- Any conclusion can be made if the initial proposition is false.
- Identification of a general pattern is a necessary step in inductive logic.

For those who are familiar with mathematical induction, it should be noted that mathematical induction and inductive reasoning (or logic) are quite different, though they sound quite similar. Mathematical induction is a method of proof while inductive logic is a no rigorous approach. In this regard, the philosophical question arises about whether inductive reasoning leads to truth. The problem can be in the initial proposition and in the pattern.

▶ Example 4

Proposition:	All birds I have ever seen can fly.
Pattern:	Birds share similar features.
Conclusion:	All birds can fly.

◀

- ***Problem in initial proposition***: I have never seen an ostrich or a penguin before. As soon as I encounter those birds, my initial proposition will become false and hence the conclusion as well.
- ***Problem in the pattern***: I made a generalizing pattern that all birds share the ability to fly.

Inductive reasoning or ***inductive logic*** starts with the property of a specific instance or instances and ends with a general conclusion about the objects of study based on recurring patterns.

Questions for Self-Review for ▶ Chap. 2

1. How would you define the term "scientific method"?
2. Is the scientific method actually a method?
3. What is the scientific method?
4. How would you define the term *hypothesis*?
5. What role do hypotheses play in research?
6. Provide an example of a hypothesis.
7. What is a counterhypothesis?
8. What is an alternative hypothesis?
9. What is hypothesis evaluation?
10. Why is hypothesis evaluation needed?
11. How can a hypothesis be verified?
12. What does it take to prove a hypothesis or to reject it?
13. What is logical hypothesis verification?
14. What is statistical hypothesis verification?
15. Does one need real-world or made-up data for hypothesis verification?

16. Are there any hypotheses that do not need real-world data for verification?
17. What is Occam's razor?
18. What is modus ponens?
19. What is inductive reasoning?
20. What is deductive reasoning?
21. What is the difference between inductive and deductive reasoning, and to what kind of problems are they applied?

The Research Process

Contents

3.1 Logical Phases of Research – 53

3.2 Phase I: Preparation for Research – 53
3.2.1 Select a Research Field Related to Your Interest and Expertise – 54
3.2.2 Formulate the Research Problem – 55
3.2.3 Formulate the Research Purpose – 57
3.2.4 Conduct a Review of the Literature – 57
3.2.5 Define the Major Terms Used in the Research – 58
3.2.6 Formulate Key Hypotheses and Models if Needed – 59
3.2.7 Develop the Research Design – 59
3.2.8 Define the Research Objectives and the Expected Results – 61
3.2.9 Write and Submit the Research Proposal for Approval – 61
3.2.10 Discussion, Negotiation, and Approval of the Research Proposal – 62

3.3 Phase II: Conducting Research – 62
3.3.1 Finalize the Models and Hypotheses for the Research if Needed – 62
3.3.2 Finalize the Data Collection Plan and Collect Data – 63
3.3.3 Organize and Process the Data, Using the Models if Appropriate – 63
3.3.4 Analyze and Interpret the Data and Verify the Hypotheses If Any – 63
3.3.5 Summarize the Research Findings and Interpret the Results – 64

S. K. Aityan, *Business Research Methodology*, Classroom Companion: Business,
https://doi.org/10.1007/978-3-030-76857-7_3

3.3.6 Derive Conclusions – 64
3.3.7 Make Recommendations and Predictions if Appropriate – 65

3.4 Phase III: Delivery of the Results – 65
3.4.1 Write the Research Report – 65
3.4.2 Develop and Make Presentations – 66
3.4.3 Defending the Project – 66

3.5 Summary of the Research Process – 67

3.6 Major Reasons for Possible Research Failures – 68
3.6.1 Ambiguous or Unclear Problem Statement – 68
3.6.2 Unclear Scope and Limitations – 68
3.6.3 Unclearly Formulated Hypotheses – 68
3.6.4 Controversial and Conflicting Terms Used in the Research – 68
3.6.5 Wrong Methods and Procedures Used in the Research – 69
3.6.6 Inaccurate or Unreliable Data – 69
3.6.7 Unclear or Inconsistent Conclusions – 69

3.1 Logical Phases of Research

A correctly established and thoroughly followed research process significantly improves the quality of the research by assuring that no steps are missing and the research is complete and credible. Though details of the research process may depend on the type of research and other related circumstances, there is a typical research process framework that can be used as a framework for almost all research projects. The typical research process consists of three distinct phases:

- Phase I: Preparation for research
- Phase II: Conducting research
- Phase III: Delivery of the research results

Each of the research phases is very important and should be given serious attention. This is especially important for applied research, including business research. Proper preparation for research, Phase I, lays a solid foundation and forms the prospective research. The better and more detailed this phase is, the fewer "unpleasant surprises" the researcher will face in the later research phases – though "surprises" in research are quite common. A comprehensive and thorough Phase II assures depth, value, completeness, and accuracy of the research, while good delivery of results, Phase III, guarantees that the research is not wasted and the results become known to others and contribute to the "pyramid of knowledge," as mentioned in ► Chap. 1 of this book, and find the fastest way to practical use of applied research.

The bottom line is that without good preparation, good research is hardly possible, and without good delivery, even perfect results might be wasted because people are unaware of them. Certainly, even perfect delivery of research results cannot offset poor or meaningless research, but a good delivery is essential for a good research.

The three phases mentioned above make common sense and are fundamentally applicable to any activity, say cooking a diner, making furniture, and many other activities.

All three phases of the research process and the steps within each phase are discussed in this chapter.

3.2 Phase I: Preparation for Research

It is common sense to get prepared for any activity. For example, if we want to fix a car, we better have the repair manual and all the needed tools and parts before we start the work; otherwise, the work will take much longer time, and the final result might be compromised. The research process is no different and should be thoroughly prepared. In the preparation for research, the following steps should be completed:

- Select a research field related to your interest and expertise.
- Formulate the research problem:
  - Ask the major question(s), to which you want to find answer(s) in your research.
  - Break the research question(s) (problem) into smaller subquestions (subproblems).
  - Evaluate the problem and define the project's scope and limitations.
- Formulate the research purpose.
- Build a preliminary bibliography and review the literature.
- Define the major terms used in the research.
- Develop the research design:
  - Formulate hypotheses and models if needed.
  - Identify the data collection plan.
  - Identify the methods and procedures to be used in the research.
  - Identify the resources and skills needed for the research.
  - Plan the project schedule and budget if required.
- Define the research objectives.
- Write and submit the research proposal for approval.
- Discuss and negotiate the research proposal with the approval body and obtain the approval.

The proposal approval step concludes the preparation phase for research. As soon as the research proposal is approved, you may move to Phase II and start conducting the research.

3.2.1 Select a Research Field Related to Your Interest and Expertise

Researchers must work in the area of their expertise, experience, and interest. If this is a group project, it applies to the group. The combination of expertise, experience, and interest is essential. Without enough knowledge and expertise in the area of research, it would be hard or even impossible to expect valuable results. This does not mean that researchers should stay away from new areas or subjects; they just need to learn the subject before jumping into research. Experience helps researchers to formulate good research problem, generate reasonable models and hypotheses, and conduct the research in the most optimal and efficient way without making mistakes that could be easily avoided if the sufficient expertise was available. For this reason, it is strongly recommended for beginners to have an advisor or consult with other people with the expertise in the research area before selecting the research area and the research problem. The researcher's interest in the subject provides motivation and driving force which is critical for good research.

3.2.2 Formulate the Research Problem

A clearly and accurately formulated and reasonably limited research problem plays a crucial role in the success of a research project. The research problem formulation step should answer the question "What?" – what are you going to do in the research project?

> The ***research problem*** formulation step should answer the question "What?" – what are you going to do in the research project?

A properly formulated research problem helps to focus on the solution, while an ambiguously or unclearly stated problem may make the research stray from the goal, take the research in a wrong direction, and lead to a significant scattering of resources and waste of time.

The research problem formulation step consists of three actions that have to be completed sequentially:

- Ask questions that lead to the problem statement.
- Break the problem into smaller subproblems.
- Evaluate the problem and define the project's scope and limitations.

These actions may be iteratively repeated several times until a clear picture of the research problem and its constraints emerges.

Ask Questions that Lead to the Problem Statement

A research problem comes from a question you want to answer, and the answer or answers to this question are unknown or unavailable. If the answer to the question can be found in existing sources in a reasonable amount of time and with a reasonable use of resources, such a question does not constitute the basis for a research problem and does not lead to research. If the answer to the question is unknown, that question is suitable for research. However, what if answers are possibly known but unavailable? Does such a question constitute a research problem? It depends on the efforts and time needed to get the answer if it is known but unavailable.

> A ***research problem*** comes from the question which you want to answer, and the answer or answers are yet unknown or unavailable.

Let's pretend we are on a desert island and there are neither clocks nor watches around. The question "What is the time now?" definitely has an accurate answer for people in Hawaii but not on that island. Thus, the answer is known but unavailable. Most likely, we would have to do some research on that island to obtain an answer to the question about time. As another example, suppose a computer chip company needs to do research on some specific properties of electronic chips. It is well known that the competitor has already done such research. However, it would be unreasonable to expect the competitor to share the results of its research. Thus, though the results are already known, they are unavailable, and the company should conduct its own research. The question leads to a viable research problem to investigate.

For fundamental research, the question is supposed to be of general interest and aimed at acquiring new knowledge or verifying or updating existing knowledge. For an applied research, the question should have practical value for the application of the research results. In the area of business research, the question must be important for business or industry or the economy in general.

The question should be original, and the answer to the question should be nontrivial (that means that the question cannot be answered just from the common sense) and not available. If the answer is easily available and easily accessible, it can be found just by search rather than research. Trivial questions, typically, have trivial answers and do not constitute a credible bases for research. For example, the question "What is the date of the first Monday after the next New Year's Day?" could be easily answered with a calendar, and for this reason, it does not constitute a basis for research. On the other hand, the question "What kind of products from my company's product line will be in highest demand in the next quarter?" has neither a known nor an available answer, and for this reason, it does constitute a basis for research.

A research problem can be formulated as a question, or the question could be transformed into a problem statement.

Break the Problem into Smaller Subproblems

It is easier to solve a number of smaller problems than one big one, just as it is easier to move a big rock by breaking it into smaller pieces. For this reason, it is recommended to break a research problem into smaller subproblems and then identify a logical way of how to form the answer to the original problem from the answers to the subproblems.

Evaluate the Problem and Define the Project's Scope and Limitations

As soon as the research problem is formulated and divided into smaller subproblems, it is important to evaluate the feasibility of finding the answers subject to the complexity of the problem, the existing knowledge in the area, and the given constraints such as available expertise, skills, time, budget, and other project constraints, both objective and subjective.

Now, it is time to evaluate the problem and realistically constrain its scale by defining its scope and limitations. As the result of problem evaluation, the scale of the research project should be realistically constrained so that it will be valuable enough to deliver value and reasonable enough to be completed under the given constraints. The scope and limitation of the problem define the boundaries and scale of the research. For example, if our research is dedicated to the correlation analysis of the stock markets in the global economy, we may define the scope as the analysis of correlations between stock markets in industrially developed countries and limit the time period of the analysis to the ten previous years.

The Critical Importance of Problem Formulation

The problem formulation step is critical for a research project. A clearly and unambiguously formulated research problem, including subproblems, scope, and limitations, assures more efficient research, helps the researchers to stay focused on the research problem, and prevents them from moving in the wrong direction or dissipating their efforts.

A detailed discussion on research problem formulation is presented in ▶ Chap. 4 of this book.

3.2.3 Formulate the Research Purpose

Anything we do must have a purpose. Doing things without purpose is a waste of time and efforts. Research must have a purpose too. The purpose of fundamental research is based on natural curiosity to learn more about our world or to verify some existing knowledge. Every applied research project must have a very clear, meaningful, and valuable practical purpose. The purpose of a research project should be worthy of the efforts and resources spent on it. Without a clearly understood and well-spelled-out purpose, the research may become an activity that has too little value to be worth pursuing.

Thus, the purpose of research should be explicitly and clearly stated. For fundamental research, the purpose should tell what kind of missing knowledge the project aims to add or what piece of the existing knowledge it aims to verify or update. For applied research, the purpose should explicitly state what practical value the results of the research will or may have and who will or may be interested in using and applying the results of the research.

The ***research purpose*** should answer the question "Why?" – why are you going to do this research?

The ***research purpose*** should answer the question "Why?" – why are you going to do this research?

For example, the purpose of research on supernova stars is to learn more about our universe and the processes in it. This is fundamental research, and the purpose of such research is to add to the common pool of knowledge without having any practical applications in mind, at least for the time being.

On the other hand, the purpose of research on consumer perception of brand goods versus generic goods belongs to the category of applied research and should have a specific practical purpose, for example, to facilitate sales of generic goods.

3.2.4 Conduct a Review of the Literature

After you have stated the research problem, you must learn first what people already know about it. Maybe some other researchers have already solved it or

3

tried to solve it. Maybe some hints for solving the problem have been given by the research community. If your problem requires a hypothesis, maybe you will find some clues and hints in the research conducted before you. You have to choose methods for solving the problem among the variety of methods that may be suitable for it. It would be helpful to analyze the approaches other researchers have already tried to use in the past to find out, which of them had been successful. You need to become familiar with the results of other research projects and results related to your research. The bottom line is that you should learn the relevant part of the pyramid of knowledge collected by the research community before you've joined in to solving the problem. That may help you to find the best research path, avoid duplicative efforts, and avoid many possible mistakes in your research. All this you can get from reviewing the related literature.

To do a comprehensive literature review, you have to select the appropriate papers, reports, books, and other sources that contain the relevant information. Such a list is called a ***bibliography***. In the preparation phase of your research, you are likely to miss some sources which you will add later. For this reason, the bibliography at this phase of research is called the ***preliminary bibliography***. Additional sources may be added to this list as your research progresses.

A detailed description of literature review is presented in ▸ Chap. 5 of this book.

3.2.5 Define the Major Terms Used in the Research

Lack of accurate definition of the major terms is a common source of confusion when people start discussing things. Different people may understand the same term differently, and that leads to mutual misunderstanding and results in confusion, disappointment, wrong interpretations, and a significant waste of time. For this reason, you need to define the major terms before you start using them. Such a seemingly trivial step will help you save a lot of time and effort and avoid misunderstandings among the research team and with other researchers and your audience.

For example, if we discuss recession in our research without clearly defining what the term ***recession*** means, we may get conflicting conclusions because the term ***recession*** has several different definitions in economics. The traditional definition of a recession is a decline in gross domestic product (GDP) for two or more successive quarters.[1] However, the National Bureau of Economic Research (NBER) has introduced another definition of ***recession*** that is frequently used by economists. According to the NBER, "a recession is a significant decline in economic activity spread across the economy, lasting more than a few months, normally visible in real GDP, real income, employment, industrial production, and wholesale-retail sales."[2] Though the traditional definition of *recession* is clear and

1 Shiskin, Julius (1 December 1974). "The Changing Business Cycle". The New York Times
2 ▸ http://www.nber.org/cycles/recessions.html

measurable while NBER's definition is fuzzy and open to speculation, both definitions can be used by economists, particularly now. It is crystal clear that if you want to avoid controversy in your analysis and conclusions, you must indicate what definition of *recession* is going to be used in your research.

3.2.6 Formulate Key Hypotheses and Models if Needed

At this stage of a research project, the researcher has clearly formulated the research problem and purpose and reviewed the related literature. The researcher is now ready to formulate a hypothesis or hypotheses needed to guide the research as well as the models that are going to be used, if models are appropriate.

Definitely, as the research progresses, the researcher may modify the hypotheses and models based on the results being discovered.

3.2.7 Develop the Research Design

Whatever we do must be planned to ensure high efficiency and good results. Research is no exception. If a research project is planned thoroughly, the project goes more smoothly, stays focused, consumes fewer resources, takes less time to complete, and delivers better results. A plan for a research project is referred to as a ***research design*** and consists of the following activities:

- Formulate hypotheses and models if needed.
- Identify the data collection plan.
- Identify the methods and procedures to be used in the research.
- Identify the resources and skills needed for the research.
- Plan the project schedule and budget if required.

> The ***research design*** should answer the question "How?" – how are you going to do this particular research?

Thus, the research purpose, the research problem, and the research design are the steps in the preparation-for-research phase that answer three very important questions summarized in ◘ Table 3.1.

In the following paragraphs, we briefly discuss the activities involved in research design, but we give a detailed description of the activities in this step in ► Chap. 6 of this book.

Formulate Hypotheses and Models if Needed

Formulation of the models and the hypotheses used in the research is a fundamental part of planning the research. A correctly defined model defines the major principles and constraints used in the research, while the hypotheses address the major explanatory perspectives of the research project.

Table 3.1 Questions to be answered in preparation for research

Step in phase I	Question	Description of the question
Research problem	*What* to research?	What is the question to be answered in the research?
Research purpose	*Why* do it?	Why is the research needed? Who might be interested in it, and who is going to use the results of the research?
Research design	*How* to do it?	How is the researcher going to find the answer to the question asked in the research problem statement?

Any analysis conducted without formulating an appropriate model cannot be focused enough to produced viable results. Not every research project needs hypotheses, but if they are needed, it is the right time to formulate them.

Identify the Data Collection Plan

Good, reliable, and accurate data are essential for the research success. If data is unreliable or inaccurate, the research results might be critically compromised. "GIGO – Garbage In, Garbage Out" is a well-known and popular slogan. For this reason, researchers must pay very serious attention to the quality of data.

The data collection plan should include the data sources and methods of collecting the data that will ensure that the data sources are reliable and the available data is accurate.

The collected data should be organized and structured to be convenient and suitable for the further processing and analysis. Even very good data may have little or no value if it is not well organized, particularly if the volume of data is huge, as it normally is in the modern research projects.

Identify the Methods and Procedures to Be Used in the Research

It is important to identify and prepare the methods and processes to be used for data collection, organization, processing, and analysis as well as the methods and processes for hypothesis verification and model analysis.

Some theoretical research is dedicated to methods and process development, so it is difficult to identify all details in the research design for such research. However, for the other kinds of research, particularly for applied research, it is important to identify the methods and procedures in advance in the research preparation phase. This makes your research planning more consistent, and you will not face an unexpected lack of methods or procedures when you move to the actual research phase.

You do not need to have real data available at the research design step for preparing methods and procedures for your research; you can do it using even made-up data structurally resembling the real data which you plan and expect to collect in your research.

Identify the Resources and Skills Needed for the Research

It would be quite embarrassing for the researcher and destructive for the project to find out in the middle of the project that the researcher does not have enough resources or lacks some critical knowledge or skills to complete the project. For this reason, it is strongly advised to conduct such analysis in advance on the research design step.

Identify the Schedule and Budget if Required

No project can be conducted endlessly and on an unlimited budget. Research projects have time and budget constraints too. These constraints must be identified in the research design step to be presented for approval.

Some student research projects, particularly graduate student research projects, may need no budget because they are conducted for free. However, all projects, including graduate student projects, have time constraints which should be clearly identified in the research design stage.

3.2.8 Define the Research Objectives and the Expected Results

To understand the degree of completeness of a project, one has to define the expected measurable types of results of the project. Such types of results are referred to as ***project objectives***. Clearly defined research objectives provide an objective measure of the research status. As soon as the objectives are defined, the progress of the research project gets boundaries and can be measured and tracked.

There is no way to predict the actual results of any research; if that was possible, such research would be meaningless. However, the researcher must clearly identify the types of results expected to be obtained in the research. For example, in competitive analysis research, nobody can predict the actual results, but the researchers must be able to describe what type of results they would expect to obtain. Say, we expect to build a chart that compares side-by-side properties of the products from our company and from other main competitors. The research objectives provide a clear picture of the kind of outcome expected from the research and how well such results would meet the research goal and answer the question in the research problem. Once again, the expected results are not the actual results but rather the types of results or a framework of the results.

Clearly formulating the research objectives will also help in the future with the acceptance of the research completeness by eliminating possible discussion on the expected results.

3.2.9 Write and Submit the Research Proposal for Approval

As the preparation for research is completed, a research proposal has to be written and submitted to the authorities or sponsors for approval. They may return the research proposal with some questions, comments, and recommendations. In this case, the proposal must be revised and resubmitted.

Upon approval of the research proposal, the researcher or the research team can jump into conducting the actual research. We will discuss the content of research proposals in a greater detail in ► Chap. 7 of this book.

3.2.10 Discussion, Negotiation, and Approval of the Research Proposal

The final step of the preparation for research phase is the final approval of the research proposal. However, the research proposal may not be suitable to the goal, objectives, and available resources of the approving body. Thus, you may negotiate the details of the research proposal with the approving body to settle and adjust the disagreement and converge on the reasonable arrangements.

3.3 Phase II: Conducting Research

At this moment, we presume that all reasonable preparations for research are made, the research proposal is approved, and "a green light" is given to the research. The researcher or the research team now is ready to move to the next phase of the research project, Phase II: Conducting Research. This phase of the research project is dedicated to actual research and comprises the following steps:

- Finalize the models and hypotheses for the research if needed.
- Finalize the data collection plan and collect data.
- Organize and process the data, using the models if appropriate.
- Analyze and interpret the data and verify the hypotheses if any.
- Summarize the research findings and interpret the results.
- Derive conclusions.
- Make predictions and recommendations if appropriate.

The research process may significantly vary subject to the problem and research design. However, the steps mentioned above constitute a framework for conducting the research phase.

3.3.1 Finalize the Models and Hypotheses for the Research if Needed

Most research need and use models for data processing, analysis, and interpretation as well as for theoretical analysis of facts, events, relationships, processes, and phenomena. Some research also need hypotheses to explain facts, events, relationships, processes, and phenomena. All models and hypotheses are supposed to be defined in Phase I: Preparation for Research, as it was discussed earlier in this chapter. Though the first round of defining the models and hypotheses was undertaken in the preparation-for-research phase, now is the time to finalize the models and hypotheses by reviewing them from the perspective of the better understanding and the new information received since the first round. Some models and hypotheses need more detailed analysis and development to be used in the research.

3.3.2 Finalize the Data Collection Plan and Collect Data

Good data is key for most research. Though the data collection plan should be developed at the research design step during the preparation for the research, a review of the plan is advisable at this step to make sure that the plan reflects the most recent understanding and status of the data sources and data acquisition methods. It is time now to finalize the plan to a very specific, detailed level by reviewing the sources and methods of data acquisition.

The quality of the data has a crucial impact on the quality of the entire research project. Accurate and reliable data acquired from reliable sources and obtained with accurate methods will provide solid support for the research findings and conclusions. On the other hand, inaccurate and unreliable data will compromise research findings and conclusions and hence the credibility of the research.

3.3.3 Organize and Process the Data, Using the Models if Appropriate

To be properly used, data collected in the course of research should be systematically structured and organized to reflect the data types, data semantics, and relationship between different data types. The data structures should also be convenient for further processing. Examples of structures for organizing data include data records, tables, graphs, charts, spreadsheets, and databases. The data can be stored in the form of paper records, which are rapidly going out of style, or in the form of computer files matching the appropriate data structures, which practically all researchers use in the modern research.

Researchers acquire data in research to verify hypotheses, to explain or predict a certain behavior, and to make decisions, among other purposes. To serve these purposes, the acquired data may be used as input for further processing, jointly or separately, to transform it into other forms more suitable for the research purpose. The models, hypotheses, methods, and procedures developed in the research design step and finalized in the early step of the conducting-research phase should be used as a framework for data processing during the research.

3.3.4 Analyze and Interpret the Data and Verify the Hypotheses If Any

As the data obtained in the research is processed, it must be analyzed and interpreted to figure out what it really means. The data must tell a story about the

3

research subject by providing information that helps the researcher to find the answer to the research problem. It is important to keep in mind that data itself is just the material basis that researchers use to discover new facts and make their conclusions about the research problem; the data is not the ultimate goal of research.

Collected and processed data is also used for hypothesis verification, if any hypothesis was formulated in the research. At this step of the research process, all data are supposed to be ready, so it is the right time to verify the hypotheses formulated in the research.

We will discuss measurements and data collection in a greater detail in ► Chap. 19 of this book.

3.3.5 Summarize the Research Findings and Interpret the Results

Now, the research process is at the point where all data are processed and interpreted and the hypotheses are accepted or rejected based on the results of verification. Now is the time to summarize all the findings of the research by putting them together. The most important part of this task is interpretation of the results. It includes building a "big picture" of the results, analyzing them from different perspectives, and understanding what story the results are telling about the subject of the research.

3.3.6 Derive Conclusions

Deriving conclusions is the climax of any research. Conclusions are the answers to the questions stated in the research problem. This is the ultimate goal of research. Conclusions must be logically derived from the research findings, summarized from the answers to the questions in the subproblems, and logically combined into the answers to the main question or questions in the research problem.

Conclusions should address all questions in the research problem and its related subproblems, leaving no questions without answers. Answers might be positive or negative, and both bring value. Without conclusions, any research is incomplete.

> ***Conclusions*** are the answers to the questions stated in the research problem. Without conclusions, research is incomplete.

It is also a good practice to mention the research problems or directions that may appear as a result of current research and that should be addressed in future research projects.

We will discuss how to derive conclusions in greater detail in ► Chap. 20 of this book.

3.3.7 Make Recommendations and Predictions if Appropriate

Finding answers to the questions is the goal of research, and some research questions aim at predictions for the future. For example, "What revenue could company XYZ expect in the next quarter?" The answer to that question is a prediction and should be covered in the research conclusions. However, some research may provide predictions even if such questions were not asked in the research problem. It is a very powerful outcome if the research results lead to predictions in addition to answering the questions asked in the research problem.

Research results may lead to practical recommendations in applied research, including business research. Practical recommendations, if they arise from the research results, bring additional value to the research.

Thus, research brings even greater value if predictions or practical recommendations can be derived from the research results. We will discuss predictions and recommendation in a greater detail in ▶ Chap. 20 of this book.

3.4 Phase III: Delivery of the Results

Now, the research conclusions have been derived, and predictions and recommendations have been made, if appropriate. Is the research complete at this point? Definitely not yet. The research results still need to be delivered to the research community or to the people or organizations for which the research was conducted. If the research results are not delivered, the research effort might be wasted because nobody will know about its results. If the results are not reported, the research will contribute neither to the common store of knowledge nor to the target people or organizations that can use those results. For this reason, the delivery of research results is a very important phase of any research project. It is the same with any other human activity. For example, if you composed a wonderful piece of music but never published or played it, the music would be wasted because nobody could enjoy it.

Only upon completion of the delivery phase can the research project be considered completed. Delivery of the research results can be done in many forms, including a research report, a research paper, a book, or a presentation.

3.4.1 Write the Research Report

Writing a research report is a common way to deliver research results. The size of report, the level of detail, the style, and the formatting depend significantly on the requirements of the organization to which the report is going to be submitted.

Publication is another form of research results delivery. It includes publishing a research paper or papers in journals, magazines, and newspapers or writing a book. The form of publication depends on the value which the research brings to the pool of knowledge, the requirements for the research project, the inclinations of the researchers who conducted the research, and many other factors. The format and size of such publication also depend on a variety of factors.

The bottom line is consider publishing your research results if they provide sufficient value, but please do not plan a publication if you have nothing to say. Contribute new knowledge to the pool of knowledge, but please refrain from contributing to "information overload" and "information noise," which level is growing too high nowadays.

We will discuss writing a research report and making publications in a greater detail in ► Chap. 22 of this book.

3.4.2 Develop and Make Presentations

Presentations at seminars, conferences, and other public or private meetings as well as project defenses, including thesis defenses, are a very powerful form of delivery of research results. In contrast to reports and publications, which are one-way communication channels, that is, without any real-time feedback from the readers, presentations establish two-way communication and allow the presenter and the audience to discuss the research in real time. Such two-way communication provides both parties with better opportunities to discuss things and address related issues which were not addressed in the presentation. On the other hand, presentations have time limits and require a more compressed delivery than can be done in some publications. For this reason, oral research presentations are quite different in structure and format from research publications. We will discuss the issue of developing and making research presentations in greater detail in ► Chap. 23 of this book.

3.4.3 Defending the Project

Some projects assume a defense procedure before the research project is considered complete. This includes thesis defense for students. Before defending a research project, the researcher submits a research report to the appropriate body responsible for the project's acceptance. The report must be submitted in advance of the defense to give the members of the acceptance body an opportunity for getting familiar with the research. The defense procedures in different organizations can vary significantly. However, a typical project defense consists of presentation, questions and answers, and comments.

In ► Chap. 23, we will discuss the thesis defense procedure in a greater detail, using the example of a student thesis defense.

3.5 Summary of the Research Process

The research process for different types of research projects may vary significantly. The higher-level and more complex projects may have more detailed and more complex structures and processes than the smaller and simpler projects. However, there is a typical framework that most research projects follow to a certain degree. This chapter has presented and discussed a typical research process. The phases and steps in the typical research project are summarized in ► Box 3.1.

Box 3.1 Typical Research Process

Phase I: Preparation for Research

- Select a research field related to your interest and expertise.
- Formulate the research problem:
  - Ask the major question(s), to which you want to find answer(s) in your research.
  - Break the research question(s) (problem) into smaller subquestions (subproblems).
  - Evaluate the problem and define the project's scope and limitations.
- Formulate the research purpose.
- Build a preliminary bibliography and review the literature.
- Define the major terms used in the research.
- Develop the research design:
  - Formulate hypotheses and models if needed.
  - Identify the data collection plan.
  - Identify the methods and procedures to be used in the research.
  - Identify the resources and skills needed for the research.
  - Plan the project schedule and budget if required.
- Define the research objectives.
- Write and submit the research proposal for approval.
- Discuss and negotiate the research proposal with the approval body and obtain the approval.

Phase II: Conducting Research

- Finalize the models and hypotheses for the research if needed.
- Finalize the data collection plan and collect data.
- Organize and process the data, using the models if appropriate.
- Analyze and interpret the data and verify the hypotheses if any.
- Summarize the research findings and interpret the results.
- Derive conclusions.
- Make recommendations and predictions if appropriate.

Phase III: Delivery of the Research Results

- Write the research report.
- Write about the research for publication.
- Develop and make presentations.
- Defend the project.

3.6 Major Reasons for Possible Research Failures

To make a research project successful takes serious efforts. Even minor errors may result in the failure of a project that initially looked very promising. In the following subsections, we list and explain some of the most important and most typical reasons for research failures.

3.6.1 Ambiguous or Unclear Problem Statement

A clearly formulated and focused problem statement is key for successful research. Any fuzziness or ambiguity in the problem statement can lead to deviation of the research focus and may easily result in research failure. Time spent on the development of a clearly formulated problem statement pays off with more efficient and focused research, prevents the research from going in a wrong direction, and makes research failure much less likely.

3.6.2 Unclear Scope and Limitations

The research scope and limitations set clear boundaries for the research project. Such boundaries prevent failure of the research efforts and focus the research on the research goal. Unclear boundaries can easily sidetrack research and lead to failure.

3.6.3 Unclearly Formulated Hypotheses

Models and hypotheses, if they are present, play central role in the research. Clearly formulated models and hypotheses help researchers to stay on track. On the contrary, unclearly or ambiguously formulated models and hypotheses sidetrack research and may even lead to wrong results.

3.6.4 Controversial and Conflicting Terms Used in the Research

Many researchers, particularly young ones, do not pay serious attention to accurate definition of terms, regarding that as a secondary issue. However, some terms are ambiguous, and sometimes, the same term may mean different things in different contexts. For example, the term volatility in the securities market means "a statistical measure of the dispersion of returns for a given security or market index."[3] However, volatility can be calculated in other ways. For example, to calculate volatility, "typically, log returns are used, where log denotes a natural loga-

3 *Investopedia,* s.v. "Volatility," ► http://www.investopedia.com/terms/v/volatility.asp

rithm. However, simple returns are sometimes used."[4] Thus, if we used that term ***volatility*** in our research without clearly defining it, we might get into a controversy trap and come up with the wrong results.

3.6.5 Wrong Methods and Procedures Used in the Research

The choice of methods and procedures used in research plays a critical role for research success. All methods and procedures must be carefully selected based on their adequacy and accuracy. Wrongly chosen, even good methods and procedures can easily lead to wrong results and in research failure.

3.6.6 Inaccurate or Unreliable Data

Data collection from reliable sources and with adequate accuracy dramatically impacts the research quality. Inaccurate or unreliable data may compromise the research regardless of how good all other steps in the research are.

3.6.7 Unclear or Inconsistent Conclusions

Deriving good conclusions is a critical task in any research. The step of deriving conclusions must be performed with extreme care because this is exactly what concludes the research. Careless work on the research conclusions can easily compromise the entire research project and diminish its value.

Questions for Self-Review for Chap. 3

1. What are the major phases of a research project?
2. What steps have to be done in the preparation-for-research phase?
3. Why is preparation for research important?
4. What does *research purpose* mean?
5. Why is it important to clearly formulate the research purpose?
6. How is a research problem formulated?
7. What is included in the research problem formulation step?
8. How does breaking down the main research problem into subproblems help in the research?
9. What does scope and limitations of the research problem mean?
10. How does a review of literature help in doing research?
11. Why is a definition of terms important for a research project?
12. When should major hypotheses and models be developed?
13. Why is research design needed?
14. What tasks are included in the research design step?

4 ► *riskglossary.com,* s.v. "Volatility," ► http://www.riskglossary.com/link/volatility.htm

15. Why is a data collection plan important?
16. What does the term *expected results* mean?
17. What purpose does a research proposal serve?
18. What do data analysis and data interpretation mean?
19. What role do research conclusions play in research?
20. Do all research projects lead to predictions and recommendations?
21. Why is the delivery phase needed in the research process?
22. In what ways can researchers deliver research results?
23. What is the difference between research publication and presentation?
24. What is research project defense?
25. What are the major reasons for research project failure?

Preparation for Research

Contents

Chapter 4 Formulating a Research Problem – 73

Chapter 5 Review of Literature – 85

Chapter 6 Research Design – 97

Chapter 7 Research Proposal – 109

Formulating a Research Problem

Contents

4.1 Research Starts with a Question – 75

4.2 Research Purpose – 75

4.3 First Ask a Question to Start Formulating a Research Problem – 75

4.4 Correctly Ask Research Questions – 77
4.4.1 Try to Avoid Questions That Allow for Just "Yes" or "No" Answer – 77
4.4.2 Phrase Questions to Deal with Cause-and-Effect Relationship – 77
4.4.3 Avoid Phrasing Value Judgment Types of Questions – 78

4.5 Factoring the Research Problem – 79
4.5.1 Subproblems – 79
4.5.2 Scope and Limitations – 80

4.6 Evaluating the Research Problem – 81
4.6.1 Scholarly Acceptability – 81
4.6.2 Depth and Complexity – 82
4.6.3 Researchability – 82
4.6.4 Researcher Accountability – 83

S. K. Aityan, *Business Research Methodology*, Classroom Companion: Business,
https://doi.org/10.1007/978-3-030-76857-7_4

4.7 Difficulties in Selecting a Research Problem – 83
4.7.1 Difficulties – 83
4.7.2 Major Advices – 83

4.1 Research Starts with a Question

Any research starts with a question, the answer to which is unknown or unavailable. The research is completed when the answer is found. Carefully selecting and developing the research problem and then clearly and accurately stating it are critical steps in the research process. These steps should include selecting a manageable portion of the research area or topic for study. Clearly, accurately, and unambiguously stated research problem is easier to solve. One can say "a problem well put is a problem half solved."

Formulating a research problem is a challenging and very important task, sometimes quite difficult. An accurately and correctly formulated problem (research question) may significantly help in finding the solution (answer to the research question). On the other hand, the problem vagueness may lead to the collection of much useless data that do not contribute to the answer to the problem. This quality of the problem statement is critical.

4.2 Research Purpose

As we have discussed in the previous chapters, researchers should clearly formulate the purpose of the research. Particularly, it is important for the applied research. The research purpose should state the following:

- Practical purpose of the research.
- Who will or may be interested and benefit from the results of the research project.

This step is interchangeable with the step of formulating the research problem. Sometimes, the research problem comes from the research purpose, but sometimes, the research purpose follows the research problem statement.

4.3 First Ask a Question to Start Formulating a Research Problem

To formulate a research problem, start asking questions about the subject. To do so, one may start thinking in terms of "I wonder …?"

Below are some examples of research questions.

▶ Examples of Research Questions

- I wonder whether the economy needs so much oil as it consumes now?
- I wonder whether the stock market is predictable?
- I wonder what guidelines are needed for management to design and develop an efficient management information system?

- I wonder what the current effects of the legal environment are on the global economy?
- I wonder how the alternative energy sources would impact on the development of public transportation?
- I wonder how feasible and difficult it is to establish a new coffee shop in my city of residence?

The question phrasing with word "I wonder" is give just for illustration. Please feel free to use any other wording.

The research question should be clearly and accurately phrased in the problem statement. The research question may be paraphrased into the form of an affirmative sentence in the problem statement or just left as is in the form of a question. Both ways are good. All depends on your taste as long as the semantics of the research question stays the same.

Below are examples of research questions listed above and converted into affirmative statements. ◀

▶ Examples of Research Questions Converted into Affirmative Statements

- We will analyze the oil consumption and oil demand in the modern economy.
- This research will study the issues related to the stock market predictability.
- Our major goal is to study the impact of guidelines for management on the design and development of an efficient management information system.
- We are interested in the current effects of the legal environment on the global economy.
- We focus on the implications of alternative energy sources on the development of public transportation.
- The goal of this study is feasibility and difficulties of establishing a new coffee shop in my city of residence.

Most of the time, research problem formulation is an iterative process. It is recommended to formulate the research problem and leave it for some time to settle in your mind. It may be for a day or two or may be for a longer time. All depends on the circumstances. Then, come back and review the research problem. You will definitely find a way for improvement. Make the appropriate corrections to the research question, and leave it again for some time. Continue with such iterations until you are satisfied with the research problem formulation. ◀

- Any research starts with a question, the answer to which is unknown or unavailable.
- The research is completed when the answer is found.

One can say "a problem well put is a problem half solved."

4.4 Correctly Ask Research Questions

There are several common sense rules for formulating research questions:

- Avoid questions that allow for just "Yes" or "No" answer.
- Phrase questions to deal with cause-and-effect relationship.
- Avoid phrasing value judgment types of questions.

The abovementioned rules are very helpful for the development of a good research problem.

4.4.1 Try to Avoid Questions That Allow for Just "Yes" or "No" Answer

Phrase the question in a form that will elicit more than a mere "yes" or "no" answer. Questions that allow for a simple "yes" or "no" answers may not lead to a detailed and deep analysis of the problem to reveal the internal structures and relationships in the field of study. The following examples illustrate the issue.

▶ Example 1

Incorrect – allows for "yes" or "no" answer:

"Do published financial statements provide relevant and adequate information to meet the needs of present and future stockholders?"

(*** A simple "yes" or "no" may lead to answering this question without a deep analysis of the problem. ***)

Correct:

"To what extent do published financial statements provide relevant and adequate information to meet the needs of present and future stockholders?" ◀

▶ Example 2

Incorrect – allows for "yes" or "no" answer:

"Can the behavior of the stock market be predicted?"

(*** A simple "yes" or "no" would answer this question without a deep analysis of the problem. ***)

Correct:

"What are the issues and problems in predicting the behavior of the stock market?"

It is evident from the examples above that the correctly asked questions, not allowing for a simple "yes" or "no" answers, lead to a more detailed and comprehensive answers. ◀

4.4.2 Phrase Questions to Deal with Cause-and-Effect Relationship

If possible, phrase the question in analytic form, one that deals with cause-and-effect relationship. It is an if-then approach. Such phrasing forces precision and furnishes a better basis for generalization in analysis.

► Example 1

Incorrect – does not require to find cause-and-effect relationship:

"What effect does digital marketing have?"

(*** Such a question leaves uncertainty on what we actually are looking for. ***)

Correct:

"What effect does digital marketing have on the sales growth?"

Also correct:

"How does digital marketing impacts on the buyers buying decisions?" ◄

► Example 2

Incorrect – does not require to find cause-and-effect relationship:

"How important is employee loyalty?"

(*** Such a question does not imply any analysis of any relationship. ***)

Correct:

"How important is employee loyalty for the company success?"

Also correct:

"What are the implications of high level of employee loyalty for the competitive power of the company?"

The examples above clearly show the weakness of questions with the cause-and-effect uncertainty. ◄

4.4.3 Avoid Phrasing Value Judgment Types of Questions

Avoid phrasing value judgment types of questions. Such questions aren't researchable – they have no answer. Research should provide comprehensive and objective analysis of the problem and provide conclusions and possible options. Value judgment is purely subjective and does not belong to research. Let's do research and leave value judgments to individuals, community, management, courts, and politicians.

Especially, value judgment is an estimate of the goodness or worth of a person, action, or event. A judgment is an expression of a person's approval or disapproval of something. A frailty of such a question is that researcher tends to ignore negative data – data that do not support the desired answer. Value judgment questions are usually prefaced with "should … ?"

► Example 1

Incorrect – a subjective judgment "should" or "should not":

"Should the federal government adopt a comprehensive program to control global warming?"

Correct:

"What are the implications and the current thoughts on the federal government adoption of a program to control global warming?" ◄

► Example 2

Incorrect – a subjective judgment "should" or "should not":

"Should nuclear energy be banned?"
"Should advertising be banned from children's television programs?"
"Should abortion be legalized?"
"Do managers need a code of ethics?"
"Should nudity be used in commercial advertising?"

Correct:

"What could be implications of banning nuclear energy?"
"What are the implications of advertising on children's television programs on children psychology?"
"What could be implications from legalization of abortion?"
"How would a formal code of ethics help managers?"
"What implication does nudity in commercial advertising have on the community?"

Answers to the value judgment questions will result in position papers rather than credible research. On the other hand, the correctly phrased questions will lead to a comprehensive research. ◄

- Avoid questions that allow for just "Yes" or "No" answer.
- Phrase questions to deal with cause-and-effect relationship.
- Avoid phrasing value judgment types of questions.

4.5 Factoring the Research Problem

A research problem may be too big to solve as one problem. Such a problem should be divided into smaller subproblems, which can be solved separately, one by one. The original problem then can be solved by combining the solutions to those smaller problems, similarly as we cannot eat a watermelon without slicing it into smaller pieces.

Factoring is a process of division and addition. Factoring a research problem involves the following:

- Identifying and formulating subproblems
- Setting up the scope and limitation to the research problem

4.5.1 Subproblems

Let's first identify subproblems (subquestions) that stem from the overall main problem (question). The subproblems (subquestions), when answered, provide the framework for the answer to the overall original problem. A logical link should be provided for the subproblems to help deriving the overall answer to the main research problem by linking the answers to the subproblems.

This activity consists of the following:

- Break the research problem into smaller subproblems in such a way that the answers to all subproblems would provide the framework for the answer to the main research problem.
- Prioritize the subproblems by their importance for the solution of the main problem.
- Define a logical process of how to build the answer to the main research question (main problem) from the answers to the subquestions (subproblems).

4.5.2 Scope and Limitations

Sometimes, the research problem is crisp and clear, but there are too many variations depending on the time period, region, or some other parameters. Setting up the scope and limitations to the research problem helps to set up the boundary and confine the main problem. The scope defines the boundaries of the research and identifies the size of the problem. Limitations, typically, reduce the size of the problem by focusing the problem on a certain period of time, certain region, or on some other parameters.

Thus,

- The scope sets up the boundaries of the research.
- The limitations confine the research.

By setting a scope of the problem, you can reduce the complexity of the problem and size the problem down to become realistic and doable.

If necessary, one can generally limit the problem in terms of the following:

- Time
- Place (geographic)
- Types (characteristics, factors, criteria, variables)
- Quantities
- Combination of the foregoing

The following examples illustrate how setting scope and limitations draws clear boundaries and confines the problem.

▶ Example 1 of a Scope

The research problem is "What is the correlation between the American and Asia Pacific Stock Markets?"

The scope of the problem could be "the correlations between the US stock indices such as Dow Jones and Nasdaq and the Japanese N225." ◀

▶ Example 2 of a Scope

The research problem is "The impact of additional unemployment benefits on the economic recovery from the pandemic of 2020."

The scope of the problem could be "in the hospitality industry." ◀

▶ Example 1 of Limitation

The problem: "What is the correlation between the American and Asia Pacific Stock Markets?"

Limitation: The research will be limited for years between 2000 and 2020. ◀

Other Examples of Limitation

- "Strategy of automotive market in Northern America." (limitation – Northern America)
- "The impact of migration of low-skilled labor force in Eastern Europe caused by globalization." (limitation – Eastern Europe)
- "Challenges in marketing of high-volume goods." (limitation – quantities: high-volume goods)

> - The scope sets up the boundaries of the research.
> - The limitations confine the research.

4.6 Evaluating the Research Problem

Every research problem needs to be evaluated to make sure that it meets the research quality requirements. The following criteria will help you to evaluate the quality of your research problem by:

- Scholarly acceptability
- Depth and complexity
- Researchability
- Researcher accountability

4.6.1 Scholarly Acceptability

To meet the criteria of scholarly acceptability, the research problem should be:

- Original to the extent that it will make a reasonable contribution to knowledge
- Concrete and explicit
- The next logical problem in the field to answer
- Of interest to the scholars and practitioners in the field

4.6.2 Depth and Complexity

The problem should be not trivial and has sufficient depth and level of complexity. The problem:

- Must be focused and narrow enough to solve it, but not too narrow as to be trivial or insignificant
- May be expandable into other fields
- Will answer a practical and immediate need when solved
- Expresses a relationship between two or more variables
- Provides a basis for analysis, not mere fact grubbing (!!!)

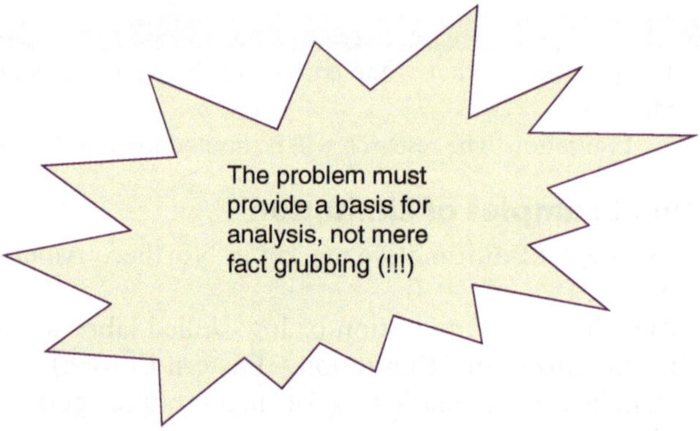

Variables and Complexity

Analytical questions involve variables, and as the number of variables increases, so does the complexity of the problem as shown in ◘ Fig. 4.1.

4.6.3 Researchability

The problem should be one of the following:

- Adequate data are available; cooperation can be obtained from those people who must participate.
- Adequate techniques or instruments or both are available.

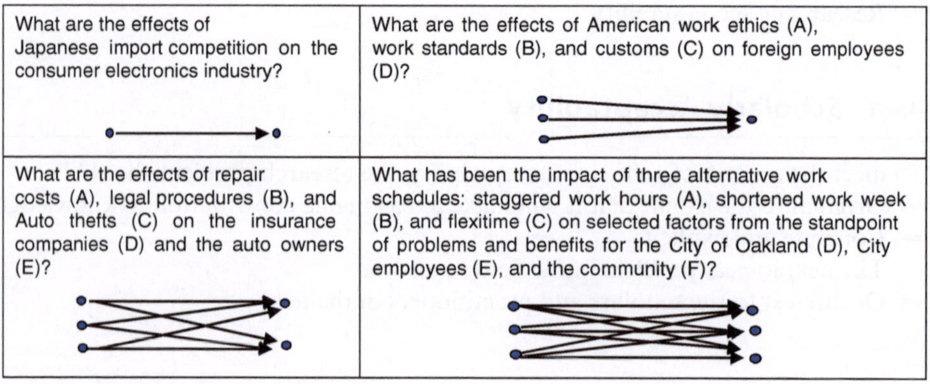

◘ **Fig. 4.1** Illustration of the complexity of a problem in terms of the number of variables and their relationship

- Data can be treated objectively, not dependent only upon value judgments.
- Research will not be too costly in time or money.
- The possibility of empirical testing is present.

4.6.4 Researcher Accountability

For the researcher, the problem:
- Is one for which the researcher has the required skills or can obtain them
- Is one in which the researcher has a personal interest
- Is closely related to the researcher's field of concentration
- Will provide experience to stimulate the researcher's intellectual growth

The following criteria will help in evaluating the quality of your research problem by:
- Scholarly acceptability
- Depth and complexity
- Researchability
- Researcher accountability

4.7 Difficulties in Selecting a Research Problem

4.7.1 Difficulties

Beginners in research often have difficulty selecting a research problem because of their lack of familiarity in a field and what has been accomplished in it.

A researcher may fail to identify a problem accurately because of the following:
- It is typical for young researcher to formulate a much broader problem than he or she can solve.
- The researcher does not perceive the problem or does not define it correctly. This dilemma stems from a problem too complex for comprehension, a closed mind, or a lack of experience in the area.
- The researcher sees the wrong problem or wrong causes or both. The situation may be a mix of several problems interwoven; the situation may be a symptom of a more complex problem, or a wrong inference may be made.
- The researcher may think that doing something is better than doing nothing; the problem identification phase is ignored.

4.7.2 Major Advices

Major advice to the researchers is work on the problem statement until the following:
- Problem and its purpose are clearly and unambiguously formulated.
- Problem is sufficiently narrowed down and focused to become solvable.
- The researcher has clear vision about data availability for the applied research.

Among other advices to the researchers are the following:
- Be a thinker.
- Keep your mind open.
- Think systemically.
- Think multidisciplinary.

4

Major advice to the researchers is work on the problem statement until the following:
- Problem and its purpose are clearly and unambiguously formulated.
- Problem is sufficiently narrowed down and focused to become solvable.
- The researcher has clear vision about data availability for the applied research.

Questions for Self-Control for ▶ Chap. 4

In all answers, provide definitions, elaborate on the concept, and provide examples. Feel free to make up the entire example and all data for your examples:

1. How to formulate a research problem?
2. Should a research problem always be expressed as a question?
3. What is research purpose?
4. What phrasing of research questions is better to avoid and why?
5. Why is it better to avoid research questions, which allow simple answers "yes" or "no"?
6. Why not to ask value judgment questions?
7. How important is it to address cause-and-effect relationship in the research question?
8. What is the scope and limitations?
9. Why are scope and limitations needed in research?
10. What are subproblems and why are they needed?
11. What logical relationship should subproblems have?
12. What is research depth and complexity?
13. How complex a research problem should be?
14. How to analyze researchability of the problem?

Practical Assignments for Chap. 4

1. Ask yourself a question and formulate a research problem of your interest. Work on the research problem until it becomes narrow and focused enough for one researcher or for a small team of researchers. Keep in mind data availability for the research problem.
2. Develop subproblems for the problem formulated in the previous assignment. Track the logical way how you will find the answer to the main research question form the answers to the subquestions.
3. Formulate the scope and limitations for the research problem formulated in the previous assignment.

Review of Literature

Contents

5.1 Continuity of Knowledge – 86

5.2 Value of Literature Review – 86

5.3 Sources of Information – 87
5.3.1 Primary and Secondary Sources – 87
5.3.2 Evaluating the Quality of Secondary Sources – 87

5.4 How to Review Literature – 88
5.4.1 The Sense of Review of Literature – 88
5.4.2 How to Write a Review of Literature – 88

5.5 Basic Terminology – 89
5.5.1 Bibliography vs. Index – 89
5.5.2 Outline vs. Table of Contents vs. Presentation Time Table – 90
5.5.3 Journal vs. Magazine – 91

5.6 List of Bibliography – 91

5.7 References, Citations, and Quotations – 92
5.7.1 Citations – 92
5.7.2 Quotations – 94

5.8 Footnotes and Endnotes – 94
5.8.1 Footnotes – 94
5.8.2 Endnotes – 95

S. K. Aityan, *Business Research Methodology*, Classroom Companion: Business,
https://doi.org/10.1007/978-3-030-76857-7_5

5.1 Continuity of Knowledge

Knowledge has been accumulated throughout a long time for thousands of years piece by piece adding up on the top of "pyramid of knowledge." Every new discovery and every new big and even small research result have been adding up a piece of new knowledge on the top of the existing knowledge pool. Every research we do is based on the previously existing knowledge and represents a continuity of the knowledge accumulation process.

Thus, it is very important to be aware of the preceding research results, which have been obtained in the area of your research interests, to provide such continuity and conduct a scholarly good, viable, and valuable research.

5.2 Value of Literature Review

It is very likely that someone else has already worked in the same area as you and, perhaps, what they have done was so close to what you plan to undertake that it is important to take it into account to avoid duplication of efforts and to learn the positive and negative experiences in that research domain. Literature review helps researchers to learn the accumulated experience and methodologies and get some hints for your efforts to make the next step in the research in this particular area of knowledge. Literature review also helps avoid the dead-end directions in research that someone else has already took. You must review literature before starting your own research to understand how your research will contribute to the knowledge pool in your research area. From literature, you may learn about specific methods successfully used in similar research project and possibly about the methods that failed in similar research.

Thus, literature review:

- Helps prevent a duplication of efforts
- Serves to orient readers on the status of the problem
- Delineates available information, books and articles related to the problem
- Relates significant opinions or perspectives about the problem area
- Develops a rationale and the significance of the research that indicates:
  - The need for additional research
  - The areas of conflict or areas of agreement or both
  - The bases for challenging accepted ideas or views
- Contributes to the research design
- Furnishes evaluative techniques or criteria
- Points out findings that will support or contrast with the findings of your study as will be described in the content chapters of your final research project report.

5.3 Sources of Information

5.3.1 Primary and Secondary Sources

Information may come to us from primary and secondary sources:
- A primary source is a source that presents information in its original form.
- A secondary source is a source that presents processed or interpreted information.

How to distinguish primary and secondary sources?

Let's consider stock quotes from Nasdaq stock exchange as an example. Nasdaq website (▶ www.nasdaq.com) or Nasdaq publications are definitely primary sources for such quotes. Stock brokerage websites (▶ www.tdameritrade.com and others) provide a network media for the quotes coming directly from Nasdaq through the information pipeline, and therefore, the quotes on that websites are also original, and such sources can be considered primary sources too.

A business magazine, say, BusinessWeek, that publishes a review on stock market together with the processed and aggregated information is a secondary source for stock market quotes because the magazine publishes its own papers where the original data were used and presented in a way different from the primary sources.

5.3.2 Evaluating the Quality of Secondary Sources

Depending upon the nature of the research, the criteria for evaluating secondary data will vary. Mainly, we will be concerned with the following factors about the data and information we collect and use:
- Reliability
- Accuracy
- Coverage
- Author qualification
- The nature of publication

Some sources pay better attention to the quality of the information they publish than other sources; thus, researchers prefer to use the most reliable sources.

The accuracy of information is a very important criteria for using the respective source of information. Most likely, you do not want to spend significant time conducting research and then find out that the information, which you used in the research, is inaccurate to the degree that compromises your research findings and conclusions.

Researchers prefer to use information sources that provide the better coverage to the subject area, thus making the coverage one of the most important criteria for the evaluation of information sources.

Different authors may have quite different level of qualification in the subject area. Some authors are well known for providing reliable and accurate information and thus are more trustworthy in the research community.

The nature of publication tells how much you can trust the information published in the source. It is clear that "The Journal of Theoretical Physics" is a more reliable source for the information about physics than, say, magazine "BusinessWeek." On the other hand, "BusinessWeek" is a more reliable source for the information about business than "The Journal of Theoretical Physics."

Researchers can equally use primary or secondary sources of information. If you use a secondary source, just make sure that it provides quality information meeting your requirements and standards.

- A ***primary source*** is a source that presents information in its original form.
- A ***secondary source*** is a source that presents processed or interpreted information

5.4 How to Review Literature

5.4.1 The Sense of Review of Literature

In a review of literature, you should learn and tell what other researchers have done so far in the area of your research and in the adjacent areas to show a "big picture" of the area of research based on the publications and other information in your possession.

A review of literature sets up a stage for the research by showing what has already been done in that area, what is still missing in that area, and what should be done next to expand the knowledge in that area, particularly in the direction of your research topic. A review of literature should also provide an analysis of the most efficient research methods and procedures used by other researchers in the research area along with the major mistakes made and dead ends faced by other researchers.

5.4.2 How to Write a Review of Literature

A review of literature is a "story" told based on the previously published results. All sources used in the review of literature must be mentioned by references or footnotes to the appropriate sources which should be listed in your bibliography. We will discuss bibliography, references, and footnotes later in this chapter. A review of literature is a story written by you rather than a collection of quotations or data from a variety of sources.

Specific quotes are welcome in a review of literature; however, the volume of quotations in the review of literature should be reasonable not to turn the review into a plagiarism. Any quotation or data from any source must be comprehensively referenced, so anyone should be able to find and review the source by the reference.

5.5 Basic Terminology

Working with different information source, it is important to become familiar with the related terminology. You must distinguish between the following:

- *Bibliography* and *index*
- *Outline*, *table of contents*, and *presentation timetable*
- *Journal* and *magazine*

5.5.1 Bibliography vs. Index

A ***bibliography*** is a specialized list of documentary sources giving author, title, publication data, and sometimes an abstract.

An ***index*** is not a data source, it is an alphabetical listing of data sources, and it tells only where the data can be found.

Thus, a bibliography is a list of specific documents that contain actual information you need, but an index is a list of sources rather than actual information. An index does not contain actual information about the particular facts, events, processes, or phenomena, but contains the list of sources where such information could be found.

The following examples help understand the difference between bibliography and index. Suppose we are reviewing literature on the theory of value in economics. The bibliography may look as the following.

▶ Example 1 – Example of Bibliography

- Aityan, Sergey K. (2020) Analysis of Competitive Strategies by Asserting General Value, *International Journal of Economics and Finance*, vol. 12, No. 5, pp. 10–21.
- Martinez-Alier, Joan; Munda, Giuseppe; and O'Neill, John (1998). Weak Comparability of Values as a Foundation for Ecological Economics, *Ecological Economics*, vol. 26, No. 3, pp. 277–286.
- Stigler, George J. (1950). The Development of Utility Theory. *International Journal of Political Economy*, vol. 58, No. 4, pp. 307–327. ◀

▶ Example 2 – Example of Index

- International Journal of Economics and Finance
- Ecological Economics
- International Journal of Political Economy ◀

As evident from the examples above, the bibliography contains the sources of actual information, but the index contains the source where the actual information could be found.

5.5.2 Outline vs. Table of Contents vs. Presentation Time Table

An ***outline*** is a content structure of a book, report, paper, presentation, or any document that consists of major chapters and sections. By this, an outline is a "skeleton" of your document.

A ***table of contents*** or just contents is an outline of the report, book, paper, presentation, or any document, along with page numbers. It is a road map of the publication.

A ***presentation timetable*** is an outline of the presentation, along with the time to spend on each item. It is a time map of the presentation.

5

▶ Example 3 – Example of an Outline

1. Introduction
2. Problem Statement
   2.1. The Problem
   2.2. Scope and Limitations
3. Results
4. Conclusions

◀

▶ Example 4 – Example of a Table of Contents

The table of contents is the outline + the respective pages.

1. Introduction.. 1
2. Problem Statement.............................. 4
   2.1. The Problem................................... 5
   2.2. Scope and Limitations.................... 7
3. Results.. 9
4. Conclusions.. 10

◀

▶ Example 5 – Example of a Presentation Timetable

The presentation timetable is the outline + the time to spend for each item.

1. Introduction.. 2
2. Problem Statement.............................. 1
   2.1. The Problem................................... 3
   2.2. Scope and Limitations.................... 2
3. Results.. 4
4. Conclusions.. 2

Total time: 15 minutes

◀

5.5.3 Journal vs. Magazine

- A ***journal*** is a scholarly publication of a learned society or profession related to research.
- A ***magazine*** is normally a popular or newsstand type of publication.

Journals are mostly professional publications focusing on certain aspects of research. Magazines, on the other hand, are publications of general purpose. It does not mean that magazines are the lower-quality publications.

Some examples of journal and magazines are shown below.

▶ Example 6 – Examples of Journals

- Journal of Econometrics
- American Journal of Business
- International Journal of Financial Markets
- European Journal of Operational Research ◀

▶ Example 7 – Examples of Magazines

- International Journal of Econometrics
- American Business Journal
- International Journal of Financial Markets
- European Journal of Business ◀

The actual difference between journals and magazines is sometimes less vivid as it looks from the definition. Sometimes, journals are very popular and generic, like Wall Street Journal. It is a general-purpose financial magazine of high-quality information and papers. Sometimes, magazines are quite focused and research-oriented publications. For example, Popular Electronics is an American magazine with quite focused and mostly high-quality professional publications. However, for majority of publications, the classification presented above makes good sense.

5.6 List of Bibliography

A bibliography is a list of references to specific publications, not just general references to the source. Each entry in the list of bibliography must be done in such a way that anyone would be able to identify the publication by the reference. There are different formatting standards for bibliography. Please refer to the guidelines of the publisher to learn the formatting standard they require. A generic example of bibliography entries is presented below.

▶ Example 8 – Bibliography Organized by the Order of the First Author Last Name

Aityan, Sergey K.; Alexey K. Ivanov-Schitz; and Sergey S. Izotov (2010). Critical Issues in Investment Strategy, Journal of International *Financial Markets, Institutions & Money*, vol. 5, pp. 590–605. ← Article

Fontanills, George A.; Tom Gentile (2001). *The Stock Market Course*, Wiley, 464p, ISBN-10: 0471393150; ISBN-13: 978-0471393153. ← Book

Baranauckas, Carla (2006). A dog's life, upgraded, at luxury pet resorts, *New York Times*. September 24, 2006, ▶ http://www.iht.com/articles/2006/09/24/america/web.0924topdog.php. ← Web

◀

▶ Example 9 – Bibliography Organized as a Numbered List

1. George A. Fontanills, Tom Gentile, (2001). *The Stock Market Course*, Wiley, 464p, ISBN-10: 0471393150; ISBN-13: 978–0471393153. ← Book

2. Sergey K. Aityan, Alexey K. Ivanov-Schitz, and Sergey S. Izotov (2010). Critical Issues in Investment Strategy, Journal of International *Financial Markets, Institutions & Money*, vol. 5, pp. 590–605. ← Article

3. Carla Baranauckas, "A dog's life, upgraded, at luxury pet resorts." New York Times. September 24, 2006, ▶ http://www.iht.com/articles/2006/09/24/america/web.0924topdog.php. ← Web

◀

5.7 References, Citations, and Quotations

5.7.1 Citations

If you use any third-party information, always refer to the document source. Referencing to the source is very important for many reasons:

- Enables information verification.
- Provides support to the information as of relevance, accuracy, and reliability of both the information and the source.
- Acknowledges the contribution by other authors.
- Assures knowledge continuity.

Using someone's information or data without reference is plagiarism which is scientifically wrong and ethically incorrect. You must provide a reference to the information or data from other sources as soon as you mentioned this information or data in your proposal, report, book, article, or any other document. Let's assume that all specific sources of the information used in your document are listed in the bibliography.

The information citations in the document are made by referencing the appropriate entry in the list of bibliography. Such a citation can be done in two different ways:

- By author name and year
- By number in the bibliography

Depending on the formal requirements or on your own choice if no specific requirements are mentioned. However, you should use one type of reference throughout the entire document, never mix the reference types.

If the bibliography is organized by the author names, then do the citation by names, but if the bibliography is organized by the numbered entries, then do the citation by numbers as shown in the example below. Suppose we would like to make a citation to the bibliography in ► Examples 1 and 2 in ► Sect. 5.6. In the citations made by name, use only the last name or names of the authors.

If the bibliography reference has a single author as in the third reference, then the citations will be looking as follows.

► Example 10 – A Citation Made to a Bibliography Organized by Name (One Author)

Pet owners spent $38.4B for their pets in 2005, and this amount increased by $2.1B in 2006 and expected to grow by $2.7 B in 2007 (Baranauckas, 2006). ◄

► Example 11 – A Citation Made to a Bibliography Organized as a Numbered List

Pet owners spent $38.4B for their pets in 2005, and this amount increased by $2.1B in 2006 and expected to grow by $2.7 B in 2007 [3].

Citations made to the bibliography organized as a numbered list are the same regardless of the number of authors.

Citations made to the bibliography are organized by name, if the bibliography entry has two authors as in the first reference; then, the citation by names uses the last names of both authors as shown below. ◄

► Example 12 – A Citation Made to a Bibliography Organized by Name (Two Authors)

Fontanills and Gentile (2001) provided a detailed description of the stock market trading process.

or

The book provided a detailed description of the stock market trading process (Fontanills and Gentile, 2001).

If the bibliography reference made by name has three or more authors, then use only the name of the first author as shown in the example below. ◄

► Example 13 – A Citation Made to a Bibliography Organized by Name (Three or More Authors)

The next-day correlation coefficients for Dow Jones and Nikkei 225 indices are higher than the same-day correlation coefficients for the same indices (Aityan et al., 2010).

Please refer to specific requirements for the structure of bibliography and citations established by the publisher or your organization before entering the bibliography and citation. ◀

5.7.2 Quotations

Precision in words sometimes is crucial, and you want to use the entire phrase from another publication or even from a verbal communication. In this case, the quoted phrase should be put in quotes, and the accurate citation should be provided.

▶ Example 14 – A Quotation Made to a Bibliography Organized by Name

It was stated that "delays in information propagation may cause a lead-lag relationship in different stock markets and in different segments of a single stock market" (Aityan et al., 2010). ◀

▶ Example 15 – A Quotation Made to a Bibliography Organized as Numbered List

A quite obvious fact that "the luxury kennels reflect the complexity of the bond between humans and dogs" [3] was widely overlooked.

Both ▶ Examples 9 and 10 provide quotation to the entire phrase taken from the cited sources. ◀

5.8 Footnotes and Endnotes

5.8.1 Footnotes

Some publishers and organizations require the references to the information sources to be made in the form of footnotes rather than in the list of bibliography. Footnotes are notes placed at the bottom of a page. In this case, the reference to the information source (a bibliography entry) is placed at the bottom of the page, where the source is cited. Each footnote has a number, and the citation is made by the number as shown in ▶ Example 11.

▶ Example 16 – A Reference (Citation) Made in the Form of Footnote

In market trend forecasting, it is essential to determine "the prevailing mood of the market"[1]. ⟵ Text in the document

⟵ Footnote at the bottom of the page

[1]George A. Fontanills, Tom Gentile, "The Stock Market Course," page 339, Wiley, 2001 (ISBN-13: 978–0471393153)

◀

Typically, footnotes are numbered continuously throughout the entire document or a section of the document and placed at the bottom of the appropriate pages of the document, where the citation is made.

5.8.2 Endnotes

Endnotes are the same as footnotes but placed at the end of the document or a section of the document.

Questions for Self-Control for Chap. 5

In all answers, provide definitions, elaborate on the concept, and provide examples. Feel free to make up the entire example and all data for your examples:

1. Describe continuity of knowledge.
2. Why is review of literature needed?
3. How to do review of literature?
4. What are primary and secondary sources of information?
5. What sources of information should be used in research: primary or secondary?
6. Why should review information be well organized?
7. What is bibliography?
8. What standards of bibliography do you know?
9. How to make citation to a source of information?
10. How to make quotation from a source?
11. What is a footnote?
12. What is the endnotes?

Practical Assignments for Chap. 5

1. Choose a topic of interest. Browse the Internet and other available sources. Read available literature, develop a list of bibliography, and write a brief literature review with proper references.

Research Design

Contents

6.1 A Good Research Deserves a Good Design – 99

6.2 Major Factors in Research Design – 100

6.3 Determining the Research Approach – 100

6.4 Construct the Models – 101

6.5 Formulate the Hypotheses if Needed – 102

6.6 Decide on Data Sources and Data Collection Methods – 102

6.7 Experiment Planning – 103

6.8 Selecting Research Methods and Procedures – 104

6.9 Skills, Expertise, and Equipment Needed for Research – 104

6.10 Size of the Research Team – 104

6.11 Budget and Timelines – 105

6.12 Pilot Study – 105

6.13 Research Plan Implementation – 105

6.13.1 The Ideal Case – 105

S. K. Aityan, *Business Research Methodology*, Classroom Companion: Business,
https://doi.org/10.1007/978-3-030-76857-7_6

6.13.2 Quite Possible Case – 106
6.13.3 Most Likely Case – 106

6.14 The Reasons of Biggest Errors in Research – 106

6.1 A Good Research Deserves a Good Design

Any activity goes more smoothly and provides better results if it is well planned and organized. It is practically impossible to build a good house in a reasonable time if it is not properly designed and the construction work is not well organized. This is applicable to each type of human activity. The same applies to research projects too. A well-planned research goes smoother, takes less times and resources, and delivers better results.

You may be wondering how research can be planned if any research project is a journey to the land of the unknown. It is true – research implies a lot of uncertainties, and the results are not known from the beginning. On the other hand, building a house looks a routine process, where all is known in advance. Yes, these two activities, conducting a research project and building a house, are two extremes, but they both have a lot in common. First, even with building a house, some unexpected things may occur during the construction, and some unexpected circumstances may come up. On the other hand, in conducting research, the results are not known, but we can plan our activities, not the results. Such a research plan is referred to as a research design.

Research design is a detailed plan of your research.

Similar to all other human activities, before getting engaged, we must answer three major questions: what are we going to do, why we are going to do it, and how we are going to do it? These questions attributed to a research projects are the research problem, the research purpose, and the research design:

- Problem statement is the "what?" of the research.
- Purpose is the "why?" of the research.
- Research design is the "how?" of the research.

Clearly formulated problem, purpose, and research design help conduct the more efficient research project and obtain the better and more reliable results.

As an example, suppose I own a small restaurant and want to conduct a research to find a better competitive positioning of my restaurant. If I jump into research without planning, it may take 3 years and enormous cost incomparably higher than the survival time for my restaurant and the total available resources, thus making the research project completely useless and unfeasible.

Thus, research projects should be planned too. Some modifications of the research design may occur in the process of conducting research due to the nature of research. However, the better research is designed, the less "surprises" may be faced during the actual research.

- Problem statement is the "what?" of the research.
- Purpose is the "why?" of the research.
- Research design is the "how?" of the research.

- The research problem statement answers the question "what?" – what we are going to do in the research?
- The research purpose answers the question "why?" of the research.
- The research design answers the question "how?" of the research.

6.2 Major Factors in Research Design

As the problem is formulated, you begin the development of the research strategy or research design which is a detailed plan of the research undertaking. You must be sure your research design is adequate to provide a specific answer to your research question. You already know what you will investigate. Now, you must decide how you will conduct the inquiry.

Research design or research plan does not mean the same as research method. The research method is only a part of the overall research design.

In the research design, we must plan the course of the prospective research project organizationally and technically. It is important to decide on the following factors on the research design step:

- Select the research approach.
- Construct the models.
- Develop hypotheses if needed, and decide on the verification methods and acceptance or rejection criteria.
- Decide about data collection sources and data collection methods.
- Decide and plan experiments if needed in the research.
- Select methods and procedures which will be used in the research.
- Identify the skill sets, expertise, and equipment needed to conduct the research.
- Decide on the size of the research team.
- Plan the timelines and budget for the research project.
- For a big-scale projects, plan for a pilot study, if needed. A pilot study can be used to determine the validity and reliability of tests.

All the abovementioned factors are the important parts of the research design. Precision in making the research design pays dividends in time saved through avoiding false starts, wrong routes, and hazy approaches.

6.3 Determining the Research Approach

As we discussed earlier in ► Chap. 1 of this book, there is a variety of research approaches:

- Exploratory research
- Descriptive research
- Theoretical research
- Experimental research

- Simulation research
- Analytic research
- Creative research

These approaches are different by their nature and methodologies. Any research project may use a single approach or a combination of approaches. For example, for the development of the advanced theory of general value, the researcher plans to use the theoretical approach. For the research on employee loyalty, the descriptive approach is the best fit. On the other hand, for the research on competitive strategy, a combination of theoretical, experimental, and simulation approaches was chosen. The researcher plans to develop the appropriate theoretical basis for the analysis of competitive strategies using the theoretical approach, to collect the real-world data using the experimental approach, and to find the optimal strategies using computer simulation.

6.4 Construct the Models

Most research need models. According to the definition given in ► Chap. 1 ► Sect. 1.4.3 of this book, a ***model*** can be defined as an abstract construct which includes major parameters and their relationships and dependencies of the related objects of interest for the purpose of the analysis.

Objects, processes, and phenomena in the real world are very complex and comprise enormous number of features and parameters. Even simple objects are too complex to be analyzed in full without constraints and limitation in a finite and concise way. Realistically, we must work with the models to be able to analyze the objects. The same object may have different models for different purposes of analysis. A model of a human for the human resource (some personal information plus work-related information) is different from the model of the same human for medical analysis (some personal information plus medical information) and also different from the model for the aircraft size design (human size and weight).

> A ***model*** can be defined as an abstract construct which includes major parameters and their relationships and dependencies of the related objects of interest for the purpose of the analysis.

Models developed on the research design step will be used in the research and needed for all other planning and design activities. The methods, procedures, devices, required team skills, project timelines, and budget will all depend on the models used in the research.

The models developed on the research design step may be modified as the research progresses. However, if the models need dramatic change and modification in the research process, it indicates a certain degree of failure in the research design step, particularly in the applied research.

6.5 Formulate the Hypotheses if Needed

Hypotheses aim to explain events, processes, or phenomena. Some research need hypotheses, but some research do not. For example, we needed a hypothesis to explain the dramatic failure of the new Coca-Cola in 1985, but we do not need a hypothesis to analyze the demography of people buying certain car models.

A ***hypothesis*** is a suggested solution to a research problem.

Hypotheses in general were discussed in ► Chap. 2 ► Sect. 2.1 of this book. We will also discuss statistical hypothesis testing in ► Chap. 14.

6

Hypotheses needed for the research should be formulated on the research design step. Some research projects are launched to verify certain hypothesis. In this case, the hypothesis is part of the problem statement, and the entire research project is dedicated to the hypothesis. However, most research project, which need hypotheses, use the hypotheses as the mechanism for solving the problems stated in the problem statement.

Hypothesis could be logical, statistical, and deterministic. Logical hypotheses can be verified by the rule of classical or nontraditional logic accepted in the research area.

Statistical hypotheses can be tested using the real-world data and statistical methods. Statistical hypotheses can be accepted or rejected only within certain allowed error. There is no way we can proof a statistical hypothesis with one hundred percent certainty. To accept a statistical hypothesis, one should not have enough evidences to reject it within the allowed error.

Deterministic hypotheses can be rejected with a single evidence contradicting the hypothesis. One can say that a deterministic hypothesis is an extreme case of the statistical hypothesis with zero allowed errors.

- A ***logical hypothesis*** is a hypothesis that can be accepted or rejected based on the rule of classical or nontraditional logic accepted in the subject area.
- A ***statistical hypothesis*** is a hypothesis that can be verified by using statistical methods based on empirical data.
- A ***deterministic hypothesis*** is a hypothesis that can be rejected based on a single evidence contradicting the hypothesis.

6.6 Decide on Data Sources and Data Collection Methods

In the research design, one must decide on major data sources, data collection and processing plan, methods, tools, and procedures, which will be used in data collection and processing:

- Identify major data sources.
- Develop data collection and processing plan.

- Identify methods, tools, and procedures, which will be used in data collection.
- Identify major data processing methods and algorithms, if such methods exist, and plan on development of new methods if such methods are not currently available.

Unavailability of reliable data can easily cause the research failure. It is strongly advisable to check and verify the availability of reliable data at the research design stage.

It is strongly advisable to identify, prepare, and test all methods and algorithms, which are planned to be used in the research. At this stage, no actual data is yet available. However, testing of methods and algorithms can be performed on dummy data, which are specifically made up for the purpose of testing.

6.7 Experiment Planning

Some research projects need experimentation. ***Experiment*** is a test set up under controlled conditions intentionally reproducing certain phenomena, events, or processes with the purpose of learning about them, including major relationships and dependencies. Experiments are typically set up under certain conditions that reproduce the conditions which are supposed to be faced in the real world. Experiments can be conducted in natural or in laboratory conditions.

> ***Experiment*** is a test set up under controlled conditions intentionally reproducing certain phenomena, events, or processes with the purpose of learning about them, including major relationships and dependencies.

Some experiments are easy to plan and conduct while some experiments need sophisticated equipment, special skills, possibly, a long time span, and incur high costs. Thus, planning experiments in advance is a crucial task in the preparation for research.

> **An Example of Experiment Planning for Data Collection**
> - ***The problem:*** Suppose the research problem is to find out the population density and the average size of fish in the SF Bay.
> - ***The purpose:*** For the purpose of fishery management.
> - ***The research design:*** To solve the problem, we plan to catch fish in several random locations in the bay at different times (as a random sample) during chosen periods of time (to assess the population density by the caught quantity) and estimate the average size of fish by measuring the mean size on the caught sample.

To complete the research design:
- We plan how we will be choosing random locations and times for the experiment.
- We choose the allowed significance level to assess the confidence intervals for the fish population and fish size estimates.
- We estimate the sample size to meet the conditions for statistical estimates.

At this stage, we should prepare all statistical methods and test them on the data, artificially made up for the testing purpose. We have not yet conducted the actual experiment, but we can test the completeness of the methods by testing them on the "dummy" data.

6.8 Selecting Research Methods and Procedures

In the research design, one must decide on adequate models and hypotheses used in the research:
- Describe all methods, procedures, techniques, data processing, and data analysis tools to be used in the research.
- Plan to develop (during the research) new methods and procedures which are needed for the research if they are not yet available.

All methods and procedures chosen at this stage should be described and tested on "dummy" data to make sure that they will work on the real data collected in the research.

6.9 Skills, Expertise, and Equipment Needed for Research

The skills and expertise needed for the research should be identified on the research design step:
- List the skills and expertise needed for the research.
- Plan to learn the skills and acquire the new expertise needed, or plan to invite additional researchers on the team with the expertise and skills needed for the research project.

6.10 Size of the Research Team

Small research projects can be conducted by a single individual. Such individual research projects are typical, for example, for student graduate projects. Large-scale or multidisciplinary projects need more researchers on the team. Some huge projects need hundreds or even thousands of people. It is very important to decide on the team size of the project in advance at the research design stage.

6.11 Budget and Timelines

Some projects like the graduate student projects can be conducted without budget if no external expenses are expected. However, most research projects need to deal with expenses, and the project budget should be addressed and planned at the research design stage.

Practically, all research projects need time scheduling. It is clear that nobody can schedule discoveries, but every project must have duration for organizational, financial, and other reasons.

Thus, the research project timing and budget (if applicable) must be addressed at the research design stage:

- The itemized budget for the project.
- In case of student research project, sometimes, budget is not needed, for example, for some graduate theses research projects.
- Timelines and schedule for the research project must be clearly identified in the research design.
- The timelines of the research project are very important for the timely completion of the project and for staying on the planned budget.

6.12 Pilot Study

Large-scale research projects imply high risk, and before launching large-scale projects, it would be necessary to conduct a pilot study to test the research feasibility and potential outcomes of the project.

This should be planned at the research design stage.

6.13 Research Plan Implementation

Any research is a journey with many unknowns. For this reason, it would be hard to predict all the details and follow all planned activities as it can be done in the routine engagements. However, we must plan the research projects too. There are three possible courses of research project implementations:

- The ideal case
- Quite possible case
- Most likely case

6.13.1 The Ideal Case

As the research plan is developed, in the ideal case, you will do no more and no less than you have planned and expected. You will solve the problem stated in your problem statement as confined by the research scope and limitation. All models, hypotheses, methods, and procedures will work well, and you complete the project on the planned time and within the budget as planned. Such situation may typically occur with rather simple research projects which are being quite smoothly conducted without any unexpected "surprises."

6.13.2 Quite Possible Case

There are a lot of unknowns in any research. Thus, your research plan, scope, and limitations can easily fail and should be changed during the research. Some methodologies, methods, and procedures may also fail or be proven inefficient. In result, you will ask for additional resources and time to complete the research. Though such situation is possible, try to avoid it.

6.13.3 Most Likely Case

Some corrections in the research plans are possible, but it occurs quite infrequently, thus, to stay more or less close to the research plan and the budget. Do not expect that everything will go perfectly smooth in your research. It is a journey to the land of the unknown.

6.14 The Reasons of Biggest Errors in Research

If choices of the problem and research methods are made wisely and the research does not imply a lot of uncertainty, data collection and analysis will be conducted by implementing the research design. However, such "ideal" research projects occur quite unfrequently. In most research projects, unexpected complications appear, and sometimes, research projects fail. The sources of the largest errors in business research are the following:

- The research questions were not formulated well enough and clear.
- The nature, boundaries, and limitations of the research were not clearly identified and stated.
- Unclear or incomplete research design led to the unexpected methodological complications.
- Data source was chosen wrongly or data availability was not verified in the research design.

Questions for Self-Control for Chap. 6

In all answers, provide definitions, elaborate on the concept, and provide examples. Feel free to make up the entire example and all data for your examples:

1. What are the "WHAT?", "WHY?", and "HOW?" of a research project?
2. List and describe the types of research.
3. What is the research design?
4. Why is the research design needed?

5. What major factors are included in research design?
6. What does the term “model” mean, and why do we need to develop models for research?
7. Does every research need hypotheses?
8. Why verification of data availability is very important at the research design stage?
9. Does every research project need budget and why?
10. How important is planning time schedule for research?
11. What are the major sources of errors in research?

Research Proposal

Contents

7.1 What Is the Research Proposal? – 111

7.2 Suggested Content of the Research Proposal – 111

7.3 Tentative Title of the Research – 112

7.4 Purpose of the Proposal – 112

7.5 Summary – 112

7.6 Writing Introduction – 113

7.7 Purpose of the Research – 114

7.8 Definition of Terms – 114

7.9 Review of Literature – 115

7.10 Problem Statement – 115

7.11 Research Objectives – 115

7.12 Research Design – 116

7.12.1 Hypotheses if Applicable – 116

7.12.2 Data Sources and Data Collection Plan – 116

7.12.3 Data Collection Methods Including Experiment Planning (if Applicable) – 116

S. K. Aityan, *Business Research Methodology*, Classroom Companion: Business,
https://doi.org/10.1007/978-3-030-76857-7_7

7.12.4 Data Processing and Data Analysis Techniques, Methods, and Procedures – 117
7.12.5 Required Knowledge, Skill Set, and Expertise – 117
7.12.6 Researcher or Research Staff Qualifications and the Team Size – 117
7.12.7 Project Timelines and Project Budget (if Applicable) – 118

7.13 Overview of Expected Outcome and the Project Acceptance Criteria – 118

7.14 Bibliography – 118

7.15 Appendices – 119

7.16 Formatting the Research Proposal – 119

7.17 Submission and Approval – 121

7.1 What Is the Research Proposal?

The proposal submission and approval are the final activities in the preparation for research. The goal of the research proposal is to present the prospective research proposal for review and approval. The research proposal is a structured document that describes what you plan to do in the research project and how you plan to do it. The proposal should include all the necessary information that allow the approval organization to make decision on the prospective research. As the proposal is approved, you get the green light to conduct the research.

7.2 Suggested Content of the Research Proposal

Proposal formats and content vary among organizations, agencies, and schools, so please refer to and follow the guidelines provided by the respective organization. However, the proposal is your document, so you decide how to present the prospective research project in the best way and follow the requirements.

The research proposal should include the information relevant to the prospective research. A suggested generic structure of a research proposal is shown in ◘ Fig. 7.1.

Tentative title of the research
Summary
1. Introduction
2. The purpose of the research and the research goal(s)
3. Definition of terms. (In this section, list and define special terms used in the proposal)
4. Review of literature
5. Problem statement. In this section the author(s) should provide and explain the research problem statement including subproblems, scope, and limitations
6. Research objectives
7. Hypotheses if applicable
8. Methods and procedures
9. Data sources, data collection plan, procedures, and experiment planning if applicable
10. Data processing and data analysis techniques and methods
11. Required knowledge, skill set, and expertise
12. Researcher or research staff qualifications and the team size
13. Project timelines and project budget (if applicable)
14. Overview of expected outcome and the project acceptance criteria

Bibliography
Appendices (if applicable)

◘ **Fig. 7.1** A suggested generic structure of a research proposal

The content and structure of the research proposal may vary subject to the type of research, specific requirement by the approval organization, and your personal writing and communication style under given requirements and constraints.

Typically, sections summary and bibliography are not numbered.

7.3 Tentative Title of the Research

The tentative title of the research is the title suggested by the author or authors of the proposal. The research title must be concise and clearly stated without ambiguity and must adequately reflect the nature of the research. It is not the problem statement but the title of the research project.

The research project title is called tentative at this stage of the project because the title may be changed after the proposal review based on the suggestions from the reviewers as well as during the research or in the delivery phases of the project. This is similar to book and movie titles, which begin with the tentative title, and the final title of the book or the movie is decided later before the book is published or the movie is released.

Normally, the title of the research is placed on a separate page referred to as the title page or the cover page. The title page shows the tentative title, author(s), organization, type of the proposal, and submission date. Some organizations may require some other information to be shown in the title page.

A typical sample title page for the graduate research proposal is presented in ◘ Fig. 7.2. The formats of the title page may vary. Different organizations, agencies, and schools may have specific requirements for the proposal title page or may leave it flexible.

7.4 Purpose of the Proposal

Don't get confused with the purpose of the proposal and purpose of the research. For example, suppose the purpose of a research is "to help build efficient international stock investment portfolios in global environment" while the purpose of the proposal is "for approval of the proposed research project by graduate committee."

7.5 Summary

Summary is a brief description of the document. Normally, people read summary first to find out if they are interested in reading the entire document. Thus, the summary should be a very compressed and brief description of the major points made in the document.

Though the summary is located first in the document, it should be written last, when the document is practically written and ready.

Fig. 7.2 A sample title page of the proposal

Lincoln University, Oakland, CA

Correlation Analysis for Managing International Investment Portfolios

Research Proposal

for

Master Thesis

(BA399, MBA Research Project)

Presented to

Graduate Committee of Lincoln University

by

John Smith

Advisor: Prof. Sam Adams

December 2021

7.6 Writing Introduction

This section of the proposal provides a comprehensive background review, description, and analysis of the current situation in the problem area. The goal of the introduction is to provide the background information and tell the reader what gave rise to the problem you are planning to investigate. The content of this chapter should set the stage, so your reader will clearly and logically see a problem evolving. Thus, the transition to the problem statement later in the proposal for the reader will be quite clear and natural.

Do not make the introduction a very long story. It should be long enough to include the background information but brief enough not to become a long boring historical novel. You should be especially alert to restrict the background information to few pages – perhaps not more than three or four pages at most.

Keep in mind that the introduction is a brief background of the proposed research rather than a complete history of the problem area and the research topic.

A good introduction should lay out a clear understanding of the area of the research and provide a background for the research problem as well as justify timeliness and necessity of the research problem. Thus, the research problem that is going to be formulated later in the proposal should be viewed as logically justified and natural.

Close this section with a transition statement that leads naturally to your research purpose and problem statement sections.

7.7 Purpose of the Research

The purpose of the research must be clearly and accurately formulated, particularly for the applied research. Provide a clear explanation who will be interested in the results of the research, how the research results will or may benefit then, and how the research will contribute to the overall knowledge in the problem area.

The purpose of the research must be clearly and accurately formulated:

- A problem is a question raised for inquiry, consideration, or solution (this question will be addressed in the problem statement section of the proposal).
- A purpose, however, is the reason for which something is done.

The purpose of the research answers to the following questions:

- Why is the research needed?
- How will the research results improve the current situation?
- Who will benefit from the research results?

This section may precede the problem statement section in the proposal or may follow the problem statement section of the proposal. This depends on the material presentation logic of the proposal.

7.8 Definition of Terms

The primary purpose of the "Definition of Terms" section is to specify the precise meaning intended for words or terms subject to different interpretations. All special terms used in the proposal or other terms that may be misinterpreted or not clear must be clearly defined in this section of the proposal before the terms are used.

Definition of terms is an important part of the proposal because, without clearly defined terms, different people might understand the terms used in the proposal differently that would lead to a confusion, misunderstanding, and misinterpretation of the proposed research and its future results.

You have several choices for placing definition of terms in your document:

- Insert as a subsection in the "Introduction" chapter.
- Insert as a separate section of the document.
- Define in apposition the first time the term is used in any narrative portion of the document.
- Include as a glossary of terms in the "Appendix."
- Use combination of the foregoing choices.

7.9 Review of Literature

This section of the proposal provides a comprehensive but focused description and analysis of the current situation in the area of research based on the data and other relevant information available in literature and other reliable sources.

The main purpose of the literature review is to identify a void in the existing knowledge. This void, when identified, will show what new knowledge is needed to complete the picture and how your effort can help to do it.

More likely, your research will fit into a broader scheme of research results.

Other purposes for the literature review are as follows:

- To contribute ideas for the research design
- To furnish evaluative techniques or criteria
- To provide opinions or perspective about your problem area

Try to keep the review of literature focused, and do not turn it into a comprehensive course on science or a detailed history of the evolution of knowledge in the problem area.

7.10 Problem Statement

In this section of research proposal, the research problem must be clearly stated, without any ambiguity and fuzziness.

Together with the main problem, all subproblems must be formulated, and the link between the subproblems must be provided. It should be clearly stated how the solution to the main problem can be derived from the solutions to the subproblems.

The problem scope and limitations must be clearly formulated.

7.11 Research Objectives

Research objectives define the planned outcome of the research. It is obvious that no one can predict the results of the research, but the types of the expected results can be described. The objectives define the type of results that are expected to obtain. For example:

The problem: Dynamics of customer demand on cars in San Francisco area.

The scope of the problem: To analyze the customer demand on passenger cars in all cities in Bay Area.

The limitations: We limit our research to the last 10 years from 2017 to 2020.

The objectives:

- To build historical charts on demand by cars and cities in San Francisco Bay Area
- To build the demand trend charts for analysis
- To build a chart for prediction of the demand on different types of cars by cities in San Francisco Bay Area

The objectives relate to what you expect to be done in the research to solve the problem formulated in the problem statement section

7.12 Research Design

Items 9–14 in the suggested generic structure of the research proposal presented above in ◘ Fig. 7.1 belong to the research design. These items can be presented combined in one chapter of the proposal or in separate chapters as shown in ◘ Fig. 7.1. This depends on the requirements of the organization and the author's presentation logic and style.

7.12.1 Hypotheses if Applicable

Hypotheses used in the research should be clearly justified and formulated. You should explicitly classify the hypothesis as logical, statistical, or deterministic. Identify the methods of hypothesis testing and verification.

7.12.2 Data Sources and Data Collection Plan

In this section, clearly identify data collection sources, and tell whether the data sources provide primary or secondary data. Data availability, data quality, and reliability of sources should be also addressed in this section.

7.12.3 Data Collection Methods Including Experiment Planning (if Applicable)

This section describes the data collection methods and techniques. It could be data collection by observation in natural conditions, survey to collect subjective opinions, collection from literature or from experiments, and actual in the real world, in the lab, or in computer simulation.

A brief description of the data collection methods should be presented in this section:

- The observation and measurement methods that will be used for data collection
- The major principles and basis for surveys and questionnaires to be used in the research (if applicable)
- The experimental and simulation methods to be used in the research

New and not yet existing or not yet developed methods, procedures, and tools, which are planned to be used for data collection in research, should be mentioned. These methods, procedures, and tools are considered a part of the research project to be done in the research phase

If a description of any methods, procedures, or tools is lengthy and requires the more detailed description, such methods, procedures, or tools should be briefly described in this section of the proposal with the reference to the appropriate literature or "Appendix" or "Appendices" of the proposal where they are described in a greater detail.

7.12.4 Data Processing and Data Analysis Techniques, Methods, and Procedures

Data processing and analysis techniques, methods, and procedures should be clearly described in the proposal. Briefly describe and explain the major approaches, mathematical equations, and techniques.

A brief description of the research methods should be presented in this section:

- The mathematical methods that will be used in the research
- The major principles of the data processing and analysis to be used in the research
- Data processing and data analysis tools to be used in the research
- The computer simulation methods to be used in the research

Do not overload this section with the detailed description of the mathematical methods, computer programs, and processing and analysis tools. Such an overload may break the logical flow of the document. Provide a brief description in the body of the document, and move the detailed description to Appendices, or refer to the appropriate literature.

7.12.5 Required Knowledge, Skill Set, and Expertise

The methods and procedures identified in the research designed require the appropriate qualifications. In this section, such qualification must be clearly described not to face an embarrassing situation in the research process by being unable to use the methods and procedures declared in the proposal or use them on a substandard level.

7.12.6 Researcher or Research Staff Qualifications and the Team Size

The researcher alone, if it is single researcher project, or the research staff in case of a larger-scale projects must possess the knowledge, skills, qualification, and expertise required for the research project. By reviewing and describing the researcher and research staff qualifications, we provide evidence and assure that the research team is capable of conducting the proposed research project.

If for any reason some required knowledge, skills, or expertise are currently missing, the author(s) of the proposal should mention that these missing skills and expertise will be acquired, or the appropriate people will be added to the project after the proposed project is approved and starts.

7.12.7 Project Timelines and Project Budget (if Applicable)

This section of the proposal should define the timelines of the project with the proposed schedule and sequence of activities.

The budget for the project should be shown and discussed with the relationship to the entire project, its phases, and activities. If the research project does not require a budget like most graduate projects, this part can be omitted in the proposal.

7.13 Overview of Expected Outcome and the Project Acceptance Criteria

Any project can be completed with different levels of results if no expectations are set. Just as the example, if we plan to build a house, we may end up with a single-story primitive house without amenities or a high-rise house with a very complex infrastructure. In this, before the approval on the construction of the house, we must specify the expected house and list the completeness and acceptance criteria.

The same should be done to a research proposal. The expected outcomes of the proposed research should be explicitly described and the acceptance criteria explicitly phrased to avoid possible misconception and misunderstanding upon the completion of the research project.

7.14 Bibliography

The bibliography section should list all sources of information used in the research proposal.

The information sources can be listed by:

- Order of first mentioning in the proposal
- Alphabetical order by first author's last name
- Any other order the author believes is the best for this proposal

Any data or specific information used in the proposal must be references by providing the appropriate link (reference number or author name and year) to the bibliography.

Different organizations, agencies, and schools may have different requirements for bibliography and cross-referencing. Most schools currently use APA style for bibliography with some minor modifications. Please refer to your organization, agency, and school requirements for details.

7.15 Appendices

An "Appendix" is a special section that contains a specific detailed or auxiliary information which is mentioned in the document (say, proposal) but should not be placed in the content body of the document (say, proposal) to keep the proposal's logical flow clear and concise.

▶ Example 1

The proposal says that a questionnaire on car preference will be used for collecting data. A complete structured text of the questionnaire is placed in Appendix 1 with the appropriate reference in the body of the proposal not to break the logical flow of the proposal's content body. ◀

▶ Example 2

The proposal says that a correlation analysis is going to be used for the data analysis. A complete and detailed description of the correlation analysis techniques is placed in the Appendix 2 with the appropriate reference in the body of the proposal not to break the logical flow of the proposal's content body. ◀

Various types of numeration of the Appendices could be used in the document:
- Numerical (Appendix 1, Appendix 2, …)
- Alphabetical (Appendix A, Appendix B, …)
- Alphanumeric (Appendix A1, Appendix A2, …)
- Others

The most typical is alphabetical numeration of the Appendices.

7.16 Formatting the Research Proposal

Different organizations may have different requirements and guidelines for the document formatting including research proposals. Some organizations are quite firm in their requirement, while some organizations are relatively flexible.

A sample section numbering guideline for documents is shown in ◘ Fig. 7.3.

Typically, sections "Summary" and "Bibliography" are not numbered as shown in ◘ Fig. 7.3. The authors may add the "Acknowledgment" section to the document, which also is not a numbered section.

Sample document formatting guidelines are shown in ◘ Fig. 7.4.

It is strongly advisable to use the styles and automated numbering and some other features of the word processing software while writing the document. This will save you a lot of time and make the document cleaner and help avoid many formatting mistakes. Beginners may review word processing tutorials available online free of charge or read introductory books on the usage of modern word processing.[1]

1 Sergey K. Aityan (2020). Practical Guide to PC and Microsoft Office 365, Amazon KDP, 180p

All sections and subsections of the proposal must have hierarchical through numeration using Arabic numbers.
Example:

Summary
1 Introduction
  1.1 The overview of the Car Sales in San Francisco Bay Area
  1.2 Current Challenges of Car Sales in San Francisco Bay Area
2 Review of Literature
…
7 Acceptance criteria
Bibliography
Appendix A. The questionnaire on car preference
Appendix B. The regression analysis method

Fig. 7.3 A sample section numbering guideline

The document formatting guidelines:

- Separate title page
- The document should be written with single spacing between the lines
- The first line in paragraph indent 0.5”
- The document is printed double-sided with 1-inch margins on all sides.
- Hierarchical numbering of the document sections with Arabic numbers
- Alphabetic numbering for appendices
- Bibliography and cross-references in APA style
- Fonts face “Times New Roman”
- Font size for
  - ✓ content text: size 12
  - ✓ The Title: size 20
  - ✓ Main Sections: size 14 bold
  - ✓ Sub-sections: size 13 bold
  - ✓ Sub-sub-sections: size 12 bold
  - ✓ Table titles, figure capture: size 12

Fig. 7.4 Sample document formatting guidelines

7.17 Submission and Approval

The completed proposal should be submitted to the approving body for review and approval. After the review, questions may arise to the authors of the proposal from the proposal approving authorities. The questions should be discussed and negotiated. The appropriate corrections should be included in the proposal. The approval body may request a revision and further improvements of the proposal with the following resubmission.

As the proposal is approved, the research may start.

Questions for Self-Control for Chap. 7

In all answers, provide definitions, elaborate on the concept, and provide examples. Feel free to make up the entire example and all data for your examples:

1. What is the goal of a research proposal?
2. Why is the proposal title considered tentative?
3. What is the typical structure of a research proposal?
4. May people vary the structure of a research proposal?
5. How to organize the proposal title page?
6. Why is the definition of terms important in the proposal?
7. What role does the review of literature play in the research proposal?
8. What should be included in the problem statement section of the proposal?
9. What are the research objectives?
10. What should be included in the research design section of the proposal?
11. What is the role of the research design in the research proposal?
12. What is the expected outcome of the research and why is it needed in the proposal?
13. What is the role of bibliography in the proposal?
14. How to organize the bibliography and citations?
15. What is an appendix in the proposal and why is it needed?
16. What is the proposal summary and when should it be written?
17. What document formatting rules should be used in the proposal?

Practical Assignments for Chap. 7

1. Choose a topic of interest. Develop an outline for a proposal for the respective research project.

Research Methods

This part of the book consists of Chapters **8** through **14** and introduces and discusses some most common and frequently used methods in business research. Though the collection of methods in this part does not cover all possible methods used in business research, this collection is quite representative. The major goal of this part is to introduce the reader to those methods with a sufficient depth, so the reader would be able to conduct business research by applying one of the methods discussed in this part.

Contents

Chapter 8 Foundations of Probability – 125

Chapter 9 Distribution, Expectation, and Risk – 153

Chapter 10 Bayesian Probability – 175

Chapter 11 Major Distributions – 191

Chapter 12 Introduction to Statistics – 217

Chapter 13 Confidence Intervals – 233

Chapter 14 Statistical Hypothesis Testing – 279

Chapter 15 Sampling Experiments – 321

Chapter 16 Survey Method – 343

Chapter 17 Linear Regression – 359

Chapter 18 Comparative Analysis – 395

Foundations of Probability

Contents

8.1 Uncertainty and Risk – 127

8.2 Fundamentals of Probability – 127
8.2.1 The Universal Sample Space – 129
8.2.2 Probability – 129

8.3 Major Properties of Probability – 132
8.3.1 Probability Is a Number Between Zero and One – 132
8.3.2 Operations on the Universal Sample Space – 133
8.3.3 The Sum of All Probabilities Equals One – 134

8.4 Operations with Probabilities – 135
8.4.1 Probability of a Negation – 135
8.4.2 Operation "AND" of Independent Events – 136
8.4.3 Operation "OR" of Independent Events – 138

8.5 Interpretations of Probability – 140
8.5.1 Classical Interpretation – 140
8.5.2 Frequential Interpretation – 140
8.5.3 Subjective Interpretation – 140

8.6 Calculating Probabilities Using Classical Interpretation – 141
8.6.1 Calculating Probability From Symmetry – 141
8.6.2 Calculating Probabilities From Content Percentage – 143

S. K. Aityan, *Business Research Methodology*, Classroom Companion: Business,
https://doi.org/10.1007/978-3-030-76857-7_8

8.7 Estimating Probabilities Using Frequential Interpretation – 143
8.7.1 Estimating Probabilities From Sampling Experiments – 143
8.7.2 Estimating Probabilities From Historical Data – 144

8.8 Subjective Determination of Probabilities – 144
8.8.1 New Product Marketing – 144
8.8.2 Business Strategy – 144

8.9 Problems for Practicing – 145
8.9.1 Flipping a Coin – 145
8.9.2 Rolling the Dice – 146
8.9.3 Electronic Devices – 147

8.10 What More to Lean About Probabilities – 150

8.1 Uncertainty and Risk

Uncertainty is an immanent property of our world. We are not going to get into a philosophical discussion whether our world is fundamentally stochastic or deterministic. However, we face uncertainty in either case. If our world is fundamentally stochastic, we evidently face uncertainty. On the other hand, even if our world is strictly deterministic, which is not true at all, a vast variety of different things are happening beyond our control and hence impacting on the occurrences of our interest, thus creating uncertainty.

Uncertainty can be caused by the state of nature, economy, business competition, human behavior, and many other factors. There is a certain degree of risk practically in any actions we take. We plan our vacation at a nice beach resort, but we are not sure about the weather at the time of the vacation. We plan our business, but we are not sure about its success. When we plan business operations and growth, nobody can predict the outcome with complete certainty. We plan our study at university, but we are not sure whether family circumstances are going to be favorable for studying. We plan our investment, but we are not sure whether the return is going to be positive and how much positive.

In this regard, a legitimate question arises whether it makes any sense to plan our future if there is so much uncertainty in it. Nevertheless, the answer to this question is quite positive. Yes, we can make predictions and plan for the future. Though we do not have a crystal ball to see into the future and cannot actually predict a precise course of events or an exact outcome from our actions, we are able to assess our expectations of the outcome and can estimate risk associated with the activity.

- How to make a prediction under uncertainty?
- How to plan our activities under uncertainty?

There are many scientific approaches that aim treatment of uncertainty. Among them, probability, statistics, fuzzy logic, game theory, and other disciplines help make decisions and operate in the world under uncertainties. None of these disciplines are the universal panaceas but have their specific areas of application and should be applied only under conditions when they make sense.

This chapter addresses probability theory that is one of the most powerful and well-accepted approaches for treatment of events under uncertainty.

8.2 Fundamentals of Probability

Suppose you roll a dice. There are six equally possible outcomes of the roll: 1, 2, 3, 4, 5, and 6. Which one will occur? Suppose you purchased a new car. How long will you drive the car until the first repair is needed? There are no definitive answers to these questions. However, sometimes, we can estimate chances for events to occur. Such chances can be presented in terms of probabilities.

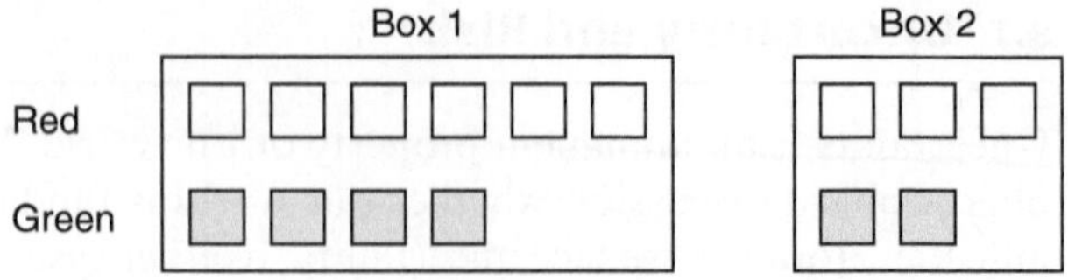

■ **Fig. 8.1** Two boxes with red and green candies

Suppose we have a box that contains six red and four green candies. All candies are thoroughly mixed in the box. You have to randomly pick one (just one) candy and you want it to be a red one. By randomly, we mean "blindly," i.e., just putting your hand in the box and picking whatever comes without any additional information about the candy. What chances do you have for getting what you want? Suppose you have another box, a smaller one that contains three red candies and two green candies. What are your chances for picking a red candy in this case? Are the chances different in these two cases?

Let's analyze the chances of picking a red candy in both cases as shown in ■ Fig. 8.1. Box 1 contains a total of ten candies, and if we have no additional information about the chances of what candy we are picking from the box, we consider equal chances for picking any candy in the box. Thus, we can conclude that our chances are six out of ten for getting a red candy from box 1. Similarly, with box 2, our chances are three out of five. If we measure our chances as a ratio of the number of all possible favorite events (picking a red candy) versus the number of all possible events (picking any candy), then we can easily conclude that our chances are the same with box 1 and box 2:

8

$$\frac{6}{6+4} = \frac{3}{3+2} \tag{8.1}$$

It means that our chances for picking a red candy can be assessed as a ratio of the number of red candies over the number of all candies in the box if the odds of picking any candy from the box are equal. Such ratio depends on the proportion of red and green candies in the box rather than on the number of candies.

Suppose we have already picked a candy from box 1 and it happened to be a green one. Then, if we pick a second candy from that box without replenishing green candies in the box, our chances are now six out of nine because one green candy is already gone and only two of them are left in the box. For the same reason, our chances for picking a red candy from box 2 if the first picked candy happened to be a green one are now two out of four. Thus, our chances for the second pick with two boxes are now different if we do not restore the box content before the second pick.

On the other hand, if we keep replenishing the boxes by returning the picked candy back to the box, the chances of picking a red candy will stay unchanged for any pick and are the same for both boxes. Let's consider just the first pick from box 1 or, what is the same, any other pick if we keep the box content replenished and carefully mixed after each pick.

Please note that so far, we use a colloquial term "chances" and did not call it "probability." We will define the term "probability" in one more step in this chapter.

8.2.1 The Universal Sample Space

Let's introduce a very helpful abstract concept of the ***universal sample space***. In probability theory, the universal sample space Ω of a random trial is the set (collection) of all possible events. Thus, for random trials with box 1 and box 2, the universal sample spaces are the sets of all possible events.

To avoid confusion, let's define some terms. ***Occurrence*** is a random draw or random action. ***Outcome*** is the result of a random occurrence. ***Event*** is the set of outcomes for which the probability is assigned. For example, if we roll a die, each possible occurrence of number 5 is a possible outcome, but the set of all possible outcomes of number "5" constitute event "5."

For the random trial with box 1 of candies, there are six possible outcomes of picking a red candy, and they all together constitute an event for picking a red candy. Let's call this event "Red." Also, there are four possible outcomes of picking a green candy, and they all constitute an event for picking a green candy. Let's call this event "Green". There are no other possible events in this trial. Both events "Red" and "Green" constitute the universal sample space Ω_1 for this random trial.

For the random trial with box 2 of candies, there are three possible outcomes of picking a red candy, and they all together constitute an event for picking a red candy, i.e., event "Red." Also, there are two possible outcomes of picking a green candy, and they all constitute an event for picking a green candy, i.e., event "Green." There are no other possible events in this trial. Both events "Red" and "Green" constitute the universal sample space Ω_2 for this random trial.

Please note that the universal sample space is an abstract concept that has no real shape and, hence, can be represented in any form that is convenient for analysis. For example, representations (a) and (b) of the universal sample space Ω in ◘ Fig. 8.2 are given in the form of countable equally possible events, while representations (c) and (d) are representations given in the form of rectangular areas proportional to the number of the appropriate equally possible events in the universal sample space. Both representations are equally good, and you can use anyone depending on the convenience. You may make some other representation if you find it more convenient for you.

In probability theory, the ***universal sample space*** of a random trial is the set of all possible events.

8.2.2 Probability

As it was noted above, we can assess the chances for picking a red candy as the ratio of the number of red candies over the number of all candies in the box. In terms of the universal sample space, such ratio can be calculated as the ratio of countable entries for the favorite events over the countable entries for all events in the universal sample space (see representations (a) and (b) in ◘ Fig. 8.2) or as the ratio of the area for favorite events over the total area in the universal sample space (see repre-

Fig. 8.2 Various representations for the universal sample space for the events Red and Green for random trials with candies in boxes 1 and 2; **a** and **b** are the representations by countable events, and **c** and **d** are the representations by area

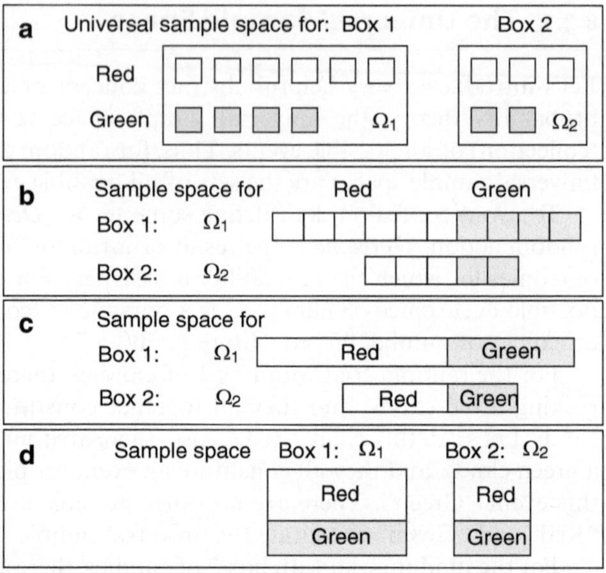

sentations (c) and (d) in Fig. 8.2). Such ratio is referred to as probability. For the countable representations (Fig. 8.2a, b), probabilities are

$$P_{\text{Red}} = \frac{N_{\text{Red}}}{N_{\text{Red}} + N_{\text{Green}}} = \frac{N_{\text{Red}}}{N_{\Omega}}$$

$$P_{\text{Green}} = \frac{N_{\text{Green}}}{N_{\text{Red}} + N_{\text{Green}}} = \frac{N_{\text{Green}}}{N_{\Omega}} \quad (8.2)$$

where P_{Red} and P_{Green} are the probabilities for events of picking red and green candies from the box, N_{Red} and N_{Green} are the numbers (count) of the appropriate entries for event "picking a red candy" and "picking a green candy" in the universal sample space, and N_{Ω} is the total count of all entries in all possible events in the universal sample space, i.e., $N_{\Omega} = N_{\text{Red}} + N_{\text{Green}}$. For the representations by area (Fig. 8.2c, d), the same probabilities can be defined as

$$P_{\text{Red}} = \frac{S_{\text{Red}}}{S_{\text{Red}} + S_{\text{Green}}} = \frac{S_{\text{Red}}}{S_{\Omega}}$$

$$P_{\text{Green}} = \frac{S_{\text{Green}}}{S_{\text{Red}} + S_{\text{Green}}} = \frac{S_{\text{Green}}}{S_{\Omega}} \quad (8.3)$$

where S_{Red} and S_{Green} are the appropriate areas for events "picking a red candy" and "picking a green candy" in the universal sample space and S_{Ω} is the total area of all possible events in the universal sample space, i.e., $S_{\Omega} = S_{\text{Red}} + S_{\text{Green}}$.

Definitely, we assume that all candies in the box are thoroughly mixed up that makes chances for picking any individual candy equal and allows us to build the universal sample space that reflects the assumption that every individual candy has equal chances to be chosen. If candies in the box are not mixed up but placed in the box by following a certain pattern, say, first green candies and then red ones on the top of the green ones without further mixing, the chances for picking red and green candies may change, and hence, the universal sample space may change too. Thus, we assume that there is no pattern of placing candies in the box by color.

Thus, now, we are ready to give a general definition of probability. In terms of the universal sample space in the form of countable events, the probability of event A equals the ratio of the number of all equally possible outcomes A over the number of all equally possible outcomes in the universal sample space, i.e.,

$$P_{\mathrm{A}} = \frac{N_{\mathrm{A}}}{N_{\Omega}} \tag{8.4}$$

where N_{A} is the number of favorite outcomes for event A in the universal sample space and N_{Ω} is the number of all equally possible outcomes in the universal sample space. Similarly, for the representation of the universal sample space in the form of areas, probability can be defined as

$$P_{\mathrm{A}} = \frac{S_{\mathrm{A}}}{S_{\Omega}} \tag{8.5}$$

where S_{A} is the area occupied by favorite event A and S_{Ω} is the total area of the universal sample space, i.e., the total area occupied by all possible events in the universal sample space.

Let's refer both N_{A} and S_{A} as ***measure*** of event A and denote it as M_{A}. Similarly, refer N_{Ω} and S_{Ω} as ***measure*** of the universal sample space Ω, i.e., measure of all possible events in the universal sample space, and denote it as M_{Ω}. The Euler diagram for event A and the universal sample space is shown in ◘ Fig. 8.3.

In general, ***measure*** can be defined as a certain numerical value assigned to an entity according to certain rules. In the application to probabilities, ***measure*** is a certain numerical value assigned to events in the universal sample space according to certain rules.

The probability of event A can be generically defined as

$$P_{\mathrm{A}} = \frac{M_{\mathrm{A}}}{M_{\Omega}} \tag{8.6}$$

The definition of probability given in Eq. (8.6) can be used for countable representation of the events in the universal sample space, for the representation by area, and for any other representation, for which measure of events is defined.

Occurrence is a random draw or random action.

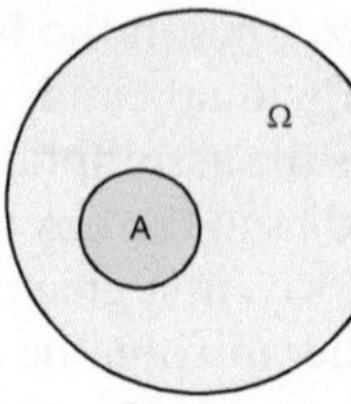

Fig. 8.3 A Euler diagram event A in universal sample space Ω

Outcome is the result of a random occurrence.

Event is the set of outcomes for which the probability is assigned.

The ***universal sample space*** is a set of all possible events.

In the application to probabilities, ***measure*** is a certain numerical value assigned to events in the universal sample space according to certain rules.

8.3 Major Properties of Probability

8.3.1 Probability Is a Number Between Zero and One

As follows from the definition given above, probability is a number between zero and one, i.e.,

$$0\,''\,P\,''\,1 \tag{8.7}$$

because a number of possible events are not negative and are always less than or equal to the number of all possible events in the universal sample space. Similarly, it is true for the representation by area too.

If event A can never occur, then the probability of such an event is zero because the number of possible events in the universal sample space is equal to zero, $N_A = 0$. On the other hand, if event B always occurs, then the probability of such event equals one, because the number of all possible events B is equal to the number of all possible events in the universal sample space.

Thus, probability is a number between zero and one. We can measure proportions of possible events in the universal sample space in percent, so it is not unusual to hear people referring probabilities in percent. However, try to use a more formal representation of probability in fraction rather than in percent.

The ***probability*** of event A is the ratio of the measure of the favorite event A to the measure of all possible events in the universal sample space:

$$P_A = \frac{M_A}{M_{All}}$$

Probability is a number between zero and one: $0 \leq P \leq 1$.

8.3.2 Operations on the Universal Sample Space

Suppose you are participating in a prize drawing. You know that there are tickets for various trips placed in the drawing box and represented in the following proportions: 30% of the tickets offer a Las Vegas trip, 10% an Alaska trip, 15% a Yellowstone trip, 20% a Grand Canyon trip, and 25% a trip to Hawaii. All tickets are thoroughly mixed. You want to win either a trip to Alaska or to Hawaii. What is the probability of such event?

$$P_{\text{Las Vegas}} = 0.30$$
$$P_{\text{Alaska}} = 0.10$$
$$P_{\text{Yellowstone}} = 0.15$$
$$P_{\text{Grand Canyon}} = 0.20$$
$$P_{\text{Hawaii}} = 0.25$$

Let's first build a universal sample space for this drawing. Presuming that all tickets in the box are well mixed up, each ticket has the same chance to be taken. For this reason, the universal sample space for picking up the trips consists of the events of picking a specific trip proportionally to the percentage of the tickets by trip in the box as shown in ◘ Fig. 8.4. Just for convenience of presentation, every rectangular block in ◘ Fig. 8.4 represents 5% of the universal sample space. According to the universal sample space, one can calculate the probabilities of events by trips as shown in ◘ Fig. 8.4.

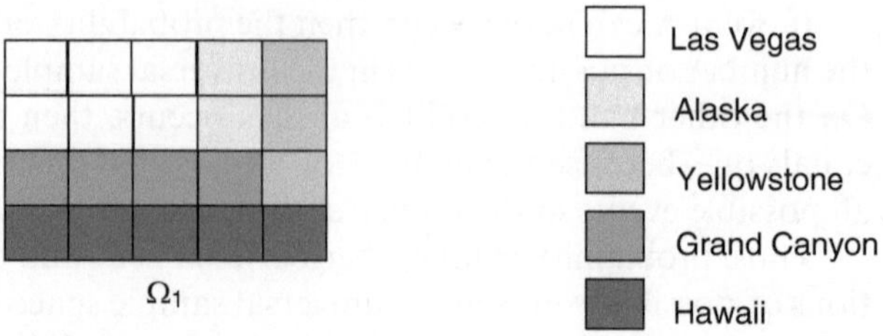

■ Fig. 8.4 The universal sample space for trip drawing

Suppose we want trips either to Alaska or to Hawaii. In terms of the universal sample space, the events that offer trips to Alaska or Hawaii are the favorite (desired) events for us. The combined percentage of the universal sample space for these events is 10% + 25% = 35% of all possible events. Thus, the measure of events "Alaska+Hawaii" $M_{\text{Alaska\&Hawaii}} = 35$, and the measure of all events $M_{\text{Alaska\&Hawaii}} = 100$, and the probability of winning either trip to Alaska or to Hawaii $P_{\text{Alaska\&Hawaii}} = 0.35$. By the definition of probability, it is

$$P_{\text{Alaska OR Hawaii}} = \frac{M_{\text{Alaska OR Hawaii}}}{M_{\Omega}} = \frac{M_{\text{Alaska}} + M_{\text{Hawaii}}}{M_{\Omega}} = \\ = \frac{M_{\text{Alaska}}}{M_{\Omega}} + \frac{M_{\text{Hawai}}}{M_{\Omega}} = P_{Alaska} + P_{\text{Hawai}} \tag{8.8}$$

Such operation is correct only if the events in the universal sample space are independent, i.e., are not overlapping. As it is clearly seen from ■ Fig. 8.4, every element of the universal sample space does not overlap with any other element. For example, every ticket in our example offers just one trip and has nothing to do with any other trips and tickets. The nonoverlapping condition means that the areas for different events have no intersection in the universal sample space.

8.3.3 The Sum of All Probabilities Equals One

Suppose the universal sample space is built of a variety of independent and non-overlapping possible events, i.e., all events are mutually exclusive. The probability of event k as defined on the universal sample space is

$$P_k = \frac{M_k}{M_{\Omega}} \tag{8.9}$$

Now, let's summarize the probabilities for all possible events. This leads to

$$\sum_{k=1}^{n} P_k = \frac{\sum_{k=1}^{n} M_k}{M_{\Omega}} = \frac{M_{\Omega}}{M_{\Omega}} = 1 \tag{8.10}$$

where n is the number of all possible events in the universal sample space. In Eq. (8.10), we used the fact that the sum of all possible events constitutes the universal space

$$\sum_{k=1}^{n} M_k = M_\Omega \tag{8.11}$$

Thus,

$$\sum_{k=1}^{n} P_k = 1 \tag{8.12}$$

That means that the sum of probabilities of all events equals one. The interpretation of this conclusion is quite clear – the sum of all probabilities includes all events whatever these events are.

> The sum of probabilities of all possible events is equal to one:
> $$\sum_{k=1}^{n} P_k = 1$$

Using the previous example about random trial on trips, we can conclude that the probability of winning a trip (does not matter which one) in the drawing is equal to one because each ticket offers a trip and there are no "empty" tickets without trips in the drawing.

8.4 Operations with Probabilities

8.4.1 Probability of a Negation

Suppose in the trip drawing discussed above you like all trips, but you've just come back from Hawaii, and for this reason, you prefer any other trip but going back to Hawaii. Thus, you want to pick a ticket with any trip but Hawaii. What is the probability of such event?

We can look at the situation just by listing all other possibilities in the universal sample space for the drawing and calculating the probability of winning any trip except the trip to Hawaii as

$$\begin{aligned} P_{\text{NOT Hawaii}} &= P_{\text{Las Vegas}} + P_{\text{Alaska}} + P_{\text{Yellowstone}} + P_{\text{Grand Canyon}} = \\ &= 0.30 + 0.10 + 0.15 + 0.20 = 0.75 \end{aligned} \tag{8.13}$$

This way of calculating the probability of "NOT Hawaii" is basically correct but sort of long and boring. By calculating the probability in such a way, we must have knowledge on all other probabilities.

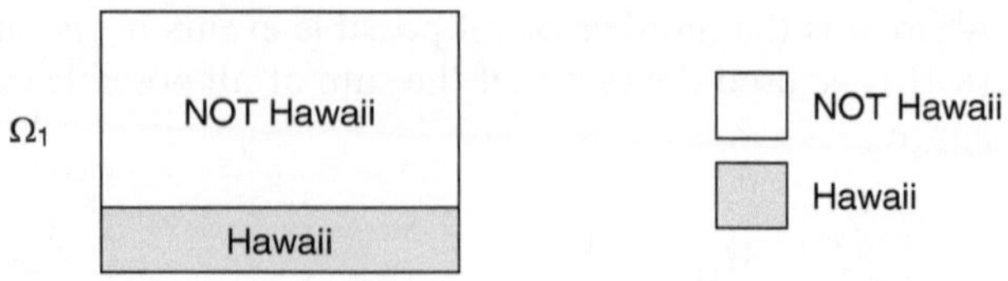

Fig. 8.5 The universal sample space for Hawaii or NOT Hawaii choices

It would be much easier to say that we consider only two events: "Hawaii" and "NOT Hawaii," where "NOT Hawaii" includes all other trips but Hawaii. The universal sample space rearranged from such perspective looks as shown in Fig. 8.5.

Now, we will utilize the property of probabilities that the sum of all probabilities is equal to one:

$$P_{\text{Hawaii}} + P_{\text{NOT Hawaii}} = 1 \tag{8.14}$$

The equation above immediately leads to

$$P_{\text{NOT Hawaii}} = 1 - P_{\text{Hawaii}} = 1 - 0.25 = 0.75 \tag{8.15}$$

Equation (8.15) leads us to the same result as Eq. (8.13), but the approach with the negation is much faster and less susceptible for mistakes by omission. In general, the probability of negation is equal to one minus the probability of the base event. Suppose we know probability P_A of event A. Then, the probability of the negation (NOT A) is

$$P_{\text{NOT A}} = 1 - P_A \tag{8.16}$$

The following notations can be equally used for negation:

$$P_{\text{NOT A}} \equiv P_{\neg A} \equiv P_{\bar{A}} \equiv \overline{P_A} \tag{8.17}$$

which are all semantically equivalent and can be used as synonyms.

> The probability of the negation for event A is
> $P_{\text{NOT A}} = 1 - P_A$
> where P_A is the probability of event A.

8.4.2 Operation "AND" of Independent Events

Suppose we have 10,000 candies in the box, 6000 of them are sweet, and 4000 of them are bitter. All candies randomly and independently of the taste are wrapped up in the red or green candy wrapper. Among them are 7000 red and 3000 green candy wrappers. You randomly pick one candy. What is the probability of picking a candy that is sweet and red?

To solve this problem, let's first build the appropriate universal sample space for events with candies as shown in Fig. 8.6.

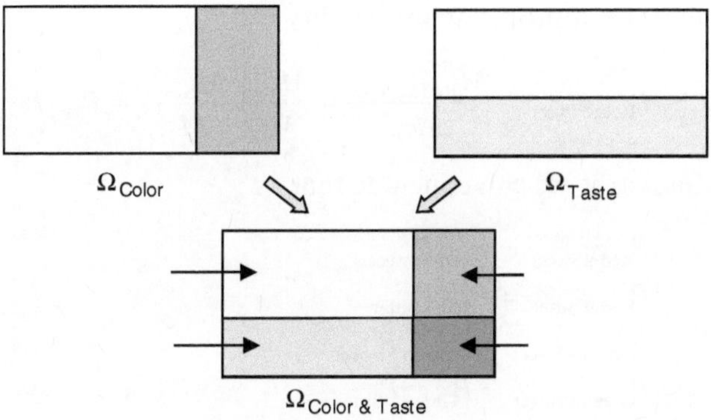

Fig. 8.6 The universal sample space for red/green and sweet/bitter candies

The universal sample space for the events with the candies of different colors (red/green), Ω_{Color}, is shown in the upper left corner of Fig. 8.6. That universal sample space allocates 70% of the space for red candies and 30% of the space for green candies based on the box content. Thus, probabilities of picking randomly a red candy is $P_{Red} = 0.7$ and a green candy is $P_{Green} = 0.3$. Similarly, the universal sample space for the same box of candies configured by taste, Ω_{Taste}, allocates 60% of the space for sweet candies and 40% of the space for bitter candies as shown in upper-right corner of Fig. 8.6. The probabilities of picking, say, a sweet candy is $P_{Sweet} = 0.6$ and a bitter one is $P_{Bitter} = 0.4$:

$$\begin{aligned} P_{Red} &= 0.7 \\ P_{Green} &= 0.3 \\ P_{Sweet} &= 0.6 \\ P_{Bitter} &= 0.4 \end{aligned} \tag{8.18}$$

Taking into account that candy's color and taste are independent parameters, they are sharing the universal sample space independently. Thus, the configuration of the universal sample space for the candy box by color and taste, $\Omega_{Color\&Taste}$, can be achieved by superposition of Ω_{Color} and Ω_{Taste}. Each quadrant in $\Omega_{Color\ \&\ Taste}$ describes a proportion of the possible events with a combination of characteristics: red and sweet, red and bitter, green and sweet, and green and bitter.

In the universal sample space $\Omega_{Color\ \&\ Taste}$, the subspace for each event by color, red or green, is divided by taste, "sweet" and "bitter," with the given proportion of sweet and bitter candies due to independence of color and taste as shown in the bottom part of Fig. 8.6. There are 70% red candies in the box, and only 60% of them are going to be sweet, and 40% of them are going to be bitter.

Thus, the measure of event for picking a red candy, which is sweet, is

$$M_{Red\&Sweet} = M_{Red} \frac{M_{Sweet}}{M_{\Omega}} \tag{8.19}$$

and the appropriate probability is

$$P_{\text{Red\&Sweet}} = \frac{M_{\text{Red\&Sweet}}}{M_{\Omega}} = \frac{M_{\text{Red}}}{M_{\Omega}} \frac{M_{\text{Sweet}}}{M_{\Omega}} = P_{\text{Red}} P_{\text{Sweet}} \tag{8.20}$$

Similarly, we can conclude that as

$$\begin{aligned} P_{\text{Red\&Sweet}} &= P_{\text{Red}} P_{\text{Sweet}} \\ P_{\text{Red\&Bitter}} &= P_{\text{Red}} P_{\text{Bitter}} \\ P_{\text{Green\&Sweet}} &= P_{\text{Green}} P_{\text{Sweet}} \\ P_{\text{Green\&Bitter}} &= P_{\text{Green}} P_{\text{Bitter}} \end{aligned} \tag{8.21}$$

Generalizing the example with candies, one can say that for any two independent events, A and B, the probability of the event, where both features occur, $P_{\text{A\&B}}$, is equal to the product of individual probabilities P_{A} and P_{B} of the events, $P_{\text{A\&B}} = P_{\text{A}} P_{\text{B}}$. Such operation is known as "AND" and is denoted as "AND" or "&" which are synonyms. Thus, the probability of A AND B for two elementary and independent events is

8

$$P_{\text{A\&B}} = P_{\text{A}} P_{\text{B}} \tag{8.22}$$

For independent events *A* and *B*, the probability of *A* "AND" *B* is

$P_{\text{A\&B}} = P_{\text{A}} P_{\text{B}}$

where P_{A} and P_{B} are the probabilities of events *A* and *B*.

8.4.3 Operation "OR" of Independent Events

With the same candy box discussed in the previous section, we are interested now in the probability of picking up a candy which is either red or sweet. Such combination can be expressed in terms of operation "OR" and written as red "OR" sweet. Operation OR can be also written as "|" which are synonyms. To answer to this question, let's come back to the universal sample space (◘ Fig. 8.6) and reconfigure it to red | sweet as shown in ◘ Fig. 8.7.

Red | sweet (the same as red "OR" sweet) means that we would be satisfied if candy is either red or sweet or both. Thus, the satisfactory combinations are red & sweet, red & bitter, and green & sweet. The only combination that does not meet the conditions red | sweet is green & bitter.

We can approach the problem of finding the probability of a candy to be red | sweet by listing all combinations of the features in the universal sample space that meet the condition, i.e.,

$$\begin{aligned} P_{\text{Red|Sweet}} &= P_{\text{Red\&Sweet}} + P_{\text{Red\&Bitter}} + P_{\text{Green\&Sweet}} = \\ &P_{\text{Red}} P_{\text{Sweet}} + P_{\text{Red}} P_{\text{Bitter}} + P_{\text{Green}} P_{\text{Sweet}} = \\ &0.7 * 0.6 + 0.7 * 0.4 + 0.3 * 0.6 = 0.88 \end{aligned} \tag{8.23}$$

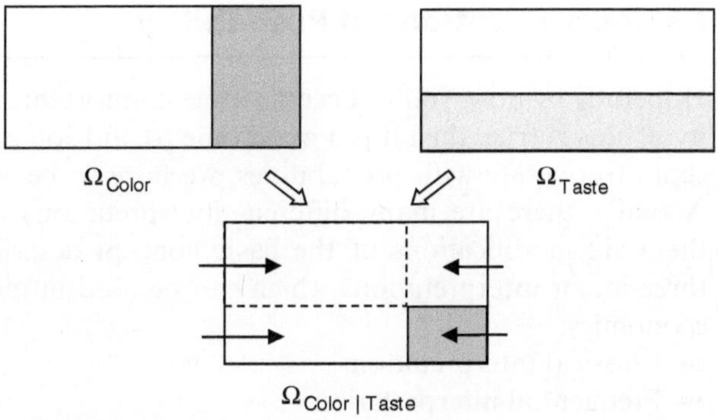

Fig. 8.7 The universal sample space for red | sweet candies

However, we can attack this problem from the negation point of view. The only combination in the universal sample space that does not meet the condition of red | sweet is green & bitter. Hence, the probability of red | sweet can be calculated as a probability of not being green & bitter which is

$$\begin{aligned} P_{\text{Red|Sweet}} &= 1 - P_{\text{Green\&Bitter}} = \\ &1 - P_{\text{Green}} P_{\text{Bitter}} = \\ &1 - 0.3 * 0.4 = 0.88 \end{aligned} \tag{8.24}$$

We can obtain the same result by taking another view at the universal sample space. Let's add up the "red" and "sweet" areas in the universal sample space. As shown clearly from Fig. 8.7, if we account for the red area and the sweet area separately in the universal sample space, then we appear to count red & sweet area twice. For this reason, we have to deduct red & sweet once from the sum of red area and sweet area in the universal sample space. The result of such operation gives us the probability of picking a red or sweet candy, $P_{\text{Red | Sweet}}$,

$$\begin{aligned} P_{\text{Red|Sweet}} &= P_{\text{Red}} + P_{\text{Sweet}} - P_{\text{Red\&Sweet}} = \\ &P_{\text{Red}} + P_{\text{Sweet}} - P_{\text{Red}} P_{\text{Sweet}} = \\ &0.7 + 0.6 - 0.7 * 0.6 = 0.88 \end{aligned} \tag{8.25}$$

This approach is the most general for calculating the probability of "OR" relationship between independent event because it deals only with the probabilities P_{Red} and P_{Sweet} and does not require any knowledge of other probabilities like P_{Green} and P_{Bitter} and others if applicable. The general rule for operation "OR" for independent events is

$$P_{\text{A|B}} = P_{\text{A}} + P_{\text{B}} - P_{\text{A}} P_{\text{B}} \tag{8.26}$$

For independent events *A* and *B*, the probability of *A* "OR" *B* is

$$P_{\text{A|B}} = P_{\text{A}} + P_{\text{B}} - P_{\text{A}} P_{\text{B}}$$

where P_{A} and P_{B} are the probabilities of events *A* and *B*.

8.5 Interpretations of Probability

Hopefully by now, you've become quite comfortable with the concept of probability. If this is true, then it is a good time to add some more complexity to this concept. To operate with probabilities, we have to be able to calculate probabilities. Actually, there are many different interpretations of probability, though all of them are modifications of the basic concept described above. Among them are three major interpretations which can be used in most problems in business and economics:

- Classical interpretation
- Frequential interpretation
- Subjective interpretation

8.5.1 Classical Interpretation

Classical interpretation of probability deals directly with the universal sample space, calculating measures in the universal sample space – counting the proportions of specific events as shown in Eq. (8.6). Cases, described in ► Sects. 8.6.1 and 8.6.2, belong to the classical interpretation.

8.5.2 Frequential Interpretation

Sometimes, it is impossible or there is not enough information to build the universal sample space to find probabilities by dealing directly with the universal sample space. However, we can generate events by counting actual outcomes in the real world, rather than in the universal sample space, and use these events to calculate probabilities using the same ratios, which we used for the universal sample space shown in Eq. (8.6). However, in this case, the count for events comes from the real-world outcomes, which can be quite different from the size of events in the universal sample space, if we would be able to build it. In this case, the probabilities calculated using this method are just estimates rather than accurate probabilities calculated in the classical interpretation. Frequential interpretation uses actual samples to estimate the parameter on the population as it is done in statistics. The accuracy of such estimates and the appropriate number of outcomes sufficient for the conclusion are discussed in ► Chaps. 13 and 15 of this book dedicated to sampling experiments in statistics. Cases described in ► Sects. 8.7 and 8.7.2 belong to the frequential interpretation.

8.5.3 Subjective Interpretation

There are some situations where neither classical nor frequential approaches would work due to impossibility of building the universal sample space or casting actual outcomes or even repeating any experiments. For example, if we are interested in the course of stock index on the next trading day, we cannot build a universal sample space for possible events, and also, we cannot conduct any actual experiment because tomorrow will be a unique tomorrow with all the factors and surprises that will come tomorrow, which cannot be sampled by previous trading days.

In this case, a decision about probabilities could be made from intuitive expectations and negotiations. This must sound a bit weird at first glance. However, such determinations of probability are happening quite often. For example, suppose we would like to determine what is the probability of the pharmaceutical company to develop a new type of medication by the next year. There is no way of formally calculating such probability, and the only way left is to collect intuitive and subjective opinions about the probability and negotiate it until all agree on the number. Such an approach, though it sounds quite weird and inaccurate, is quite reasonable because, through negotiations, people account for most informal parameters and most subjective opinions based on understanding of the discussed matter. Subjective interpretation of probability reflects individual opinions and, hence, is susceptible to individual biases. An example of the subjective interpretation of probabilities is discussed in ► Sect. 8.8.

8.6 Calculating Probabilities Using Classical Interpretation

To work with probabilities, we first have to be able to find them. How can we do it in the real-world situations? Often finding probabilities is not an easy task, but in many cases, it can be done.

8.6.1 Calculating Probability From Symmetry

Tossing a Coin

Source: Image by Alexander Lesnitsky from Pixabay

Suppose we toss an ideal coin that is symmetric, i.e., there is no physical difference between heads and tails. In this case, just from the consideration of symmetry, we can assume that there are only two events in the universal sample – heads and tails. The universal sample space for these events is divided into two equal parts, one for heads and another one for tails, and there are no other possible events.

We can find the probabilities P_{Heads} and P_{Tail} for heads and for tails using the definition given in Eq. (8.6) and the assumption that both events have the same measure, i.e., $M_{\text{Heads}} = M_{\text{Tails}}$:

$$\begin{aligned} M_{\text{Heads}} &= M_{\text{Tails}} \\ P_{\text{Heads}} &= \frac{M_{\text{Heads}}}{M_{\text{Heads}} + M_{\text{Tails}}} = \frac{1}{2} \\ P_{\text{Tails}} &= \frac{M_{\text{Tails}}}{M_{\text{Heads}} + M_{\text{Tails}}} = \frac{1}{2} \end{aligned} \tag{8.27}$$

We can also calculate probabilities P_{Heads} and P_{Tails} using a presumption that the probabilities of heads and tails are equal and the fact that the sum of probabilities of all possible events is equal to one:

$$\begin{aligned} P_{\text{Heads}} &= P_{\text{Tails}} \\ P_{\text{Heads}} + P_{\text{Tails}} &= 1 \end{aligned} \tag{8.28}$$

8

Solution to this set of equations results in

$$P_{\text{Heads}} = P_{\text{Tails}} = \frac{1}{2} \tag{8.29}$$

Rolling a Die

Source: Image by taintedtextures from Pixabay

Suppose we roll an ideal dice for which all six faces are physically similar. Thus, the chances of getting the dice to roll face up on any of its six faces are the same, and there are no other events. Thus, the measures of all possible events are the same and hence

$$\begin{aligned} &M_1 = M_2 = M_3 = M_4 = M_5 = M_6 \\ &M_\Omega = M_1 + M_2 + M_3 + M_4 + M_5 + M_6 \\ &P_1 = P_2 = P_3 = P_4 = P_5 = P_6 = \frac{1}{6} \end{aligned} \tag{8.30}$$

Another way to calculate the probabilities of getting a face up after a roll of the die, 1, 2, 3, 4, 5, or 6, are equal and the sum of all these probabilities is equal to one is

$$\begin{aligned} P_1 = P_2 = P_3 = P_4 = P_5 = P_6 \\ P_1 + P_2 + P_3 + P_4 + P_5 + P_6 = 1 \end{aligned} \quad (8.31)$$

Solving these equations results in

$$P_1 = P_2 = P_3 = P_4 = P_5 = P_6 = \frac{1}{6} \quad (8.32)$$

Thus, if we have information on symmetry or any specific relationship of a set of possible events or which is the same on the symmetry or any specific relationship in the universal sample space, we may be able to calculate the appropriate probabilities from pure theoretical point of view without collecting any empirical data.

8.6.2 Calculating Probabilities From Content Percentage

Probabilities can be found form content percentage as it was described for the candy box in ► Sect. 8.2. The content can be used for the generation of events and the universal sample space and then assessing the probabilities for different events by the proportion of the universal sample space occupied by that event with the appropriate outcomes over the entire universal sample space as shown in Eq. (8.6) and ◘ Fig. 8.3.

8.7 Estimating Probabilities Using Frequential Interpretation

8.7.1 Estimating Probabilities From Sampling Experiments

Suppose we have a big supply of chestnuts. We expect some of the chestnuts can be rotten. What is the probability of getting a rotten chestnut? To solve this problem with a 100% accuracy, we have to crack all chestnuts and calculate the probability using the universal sample space. However, such experiment makes no sense because we would destroy all chestnuts to find the probability and we will not be able to use the results as no chestnuts are left. Instead, we may crack some chestnuts and calculate how many of them were rotten. Then based on the result, we can estimate the probability of getting a spoiled chestnut as

$$P_{\text{Rotten}} \oplus \frac{N_{\text{Spoiled}}}{N_{\text{All Tested}}} \quad (8.33)$$

This approach is not 100% accurate but it would give us a reasonable perspective. This is a statistical approach, where the collection of chestnuts for testing is called a sample, and the testing experiment is referred to as sampling experiment. We will discuss sampling experiments and their accuracy in ► Chap. 15 of this book.

8.7.2 Estimating Probabilities From Historical Data

Suppose we plan some outdoor activities for July next year and we would like to know what probability we have for a good weather without rain. Nobody has a "crystal ball" to see into the future, but there is a way we can estimate such probability. In presumption that climate has not significantly changed for the last several years, we can collect historical data on the weather in July for the past several years and estimate the probability of a good weather as

$$P_{\text{GoodDays}} \oplus \frac{N_{\text{GoodDays}}}{N_{\text{AllDays}}} \tag{8.34}$$

Such approach belongs to the category of sampling experiments too, similar to the previous example.

8.8 Subjective Determination of Probabilities

8.8.1 New Product Marketing

Suppose a company has developed a new product and starts marketing the product. There are a number of possible marketing scenarios the company can pursue. Which scenario has better chances to succeed? There is no way to experiment with all scenarios in full scale first and then estimate the probabilities for each scenario. The most practical way is to evaluate the probabilities by collecting expert opinions about those probabilities and negotiate them. This is a typical subjective approach for determining the probabilities.

8.8.2 Business Strategy

Suppose a company is developing its strategy for the future. Typically, every strategy considers success and risk factors. What is the probability for the success with the developed strategy? In most cases, it is practically impossible to calculate such probability using any but subjective approach. People, who have experience and a good judgment in the situation, discuss their opinions, suggest the probability, and negotiate them if their suggestions are different.

8.9 Problems for Practicing

8.9.1 Flipping a Coin

Problem 1

What is the probability of getting three heads in a row?

Every new flip of the coin is independent from the other flips, i.e., the coin does not "remember" the results of the previous flips; thus, the probability of getting the heads on the first, second, and third flip is the same and equals 1/2. The probability of getting three heads in a row is

$$P_{3H} = P_{H\&H\&H} = P_H P_H P_H = P_H^3 = \left(\frac{1}{2}\right)^3 = \frac{1}{8} \tag{8.35}$$

Problem 2

What is the probability of getting at least one tail from three flips of a coin?

Let's first build the universal sample space for flipping a coin three times (or flipping three coins, which is the same) as shown in ◘ Fig. 8.8.

Solution 1 to Problem 2

There are a total of eight possible outcomes in the universal sample space for flipping a coin three times: HHH, HHT, HTH, THH, HTT, THT, TTH, and TTT where "H" stands for heads and "T" stands for tails. Only the first combination, HHH, does not include any tails, while other combinations meet the condition of containing at list one tails.

We can solve this problem in two different ways. The first approach is to count all favorite combinations of three flips in the universal sample space for three coins:

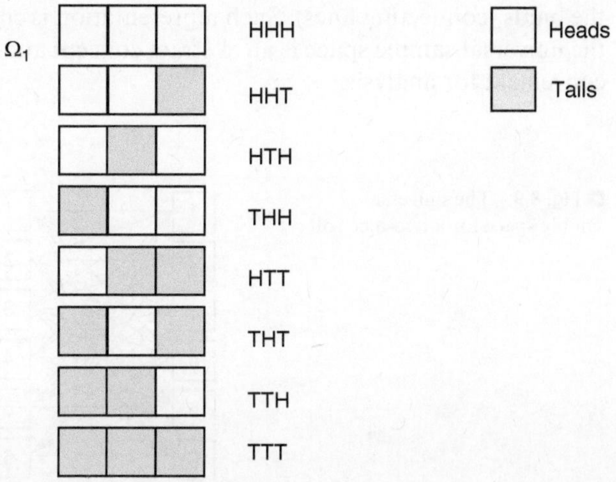

◘ **Fig. 8.8** The universal sample for flipping a coin three times

$$P_{\text{atleast1T}} = P_{\text{HHT}} + P_{\text{HTH}} + P_{\text{THH}} + P_{\text{HTT}} + P_{\text{THT}} + P_{\text{TTH}} + P_{\text{TTT}} = 7 * \left(\frac{1}{2}\right)^3 = \frac{7}{8} \tag{8.36}$$

Solution 2 to Problem 2

The second approach employs the negation. We can say that out of all combinations, only HHH does not meet the condition. Taking into account that all combinations are equally probable, we can conclude that

$$P_{\text{atleast1T}} = 1 - P_{\text{HHH}} = 1 - \left(\frac{1}{2}\right)^3 = \frac{7}{8} \tag{8.37}$$

As evident from the Eqs. (4.36) and (4.37), both approaches lead to the same result; however, the second approach is shorter and more elegant.

8.9.2 Rolling the Dice

Suppose we roll two dice.

Problem 3

What is the probability of getting 3 and 5?

Each die has six faces and for this reason offers six possible outcomes. The universal sample space for a two-dice roll is shown in ◘ Fig. 8.9 in the form of binds (connecting lines) between the possible outcomes of each dice:

$$P_{3\&5} = \frac{2}{36} = \frac{1}{18} \tag{8.38}$$

The number of all possible outcomes for a two-dice roll is equal to the number of the binds (connecting lines). Such representation is chosen to illustrate the fact that the universal sample space is an abstract concept and can be presented in any form convenient for analysis.

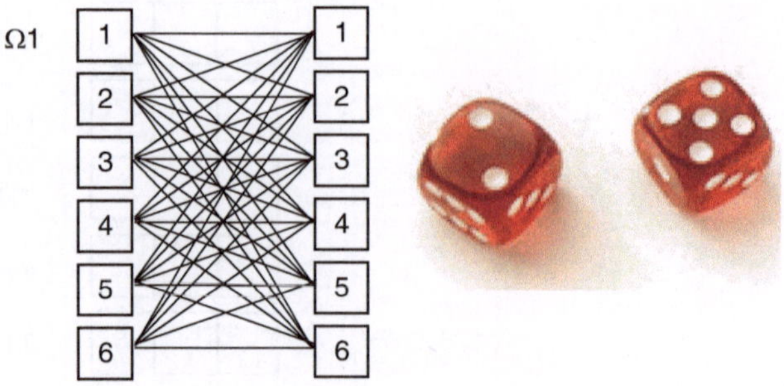

◘ **Fig. 8.9** The universal sample space for a two-dice roll

What is the probability of getting 5 and 3 in any order from rolling two dice? As it follows from the universal sample space, there are a total of 6 * 6 = 36 possible outcomes from rolling two dice, and only two of them, (3, 5) and (5, 3), are what we want. Thus, the probability of getting 3 and 5 is 1/18 as two possible favorite events in the universal sample space out of totally 36 equally possible events.

We can address this problem also from a different perspective. The probability of getting first 3 and second 5 is 1/6*1/6 = 1/36, and the probability of getting first 5 and second 3 is 1/6*1/6 = 1/36 too. We have to add these two probabilities because we are not interested in the order, both outcomes meet our condition, and the outcomes are independent. The result is

$$P_{3\&5} = P_{35} + P_{53} = P_3P_5 + P_5P_3 = 2P_3P_5 = 2\frac{1}{6}*\frac{1}{6} = \frac{1}{18} \tag{8.39}$$

Thus, both results are the same regardless of the approach.

Problem 4

What is the probability of getting at least one 4 in a two-dice roll?

Definitely, we can count all favorite outcomes that contain at least one 4 in the universal sample space shown in ◘ Fig. 8.9 and then divide this number over the number of all equally possible outcomes. Let's instead engage some more analytic approach. If the first dice shows 4 (let's call it case A), then we should not worry about the outcome on the second dice. The probability of getting 4 on the first dice is 1/6. Similarly, if the second dice shows 4 (let's call it case B), then we should not worry about the outcome on the first dice. The probability of getting 4 with the second dice with any number on the first is 1/6 too. It looks that we may just add up these probabilities too. However, it is not as easy. Outcome 4 on the first dice and 4 on the second dice have probability 1/6*1/6 = 1/36 and belong to both cases, A and B; thus, it was counted twice. For this reason, we have to subtract the probability of the double 4 from the sum of probabilities of cases A and B. The result will be the following:

$$P_{\text{at least one 4}} = P_4 + P_4 - P_{44} = 2P_4 - P_{44} = 2P_4 - P_4P_4 = 2\frac{1}{6} - \frac{1}{6}*\frac{1}{6} = \frac{11}{36} \tag{8.40}$$

The bottom line of the problems above is the following – always think first about the most elegant solution which normally is the easiest and the shortest one.

8.9.3 Electronic Devices

Suppose there is a box that contains AMD and Intel microprocessors. Sixty percent of the processors are AMD, and 40% are Intel, all randomly distributed in the box. The number of microprocessors in the box is so high that removing several of them from the box does not change the content percentage to any noticeable degree; hence, we can consider probabilities of getting an AMD processor, $P_A = 0.6$, and getting a Intel processor, $P_N = 0.4$, for a number of draws. Thus,

$$\begin{aligned} P_A &= 0.6 \\ P_N &= 0.4 \end{aligned} \tag{8.41}$$

Problem 5

You randomly take two processors from the box.

What is the probability that at least one of the processors is AMD?

Solution 1 to Problem 5

We can solve this problem by listing all possible combinations that meet the condition of at least one AMD as shown in ◘ Fig. 8.10 where "A" stands for AMD and "N" stands for Intel. Those combinations are AA, AN, and NA and NN. Combination NN does not contain any A and for this reason does not meet the condition. Thus, the probability of getting at least one AMD out of two processors is

$$\begin{aligned} P_{\text{at least one A}} &= P_A P_A + P_A P_N + P_N P_A = \\ &0.6 * 0.6 + 0.6 * 0.4 + 0.4 * 06 = 0.84 \end{aligned} \tag{8.42}$$

Solution 2 to Problem 5

Instead of listing all combinations that meet the condition, we can list the combinations that do not meet the condition and then apply the negation. In this case, the only combination that does not meet the condition is NN. Thus,

$$P_{\text{at least one A}} = 1 - P_N P_N = 1 - 0.4 * 0.4 = 0.84 \tag{8.43}$$

The second solution is shorter than the first one because the number of combinations that do not meet the condition "at least one AMD" is less than the number of combinations that meet the condition.

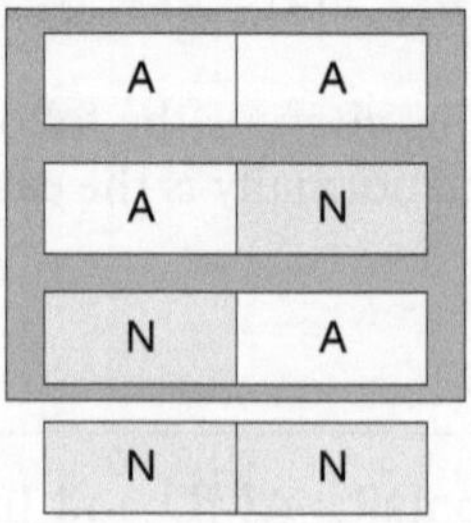

◘ **Fig. 8.10** Possible combinations of AMD or Intel processors out of two

Problem 6

You take three randomly chosen processors from the box.

What is the probability of picked two AMD and one Intel processors?

Solution 1 to Problem 6

The problem can be solved in a straightforward way by listing all matching combinations AAI, ANA, and NAA from all possible combinations in the universal sample space as shown in ◘ Fig. 8.11 and then calculating the probability of those events, P_{2A1N}:

$$P_{2A1N} = P_A P_A P_N + P_A P_N P_A + P_N P_A P_A = \\ 0.6 * 0.6 * 0.4 + 0.6 * 0.4 * 0.6 + 0.4 * 06 * 06 = 0.432 \tag{8.44}$$

With this approach, one has to list all possible combinations of two AMDs and one Intel that contribute to the universal sample space for this problem. Even with three totally picked processors, it is a little challenge not to miss some of the combinations. The complexity of the problem will grow if there are more processors to pick.

Solution 2 to Problem 6

It is easy to notice that all three possible combinations in Eq. (8.44) have equal probabilities

$$P_A P_A P_N = P_A P_N P_A = P_N P_A P_A \tag{8.45}$$

because the only difference between those combinations is in the order in which A and N come up, two A and one N from three trials: AAN, ANA, and NAA.

The number of combinations from n elements by k is equal to

$$\binom{n}{k} = \frac{n!}{k!(n-k)!} \tag{8.46}$$

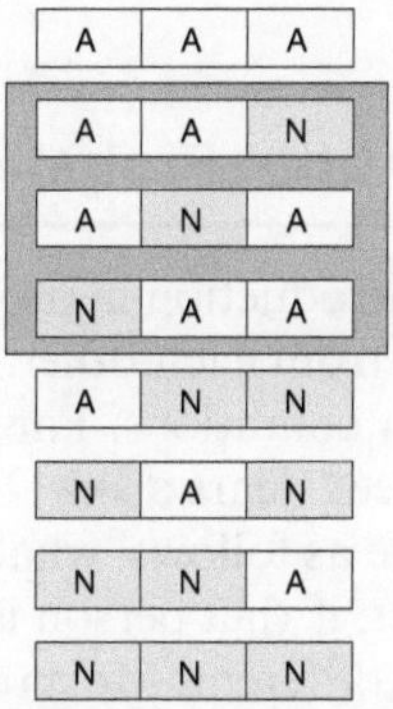

◘ **Fig. 8.11** Possible combinations of three processors

where $n \geq k \geq 0$ and

$$n! = 1 * 2 * \ldots * n \quad \text{and} \quad 0! = 1 \tag{8.47}$$

Function $n!$ is referred to as ***n-factorial***. It is easy to figure out from Eq. (8.46) that

$$\binom{n}{k} = \binom{n}{n-k} = \frac{n!}{k!(n-k)!} \tag{8.48}$$

Coming back to the solution of the problem, we need two A and one N from the set of three trials. Let's take it as AAN; it does not really matter what order we use. The probability of such combination is

$$P_A P_A P_N \tag{8.49}$$

The number of all possible combinations of two A and one N out of three is

$$\binom{3}{2} = \frac{3!}{2!(3-2)!} = \frac{3!}{2!(1)!} = \frac{1*2*3}{(1*2)(1)} = 3 \tag{8.50}$$

8

These combinations are AAN, ANA, and NAA. Thus, the probability of getting two A and one C out of three trials is

$$P_{2A1C} = \binom{3}{2} P_A P_A P_N = \\ 3 * 0.6 * 0.6 * 0.4 = 0.432 \tag{8.51}$$

Solution 2 gives the same result as solution 1; however, with solution 2, we do not need explicitly to list all possible combinations, but use just one of them and multiply the probability of it by the number of similar combinations as of Eq. (8.49). With such an approach, we have much less chances to miscount some of the combination by just forgetting to list them. Can you imagine how convenient such approach is in case of large sets, suppose 63 AMDs and 37 Intel out of 100 processors?

8.10 What More to Lean About Probabilities

This chapter presented just an introduction in probabilities. We presumed that random outcomes are independent from each other. In the real world, outcomes and events may be subject to certain conditions. For example, what is the probability that a random person on the street wears a skirt? A similar question with an additional condition could sound like as follows: what is the probability that a random person on the street wears a skirt, if that person is a female? It would be correct to assume that the probabilities are different. Most random cases and situations imply certain conditions.

The probability of events under certain conditions are referred to as Bayesian probabilities. Unfortunately, the size and scope limitations of this book do not allow us to address this exciting part of probability. We leave this part for your additional study.

Questions for Self-Control for Chap. 8

1. What is random trial?
2. What is the difference between random occurrence, outcome, and event?
3. What is the universal sample space?
4. What is measure for events and the universal sample space?
5. What is the definition of probability?
6. Does the sum of all probabilities of independent events have any limitations or constraints?
7. What are classical, frequential, and subjective interpretations of probability?
8. At what circumstances should classical interpretation of probability be used?
9. At what circumstances should frequential interpretation of probability be used?
10. At what circumstances should subjective interpretation of probability be used?
11. What logical operations on probabilities do you know?
12. How to calculate the probability of a negation?
13. How to calculate the probability of two independent events associated by logical “AND”?
14. How to calculate “OR” on two independent events?

Problems for Chap. 8

1. What is the probability of getting 2 and 4 when you roll two dice?
2. You flip a coin. What probability is higher, to get five heads in a row or to get three heads and two tails in any sequence?
3. You flip a fair coin (fair coin means $P_{\text{Heads}} = P_{\text{Tails}}$) and get six heads in a row. What chances do you have for heads and tails in the next flip of the coin?
4. In the game of rolling two dice, you will get \$10 for a double ($1 \times 1, \ldots, 6 \times 6$) and lose \$1 for any other combination. What are the expectations and risks associated with the game? Would you play the game or reject it?
5. The probability of picking a defective device is 0.2. What is the probability that there are two defective devices out of five you get?
6. Twenty-five students are registered for a class. What is the probability that at least two students have their birthday on the same day?

Distribution, Expectation, and Risk

Contents

9.1 Random Variables – 154

9.2 Probability Distribution – 155
9.2.1 Notation Convention for Random Variables – 155
9.2.2 Probability Distribution for a Discrete Random Variable – 155
9.2.3 Probability Distribution for a Continuous Random Variable – 156

9.3 Expectation and Risk – 159
9.3.1 What to Expect From a Random Draw – 159
9.3.2 Expected Value – 160
9.3.3 Standard Deviation and Risk – 162
9.3.4 Coefficient of Variation – 166
9.3.5 Risk-Reward Analysis – 166

9.4 Case 1: Beach Café – 167

9.5 Case 2: Investment Risk and Decision-Making – 168

9.6 A Decision Tree – 169

S. K. Aityan, *Business Research Methodology*, Classroom Companion: Business,
https://doi.org/10.1007/978-3-030-76857-7_9

9.1 Random Variables

A ***random variable*** is a variable whose values randomly take numerical values. Thus, a random variable is a measurement of the numerical outcome of a random situation.

A ***discrete random variable*** is a random variable that can take discrete values, for example, a number of times you hit a target out of five attempts when shooting. This variable can take values zero, one, two, three, four, and five, and for this reason, it is a discrete random variable.

If a random variable can take any value from a continuous interval of numbers, such variable is called a ***continuous random variable***. For example, a weight of an apple could be any from the interval between 0 and 3 lb if all apples are within this weight range. We will discuss continuous random variables in a greater detail a little bit later in this chapter.

However, it is possible that the outcomes of a random trial are not numbers. For example, a name of a randomly chosen person could be any name, but it is not a number. Such outcome is referred to as ***categorical variables***.

If we measure the heights of individuals, we are dealing with a random variable because all measurements are numbers. When we roll a dice, the outcomes are also numbers; thus, the outcome is also a random variable. In contrast, when we flip a coin, the possible outcomes could be "heads" or "tail" that are not numbers; hence, the measurements belong to a categorical variable. We can easily turn such a categorical variable into a random variable if we assign a number to every possible outcome, say one for the heads and zero for the tails. It is not clear how to process categorical random values without assigning numerical values to the outcomes and converting the categorical variable into a numerical random variable.

A ***random variable*** is a variable whose values randomly take numerical values.

A ***discrete random variable*** is a random variable that can take discrete values.

A ***continuous random variable*** is a random variable that randomly takes value from an interval of continuous numbers.

A ***categorical random variable*** is a measurement of the outcome of a random situation which is not numerical.

9.2 Probability Distribution

9.2.1 Notation Convention for Random Variables

Typically, every random variable is given an identifier, for example, variable X. It could be any character or any combination of characters, numbers, and some special signs. Typically, capital letters are used for naming random variables. A value that variable X takes is normally denoted with lower case, say value x for random variable X. Suppose we have function $f(X)$. This function is identified as $f(X)$, where X is the variable. If we want to show value of the function at variable equal x, i.e., $X = x$, the value of function f at $X = x$ can be written as $f(x)$.

Thus, probability of a random variable X to take value x can be written as $P(x)$ or $P(X = x)$. For example, the probability that X takes value of five can be written as $P(5)$ or $P(X = 5)$. Probabilities for random variable X are labeled as $P(X)$. To avoid any confusion in the future, let's reiterate the notation convention. The notation and their meanings are shown in ◘ Table 9.1.

9.2.2 Probability Distribution for a Discrete Random Variable

A ***probability distribution*** for a discrete random variable, X, is a set of all possible values X together with the associated probabilities for those values, $P(X)$. In other words, probability P is a function of random value X.

Suppose we have a supply of watermelons with the weights from 15 to 25 lb. The probability of a watermelon to have weight x is $P(x)$. The scale on which we weigh watermelons works with the accuracy of 1 lb. Thus, if a watermelon weight

◘ Table 9.1 Notation for random variables, their values, and probabilities

Notation	Meaning	Comments
X	An identifier for a random variable	It is just a label (identifier) for a random variable rather than its value
x	A value that random variable X takes	It is a specific number. For example, five
$P(X)$	An identifier for probability distribution for random variable X	It is just a label for function P of variable X rather than any specific probability or any specific value
$P(x)$ or $P(X = x)$	A probability of random variable X to take value, i.e., $X = x$	For every x, probability $P(x)$ is a number $0 \le P(x) \le 1$

X	P(X)
15	0.001
16	0.008
17	0.038
18	0.111
19	0.211
20	0.261
21	0.211
22	0.111
23	0.038
24	0.008
25	0.002

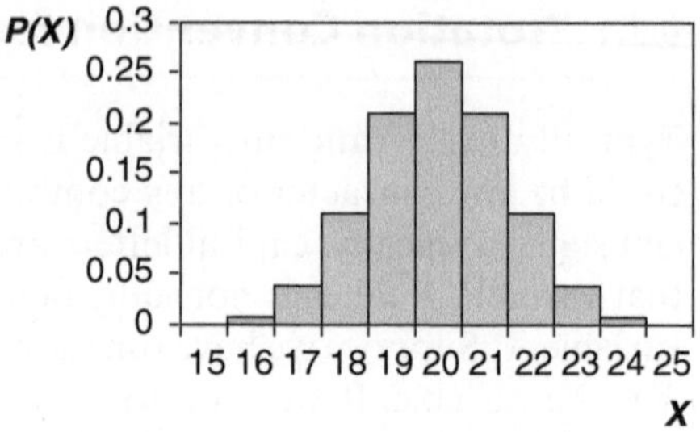

Fig. 9.1 An example of a probability distribution

shows, say, 19 lb, the actual weight is rounded to integers, i.e., it is somewhere between 18.5 lb and 19.5 lb. It means that $P(19)$ actually means $P(18.5 < x \leq 19.5) = P(19 \pm 0.5)$. We use interval (18.5, 19.5] that does not include point 18.5 but includes point 19.5 for the reason not to count for the same point two times in the adjacent intervals. Thus, for any integer x, $P(x)$ actually means $P(x \pm 0.5)$. We denote intervals $a < x \leq b$ as $(a,b]$, where a round bracket "(" indicates that the end point is not included into the interval while the square bracket indicates that the end point is included into the interval. It is very important to understand that no measurement can be done with the perfect precision and any value is measured only with a certain accuracy, which is ±0.5 in this particular case. The example of a probability distribution for the watermelon weights is shown in the table and in the chart in Fig. 9.1. The sum of all probabilities for the watermelon weights equals to one.

The ***probability distribution*** of a discrete random variable, X, is a set of all possible values X together with the associated probabilities of these values, $P(X)$.

9.2.3 Probability Distribution for a Continuous Random Variable

Assume we have improved the accuracy of the scale and now we can weigh watermelons with the accuracy of 0.25 lb. Then, we'll get a similar distribution but with the values $X = \{15, 15.25, 15.5, 15.75, 16, \ldots\}$ with the increment $\Delta x = 0.25$ as shown in Fig. 9.2. Now, every value x actually means $x \pm \Delta x/2 = x \pm 0.125$, and the associated probability $P(x)$ is the probability of x to be between $x - 0.125$ and $x + 0.125$ that is $P(x \pm 0.125)$.

You might have already noticed that the probability of $x = 19$ in this case when we measure the weight with the accuracy of ±0.125 is 0.053 (see table in Fig. 9.2), while in the previous case when the weight was measured with accuracy ±0.25, the probability of $x = 19$ was 0.211 (see table in Fig. 9.2). Is there any problem with the probabilities? Not at all. The probability of $x = 19$ in case of measurement

Fig. 9.2 Probability distribution $P(X)$ with the more but smaller intervals for x from X

X	P(X)	X	P(X)	X	P(X)	X	P(X)
15	0.000	17.5	0.017	20	0.066	22.5	0.017
15.25	0.001	17.75	0.022	20.25	0.065	22.75	0.012
15.5	0.001	18	0.027	20.5	0.063	23	0.009
15.75	0.002	18.25	0.034	20.75	0.059	23.25	0.006
16	0.002	18.5	0.040	21	0.053	23.5	0.004
16.25	0.003	18.75	0.047	21.25	0.047	23.75	0.003
16.5	0.004	19	0.053	21.5	0.040	24	0.002
16.75	0.006	19.25	0.059	21.75	0.034	24.25	0.002
17	0.009	19.5	0.063	22	0.027	24.5	0.001
17.25	0.012	19.75	0.065	22.25	0.022	24.75	0.001

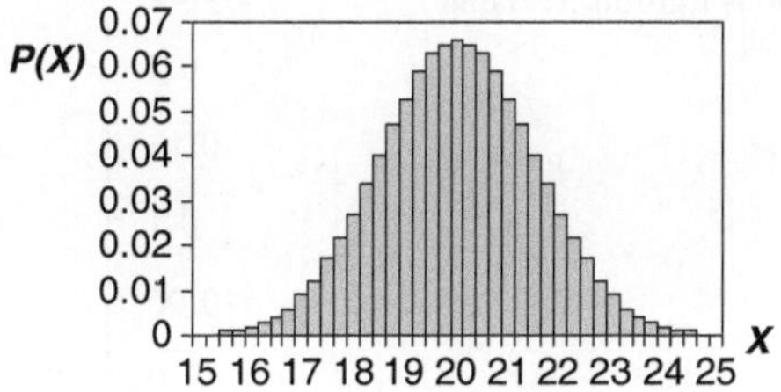

accuracy of ±0.50 accounts for the watermelons with the weights from in the interval (18.5, 19.5], while the probability of $x = 19$ in case of measurement accuracy of ±0.125 accounts for the watermelons with the weights from 18.875 to 19.125 which is expected to be much less than the probability in the previous case because the measurement interval now is $18.875 < x \leq 19.125$ which is four times smaller than interval $18.875 < x \leq 19.125$ in the previous case. Note that the sum of all probabilities is equal to one in both cases because it is a fundamental feature of probabilities in the interval (18.875, 19.125]. Interval (18.5, 19.5] is now broken into four intervals, and interval (18.875,19.125] is just one of them. Thus, the smaller intervals of X, the lower is the probability of $P(X)$ for variable X to be in this interval.

We may reduce the intervals more and get some other numbers for the even smaller probabilities. However, if we count probabilities for any for each interval ($x1$, $x2$) using any accuracy, the total probability of the random variable to be within such interval would stay the same regardless of the accuracy.

Please think thoroughly about it because it is very important to understand that in contrast to the discrete random variables, probabilities of continuous random variable, X, are being measured on intervals of x rather than on the precise values of x.

If we keep increasing the accuracy of the scale, i.e., indefinitely reducing intervals Δx along the X axis, the associated probabilities start covering the smaller and smaller intervals. Finally, as interval Δx of random variable tends to zero, X no longer takes discrete values, it becomes continuous, and we come up with $P(X)$ becomes a smooth distribution function on continuous variable. ◘ Figure 9.3 shows the values of X in three cases considered above. In case (a), the watermelon weight is measured with the accuracy of 1 lb, so $X = \{15, 16, \ldots, 25\}$. In case (b), the weight is measured with the accuracy of 0.25 lb, so $X = \{15, 15¼, 15½, 15¾, 16, \ldots 25\}$, while in case (c), the measurements can be performed with the continu-

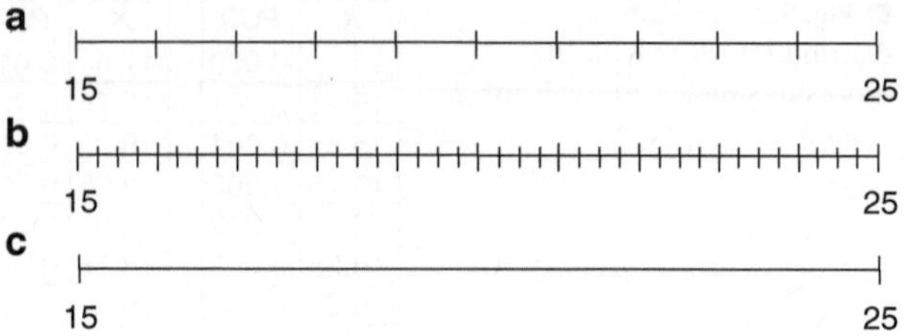

Fig. 9.3 Discrete and continuous random variables: (**a**) a larger scale discrete random variable; (**b**) a smaller scale discrete random variable; (**c**) a continuous random variable

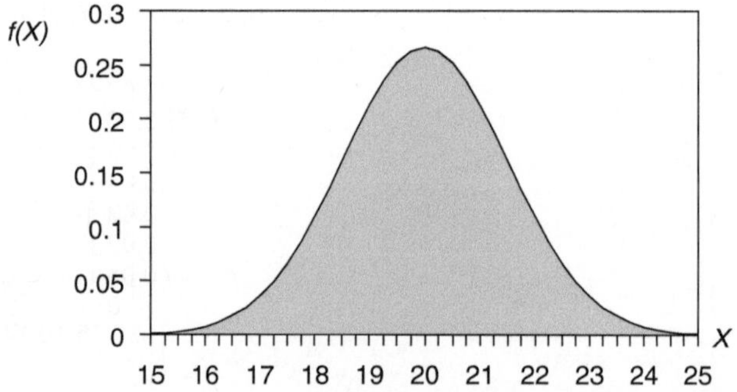

Fig. 9.4 Probability distribution density for a continuous random variable

ous accuracy, and X can take any value from the interval from 15 to 25. Please note that nobody can make measurements with the continuous accuracy. The accuracy can be very low but still finite. Thus, continuous variable is an abstraction. In Fig. 9.3, we are dealing with the discrete random variable X in cases (a) and (b) and with the continuous random variable X in case (c).

For the continuous random variable, the probability distribution turns into a curve as shown in Fig. 9.4. For continuous random variable X, the curve $f(X)$ is referred to as probability distribution density. The total area under the curve $f(X)$ is equal to one because it represents the total probability of all possible values of X that is the same as the sum of all probabilities in case of discrete random variable.

The probability $P(x_1 < x < x_2)$ of the continuous random variable X takes values within an interval between x_1 and x_2 and is equal to the area under the curve $f(X)$ constrained by these two values, x_1 and x_2, as shown in Fig. 9.5.

It is interesting to notice that probability of any precise number, say $x = 21$, is equal to zero for a continuous random variable because any precise number x is the same as the interval of a zero length that results in a zero area under the curve $f(x)$. For this reason, we now start using simple open intervals for X like $x_1 < x < x_2$ instead of the intervals with one open and another closed ends.

There are some exceptions from this trait that lie in specific areas of mathematics dealing with Lebesgue measure and generalized functions that are far beyond the scope of this book and typical applications of probabilities in business. You may face this situation only if you work in mathematics and theoretical physics.

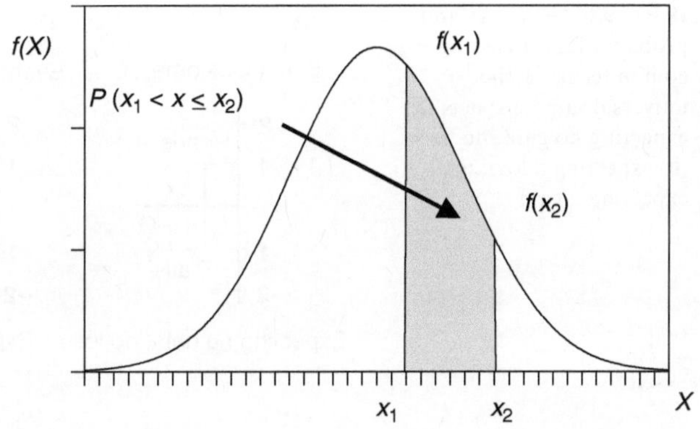

Fig. 9.5 Probability for interval of $x_1 < x < x_2$

9.3 Expectation and Risk

The power of the probability theory is that we can use probabilities to estimate expectations and risks when we act under uncertainty.

9.3.1 What to Expect From a Random Draw

Suppose you flip a coin and, if it lands on heads, you get 1 cent but, if it lands on tails, you lose 1 cent. Would you play such game? Nobody can predict whether it is going to be heads or tails in the next flip of the coin, so you may win or lose. However, from the common sense, most likely, you would believe that this game is fair, i.e., no win/no lose, and do not hesitate to play if you have a mood for that. Let's change the rule of the game. Now, if it is heads, you win 1 cent, but if it is tails, you lose 2 cents. Though this game is not about big money and the coin may land on heads, most likely, you would not play because you sense a loss. On the other hand, if you get 2 cents in case of heads and lose 1 cent in case of tails, you would be more willing to play because you expect a gain. Somehow, you intuitively expect a gain, though anything may occur.

How do you sense gain or loss given that you are not a clairvoyant and have no crystal ball to see into the future? You can make some estimates about your expectations of the game based on probabilities and outcomes. The game may go any way different from the expectation, but the basic expectation gives you some hints whether the game is worth trying. Possibly, you were intuitively thinking in terms of rewards on the universal sample space for the assessment of your expectations as shown in Fig. 9.6.

Probabilities and rewards are shown in Fig. 9.6 in the form of bars in which width represents the probabilities in terms of the universal sample space Ω while the heights of the bars represent the appropriate rewards. As we remember from the definition of random variables given in the previous section, the rewards X_{Heads}

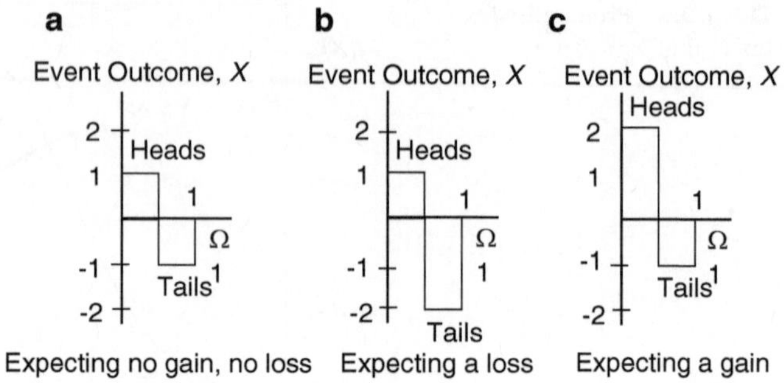

Fig. 9.6 Rewards and probabilities for tossing a coin in terms of the universal sample space: (**a**) expecting no gain, no loss; (**b**) expecting a loss; (**c**) expecting a gain

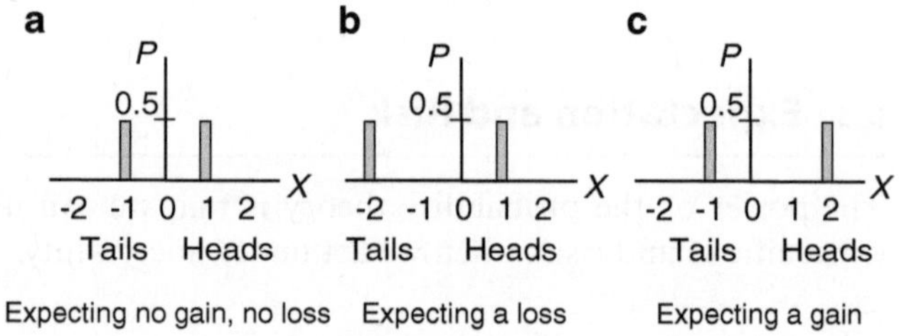

Fig. 9.7 Rewards and probabilities for tossing a coin in terms of probability distribution: (**a**) expecting no gain, no loss; (**b**) expecting a loss; (**c**) expecting a gain

9

and X_{Tails} are random variables that assigned the appropriate probabilities P_{Heads} and P_{Tails}. We can rearrange the presentation given in Fig. 9.6 by showing it in terms of probability distribution, i.e., as random variables, X, versus the appropriate probabilities, P. Such representation is shown in Fig. 9.7.

Perhaps, you intuitively already figured out how convenient such representation is for assessing your expected gain or loss. The probability distribution in Fig. 9.7 indicates the shifts in gain/loss expectation in the coin-flipping game.

9.3.2 Expected Value

Suppose we have a probability distribution for a random drawing in the form of outcomes for discrete random variable $X = \{x_1,\ldots, x_n\}$ associated with the appropriate probabilities $P = \{P_1,\ldots, P_n\}$ as shown in Fig. 9.8. Outcome, X, could represent business revenue, profit, game gain, return on investment, and any numeric outcomes associated with the appropriate probabilities $P(X)$.

Note that the distances between the values on the X axis are different. It is quite normal because random variable may take values not necessarily showing equal increments. As soon as the events are random, we do not know which of the events may occur, and hence, we do not know what value of X will come up as the outcome of the random situation.

The ***expected value***, μ, of the outcome on a random drawing can be determined as the mean value of all outcome in the universal sample space as

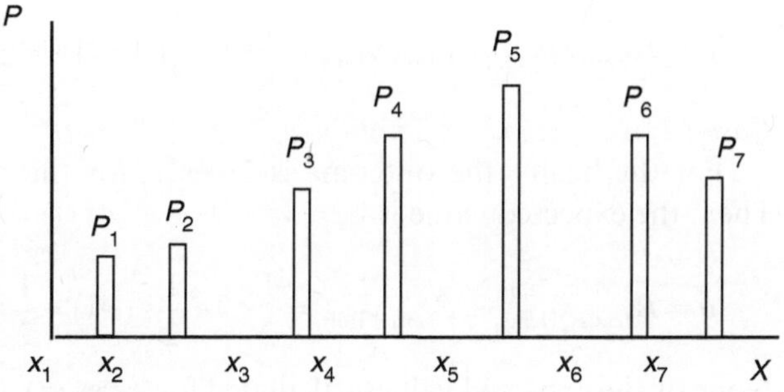

Fig. 9.8 Probability distribution, $\{P_k(X)\}$, and outcomes, x_k, in the universal sample space, Ω

$$\mu = \sum_{k=1}^{n} P_k x_k \tag{9.1}$$

(μ is a Greek character pronounced mu).

The expected value shows the expectation rather than any actual outcome. By no means can you count on making the outcome precisely equal the expected value in any occurrence of the random drawing. The expected value is the mean of all possible outcomes in the universal sample space rather than any instance of the outcome.

Let's go back to the example of tossing a coin discussed in the previous section. The expected value in this game is

$$\mu = P_{\text{Head}} x_{\text{Head}} + P_{\text{Tail}} x_{\text{Tail}} \tag{9.2}$$

where P_{Heads} and P_{Tails} are the probabilities of getting heads and tails and x_{Head} and x_{Tail} are the appropriate rewards. We presume that we are dealing with a fair coin that has equal probabilities for getting heads or tails

$$P_{\text{Heads}} = P_{\text{Tails}} = \frac{1}{2} \tag{9.3}$$

There were three different cases of the reward rules in the coin-flipping game as described in the previous section and shown in Fig. 9.6:

Case (a)

For the heads, the outcome is 1 cent; for the tails, the outcome is −1 cent. Then, the expected value is

$$\mu = P_{\text{Heads}} x_{\text{Heads}} + P_{\text{Tails}} x_{\text{Tails}} = \frac{1}{2} * 1 + \frac{1}{2} * (-1) = 0 \tag{9.4}$$

Case (b)

For the heads, the outcome is 1 cent; for the tails, the outcome is −2 cents. Then, the expected value is

$$\mu = P_{\text{Heads}} x_{\text{Heads}} + P_{\text{Tails}} x_{\text{Tails}} = \frac{1}{2} * 1 + \frac{1}{2} * (-2) = -\frac{1}{2} \tag{9.5}$$

Case (2)

For the heads, the outcome is 2 cents; for the tails, the outcome is −1 cent. Then, the expected value is

$$\mu = P_{\text{Heads}} x_{\text{Heads}} + P_{\text{Tails}} x_{\text{Tails}} = \frac{1}{2} * 2 + \frac{1}{2} * (-1) = \frac{1}{2} \tag{9.6}$$

None of the expected values calculated for cases (a), (b), and (c) equal to any of the outcomes.

Now, it looks quite reasonable why the intuitive reaction in case (a) is neutral, negative in case (b), and positive in case (c). Key is in the expected value. It should be noted one more time that a real game can go anyway because it is fundamentally random. The expected value is only a direction where it will most likely to go but not the guaranteed outcome.

Expected value of a random drawing is

$$\mu = \sum_{k=1}^{n} P_k x_k$$

where P_k is the probability of event k and x_k is the outcome of event k.

9

9.3.3 Standard Deviation and Risk

The Concept of Risk

Let's continue playing the coin-flipping game and concentrate on the fair game in case (a) where the bet is 1 cent for the heads and −1 cent for the tails. The expected value $\mu = 0$. Thus, the game looks neutral, and you would be willing to play just for fun, if the bet is 1 cent! How about changing the bet to $1? Would you be willing to keep playing the game? Possibly! How about increasing the bet to $one million? If you are a person of reason and do not have a stash of money to waste, you must refuse playing the game. Why? I hope you say, "Risk is too high." By the way, even with the one million dollars bet for both, heads and tails, the expected value of the game is zero. What are you afraid of?

Most likely, your reasoning goes as follows: "Yes, the expected value is zero, but if at least the first flip of the coin goes wrong, my life is ruined. I don't want it because risk is too high." However, the game still has zero expected value similarly to the game with just 1 cent bet. What does the term risk mean?

Risk is a complex concept that could be taken in quite a few different ways. We will engage one of them, which is typical in finance.

Let's analyze what is the difference between betting 1 cent, 1 dollar, and one million dollars in the coin-flipping game. The expected value in all cases is the same and equals zero. However, as the bet goes, we get more reluctant to play because

Fig. 9.9 A schematic illustration of risk as the expected distance from the expected value

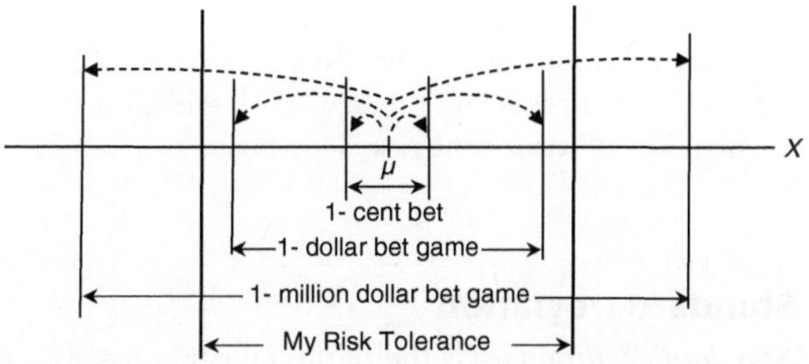

any wrong outcome can hurt us more and more severely. Thus, in addition to the expected value for the game that shows whether the game is overall promising for us, we are assessing the risk of the game by estimating how far from the expected value we may expect to deviate. Though the game with all three bets has the same zero expected value, the game with 1 cent bet could bring us to the loss of a couple of cents that is no issue at all; the $1 bet could randomly bring us to the loss of a couple of dollars that is not pleasant but quite tolerable. The one million dollars bet can easily bring us to a disastrous end.

So, what was our consideration and concerns when you agreed to play a 1 cent bet coin-tossing game, less agreed to play a 1 dollar bet game, and completely opposed playing one million dollar bet game? The expected value for all three games was the same and equal to zero, so you were comfortable with the expected value. However, understanding that it is a random draw game and actual results are not going to be zero, you asked yourself a question – what is the expected value of the distances between the outcomes and the expected value of the outcomes? If the expected deviation (distance) from the expected value was low (plus-minus 1 cent), you considered it low risk and agreed to play. If the expected deviation from the expected value was moderately low (plus-minus 1 dollar), you considered the risk to be moderately low and agreed to play. However, as the expected deviation from the expected value became intolerably big (plus-minus one million dollars), you refused to play the game. This consideration is illustrated in Fig. 9.9.

Let's try now to convert the risk assessment approach discussed above into a mathematical expression.

Concept of risk

What is the expected value of the distances between the outcomes and the expected value of the outcomes?

Risk assessment

> If the expected value of the distances between the outcomes and the expected value of the outcomes is lower than our risk tolerance, we accept the challenge; otherwise, we refuse it because the risk is too high.

Standard Deviation

Standard deviation, σ, is the parameter that assesses the risk for a random draw

$$\sigma = \sqrt{\sum_{k=1}^{n} P_k \left(x_k - \mu\right)^2} \tag{9.7}$$

where x_k is the outcome of event k with probability P_k, μ is the expected value, and σ is the standard deviation (σ is a Greek character pronounced sigma).

Standard deviation is a measure of risk and shows the expected value for the deviation of the outcome of the events from the expected value of the outcomes. This might sound confusing at first glance. Let's elaborate on it. The expected value μ shows the outcome we expect from the random drawing. Expected value determines what we expect rather what we will really get.

Let's now refer to our risk analysis in the coin-flipping game analyzed in the previous section. However, just having the expected value is not enough to assess our desire to get engaged in the random draw. We assess risk by answering the following question, phrase in the previous section:

What is the expected value of the distances between the outcomes and the expected value of the outcomes? (9.8)

By outcomes, we understand here the outcomes of the possible events. We will use this question to formalize the concept of risk.

We numbered this question as a mathematical expression because, as we will see in a couple of paragraphs from here, this phrase is the same as Eq. (9.7) but just expressed in the human natural language rather than in the mathematical language as in Eq. (9.7).

How can we express the distance between a possible outcome x_k and the expected value of the outcomes μ? If we express it simply as a difference $x_k - \mu$, then some distances may be negative, if a certain outcome is less than the expected value (on the left of μ in ■ Fig. 9.10). This is not correct because distances cannot be negative. If we allow distances to be negative, then two distances, positive and negative, even big ones may compensate to zero, which is wrong. Thus, to make distances positive when x_k is lower than μ, we can use the absolute value of the difference $| x_k - \mu |$. However, it is hard to work with the

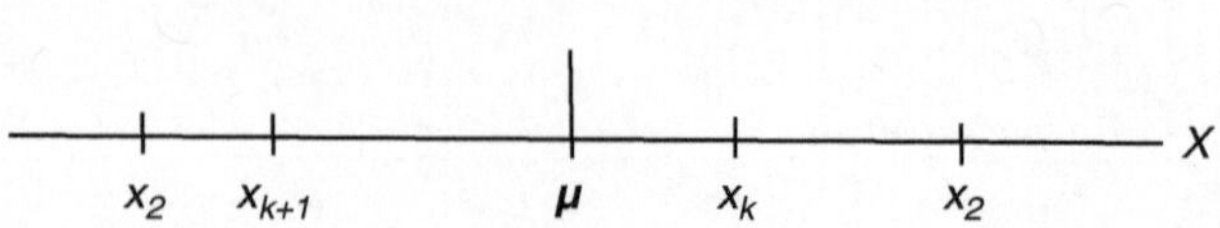

■ **Fig. 9.10** Illustration of event outcomes to be on the both sides from the expected value of the outcomes

absolute value function. For this reason, square differences $(x_k - \mu)^2$ are most of the time used in mathematics to make their value positive. As soon as we use square distance, we should take a square root, when the operations are completed. Keep this in mind.

The square distance $(x_k - \mu)^2$ is a random variable because x_k is the random variable. The expected value of the random variable $(x_k - \mu)^2$ can be calculated using Eq. (9.1) with the square distance $(x_k - \mu)^2$ as the random variable instead of just outcome x_k in Eq. (9.1). In result, we obtain

$$\sigma^2 = \sum_{k=1}^{n} P_k (x_k - \mu)^2 \tag{9.9}$$

where σ^2 is referred to as the variance. Remember that we used a square of the differences and kept in mind that we have to take a square root of the result. Taking a square root of Eq. (9.9), we come up with Eq. (9.7), which says exactly the same as in our risk-defining question in Eq. (9.8).

Equation (9.7) for standard deviation looks much clearer now and starts making the better sense. Standard deviation measures risk associated with random drawing. Standard deviation measures risk with the same units of measurement as the units for gain/loss (reward).

Let's analyze the coin-flipping game from the perspective of the expected value and the associated risk in terms of standard deviation. We flip a fair coin that has $P_{Heads} = P_{Tails} = ½$ and place equal bets. It means that in case of heads, you win A (outcome is A), but in case of tails, you lose A (outcome is –A). As we discussed in the previous section, if A = 1 cent (bet 1), you would gladly play; if A = $1 (bet 2), you may be playing, but if A = one million dollars (bet 3), you will reject the game because it poses too much risk. Remember that the expected value of the game with all three bets is the same and equals to zero, $\mu = 0$. However, the game differs by the standard deviation, which in the coin-tossing game is

$$\begin{aligned}\sigma &= \sqrt{P_{\text{Heads}}(A-\mu)^2 + P_{\text{Tails}}(A-\mu)^2} = \sqrt{P_{\text{Heads}}A^2 + P_{\text{Tails}}A^2} = \\ &= \sqrt{(P_{\text{Heads}} + P_{\text{Tails}})A^2} = \sqrt{A^2} = A\end{aligned} \tag{9.10}$$

because $\mu = 0$, and $P_{Heads} + P_{Tails} = 1$.

Thus, as it becomes clear from Eq. (9.10), the standard deviation that means risk is higher with the higher bets. Now, it is quite clear why we made very good intuitive judgments on these different bets which are illustrated in ▫ Fig. 9.9.

> ***Standard deviation*** measures risk associated with random draw
>
> $$\sigma = \sqrt{\sum_{k=1}^{n} P_k (x_k - \mu)^2}$$
>
> where μ is the expected value, P_k is the probability of event k, and x_k is the outcome of event k.

9.3.4 Coefficient of Variation

Suppose for an investment opportunity standard deviation, σ, is equal to \$100,000. Is it a high risk or not? You probably already figured out that there is no answer to that question unless you know something else. It depends on the expected gain (reward) which is measured by expected value, μ. If a big company, say IBM, invests \$100,000 in business expecting \$10M return, probably, the risk is not too high relative to the expected gain. On the other hand, if the return on investment is expected to be only \$10,000, probably, it is not a good idea to invest such money and the risk is too high. Thus, the ratio of standard deviation over the expected value would be a reasonable parameter that measures how high the risk is relative to the expected gain. This parameter is referred to as the ***coefficient of variation***

$$\nu = \frac{\sigma}{\mu} \tag{9.11}$$

("ν" is a Greek character and is pronounced as nu).

9

Coefficient of variation of a random drawing is

$$\nu = \frac{\sigma}{\mu}$$

where σ is standard deviation and μ is the expected value. Coefficient of variation measures risk relative to the expected gain (expected value).

9.3.5 Risk-Reward Analysis

Now, we are armed for making a decision under uncertainty if we know or can calculate the expected value, standard deviation, and coefficient of variation. Definitely, these three parameters, though do not provide comprehensive information for risk-reward analysis, are quite handy for helping make right decisions in many situations under uncertainty. Remember that there is no panacea in our world. Do not become a slave of formal parameters in your decisions, use these parameters as a decision support tool that helps you make thoughtful decision, and keep your mind open and common sense up.

$$\mu = \sum_{k=1}^{n} P_k x_k \qquad \sigma = \sqrt{\sum_{k=1}^{n} P_k (x_k - \mu)^2} \qquad \nu = \frac{\sigma}{\mu}$$

Expected value (μ) is the expected value outcome.

Standard deviation (σ) is the expected deviation from the expected value expected value.

Coefficient of variation (ν) is the standard deviation normalized to the expected value.

Do not become a hostage of formal parameters in your decisions, use these parameters as a decision support tool that helps you make thoughtful decision, and keep your mind open and common sense up.

In the next sections of this chapter, we will go through several examples that demonstrate how to apply the notion of expected value, standard deviation, and coefficient of variation to the decision-making processes in business.

9.4 Case 1: Beach Café

Suppose you are operating a beach café and would like to find out whether this business is going to be profitable next July. How would you do it?

Assume you know from the previous experience with the café that there are basically three scenarios. If the weather is good, then the café makes $2000 daily profit; if the weather is excellent, daily profit is $3000, but if the weather is bad, the café loses $700 per day. However, we are unable to predict the weather for so long in advance, but we would be able to calculate the expected value of profit, standard deviation, and coefficient of variation if you know the probabilities of different types of weather. We can get the appropriate probabilities from historical data for the last several years presuming that the climate has not changed significantly for that period. With all information collected, we have outcomes along with the probabilities as show in ◘ Table 9.2.

Now, we are ready for calculations of the expected value for the café profit, standard deviation, and coefficient of variation. We can do the calculations manually with a pen and paper or with a calculator or even using spreadsheet software. The result is

◘ **Table 9.2** Weather-based scenarios for beach café

Weather scenario	Probability	Daily profit
Good weather	0.5	$2000
Excellent weather	0.2	$3000
Bad weather	0.3	−$700

$$\mu = 0.5 * \$2{,}000 + 0.2 * \$3{,}000 + 0.3 * (-\$700) = \$1{,}390$$

$$\sigma = \sqrt{0.5 * (\$2{,}000 - \$1{,}390)^2 + 0.2 - (\$3{,}000 - \$1{,}390)^2 + 0.3 * (-\$700 - \$1{,}390)^2} = \$1{,}419$$

$$v = \frac{\sigma}{\mu} = \frac{\$1{,}419}{\$1{,}390} = 1.02$$

As we see from the calculations, the expected daily profit is $1390 which is not bad at all. However, standard deviation is quite high that means you may expect significant deviation from the expected profit and such expected deviation can even bring your profit to the negative territory. This fact is clearly reflected by the coefficient of variation which a higher than one. However, don't let the numbers make a decision for you. Remember that the numbers can justify your decision, but the decision itself is all up to you. It would be no surprise if different people make different decisions upon the same supporting numbers.

9.5 Case 2: Investment Risk and Decision-Making

Suppose you have one hundred thousand dollars and consider two investment opportunities shown in the form of two investment scenarios in ◘ Table 9.3.

From the due diligence of the investment scenarios, the conclusion was made that Scenario 1 may offer $60 K in return if inflation is slow and $25 K if inflation is moderate, and the investment will result in $14 K loss if inflation is rapid. Accordingly, with Scenario 2, gain of $20 K is expected if inflation is slow, $15 K if inflation is moderate, and $1 K loss in case of rapid inflation. The probabilities of different occurrence by inflation are assessed from the economy analysis and are 0.2 for slow inflation, 0.5 for moderate inflation, and 0.3 for rapid inflation. The question is what investment scenario is better?

We calculate expected value for the return on investment (μ), standard deviation (σ), and coefficient of variation (ν) for both investment scenarios. The calculated parameters are shown in ◘ Table 9.4.

The risk/reward analysis of the investment scenarios leads to the following conclusions:

- Expected return with Scenario 1 (μ = $20 K) is higher than the return with Scenario 2 (μ = $11 K).

◘ **Table 9.3** Investment opportunities

Inflation rate	Probability	Return on investment ($K)	
		Scenario 1	Scenario 2
Slow inflation	0.2	60	20
Moderate inflation	0.5	25	15
Rapid inflation	0.3	−14	−1

Table 9.4 Expected value, standard deviation, and coefficient of variation for investment scenarios

Investment scenarios	μ	σ	ν
Scenario 1	20	26	1.3
Scenario 2	11	8.2	0.73

- Risk with Scenario 1 (σ = \$26 K) is significantly higher than the risk with Scenario 2 (σ = \$8.2 K).
- Risk per expected return with Scenario 1 (ν = 1.3) is higher than the risk per expected return with Scenario 2 (ν = 0.73).

Which scenario is better? There is no straight answer to this question that would come just from the numbers. Every scenario has it cons and pros. Scenario 1 is more aggressive and more risky, but the expected return is much higher, while Scenario 2 is more conservative with less risk and less expected return. This is up to the investor to make a decision proceeding from the investor's preference for risk and other circumstances. Unfortunately, the higher returns on investment are usually associated with the higher risk. The bottom line is that investors better make their choice based on a comprehensive risk analysis rather than just picking a scenario with a higher expected return.

9.6 A Decision Tree

Suppose Pacific Eagle Company based in Australia considers expansion to a foreign market. The company has three possible choices for the expansion: the USA, Europe, and Asia.

There is uncertainty with general economic conditions of the markets, so it could be either economic growth or recession. Independently of economic conditions, the company products may be either competitive or not competitive on the market. All such possibilities are shown in the decision tree for the company expansion shown in Fig. 9.11.

Please note that the decision tree in Fig. 9.11 is a simplification for the sake of illustration. Market conditions in the real world could be much more complex than just showing growth or recession, and competitive conditions could be more diverse than just to be competitive or not competitive. The company and all economic data and market condition used in Fig. 9.11 and in the example are made up for illustration and do not reflect the actual real-world economic conditions.

The decision tree in Fig. 9.11 has three branches; each represents an appropriate choice of markets for business expansion: the USA, Europe, and Asia. The probabilities of economic conditions, P_e, for growth or recession in each market,

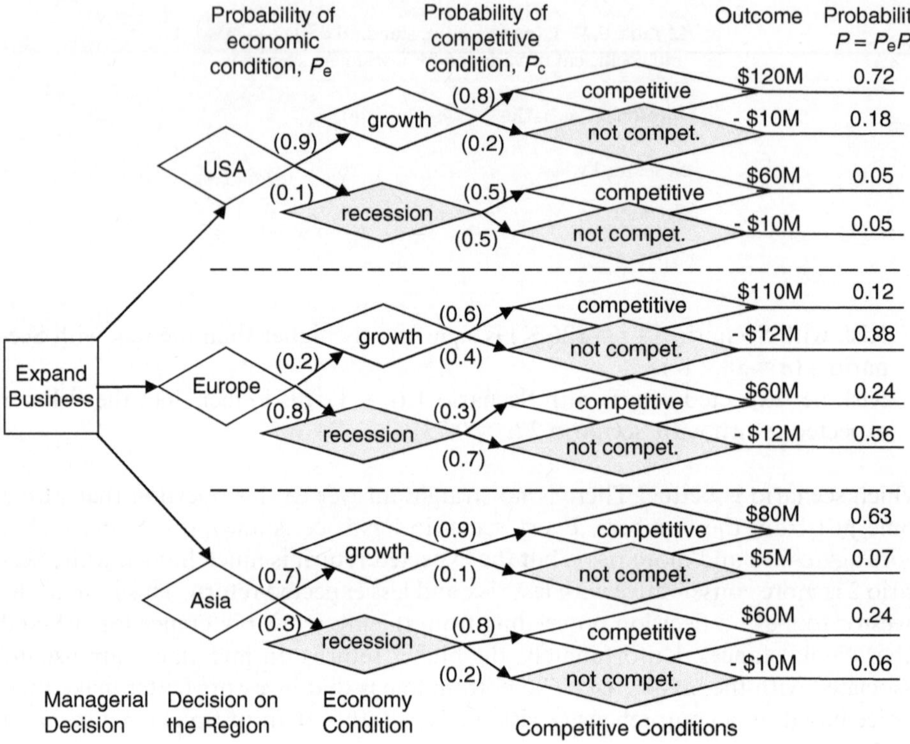

Fig. 9.11 A decision tree for expansion of Pacific Eagle Company (All data in this decision tree were taken arbitrarily for the illustration purpose only and have no relevance to the actual economic and market conditions.)

9

0.9 versus 0.1 for the USA, 0.2 versus 0.8 for Europe, and 0.7 versus 0.2 for Asia, could be obtained as subjective probabilities from expert assessments. The probabilities of competitive conditions, P_c, could be estimated from comparative product analysis and marketing research. The column "Outcome" in Fig. 9.11 showed expected gain/loss in each occurrence of economy and competitive condition in the appropriate market choice. For example, in case of expansion to the USA, if economy shows growth and company products are competitive, the company expects to get $120M profit versus $10M loss if the products occurred to be not competitive. In the same case, if economy shows recession, the company expects $60M profit if its products are competitive and $10M loss otherwise. These amounts of profit/loss can be estimated by the company operations and production analysis. The last column in Fig. 9.11 shows the total probabilities of each occurrence as a product of the respected probabilities of the economic and competitive conditions, $P = P_e P_c$. For example, the total probability of the first occurrence in the branch of expansion to the USA is $P = P_e P_c = 0.9*0.8 = 0.72$.

Pacific Eagle Company can calculate the expected value μ, standard deviation σ, and coefficient of variation ν for each branch of the decision tree, i.e., for each expansion choice as shown below:

$$\mu_{\text{USA}} = 0.72*\$120\text{M} + 0.18*(-\$10\text{M}) + 0.05*\$60\text{M} + 0.05(-\$10\text{M}) = \$87.1\text{M}$$

$$\sigma^2_{\text{USA}} = 0.72*(\$120\text{M} - \$87.1\text{M})^2 + 0.18*(\$-10\text{M} - \$87.1\text{M})^2 + \\ +0.05*(\$60\text{M} - \$87.1\text{M})^2 + 0.05*(-\$10\text{M} - \$87.1\text{M})^2 = \$2984\text{M}^2$$

$$\sigma_{\text{USA}} = \sqrt{\$2984\text{M}^2} = \$54.6\text{M}$$

$$v_{\text{USA}} = \frac{\sigma_{\text{USA}}}{\mu_{\text{USA}}} = \frac{\$54.6\text{M}}{\$87.1\text{M}} = 0.63$$

$$\mu_{\text{Europe}} = 0.12*\$110\text{M} + 0.08*(-\$12\text{M}) + 0.24*\$60\text{M} + 0.56(-\$12\text{M}) = \$19.9\text{M}$$

$$\sigma^2_{\text{Europe}} = 0.12*(\$110\text{M} - \$19.9\text{M})^2 + 0.08*(-\$12\text{M} - \$19.9\text{M})^2 + \\ +0.24*(\$60\text{M} - \$19.9\text{M})^2 + 0.56*(-\$12\text{M} - \$19.9\text{M})^2 = \$2011\text{M}^2$$

$$\sigma_{\text{Europe}} = \sqrt{\$2011\text{M}^2} = \$44.8\text{M}$$

$$v_{\text{Europe}} = \frac{\sigma_{\text{Europe}}}{\mu_{\text{Europe}}} = \frac{\$44.8\text{M}}{\$19.9\text{M}} = 2.25$$

$$\mu_{\text{Asia}} = 0.63*\$80\text{M} + 0.07*(-\$5\text{M}) + 0.24*\$60\text{M} + 0.06*(-\$10\text{M}) = \$63.8\text{M}$$

$$\sigma^2_{\text{Asia}} = 0.63*(\$80\text{M} - \$63.8\text{M})^2 + 0.07*(-\$5\text{M} - \$63.8\text{M})^2 + \\ +0.24*(\$60\text{M} - \$63.8\text{M})^2 + 0.06*(-\$10\text{M} - \$63.8\text{M})^2 = \$8269\text{M}^2$$

$$\sigma_{\text{Asia}} = \sqrt{\$8269\text{M}^2} = \$29.8\text{M}$$

$$v_{\text{Asia}} = \frac{\sigma_{\text{Asia}}}{\mu_{\text{Asia}}} = \frac{\$29.8\text{M}}{\$63.8\text{M}} = 0.45$$

The results of the calculations are presented in ◘ Table 9.5. To make decision, Pacific Eagle Company must first interpret the results. The appropriate interpretations of the results are presented in ◘ Table 9.6.

Business expansion to the USA promises high business potential along with a relatively high absolute risk with moderate relative risk per expected profit. Expansion to Europe has low potential and high absolute and relative risks, while expansion to Asia has a moderate potential and the lowest absolute and relative risks. Proceeding from the calculated expected values, standard deviations, and coefficients of variations and their interpretations, Pacific Eagle Company can now make a decision on the region for the business expansion. The decision cannot be formally derived from the expected values, standard deviations, coefficients of variations, their interpretations, and risk analysis but significantly depends on risk-taking attitude of the decision-makers. Some people may prefer to expand to the USA because of a higher expected profit and despite a higher risk than in Asia. Some other people would prefer to expand to Asia because of its lower risk and despite of a moderate expected profit lower than in case of the expansion to the USA. There are no right and wrong decisions, and all depends on the tolerance of people toward risk.

Table 9.5 Expected values, standard deviations, and coefficients of variation for the decision tree of Pacific Eagle Company

Region	Economy condition		Competitive condition		Expected outcome		Expected value, μ ($M)	Standard deviation, σ ($M)	Coefficient of variation, ν
	Status	Prob	Status	Prob	$M	Total Prob			
USA	Growth	0.9	Competitive	0.8	120	0.72	87.1	54.6	0.63
			Not Comp.	0.2	−10	0.18			
	Recession	0.1	Competitive	0.5	60	0.05			
			Not Comp.	0.5	−10	0/05			
Europe	Growth	0.9	Competitive	0.8	120	0.72	19.9	44.8	0.2.25
			Not Comp.	0.2	−10	0.18			
	Recession	0.1	Competitive	0.5	60	0.05			
			Not Comp.	0.5	−10	0/05			
Asia	Growth	0.9	Competitive	0.8	120	0.72	63.8	29.8	0.45
			Not Comp.	0.2	−10	0.18			
	Recession	0.1	Competitive	0.5	60	0.05			
			Not Comp.	0.5	−10	0/05			

Table 9.6 Interpretation of expected values, standard deviations, and coefficients of variation for the decision tree of Pacific Eagle Company

Region	Expected value, μ ($M)	Standard deviation, σ ($M)	Coefficient of variation, ν	Interpretation
USA	87.1	54.6	0.63	High potential, high absolute risk, and moderate relative risk per expected profit
Europe	19.9	44.8	2.25	Low potential, moderate absolute risk, and high relative risk per expected profit
Asia	63.8	29.8	0.45	Moderate potential, low absolute risk, and low relative risk per expected profit

Questions for Self-Control for Chap. 9

1. What is random variable?
2. What is discrete random variable?
3. What is continuous random variable?
4. What is categorical random variable?
5. What is a probability distribution?
6. How would you describe the probability density?
7. What does it mean that probability is measured on an interval?
8. How to calculate the expected value?
9. What is the meaning of expected value?
10. How would you define risk?
11. How to calculate standard deviation?
12. What is the meaning of standard deviation?
13. How to calculate the coefficient of variation?
14. What is the meaning of the coefficient of variation?
15. What information can help you in making a risk-related decision?
16. What is a decision tree?

Problems for Chap. 9

1. Your company plans a marketing campaign and should select one of two suggested scenarios. With Scenario 1, the company may gain $10M with probability of 0.4 but may lose $5M with probability of 0.6. On the other hand, with Scenario 2, the company may gain $15 with probability of 0.7 but may lose $8M with probability of 0.3. What scenario and why would you believe is better?
2. You plan to invest in real estate with $1M. If interest rates will stay low, you may gain $200 K, but if interest rates will go higher, you may lose $50 K. The probability for the interest rate to stay low is 0.4 and to go higher is 0.6. Please analyze your expectation and risk and make a decision whether you want to invest or not.

Bayesian Probability

Contents

10.1 Conditional Probability – 176

10.2 Bayes' Theorem – 177
10.2.1 Conditional, Marginal, and Joint Probabilities – 177
10.2.2 Analysis of the Inverse Conditional Probabilities – 180

10.3 Bayesian Probability and Information – 181

10.4 The Monty Hall Problem – 181
10.4.1 Bayesian Solution to the Monty Hall Problem – 183
10.4.2 Decision Tree Solution to the Monty Hall Problem – 184

10.5 Analysis of Posterior Probabilities – 185

10.6 General Form of Bayes' Theorem – 187

10.7 Further Probability Revisions – 188

S. K. Aityan, *Business Research Methodology*, Classroom Companion: Business,
https://doi.org/10.1007/978-3-030-76857-7_10

10.1 Conditional Probability

In the previous chapter, we discussed independent events. Independent events are events probability that does not depend on the occurrence of some other events. If we toss a fair coin, the probability of heads and tails does not depend on the results of the previous flips of the coin. Thus, a coin tossing is an independent event.

▶ Example 1: Ten Candies

Suppose we have a jar with ten candies of different wrapper color (red and green) and taste (sweet and bitter). Among those candies are as follows:
- Four red (*R*) and sweet (*S*)
- Two red (*R*) and bitter (*B*)
- Three green (*G*) and sweet (*S*)
- One green (*G*) and bitter (*B*) ◀

The probabilities of randomly drawing a candy of a specific color regardless of the taste are

$$\begin{aligned} P(R) &= 6/10 \\ P(G) &= 4/10 \end{aligned} \tag{10.1}$$

where $P(R)$ and $P(G)$ are the probabilities of drawing a red and a green candy, respectively.

10

These probabilities of randomly drawing a candy of a specific taste regardless of the color are

$$\begin{aligned} P(S) &= 7/10 \\ P(B) &= 3/10 \end{aligned} \tag{10.2}$$

where $P(S)$ and $P(B)$ are the probabilities of drawing a sweet and a bitter candy, respectively.

The probabilities of drawing a candy with the matching color and taste are

$$\begin{aligned} P(RS) &= 4/10 \qquad P(RB) = 2/10 \\ P(GS) &= 3/10 \qquad P(GB) = 1/10 \end{aligned} \tag{10.3}$$

where $P(RS)$, $P(RB)$, $P(GS)$, and $P(GB)$ are the probabilities of drawing a red-sweet, red-bitter, green-sweet, and green-bitter candy, respectively.

Now, let's ask a question about the probability under condition that one of the parameters is known. Suppose we can look at the jar and take a candy of a specified color, but we do not know the taste. What is the probability of taking a sweet candy if it is red? The probabilities are

$$\begin{aligned} P(S|R) &= 4/6 \\ P(B|R) &= 2/6 \end{aligned} \tag{10.4}$$

because there are a total of six red candies, four of them are sweet and two are bitter. Thus, $P(S|R)$ and $P(B|R)$ are the probabilities of taking a sweet and bitter

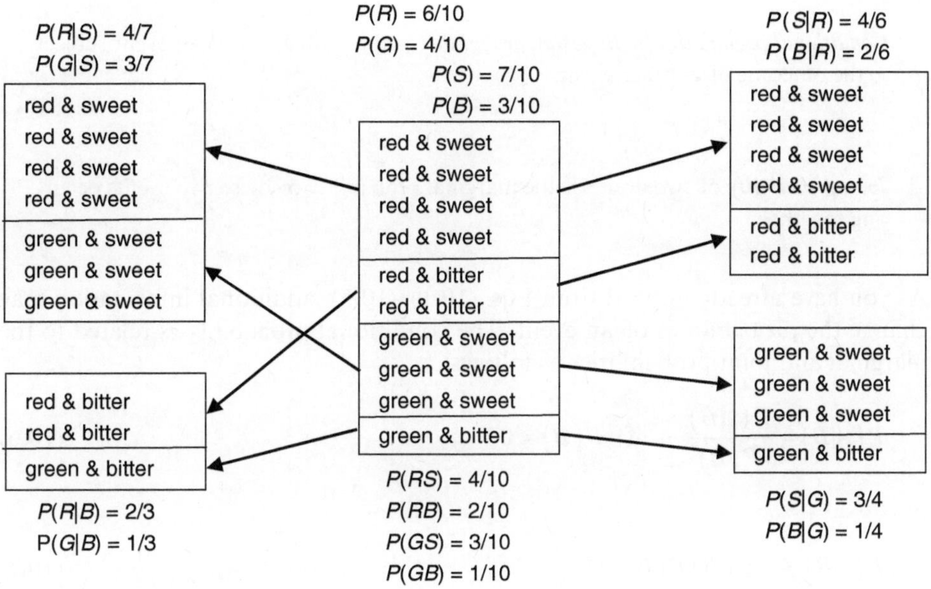

Fig. 10.1 Universal sample spaces and respective marginal, conditional, and joint probabilities for red/green and sweet/bitter candies

candy, respectively, if the candy is red. Similarly, for the green candies, the probabilities of taking a sweet $P(S|G)$ and a bitter $P(B|G)$ candy, respectively, are

$$\begin{aligned} P(S|G) &= 3/4 \\ P(B|G) &= 1/4 \end{aligned} \tag{10.5}$$

The universal sample spaces and respective marginal, conditional, and joint probabilities for red/green and sweet/bitter candies are shown in Fig. 10.1.

10.2 Bayes' Theorem

10.2.1 Conditional, Marginal, and Joint Probabilities

The notation $P(A|B)$ means the probability of event A when event B occurred. Such a probability is referred to as a ***conditional probability*** or ***Bayesian probability***. The probability of event A irrespective of the outcome of other events is referred to as ***marginal probability***. The notation for marginal probability of event A is $P(A)$. $P(AB)$ is the marginal probability of events A and B occurring together, also called the ***joint probability*** of two events, A and B.

> ***Marginal probability*** is the probability of an event irrespective of the outcome of other events.

Conditional probability or ***Bayesian probability*** is the probability of an event subject to the outcome of another event.

Joint probability of two events is the marginal probability of these two events occurring together.

As you have already noticed from Eqs. (10.1)–(10.5), additional information may change the probabilities of an event. The conditional probability is related to the marginal and joint probabilities as follows:

$$P(A|B) = \frac{P(AB)}{P(B)} \quad \text{if} \quad P(B) \neq 0 \tag{10.6}$$

or

$$P(AB) = P(A|B)P(B) \tag{10.7}$$

Taking into account that $P(AB) = P(BA)$, Eq. (10.7) can be rewritten as

$$\left.\begin{array}{l} P(AB) = P(A|B)P(B) \\ P(BA) = P(B|A)P(A) \end{array}\right\} \text{then } P(A|B)P(B) = P(B|A)P(A) \tag{10.8}$$

Thus,

$$P(A|B) = \frac{P(B|A)}{P(B)} P(A) \tag{10.9}$$

The relationship in Eq. (10.9) is known as ***Bayes' theorem***. The conditional probability $P(A|B)$ is called the ***posterior probability*** (or ***revised probability***), marginal probability $P(A)$ is called the ***prior probability***, and the ratio $P(B|A)/P(B)$ is called the ***likelihood ratio***. Bayes' theorem can be phrased as the posterior probability equals the prior probability times the likelihood ratio.

The marginal probability of an event $P(A)$ equals the weighted sum of the conditional probability of that event $P(A|B)$ weighted (multiplied) by the marginal probability $P(B)$ of the condition event B and the conditional probability $P(A|B')$ of that event conditioned by the complement of the first condition event (B') weighted (multiplied) by the marginal probability of the complement to condition event $P(\neg B)$, i.e.,

$$P(A) = P(A|B)P(B) + P(A|B')P(B') \tag{10.10}$$

where event B is a condition event for event A and $\neg B$ is the complement to the condition event B, so $P(B) + P(B') = 1$. Do not get confused with the description of Eq. (10.10) given in the paragraph above. It may look very complex, but actually, it is a narrative description of Eq. (10.10).

The rule in Eq. (10.10) can also be expressed in terms of explicitly listing all possible condition events as

$$P(A) = \sum_{k=1}^{n} P(A|B_k)P(B_k) \quad \text{such as} \quad \sum_{k=1}^{n} P(B_k) = 1 \tag{10.11}$$

- Conditional probability $P(A|B)$ is called the ***posterior probability*** (or ***revised probability***).
- Marginal probability $P(A)$ is called the ***prior probability***.
- Marginal probability $P(AB)$ of events A and B occurring together is called the ***joint probability*** of two events, A and B.

Bayes' theorem

$$P(A|B) = \frac{P(B|A)}{P(B)} P(A)$$

- ***Marginal probability*** of an event is the weighted sum of the conditional probability of that event weighted by the marginal probability of the condition event and the conditional probability of that event to the complement to the first condition weighted by the marginal probability of the complement to the first condition:

$$P(A) = P(A|B)P(B) + P(A|B')P(B')$$

- ***Marginal probability*** of an event is the weighted sum of the conditional probabilities of that event weighted by the marginal probabilities of the condition events over all condition events:

$$P(A) = \sum_{k=1}^{n} P(A|B_k)P(B_k) \quad \text{such as} \quad \sum_{k=1}^{n} P(B_k) = 1$$

Let's apply the relationship described in Eq. (10.6) to the conditional, joint, and marginal probabilities in Example 1 with the red/green and sweet/bitter candies:

$$P(S|R)=\frac{P(RS)}{P(R)}=\frac{4/10}{6/10}=\frac{4}{6} \quad \text{and} \quad P(B|R)=\frac{P(RB)}{P(R)}=\frac{2/10}{6/10}=\frac{2}{6}$$

$$P(S|G)=\frac{P(GS)}{P(G)}=\frac{3/10}{4/10}=\frac{3}{4} \quad \text{and} \quad P(B|G)=\frac{P(GB)}{P(G)}=\frac{1/10}{4/10}=\frac{1}{4} \tag{10.12}$$

That perfectly matches the probabilities shown in Fig. 10.1.

▶ Example 2: Buying New Home Subject to Mortgage Rates

If the mortgage rates at least will stay as they are now, there is a 0.8 probability that I will be able to buy a new home next year. There is 0.9 probability that the mortgage rates will not go up till next year:

Probability of mortgage to stay unchanged till next year $P(M)=0.9$.
Probability of buying home next year if mortgage rates stay $P(H|M)=0.8$
Probability of buying home next year is $P(HM)=P(H|M)*P(M)=0.9*0.8=0.72$. ◀

10.2.2 Analysis of the Inverse Conditional Probabilities

Bayes' theorem offers a very convenient approach for assessing conditional probabilities of events through the inverse conditional probabilities.

▶ Example 3: Probability of a Loan Default

A bank considers a loan to a person. Before issuing the loan, a bank wants to assess the probability of failure for the loanee (loanee is a person who receives a loan).

The probability of a person to be a resident of an urban area with the population over 500,000 (event U_{500}) if the person defaulted in a loan (event F) is $P(U_{500}| F) = 0.2$. The marginal probability of a person to live in the urban area with the population over 500,000 (event U_{500}) is $P(U_{500}) = 0.4$. The marginal probability of a loan default for a general loanee regardless of the place of residence is $P(F) = 0.3$. The bank wants to know what is the probability of a person to default in a loan if the person resides in the urban area with the population over 500,000, i.e., $P(F|U_{500}) = ?$

The solution: According to the Bayes' theorem in Eq. (10.9),

$$P(F|U_{500})=\frac{P(U_{500}|F)}{P(U_{500})}P(F)=\frac{0.2}{0.4}*0.3=0.15 \tag{10.13}$$

Please be advised that the numbers used in this example do not reflect any specific community and do not relate to any specific urban geographic area. ◀

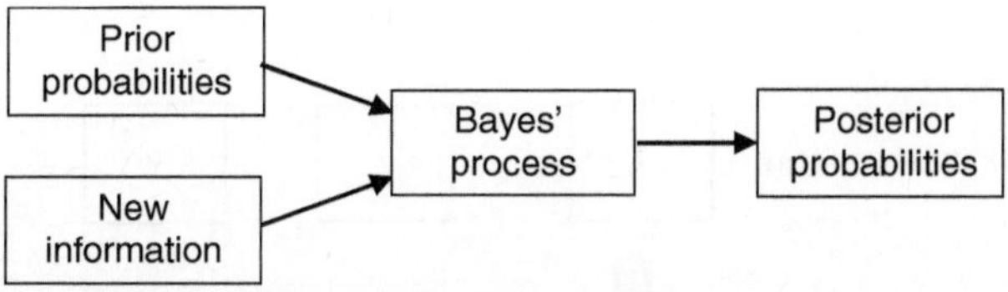

Fig. 10.2 The impact of additional information on posterior probabilities

10.3 Bayesian Probability and Information

Occurrence of a condition event in dependent events may change the probability of condition events (conditional probability), i.e., new information may change the posterior probability of condition events as is schematically illustrated in Fig. 10.2.

▶ Example 4: Probability of Small Business Survival

The probability of a small business to survive in the first year in business is $P(S|T < 1) = 0.4$, and the probability for the same business to survive in general (the survival rate) is $P(S) = 0.6$. It is known that the number of new small businesses established every year equals 20% of the existing new business. What is the probability of a small business to survive if the business already survived the first year, i.e., $P(S|T > 1) = ?$

According to Eq. (10.10), we can write

$$P(S) = P(S|T<1)P(T<1) + P(S|T>1)P(T>1) = 0.6 \tag{10.14}$$

The marginal (prior) probability of a business to be in the first year is $P(T < 1) = 20/(100 + 20) = 20/120 = 1/6$. Note that the probability is not 0.2 as may wrongly appear from the statement above that the number of new small businesses formed every year equals 20% of the existing small businesses. Thus, the probability of a small business to be new among all small businesses can be calculated as the proportion of new business among old and new business, i.e., $P(T < 1) = 20/(100 + 20) = 20/120 = 1/6$. Thus,

$$P(T<1) = \frac{1}{6} \quad \text{and} \quad P(T>1) = \frac{5}{6} \tag{10.15}$$

We can derive from Eq. (10.13) that

$$P(S|T>1) = \frac{P(S) - P(S|T<1)P(T<1)}{P(T>1)} = \frac{0.6 - 0.4 * \frac{1}{6}}{\frac{5}{6}} = 0.64 \tag{10.16}$$

that answers our question. ◀

10.4 The Monty Hall Problem

The Monty Hall problem is a paradoxical problem in conditional probability and reasoning using Bayes' theorem. This problem explicitly shows how information may impact on decision, which at first glance looks impossible.

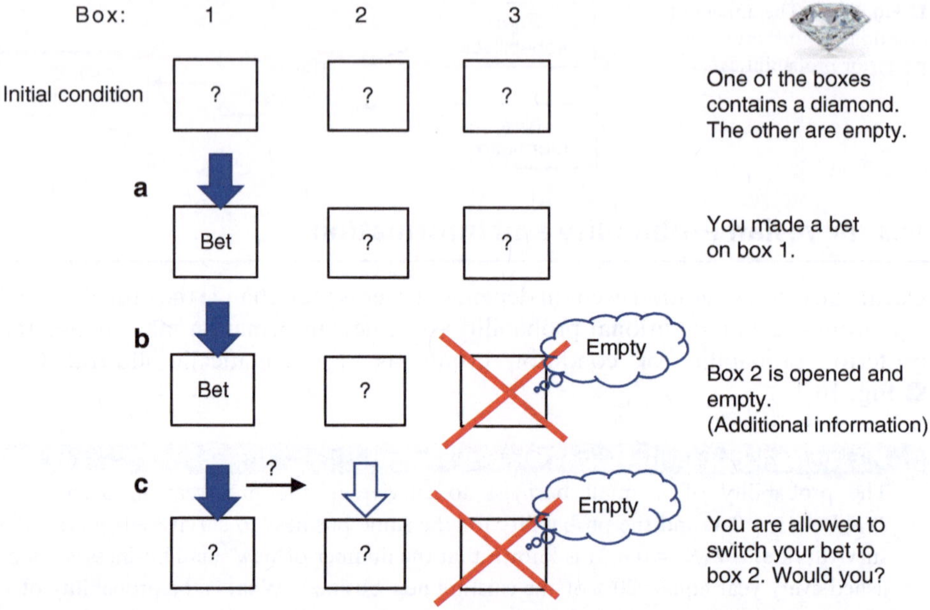

■ **Fig. 10.3** The Monty Hall problem step by step

The problem is illustrated in ■ Fig. 10.3 step by step.

Initial condition: There are three identical closed boxes, and one of them contains a diamond, but you do not know in what box the diamond is. The host knows where the diamond is:[1]

- Step (a): You are offered to choose one of the boxes. From your perspective, the probability for each box to contain a diamond is 1/3 because there is no additional information. Suppose you chose box 1.
- Step (b): The host is a nice person, and he opened box 3 and demonstrated that the box is empty. No diamond in the box. It is a new information for you.
- Step (c): The host offers you a choice. You may stay with your bet on box 1 or you can switch to box 2. Is it any difference for you from the perspective of the probability to get a diamond? Will you switch to box 2 or stay with box 1?

The Monte Hall problem is shown in ■ Fig. 10.1. At first glance, it looks like there is no reason to switch the bet to box 2. There is no difference between two remaining boxes 1 and 2. However, let's do not rush with the judgment and analyze the probabilities.

---

1 The original Monty Hall problem deals with three doors and a car behind one of the doors. We chose to formulate the problem using three boxes and a diamond just for fun. This choice does not change the solution and does not take the authorship of this game away from TV host Monty Hall and statistician Steve Selvin (1975), who introduced this mind-blowing problem.

10.4.1 Bayesian Solution to the Monty Hall Problem

First, let's define terms. C_k indicates the event that the diamond is in box k; H_k is the event of the opening box k by the dealer in step (b).

In Step (a), you choose a box and make a bet on it. You would choose any box, because you have no additional information, and therefore, all three boxes have equal probability for you to contain the diamond, i.e.,

$$P(C_1) = P(C_2) = P(C_3) = \frac{1}{3} \tag{10.17}$$

Suppose you chose box 1 as shown in ◘ Fig. 10.1a.

In Step (b), the host opens box 3. Let's work on the probabilities. The host can open either box 2 or box 3. The conditional probabilities for these events are as follows:

$$\begin{array}{ll} P(H_3|C_1) = \frac{1}{2} & P(H_2|C_1) = \frac{1}{2} \\ P(H_3|C_2) = 1 & P(H_2|C_2) = 0 \\ P(H_3|C_3) = 0 & P(H_2|C_3) = 1 \end{array} \tag{10.18}$$

The explanation of Eq. (10.13) is the following. $P(H_3|C_1)$ is the probability of opening box 3 by the host (event H_3) if the diamond is in box 1 (event C_1), and $P(H_2|C_1)$ is the probability of opening box 2 by the host (event H_2) if the diamond is in box 1 (event C_1). The host can open either box (2 or 3) with equal chances because the diamond is in box 1 (event C_1). Thus, $P(H_3|C_1) = P(H_2|C_1) = ½$.

If the diamond is in box 2 (event C_2), then the host will never open this box (event H_2) and has no choice but to open box 3 (event H_3). Thus, $P(H_3|C_2) = 1$ and $P(H_3|C_3) = 0$.

If the diamond is in box 3 (event C_3), then the host will never open this box (event H_3) and has no choice but to open box 3 (event H_2). Thus, $P(H_2|C_2) = 0$ and $P(H_3|C_2) = 1$.

Now, we can move to step (c) and discuss the probabilities of the diamond to be in box 1 (event C_2) or in box 2 (event C_3) given the fact that box 3 (event H_3) is empty (new information). The probability for the diamond to be in box 1 (event C_1) if the host opened box 3 (event H_3) and showed it was empty, $P(C_1|H_3)$, and the probability for the diamond to be in box 2 (event C_2) if the host opened box 3 (event H_3) and showed it was empty, $P(C_2|H_3)$, can be expressed as

$$P(C_1|H_3) = \frac{P(H_3|C_1)}{P(H_3)} P(C_1) \quad \text{and} \quad P(C_2|H_3) = \frac{P(H_3|C_2)}{P(H_3)} P(C_2) \tag{10.19}$$

According to Eq. (10.17), $P(C_1) = P(C_2) = 1/3$, and according to Eq. (10.18), $P(H_3|C_1) = ½$, and $P(H_3|C_1) = 1$. The marginal (overall) probability $P(H_3)$ of opening box 3 can be expressed as

$$P(H_3) = P(H_3|C_1)P(C_1) + P(H_3|C_2)P(C_2) + P(H_3|C_3)P(C_3) = \\ = \frac{1}{2} * \frac{1}{3} + 1 * \frac{1}{3} + 0 * \frac{1}{3} = \frac{1}{2} \tag{10.20}$$

Finally, substitution all conditional and marginal probabilities in Eq. (10.19), we can calculate the probability for the diamond to be in box 1 (event C_1) and box 2 (event C_3) given that box 3 was opened and was empty (event H_3):

$$\begin{aligned} P(C_1|H_3) &= \frac{P(H_3|C_1)}{P(H_3)} P(C_1) = \frac{1/2}{1/2} * \frac{1}{3} = \frac{1}{3} \\ P(C_2|H_3) &= \frac{P(H_3|C_2)}{P(H_3)} P(C_2) = \frac{1}{1/2} * \frac{1}{3} = \frac{2}{3} \end{aligned} \tag{10.21}$$

To our great surprise, we found out that with the given information that box 3 is empty, the probability for the diamond to be in box 2 is twice as higher than on box 1. Thus, if you want to win the diamond, you better switch your bet from box 1 to box 2 as the new information was given that box 3 is empty.

Your sense of confusion is clearly understood. Do not worry. Go through the Bayesian inference above one more time, and all will come together.

The Monty Hall problem explicitly illustrates how additional information may change the probabilities. The initial probability 1/3 for the diamond to be in box 3 turns into zero as the host opened box 3, and that probability 1/3 is not shared between the two remaining options but migrates to one option only – box 2. Think about it.

10.4.2 Decision Tree Solution to the Monty Hall Problem

Let's try to solve the Monty Hall problem (■ Fig. 10.1) using the decision tree methodology as shown in ■ Fig. 10.4.

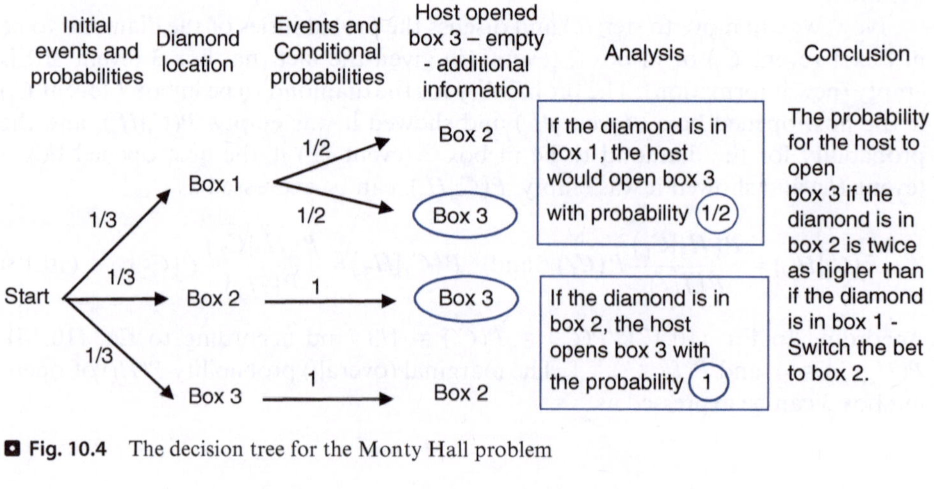

■ **Fig. 10.4** The decision tree for the Monty Hall problem

Initially, all three boxes have the same probability of containing the diamond. These probabilities equal to 1/3 for each initial branch of the tree in ◘ Fig. 10.4 as indicated in the beginning of the decision tree in ◘ Fig. 10.1a, so you chose box 1 just randomly without any preferences in step (a).

In step (b), the host opened box 3 and demonstrated that the diamond was not there. Let's analyze the conditional probabilities of this action. The diamond, for sure, was not in box 3; otherwise, the host would not open it. If the diamond was in box 1, then the host could open either box 2 or box 3 with the equal probabilities of ½. However, if the diamond was in box 2, the host could open box 3 with probability of 1 as shown in the decision tree in ◘ Fig. 10.4.

Thus, the probability for the host to open box 3 if the diamond is in box 2 is twice as higher than if the diamond is in box 1. The conclusion is clear – switch your bet from box 1 to box 2 if you want to double your probability of winning the diamond.

10.5 Analysis of Posterior Probabilities

Suppose we have a die and there is a fifty-fifty chance that the die is fair or loaded. Formally, the probability of the die to be fair and to be loaded is ½, i.e.,

Source: Image by Fernando Latorre from Pixabay

$$P(\text{fair}) = \frac{1}{2} \quad \text{and} \quad P(\text{loaded}) = \frac{1}{2} \tag{10.22}$$

We also know that the die rolls the number 3 with probability of 1/6 if the die is fair and with probability of 3/5 if the die is loaded, i.e.,

$$P(3|\text{fair}) = \frac{1}{6} \quad \text{and} \quad P(3|\text{loaded}) = \frac{3}{5} \tag{10.23}$$

The joint probability that the die rolls the number 3 and the die is fair, $P(3 \,\&\, \text{fair})$, and the joint probability that the die rolls the number 3 and the die is loaded can be calculated using Eq. (10.7) as

$$P(3\,\&\,\text{fair}) = P(3|\text{fair}) * P(\text{fair}) = \frac{1}{6} * \frac{1}{2} = \frac{1}{12}$$
$$P(3\,\&\,\text{loaded}) = P(3|\text{loaded}) * P(\text{loaded}) = \frac{3}{5} * \frac{1}{2} = \frac{3}{10} \quad (10.24)$$

The sum of these probabilities gives us the marginal probability of rolling the number 3:

$$P(3) = P(3\,\&\,\text{fair}) + P(3\,\&\,\text{loaded})$$
$$= P(3|\text{fair}) * P(\text{fair}) + P(3|\text{loaded}) * P(\text{loaded}) = \frac{1}{12} + \frac{3}{10} = \frac{23}{60} \quad (10.25)$$

If the die rolled on the number 3, the probability that the die was the fair one can be calculated from Eqs. (10.24) and (10.25) as

$$P(\text{fair}|3) = \frac{P(\text{fair}\,\&\,3)}{P(3)} = \frac{1/12}{23/60} = \frac{5}{23} = 0.22 \quad (10.26)$$

The probability that the die was loaded if it rolls the number 3 is also calculated from the same equations as

$$P(\text{loaded}|3) = \frac{P(\text{loaded}\,\&\,3)}{P(3)} = \frac{3/10}{23/60} = \frac{18}{23} = 0.78 \quad (10.27)$$

10

In Eqs. (10.26) and (10.27), we used commutativity of logical operation "&" (logical "and"), i.e., $P(A\&B) = P(B\&A)$ or the more specific $P(3\ \&\ \text{fair}) = P(\text{fair}\ \&\ 3)$ and $P(3\ \&\ \text{loaded}) = P(\text{loaded}\ \&\ 3)$.

Equations (10.26) and (10.27) provide the revised or ***posterior probabilities*** for the next roll of the die. We can use them to revise our prior probability estimates.

The relationship between the conditional, prior, joint, and posterior probabilities is shown in ◘ Table 10.1. By state *A'*, we denote the complement to state *A*.

◘ Table 10.2 shows the same relationships in ◘ Table 10.1 applied to the states "fair die" and "loaded die" conditioned that it rolls the number 3.

◘ Table 10.1 Relationship between conditional, prior, joint, and posterior probabilities

State of nature	*P(B | state of nature)*	Prior probability	Joint probability	Posterior probability
A	$P(B\|A)$	$P(A)$	$= P(B\&A)$	$P(A\|B) = P(B\&A)/P(B)$
A'	$P(B\|A')$	$P(A')$	$= P(B\&A')$	$P(A'\|B) = P(B\&A')/P(B)$
			$P(B)$	

Table 10.2 Relationship between conditional, prior, joint, and posterior probabilities if the die rolls the number 3

State of nature	*P(B | state of nature)*	Prior probability	Joint probability	Posterior probability
Fair die	1/6	* 1/2	= 1/12	(1/12)/(23/60) = 5/23
Loaded die	3/5	* 1/2	= 3/10	(3/10)/(23/60) = 18/23
			23/60	

10.6 General Form of Bayes' Theorem

Bayes' theorem formulated in Eq. (10.9) can be rewritten by using the relationship in Eq. (10.10) as

$$P(A|B)=\frac{P(B|A)P(A)}{P(B|A)P(A)+P(B|A')P(A')} \tag{10.28}$$

where event (state) A' is the complement to event (state) A. Bayes' theorem in the form of Eq. (10.28) is called the general form of Bayes' theorem.

Bayes' theorem in the general form

$$P(A|B)=\frac{P(B|A)P(A)}{P(B|A)P(A)+P(B|A')P(A')}$$

▶ Example 5: Conditional Probability of a Fair Die

As an example of the Bayes' theorem in its general form, the conditional probability that it was a fair die, given that it rolls the number 3, in Eq. (10.26) can be written as

$$P(\text{fair}\,|\,3)=\frac{P(\text{fair}\ \&\ 3)}{P(3)}=\frac{P(3\,|\,\text{fair})P(\text{fair})}{P(3\,|\,\text{fair})P(\text{fair})+P(3\,|\,\text{loaded})P(\text{loaded})}=$$
$$=\frac{(1/6)(1/2)}{(1/6)(1/2)+(3/5)(1/2)}=\frac{1/3}{1/6+3/5}=\frac{5}{23} \tag{10.29}$$

and Eq. (10.27) as

$$P(\text{loaded}\,|\,3)=\frac{P(\text{loaded}\ \&\ 3)}{P(3)}=\frac{P(3\,|\,\text{loaded})P(\text{loaded})}{P(3\,|\,\text{fair})P(\text{fair})+P(3\,|\,\text{loaded})P(\text{loaded})}=$$
$$=\frac{(3/5)(1/2)}{(1/6)(1/2)+(3/5)(1/2)}=\frac{3/5}{1/6+3/5}=\frac{18}{23}=0.78 \tag{10.30}$$

It is evident that the results obtained in Eqs. (10.29) and (10.30) are the same as the results obtained in Eqs. (10.26) and (10.27). ◀

10.7 Further Probability Revisions

We can obtain additional information by performing the experiment the second time, the third time, and so on. Each new experiment will help us revise the posterior probability.

Suppose we rolled the die two times and the die rolled twice in the number 3. Our initial presumptions expressed in Eqs. (10.22) and (10.23) are the same, so

$$P(\text{fair}) = \frac{1}{2} \quad \text{and} \quad P(\text{loaded}) = \frac{1}{2} \tag{10.31}$$

$$P(3|\text{fair}) = \frac{1}{6} \quad \text{and} \quad P(3|\text{loaded}) = \frac{3}{5} \tag{10.32}$$

Then, due to the independence of the die rolls, the probabilities of rolling two times in a row the number 3 if the die is fair and if the die is loaded are

$$\begin{aligned} P(3,3,|\text{fair}) &= P(3|\text{fair})\,P(3|\text{fair}) = \frac{1}{6} * \frac{1}{6} = \frac{1}{36} \\ P(3,3,|\text{loaded}) &= P(3|\text{loaded}) * P(3|\text{loaded}) = \frac{3}{5} * \frac{3}{5} = \frac{9}{25} \end{aligned} \tag{10.33}$$

Then, the joint probabilities of getting two times the number 3 and the die is fair and getting two times the number 3 and the die is loaded are

$$\begin{aligned} P(\text{fair} \,\&\, 3{,}3) &= P(3{,}3 \,\&\, \text{fair}) = P(3,3,|\text{fair})\,P(\text{fair}) = \\ &= \frac{1}{36} * \frac{1}{2} = \frac{1}{72} = 0.014 \\ P(\text{loaded} \,\&\, 3{,}3) &= P(3{,}3 \,\&\, \text{loaded}) = P(3,3,|\text{loaded})\,P(\text{loaded}) = \\ &= \frac{3}{5} * \frac{1}{2} = \frac{3}{10} = 0.30 \end{aligned} \tag{10.34}$$

and in the final step, we can calculate the posterior probability of the die being fair if it rolled twice the number 3:

$$\begin{aligned} P(\text{fair}|3,3) &= \frac{P(\text{fair} \,\&\, 3{,}3)}{P(3{,}3)} = \frac{P(3{,}3 \,\&\, \text{fair})}{P(3{,}3)} = \\ &= \frac{P(3,3,|\text{fair})\,P(\text{fair})}{P(3,3,|\text{fair})\,P(\text{fair}) + P(3,3,|\text{loaded})\,P(\text{loaded})} = \\ &= \frac{(1/36)(1/2)}{(1/36)(1/2) + (9/25)(1/2)} = \frac{25}{25+324} = \frac{25}{349} = 0.072 \end{aligned} \tag{10.35}$$

Similarly, the posterior probability of the die being loaded if it rolled twice the number 3 is

Table 10.3 Changes of the posterior (revised) probabilities with the additional information

Information	Posterior probability of a die to be fair *P(fair | information)*	Posterior probability of a die to be loaded *P(fair | information)*
No info (initial state before die rolls)	0.5	0.5
Rolled number 3 once	0.22	0.78
Rolled number 3 second time in a row	0.072	0.928

$$P(\text{loaded}\,|,3,3)=\frac{P(\text{loaded}\,\&\,3{,}3)}{P(3{,}3)}=\frac{P(3{,}3\,\&\,\text{loaded})}{P(3{,}3)}=$$
$$=\frac{P(3,|3,|\text{loaded})\,P(\text{loaded})}{P(3,3,|\text{fair})\,P(\text{fair})+P(3,3,|\text{loaded})\,P(\text{loaded})}= \tag{10.36}$$
$$=\frac{(9/25)(1/2)}{(1/36)(1/2)+(9/25)(1/2)}=\frac{324}{25+324}=\frac{324}{349}=0.928$$

Comparing the results in Eqs. (10.35) and (10.36) with Eqs. (10.26), (10.27), and (10.22), we can conclude that with the initial assumption that the die can be fair or loaded with the probabilities of ½ (Eq. (10.22)) for each option, the posterior (revised) probability for the die to be fair or loaded has changed as the first information arrived that the die rolled the number 3 in the first roll. With this new fact, the probability of the die to be fair decreased from 0.5 to 0.22, while the probability of the die to be loaded increased from 0.5 to 0.78. The repeating evidence that the die rolled the number 3 for the second time in a row has further changed the probabilities of the die to be fair or loaded. With this second portion of additional information, the probability of the die to be fair further decreased from 0.22 to 0.072, while the probability of the die to be loaded further increased from 0.78 to 0.92. These results are tracked in Table 10.3.

The results shown in Table 10.3 clearly indicate that additional information may change the posterior probabilities.

Questions for Self-Control for Chap. 10

1. What is the conditional probability?
2. What is the difference between conditional, revised, and Bayesian probabilities?
3. What is the marginal probability?
4. What is the joint probability?
5. What is the difference of the following two joint probabilities, *P*(*A*&*B*) and *P*(*B*&*A*)?

6. How are the conditional, marginal, and joint probabilities related?
7. What can you say about conditional probability $P(A|B)$ if $P(B|A)$ is known?
8. How is Bayes' theorem formulated and what does it mean?
9. How does marginal probability relate to the conditional probabilities?
10. What is Bayes' theorem in the general form?
11. Can additional information change probabilities of events?
12. How does additional information change probabilities of events?
13. What is the Monty Hall problem and what is puzzling in it?
14. How can you explain the puzzle in the Monty Hall problem?
15. What can you say about the probability of a dice to be fair or loaded depending on the results of the die rolls?

Problems for Chap. 10

1. The probability of wine to be good if it comes from region A is 0.9, while the probability of wine to be good if it comes from region B is 0.7. Sixty percent of the total wine supply comes from region A, and 40% of the total supply comes from region B. What is the probability to buy a good wine without any knowledge about the supplier?
2. The probability of buying a defective part is 0.3. This part is supplied by two manufacturers. The first manufacturer holds 70% and the second 30% of the market by the number of sold units. The percent of the defective parts supplied by the first manufacturer is twice as higher than the percent of the defective parts supplied by the second manufacturer. You bought two parts with no knowledge about the manufacturer, and both parts occurred to be defective. What is the probability that you bought both parts from the first manufacturer?
3. The probability of finding an employment candidate, who has both a business degree and good computer skills, is 0.3, while the probability of finding an employment candidate with a business degree is 0.6. What is the probability for an employment candidate to possess good computer skills if the candidate has a business degree?
4. You suspect that a coin is loaded. The initial probability of the coin to be fair is 0.6 and to be loaded is 0.4. If the coin is fair, then the probability of its landing on heads is ½, but if the coin is loaded, the probability of landing on heads is 2/3. The coin in three flips has landed on heads three times in a row. What is the posterior probabilities of the coin to be fair and to be loaded given that it landed on heads three times in a row?
5. The probability of a car model to be successful in the competition in the market is 0.8 if the gas mileage of the car model meets the market average. The probability of meeting the gas mileage market average is 0.9. In fact, the car model became successful in the market. What was the probability that the car model met the gas mileage average if it became successful in the market?

Major Distributions

Contents

11.1 Probability Density Versus Probability Distribution – 193

11.2 Normal Distribution – 196

11.3 Cumulative Normal Probability – 198

11.4 The Normal Distribution and the Real World – 199

11.5 The Standard Normal Distribution – 200

11.6 Calculating Standard Normal Cumulative Probabilities Using Tables – 201

11.6.1 Cumulative Standard Normal Probabilities Tables – 202

11.6.2 Centered Cumulative Standard Normal Probabilities Table – 202

11.7 Transformation to the Standard Normal Distribution – 204

11.8 The Importance and Utility of the Standard Normal Distribution – 204

11.9 Calculating Normal Distribution with Computers – 205

11.9.1 NORMDIST: Normal Distribution Density and Cumulative Probability – 206

11.9.2 NORM.INV: Inverse Calculation of Cumulative Normal Probabilities – 207

S. K. Aityan, *Business Research Methodology*, Classroom Companion: Business,
https://doi.org/10.1007/978-3-030-76857-7_11

11.9.3 NORM.S.DIST: Cumulative Standard Normal Probabilities – 208
11.9.4 NORMSINV: Inverse Cumulative Standard Normal Probabilities – 209
11.9.5 STANDARDIZE: Transformation From Normal Distribution to Standard Normal Distribution – 210

11.10 Binomial Distribution – 211

11.11 Calculating Binomial Distribution with Computers – 214

11.12 Relationship Between Normal and Binomial Distributions – 214

11.1 Probability Density Versus Probability Distribution

Suppose we measure the weight of watermelons at our farm. We denote the watermelon weight with the random variable X. We measured weights of the watermelons with the accuracy of $\Delta X = 2$ kg, i.e., the watermelon weights were categorized between 0–2, 2–4, 4–6, 6–8, 8–10, 10–12, 14–16, 16–18, and 18–20 kg of weight. The probability distribution of a watermelon to have the respective weight is shown in the histogram in ◘ Fig. 11.1a. For example, the probability of a watermelon to have the weight between 12 and 14 kg is 0.208. If we categorize the watermelons with the accuracy of 1 kg, i.e., $\Delta X = 1$, the probability of the watermelons to have the weight within the respective intervals of weight is shown in the histogram in ◘ Fig. 11.1b. For example, the probability of a watermelon to have the weight between 12 and 13 kg is 0.104. Similarly, if we measure the watermelon weights with the accuracy of one-half kilogram, i.e., $\Delta X = 0.05$, the probability of the watermelons to have the weight within the respective intervals of weight is shown in the histogram in ◘ Fig. 11.1c. For example, the probability of a watermelon to have the weight between 12 and 12.5 kg is 0.052. It is evident that the smaller the interval, the lower the probability of having the weight within the interval, because the less number of watermelons has the weight within each smaller interval.

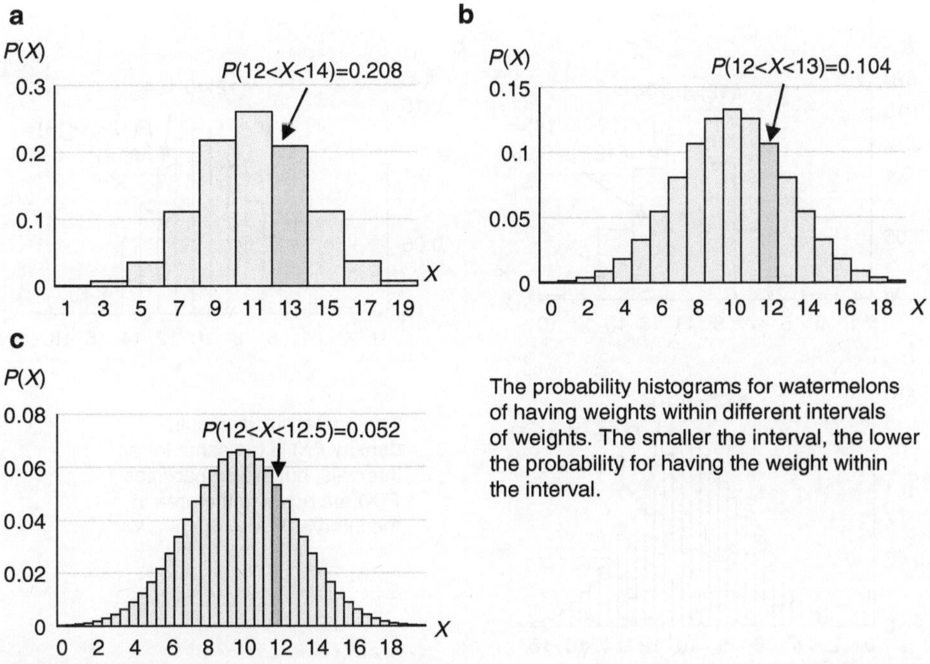

◘ **Fig. 11.1** Probability distribution histogram for different intervals of random variable X; **a** for interval $\Delta X = 2$, **b** for interval $\Delta X = 1$, and **c** for interval $\Delta X = 0.5$

Let's introduce probability density. ***Probability density*** $f(X)$ is defined as

$$f(X) = \frac{dP(X)}{dX} \tag{11.1}$$

which can be interpreted as the probability for the random variable to be within the unit interval. Thus, the probability of the random variable $P(X)$ within interval dx is the product of the density $f(X)$ multiplied by the interval ΔX

$$P(x < X < x + dX) = f(x)dX \tag{11.2}$$

or for $X = x$ within interval ΔX

$$P(x < X < x + \Delta x) \approx f(x)\Delta x \tag{11.3}$$

where x is a given number of the random variable X and ΔX is the interval. Please do not get confused with X and x. The capital character X (capital X) denotes the variable, and x (lowercase x) denotes a value of this variable.

The probabilities for different intervals ΔX were shown in ◘ Fig. 11.1. The same distribution in terms of probability density $f(X)$ is shown in ◘ Fig. 11.2. The probability density $f(X)$ is the same for the same weight $X = 12$ kg regardless of the chosen intervals ΔX shown in ◘ Fig. 11.2a–c, but the probabilities are different for different intervals and equal to the area in the interval calculated as $P(X) = f(X)^* \Delta X$.

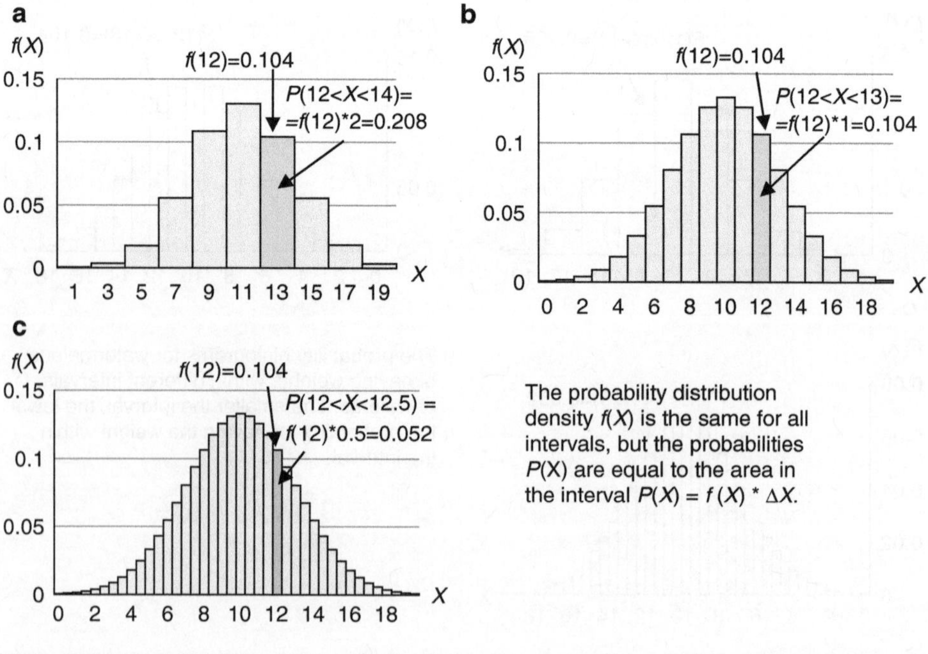

◘ **Fig. 11.2** Probability distribution density $f(X)$ and the probabilities $P(X)$ for different intervals of random variable X as the area in the intervals; **a** for interval $\Delta X = 2$, **b** for interval $\Delta X = 1$, and **c** for interval $\Delta X = 0.5$

If interval ΔX tends to zero, i.e., $\Delta X \rightarrow 0$, the discrete probability density turns into a continuous probability density distribution as illustrated in ◘ Fig. 11.3. ◘ Figure 11.3a illustrates a discrete distribution density with intervals ΔX, and ◘ Fig. 11.3b shows the continuous probability density distribution when $\Delta X \rightarrow 0$. In both cases, the probability distribution for any interval is equal to the areas under the probability density distribution curve.

The probability of random variable within certain interval (x_1, x_2) of the random variable, i.e., $P(x_1 < X < x_2)$, is equal to the area under the probability density distribution curve as shown in ◘ Fig. 11.4. The total area under the curve $f(X)$ equals to one. This reflects the fact that the entire X axis represents all possible values of the continuous random variable X:

$$P(\text{for all}X) = 1 \tag{11.4}$$

The cumulative probability $P(x)$ is the probability for all $x < X$, i.e., the area under $f(X)$ curve for all $x < X$:

$$P(x) = P(X < x) \tag{11.5}$$

as illustrated in ◘ Fig. 11.5.

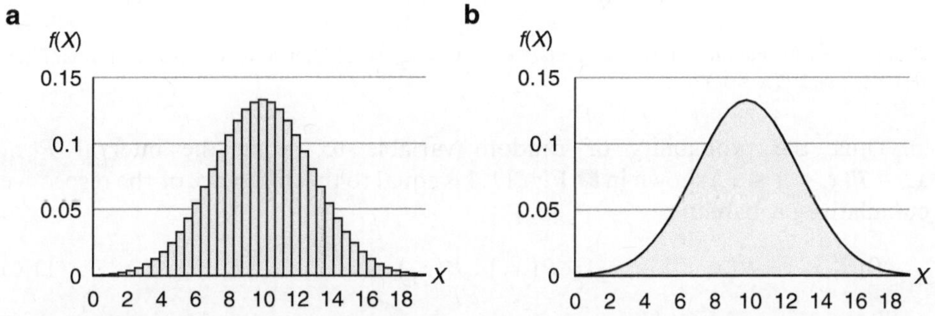

◘ **Fig. 11.3** Probability distribution density $f(X)$ and the probabilities $P(X)$ for different intervals of random variable X as the area in the intervals; **a** for interval $\Delta X = 2$, **b** for interval $\Delta X = 1$, and **c** for interval $\Delta X = 0.5$

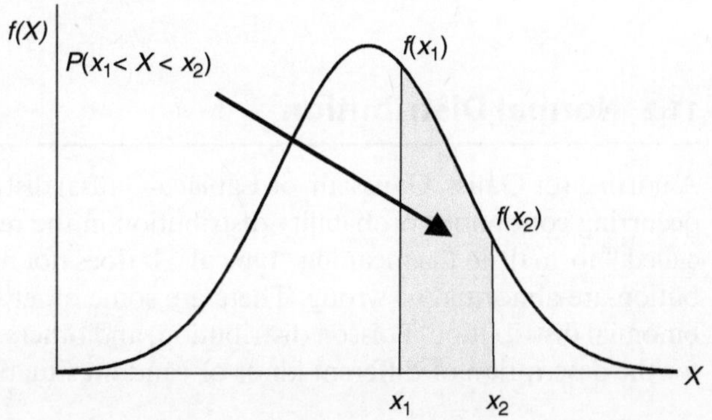

◘ **Fig. 11.4** Probability $P(x_1 < X < x_2)$ for X in the interval (x_1, x_2)

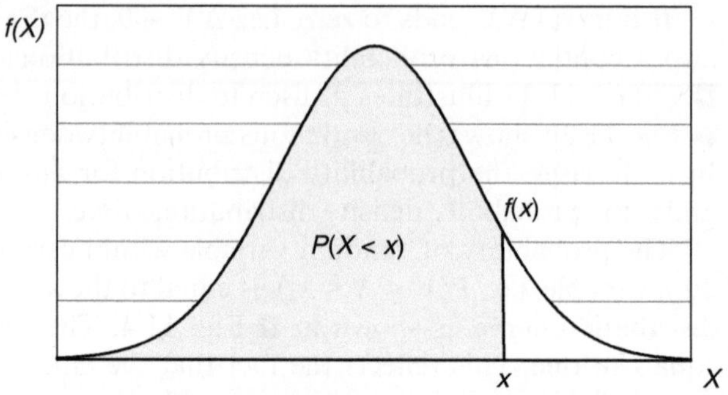

Fig. 11.5 Cumulative probability $P(x) = P(X < x)$

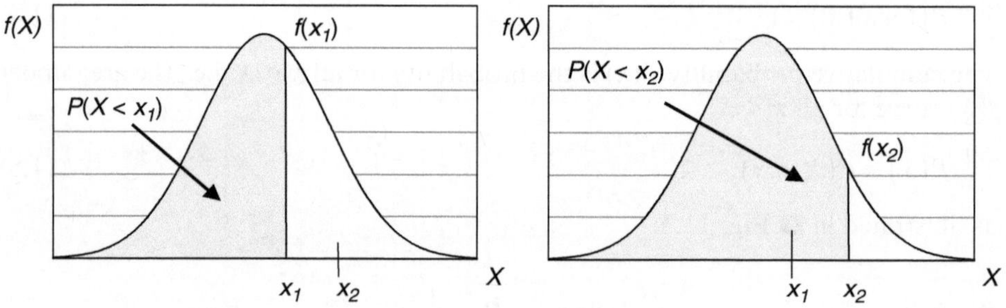

Fig. 11.6 Probability of the interval $P(x_1 < X < x_2)$ as difference of cumulative probabilities $P(X < x_1)$ and $P(X < x_2)$

Thus, the probability of random variable to be in the interval $P(x_1, x_2) = P(x_1 < X < x_2)$ shown in Fig. 11.4 is equal to the difference of the respective cumulative probabilities:

$$P(x_1,x_2) = P(x_1 < X < x_2) = P(x_2) - P(x_1) \tag{11.6}$$

as illustrated in Fig. 11.6.

The following notations $P(x_1)$, $P(X = x_1)$ and $P(X < x_1)$ are just synonymous:
$P(x_1) \equiv P(X = x_1) \equiv P(X < x_1)$

11.2 Normal Distribution

A normal (or Gauss, Gaussian, or Laplace-Gauss) distribution is the most frequently occurring continuous probability distribution in the real world. For this reason, it is called "normal" in the meaning "typical." It does not mean that other types of distribution are abnormal or wrong. There are some other quite useful distributions, like binomial distribution, Poisson distribution, and others which are also very important for the description of different kinds of random situations in the real world.

Normal distribution $f(X)$ is a family of probability density distribution shown in Eq. (11.7) and ◘ Fig. 11.7:

$$f(X) = \frac{1}{\sqrt{2\pi\sigma^2}} e^{-\frac{(X-\mu)^2}{2\sigma^2}} \tag{11.7}$$

Random variable X is defined on all real numbers, i.e., $-\infty < X < \infty$. It has a symmetric bell-shaped form with maximum at $X = \mu$, and its width (spread of its wings) is controlled by parameter σ. Parameter μ is the ***mean***, σ is its ***standard deviation***, and σ^2 is referred to as ***variance***. You must have already noticed the association of these parameters with the expected value and standard deviation in probability theory. ◘ Figure 11.8 illustrates how the variation of mean μ and standard deviation σ (variance σ^2) influence the normal distribution. Four normal distribution curves are shown in the ◘ Fig. 11.8 as examples of the family of normal distribution with different parameters μ and σ.

Curves (a), (b), and (c) in ◘ Fig. 11.8 all centered at $\mu = 15$, but their "spread" is different and depends on parameter σ. The higher the σ, the wider the spread is. Curves (a) and (d) are identical by shape but centered at $\mu = 15$ and $\mu = 10$ correspondently.

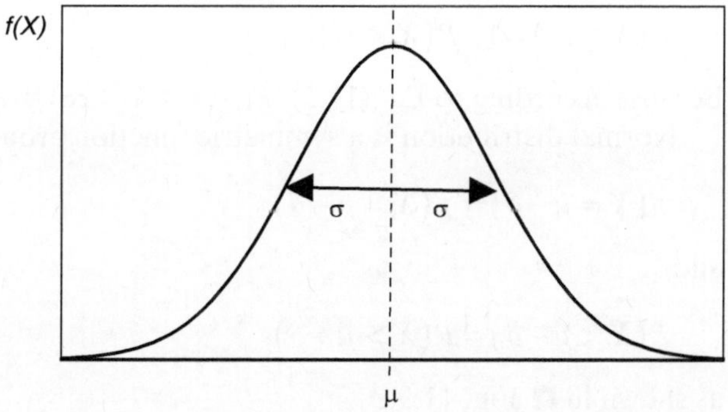

◘ **Fig. 11.7** A normal distribution

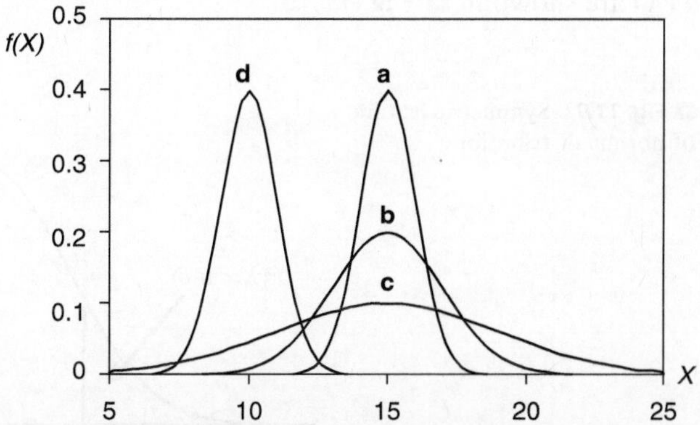

◘ **Fig. 11.8** Examples of normal distribution with different mean μ and standard deviation σ; **a** $\mu = 15$ and $\sigma = 1$, **b** $\mu = 15$ and $\sigma = 2$, **c** $\mu = 15$ and $\sigma = 3$, and **d** $\mu = 10$ and $\sigma = 1$

The conventional notation for a normally distributed random variable X is

$$X \sim N\left(\mu, \sigma^2\right) \tag{11.8}$$

This notation means that X is a continuous random variable distributed normally with mean μ and variance σ^2.

11.3 Cumulative Normal Probability

As we already discussed, the probability of the continuous random variable X to be found within interval $x_1 < X < x_2$ is equal to the area under the probability distribution density curve, $f(X)$, in the interval from x_1 to x_2 as shown in ◘ Fig. 11.4.

The cumulative probability for normal distribution is referred to as the ***cumulative normal probability***.

The total area under function $f(X)$ equals to one, because it represents the probability of having any of the values of the continuous random variable X:

$$P(\text{for all} X) = P(-\infty < X < \infty) = 1 \tag{11.9}$$

Taking into account Eq. (11.9), it is clear that

$$P(X > x_1) = 1 - P(X < x_1) \tag{11.10}$$

Because according to Eq. (11.9), $P(-\infty < X < \infty) = P(X < x_1) + P(X > x_1) = 1$.

Normal distribution is a symmetric function around its mean μ; hence,

11

$$f(X = \mu - \delta) = f(X = \mu + \delta) \tag{11.11}$$

and

$$P(X < \mu - \delta) = P(X > \mu + \delta) \tag{11.12}$$

as shown in ◘ Fig. 11.9.

The distribution density $f(X)$ and the cumulative normal probability function $P(X)$ are shown in ◘ Fig. 11.10.

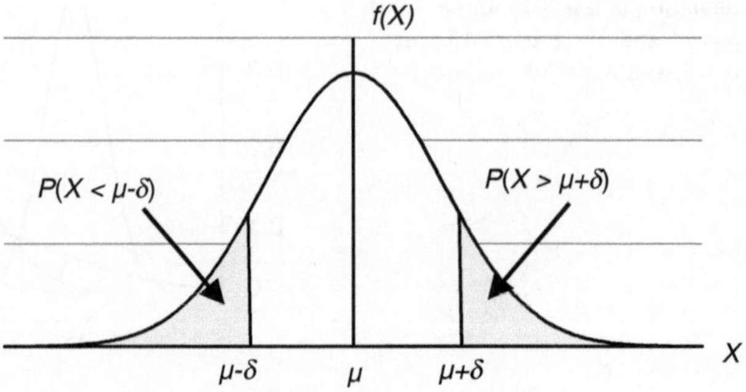

◘ **Fig. 11.9** Symmetric feature of normal distribution

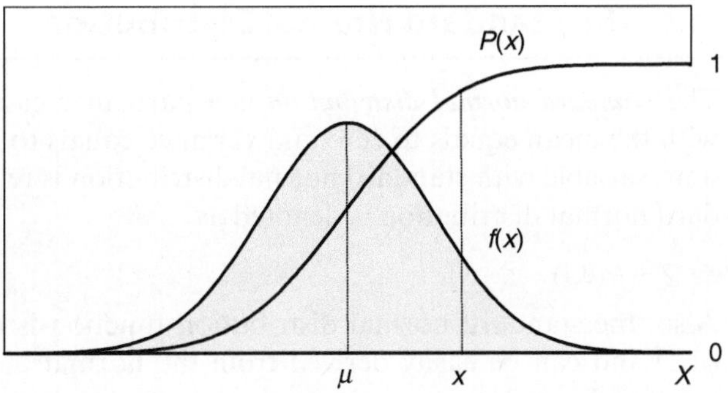

Fig. 11.10 The normal distribution $f(X)$ and cumulative normal probability $P(X)$

11.4 The Normal Distribution and the Real World

The central limit theorem (CLT) in probability theory states that under certain conditions, the sum of a sufficiently large number of independent random variables, each with finite mean and variance, will be approximately normally distributed (Rice 1995). The central limit theorem also requires the random variables to be identically distributed, unless certain conditions are met.

The central limit theorem was first proved by the French mathematician Pierre-Simon Laplace in 1810. It would not be an exaggeration to say that it is one of the most powerful theorems in probability and statistic that lays foundations for many concepts and applications in those areas.

The two of the most important conclusions from the CLT are as follows:

- Most variations in the real world are normally distributed.
- The means of all possible samples of a population are distributed normally with the mean and variance equal to the mean and variance on the population.

Measurable parameters of any object or subject may vary according to many random causes. For example, the height of different people in a community is varying around certain mean height. A weight of watermelons from the same farm is varying around their mean weight. The kinetic energy of molecules in the air is varying around their mean energy (the air temperature). All these variations are caused by many independent random events which are difficult or practically impossible to observe independently. For this reason, we often observe and measure random variables that are very close to normally distributed. The example of measuring weight of watermelons discussed above, most likely, deals with normal distribution because there are many independent factors that impact on the watermelon weight which we are unable to take into account. These factors could be local differences in soil at every watermelon plant location, differences in local water supply for each watermelon, lighting, and many other factors. Similarly, the daily revenue of a restaurant would be different every day but most likely be distributed normally due to many independent factors impacting on it.

Thus, we can consider the most natural random parameters in the real world, which are caused by many independent random events distributed normally.

11.5 The Standard Normal Distribution

The ***standard normal distribution*** is a particular case of the normal distribution with the mean equals to zero and variance equals to one. Conventionally, the random variable with standard normal distribution is referred to as Z. Thus, the standard normal distribution is denoted as

$$Z \sim N(0,1) \tag{11.13}$$

Also, the standard normal distribution function is conventionally referred to as $\varphi(Z)$ and can be easily derived from the normal distribution function $f(X)$ with $\mu = 0$ and $\sigma^2 = 1$ as

$$\phi(Z) = \frac{1}{\sqrt{2\pi}} e^{-\frac{Z^2}{2}} \tag{11.14}$$

The standard normal distribution density function $\varphi(Z)$ is shown in ◘ Fig. 11.11.

The standard normal distribution is a very important case of a normal distribution. As we will discuss later in this chapter, any normal distribution can be transformed into the standard normal distribution and, thus, be analyzed based on the properties of the standard normal distribution. This is particularly important:

- To compare normal distributions with different means and variances
- If no computer programs are used for calculation but only tables of the standard normal distribution

Let's discuss some helpful features of the standard normal distribution which will find practical application in a hypothesis testing and sampling experiment analysis discussed in ► Chaps. 13, 14, and 15.

It is evident that the standard normal distribution is symmetric around zero because its mean value $\mu = 0$. Hence, the following relationship is correct:

$$P(Z < -z_a) = P(Z > z_a) \tag{11.15}$$

as shown in ◘ Fig. 11.12.

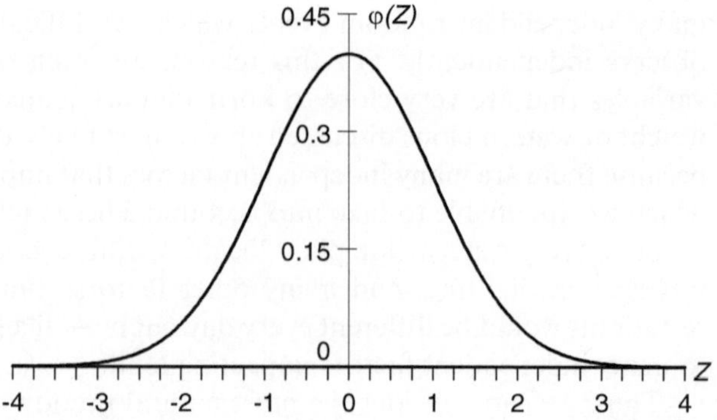

◘ **Fig. 11.11** Standard normal distribution function

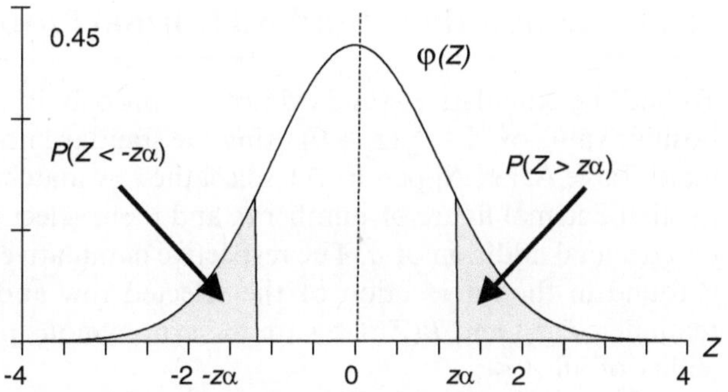

Fig. 11.12 Symmetry of the standard normal probabilities $P(Z < -z_\alpha)$ and $P(Z > z_\alpha)$

Taking into account the property in Eq. (11.15), one can write

$$P(Z < -z_\alpha) = 1 - P(Z < z_\alpha) \tag{11.16}$$

Quite often, we need to find $P(-z_\alpha < Z < z_\alpha)$ when $P(Z < z_\alpha)$ is known. It could be easily derived that

$$P(-z_\alpha < Z < z_\alpha) = 1 - P(Z > z_\alpha) - P(Z < -z_\alpha) = 1 - 2P(Z > z_\alpha) \tag{11.17}$$

The properties of the standard normal distribution described above are very helpful in calculating the cumulative standard normal probability values by using tables.

Similarly, as for the normal distribution, the notations $P(z_\alpha)$, $P(z = z_\alpha)$, and $P(z < z_\alpha)$ are considered synonymous, i.e.,

$$P(z_\alpha) \equiv P(Z = z_\alpha) \equiv P(Z < z_\alpha) \tag{11.18}$$

The following notations $P(z_\alpha)$, $P(z = z_\alpha)$, and $P(z < z_\alpha)$ and $P(Z < z_\alpha)$ are just synonymous:

$$P(z_\alpha) \equiv P(Z = z_\alpha) \equiv P(Z < z_\alpha)$$

Thus, the notation $P(z)$ means the cumulative standard normal probability at point z, i.e., the area under the standard normal distribution density curve, $\varphi(Z)$, on the left from point $Z = z$.

11.6 Calculating Standard Normal Cumulative Probabilities Using Tables

Precalculated tables for the standard normal distribution are commonly available. The tables and detailed instructions are available in Appendix A in this book.

11.6.1 Cumulative Standard Normal Probabilities Tables

To find the cumulative standard normal probability $P(z_\alpha) = P(Z < z_\alpha)$ for a given positive value of $Z = z_\alpha$ ($z_\alpha > 0$) using the standard normal cumulative probabilities table (Table A.1 in Appendix A), select the row matching the value of Z trimmed to the first decimal figure of number a, and then, select the column matching the second decimal addition of a. The respective cumulative probability $P(z_\alpha) = P(Z < z_\alpha)$ is found in the intersection of the selected row and the selected column. Just a reminder, $P(z_\alpha)$ and $P(Z < z_\alpha)$ are the synonymous notations that mean the probability of all $Z < z_\alpha$.

For example, if $z_\alpha = 1.27$, then z_α trimmed to the first decimal figure is 1.2, and the second decimal addition is 0.07. The overall z_α is $1.2 + 0.07 = 1.27$. The method of finding the cumulative standard normal probability using the standard table $P(1.27) = P(z_\alpha < 1.27)$ is shown in ◘ Fig. 11.13. $P(1.27) = P(Z < 1.27) = 0.8980$.

The cumulative standard normal probabilities for negative values of Z can be found from the same table utilizing the symmetry of the standard normal distribution around $Z = 0$, i.e.,

$$P(-z_\alpha) = 1 - P(z_\alpha) \tag{11.19}$$

11.6.2 Centered Cumulative Standard Normal Probabilities Table

The standard normal distribution $\varphi(Z)$ is a symmetric function with the symmetry around $Z = 0$, i.e., $\varphi(-Z) = \varphi(Z)$. For this reason, the $P(Z < 0) = 0.5$, because the area under $\varphi(Z)$ for all $Z < 0$ equals exactly area under $\varphi(Z)$ for all

zα	0	0.01	0.02	0.03	0.04	0.05	0.06	0.07	0.08	0.09
0.0	0.5000	0.5040	0.5080	0.5120	0.5160	0.5199	0.5239	0.5279	0.5319	0.5359
0.1	0.5398	0.5438	0.5478	0.5517	0.5557	0.5596	0.5636	0.5675	0.5714	0.5753
0.2	0.5793	0.5832	0.5871	0.5910	0.5948	0.5987	0.6026	0.6064	0.6103	0.6141
0.3	0.6179	0.6217	0.6255	0.6293	0.6331	0.6368	0.6406	0.6443	0.6480	0.6517
0.4	0.6554	0.6591	0.6628	0.6664	0.6700	0.6736	0.6772	0.6808	0.6844	0.6879
0.5	0.6915	0.6950	0.6985	0.7019	0.7054	0.7088	0.7123	0.7157	0.7190	0.7224
0.6	0.7257	0.7291	0.7324	0.7357	0.7389	0.7422	0.7454	0.7486	0.7517	0.7549
0.7	0.7580	0.7611	0.7642	0.7673	0.7704	0.7734	0.7764	0.7794	0.7823	0.7852
0.8	0.7881	0.7910	0.7939	0.7967	0.7995	0.8023	0.8051	0.8078	0.8106	0.8133
0.9	0.8159	0.8186	0.8212	0.8238	0.8264	0.8289	0.8315	0.8340	0.8365	0.8389
1.0	0.8413	0.8438	0.8461	0.8485	0.8508	0.8531	0.8554	0.8577	0.8599	0.8621
1.1	0.8643	0.8665	0.8686	0.8708	0.8729	0.8749	0.8770	0.8790	0.8810	0.8830
1.2	0.8849	0.8869	0.8888	0.8907	0.8925	0.8944	0.8962	0.8980	0.8997	0.9015
1.3	0.9032	0.9049	0.9066	0.9082	0.9099	0.9115	0.9131	0.9147	0.9162	0.9177
1.4	0.9192	0.9207	0.9222	0.9236	0.9251	0.9265	0.9279	0.9292	0.9306	0.9319

◘ **Fig. 11.13** Finding the cumulative standard normal probability for $Z = 1.27$ using the cumulative standard normal probabilities table (Appendix A)

$Z > 0$. Thus, the centered standard normal probability calculated for the interval $P_C(Z < z_\alpha) = P(0 < Z < z_\alpha)$ is exactly by 0.5 less than the cumulative standard normal probability $P(Z < z_\alpha)$:

$$PC(Z < z_\alpha) = P(0 < Z < z_\alpha) = P(Z < z_\alpha) - 0.5 \tag{11.20}$$

Such a probability is referred to as centered cumulative standard normal probability (Table A.2 in Appendix A) and presents the centered cumulative standard normal probabilities. It becomes evident by comparing the probabilities in Tables A.1 and A.2 that all probabilities in Table A.2 are by 0.5 less than the probabilities shown in Table A.1.

Centered cumulative standard normal probabilities can be found from Table A.2 using the same method as for Table A.1 described above.

▶ Example

For example, if $z_a = 1.27$, then Z trimmed to the first decimal figure is 1.2, and the second decimal addition is 0.07. The overall $z_a = 1.2 + 0.07 = 1.27$. The method of finding the centered cumulative standard normal probability $P_C(1.27) = P_C(0 < Z < 1.27)$ is shown in ◘ Fig. 11.14. $P_C(1.27) = P_C(0 < Z < 1.27) = 0.3980$.

The cumulative standard normal probabilities $P(Z)$ can be found for positive Z from the centered cumulative standard normal probabilities as

$$P(Z) = P_C(Z) + 0.5 \tag{11.21}$$

For example, $P(Z = 1.27) = P_C(Z = 1.27) + 0.5 = 0.3980 + 0.5000 = 0.8980$. ◀

z_a	0	0.01	0.02	0.03	0.04	0.05	0.06	0.07	0.08	0.09
0.0	0.0000	0.0040	0.0080	0.0120	0.0160	0.0199	0.0239	0.0279	0.0319	0.0359
0.1	0.0398	0.0438	0.0478	0.0517	0.0557	0.0596	0.0636	0.0675	0.0714	0.0753
0.2	0.0793	0.0832	0.0871	0.0910	0.0948	0.0987	0.1026	0.1064	0.1103	0.1141
0.3	0.1179	0.1217	0.1255	0.1293	0.1331	0.1368	0.1406	0.1443	0.1480	0.1517
0.4	0.1554	0.1591	0.1628	0.1664	0.1700	0.1736	0.1772	0.1808	0.1844	0.1879
0.5	0.1915	0.1950	0.1985	0.2019	0.2054	0.2088	0.2123	0.2157	0.2190	0.2224
0.6	0.2257	0.2291	0.2324	0.2357	0.2389	0.2422	0.2454	0.2486	0.2517	0.2549
0.7	0.2580	0.2611	0.2642	0.2673	0.2704	0.2734	0.2764	0.2794	0.2823	0.2852
0.8	0.2881	0.2910	0.2939	0.2967	0.2995	0.3023	0.3051	0.3078	0.3106	0.3133
0.9	0.3159	0.3186	0.3212	0.3238	0.3264	0.3289	0.3315	0.3340	0.3365	0.3389
1.0	0.3413	0.3438	0.3461	0.3485	0.3508	0.3531	0.3554	0.3577	0.3599	0.3621
1.1	0.3643	0.3665	0.3686	0.3708	0.3729	0.3749	0.3770	0.3790	0.3810	0.3830
1.2	0.3849	0.3869	0.3888	0.3907	0.3925	0.3944	0.3962	0.3980	0.3997	0.4015
1.3	0.4032	0.4049	0.4066	0.4082	0.4099	0.4115	0.4131	0.4147	0.4162	0.4177
1.4	0.4192	0.4207	0.4222	0.4236	0.4251	0.4265	0.4279	0.4292	0.4306	0.4319

◘ **Fig. 11.14** Finding the centered cumulative standard normal probability for $z_a = 1.27$ using the centered cumulative standard normal probabilities table (Appendix B)

11.7 Transformation to the Standard Normal Distribution

Any normal distribution $X \sim N(\mu, \sigma^2)$ can be transformed to the standard normal distribution $Z \sim N(0,1)$ by applying the following transformation:

$$Z = \frac{X - \mu}{\sigma} \tag{11.22}$$

that results in

$$f(X) = \frac{1}{\sqrt{2\pi\sigma^2}} e^{-\frac{(X-\mu)^2}{2\sigma^2}} = \frac{1}{\sqrt{2\pi}} e^{-\frac{Z^2}{2}} = \phi(Z) \tag{11.23}$$

The standard normal distribution is a very convenient form of the normal distribution for the following reason. By studying the properties of the standard normal distribution and taking into account that any normal distribution can be easily converted into the standard normal distribution, one can analyze properties of any normal distribution.

The inverse transformation from the standard normal distribution $Z \sim N(0,1)$ to a normal distribution $X \sim N(\mu, \sigma^2)$ can be performed as

$$X = \mu + Z\sigma \tag{11.24}$$

11

11.8 The Importance and Utility of the Standard Normal Distribution

The cumulative normal probability $P(X)$ is not an analytic function. It means that there is no analytic expression, which can be used to calculate it. It can be calculated either using computer algorithms or specially designed precalculated tables. It is practically impossible to prepare the precalculated tables for the entire family of normal distributions with all possible means and variances. On the other hand, the standard normal distribution is well analyzed, its properties are well known, and the precalculated tables for standard cumulative probabilities are developed. Therefore, typical operations with any normal distribution $X \sim N(\mu, \sigma^2)$, unless done with the help of computer algorithms, are performed in the following steps:

- Transform the normal distribution to the standard normal distribution $X \sim N(\mu, \sigma^2) \rightarrow Z \sim N(0,1)$ using Eq. (11.22).
- Analyze and solve the problem using standard normal distribution $Z \sim N(0,1)$.
- Then, if needed, perform the inverse transformation from the standard normal distribution to the original normal distribution $Z \sim N(0,1) \rightarrow .X \sim N(\mu, \sigma^2)$ using Eq. (11.24).

To find cumulative normal probability $P(x_a)$ for value x_a of the normally distributed random variable $X \sim N(\mu, \sigma^2)$ with mean μ and variance σ^2 using the standard normal distribution tables, one can convert the normally distributed random variable X to the standard normally distributed random variable Z by using z-transform in Eq. (11.22):

$$Z_a = \frac{x_a - \mu}{\sigma} \tag{11.25}$$

Then, find cumulative standard probability $P(z_a)$ for z_a using the standard normal distribution tables. In result,

$$P(x_a) = P(z\alpha) \tag{11.26}$$

If you need to continue the analysis with random variable X, then perform the inverse transformation $z_a \to x_a$ using Eq. (11.24).

▶ Example

For example, we want to calculate the cumulative normal probability $P(x_a)$ for normally distributed random variable $X \sim N(20, 25)$ at $x_a = 23.4$. Thus, the normal distribution has mean $\mu = 20$ and variance $\sigma^2 = 25$; hence, the standard deviation $\sigma = 5$. First, perform the z-transform $x_a \to z_a$ by applying Eq. (11.21):

$$z_a = \frac{x_a - \mu}{\sigma} = \frac{23.4 - 20}{5} = 0.68 \tag{11.27}$$

We can find $P(z_a)$ by using the special table of cumulative standard normal probabilities or a computer algorithm. From the table, we find $P(z_a = 0.68) = 0.7517$ for $z_a = 0.68$. The problem is solved, and $P(x_a)$ is found:

$$P(X < 23.4) = P(Z < 0.68) = 0.7517 \tag{11.28}$$

Just reminding that notations $P(x_a)$, $P(x = x_a)$, and $P(x < x_a)$ are identical.

The normal distribution tables and their operation description are available in Appendix A at the end of this book.

The result will be the same regardless of whether we used the special tables or computer applications for the calculation. Computer algorithms can calculate cumulative normal probabilities for any normal distribution, i.e., for normally distributed random variable with any possible values of mean and variance. ◀

11.9 Calculating Normal Distribution with Computers

Cumulative normal probabilities and, hence, the cumulative standard normal probabilities cannot be calculated analytically. It means that there are no explicit formulas to calculate these values. However, the values of cumulative normal probabilities can be calculated numerically for each value of random variable. Special tables have been developed that present the calculated values for the cumulative standard normal distribution.

In the twenty-first century, when computers are widely available, calculating cumulative normal distribution has become an easy task. A variety of software algorithms and products can perform computation for normal distributions with various means and variances. For example, Microsoft Excel and OpenOffice Calc have built-in functions for such calculations.

In this section, we will discuss some of the most frequently used built-in functions in Microsoft Excel and OpenOffice Calc for normal and standard normal distribution. In the examples, we will keep the six-digit accuracy of calculations.

11.9.1 NORMDIST: Normal Distribution Density and Cumulative Probability

As we already know, the normal distribution $X \sim N(\mu, \sigma^2)$ is

$$f(X) = \frac{1}{\sqrt{2\pi\sigma^2}} e^{-\frac{(X-\mu)^2}{2\sigma^2}} \tag{11.29}$$

The function for the calculation of the normal distribution density and the cumulative normal probabilities is NORMDIST.[1]

Product	Function syntax
Microsoft Excel	NORM.DIST(X, μ, σ, c)
OpenOffice Calc	NORMDIST(X; μ; σ; c)

Functions NORM.DIST and NORMDIST return the following values.

Description of NORMDIST	Parameter
Returns the value of the normal distribution density $f(X)$ for any x from $X \sim N(\mu, \sigma^2)$.	c = FALSE
Returns the value of the cumulative normal probability $P(X)$ for any x from $X \sim N(\mu, \sigma^2)$.	c = TRUE

The values of X could be any, positive, negative, or zero. To avoid confusion with $P(X)$, it is the cumulative normal probability for the random value z that means the area under the normal distribution density curve $f(X)$ for all values lower than x as shown in ◘ Fig. 11.10.

1 MS Excel uses both NORM.DIST and NORM.DIST, and OO Calc uses NORMDIST name for this function. We will be using NORM.DIST and NORMDIST interchangeably in this book.

► **Example 1**

In this example, we use three normal distributions, $X \sim N(10,16)$, with the mean μ,= 10 and the standard deviation $\sigma = 4$, $X \sim N(-2,25)$ with the mean μ,= −2 and the standard deviation $\sigma = 5$, and $X \sim N0,1)$ with the mean μ,= 0 and the standard deviation $\sigma = 1$. The last one is actually the standard normal distribution. Function NORM.DIST returns the appropriate values of the normal distribution density and the cumulative normal probability. All calculations were performed with the six-digit accuracy.

Function NORM.DIST

x	μ	σ	**Returned value** $f(X)$ **if** c **= FALSE**	$P(X)$ **if** c **= TRUE**
11	10	4	0.096667	0.598706
5.12345	10	4	0.047436	0.111396
−1	10	4	0.002273	0.002980
−3	−2	5	0.078209	0.420740
−2	−2	5	0.079788	0.500000
0	−2	5	0.073654	0.655422
−1.96	0	1	0.058441	0.024998
0	0	1	0.398942	0.500000
1.96	0	1	0.058441	0.975002

◄

11.9.2 NORM.INV: Inverse Calculation of Cumulative Normal Probabilities

Suppose we know the cumulative normal probability p for $X \sim N(\mu, \sigma^2)$ and would like to find the corresponding x. Such calculation could be done by using built-in function NORM.INV.

Product	Function syntax
Microsoft Excel	NORMINV(p, μ, σ)
OpenOffice spreadsheets	NORMINV(p; μ; σ)

Function NORM.INV returns the value of x for which $P(x) = p$ for normally distributed random variable $X \sim N(\mu,\sigma^2)$ with the mean μ and standard deviation σ.

► Example 2

For $X \sim N(10,16)$, with the mean μ,= 10 and the standard deviation σ = 4 and for $X \sim N(-2,25)$ with the mean μ,= −2 and the standard deviation σ = 5, function NORMINV returns the values of x for which $P(x) = p$. All calculations were performed with the six-digit accuracy.

Function NORM.INV

p	μ	σ	**Returns x for which $P(x) = p$**
0.598706	10	4	11.0000
0.111396	10	4	5.12345
0.002980	10	4	−1.00000
0.420740	−2	5	−3.00000
0.500000	−2	5	−2.00000
0.655422	−2	5	0.00000
0.024998	0	1	−1.960000
0.500000	0	1	0.000000
0.975002	0	1	1.960000

◄

11.9.3 NORM.S.DIST: Cumulative Standard Normal Probabilities

11

Function NORM.S.DIST calculates the cumulative standard normal probability for the standard normal distribution $Z \sim N(0,1)$. Function NORMSDIST is a special case of function NORMDIST described above with $\mu = 0$ and $\sigma = 1$ and c = TRUE. In function NORM.S.DIST, the distribution is assumed to be standard normal rather than any normal distribution as in the function NORM.DIST. In contrast to NORM.DIST, function NORM.S.DIST calculates only cumulative standard probabilities, and therefore, the function does not have any control parameters.

Product	**Function syntax**
Microsoft Excel	NORM.S.DIST(Z)
OpenOffice spreadsheets	NORMSDIST(Z)

Function NORM.S.DIST returns the value of the cumulative standard normal probability for any value of z, positive, negative, or zero.

▶ Example 3

For $Z \sim N(0,1)$, function NORM.S.DIST returns the appropriate values of the normal distribution density and the cumulative normal probability. All calculations were performed with the six-digit accuracy.

Function NORM.S.DIST

Z	*P(Z)*
−1.96	0.024998
0	0.500000
1.96	0.975002

◀

11.9.4 NORMSINV: Inverse Cumulative Standard Normal Probabilities

Function NORMSINV calculates the percentage points for standard normal distribution $Z \sim N(0,1)$. The percentage point is the value of z for which the cumulative standard normal probability $P(z)$ equals to the given value p.

Product	Function syntax
Microsoft Excel	NORMSINV(*p*)
OpenOffice spreadsheets	NORMDINV(*p*)

Function NORMSINV returns the value of z for which $P(z) = p$ for the random variable z.

▶ Example 4

For $Z \sim N(0,1)$, function NORM.INV returns the values of z for which $P(z) = p$. All calculations were performed with the six-digit accuracy.

Function NORM.S.INV

p	***Returns Z for which P(Z) = p***
0.005	−2.57583
0.025	−1.95996
0.05	−1.64485
0.1	−1.28155

Function NORM.S.INV

p	*Returns Z for which P(Z) = p*
0.5	0.00000
0.9	1.28155
0.95	1.64485
0.975	1.95996
0.995	2.57583

◀

11.9.5 STANDARDIZE: Transformation From Normal Distribution to Standard Normal Distribution

Function STANDARDIZE transforms a value of random variable x with normal distribution $X \sim N(\mu, \sigma^2)$ to the appropriate value of random variable z with standard normal distribution $Z \sim N(0,1)$.

Product	Function syntax
Microsoft Excel	STANDARDIZE(x, μ, σ)
OpenOffice spreadsheets	STANDARDIZE(x; μ; σ)

11

Function STANDARDIZE performs the transformation

$$z = \frac{x - \mu}{\sigma} \tag{11.30}$$

and returns the appropriate value z for the random variable with the standard normal distribution $Z \sim N(0,1)$ calculated from the value x for normally distributed random variable $X \sim N(\mu, \sigma^2)$ with the mean μ and standard deviation σ.

▶ Example 5

In this example, we use three normal distributions, $X \sim N(10,16)$, $X \sim N(-2,25)$, and $X \sim N(0,1)$. The last one is actually the standard normal distribution. Function STANDARDIZE returns the value of the random variable transformed from the given normal distribution to the standard normal distribution. All calculations were performed with the six-digit accuracy.

Function STANDARDIZE

x	μ	σ	**Returned value: z**
11	10	4	0.25000
5.12345	10	4	−1.21914
−1	10	4	−2.75000

Function STANDARDIZE

x	μ	σ	Returned value: z
−3	−2	5	−0.20000
−2	−2	5	0.00000
0	−2	5	0.40000
−1.96	0	1	−1.96000
0	0	1	0.00000
1.96	0	1	1.96000

◀

11.10 Binomial Distribution

Suppose there is a random dichotomous trial with two possible Boolean outcomes: one or zero. Such one/zero trial outcome can be synonymously classified as true/false, yes/no, success/failure, or other Boolean outcomes. The probability of the positive outcome one/true/yes/success is p, and the probability of the negative outcome zero/false/no/failure is $q = 1 - p$. Suppose, in a series of n independent trials, k trials end up with the success and n–k trials end up with the failure. The term "independent" means that the probability of a trial outcome does not depend on the outcome of the previous trials. A single success/failure trial is also called a Bernoulli trial or Bernoulli experiment.

Let's define a discrete random variable $X = (0, 1, 2, \ldots, k, \ldots, n)$ that takes integer values indicating the number of successful trial out of total n trials. The probability distribution by X successes out of n trials is called binomial distribution and is denoted as

$$X \sim B(n, p) \tag{11.31}$$

The probability of k successes and n–k failures out of the series of total n trials is

$$P(X, n, p) = \binom{n}{X} p^X (1-p)^{n-X} = \frac{n!}{X!(n-X)!} p^X (1-p)^{n-X} \tag{11.32}$$

where $\binom{n}{X}$ is the number of combination from n by X from where $X = (0, 1, 2, \ldots, k, \ldots, n)$:

$$\binom{n}{X} = \frac{n!}{X!(n-X)!}, \quad \text{where} \quad X! = 1*2*\ldots*k \quad \text{and} \quad 0! = 1 \tag{11.33}$$

Discrete probability $P(X, n, p)$ of X successful trials in the series of total n independent trials regardless of the sequencing (combination) of successes and failures in the series of n trials with the probability p of a success for each trial forms a distribution, which is called binomial distribution and shown in ◘ Fig. 11.15a.

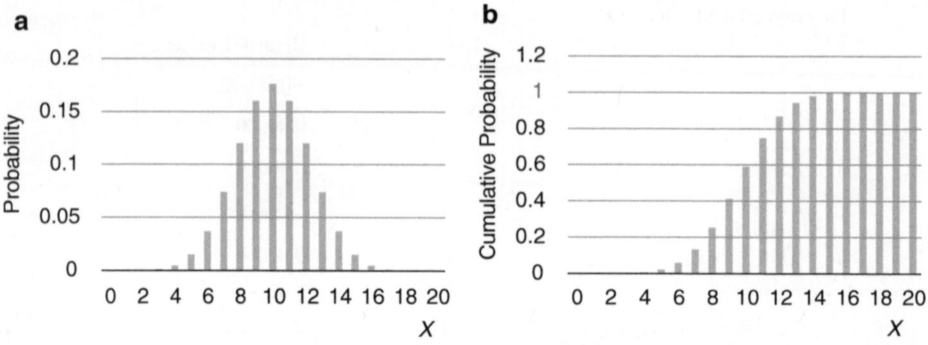

Fig. 11.15 Binomial **a** probability distribution and **b** cumulative probability distribution for the series of 20 independent trials with the probability of success of each trial $p = 0.5$

The sum of probabilities for number of all successful outcomes X equal or less than k for the series of n tests with the probability p for each successful outcome is

$$P(X \le k, n, p) = \sum_{X=0}^{k} P(X, n, p) = \sum_{X=0}^{k} \binom{n}{X} p^X (1-p)^{n-X} = \sum_{X=0}^{k} \frac{n!}{X!(n-X)!} p^X (1-p)^{n-X} \tag{11.34}$$

and is referred to as cumulative probability as shown in Fig. 11.15b. It is evident that the total cumulative probabilities for all possible numbers of successful outcomes equal to one, i.e.,

$$\sum_{X=0}^{n} P(X, n, p) = 1 \tag{11.35}$$

The probability peak of binomial distribution depends on the probability p. If $p = 0.5$, the distribution is centered. If $p < 0.5$, the distribution peak is shifted to the left, and if $p > 0.5$, the distribution peak is shifted to the right as shown in Fig. 11.16.

If the value of each successful outcome is one and failure is zero, then the expected value of μ for the binomial distribution is equal to the mean number of successful trials, i.e.,

$$\mu_X = \sum_{X=0}^{n} P(X, n, p) X = \sum_{X=0}^{n} \binom{n}{X} p^X (1-p)^{n-X} X = \sum_{X=0}^{n} \binom{n}{X} p^X (1-p)^{n-X} X = np \tag{11.36}$$

the standard deviation of the binomial distribution is

$$\sigma_X^2 = E(X-\mu)^2 = \sum_{X=0}^{n} P(X,n,p) * (X-np)^2 = \sum_{X=0}^{n} \binom{n}{X} p^X (1-p)^{n-X} (X-np)^2 =$$
$$= \sum_{X=0}^{n} \frac{n!}{X!(N-x)!} p^X (1-p)^{n-X} (X-np)^2 = np(1-p) \tag{11.37}$$

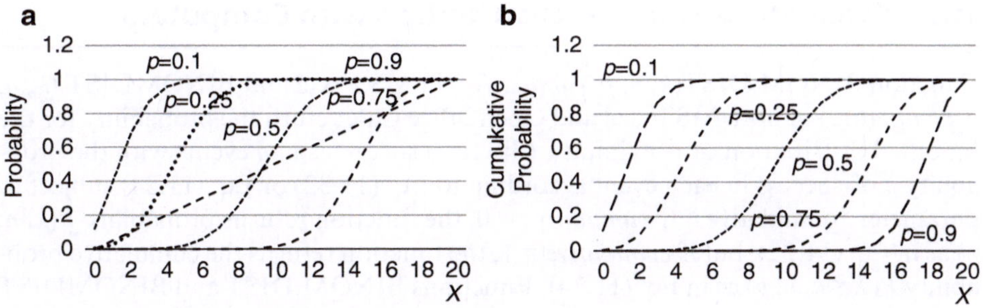

Fig. 11.16 The binomial **a** probability distribution and **b** cumulative distributions for 20 trials with different probabilities of successful outcome in each trial $p = 0.1, p = 0.25, p = 05, p = 0.75$, and $p = 0.9$

Fig. 11.17 Sequence of trials and probabilities for three heads and one tail of total of four flips of a coin

$$\binom{4}{3} = \frac{4!}{3!1!} = \frac{1*2*3*4}{1*2*3*1} = 4$$

Sequence of events	Probability
HHHT	$p^3(1-p)^1$
HHTH	$p^3(1-p)^1$
HTHH	$p^3(1-p)^1$
THHH	$p^3(1-p)^1$

and hence, the standard deviation is

$$\sigma_X = \sqrt{np(1-p)} \tag{11.38}$$

▶ Example 6

Consider tossing a coin with the probability of heads $p_{\text{Heads}} = p$ and the probability of tails $p_{\text{Tails}} = 1 - p$. Suppose the coin is possibly loaded, i.e., $p \neq 1/2$. After four flips of the coin, we have three heads and one tails. Such a result can be obtained with various sequences of outcomes of each flip of the coin, which are shown in Fig. 11.17: The total probability of getting three heads and one tails from four flips of the coin regardless of the sequencing of getting heads and tails is

$$P(3, 4, p) = \binom{4}{3} p^3 (1-p)^{4-3} = \frac{4!}{3!1!} p^3 (1-p)^1 = 4p^3 (1-p)^1 \tag{11.39}$$

With the increase of the number of trial, n, the binomial distribution becomes closer to the normal distribution with the appropriate mean and variance, $\mu_X = np$ and $\sigma_X^2 = np(1-p)$. ◀

For the binomial distribution $X \sim B(n, p)$:

$\mu_X = np$

$\sigma_X^2 = np(1-p)$

$\sigma_X = \sqrt{np(1-p)}$

11.11 Calculating Binomial Distribution with Computers

Function BINOM.DIST(*k*, *n*, *p*, *cumulative*) in MS Excel and BINOMDIST (*k*, *n*, *p*, *cumulative*) in both MS Excel and OpenOffice Calc return the probability for the binomial distribution of obtaining *k* (discrete) successes in *n* events with the probability *p* of success in each event according to Eq. (11.32) or Eq. (11.34) subject to parameter "cumulative." If *cumulative* = 0, the function returns probability $P(k, n, p)$ as in Eq. (11.32), but if *cumulative* = 1, the function returns the cumulative probability $P(X \le k, n, p)$ as in Eq. (11.34). Functions BINOM.DIST and BINOMDIST are identical.

Product	Function syntax
Microsoft Excel	BINOM.DIST(*X*, *n*, *p*, *cumulative*) BINOMDIST(*X*, *n*, *p*, *cumulative*)
OpenOffice spreadsheets	BINOMDIST(*X*, *n*, *p*, *cumulative*)

11.12 Relationship Between Normal and Binomial Distributions

11

Normal distribution is defined on a continuous random variable *X* with the distribution density as in Eq. (11.7), while binomial distribution is defined on a discrete random variable *X* with the distribution as in Eq. (11.32). Both distributions look similar, and with a big number of total events *n*, the binomial distribution becomes very close to the normal distribution.

Questions for Self-Control for Chap. 11

1. What is the difference between probability and probability density distributions?
2. What are distribution density and cumulative probability?
3. What is the definition of the normal distribution?
4. What are the mean, variance, and standard deviation?
5. Where can the normal distribution be found in the real life?
6. What shape does the normal distribution density curve have?
7. What is the standard normal distribution?
8. How is the difference between the normal distribution and the standard normal distribution?
9. What is the notation for the normal distribution?
10. What are the properties of the standard normal distribution?
11. How to calculate the cumulative standard normal probabilities by using the tables?
12. How to calculate the normal standard distribution density and cumulative probabilities by using the built-in functions in MS Excel and OpenOffice Calc?

13. How to transform the normal distribution to the standard normal distribution?
14. Why is the standard normal distribution important?
15. What is binomial distribution?
16. What is the expected value and standard deviation for the binomial distribution?
17. What is the relationship between normal and binomial distributions?

Problems for Chap. 11

1. Using MS Excel or OO Calc, calculate the cumulative standard probabilities, and calculate the probability of $Z < 1.52$ for $Z \sim N(0,1)$.
2. Using MS Excel or OO Calc, calculate the cumulative standard probabilities, and calculate the probability of $0.5 < Z < 1.52$ for $Z \sim N(0,1)$.
3. Using MS Excel or OO Calc, calculate the cumulative standard probabilities, and calculate the probability of $1.96 < Z$ for $Z \sim N(0,1)$.
4. Calculate the probability of continuous random variable with normal distribution $X \sim N(1,4)$ to be less than two (i.e., $X < 2$) by using MS Excel or OO Calc functions for the cumulative standard normal probabilities.
5. For $X \sim N(1,4)$, calculate the probability of $0 < X < 1$.
6. Transform $X \sim N(3,9)$ to $Z \sim N(0,1)$.
7. By using MS Excel or OpenOffice Calc, calculate the cumulative probability for the continuous random variable $X \sim N(3,9)$ to be less than 0.975, i.e., $X < 0.974$.
8. By using MS Excel or OpenOffice Calc, calculate the cumulative probability for the continuous random variable $X \sim N(3,9)$ to be greater than 0.025, i.e., $X < 0.025$.
9. Probability of a defective part in large supply of parts is $p = 0.1$. What is the probability of having five defective parts in randomly chosen ten parts? The term large supply means that the probability of taking a defective part does not change with the number of parts taken from the supply.
10. Probability of heads in flipping a fair coin is $p = 0.5$. What is the probability of having no less than four heads in a series of six flips of the coin?
11. The probability of a cat to be white in color is $p = 0.1$. Calculate using MS Excel of OpenOffice the probability of seeing three white cats of in total of ten cats you watched.

Introduction to Statistics

Contents

12.1 The Sense of Statistics – 218

12.2 Sample Versus Population – 218

12.3 Types of Statistics – 221

12.4 Statistical Nature of Samples – 222

12.5 Major Parameters on Population – 223

12.6 Population Parameters Versus Sample Statistic – 226

12.7 Sample Statistic: Measuring Car Mileage – 228
12.7.1 The Range, Median, Mode, Mean Variance, and Standard Deviation – 228
12.7.2 Covariance and Coefficient of Correlation – 229

12.8 Calculations with the Microsoft Excel and OpenOffice Calc – 231

S. K. Aityan, *Business Research Methodology*, Classroom Companion: Business,
https://doi.org/10.1007/978-3-030-76857-7_12

12.1 The Sense of Statistics

We live in a big world and constantly face the necessity of making generalized conclusions about it based on limited observations and measurements. For example, a retail store would like to understand consumer purchasing patterns based on what their customers have purchased in the past. Most likely, the actual purchases at a store reflect the general purchase patters but only to a certain degree. What can we say about such patterns in general? Health-care organizations would like to learn what major health problems the population has, based on the data about patients who received medical treatment with that organization. In politics, national polls include a limited number of respondents but are supposed to reflect the opinion of the entire population. The bottom line is that statistics deals with measurements on a limited number of objects of interest and has a goal of generalizing the results of such measurements to all objects of that category.

The term ***statistics*** can be used either in singular or in plural form. In its plural form, ***statistics*** refer to the mathematical discipline including different branches like descriptive, inferential, predictive, and mathematical statistics. In its singular form, term ***statistic*** refers to a quantity, such as mean or other quantitative values, calculated from a set of data, typically from a sample.

Probability and statistics are two different disciplines, though they may look quite similar and both use quite similar equations. Probabilities are deductive by its nature while statistics is inductive. In probabilities, we presume that we start from a general rule and try to apply it to learn what may occur in the coming event. In statistics, on the other hand, we say that we know only what we have observed and try to generalize this knowledge. This makes statistics inductive.

- ***Statistics*** (plural) refer to the mathematical discipline.
- ***Statistic*** (singular) refers to a quantity, such as mean or other quantitative values, calculated from a set of data, typically from a sample.

12.2 Sample Versus Population

The term ***population*** is used in statistics to represent all possible elements that are of interest in a given study. However, sometimes, the population is too big that whatever measurements we can actually make normally cover only a part of the population. For example, in national polls, it would be unfeasible to ask all people in the country. Instead, a poll covers only a limited number of people, and the results of the poll are generalized to represent the opinion of the entire population.

The term ***sample*** is used in statistics to represent a limited number of measurements on a part of a population, i.e., on a subset of a population. A sample consists of limited number of elements from the population.

Most likely, all this sounds confusing because we have no idea about the results of measurements on the entire population if getting such measurements is practically unreal. However, we live in the real world, and it is a matter of fact that, from time to time, we have to estimate certain parameters on the population based on limited measurements, because we have no other choice. Let's face the reality and use statistics to help us do it.

First of all, let's discuss the terms population and sample in a greater detail

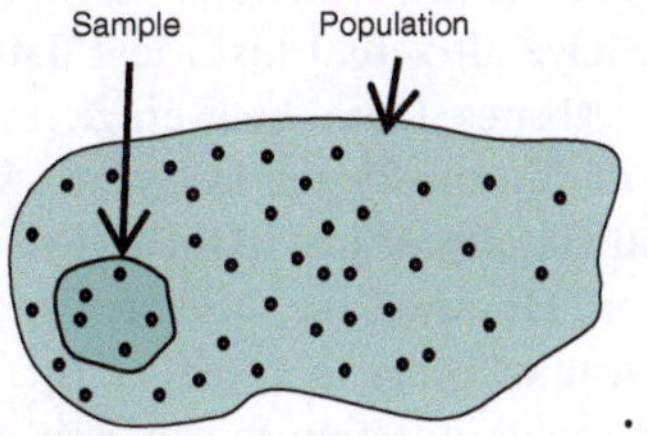

▶ Example 1

A doctor collects the body temperature of all his patients in the hospital. This measurement was conducted on the population of the patients of this doctor. However, if the results of these measurements will be generalized to the entire hospital, it becomes a sample. ◀

▶ Example 2

A computer company received a supply of electronic chips from the supplier. All received chips were tested at the company. For this computer company, it was a population, but for the supplier, it was a sample. If the computer company wants to analyze the received chips, the supply is considered a population of the received chips. However, if the computer company aims to generalize their conclusions to build their opinion about the supplier, the received chip should be considered a sample. ◀

▶ Example 3

Suppose you have to measure the average weight of the people on planet Earth and even assume that you really want to do it. You would spent enormous amount of time for measuring all people, but by the time you completed the measurement, some people have grown taller, some new people were born, and some people have died since you started the measurements.

Thus, performing measurements on the population of people on the Earth is practically impossible, and we must use samples. ◀

▶ **Example 4**

Suppose you have a large storage of bottled wine and would like to figure out the percentage of the bottles in which the wine is spoiled. Even you have all bottles open, which is unreasonable action because you would spoil the wine by opening the bottle; this is not the population. Guess why? – because you will spoil the wine by opening the bottles and your results no longer make any sense. Thus, we have to use a sample that consist of a limited number of bottles for testing the wine. ◀

▶ **Example 5**

You want to measure the average daily return of the stock market index, say Dow Jones for the last year, to make some predictions for your future investment. All sounds just straightforward; you have all actual historical daily returns of Dow Jones that are available on financial websites. Does the average return calculated form that data represent the population of returns for the last year? All depends on the purpose of the measurement. If you are interested just in the last year's returns, then you are right; it represents the population. However, the measurements are supposed to be used for predictions for the next year or years to come. In this case, the measurements were made on a sample. A legitimate question is why is it a sample if we performed the measurement every day and did not miss a single day when the stock market operated in the last year and the daily returns neither changed nor can be varied by any means? All this is true, but if we are going to use the result of measurement for the predictions to the future, we may consider that the actual results were reflecting very specific series of circumstances in the economy, finances, and business and virtually might be different if some circumstances differ. Thus, even in this case, if we use the measurement for reasons that make sense, the measurements were considered on a sample rather than on the population. ◀

The conclusion that comes from the examples above says that the measurement on a population is a much more complex concept than just measuring all the elements on the population. Therefore, we use the qualifier "all possible" in the definition of the term population rather than just "all." Thus, let's agree that any measurements performed in the real world for practical purposes are made on a sample rather than on a population.

- A ***population*** consists of all elements that are of interest for a given study.
- A ***sample*** is a subset of a population.

A ***population parameter*** is an aggregate number calculated from measurements on the entire population that describes specific property of the population. A ***sample statistic*** is an aggregate number calculated from measurements on a sample that describes the same property of the sample. Parameters are typically unknown but can be estimated based on statistic measured and calculated on a sample. For example, the mean value calculated on a sample is statistic, because the mean val-

■ **Table 12.1** Notation for population parameters and sample statistic

Aggregate feature	Population	Sample
Mean	μ	$\overline{x}$
Variance	σ^2	s^2
Standard deviation	σ	s
Covariance between X and Y	σ_{XY}	s_{XY}
Correlation coefficient between X and Y	ρ_{XY}	r_{XY}

ues could vary on different samples. The mean value on the population is the parameter. The commonly used notation for parameters on the population and statistic on samples is presented in ■ Table 12.1.

- A ***parameter*** is a value that describes an aggregate feature of the entire population.
- A ***statistic*** represents value that describes an aggregate feature measured on a sample.

12.3 Types of Statistics

There are two major branches of statistics as a discipline:
- Descriptive statistics
- Inferential statistics

Descriptive statistics implies analyzing, summarizing, and describing the main features of a collection of data. Descriptive statistics is concerned with properties of the observed data. ***Inferential statistics*** implies application of statistical methods to random sampling to make conclusions about some unknown aspects of a population, for example, by testing hypotheses and making estimates.

Two major branches of statistics:
- ***Descriptive statistics*** implies analyzing, summarizing, and describing the main features of a collection of data. Descriptive statistics is concerned with properties of the observed data.
- ***Inferential statistics*** implies application of statistical methods to random sampling to make conclusions about some unknown aspects of a population, for example, by testing hypotheses and making estimates.

12.4 Statistical Nature of Samples

Suppose we want to learn a specific quantitative feature of a population, but we are unable to perform the measurements on the entire population. For example, we need to find the average weight of people to use the information in the aircraft design. It is practically impossible to measure the weight of the entire population. It is quite natural to measure the weight of a certain number of randomly selected people to find their average weight. Assume we performed the measurement on a sample that consists of randomly selected 45 people as shown in ◘ Table 12.2 and found out that the mean weight is 165 lb for this group of people.

However, a quite legitimate question arises in this regard – how does the mean weight measured on the sample of 45 people relate to the mean weight for the population of people?

How does the mean measured on a sample relate to the mean of the population?

This is not an easy question for many reasons. First of all, a random sample may occasionally include a proportionally higher number of heavier (or lighter) people than in the entire population. This would directly impact on the mean weight measured on the sample. On the other hand, if we perform the measurement on different samples, we might get different results. Suppose three different researchers were given the same task of measuring the mean on a sample of 45 people (or one researcher did it three different times) as presented in ◘ Tables 12.1, 12.2, 12.3, and 12.4. It is clear that the samples are different because every time people included into a sample were selected randomly.

Thus, different samples may show different means. What can we say about the mean on the population based on a single sample mean? We will discuss this problem below in this chapter.

◘ **Table 12.2** Weights in Sample 1 (in lb). Average weight is 165 lb

165	135	181	163	147	117	182	157	177	153	201	171	131	184	149
140	174	104	191	156	178	162	194	188	168	221	154	200	134	217
175	158	133	168	144	190	114	210	152	195	108	173	169	146	183

◘ **Table 12.3** Weights in Sample 2 (in lb). Average weight is 163 lb

122	160	154	178	205	149	175	168	140	192	130	155	118	177	139
185	195	110	165	235	215	125	160	189	188	171	215	156	170	167
156	144	182	135	175	159	136	105	162	145	199	138	187	128	158

Table 12.4 Weights in Sample 3 (in lb). Average weight is 169 lb

125	190	145	200	151	185	171	228	159	201	168	135	191	153	125
180	177	189	140	215	103	205	175	185	188	148	210	179	225	180
165	131	175	155	155	195	169	128	180	165	115	185	110	148	165

12.5 Major Parameters on Population

Major parameters on a population include the mean, median, mode, variance, and standard deviation for a single random variable and covariance and correlation coefficient for the joined behavior of two random variables.

The ***mean***, μ, is the average value of all values of the random variables comprising the population, which is calculated as

$$\mu = \frac{1}{N}\sum_{k=1}^{N} x_k \qquad (12.1)$$

The ***median***, c, is the middle value of random variable X, for which the same number of the elements on the population has value of X higher and lower than the median, c,

$$c : \sum_{k=1}^{N} k\left(x_k < c\right) = \sum_{k=1}^{N} k\left(x_k > c\right) \qquad (12.2)$$

The ***mode***, m, is the most frequent value of X in the population:

$$m = \text{the most frequesnt value of the random variable} \qquad (12.3)$$

The mode can be calculated for discrete random variables or for the equal intervals for the continuous random variable.

The ***variance***, σ^2, is the mean squared distance between the values of random variable X and the mean value μ on the population, calculated as

$$\sigma^2 = \frac{1}{N}\sum_{k=1}^{N}\left(x_k - \mu\right)^2 \qquad (12.4)$$

The ***standard deviation***, σ, is the mean distance between the values of random variable X and the mean value μ on the population, calculated as a square root of the variance

$$\sigma = \sqrt{\frac{1}{N}\sum_{k=1}^{N}\left(x_k - \mu\right)^2} \qquad (12.5)$$

The ***covariance***, σ_{XY}, is the statistical measure of mutual relationship between two random variables X and Y, calculated as

$$\sigma_{XY} = \frac{1}{N}\sum_{k=1}^{N}(x_k - \mu_X)(y_k - \mu_Y) \tag{12.6}$$

If the values of both variables are going above or below their respective mean values synchronously or almost synchronously, the covariance is positive. If the values of both variables are going above or below their respective mean values mostly in opposite directions, the covariance is negative. If the values of both variables vary without any relationship to each other, then the covariance is zero. Note that according to Eqs. (12.6) and (12.4), the covariance of random variable X with itself is identical to the variance X. Therefore, the notations σ^2 and σ_{XX} are considered synonymous.

The sign of the covariance σ_{XY}, positive and negative, indicates the directions of relative variations of the values of both variables. However, the value of the covariance does not explicitly indicate the degree of synchronicity in any direction. For example, if we measure the relationship between prices on gasoline and food, the value of the covariance will be 10,000 times higher if we measure prices in cents rather than in dollars, because 1 dollar equals to 100 cents, though the relationship between the prices stays the dame regardless of the units of measurement.

Covariance indicates linear relationship between two random variables X and Y. Covariance on a population (Eq. (12.6)) and on a sample (Eq. 12.9)) are compared in Table 12 5. A positive covariance indicates a positive linear relationship between X and Y, i.e.,

- X increases as Y increases.
- X decreases as Y decreases.

12

A negative covariance indicates a negative linear relationship between X and Y, i.e.,

- X increases as Y decreases.
- X decreases as Y increases

The ***correlation coefficient*** was introduced to provide the explicit numerical measure of the strength of the relationship between two random variables. The ***correlation coefficient*** is calculated as the covariance normalized by the standard deviations of both variables as

$$\rho_{XY} = \frac{\sigma_{XY}}{\sigma_X \sigma_Y} \tag{12.7}$$

where σ_X and σ_Y are the standard deviations of variables X and Y, respectively. If we substitute the covariance and the standard deviations in Eq. (12.7) with the expressions from Eqs. (12.5) and (12.5), then the correlation coefficient can be calculated as

$$\rho_{XY} = \frac{\sum_{k=1}^{N}(x_k - \mu_X)(y_k - \mu_Y)}{\sum_{k=1}^{N}(x_k - \mu_X)^2 \sum_{k=1}^{N}(y_k - \mu_Y)^2} \tag{12.8}$$

The correlation coefficient is a number that varies between minus one and one:

$$-1 \le \rho_{XY} \le 1 \tag{12.9}$$

If both variables are synchronously moving in the same direction, the correlation coefficient is equal to one. If the both variables are synchronously moving in the different directions, the correlation coefficient is equal to minus one. If both variables are moving completely independently of each other, the correlation coefficient is equal to zero. In all other cases, it takes values between minus one and one indicating the degree of synchronicity between both variables. The correlation coefficient σ_{XX} of random variable X with itself is called the autocorrelation coefficient and according to Eq. (12.8) equals to one because variations of variable X are perfectly synchronous to itself. Thus, if the correlation coefficient is

- near −1 shows strong negative correlation
- near 0 shows no correlation
- near +1 shows strong positive correlation

▶ Example 1 of the Mean, Median, Mode, and Variance on a Population

Suppose a population X consists of nine elements as

$$X = \{1,2,5,4,2,5,3,2,6\} \tag{12.10}$$

The range in the population

$$\text{Range} = \max(X) - \min(X) = 6 - 1 = 5 \tag{12.11}$$

The median on the population equals to three as shown below:

$$c : \sum_{k=1}^{N/2} k(x_k < c) = \sum_{k=(N/2)+1}^{N} k(x_k > c) \Rightarrow c = 3 \tag{12.12}$$

The mode on the population equals to two, because $X = 2$ is the most frequent value of variable X on the population:

$$m = 2 \tag{12.13}$$

The mean on the population is

$$\mu = \frac{1}{N}\sum_{k=1}^{N} x_k = \frac{1+2+5+4+2+5+3+2+6}{9} = 3.3 \tag{12.14}$$

Actually, $\mu = 3.3333 \ldots$, but we rounded it in Eq. (12.14) to one decimal figure.

The variance on the population is

$$\begin{aligned}\sigma^2 &= \frac{1}{N}\sum_{k=1}^{N}(x_k - \mu)^2 = \\ &= \frac{(1-3.3)^2 + (2-3.3)^2 + (5-3.3)^2 + (4-3.3)^2 + (2-3.3)^2}{9} + \\ &+ \frac{(5-3.3)^2 + (3-3.3)^2 + (2-3.3)^2 + +(6-3.3)^2}{9} = 2.7\end{aligned} \tag{12.15}$$

and $\sigma = 1.6$.

The population mean, median, mode, range, and standard deviation are shown in ◘ Fig. 12.1. ◀

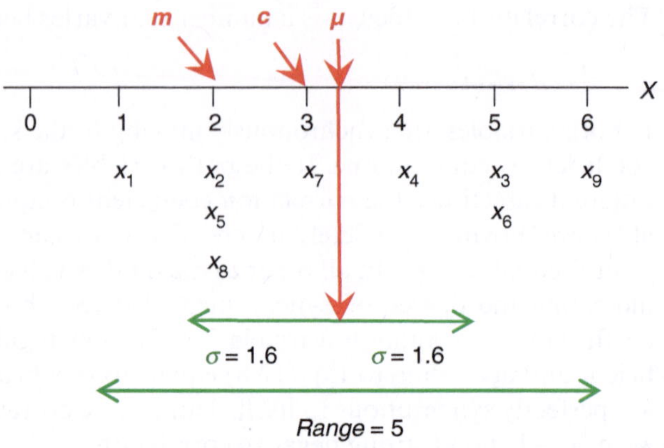

Fig. 12.1 The population mean, median, and mode

12.6 Population Parameters Versus Sample Statistic

In the analysis of a population, we need to know certain aggregate values on the population, called population parameters. However, most of the time, it is hard or even impossible to conduct measurements on the entire population and calculate the population parameters. Instead, we calculate the same aggregate values from the measurements conducted on a sample. These aggregate values calculated on a sample are called statistic. The commonly used notation for the aggregate value calculated on a population or on a sample is shown in Table 12.1.

The difference in the notation for the population parameters and the sample statistic is used to avoid confusion between population and its samples. You probably noticed that the denominator for the mean, variance, standard deviation, and covariance on the population is equal to the total size of the population, N, while the same denominator for the sample mean, variance, standard deviation, and covariance is by the unit less than the size of the sample, i.e., equals to $n - 1$. This is done to avoid a biased estimation of the population parameters from the sample statistic.

12

The major parameters on a population, such as the range, median, mode, mean, variance, standard deviation, covariance, and coefficient of correlation, are shown in Eqs. (12.1)–(12.8). The range, median, and mode on a sample are defined the same as on the population. The mean on a sample, $\overline{x}$, is calculated as

$$\overline{x} = \frac{1}{n}\sum_{k=1}^{n} x_k \tag{12.16}$$

The variance, s^2, and standard deviation, s, on a sample are calculated as

$$s^2 = \frac{1}{n-1}\sum_{k=1}^{n}\left(x_k - \overline{x}\right)^2 \tag{12.17}$$

$$s = \sqrt{\frac{1}{n-1}\sum_{k=1}^{n}\left(x_k - \overline{x}\right)^2} \tag{12.18}$$

The covariance and correlation coefficient, r_{XY}, on a sample are calculated as

$$s_{XY} = \frac{1}{n-1}\sum_{k=1}^{n}(x_k - \bar{x})(y_k - \bar{y}) \tag{12.19}$$

$$r_{XY} = \frac{s_{XY}}{s_X s_Y} \tag{12.20}$$

The correlation coefficient is always between −1 and +1, i.e., $-1 \le r_{XY} \le 1$. If the correlation coefficient is near,

- −1 shows strong negative correlation.
- 0 shows no correlation.
- +1 shows strong positive correlation.

The expressions for the population parameters and sample statistic side by side are shown in ◘ Table 12.5.

◘ **Table 12.5** Notations and expressions for the population parameters and the sample statistic

Aggregate value	**Sample statistic**	**Population parameter**
Range	The range is the difference between the largest and smallest values in the sample	The range is the difference between the largest and smallest values in the population
Median	$c:\sum_{k=1}^{n}k(x_k < c) - \sum_{k=1}^{n}k(x_k > c)$	$c:\sum_{k=1}^{N}k(x_k < c) = \sum_{k=1}^{N}k(x_k > c)$
Mode	m = the most frequent value of X in the sample	m = the most frequent value of X in the population
Mean	$\bar{x} = \frac{1}{n}\sum_{k=1}^{n}x_k$	$\mu = \frac{1}{N}\sum_{k=1}^{N}x_k$
Variance	$s^2 = \frac{1}{n-1}\sum_{k=1}^{n}(x_k - \bar{x})^2$	$\sigma^2 = \frac{1}{N}\sum_{k=1}^{N}(x_k - \mu)^2$
Standard deviation	$s = \sqrt{\frac{1}{n-1}\sum_{k=1}^{n}(x_k - \bar{x})^2}$	$\sigma = \sqrt{\frac{1}{N}\sum_{k=1}^{N}(x_k - \mu)^2}$
Covariance	$s_{XY} = \frac{1}{n-1}\sum_{k=1}^{n}(x_k - \bar{x})(y_k - \bar{y})$	$\sigma_{XY} = \frac{1}{N}\sum_{k=1}^{N}(x_k - \mu_X)(y_k - \mu_Y)$
Correlation coefficient	$r_{XY} = \frac{s_{XY}}{s_X s_Y}$	$\rho_{XY} = \frac{\sigma_{XY}}{\sigma_X \sigma_Y}$

12.7 Sample Statistic: Measuring Car Mileage

12.7.1 The Range, Median, Mode, Mean Variance, and Standard Deviation

Suppose we want to analyze the car mileage for a certain car model. Each individual car shows different gas mileage on the car itself and the driver's driving style, so we want to find the average (mean) gas mileage for the population of that car. We are unable to make the gas mileage measurements on the entire population of that cars, but instead, we select a sample and conduct all required measurements on that sample. In our example, we chose seven cars as a sample. Such a sample would be too small for the actual study, but it works fine as an illustration. Our sample measures the following gas mileage (miles per gallon):

$$X = \{30,27,32,35,33,29,33\} \tag{12.21}$$

The sample size n is

$$n = 7 \tag{12.22}$$

The range is

$$\text{Range} = \max(X) - \min(X) = 35 - 27 = 8 \tag{12.23}$$

The median, c, and the mode, m, are

$$c = 32; m = 33 \tag{12.24}$$

The mean value on the sample, $\overline{x}$, is

$$\begin{aligned} \overline{x} &= \frac{1}{n}\sum_{k=1}^{n} x_k = \frac{1}{7}\sum_{k=1}^{7} x_k = \frac{x_1 + x_2 + x_3 + x_4 + x_5 + x_6 + x_7}{7} = \\ &= \frac{30+27+32+35+33+29+33}{7} = \frac{219}{7} = 31.29 \approx 31 \end{aligned} \tag{12.25}$$

The variance is

$$\begin{aligned} s^2 &= \frac{1}{n-1}\sum_{k=1}^{n}(x_k - \overline{x})^2 = \\ &= \frac{1}{6}\Big((30-31.29)^2 + (27-31.29)^2 + (32-31.29)^2 + (35-31.29)^2 \\ &\quad + (33-31.29)^2 + (29-31.29)^2 + (33-31.29)^2\Big) = 7.57 \end{aligned} \tag{12.26}$$

and the standard deviation is

$$s = \sqrt{s^2} = \sqrt{7.57} = 2.75 \tag{12.27}$$

12

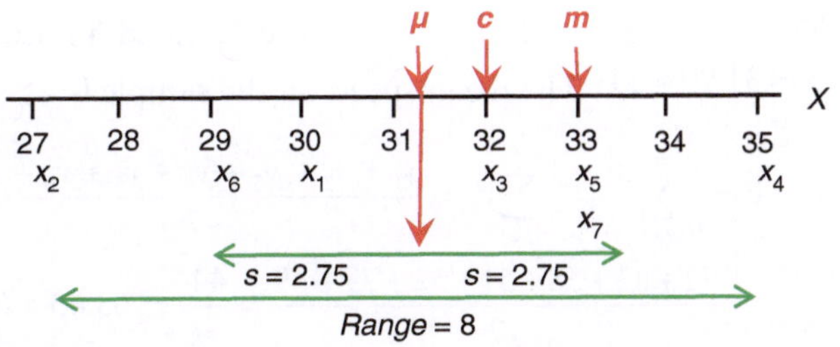

Fig. 12.2 The sample mean, median, mode, range and standard deviation

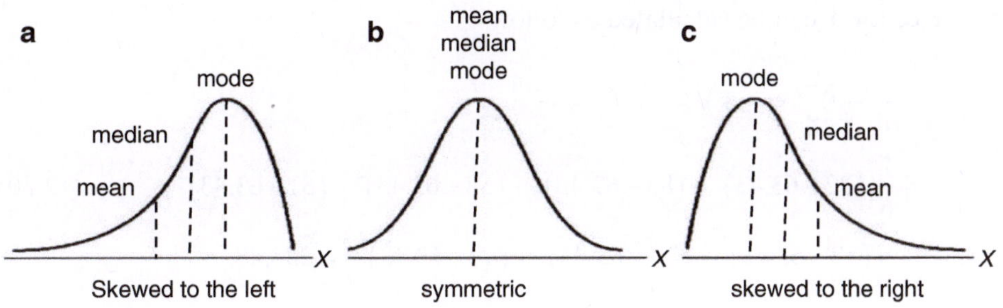

Fig. 12.3 The relationship between the sample mean, median, and mode for the distributions **a** skewed to the left, **b** symmetric, and **c** skewed to the right

The sample mean, median, mode, standard deviation, and range are shown in Fig. 12.2.

As you have most likely already noticed from Figs. 12.1 and 12.2, the median is between the mean and the mode. It is not an occasion. The relationship among mean, median, and mode depends on the shape of distribution, but the median is always between the mean and the mode. If the distribution is symmetric, then the mean, median, and mode have the same value. If the distribution is skewed to the right, then the mean is greater than the median and the median is greater than the mode. If the distribution is skewed to the left, then the mean is less than the median and the median is less than the mode. This relationship is illustrated in Fig. 12.3.

12.7.2 Covariance and Coefficient of Correlation

To continue with the example about the car gas mileage, we would like to analyze how the gas mileage depends on the driving speed. On our sample in addition to the gas consumption, we collected the average speed for each car. Thus, our sample has two random variables, X (gas mileage) and Y (average speed):

$$\begin{aligned} X &= \{30,27,32,35,33,29,33\} \quad \text{miles / gallon} \\ Y &= \{72,83,58,51,52,79,49\} \quad \text{miles / hour} \end{aligned} \tag{12.28}$$

The mean gas mileage, $\bar{x}$, was calculated in Eq. (12.25) for this case and $\bar{x} = 31.29 \approx 31$. The mean speed on the sample is

$$\begin{aligned}\bar{y} &= \frac{1}{n}\sum_{k=1}^{n} y_k = \frac{1}{7}\sum_{k=1}^{7} y_k = \frac{y_1 + y_2 + y_3 + y_4 + y_5 + y_6 + y_7}{7} = \\ &= \frac{72+83+58+51+52+79+49}{7} = \frac{444}{7} = 63.43 \approx 63\end{aligned} \tag{12.29}$$

The standard deviations s_X for X were calculated in Eq. (12.27) and $s_X = 2.75$. The variance for Y can be calculated as follows:

$$\begin{aligned}s_Y^2 &= \frac{1}{n-1}\sum_{k=1}^{n}(y_k - \bar{y})^2 = \\ &= \frac{1}{6}\Big((72-63.43)^2 + (83-63.43)^2 + (58-63.43)^2 + (51-63.43)^2 + \\ &\quad + (52-63.43)^2 + (79-63.43)^2 + (49-63.43)^2\Big) = 258.48\end{aligned} \tag{12.30}$$

and the standard deviation s_Y is

$$s_Y = \sqrt{s_Y^2} = \sqrt{258.48} = 16.08 \approx 16 \tag{12.31}$$

The covariance s_{XY} on the sample is

$$\begin{aligned}s_{XY} &= \frac{1}{n-1}\sum_{k=1}^{n}(x_k - \bar{x})(y_k - \bar{y}) = \\ &= \frac{1}{6}\big((30-31.29)(72-70.29) + (27-31.29)(83-70.29) + \\ &\quad + (32-31.29)(58-70.29) + (35-31.29)(51-70.29) + \\ &\quad + (33-31.29)(52-70.29) + (29-31.29)(79-70.29) + \\ &\quad + (33-31.29)(49-70.29)\big) = -37.48 \approx -37\end{aligned} \tag{12.32}$$

12

Now, we can calculate the correlation coefficient r_{XY} as

$$r_{XY} = \frac{s_{XY}}{s_X s_Y} = \frac{-37.48}{2.75 * 16.08} = -0.85 \tag{12.33}$$

The correlation coefficient $r_{XY} = -0.85$ indicates a strong negative correlation between the measured car gas mileage (X) and the average speed of the car (Y). It means that with the higher speed, the gas mileage decreases.

Table 12.6 Microsoft Excel and OpenOffice Calc functions to calculate the size, mean, standard deviation, covariance, and correlations coefficient

Function	Function returns
Count(array)	The number of cells (elements) in a specified array that contain numbers. The other elements are ignored
Average(array)	The mean value on a specified array of data
Stdev.p(array)	The standard deviation on the specified array as a population
Stdev.s(array)	The standard deviation on the specified array as a sample
Covariance.p(array1,array2)	The covariance of two specified arrays as a population
Covariance.s(array1,array2)	The covariance of two specified arrays as a sample
Correls(array1,array2)	The correlation coefficient on two specified arrays as a sample

12.8 Calculations with the Microsoft Excel and OpenOffice Calc

Both Microsoft Excel and OpenOffice Calc have similar functions for calculating the mean values, standard deviation, covariance, and correlation coefficient. The syntax and brief description of the functions are presented in Table 12.6.

The empty or nonnumerical cells (elements) in the arrays are automatically ignored. For the more detailed description of the functions, refer to the respective software application.

These functions are available in some other software applications too.

Questions for Self-Control for Chap. 12

1. What is the sense and the goal of statistics?
2. What is the difference between the terms "statistics" (plural) and "statistic" (singular)?
3. What is the difference between the population and a sample?
4. What is the difference between a parameter and a statistic?
5. What is the range, median, and mode on a population or a sample?

6. What is the relationship between the mean, median, and mode on a population or a sample?
7. How do you define and interpret mean, variance, and standard deviation on a population and on a sample?
8. How do you define and interpret covariance and correlation coefficient on a population and on a sample?
9. What is the difference between the correlation coefficient on a population and on a sample?
10. What types of statistics do you know and what is the difference between them?

Problems for Chap. 12

1. You have a collection of data $X = \{12, 16, 12, 11, 15, 11, 18, 13, 12, 15, 16, 18\}$. What is the mean, median, and mode on the sample?
2. You have a collection of data $X = \{12, 16, 12, 11, 15, 11, 18, 13, 12, 15, 16, 18\}$. What is the variance and standard deviation if this collection if data is treated as a population or as a sample?
3. Calculate and interpret the covariance for two arrays of data (X) and (Y): $X = \{12, 16, 12, 11, 15, 11, 18, 13, 12, 15\}$ and $Y = \{7, 7, 8, 8, 11, 6, 12, 8, 6, 9\}$ as a population.
4. Calculate and interpret the covariance for two arrays of data (X) and (Y): $X = \{12, 16, 12, 11, 15, 11, 18, 13, 12, 15\}$ and $Y = \{7, 7, 8, 8, 11, 6, 12, 8, 6, 9\}$ as a sample.
5. Calculate and interpret the correlation coefficient for two arrays of data (X) and (Y): $X = \{12, 16, 12, 11, 15, 11, 18, 13, 12, 15\}$ and $Y = \{7, 7, 8, 8, 11, 6, 12, 8, 6, 9\}$.
6. You have the measurements of the height (X) in cm and the weight (Y) in kg on a sample of people: $X = \{180, 165, 169, 185, 164, 178, 188, 172\}$ and $Y = \{85, 68, 75, 79, 60, 71, 82, 75\}$. How strong is the relationship of the weight and the height of people on the sample?

Confidence Intervals

Contents

13.1 Simple Random Sampling – 236
13.1.1 A Simple Random Sample – 236
13.1.2 The Mean on a Sample Versus the Mean on a Population – 237

13.2 A Sample as an Estimator for the Population – 239
13.2.1 Central Limit Theorem – 240

13.3 Confidence Level, Margin of Error, and Confidence Interval – 243
13.3.1 Meaning of Confidence Level – 245
13.3.2 Margin of Error and Confidence Interval – 246

13.4 *Critical Value* for Confidence Interval – 247

13.5 Student's *t*-Distribution – 252

13.6 *T*-Distribution Versus *Z*-Distribution for Large Samples – 254

13.7 Confidence Intervals for Two Unpaired Samples – 257
13.7.1 The Confidence Interval for Two Unpaired Large Samples – 258
13.7.2 The Confidence Interval When at Least One Sample Is Small – 259

S. K. Aityan, *Business Research Methodology*, Classroom Companion: Business,
https://doi.org/10.1007/978-3-030-76857-7_13

13.7.3 Both Samples Have the Same Standard Deviation – 260
13.7.4 Both Samples of the Same Size – 260

13.8 Confidence Interval for Paired Samples – 261
13.8.1 Confidence Interval for a Large Paired Sample – 262
13.8.2 Confidence Interval for a Small Paired Sample – 262

13.9 Confidence Interval for Binomial Distribution – 264
13.9.1 Large Sample – 265
13.9.2 Small Sample – 266

13.10 Confidence Interval for Probability or Percentage Difference from Two Independent Samples – 267
13.10.1 Large Samples – 268
13.10.2 Small Samples – 268

13.11 Most Popular Confidence Levels and Respective *Z*-Scores – 269
13.11.1 1-Sigma, 2-Sigma, and 3-Sigma Rule for Confidence Intervals – 269

13.12 Interpretation of Confidence Intervals – 270

13.13 One-Sided and Two-Sided Tests – 271

13.14 Summary of Confidence Intervals – 272
13.14.1 Confidence Interval for the Mean on One Sample – 272
13.14.2 Confidence Interval for the Difference of Means of Two Unpaired Samples – 273

13.14.3 Confidence Interval for the Difference of Means on Two Paired Samples – 273
13.14.4 Confidence Interval for the Binomial Distribution – 274
13.14.5 Confidence Interval for Probability or Percentage Difference on Two Samples – 275

13.1 Simple Random Sampling

13.1.1 A Simple Random Sample

The most straightforward way of forming a sample is to select it randomly from the population. Such a sample is referred to as a ***simple random sample*** or a ***random sample***, and the approach of forming such a sample is called ***simple random sampling*** or ***random sampling***. Thus, each simple random sample of the same size has an equal probability of being selected from the same population.

A ***simple random sample*** or a ***random sample*** is a sample selected in such a way that every possible sample of the same size has an equal probability of being chosen.

Suppose a finite population contains total N elements, and we want to select a sample that contains n of those elements. We may form $\binom{N}{n}$ possible combinations from N elements by n for such a sample:

$$\binom{N}{n} = \frac{N!}{n!(N-n)!} \tag{13.1}$$

in which

$$n! = 1*2*\ldots*n \quad \text{and} \quad 0! = 1 \tag{13.2}$$

where N and n are integer numbers, $0 \leq n \leq N$. Function $n!$ is referred to as ***n-factorial***.

Suppose we have a box that contains N = 10 parts, and we would like to select a sample of n = 3 parts for testing. How many possibilities for choosing a simple random sample do we have? In this example, numbers N and n are unreasonably low for a good statistical analysis, but we use these numbers for the sake of simplicity for manual calculation and illustration. The number of combinations for selecting a simple random sample in this case is

13

$$\binom{10}{3} = \frac{10!}{3!(10-3)!} = \frac{10!}{3!7!} = \frac{8*9*10}{1*2*3} = 120 \tag{13.3}$$

In processing Eq. (13.3), we used the fact that 10! = 1*2*3*4*5*6*7*8*9*10 = 7!*8*9*10 according to the definition given in Eqs. (13.1) and (13.2). Thus, one can form 120 different simple random samples by three elements out of ten. Now, you can easily imagine how many simple random samples by 45 people can be selected from the population of people, even in a small town with a population of 1000 people. The number of combinations by 45 people from 1000 is about $3*10^{78}$, a huge number!

13.1.2 The Mean on a Sample Versus the Mean on a Population

On any finite population $X = \{x_1, x_2, \dots, x_N\}$, one can choose $\binom{N}{n}$ different random samples by n elements in each. Every sample has its own mean, and the mean on each sample can be different from the means on other samples.

Similarly, as it was done for the probability distributions, we will denote the population mean μ ("mu") and the population variance σ^2 ("sigma squared"). The square root of the variance, σ^2, is referred to as standard deviation, σ ("sigma"). Thus, μ is the average value of all elements that the population has and σ^2 is the variance of those values on the population. For a finite population $X = \{x_1, x_2, \dots, x_N\}$,

$$\mu = \frac{1}{N}\sum_{K=1}^{N} x_k \quad \text{and} \quad \sigma^2 = \frac{1}{N}\sum_{K=1}^{N}(x_k - \mu)^2 \tag{13.4}$$

We will use a different notation for the mean and the variance on a sample (statistic) to distinguish them from the mean and the variance on the population. The mean $\bar{x}$ and the variance s^2 on a sample can be calculated as

$$\bar{x} = \frac{1}{n}\sum_{k=1}^{n} x_k \quad \text{and} \quad s^2 = \frac{1}{n-1}\sum_{k=1}^{n}(x_k - \bar{x})^2 \tag{13.5}$$

where n is the number of elements in the sample. The number of elements in a sample $n < N$ because a sample should have less elements than the population. Please note that the denominator in a sample variance s^2 is $n - 1$ rather than n for the purpose of making s^2 an unbiased estimator for the population variance σ^2. This result comes from mathematical statistics to make expected value of sample variances S^2 on all possible samples to be equal to the variance on the population σ^2. Note that s^2 denotes the value of the variance on a given sample while S^2 is used as a notation for the variance on samples as a random variable.

The mean μ and the variance σ^2 for a finite population are

$$\mu = \frac{1}{N}\sum_{k=1}^{N} x_k \quad \text{and} \quad \sigma^2 = \frac{1}{N}\sum_{k=1}^{N}(x_k - \mu)^2$$

The mean $\bar{X}$ and the variance s^2 for a given sample are

$$\bar{x} = \frac{1}{n}\sum_{k=1}^{n} x_k \quad \text{and} \quad s^2 = \frac{1}{n-1}\sum_{k=1}^{n}(x_k - \bar{x})^2$$

A crucial question is how to estimate the population mean μ which we do not know, using the mean $\bar{x}$ measured on a sample. The second question is how good such an estimate is.

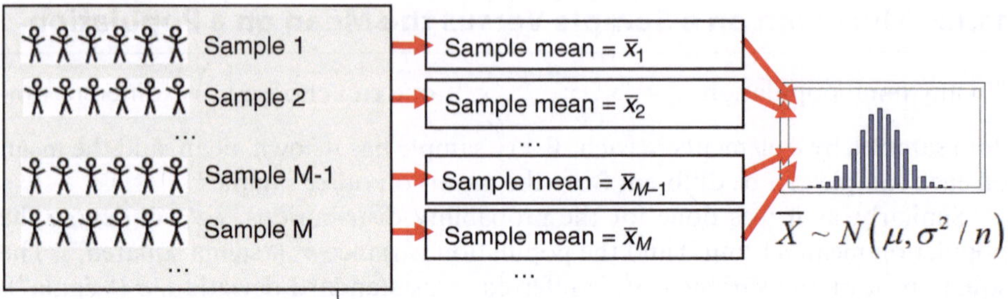

■ **Fig. 13.1** A variety of samples selected from the population of people

One can select a variety of different samples from the population. Every sample may have its own mean, and that mean may vary from sample to sample. For example, three samples presented in ▶ Tables 12.2 and 12.3 in ▶ Chap. 12 for measuring weights of people have different means as shown in ■ Fig. 13.1.

To find the mean value of the population, the mean value is measured on a randomly selected sample, which is one of all possible samples of a chosen size. Thus, the mean value on a sample is a random variable $\bar{X}$ in the variety of all possible samples, because the means on different samples may vary. Variable $\bar{X}$ can take values of the means on different samples, i.e., $\bar{X} = \{\bar{x}_m\}$, where $\bar{x}_m$ is the mean value on sample m. It is a convention to denote variables by capital letters and their values by lowercase letters. Please be careful not to get confused with all these variables and their values. ■ Table 13.1 describes the notation for variables and values on populations and samples to avoid any possible confusion.

Thus, variables $\bar{X}$ and S^2 are defined on a set of all possible samples of a given size and take values of the mean $\bar{x}$ and the variance s^2 a possible sample of a given size, i.e., $\bar{X} = \{\bar{x}_1, \bar{x}_2, \ldots, \bar{x}_m, \ldots\}$ and $S^2 = \{s_1^2, s_2^2, \ldots, s_m^2, \ldots\}$. Thus, $\bar{X}$ is the population of the mean values on all possible samples of a given size, and $\bar{X}$ is the mean of those means. All possible samples of a given size are a virtual concept because nobody really forms all possible samples and conducts measurements on all such samples. This set of all possible samples is used for deriving mathematical properties of the means and the variances of this set and their relationship with the mean and the variance on the original population X. Values $\bar{x}$ and s_m^2 are associated with a specific sample m in the set of possible samples.

A set of the means on all possible samples of size n is actually a population $\bar{X}$ of sample means on all possible samples of size n. We call this population $\bar{X}$ the ***variety*** of all possible samples of size n to avoid a possible confusion with the original ***population***, X, for which we want to find the mean. The mean μ and the variance σ^2 are the numbers which represent parameters of the population. Hopefully, the descriptions given in ■ Table 13.1 and the explanation above have clarified the situation and helped the reader to avoid confusion that is quite natural for the beginners in statistics.

13

Table 13.1 Description of parameters and variables on population, samples, and the variety (population) of all possible samples

Notation	Type	Meaning
N	Number	Size of the population
n	Number	Size of a sample
X	Variable	Random variable defined on a population and also used in samples which are subsets of the population
μ	Number	The mean of a population
$\overline{X}$	Variable	Random variable for means on all possible samples of a given size
$\overline{\overline{X}}$	Number	The mean of means of all possible samples of a given size
$\overline{x}$	Number	The mean on a given sample
$\overline{x}_m$	Number	The mean on sample m
σ^2	Number	The variance on a population
S^2	Variable	Random variable for the variance on all possible samples
s^2	Number	The variance on a given sample
s_m^2	Number	The variance on sample m

13.2 A Sample as an Estimator for the Population

We will never physically build the variety of all possible samples $\overline{X} = \{\overline{x}_m\}$ as we never know the actual mean μ of the original population for a reasonably large population $X = \{x_k\}$. The mean of the original population μ is estimated by using the mean on one randomly selected sample $\overline{x}$. With this regard, a legitimate question arises, how good such estimation is.

The larger a sample is, the closer we expect the measured mean on a sample $\overline{x}$ would be to the mean of the population μ. In the extreme, if the sample size is equal to the size of the population, i.e., $n = N$, the sample becomes identical to the population, and the mean on the sample is equal to the size of the population $\overline{x} = \mu$. However, in most real-world situations, the sample size is much smaller than the size of the population, i.e., $n << N$, and we do not know how close the mean measured on a sample is to the mean of the population.

13.2.1 Central Limit Theorem

The mean values on each sample are random variable $\overline{X}$ in the variety (population) of all possible samples of size n. The distribution of $\overline{X}$ is referred to as the ***sampling distribution of the mean*** in the variety (population) of all possible sample of the chosen size. For simplicity, the ***sampling distribution of the mean*** is also referred to as the ***sampling distribution***. That one sample, which is selected and used for the estimation of the mean on the original population, is one of those possible samples.

The ***central limit theorem*** (CLT) states that regardless of the distribution of random variable X in the original population, for reasonably large samples, $n \geq 30$, the sampling distribution of the mean becomes quite close to the normal distribution with the mean $\overline{\overline{X}}$ (mean of the mean values of $\overline{X}$ on all possible samples) equals to the mean of the original population μ and the variance equals to the variance of the original population σ^2 divided by the sample size n, i.e.,

$$\overline{X} \sim N\left(\mu, \frac{\sigma^2}{n}\right) \tag{13.6}$$

where μ and σ^2 are the mean and the variance of the original population X and n is the sample size. This is illustrated in ◘ Fig. 13.2.

If the original population is distributed normally, i.e., $X \sim N(\mu, \sigma^2)$, then the sampling distribution of the mean is always normal regardless of the sample size as is illustrated in ◘ Fig. 13.3.

Thus, for reasonably large samples ($n \geq 30$) or if the random variable in the original population X is normally distributed, the means on the variety of all possible samples $\overline{X}$ of a given size n are distributed approximately normally with the mean of the means on all possible samples $\overline{\overline{X}} = \text{mean}\left(\overline{X}\right) = \text{mean}\left\{\overline{x}_1, \overline{x}_2, \ldots, \overline{x}_m, \ldots\right\}$ equals mean μ of the original population X:

13

$$\overline{\overline{X}} = \mu \tag{13.7}$$

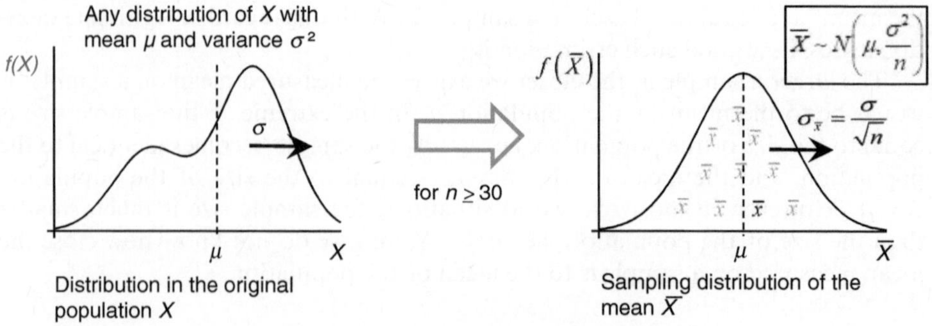

◘ **Fig. 13.2** Sampling distribution of the mean for a reasonably large samples, $n \geq 30$, becomes close to the normal distribution regardless of the distribution in the original population

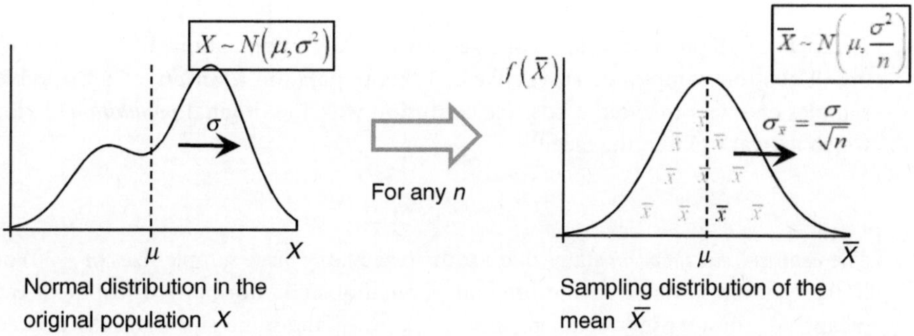

Fig. 13.3 Sampling distribution of the mean for a normally distributed population X becomes close to the normal distribution regardless of the sample size

Fig. 13.4 Population mean, μ, and mean of all possible sample means

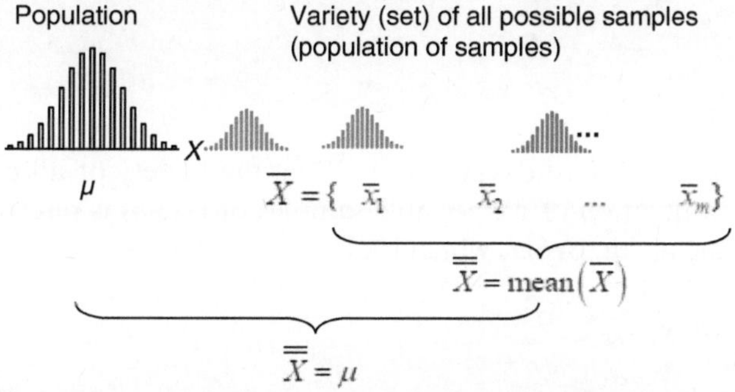

with the variance of the means in the variety of all possible samples $\sigma_{\overline{X}}^2$ approximated as

$$\sigma_{\overline{X}}^2 \equiv \mathrm{var}\left(\overline{X}\right) = \frac{\sigma^2}{n} \tag{13.8}$$

It is a very powerful result that helps estimating the unknown mean of the original population μ by measuring the mean on a random sample as illustrated in Fig. 13.4.

The essence of this result is that:

(a)	One can estimate the mean on a population by measuring the mean on a sample from the population.
(b)	The accuracy of such estimate depends on the sample size. The larger the sample, the more accurate the estimate.

A variety of all possible samples of size n are actually a population $\overline{X}$ of the means on all possible samples of size n. We call this population a ***variety*** of all possible samples of size n to avoid a possible confusion with the original ***population***, X, for which we want to find the mean.

The ***central limit theorem*** states that for the reasonably large sample sizes ($n \geq 30$) or if the random variable in the original population X is normally distributed, the means $\overline{X}$ in a variety of all possible samples of the same size n are distributed approximately normally with the mean $\overline{X}$ equals the mean of the original population μ and the variance $\sigma_{\overline{X}}^2$ equals the variance of the original population σ^2 divided by the sample size n, i.e.,

$$\overline{X} \sim N\left(\mu, \frac{\sigma^2}{n}\right)$$

The standard deviation of $\overline{X}$ on the variety of all possible samples of size n (the population of all possible samples of size n) is referred to as the ***standard error*** of the mean, $StErr$, which is

$$StErr = \frac{\sigma}{\sqrt{n}} \tag{13.9}$$

where σ is the standard deviation on the original population X and n is the size of the samples in the variety of all possible samples.

The ressults of the central limit theorem regarding the normality of the sampling distribution of the mean are summarized in ◘ Table 13.2.

13 The bottom line of this rule is that, if a sample size is 30 or higher, the sampling distribution (the distribution of $\overline{X}$) is quite close to normal regardless of the dis-

◘ Table 13.2 Dependence of sampling distribution on the population distribution and the sample size

		Sample size, *n*	
		$n < 30$	$n \geq 30$
		Sampling distribution	
Population distribution	Normal	Normal $\overline{X} \sim N\left(\mu, \frac{\sigma^2}{n}\right)$	Normal $\overline{X} \sim N\left(\mu, \frac{\sigma^2}{n}\right)$
	Unknown	Unknown	Normal $\overline{X} \sim N\left(\mu, \frac{\sigma^2}{n}\right)$

tribution in the original population X. This is a very powerful result that means that, if we select a sample large enough ($n \geq 30$), we can apply the features of normal distribution to the sampling distribution.

13.3 Confidence Level, Margin of Error, and Confidence Interval

We use the mean on a sample $\bar{x}$ to estimate the mean of the population μ. However, the mean and the variance on a sample may vary from sample to sample, and it would be good to find out how accurate is the estimation of the population mean, i.e., how close is the measured mean on a sample to the mean on the population, which is unknown. We select a random sample to estimate the mean of the population. However, we have no idea how close the statistic measured on this selected sample is to the parameters on the original population. The selected sample is just one of many possible samples; thus, it would be strange to expect that the measured mean on the sample is a completely accurate estimate of the mean on the original population.

According to the central limit theorem, under the condition shown in ◘ Table 13.2, the mean values of all possible samples of the same size $\bar{X} = \{\bar{x}_1, \bar{x}_2, \ldots, \bar{x}_k, \ldots\}$ are distributed normally around the mean of the population μ with the standard deviation referred to as the standard error, $StErr = \sigma / \sqrt{n}$ (Eq. (13.9)), where σ is the standard deviation on the original population and n is the sample size, i.e., $\bar{X} \sim N\left(\mu, \sigma^2 / n\right)$. The normal distribution of the sample means $\bar{X}$ implies that for each positive margin δ, there is a portion of samples equal to the area P ($0 < P < 1$) under the distribution density curve for $\bar{X}$, in which means $\bar{x}$ are within margin $\pm\delta$ from the mean μ of the original population X as illustrated by the gray area in ◘ Fig. 13.5. This area presents the probability P of randomly selecting a sample, in which means $\bar{x}$ are within margin $\pm\delta$ form the mean μ of the original population X, i.e.,

$$\mu - \delta < \bar{x} < \mu + \delta \tag{13.10}$$

The mean on a sample from this category of samples can be anywhere within the interval defined in Eq. (13.10).

Taking into account that the mean μ of the original population X is unknown and we want to estimate it by measuring the mean on the selected sample, Eq. (13.10) can be rewritten as

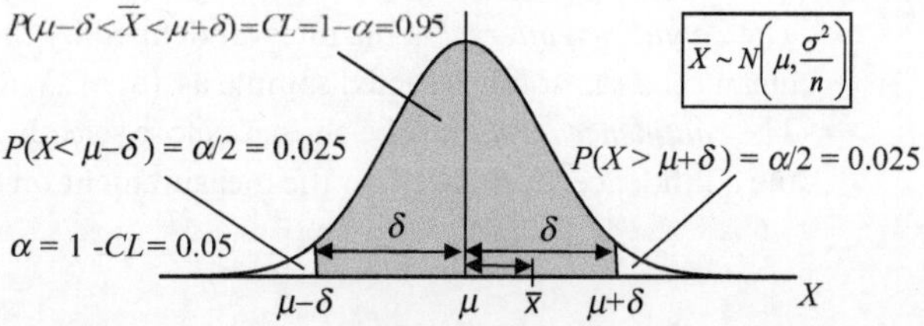

◘ **Fig. 13.5** Probabilities CL of selecting plausible samples and α of selecting extreme samples

$$\bar{x} - \delta < \mu < \bar{x} + \delta \quad (13.11)$$

or

$$\mu = \bar{x} \pm \delta \quad (13.12)$$

where P is referred to as the ***confidence level*** (CL), $\bar{x}$ is the mean measured on the sample and used as an ***estimate*** for the mean of the population μ, and margin δ is referred to as the ***margin of error*** (MOE). The interval defined in Eqs. (13.11) and (13.12) is referred to as the ***confidence interval*** and can be denoted as $(\bar{x} - \delta, \bar{x} + \delta)$.

The probability of a randomly selected sample to have its mean within the confidence interval is equal to CL. On the other hand, the probability of randomly selecting a sample in which the mean is outside that interval is $\alpha = 1 - \text{CL}$, which is referred to as the ***sampling error*** or the ***significance level.***

The process of estimating the mean of the population by the mean on a random sample is the following:

- The investigator chooses the confidence level (CL) prior to conducting any measurements.
- A random sample is selected and the mean on that sample is calculated.
- The margin of error (MOE) δ for the confidence interval is calculated matching the chosen confidence level.
- The mean of the original population is estimated as the mean measured on the selected sample plus/minus the MOE from the measured mean on the sample. Such an estimate can be presented in the form of the confidence interval.

It is important to realize that the confidence level (CL) should be chosen before selecting a sample and conducting measurements. Doing it in an inverse order is conceptually wrong because the selected sample is randomly selected. The mean value measured on the selected sample $\bar{x}$ can be any according to the sampling distribution $\bar{X}$; thus, the confidence level cannot be chosen based on the statistic measured on the selected sample.

- The ***confidence level*** (CL) is the probability of randomly selecting a plausible sample form of all possible samples of the same size, in which the mean lies within a respective margin of error from the mean of the population.
- The ***estimate*** for the mean of the population μ in the mean measured is on a randomly selected sample $\bar{x}$.
- The ***margin of error*** (MOE) is the margin δ matching the chosen confidence level.
- The *confidence interval* is the interval defined by the MOE around the measured mean on a randomly selected sample as $(\bar{x} - \delta, \bar{x} + \delta)$.
- The ***confidence level*** must be chosen before selecting a random sample. Choosing the confidence level based on the measurement on a selected sample is wrong.

13.3.1 Meaning of Confidence Level

Given the fact that a sample was randomly selected from the population, the sample may occasionally well represent the population or may occasionally consist of unusually extreme elements from the population outliers not quite typical for the population, showing the mean values quite different from the actual mean value on the population. Thus, we can never say with full certainty that the estimate of the mean of the population by the mean on a random sample is plausible. However, we may hope with a specified level of confidence that, most likely, the selected sample adequately enough represents the population rather than an extreme sample and that the mean value calculated on the sample is close enough to the mean of the population.

For example, sometimes, though very seldom, people have unusually heavy weight, say 600 lb, that goes far beyond the common weight. A randomly selected sample may occasionally consist mostly of the heavy-weight people that results in a quite unusually extreme value of the sample mean $\bar{x}$ relative to the mean of the population. For this reason, we would like to assess the chances that a selected sample, say the sample shown in ► Table 12.2 in the previous chapter, does not belong to such extreme samples. We may say that we consider 5% of all possible samples to be extreme and would like to count on 95% of the other possible samples which we consider to be more or less plausible, i.e., to belong to the category of plausible samples adequately representing the population. In this case, we can say that we have ***confidence level*** of 95% that a randomly selected sample belongs to the category of plausible samples, i.e., to the category of samples which we consider represent the population well enough. It is up to our decision to choose the confidence level. The ***confidence level*** of 95% means that we are considering 95% of all possible samples to belong to the category of plausible and 5% of all possible samples to the category of extreme outliers.

The confidence level is not a calculable value. The ***confidence level*** should be chosen and assigned from understanding of the importance of our judgment to be correct that comes from the real-world problem and from the troubles and costs of being wrong in the estimation of the mean value on the population. For example, if we are aiming to find the average size of fish in a lake for the purpose of recreational fishing, we may assign confidence level, say, 80% because there would be no serious consequences, if our estimate happens to be wrong. On the other hand, if we are analyzing life-critical medical procedures, we better leave ourselves very little chances to be wrong in our conclusions, and therefore, the confidence level should be set high, say 95%, 99%, or even higher subject to the possible consequences caused by a wrong estimate.

Thus, the confidence level is not a measurable but a chosen parameter that reflects the importance to be right in the judgment or understanding the seriousness of consequences or costs of possibly being wrong in judgment. The confidence level is chosen based on the nature of the original population and possible consequences from being wrong with the estimate. If we assess the mean value of the size of the apples, we may choose a lower confidence level, but if we talk about surgery or safety of nuclear power station, we must choose a very high confidence level.

13.3.2 Margin of Error and Confidence Interval

Choosing 95% confidence level means that we believe that a selected sample belongs to 95% of all possible samples of the same size, which we decided to consider plausible. On the other hand, the remaining 5% of all possible samples belong to the category of extreme samples, which we hope not occasionally to select. In terms of probabilities, it means that the probability of randomly selecting a sample, which we decided to consider (in our opinion) a plausible sample, is 0.95 while there is 0.05 probability to randomly select a sample which is in our opinion extreme, and its mean is too far from the mean of the population.

With the confidence level of 95%, we decided to consider 95% of possible samples to belong to the category of plausible samples, i.e., well enough represent the mean of the population for the purpose of the investigation as indicated by the gray area in ◘ Fig. 13.5. The probability of a randomly selected sample to be plausible, i.e., to be a sample, in which the mean value is no farther than by δ from the mean value of the population, i.e., $|\overline{X} - \mu| \leq \delta$, is $P(\mu - \delta < \overline{X} < \mu + \delta) = 0.95$. On the other hand, we leave the probability of $\alpha = 1 - P(\mu - \delta < \overline{X} < \mu + \delta) = 0.05$, for occasionally selecting a sample from the category of extreme samples with $|\overline{X} - \mu| > \delta$, i.e., for a sample to belong to one of the tails in the distribution of the means $\overline{X}$ on all possible samples of a given size.

13 With the confidence level CL = 0.95, the probability of samples to be in each tail of the sampling distribution is $\alpha/2 = 0.05/2 = 0.025$. The means on those extreme samples are farther than by δ from the mean value of the population, i.e., the probability of selecting a random sample from the left tail of the sampling distribution $P(\overline{X} < \mu - \delta) = \alpha/2$ and the probability of selecting a random sample from the right tail of the sampling distribution $P(\overline{X} > \mu + \delta) = \alpha/2$ as shown in ◘ Fig. 13.5.

Thus, we believe that, with the probability of 0.95, the mean value on a randomly selected sample, $\overline{x}$, is within δ from the mean value of the population. This is also referred to as the ***margin of error*** (MOE).

Reiterating the task of finding the mean of the population, it is estimated by the mean measured on a random sample selected from the population within the confidence interval according to the chosen confidence level.

The margin of error δ and the confidence interval $(\overline{x} - \delta, \overline{x} + \delta)$ show the maximum deviation of the mean of the population from the measured mean on samples, which are considered plausible according to the chosen confidence level (CL) (or sampling error $\alpha = 1 - \text{CL}$) as shown in ◘ Figs. 13.5 and ◘ 13.6. Please do not get confused about the meaning of δ. It is not the standard deviation on the population or on the sample, but the allowed variation of the mean on the population relative to the mean measured on the selected sample, if the selected sample

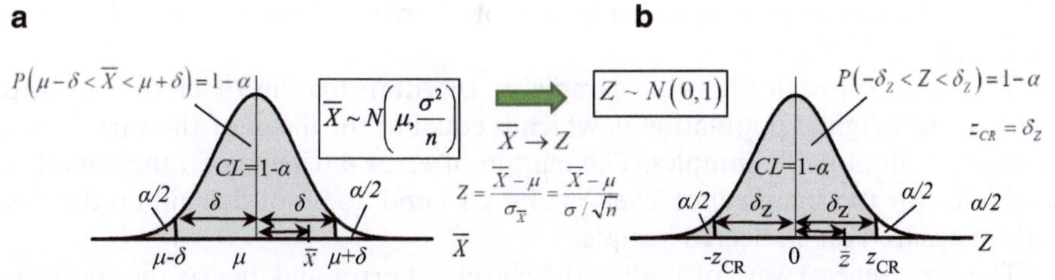

Fig. 13.6 The probability of plausible samples CL, sampling error α, and critical values for **a** sampling distribution and **b** after z-transformation $\overline{X} \to Z$

belongs to plausible samples. However, there is a chance assigned by the chosen sampling error α that we are completely wrong in our judgment about the mean on the population. Thus, if we are right in our judgment about the mean on the population according to the assigned confidence level, the mean on the population is within the margin of error from the mean measured on the selected sample or inside the confidence interval. However, if we are wrong in our judgment according to the sampling error, the mean on the population can be at any distance from the mean on the sample.

- Parameters δ and *StErr* are typically referred to as ***margin of error*** and abbreviated as MOE.
- Please do not get confused about the meaning of margin of error δ. It is not the standard deviation on the population or on the sample, but the allowed variation of the mean on the population relative to the measurement on the selected sample, if the selected sample belongs to plausible samples.
- However, there is a chance assigned by the chosen sampling error α that we are completely wrong in our judgment about the mean on the population.
- If we are right in our judgment about the mean on the population according to the assigned confidence level, the mean on the population is within the margin of error from the mean measured on the selected sample or inside the confidence interval.
- However, if we are wrong in our judgment according to the sampling error, the mean on the population can be at any distance from the mean on the sample.

13.4 *Critical Value* for Confidence Interval

According to the central limit theorem, the mean values of all possible samples $\overline{X}$, for large samples ($n \geq 30$) or for the population with normal distribution of the random variable X, are distributed normally with the mean equals to the mean on the population, i.e. $\mu_{\overline{X}} = \mu$, and the standard deviation of the mean values on all possible samples of size n equal to the standard error $\sigma_{\overline{X}} = StErr = \sigma / \sqrt{n}$ defined in Eq. (13.9) according to the distribution of the means in the variety of all possible samples as in Eq. (13.8).

The mean on each plausible sample $\bar{x}$ is within margin of error δ from the mean of the original population μ, which is equal to the mean of the variety (population) of all possible samples. The margin of error δ depends on the confidence level (CL) (or the significance level $\alpha = 1 - \text{CL}$) and does not depend on the mean value measured on a selected sample.

There are several ways of finding the margin of error and, hence, the confidence interval, which depend on the confidence level and the sample size n (◘ Fig. 13.7(a)).

Transformation of the normally distributed mean values $\bar{X} \sim N\left(\mu, \sigma^2 / n\right)$ to the standard normal distribution $Z \sim N(0, 1)$, $\bar{X} \rightarrow Z$:

$$Z = \frac{\bar{X} - \mu_{\bar{X}}}{\sigma_{\bar{X}}} = \frac{\bar{X} - \mu}{\sigma / \sqrt{n}} \tag{13.13}$$

leads to the following results shown in Eq. (13.14) and illustrated in ◘ Figs. 13.7(a) and (b):

$$\bar{X} \left\{ \begin{array}{lll} \mu & \rightarrow & 0 \\ \sigma_{\bar{X}} = \dfrac{\sigma}{\sqrt{n}} & \rightarrow & 1 \\ \bar{x} & \rightarrow & \bar{z} \\ \delta & \rightarrow & z_{CR} \\ \mu + \delta & \rightarrow & z_{CR} \\ \mu - \delta & \rightarrow & -z_{CR} \end{array} \right\} Z \tag{13.14}$$

The margin of error δ of the estimate of the mean on the original population X is transformed to the margin of error in the z-space δ_z which is defined by the ***critical value*** z_{CR}. Thus, the critical value z_{CR} represents the error of margin in the z-space. All transformations in Eq. (13.14) are shown for the explanation and reference and are not needed to be actually performed. The term critical value is very important in statistics, and for this reason, let us discuss it in a greater detail. The ***critical value*** in z-distribution is the value of random variable $Z = z_{\text{CR}}$ that depends on the significance level α (and, hence, the confidence level (CL) $= 1 - \alpha$), at which the probability of the random variable Z to be inside interval $(-z_{\text{CR}}, z_{\text{CR}})$ is equal to CL = 1

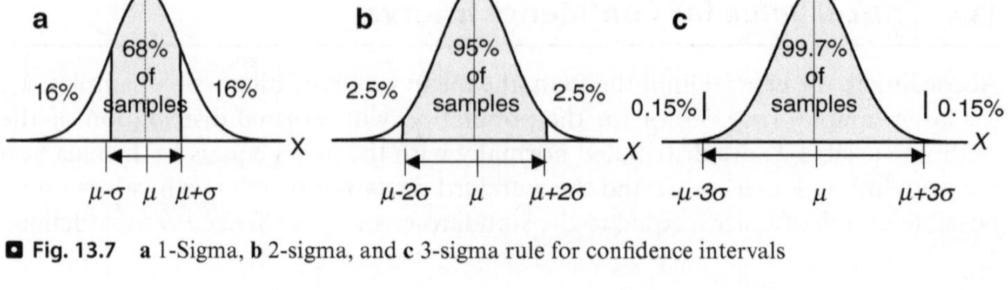

◘ **Fig. 13.7** **a** 1-Sigma, **b** 2-sigma, and **c** 3-sigma rule for confidence intervals

– α. On the other hand, critical value z_{CR} is the value of random variable Z for which the probability of the sample mean to be found outside the confidence interval is equal to α, i.e.,

$$P(-z_{CR} < Z < z_{CR}) = 1-\alpha; \quad \text{or} \quad P(-z_{CR} > Z, Z > z_{CR}) = \alpha \tag{13.15}$$

The critical values are found from the confidence level (or the significance level) and do not depend on the measurements on a sample. The critical values are illustrated in ◻ Figs. 13.6 and 13.7(b).

The ***critical value*** in z-distribution is the value of random variable z_{CR} that depends on the significance level α (and, hence, the confidence level (CL) = 1 – α), at which the probability of the random variable Z to be within interval ($-z_{CR}$, z_{CR}) is equal to CL = 1 – α or, for Z to be outside that interval, i.e., in the tails of the distribution, is equal to the significance level α:

$$P(-z_{CR} < Z < z_{CR}) = 1-\alpha; \quad \text{or} \quad P(-z_{CR} > Z, Z > z_{CR}) = \alpha$$

Critical values z_{CR} can be found for specified significance level α using the precalculated z-distribution tables (see Appendix A) or appropriate functions CONFIDENCE.NORM in MS Excel and OpenOffice Calc.

The critical value represents the margin of error $\delta_z = z_{CR}$ in the z-distribution, which can be transformed to the actual margin of error δ in the $\bar{X}$-distribution by the inverse transformation $Z \rightarrow \bar{X}$:

$$\left|\bar{X} - \mu_X\right| = Z\frac{\sigma}{\sqrt{n}} \tag{13.16}$$

Thus, the margin of error δ corresponding the chosen confidence level is calculated as

$$\delta = \delta_Z \frac{\sigma}{\sqrt{n}} = z_{CR}\frac{\sigma}{\sqrt{n}} \tag{13.17}$$

and then, the estimate of the mean of the population μ can be made by the measured mean on a random sample $\bar{x}$ and the margin of error δ as

$$\mu = \bar{x} \pm \delta = \bar{x} \pm z_{CR}\frac{\sigma}{\sqrt{n}} \tag{13.18}$$

where σ is the standard deviation on the population and n is the sample size. Equation (13.18) presents the estimate of the mean on the population including the confidence interval. The confidence interval for this estimate can also be presented as

$$\mu \in \left(\bar{x} - z_{CR}\sigma/\sqrt{n}, \bar{x} + z_{CR}\sigma/\sqrt{n}\right) \tag{13.19}$$

The sign "∈" in Eq. (13.19) means that μ belongs to the interval on the right-hand side of the expression. Hence, the mean value of the population μ can be estimated by the mean value on a random sample as

$$\mu = \overline{x} \pm \delta = \overline{x} \pm z_{CR}\frac{\sigma}{\sqrt{n}} \tag{13.20}$$

To calculate the margin of error δ and the related confidence interval according to Eqs. (13.17, 13.18, and 13.19), one needs to know the standard deviation σ on the original population X. The standard deviation on the original population may be known from the previous tests or some other considerations.

Thus, the confidence interval for the mean value on a population can be estimated as an interval defined as $(\overline{x} - \delta, \overline{x} + \delta)$ or equally as $\mu = \overline{x} \pm \delta$, where $\overline{x}$ is the mean measured on a randomly selected sample and δ is the margin of error for large samples ($n \geq 30$) or for populations with normal distribution:

- Choose the confidence level (CL) or choose sampling error $\alpha = 1 - CL$.
- Select a random sample and calculate the mean value on the sample.
- Find the *critical value* (z_{CR}) according to the confidence level by using the standard normal distribution tables or the appropriate software function.
- According to the *critical value* (z_{CR}), calculate the margin of error as

$$\delta = z_{CR}\frac{\sigma}{\sqrt{n}} \tag{13.21}$$

where σ is the standard deviation on the original population X.

- The estimate for the mean of the original population is

$$\mu = \overline{x} \pm \delta = \overline{x} \pm z_{CR}\frac{\sigma}{\sqrt{n}} \tag{13.22}$$

and the respective confidence interval also can be written as

13

$$(\overline{x} - \delta, \overline{x} + \delta) \tag{13.23}$$

The confidence interval can be equally denoted either in the form of Eq. (13.22) or Eq. (13.23).

The confidence interval is not the accuracy of measurement of the value of the mean on the population. Also, it is not a spread of the values of the random variable in the population. The confidence interval is the accuracy of the estimation of the mean value on the population, matching the assigned confidence level. It is an interval within which we believe the mean value is according to the chosen confidence level. We may be completely wrong with the estimate if a selected sample belongs to the extreme outliers. The probability of selecting such a sample is $\alpha = 1 - CL$.

The greater the sample size is, the smaller the confidence interval, i.e., the range of the estimation of the mean of the population by the mean on a random sample among the plausible samples according to the chosen confidence level. The probability of being right or wrong with the assessment does not change with the sample size because it is set by the chosen confidence level, which depends only on the confidence level for the judgment that is chosen and assigned prior to sample selection and any measurements on the sample. It means that with greater sample size, the range of the estimate of the mean of the population is narrower but the chances to being right or wrong with the assessment stay unchanged.

- The ***margin of error*** is how far from the ***estimate*** we think the true value might be (in either direction).
- The ***confidence interval*** is the ***estimate ± the margin of error***.

The margin of error can be calculated by the ***critical value*** (z_{CR}) on z-***distribution*** (the standard normal distribution) for large samples ($n \geq 30$) or for populations with normal distribution using the following procedure:

- Choose the confidence level (CL) by setting sampling error $\alpha = 1 - CL$.
- Select a random sample and calculate the mean value on the sample.
- Find the *critical value* (z_{CR}) according to the confidence level by using the standard normal distribution tables or the appropriate software function.
- Calculate the *z*-score (z_{CR}) according to the confidence level by using the standard normal distribution tables or the appropriate software function.
- According to the *z*-score (z_{CR}), calculate the margin of error as

$$\delta = z_{CR}\frac{\sigma}{\sqrt{n}}$$

- The estimate for the mean of the original population is

$$\mu = \overline{x} \pm \delta = \overline{x} \pm z_{CR}\frac{\sigma}{\sqrt{n}}$$

and the respective confidence interval also can be written as

$$(\overline{x} - \delta, \overline{x} + \delta)$$

The confidence interval for the estimate for a normally distributed population can also be calculated by using the MS Excel or OpenOffice Calc function CONFIDENCE.NORM(α,s,n).

▶ Example 1: Finding the average weight of apples when the standard deviation is known

A new harvest of apples has arrived, and we want to find the average weight of an apple in the new harvest. A sample of 100 apples was selected and results in an average (mean) weight of $\bar{x}$ = 230 g per apple. We chose the confidence level (CL) = 90%, i.e., $\alpha = 0.1$. The standard deviation of weights of apples from previous years was $\sigma = 50$ g:

$$n = 100; \quad \bar{x} = 230g; \quad \sigma = 50g; \quad \alpha = 0.1 \tag{13.24}$$

The apple weight may vary in either direction from the average weight. Thus, we use the two-tailed normal distribution with $\alpha/2 = 0.05$ for each tail. The sample size is $n = 100$. As soon as $n \geq 30$, we can use the z-score to find the critical value (◘ Table 13.2). The z-score for the critical value matching $\alpha = 0.1$ is found from the standard normal distribution table, $z_{CR} = 1.645$, for the two-tailed distribution. According to Eq. (13.21), the margin of error

$$\delta = z_{CR}\frac{\sigma}{\sqrt{n}} = 1.645 * \frac{50}{\sqrt{100}} = 8.2 \approx 8 \tag{13.25}$$

Thus, the average weight of apples μ in the new harvest with the confidence level of 90% is

$$\mu = \bar{x} \pm \delta = 230 \pm 8g \tag{13.26}$$

It means that the average weight of apples is assessed with accuracy of 8.2 grams, if we are not wrong with our assessment, i.e., if the selected sample belongs to the category of plausible samples. However, there is the probability of $\alpha = 0.1$ that we are just wrong with our judgment and the average weight of apples can be anything beyond the estimated average weight and the estimated accuracy.

The confidence interval with the normal distribution can be also calculated by using the MS Excel or OpenOffice Calc function CONFIDENCE.NORM(α,s,n). ◀

13.5 Student's *t*-Distribution

13

As indicated in ◘ Table 13.2, the sampling distribution (the distribution of means on all possible samples of a given size) is normal $\bar{X} \sim N\left(\mu, \sigma^2/n\right)$, if the sample size is reasonably big, i.e., $n \geq 30$, or the original population X is distributed normally for any sample size. Under such conditions, the z-distribution can be used to find critical values. The margin of error for the chosen confidence level is calculated based on the critical value in z-transform and using the standard deviation on the original population and the sample size. However, we may not be sure that the original population is distributed normally, or the sample size may not be big enough, i.e., $n < 30$, or the standard deviation on the original population is unknown.

Student's t-distribution or simply the t-distribution is a continuous probability distribution, which was introduced by statistician William Sealy Gosset and took its name from the pseudonym "Student" under which he published his paper. Student's t-distribution helps in the calculation of confidence intervals for small samples, $n < 30$, or for populations with unknown standard deviation.

The t-distribution is a distribution, with the random variable t as

$$t = \frac{\overline{x} - \mu}{s / \sqrt{n}} \quad (13.27)$$

where $\overline{x}$, s, and n are the sample mean, the standard deviation on the selected sample, and the sample size, respectively. The t-distribution is used together with the degree of freedom, df, calculated for a single sample (we will discuss two samples later in this chapter) as follows:

$$df = n - 1 \quad (13.28)$$

The t-distribution is a symmetric bell-shaped function that looks quite like the normal distribution but has heavier tails and has the following properties. The mean of the distribution equals to zero. The variance is equal to $df/(df - 2)$, where df is the degree of freedom and $df > 2$. The variance of the t-distribution is always greater than one, although it is close to one when there are many degrees of freedom. Thus, with high degrees of freedom, i.e., for large samples, the t-distribution is close to the standard normal distribution.

For large samples, i.e., for large degrees of freedom, the t-distribution becomes practically identical with the standard normal distribution.

The t-distribution can be used in all cases described in ◘ Table 13.2 particularly for small samples with unknown standard deviation on the population. However, for large samples, $n \geq 30$, the t-distribution is very close to the standard normal distribution that makes z-distribution work fine in this case too.

The t-distribution is typically used when the sample size is small ($n < 30$) or the standard deviation on the population is unknown.

The methodology described above in this chapter for the z-distribution is applied for the t-distribution. The critical value for t-distribution t_{CR} can be found from the appropriate tables for t-distribution (see Appendix B) or by using the appropriate computer algorithms.

The confidence interval can be calculated by finding t_{CR} on ***t-distribution*** using the following procedure:

- Choose the confidence level (CL) or choose sampling error $\alpha = 1 - CL$.
- Select a random sample, and calculate the mean value, the standard deviation, and the degree of freedom ($df = n - 1$) for one sample. We will discuss two samples later in this chapter.
- Find the t_{CR} according to the confidence level and the degree of freedom for the selected sample by using the t-distribution tables or the appropriate software function.
- According to the t_{CR}, calculate the margin of error δ as

$$\delta = t_{CR} \frac{s}{\sqrt{n}} \quad (13.29)$$

where s is the standard deviation on the selected sample.

- The estimate for the mean of the original population is

$$\mu = \overline{x} \pm \delta = \overline{x} \pm t_{\text{CR}} \frac{s}{\sqrt{n}} \tag{13.30}$$

and the respective confidence interval also can be written as

$$\left(\overline{x} - \delta, \overline{x} + \delta\right) \tag{13.31}$$

where s is the standard deviation measured on the selected sample and n is the size of the sample.

The confidence interval with Student's t-distribution can be also calculated by using the MS Excel or OpenOffice Calc function CONFIDENCE.T(α,s,n).

► Example 2: Finding the average weight of apples with a small sample ($n < 30$)

Let's solve the previous problem, if the sample size is small. We want to find the average weight of an apple in the supply. We chose the confidence level (CL) = 90%, i.e., $\alpha = 1 - \text{CL} = 0.1$. A sample of 25 apples was selected and results in an average (mean) weight of $\overline{x} = 230$ g per apple. The standard deviation of weights of apples in the original population is unknown, but the standard deviation of weights of apples in the sample is $s = 50$ g:

$$n = 25;\ \ \overline{x} = 230g;\ \ s = 50g;\ \ \alpha = 0.1 \tag{13.32}$$

We use the t-distribution because $n < 30$, and the standard deviation on the original population is unknown (■ Table 13.2). The degree of freedom is

$$df = n - 1 = 24 \tag{13.33}$$

The t_{CR} for $\alpha = 0.1$ and $df = 24$ can be found from the t-distribution table (Appendix B) and $t_{\text{CR}} = 1.708$ for the two-tailed distribution. According to Eq. (13.29), the margin of error δ is

$$\delta = t_{CR} \frac{s}{\sqrt{n}} = 1.708 \frac{50}{\sqrt{25}} = 17.1 \approx 17 \tag{13.34}$$

13

Thus, with the confidence level of 90%, the average weight of apples μ in the supply with the confidence level of 90% is

$$\mu = \overline{x} \pm \delta = 230 \pm 17g \tag{13.35}$$

The confidence interval in this example is wider than the confidence intervals in ■ Example 1 because the sample size in this example is four times smaller than in ■ Example 1. ◄

13.6 *T*-Distribution Versus *Z*-Distribution for Large Samples

As was noted in the previous section, t-distribution with high degrees of freedom, i.e., for large samples, is close to the standard normal distribution. Thus, for large samples with $n \geq 30$, t-distribution is very close to z-distribution, and therefore, either distribution can be used for large samples.

▶ Example 3: Finding the average weight of apples with a large sample using t-distribution when the standard deviation on the population is unknown

Let's find the confidence interval for the mean weight of apples for a large sample, $n = 100$, when the standard deviation on the population is unknown. In this case, the standard deviation s measured on the selected sample will be used. Suppose $s = 51$ g, i.e.,

$$n = 100; \quad \overline{x} = 230g; \quad s = 51g; \quad \alpha = 0.1 \tag{13.36}$$

The degree of freedom is

$$df = n - 1 = 99 \tag{13.37}$$

The critical value t_{CR} for $\alpha = 0.1$ and $df = 99$ can be found from the t-distribution table (Appendix B) and $t_{CR} = 1.660$ for the two-tailed distribution. According to Eq. (13.30), the margin of error δ is

$$\delta = t_{CR}\frac{s}{\sqrt{n}} = 1.660\frac{51}{\sqrt{100}} = 8.46 \approx 8 \tag{13.38}$$

Thus, with the confidence level of 90%, the average weight of apples μ in the supply with the confidence level of 90% is

$$\mu = \overline{x} \pm \delta = 230 \pm 8g \tag{13.39}$$ ◀

▶ Example 4: Finding the average weight of apples with a large sample using z-distribution when the standard deviation on the population is unknown

Let's solve the previous problem, if the standard deviation on the population is unknown. In this case, the standard deviation on the selected sample s will be used. Suppose $s = 51$ g, i.e.,

$$n = 100; \quad \overline{x} = 230g; \quad s = 51g; \quad \alpha = 0.1 \tag{13.40}$$

The critical value z_{CR} for $\alpha = 0.1$ can be found from the z-distribution table (Appendix A) and $t_{CR} = 1.645$ for the two-tailed distribution. According to Eq. (13.22) for z-distribution, the margin of error δ is

Then, the critical value margin of error with the sampling error $\alpha = 0.1$ is

$$\delta = z_{CR}\frac{s}{\sqrt{n}} = 1.645\frac{51}{\sqrt{100}} = 8.4 \approx 8 \tag{13.41}$$

and the average weight of apples is estimated with the same confidence level of 90% is:

$$\mu = \overline{x} \pm \delta = 230 \pm 8g \tag{13.42}$$ ◀

Student's t-distribution uses the standard deviation on a sample s rather than the standard deviation on the population σ. Actually, the standard deviation on the population is unknown, and the standard deviation on a sample is used for the calculation of the confidence intervals. It is expected that for large samples, the standard deviation on a random sample is getting closer to the standard deviation on the population; thus, it is quite safe to use the standard deviation on a sample for estimating confidence intervals based on large samples.

In summarizing calculation of confidence intervals, z-distribution versus t-distribution, one can conclude that most of the time, standard deviation on the population is unknown and therefore the standard deviation on a random sample is used for the estimate. Thus:

- For large samples ($n \geq 30$), the standard deviation on a random sample is quite close to the standard deviation on the population, and therefore, the z-distribution or the t-distribution can be equally used assessing the confidence intervals.
- For small samples ($n < 30$), Student's t-distribution should be used in assessing the confidence intervals.

The t-distribution is a probability distribution, with the random variable t as

$$t = \frac{\overline{x} - \mu}{s / \sqrt{n}}$$

and the degree of freedom calculated for a single sample as $df = n - 1$. (We will discuss two samples later in this chapter.)

The mean of the distribution equals to zero. The variance equals to $df/(df - 2)$ for $df > 2$.

The variance of the t-distribution is always greater than one, although it is close to one when there are many degrees of freedom. Thus, with high degrees of freedom, the t-distribution is close to the standard normal distribution that makes z-distribution work fine in this case too.

13

Student's t-distribution helps in the calculation of confidence interval for the populations with unknown standard deviation and in case of small samples from the population with unknown distribution.

If the standard deviation on the population is unknown, the confidence interval can be calculated by ***t-score*** on ***t-distribution*** using the following procedure:

- Choose the confidence level (CL) by setting sampling error $\alpha = 1 - CL$.
- Select a random sample, and calculate the mean value, the standard deviation, and the degree of freedom ($df = n - 1$) for one sample. We will discuss two samples later in this chapter.
- Find the t_{CR} according to the confidence level and the degree of freedom for the selected sample by using the t-distribution tables or the appropriate software function.
- According to the t-score, calculate margin of error

$$\delta = t_{CR}\frac{s}{\sqrt{n}}$$

where s is the standard deviation on the selected sample.

- The estimate for the mean of the original population is

$$\mu = \overline{x} \pm \delta = \overline{x} \pm t_{CR}\frac{s}{\sqrt{n}}$$

and the respective confidence interval is

$$(\overline{x} - \delta, \overline{x} + \delta)$$

For large samples, i.e., for large degrees of freedom, the t-distribution becomes practically identical with the standard normal distribution.

- For large samples ($n \geq 30$), the standard deviation on a random sample is quite close to the standard deviation on the population, and therefore, the z-distribution or the t-distribution can be equally used assessing the confidence intervals.
- For small samples ($n < 30$), Student's t-distribution should be used in assessing the confidence intervals.

The confidence interval with Student's t-distribution can be calculated by using the MS Excel or OpenOffice Calc function CONFIDENCE.T(α,s,n).

13.7 Confidence Intervals for Two Unpaired Samples

In some situations, there is an interest to compare the means on two independent populations. For example, we might be interested in comparing average salary of the same category of employees in two different cities. Employees in these two cities represent two independent populations of people.

To conduct such a comparison, we select two random samples, one for each city. Suppose the sample sizes are n_1 and n_2 and the means on the samples are $\overline{x}_1$ and $\overline{x}_2$. Such samples are called ***independent samples*** or ***unpaired samples***.

The question is to assess the difference of the means of these two populations, i.e., $\Delta\mu = \mu_1 - \mu_2$. The difference of the means on two samples $\Delta\overline{x} = \overline{x}_1 - \overline{x}_2$ and the standard deviations measured on these samples are s_1 and s_2, respectively.

13.7.1 The Confidence Interval for Two Unpaired Large Samples

If both samples are reasonably large, i.e., $n_1 \geq 30$ and $n_2 \geq 30$, then, according to ◘ Table 13.2, we can use the z-distribution to calculate the margin of error for the confidence interval as

$$\delta = z_{\mathrm{CR}} \frac{S_P}{\sqrt{n_P}} \tag{13.43}$$

where S_P is the pooled common standard deviation for two samples, which can be estimated as

$$S_P = \sqrt{\frac{(n_1 - 1)s_1^2 + (n_2 - 1)s_2^2}{n_1 + n_2 - 2}} \tag{13.44}$$

and

$$\frac{1}{\sqrt{n_P}} = \sqrt{\frac{1}{n_1} + \frac{1}{n_2}} \tag{13.45}$$

The z-score z_{CR} can be found using the standard normal distribution table to match the assigned confidence level by choosing standard error α. Thus, the difference of the mean values of these two populations with the confidence level (CL) = $1 - \alpha$ is

$$\mu_1 - \mu_2 = \bar{x}_1 - \bar{x}_2 \pm z_{\mathrm{CR}} S_P \sqrt{\frac{1}{n_1} + \frac{1}{n_2}} \tag{13.46}$$

13

The margin of error in the confidence interval for the difference of two independent populations with both large samples ($n_1 \geq 30$ and $n_2 \geq 30$) can be calculated as

$$\delta = z_{\mathrm{CR}} S_P \sqrt{\frac{1}{n_1} + \frac{1}{n_2}}$$

where S_P is the pooled common standard deviation

$$S_P = \sqrt{\frac{(n_1 - 1)s_1^2 + (n_2 - 1)s_2^2}{n_1 + n_2 - 2}}$$

Thus, the difference of the means of two independent populations can be estimated as

$$\mu_1 - \mu_2 = \bar{x}_1 - \bar{x}_2 \pm z_{\mathrm{CR}} S_P \sqrt{\frac{1}{n_1} + \frac{1}{n_2}}$$

13.7.2 The Confidence Interval When at Least One Sample Is Small

If at least one of the samples is small, i.e., either $n_1 < 30$ or $n_2 < 30$, or both samples are small, then the margin of error in the confidence interval for the difference of the means on these two populations can be found using Student's t-distribution as

$$\delta = t_{\mathrm{CR}} \frac{S_P}{\sqrt{n_P}} = t_{\mathrm{CR}} S_P \sqrt{\frac{1}{n_1} + \frac{1}{n_2}} \tag{13.47}$$

where S_p is the pooled common standard deviation for two samples as in Eq. (13.41), n_{p} is calculated according Eq. (13.45), and the degree of freedom for two samples is

$$df = n - 2 \tag{13.48}$$

The t-score for the chosen confidence level expressed with sampling error α and the degree of freedom df as in Eq. (13.48) can be found from the t-distribution table. According to Eq. (13.46), the difference of the means of these two populations with the confidence level (CL) = 1 − α is estimated as

$$\mu_1 - \mu_2 = \bar{x}_1 - \bar{x}_2 \pm t_{df} S_P \sqrt{\frac{1}{n_1} + \frac{1}{n_2}} \tag{13.49}$$

The margin of error in the confidence interval for the difference of two unpaired (independent) populations when at least one of two samples is small ($n_1 < 30$ or $n_2 < 30$) can be calculated as

$$\delta = t_{\mathrm{CR}} S_P \sqrt{\frac{1}{n_1} + \frac{1}{n_2}}$$

where S_p is the pooled common standard deviation

$$S_P = \sqrt{\frac{(n_1 - 1)s_1^2 + (n_2 - 1)s_2^2}{n_1 + n_2 - 2}}$$

Thus, the difference of the means of two independent populations can be estimated as

$$\mu_1 - \mu_2 = \bar{x}_1 - \bar{x}_2 \pm t_{\mathrm{CR}} S_P \sqrt{\frac{1}{n_1} + \frac{1}{n_2}}$$

13.7.3 Both Samples Have the Same Standard Deviation

If both samples have the same standard deviation, i.e., $s_1 = s_2 = s$, then, according to Eq. (13.44),

$$S_P = \sqrt{\frac{(n_1 - 1)s^2 + (n_2 - 1)s^2}{n_1 + n_2 - 2}} = s \tag{13.50}$$

and n_p is calculated according to Eq. (13.45).

13.7.4 Both Samples of the Same Size

If both samples have the same size, i.e., $n_1 = n_2 = n$, then, according to Eqs. (13.44) and (13.45),

$$S_P = \sqrt{\frac{s_1^2 + s_2^2}{2}} \quad \text{and} \quad n_P = n \tag{13.51}$$

▶ Example 5: Finding the difference of the salaries in two cities with large samples

We want to compare average annual salaries of the same category of employees in two different cities. Employees in these two cities represent two independent groups of people. Two samples were selected, one for each city. The confidence level is chosen CL = 95%, i.e., $\alpha = 0.05$. The statistic on the samples for two cities is

$$\begin{aligned} &n_1 = 50; \quad \bar{x}_1 = \$65{,}346; \quad s_1 = \$5{,}123 \\ &n_2 = 40; \quad \bar{x}_2 = \$57{,}482; \quad s_2 = \$4{,}321 \end{aligned} \tag{13.52}$$

Both samples are large, i.e., $n_1 \geq 30$ and $n_2 \geq 30$; then, we will use *z*-score for calculating the confidence interval for the estimation of the difference of the mean annual salaries.

13

The pooled standard deviation for these two samples is

$$\begin{aligned} S_P &= \sqrt{\frac{(n_1 - 1)s_1^2 + (n_2 - 1)s_2^2}{n_1 + n_2 - 2}} = \\ &= \sqrt{\frac{(50 - 1) * 5{,}123^2 + (40 - 1) * 4{,}321^2}{50 + 40 - 2}} = 4{,}784 \end{aligned} \tag{13.53}$$

The *z*-score for $\alpha = 0.05$ is $z_{CR} = 1.96$. Thus, the difference on the mean annual salaries is estimated as

$$\begin{aligned} \mu_1 - \mu_2 &= \bar{x}_1 - \bar{x}_2 \pm z_{CR} S_P \sqrt{\frac{1}{n_1} + \frac{1}{n_2}} = \\ &= \$65{,}346 - \$57{,}482 \pm 1.96 * \$4{,}784 * \sqrt{\frac{1}{50} + \frac{1}{40}} = \\ &= \$7{,}864 \pm 1{,}989 \end{aligned} \tag{13.54}$$

The difference between the annual salaries in two cities is \$7,864 with the confidence interval δ = \$1,989 with the confidence level of 95%. It means that with the probability of 0.95, the estimated difference of the means is within \$\$7,864±1,989, but there is still the probability of 0.05 that the difference is different than the estimated. ◀

▶ Example 6: Finding the difference of the salaries in two cities with small samples

Let's solve the same problem as in ◘ Example 4 but with small samples. We want to compare average annual salaries of the same category of employees in two cities with the confidence level of 95%, i.e., $\alpha = 0.05$. The statistic on the samples for two cities is

$$\begin{aligned} n_1 &= 20; \quad \bar{x}_1 = \$65{,}346; \quad s_1 = \$5{,}123 \\ n_1 &= 12; \quad \bar{x}_1 = \$57{,}482; \quad s_1 = \$4{,}321 \end{aligned} \tag{13.55}$$

The only difference from ◘ Example 4 is that the samples are twice as smaller. Both samples are small, i.e., $n_1 < 30$ and $n_2 < 30$, so we will use Student's *t*-distribution.

The pooled common standard deviation for two samples is

$$\begin{aligned} S_P &= \sqrt{\frac{(n_1-1)s_1^2 + (n_2-1)s_2^2}{n_1+n_2-2}} = \\ &= \sqrt{\frac{(20-1)*5{,}123^2 + (12-1)*4{,}321^2}{20+12-2}} = 4{,}844 \end{aligned} \tag{13.56}$$

and the degree of freedom is

$$df = n_1 + n_2 - 2 = 20 + 12 - 2 = 30 \tag{13.57}$$

The *t*-score for $\alpha = 0.05$ and $df = 30$ is found by using the *t*-distribution table (Appendix A), $t_{df} = 2.042$. Thus, the difference on the mean annual salaries is estimated as

$$\begin{aligned} \mu_1 - \mu_2 &= \bar{x}_1 - \bar{x}_2 \pm t_{df} S_P \sqrt{\frac{1}{n_1} + \frac{1}{n_2}} = \\ &= \$65{,}346 - \$57{,}482 \pm 2.042 * \$4{,}844 * \sqrt{\frac{1}{20} + \frac{1}{12}} = \\ &= \$7{,}864 \pm 3{,}612 \end{aligned} \tag{13.58}$$

The difference between the annual salaries in two cities is \$7,864 with the confidence interval δ = \$3,612 with the confidence level of 95%. The confidence interval in this case is greater than in ◘ Example 4 because the samples are smaller. ◀

13.8 Confidence Interval for Paired Samples

There are situations in which the same population is compared with itself under different conditions by using measurements on the same sample under different conditions. For example, vital parameters are measured on the same patients before or after the treatment with the goal to identify the difference. Another example, performance of employees, is measured before and after the training with the goal to find the difference in the employee performance as a result of the training. Both samples are composed of the same elements from the population under different conditions and referred to as ***paired samples***.

Suppose there are two different conditions A and B applied to population X. A random sample is selected from the population. The value of variable x_k is measured twice for each element k on the sample, under conditions A and B. The difference of the values for each element is

$$\Delta x_k = x_k^A - x_k^B \tag{13.59}$$

The question is to find the mean difference of the values of the variable under different conditions for the population:

$$\mu_{\Delta x} = \frac{1}{N}\sum_{k=1}^{N}\Delta x_k = \frac{1}{N}\sum_{k=1}^{N}x_k^A - x_k^B \tag{13.60}$$

where N is the size of the population. The mean difference on the population is estimated by the mean difference on a random sample. The mean difference of the values of variable X on the sample is

$$\overline{\Delta x} = \sum_{k=1}^{n}\Delta x_k = \sum_{k=1}^{n}x_k^A - x_k^B \tag{13.61}$$

where n is the size of each sample.

To find the mean of the differences, we form a new population ΔX that is composed of the differences of the elements of population X under different conditions, $\Delta X = (\Delta x_1, \Delta x_2, \ldots, \Delta x_N)$. Then, we select a random sample and measure the mean on it, i.e., $\overline{\varnothing x}$.

13.8.1 Confidence Interval for a Large Paired Sample

13

For a large paired sample, $n \geq 30$, we use the z-score similarly to the single large sample described in ► Sect. 13.4:

$$\mu_{\Delta X} = \overline{\Delta x} \pm z_{\mathrm{CR}}\frac{s_{\Delta X}}{\sqrt{n}} \tag{13.62}$$

where $s_{\Delta X}$ is the standard deviation on the sample of differences.

13.8.2 Confidence Interval for a Small Paired Sample

For a large paired sample, $n \geq 30$, we use the t-score similarly to the single small sample described in ► Sect. 13.5:

$$\mu_{\Delta X} = \overline{\Delta x} \pm t_{\mathrm{CR}}\frac{s_{\Delta X}}{\sqrt{n}} \tag{13.63}$$

with the degree of freedom $df = n - 1$, because it is actually one sample.

▶ Example 7: Finding the difference in sales performance before and after the training

Company XYZ performed the sales staff training. The staff performance was measured before and after the training for each salesperson. The question is to find out the difference in performance before and after the conducted training.

A sample of ten employees was randomly selected, and their performance was registered in the company-specific units of measurement before and after the training with the confidence level (CL) = 95%:

$$\begin{aligned} &\text{Sample A "before the training"} = (15,14,10,16,14,16,15,14,13,17) \\ &\text{Sample B "after the training"} = (16,16,14,17,15,16,17,15,15,16) \end{aligned} \quad (13.64)$$

A sample of differences in performance before and after the training is

$$\text{Sample } \Delta X \text{ "after before the training"} = (1,2,4,1,1,0,2,1,2,-1) \quad (13.65)$$

The mean difference $\overline{\varnothing x}$ and the standard deviation of the differences $s_{\Delta X}$ on the sample of differences in Eq. (13.65) are

$$\overline{\Delta x} = 1.30; \quad s_{\Delta x} = 1.38 \quad (13.66)$$

The sample is small, $n = 10$, which is less than 30, so we use the t-score to find the confidence interval. The degree of freedom $df = n - 1 = 9$, and the sampling error $\alpha = 0.05$ matching the 95% confidence level. According to t-distribution table, the t-score for $\alpha = 0.05$ and $df = 9$ is $t_{df} = 1.833$ that leads to the following estimate of the mean of the differences on the population:

$$\mu_{\Delta X} = \overline{\Delta x} \pm t_{CR} \frac{s_{\Delta X}}{\sqrt{n}} = 1.30 \pm 1.83 \frac{1.38}{\sqrt{10}} = 1.30 \pm 0.78 \quad (13.67)$$

◀

The confidence interval for two paired (dependent) populations is the confidence interval of the differences of the random variable on the same population under two conditions A and B:

$$\Delta x_k = x_k^A - x_k^B$$

Thus, both samples are of the same size n.

If $n \geq 30$, use the z-score

$$\delta = t_{CR} \frac{s_{\Delta X}}{\sqrt{n}}$$

If $n < 30$, use the t-score

$$\delta = t_{CR}\frac{s_{\Delta X}}{\sqrt{n}}$$

and the estimate of the mean of the population is

$$\mu_{\Delta X} = \overline{\Delta x} \pm \delta$$

similarly to the single sample tests.

13.9 Confidence Interval for Binomial Distribution

Estimating the probability on a population by the frequency on a sample is a quite common task. For example, the probability of "yeas" in the forthcoming election is estimated by the frequency of "yeas" in a poll.

Binary outcomes true/false (or yes/no or success/failure or one/zero or any other binary outcomes) of each event imply the binomial distribution on the population and on a random sample for this population with probabilities p for outcome "true" and probability $q = 1 - p$ for outcome "false" for each single event. The mean value and variance on a sample of n trials (a sample of n elements from the population) with the binomial distribution are (► Chap. 11)

$$\mu_n = np; \qquad \sigma_n^2 = np(1-p) \tag{13.68}$$

where μ_n is the mean value and σ_n^2 is the variance of the number of outcomes "true" on the binomial sample of size n.

As evident from Eq. (13.66), the expected value and variance on the sample per each trial (for each element in the sample) are

13

$$\mu_p = \frac{\mu_n}{n} = p; \qquad \sigma_p^2 = \frac{\sigma_n^2}{n} = p(1-p) \tag{13.69}$$

where p is the probability of outcome "true."

Binary outcomes are measured on a sample of n elements from the population. The ratio $\hat{p} = n_{\text{True}} / n$ of the number of outcomes "True," n_{True}, to the total number of elements n in the sample is taken as an estimate for probability p on the population. Similarly, the ratio $\hat{q} = n_{\text{False}} / n = 1 - \hat{p}$ of the number of outcomes "False," n_{False}, to the total number of elements n in the sample is taken as an estimate for probability $q = 1 - p$ on the population. Thus, the mean ratios for $\hat{p}$ and $\hat{q} = 1 - \hat{p}$ measured on the sample are

$$\hat{p} = \frac{n_{\text{True}}}{n}; \qquad \hat{q} = \frac{n_{\text{False}}}{n} = 1 - \hat{p}; \tag{13.70}$$

and the variance and standard deviation $\hat{s}^2$ and $\hat{s}$ of that ratio per one trial are calculated using measured $\hat{p}$ according to Eq. (13.70). Thus,

$$\hat{s}^2 = \hat{p}(1-\hat{p}); \qquad \hat{s} = \sqrt{\hat{p}(1-\hat{p})} \tag{13.71}$$

The binomial probability p is estimated based on the measured ratio $\hat{p}$ as in Eq. (13.67) with the confidence interval δ estimated by the standard deviation $\hat{s}$, calculated using the measured $\hat{p}$ according to Eq. (13.70), and the chosen confidence level using the appropriate z-score or t-score depending on the sample size n:

$$p = \hat{p} \pm \delta \tag{13.72}$$

The values of p, $\hat{p}$, σ, $\hat{s}$, and δ are expressed in terms of fraction or percentage.

If the sample size is big enough, the binomial distribution is getting close to the normal distribution, and thus, the z-score can be used for finding the critical value. The condition of being "big enough" is expressed as

$$np > 5 \quad \text{and} \quad nq = n(1-p) > 5 \tag{13.73}$$

The condition for a large sample in Eq. (13.73) can be rewritten as

$$n * \min(p, 1-p) > 5 \tag{13.74}$$

We estimate the probability p with the ratio calculated on the sample $\hat{p}$. Therefore, the condition in Eq. (13.71) can be approximated by

$$n\hat{p} > 5 \qquad \text{and} \qquad n\hat{q} = n(1-\hat{p}) > 5 \tag{13.75}$$

and the condition for a sample to be considered large in Eq. (13.74) can be rewritten as

$$n * \min(\hat{p}, 1-\hat{p}) > 5 \tag{13.76}$$

The condition for a small sample, i.e., when at least one of the following is true, is

$$n\hat{p} \le 5 \qquad \text{or} \qquad n\hat{q} = n(1-\hat{p}) \le 5 \tag{13.77}$$

or

$$n * \min(\hat{p}, 1-\hat{p}) \le 5 \tag{13.78}$$

13.9.1 Large Sample

If the condition in Eq. (13.73) is met, i.e., $n * \min(\hat{p}, 1-\hat{p}) > 5$, then the z-score can be used to find the critical value z_{CR} according to the chosen confidence level $(1 - \alpha)$. Thus, the probability or the percentage content p can be estimated as

$$p = \hat{p} \pm z_{CR}\sqrt{\frac{\hat{p}(1-\hat{p})}{n}} \tag{13.79}$$

13.9.2 Small Sample

If the sample size is not big enough, i.e., $n * \min(\hat{p}, 1-\hat{p}) \leq 5$, then the *t*-score t_{CR} should be used for the chosen confidence level (1 – *α*) and the degree of freedom

$$df = n - 1 \tag{13.80}$$

Thus, the probability or the percentage content *p* can be estimated as

$$p = \hat{p} \pm t_{df} \sqrt{\frac{\hat{p}(1-\hat{p})}{n}} \tag{13.81}$$

▶ Example 8: Finding the percentage of defective parts

An assembly plant uses parts supply from a vendor. We would like to identify the percentage of defective parts in the supply with the confidence level of 95%. A random sample of 100 parts was selected form the supply, *n* = 100, and tested for quality of the pats on the sample. It was detected that $n_D = 12$ (defective parts) and $n_G = 88$ (good parts). Evidently, $n_D + n_G = n$. The frequency ratio of the defective parts $\hat{p}$ on the sample is

$$\hat{p} = \frac{n_D}{n} = \frac{12}{100} = 0.12 = 12\% \qquad \text{and} \qquad \hat{q} = 1 - \hat{p} = 0.88 = 88\% \tag{13.82}$$

The sample is big enough because $n * \min(\hat{p}, 1-\hat{p}) = 100 * 0.12 = 12 > 5$, so we can use the *z*-distribution. The *z*-score matching 95% confidence level (*α* = 0.05) is $z_{CR} = 1.96$. Thus, the percentage of defective parts can be estimated as

$$p = \hat{p} \pm z_{CR} \sqrt{\frac{\hat{p}(1-\hat{p})}{n}} = \\ = 0.12 \pm 1.96 \sqrt{\frac{0.12 * 0.88}{100}} = 0.12 \pm 0.06 = 12\% \pm 6\% \tag{13.83}$$

◀

13

▶ Example 9: Finding the probability for management trainees of making a wrong decision

The task is to find out with confidence level of 90% the probability of management trainees of making wrong decisions. During the management training, a sample of 20 management trainees was tested on their decision-making skills by asking each trainee to make a decision in a given situation. The trainer judges their decision as correct or wrong. Sixteen trainees made correct decision, $n_C = 16$, but four of them made a wrong decision, $n_W = 4$. The frequency ratio wrong decision $\hat{p}$ on the sample is

$$\hat{p} = \frac{n_W}{n} = \frac{4}{20} = 0.20 \qquad \text{and} \qquad \hat{q} = 1 - \hat{p} = 0.80 \tag{13.84}$$

The sample is small because $n * \min(\hat{p}, 1-\hat{p}) = 20 * 0.20 = 4 < 5$, so we should use the *t*-distribution. The degree of freedom *df* is

$$df = n - 1 = 20 - 1 = 19 \tag{13.85}$$

The t-score matching 90% confidence level ($\alpha = 0.10$) and the degree of freedom $df = 19$ is $t_{df} = 1.33$. Thus, the probability of making a wrong decision is

$$p = \hat{p} \pm t_{df}\sqrt{\frac{\hat{p}(1-\hat{p})}{n}} = 0.20 \pm 1.33\sqrt{\frac{0.20 * 0.80}{20}} = 0.20 \pm 0.12 \tag{13.86}$$

◀

In binomial distribution, the values of p, $\hat{p}$, σ, $\hat{s}$, and δ are expressed in terms of fraction or percentage.

The probability or the percentage content p for a large sample, $n * \min(\hat{p}, 1-\hat{p}) > 5$, with binomial distribution, can be found using z-score z_{CR} for the chosen confidence level $(1 - \alpha)$ as

$$p = \hat{p} \pm z_{CR}\sqrt{\frac{\hat{p}(1-\hat{p})}{n}}$$

For a small sample, $n * \min(\hat{p}, 1-\hat{p}) \le 5$, the probability or the percentage content p can be found using the t-distribution with the t-score t_{df} for the chosen confidence level $(1 - \alpha)$ and the degree of freedom $df = n - 1$ as

$$p = \hat{p} \pm t_{CR}\sqrt{\frac{\hat{p}(1-\hat{p})}{n}}$$

13.10 Confidence Interval for Probability or Percentage Difference from Two Independent Samples

Suppose we need to compare probabilities or percentage contents on two independent populations X_1 and X_2. This problem is a combination of two problems discussed above in this chapter:

- The problem of estimating the difference of means on two independent populations based on two independent (unpaired) samples discussed in ► Sect. 13.7 of this chapter.
- The problem of estimating the probability or percentage content on binomial distribution discussed in ► Sect. 13.9 of this chapter.

The difference of probabilities or percentage contents can be estimated from two independent (unpaired) samples.

13.10.1 Large Samples

For both large samples, i.e., when $n_1 * \min(\hat{p}_1, 1-\hat{p}_1) > 5$ and $n_2 * \min(\hat{p}_2, 1-\hat{p}_2) > 5$, where $\hat{p}_1$ and $\hat{p}_2$ are the percentage ratios calculated on the samples, the difference of the probabilities or percentage contents on two independent populations can be estimated using the *z*-score z_{CR} found for the chosen confidence level (1 – α) as

$$p_1 - p_2 = \hat{p}_1 - \hat{p}_2 \pm z_{CR}\sqrt{\frac{\hat{p}_1(1-\hat{p}_1)}{n_1} + \frac{\hat{p}_2(1-\hat{p}_2)}{n_2}}. \tag{13.87}$$

13.10.2 Small Samples

If at least one of the samples is small, i.e., $n_1 * \min(\hat{p}_1, 1-\hat{p}_1) \le 5$ or $n_2 * \min(\hat{p}_2, 1-\hat{p}_2) \le 5$, the difference of the probabilities or percentage contents on two independent populations is estimated using *t*-score t_{df} found for the chosen confidence level (1 – α) and the degree of freedom $df = n_1 + n_2 - 2$ as

$$p_1 - p_2 = \hat{p}_1 - \hat{p}_2 \pm t_{df}\sqrt{\frac{\hat{p}_1(1-\hat{p}_1)}{n_1} + \frac{\hat{p}_2(1-\hat{p}_2)}{n_2}}. \tag{13.88}$$

▶ Example 10: Finding the difference in the percentage of spoiled fruits

There are two supplies of fruits. Each supply has a certain percentage of spoiled fruits. The task is to identify the difference between the percentage of spoiled fruits in these two supplies with confidence level of 90%.

Two samples of size $n_1 = n_2 = 100$ units of fruits each. The measure percentage of the spoiled fruits on the samples is $\hat{p}_1 = 23\%$ and $\hat{p}_2 = 18\%$, respectively. Both samples are large enough because

13

$$\begin{aligned} n_1 * \min(\hat{p}_1, 1-\hat{p}_1) &= 100 * \min(0.23, 0.77) = 23 > 5 \\ n_2 * \min(\hat{p}_2, 1-\hat{p}_2) &= 100 * \min(0.18, 0.82) = 18 > 5 \end{aligned} \tag{13.89}$$

Thus, we use the *z*-score. For (1 – α) = 0.90, z_{CR} = 1.645. The difference of the spoiled fruits in both supplies can be estimated as

$$\begin{aligned} p_1 - p_2 &= \hat{p}_1 - \hat{p}_2 \pm t_{df}\sqrt{\frac{\hat{p}_1(1-\hat{p}_1)}{n_1} + \frac{\hat{p}_2(1-\hat{p}_2)}{n_2}} = \\ &= 23\% - 18\% \pm 1.645\sqrt{\frac{0.23 * 0.77}{100} + \frac{0.18 * 0.82}{100}} = . \\ &= 5\% \pm 9\% \end{aligned} \tag{13.90}$$

It is hard to say which supply has a higher percentage of spoiled fruits because the percentage difference by the measurements on the samples is 5% but the confidence interval for the difference is 9%. ◀

13.11 Most Popular Confidence Levels and Respective *Z*-Scores

Some most popular confidence levels and their respective *z*-scores are shown in Table 13.3. Therefore, we can use the *z*-scores from the table, and there is no need to use the standard normal distribution table or computer algorithms to find those *z*-scores every time we use the confidence levels presented in Table 13.3.

The standard normal distribution is a symmetric function with the symmetry around zero, i.e., $\varphi(-z) = \varphi(z)$.

13.11.1 1-Sigma, 2-Sigma, and 3-Sigma Rule for Confidence Intervals

There are some most popular confidence levels related to the multiples of the standard deviation for any normal distribution shown in Fig. 13.7. As is clear from the figure, 68% of all possible samples fit within the interval of one standard deviation, σ, from the mean value μ, i.e., $(\mu - \sigma, \mu + \sigma)$; 95% of all possible samples fit in the interval of two standard deviations $(\mu - 2\sigma, \mu + 2\sigma)$; and 99.7% of all possible samples fit in the interval of three standard deviations $(\mu - 3\sigma, \mu + 3\sigma)$.

The more accurate values of the areas in the 1-, 2-, and 3-sigma intervals are shown below:

$$\begin{aligned} &P(\mu - 1\sigma < X < \mu + 1\sigma) \approx 0.6827 \\ &P(\mu - 2\sigma < X < \mu + 2\sigma) \approx 0.9545 \\ &P(\mu - 3\sigma < X < \mu + 3\sigma) \approx 0.9973 \end{aligned} \tag{13.91}$$

Thus, if you want to assess the confidence intervals for 68%, 95%, and 99.7% confidence levels, just use 1σ, 2σ, and 3σ, respectively.

Table 13.3 Most popular confidence levels and their respective z-scores

Confidence level (CL)	*Z*-score (z_{CR})	Area in interval ($-z_{CR}$, z_{CR})	Area in both tails (alpha)	Area in one tail (alpha/2)
80%	1.282	0.8000	0.2000	0.1000
90%	1.645	0.9000	0.100	0.0500
95%	1.960	0.9500	0.0500	0.0250
98%	2.326	0.9800	0.0200	0.0100
99%	2.576	0.9900	0.0100	0.0050

13.12 Interpretation of Confidence Intervals

Statistics is a complex and sophisticated discipline, and the correct interpretations of the results are critical. Properly understanding confidence levels and interpreting confidence intervals are critical for the understanding and using of confidence intervals.

Avoid a possible confusion with the confidence interval δ. The confidence interval is not the accuracy of measurement of the value of the random variable. It is not also a spread of values of the random variable in the population, not at all. The confidence interval is the accuracy of the estimation of the mean value of the population matching the assigned confidence level.

The greater the sample size is, the smaller the confidence interval, i.e., the accuracy of the estimation of the mean of the population by the mean of a random sample, if we are not wrong with our assessment. The probability of being right or wrong with the assessment does not change with the sample size because it is set by the chosen confidence level, which depends only on our level of judgment which is chosen and assigned prior to sample selection and any measurements. It means that with greater sample size, the estimate of the mean of the population is more accurate but the chances to be right or wrong with the assessment stay unchanged.

The ***confidence level*** is not a calculable value. The confidence level should be assigned from the clear understanding of the importance of the real-world problem, which we are solving possible troubles in case of a wrong conclusion, and the cost of being wrong in the estimate of the mean value on the population.

The ***confidence interval*** matching the assigned confidence level means that we are confident to the degree represented by the confidence level that the confidence interval captured the true situation.

Let's interpret the confidence interval calculated in ◘ Example 1 (▶ Sect. 13.4) for measuring the mean weight of apples in the supply. Estimation of the mean was
13 (230 ± 8) gram, where the confidence interval was 8 grams.

This value does not mean that 8 grams is the accuracy of the measurement, not at all!

It also does not mean that we have 90% chances to measure the mean on samples within this interval, if we repeat the experiment on other samples, not at all!

The interpretation of the result is that we are 95% confident that interval (230 ± 8) gram captures the true mean weight of the apples. However, we still may be completely wrong with our estimate.

> The ***confidence level*** is not a calculable value. The confidence level should be assigned from the understanding of the importance of the real-world problem we are solving and from the troubles and cost of being wrong in the estimate of the mean value on the population.

Choosing ***confidence level*** (CL) means that we agree that CL percentage of all possible random samples is reasonably common (typical) and $\alpha = 1 - \text{CL}$ of all possible samples are unreasonably extreme. It means that probability of randomly selecting a reasonable sample is CL and the probability of selecting an unreasonably extreme sample is
$\alpha = 1 - \text{CL}$. It is referred to as the ***significance level***.

Choosing confidence level of 95% means that we agree to consider that 95% of all possible random samples are plausible and 5% of the samples are unreasonably extreme. It means that the probability of randomly selecting a plausible sample is 0.95 and the probability of selecting an unreasonably extreme sample is 0.05.

The choice of a confidence level depends on the object and purpose of the analysis.

The interpretation of the ***confidence interval*** suiting ***confidence level*** (CL) is that we are confident with degree CL that the confidence interval captures the true mean of the population. However, we still may be completely wrong with our estimate.

Avoid a possible confusion with the confidence interval δ:

- The confidence interval is not the accuracy of measurement of the value of the random variable.
- Also, it is not a spread of values of the random variable in the population.

Not at all!

- The confidence interval is the accuracy of the estimation of the mean value on the population, if we are not wrong in our judgment, according to the chosen confidence level.

13.13 One-Sided and Two-Sided Tests

The normal distribution is a symmetric function with the symmetry around its mean. Therefore, we typically consider tails of the distribution from both sides of the function. The tails (also referred to as outliers) are parts of the distribution function that go beyond the plausible interval of the variable. The two-sided confi-

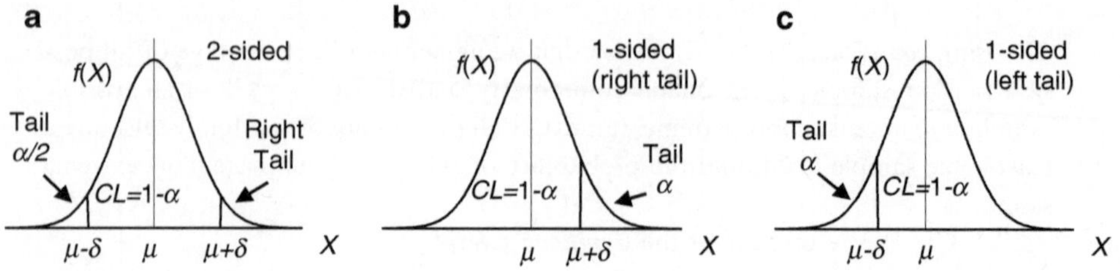

Fig. 13.8 Confidence intervals **a** two-sided, **b** one-sided right, and **c** one-sided left

dence interval $\mu \pm \delta$, i.e., the confidence interval calculated with two tails, is shown in Fig. 13.8(a). As soon as we have two symmetric tails, alpha ($\alpha = 1 - \text{CL}$) is equally shared between them by $\alpha/2$ for each tail. Such a distribution is referred to as a two-tailed or two-sided.

Sometimes, the plausible range is not symmetric because the values of the random variable on one of the tails may become always plausible. For example, if a worker has a fixed salary but paid extra for the overtime, the only plausible variation is the increase of the received money, thus making the left tail not needed. Such tests and the appropriate confidence intervals are referred to as one-tailed or one-sided. In this case, the full alpha ($\alpha = 1 - \text{CL}$) goes to the one side of the distribution as shown in Fig. 13.8(b and c) for one-sided tests.

13.14 Summary of Confidence Intervals

The following summary provides the key approaches in the estimation of confidence intervals described above. The critical z-score and t-score can be found for the respective confidence levels using the z- and t-tables or the appropriate software programs.

13

13.14.1 Confidence Interval for the Mean on One Sample

Large Sample $n \geq 30$

For a large sample $n \geq 30$ and known standard deviation on the population σ, use z-score

$$\mu = \overline{x} \pm z_{\text{CR}} \frac{\sigma}{\sqrt{n}} \tag{13.92}$$

For a large sample $n \geq 30$ and unknown standard deviation on the population, use z-score with the standard deviation on the sample

$$\mu = \overline{x} \pm z_{\text{CR}} \frac{s}{\sqrt{n}} \tag{13.93}$$

Small Sample $n < 30$ and Unknown Distribution on Population

(a) For a small sample $n < 30$ or unknown distribution on the population, use t-score with the degree of freedom $df = n - 1$:

$$\mu = \overline{x} \pm t_{df} \frac{s}{\sqrt{n}} \tag{13.94}$$

13.14.2 Confidence Interval for the Difference of Means of Two Unpaired Samples

The difference of means of two independent populations can be estimated by the difference of means of two independent sample, one from each population, $\overline{X}$ and $\overline{Y}$. This sample is referred to as unpaired samples.

Large Samples $n_1 \geq 30$ and $n_2 \geq 30$ ($\min(n_1, n_2) \geq 30$)

For large samples $n_1 \geq 30$ and $n_2 \geq 30$, use either z-score

$$\mu_X - \mu_Y = \overline{x} - \overline{y} \pm z_{\text{CR}} S_P \sqrt{\frac{1}{n_1} + \frac{1}{n_2}} \tag{13.95}$$

where S_p is the pooled estimate of the common standard deviation

$$S_P = \sqrt{\frac{(n_1 - 1)s_1^2 + (n_2 - 1)s_2^2}{n_1 + n_2 - 2}} \tag{13.96}$$

Small Sample $n_1 < 30$ or $n_2 < 30$ ($\min(n_1, n_2) < 30$)

If at least one of the samples is small, i.e., $n_1 < 30$ or $n_2 < 30$, use t-score

$$\mu_X - \mu_Y = \overline{x} - \overline{y} \pm t_{\text{CR}} S_P \sqrt{\frac{1}{n_1} + \frac{1}{n_2}} \tag{13.97}$$

with the pooled estimate for the common standard deviation as in Eq. (13.94) and the degree of freedom $df = n_1 + n_2 - 2$.

13.14.3 Confidence Interval for the Difference of Means on Two Paired Samples

The difference of means of the same population under different conditions can be estimated by two samples measured on the same elements under different conditions from the population. Such samples are referred to as paired samples. Actually, it is one sample on population X with two sequential measurements X^{A}

and X^B under different conditions A and B. The difference is measured for each element in the sample and $\Delta x_k = x_k^A - x_k^B$. We denote the population of such differences as ΔX.

The problem of estimating the mean of differences ΔX on the population X actually converges to the problem of estimating the mean on a single sample of population ΔX.

Large Sample $n \geq 30$

For a large sample $n \geq 30$, use z-score

$$\mu_{\Delta X} = \overline{\Delta x} \pm z_{\text{CR}} \frac{s_{\Delta X}}{\sqrt{n}} \tag{13.98}$$

Small Sample $n < 30$

For a small sample $n < 30$, use t-score with the degree of freedom $df = n - 1$:

$$\mu_{\Delta X} = \overline{\Delta x} \pm t_{\text{CR}} \frac{s_{\Delta X}}{\sqrt{n}} \tag{13.99}$$

13.14.4 Confidence Interval for the Binomial Distribution

Large Sample $n * \min(\hat{p}, 1 - \hat{p}) > 5$

For large enough samples, i.e., $n * \min(\hat{p}, 1 - \hat{p}) > 5$, use z-score for the chosen confidence level $(1 - \alpha)$. The probability or the percentage content p can be estimated as

$$p = \hat{p} \pm z_{CR} \sqrt{\frac{\hat{p}(1 - \hat{p})}{n}} \tag{13.100}$$

13

Small Sample $n * \min(\hat{p}, 1 - \hat{p}) \leq 5$

If the sample is not big enough, i.e., $n * \min(\hat{p}, 1 - \hat{p}) \leq 5$, use t-score for the chosen confidence level $(1 - \alpha)$ and the degree of freedom $df = n - 1$. The probability or the percentage content p can be estimated as

$$p = \hat{p} \pm t_{df} \sqrt{\frac{\hat{p}(1 - \hat{p})}{n}} \tag{13.101}$$

13.14.5 Confidence Interval for Probability or Percentage Difference on Two Samples

Large Samples $n_1 * \min(\hat{p}_1, 1-\hat{p}_1) > 5$ and $n_2 * \min(\hat{p}_2, 1-\hat{p}_2) > 5$

For both large samples, i.e., when $n_1 * \min(\hat{p}_1, 1-\hat{p}_1) > 5$ and $n_2 * \min(\hat{p}_2, 1-\hat{p}_2) > 5$, the difference of the probabilities or percentage contents on two independent populations can be estimated using the *z*-score z_{CR} found for the chosen confidence level $(1-\alpha)$ as

$$p_1 - p_2 = \hat{p}_1 - \hat{p}_2 \pm z_{CR}\sqrt{\frac{\hat{p}_1(1-\hat{p}_1)}{n_1} + \frac{\hat{p}_2(1-\hat{p}_2)}{n_2}} \tag{13.102}$$

Small Sample $n_1 * \min(\hat{p}_1, 1-\hat{p}_1) \le 5$ or $n_2 * \min(\hat{p}_2, 1-\hat{p}_2) \le 5$

If at least one of the samples is small, i.e., $n_1 * \min(\hat{p}_1, 1-\hat{p}_1) \le 5$ or $n_2 * \min(\hat{p}_2, 1-\hat{p}_2) \le 5$, the difference of the probabilities or percentage contents on two independent populations is estimated using *t*-score t_{df} found for the chosen confidence level $(1-\alpha)$ and the degree of freedom $df = n_1 + n_2 - 2$ as

$$p_1 - p_2 = \hat{p}_1 - \hat{p}_2 \pm t_{df}\sqrt{\frac{\hat{p}_1(1-\hat{p}_1)}{n_1} + \frac{\hat{p}_2(1-\hat{p}_2)}{n_2}} \tag{13.103}$$

Questions for Self-Control for Chap. 13

1. What is a random sample?
2. How to find the mean on the population by the measured mean on a sample?
3. How are all random samples distributed?
4. How does the mean on a sample relate to the mean on the population?
5. How does central limit theorem help in finding the mean on the population?
6. Are the means on all possible samples distributed normally?
7. How do the means on all possible samples distributed for different samples sizes and different distribution on the original population?
8. How to estimate the mean on the population by the mean on a random sample?
9. What are the confidence level, the margin of error, and the confidence interval?
10. How to choose the confidence level?
11. How can the confidence level be calculated?
12. How to find the margin of error and the confidence interval?

13. What does the confidence interval mean?
14. What is z-score for the confidence interval?
15. How to calculate the confidence interval using the z-score?
16. What is the 1-sigma, 2-sigms, and 3-sigma rule for the confidence interval?
17. How can you interpret the confidence interval?
18. What is the t-distribution and why is it needed?
19. What is the degree of freedom for Student's t-distribution?
20. How to calculate the confidence interval using Student's t-distribution?
21. What does the term "unpaired" samples mean?
22. How to calculate the confidence interval for the difference of means on two independent samples?
23. What does the term "paired" samples mean?
24. How to calculate the confidence interval for the difference of means on two dependent samples?
25. How to calculate the confidence interval for binomial distribution?
26. How to calculate the confidence interval for the difference of means of probabilities or percentage contents for two samples with binomial distribution?
27. What does one-sided and two-sided distributions mean and why are they needed?

? Problems for Chap. 13

1. You want to find an average weight of apples in the huge supply of apples. A random sample of 100 apples measures the mean weight 150 grams on a sample and 20 grams on standard deviation. How do you solve the problem?
2. A random sample of 50 people shows the mean height of people equals to 170 cm with the standard deviation of 20 cm. What is the average height of people on the population with the confidence level of 90%?
3. The task is to find the average time people spend on physical exercises per week. The mean time on a random sample of 75 people is 7 hours per week with standard deviation of 3 days. The confidence level is 95%.
4. A random sample shows the mean equals to 25 and the standard deviation is seven, and you found that the confidence interval is 11 and 36. What was the confidence level?
5. You need to find the mean fuel consumption for the car model XYZ. It is known that the standard deviation for the fuel consumption is 2 miles/gallon. How big should the sample size be, if the confidence interval length should be no greater than 1 mile/gallon with the confidence level of 95%? The interval length is the difference between the upper and the lower borders of the interval.
6. A small sample of ten (n = 10) manufactured parts was collected form a large supply. The mean weight of the part on the sample $\overline{x} = 24$, and the standard deviation on the sample $s = 2$. What is the estimate of the mean weight of the part on the population, and what is the confidence interval with the confidence level of 90%?

13

7. The number of successful events in $n_G = 25$ is detected on a random sample of size $n = 100$. What is the estimate with the confidence level of 95% of the probability of the successful events on the respective population from which the sample was selected?
8. A random sample of size $n = 144$ was selected from the entire supply of parts. The ratio of defective parts over all parts on the sample is 0.20. What is the percentage content with the confidence level of 90% of defective parts in the whole supply of parts?
9. The percentage ratio of obese men on a random sample of men was 0.25, and the percentage ratio of obese women on a random sample of women was 0.18. Both samples had size $n_1 = n_2 = 100$. What is the percentage difference of the obese men and women in the population?

Statistical Hypothesis Testing

Contents

14.1 The Philosophy of Statistical Hypothesis Testing – 282
14.1.1 Hypothesis Formulation and Acceptance/Rejection Framework – 284
14.1.2 Hypothesis Testing Method – 284

14.2 The Null and Alternative Hypotheses – 288
14.2.1 Examples: The Null and Alternative Hypotheses – 288

14.3 Significance Level and *p*-Value – 288
14.3.1 Significance Level – 288
14.3.2 *p*-Value – 289

14.4 The Null Hypothesis Acceptance/Rejection Rule – 290
14.4.1 Examples: Acceptance or Rejection of the Null Hypothesis – 290

14.5 Two-Tailed and One-Tailed Tests – 292

14.6 Unpaired and Paired Tests – 293
14.6.1 The Null Hypothesis Is the Focus of the Test – 293

14.7 Critical Value – 294
14.7.1 Calculating Critical Values Using Distribution Tables – 295
14.7.2 Calculating Critical Values Using Software Algorithms – 295

S. K. Aityan, *Business Research Methodology*, Classroom Companion: Business,
https://doi.org/10.1007/978-3-030-76857-7_14

14.8 Conducting the z-Test – 295
14.8.1 Calculating *p*-Values Using the Standard Normal Distribution Table – 296
14.8.2 Calculating *p*-Values Using Software Algorithms – 297

14.9 The Student's *t*-Test – 300
14.9.1 *t*-Distribution and *t*-Test – 300
14.9.2 Unpaired and Paired Two-Sample *t*-Tests – 301

14.10 *t*-Test Technique and Degrees of Freedom – 301
14.10.1 One-Sample *t*-Test – 302
14.10.2 Independent (Unpaired) Two-Sample *t*-Test – 302
14.10.3 Dependent Two-Sample *t*-Test (Paired) – 304
14.10.4 Calculating *p*-Value for the Student's *t*-Test – 304

14.11 The Statistical Hypothesis Testing Process – 306
14.11.1 First Comes Research Question – 307
14.11.2 Formulate the Null Hypothesis (H_0) and the Alternative Hypothesis (H_1) – 308
14.11.3 Choose the Significance Level – 309
14.11.4 Decide About Two-Tailed or One-Tailed Test – 309
14.11.5 Select a Random Sample and Collect Data – 310
14.11.6 Decide About the Test Type – 310
14.11.7 Conduct the Test and Calculate *p*-Value for H_0 – 311
14.11.8 Reject or Accept H_0 by Comparing the *p*-Value Against the Significance Level – 311

14.12 Type I and Type II Errors – 312
14.12.1 False Positive and False Negative Judgments – 312
14.12.2 Type I Error – 313
14.12.3 Type II Error – 314
14.12.4 Relationship Between the Type I and Type II Errors – 315

14.13 Statistical Power vs. Significance of a Hypothesis Test – 317
14.13.1 Significance vs. Power – 317
14.13.2 Calculating the Statistical Power – 318
14.13.3 The Reasons to Analyze the Test Power – 318

14.1 The Philosophy of Statistical Hypothesis Testing

A hypothesis is a tentative answer to a research question, as we discussed in ► Sect. 1.7.2 in ► Chap. 1 of this book. One can also say that a hypothesis is an educated guess.

Statistical hypothesis testing is used for making a judgment on a statement made in a statistical hypothesis about a respective population based on a statistic collected on a sample in a survey, experiment, comparative analysis, impact from specified conditions, or any other related activities.

A hypothesis is a statement, which logical value can be True, False, or Unknown. The initial status of any hypothesis is Unknown, which later can be changed to True or False. The hypothesis status turns to True, if the hypothesis is accepted; turns to False, if the hypothesis is rejected; and stays Unknown otherwise. However, we must keep in mind that statistical hypothesis status True or False is not absolute but is a judgment subjected to the chosen significance level α (or a confidence level $CL = 1-\alpha$). The significance level shows the degree of doubt in the final judgment about the hypothesis, which we chose to use in our judgment. Thus, a hypothesis can be accepted, i.e., receive the status True at one chosen significance level, while under another significance level, the same hypothesis with the same supporting evidences may be rejected, i.e., assigned status False. You will figure out "why" and "how" it may happen after reading this chapter.

The following statements represent examples of statistical hypotheses:

- The mean height of trees in the park is 30 feet.
- The mean income in city A is higher than in city B.
- The mean daily output of the firm is greater than 50 units.
- The blood pressure is reduced after the treatment course.

A statistical hypothesis is accepted (its status becomes True), when there is not enough evidence to reject it. In the jurisprudence, we can refer this principle to the "presumption of innocence." A certain degree of doubt always stays with judgments on statistical hypotheses, and this doubt is reflected in the chosen significance level, which is known in jurisprudence as judging "beyond reasonable doubt." Nobody can ever say that a statistical hypothesis is proven True. There is always a doubt. If we have enough doubt, we reject the hypothesis, but if we don't, we accept it. Deterministic hypotheses can be considered an extreme case of statistical hypotheses with zero degree of doubt. It is a fundamentally important principle in statistical hypothesis testing – we first choose and assign the agreed level of reasonable doubt referred to as the significance level and then test the hypotheses to accept or reject it. Never test the hypothesis first and then adjust the significance level for a desired acceptance or rejection; it is fundamentally wrong.

> Statistical hypothesis status True or False is not absolute but is a judgment, subjected to the chosen significance level α (or a confidence level $CL = 1-\alpha$).

- First choose and assign the agreed level of reasonable doubt referred to as the significance level and then test the hypotheses to accept or reject it.
- Never test the hypothesis first and then adjust the significance level for a desired acceptance or rejection; it is fundamentally wrong.

To make a judgment about the mean value of a random variable on a population, we select a random sample from the population, measure the mean on the sample, and then make a judgment about the mean of the population based on the mean on the sample. We hope that the selected sample adequately represents the population; however, it is just a hope. As soon as the sample is randomly selected, the statistic measured on the sample can be very close to the mean on the population or, possibly, can be quite different from it. We will never know about it with full certainty. However, we may estimate the probability of getting a random sample, which has the mean close to or very different from the mean on the population. The central limit theorem comes to help us in this challenge.

Suppose $X = \{x_1, x_2, \ldots, x_k, \ldots\}$ a random variable on a population of with mean μ and standard deviation σ, and there is a variety of all possible samples of a given size, which can be built from population X. Each sample k for population X has its own mean value $\overline{x}_k$ which may vary from sample to sample because samples are formed from different elements of the population. Actually, the means on each of all possible samples form a population of means on all possible samples of the given size $\overline{X} = \{\overline{x}_1, \overline{x}_2 \ldots, \overline{x}_k, \ldots\}$. The population of all possible samples of a given size is referred to as the variety of all possible samples formed from the original population X. We use term "variety" for the population of all possible samples $\overline{X}$ not to get confused with the original population X and clearly distinguish between two populations – the original population X (the populations) and the population of all possible samples $\overline{X}$ (the variety). The random variable $\overline{X}$ on the variety of all possible samples has mean value $\mu_{\overline{X}}$ and standard deviation $\sigma_{\overline{X}}$.

The ***central limit theorem***, as discussed in the previous chapter, states that the sample means $\overline{X}$ on the variety of all possible samples of a given size, if consists of a sufficiently large samples, are approximately normally distributed with the mean $\mu_{\overline{X}} = \mu$ and standard deviation $\sigma_{\overline{X}} = \sigma / \sqrt{n}$, i.e.,

$$\mu_{\overline{X}} = \mu \quad \text{and} \quad \sigma_{\overline{X}} = \frac{\sigma}{\sqrt{n}} \tag{14.1}$$

where μ is the mean and σ is the standard deviation of the original population X and n is the sample size.

The normal distribution of the sample means $\overline{X}$ with the mean $\mu_{\overline{X}}$, which equals the mean μ of the original population X, is a bell-shape distribution with the majority of samples having their means $\overline{X} = \{\overline{x}_1, \overline{x}_2, \ldots, x_k, \ldots\}$ close to the mean of the variety (population) of all possible samples $\mu_{\overline{X}}$ and hence to the mean on the original population μ. However, some extreme samples may have their means quite far from the mean of variety (population) and $\bar{X}$ hence from the mean of the original population X.

The major point is that you will never know how adequately a sample you selected for testing the hypothesis represents the population. Statistical hypothesis testing philosophy is based on the following.

14.1.1 Hypothesis Formulation and Acceptance/Rejection Framework

- An educated guess is made about the relationship (greater, equal, or less) between the mean values of a population with a specified number or between the mean values on two populations.
- To make a judgment about this relationship, two hypotheses are formulated – the null hypothesis and the alternative hypothesis. The null hypothesis states that there is no difference between the mean value of the population and the specified number or between the means on two populations. The alternative hypothesis is the hypothesis, which will be accepted if the null hypothesis is rejected. The alternative hypothesis is not just the negation of the null hypothesis but reflects the initial guess about the relationship.
- The null hypothesis is tested with the collected statistic on a random sample. If enough evidence is collected to reject the null hypothesis, then the null hypothesis is rejected, and the alternative hypothesis is accepted. If there is not enough evidence to reject the null hypothesis, then the null hypothesis is accepted.

14.1.2 Hypothesis Testing Method

- You want to judge about the mean value on the population, but you can only measure the mean on a sample selected from the population.
- You do not know what kind of sample you selected for the test. It could be a plausible sample (from the majority of samples) with the mean value close to the mean of the population or an extreme sample from the outliers in the tails of the sampling distribution (of samples by their mean values) with the extreme mean value.
- You hope that the selected sample is a typical sample, but there is a chance that the sample is an extreme sample. Thus, you choose and assign a degree of doubt about your judgment based on a chance that the sample was selected from the extreme outliers, and hence, your judgment about the population based on the sample is wrong. This degree is defined by the significance level that reflects the probability α (alpha) of randomly getting the outlier samples. The significance level is chosen by the investigator based on the understanding of the consequences to be wrong in the judgment. It is not a calculatable parameter and should be chosen before the statistic (the data) is collected.

- You calculate the probability of a selected sample to be selected from the category of extreme samples from the sampling distribution outliers. Such a probability is referred to as the *p*-value.
- If the *p*-value is less than the chosen significance level α (alpha), *p*-value < α, it means that the selected sample is less probable than the level α you allowed yourselves for selecting extreme samples and hence, most likely, it belongs to the category of extreme samples. This provides enough evidence to reject the null hypothesis. Thus, you reject the null hypothesis and accept the alternative hypothesis.
- If the *p*-value is greater than the chosen significance level α (alpha), *p*-value > α, it means that the selected sample is more probable than the level α you allowed yourselves for selecting extreme samples and hence, most likely, it belongs to the category of plausible samples. This does not provide enough evidence to reject the null hypothesis. Thus, you accept the null hypothesis and reject the alternative hypothesis.

The *central limit theorem*, as discussed in the previous chapter, states that the sample means $\overline{X}$ on the variety of all possible samples of a given size, if consists of a sufficiently large samples, are approximately normally distributed with the mean $\mu_{\overline{X}} = \mu$ and standard deviation $\sigma_{\overline{X}} = \sigma / \sqrt{n}$, i.e.,

$$\mu_{\overline{X}} = \mu \quad \text{and} \quad \sigma_{\overline{X}} = \frac{\sigma}{\sqrt{n}}$$

where μ is the mean and σ is the standard deviation of the original population X and n is the sample size.

We will discuss statistical hypothesis testing in a greater detail step-by-step in this chapter. First, let's illustrate it in a simple example.

▶ Example 1: Flipping a Coin

A coin was flipped 20 times, and 14 times landed heads up and 6 times tails up. We would expect the number of flips with heads and tails would be approximately the same, but we had 14:6 heads to tails. A legitimate question arises – Is the coin good or loaded?

Let's presume that the coin was good and 14 heads and 6 tails occurred just by chance as one of the random occasions. Each flip of a coin is an event that randomly results in the heads or tails. Thus, anything may happen. The result of 20 flips of the coins is one of the possible samples that could occur in 20 random flips of the coin. The result obtained on actual sample, which we have, looks quite unusual or extreme.

Our main hypothesis, let's call it the null hypothesis, H_0, is "The coin is good." This means that the coin has equal probabilities of landing on the heads and on the tails. If we accept the null hypothesis, then we consider the coin is good and the 14-6 heads to tails result occurred just occasionally. If we reject the null hypothesis, we accept the alternative hypothesis, called H_1 (or H_A), that states "The coin is loaded." This means that the coin has unequal probabilities of landing on the heads and on the tails.

As soon as random events may end up with any results and 20 flips of a coin, even if the coin is good, may end up with any number $k < 20$ of landing heads up and $20 - k$ of tails up, we would like to choose and assign the degree of doubt we may have in the final judgment about the null hypothesis. Suppose we assigned the significance level (alpha) $\alpha = 0.05$ (confidence level $CL = 1 - \alpha = 0.95$ or 95%). The significance level indicates the maximum probability we allow to the extreme samples, like our actual sample, and the more extreme samples, to occur just randomly if by our judgment the coin is considered good, i.e., to be occasionally extreme and to belong to the tails of the distribution of all possible samples. This represents our chosen degree of doubt in our final judgment. Please read two previous sentences about the meaning of the significance level one more time and think about it before proceeding further.

Once we have the null, H_0, and the alternative, H_1, hypotheses formulated, and the degree of doubt in the final judgment (significance level alpha) chosen, we may test the null hypothesis.

A coin lands heads up or tails up randomly with probability P_{Heads} and P_{Tails}, respectively, where $P_{\text{Tails}} = 1 - P_{\text{Heads}}$ because no other events are possible. A combination of k heads and $(n - k)$ tails out of n flips of the coin has the probability $P_{\text{Heads}}(n, k)$ calculated as

$$P_{\text{Heads}}(n,k) = \binom{n}{k} P_{\text{Heads}}^{k} P_{\text{Heads}}^{n-k} = \frac{n!}{k!(n-k)!} P_{\text{Heads}}^{k} P_{\text{Heads}}^{n-k} \tag{14.2}$$

Such a distribution is called a ***binomial distribution***. If the coin is good, then the probabilities of heads and tails are the same and equal $P_{\text{Heads}} = P_{\text{Tails}} = 1/2$. The probability of occasionally having an extreme sample with the 14 or more heads out of 20 flips is

$$\begin{aligned} P_{\text{Heads}}(20, k \geq 14) &= \sum_{k=14}^{20} P_{\text{Heads}}(20, k) = \left(\frac{1}{2}\right)^{20} \sum_{k=14}^{20} \binom{20}{k} = \\ &= \left(\frac{1}{2}\right)^{20} \left(\binom{20}{14} + \binom{20}{15} + \binom{20}{16} + \binom{20}{17} + \binom{20}{18} + \binom{20}{19} + \binom{20}{20} \right) = 0.058 \end{aligned} \tag{14.3}$$

The probability of k heads is equal to the probability of k tails in n coin flips. Just a reminder, $\binom{n}{k} = \binom{n}{n-k}$. Thus,

14

$$P_{\text{Tails}}(20, k \geq 14) = P_{\text{Heads}}(20, k \leq 6) = P_{\text{Heads}}(20, k \geq 14) = 0.058 \tag{14.4}$$

The total probability of a sample to have 14 or more heads or tails out of total 20 flips of a coin is equal to

$$\begin{aligned} &P_{\text{Tail}}(20, k \geq 14) + P_{\text{Head}}(20, k \geq 14) = \\ &= P_{\text{Head}}(20, k \leq 6) + P_{\text{Head}}(20, k \geq 14) = 0.058 + 0.058 = 0.115 \end{aligned} \tag{14.5}$$

because having more than 14 tails out of 20 flips of a coin is identical to having less than 6 heads. ◀

There is no typo in the last decimal of the sum in Eq. (14.5) because the result is rounded to three decimal figures. A probability of randomly having a sample which we consider extreme is called *p*-value. The *p*-value = 0.115 in our case. The *p*-value provides the probability of the actual and all other similar and more extreme samples to occur occasionally with a fair (good) coin.

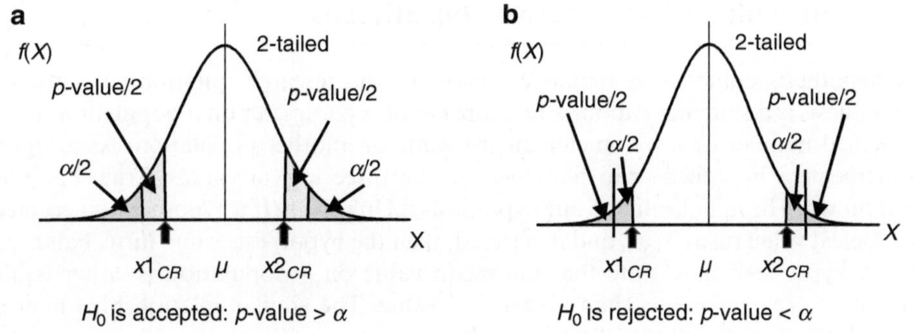

Fig. 14.1 Significance level α and p-value for a symmetric two-tailed distribution. **a** H_0 is accepted: p-value > α; and **b** H_0 is rejected: p-value < α

If the calculated p-value < α (alpha), it means that the actual sample belongs to the category of implausibly extreme samples (distribution tails or outliers) as illustrated in Fig. 14.1(b), because the probability of having such a sample occasionally, if the null hypothesis is true, is less than the accepted level of reasonable doubt we assigned by choosing the significance level α (alpha). The probability of randomly selecting a sample from the category of the implausibly extreme samples is defined by the chosen significance level. Thus, if p-value < α (alpha), the occasionally occurred extreme sample most likely belongs to the tail of the distribution, it is from the extreme outlier, and we have collected enough evidence to reject the null hypothesis. If we reject a null hypothesis, we accept the alternative hypothesis.

If the calculated p-value > α (alpha), it means that the probability of our sample to occur (p-value) is higher than the criteria for the implausible samples established by the chosen significance level α (alpha). According to the criteria, the actual sample, most likely, does not belong to the category of implausibly extreme samples (see Fig. 14.1a), and we do not have enough evidence to consider this sample to be an extreme sample. Thus, we accept the null hypothesis.

In our case, p-value = 0.115 and $\alpha = 0.05$; hence, p-value > α (alpha). The actual sample, most likely, is not an extreme sample within the chosen significance level, and there is not enough evidence to reject the null hypothesis. Thus, we accept the null hypothesis H_0 and consider the coin is good. However, there is a chance, assigned by the significance level $\alpha = 0.05$ that we completely wrong in our judgment and the coin is not good but loaded.

Statistical hypothesis status True or False is not absolute but is a judgment, subjected to the chosen significance level α (or a confidence level $CL = 1-\alpha$).

- First choose and assign the agreed level of reasonable doubt referred to as the significance level and then test the hypotheses to accept or reject it.
- Never test the hypothesis first and then adjust the significance level for a desired acceptance or rejection; it is fundamentally wrong.

14.2 The Null and Alternative Hypotheses

A hypothesis comes as a tentative answer to the research question. A statistical hypothesis is a statement about a relationship of a parameter on a population with a specified number or a parameter on the same or another population. As a logical statement, a hypothesis can have one of the three logical values: True, False, or Unknown. The initial value of any hypothesis is Unknown. If a hypothesis is accepted, its logical value turns True, and if rejected, then the hypothesis value turns False.

A hypothesis may state that the mean value on a population is either equal, unequal, greater, or less than a specified value. The similar relationships may be stated between the means of two populations.

Actually, two hypotheses are formulated: the null hypothesis and the alternative hypothesis. The ***null hypothesis*** H_0 states that there is no significant relationship between the mean on one population and on different populations as claimed in the research question.

The ***alternative hypothesis*** H_1 states the difference phrased in the research question. The alternative hypothesis is not just a negation of the null hypothesis but reflects the sense of the research question. The alternative hypothesis will be accepted if the null hypothesis is rejected in the test.

14.2.1 Examples: The Null and Alternative Hypotheses

- Problem 1: We are interested whether the students' GPA (average grade) is the same at two schools A and B.
  - H_0: Both schools, A and B, have the same average GPA, $\mu_A = \mu_B$.
  - H_1: Schools A and B have different average GPA, $\mu_A \neq \mu_B$.
- Problem 2: We anticipate that students at school A have a higher GPA than students at school B.
  - H_0: Both schools, A and B, have the same average GPA, $\mu_A = \mu_B$.
  - H_1: Students at school A have a higher GPA than students at school B, $\mu_A > \mu_B$.
- Problem 3: We wonder whether the average GPA in the Spring semester is less than the average GPA in the Fall semester.
  - H_0: The average GPA in the Spring and Fall semesters are the same, $\mu_S = \mu_F$.
  - H_1: The average GPA in the Spring semester is less than the average GPA in the Fall semester, $\mu_S < \mu_F$.

14.3 Significance Level and *p*-Value

14.3.1 Significance Level

The ***significance level***, denoted as α (alpha), is the probability chosen by the investigator for a random sample to belong to the category of the extreme samples. This reflects a degree of doubt of being wrong in the judgment about the null hypothesis. The significance level should be chosen by the investigator prior to looking into the data and conducting the hypothesis test. This level is selected from the sense of the real-world problem, conditions, and possible consequences of being wrong in the judgment. Similar to the selection of the confidence level, CL, the choice of the significance level α (alpha) reflects the troubles of being wrong with the judgment about the hypothesis. The significance level and the confidence level are related as

$$CL = 1 - \alpha \qquad (14.6)$$

It means that if the significance level $\alpha = 0.05$, then the confidence level is chosen CL = 1 – 0.95 or 95%, and vice versa. If we select the confidence level 0.9 or 90%, the significance level $\alpha = 0.1$.

The significance level is the threshold probability criteria set up by the investigator to consider a random sample to belong to the category of the extreme samples.

Remember! The significance level is not a calculatable value. It is chosen by the investigator from business and other real-world perspectives before the data on a sample is collected and analyzed. It is the degree of tolerance for being mistaken in the judgment.

Examples: Choosing the Significance Level

- Problem 1: We are curious whether trees in our park are taller than 60 feet.
- The significance level for this problem can be chosen 20%, i.e., $\alpha = 0.2$, because nothing serious will happen if I am wrong in my judgment.
- Problem 2: We are interested in the recovery rate resulted from the treatment with medication A versus medication B.
- The significance level for this problem can be chosen 1%, i.e., $\alpha = 0.01$, because being wrong in judgment may compromise human lives.

14.3.2 p-Value

The ***p-value*** is the probability for a random sample to be selected from the category of extreme samples that provide enough evidence for rejecting the null hypothesis. This probability is assessed from the variety of all possible samples $\bar{X}$.

In contrast to the significance level α, which is chosen by the investigator, as the judgment tolerance criteria for the sample to belong to the category of extreme samples, the *p*-value is a calculated value, which is used for the comparison with the chosen tolerance expressed with the significance level to make the judgment "beyond reasonable doubt."

The *p*-value for a sample can be calculated using the distribution of the sample means on the variety of all possible samples $\bar{X}$.

Examples: Calculating the *p*-Value

- Problem 1: We wonder whether the coin is fair or loaded if there were 14 heads from 20 flips. We solved this problem in the beginning of this chapter.

The p-value for the coin flipping problem was calculated as the probability of randomly selecting a group of samples with 14 and more heads or tails out of 20 coin tosses as shown in Eq. (14.5).

- Problem 2: We are interested in the recovery rate resulted from the treatment with medication A versus medication B.

  We calculate the p-value using real-world data and the normal distribution.

14.4 The Null Hypothesis Acceptance/Rejection Rule

If the p-value is less than the significance level, i.e., p-value $< \alpha$, it means that the sample fits well in the category of extreme samples defined by the significance level (the tolerance threshold). Fitting well implies that the selected sample, most likely, belongs to the category of extreme samples, according to the tolerance threshold defined by the investigator with the chosen significance level. The hypothesis test is considered statistically significant to provide enough evidence for rejecting the null hypothesis, then the null hypothesis is rejected, and the alternative hypothesis is accepted.

If the p-value calculated for the sample exceeds the significant level, i.e., p-value $> \alpha$, it means that the probability of occasionally getting such a sample is higher than the threshold probability α (alpha) defined by the investigator. Such a sample is not extreme enough and, most likely, can be considered occurred occasionally with the precepts of the null hypothesis. Thus, the sample does not provide enough evidence to reject the null hypothesis, the hypothesis test is considered statistically insignificant, and hence, the null hypothesis is accepted.

However, we may be completely mistaken with our judgment. The judgment was made "beyond reasonable doubt," but there is a chance measured with significance level that the judgment was wrong.

14

14.4.1 Examples: Acceptance or Rejection of the Null Hypothesis

- Problem 1: We wonder whether the coin is fair or loaded with significance level $\alpha = 0.05$ if there were 14 heads from 20 flips. We solved this problem in the beginning of this chapter.

  The null hypothesis H_0: The coin is fair, i.e., $\mu_H = \mu_T$.

  The alternative hypothesis H_1: The coin is loaded, i.e., $\mu_H > \mu_T$.

  The p-value for the coin flipping problem was calculated as the probability of randomly selecting a group of samples with 14 and more heads or tails out of 20 coin tosses as shown in Eq. (14.5).

  The calculated p-value = 0.115 (Eq. 14.5) is greater than the chosen significance level $\alpha = 0.05$; thus, sample with 14-6 heads and tails, most likely, occasionally occurred with the fair coin.

- Problem 2: We are interested whether with the significance level $\alpha = 0.01$, the recovery rates resulted from the treatment with medication A higher than with medication B.

  The null hypothesis H_0: Both medication result in the same recovery rate, $\mu_A - \mu_B = 0$.

  The alternative hypothesis H_1: The recovery rates resulted from the treatment with medication A higher than with medication B, $\mu_A - \mu_B > 0$.

  The *p*-value for the difference of the mean recovery rates equals 0.008.

  As *p*-value < α, the null hypothesis is rejected and the alternative hypothesis is accepted.

A null hypothesis is rejected if there is enough evidence to reject it; otherwise, the null hypothesis is accepted.

A null hypothesis is accepted if there is not enough evidence to reject it.

The *significance level*, denoted as α (alpha), is the probability chosen by the investigator for a random sample to belong to the category of the extreme samples. This reflects a degree of doubt of being wrong in the judgment about the null hypothesis.

The *p-value* is the probability for a random sample to be selected from the category of extreme samples that provide enough evidence for rejecting the null hypothesis. This probability is assessed from the variety of all possible samples $\bar{X}$.

In contrast to the *significance level* α, which is chosen by the investigator, as the judgment tolerance criteria for the sample to belong to the category of extreme samples, the *p-value* is a calculated value, which is used for the comparison with the chosen tolerance expressed with the significance level to make the judgment "beyond reasonable doubt."

If *p-value* > α, the null hypothesis is accepted and the alternative hypothesis is rejected.

If *p-value* < α, the null hypothesis is rejected and the alternative hypothesis is accepted.

14.5 Two-Tailed and One-Tailed Tests

In the assessment of extreme samples or outliers in the sampling distribution tails for hypothesis testing, we may use both tails or just one tail in the distribution depending on the testing assumption about the meaning of the tails of the distribution. This is illustrated in ◘ Fig. 14.1 for the two-tailed test for a symmetric variations of the mean, in ◘ Fig. 14.2 for the one-tailed right test, and in ◘ Fig. 14.3 for the one-tailed left test.

The two-tailed and the left or right one-tailed tests are chosen by the meaning of the test and mostly by the sense of the alternative hypothesis. If the alternative hypothesis makes a symmetric claim possible on the both tails of the distribution, as in our example with tossing a coin, then it is natural to use a two-tailed test because extreme samples may occur on the both sides of the distribution as shown in ◘ Fig. 14.1.

On the other hand, if the alternative hypothesis claims that a population parameter is greater or lower than a certain value, then the variations on the opposite tail of the distribution would not impact on the judgment; thus, it would be reasonable to use the appropriate one-tailed test as shown in ◘ Figs. 14.2 and 14.3.

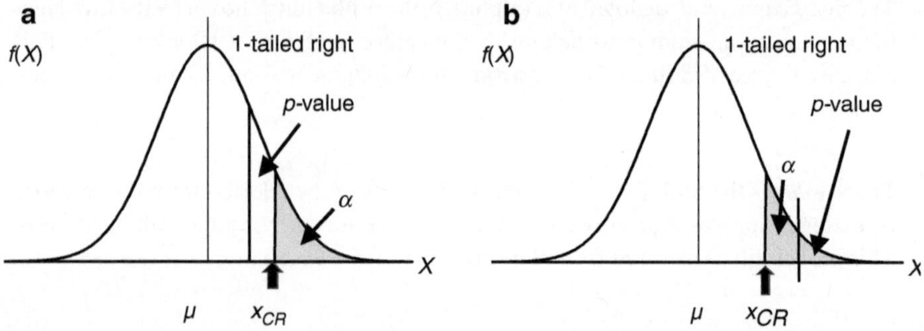

◘ **Fig. 14.2** Significance level α and p-value for a one-tailed right distribution. **a** H_0 is accepted: p-value $> \alpha$; and **b** H_0 is rejected: p-value $< \alpha$

14

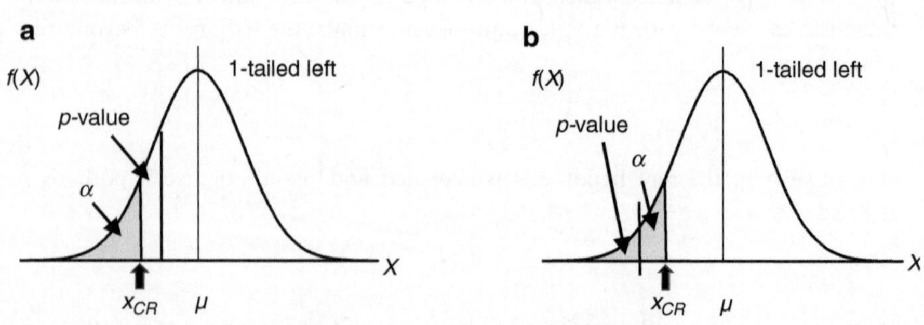

◘ **Fig. 14.3** Significance level α and p-value for a one-tailed left distribution. **a** H_0 is accepted: p-value $> \alpha$; and **b** H_0 is rejected: p-value $< \alpha$

As is evident from ◻ Fig. 14.1, in the case of a two-tailed test, significance level, α, and p-value are shared between two tails. On the other hand, in the case of a one-tailed test, significance, α, and p-value are fully applied on the appropriate tail of the distribution as is illustrated in ◻ Figs. 14.2 and 14.3.

14.6 Unpaired and Paired Tests

14.6.1 The Null Hypothesis Is the Focus of the Test

The null hypothesis is the main hypothesis to test for the acceptance or rejection. The alternative hypothesis is formulated proceeding from the understanding of the problem domain and is accepted without testing if the null hypothesis is rejected. Thus, the entire hypothesis testing process is focused on the null hypothesis.

Most Frequent Types of Problems and Hypotheses

As was discussed above, statistical hypotheses are dealing with the comparison of the mean value on the population with a specified number or the comparison on the mean values in two populations. The most frequent problems and the respective null hypothesis for them are:

- Problem 1: Can we believe that the mean value of the random variable on the population is equal to a specified value μ if the mean value on a selected sample is $\overline{x}$?

  H_0: The mean value on the population equals μ.

  H_1: The mean value on the population is not equal to, greater than, and less than μ for the two-tailed, one-tailed right, and two-tailed left test, respectively.
- Problem 2: Are the means of two random variables in two or one sample equal if their respective mean values on the sample(s) equal $\overline{x}_1$ and $\overline{x}_2$?

  H_0: The mean values of two random variables on one population (paired) or two populations (unpaired) are equal.

  H_1: *The* mean value of one random variable is not equal to, greater than, and less than the mean value of another random variable on the population(s) for the two-tailed, one-tailed right, and two-tailed left test, respectively.

Unpaired and Paired Samples

Statistical tests that involve two random variables are measured on two samples if two independently different populations are compared or on one sample if the variables are measured on the same elements of the population subject to certain conditions. The two random variable tests can be, respectively, characterized as ***unpaired*** or ***paired***.

The ***unpaired*** two-sample test (also known as ***independent*** two-sample test) is conducted to test the null hypothesis that states that the populations represented by two independent random variables in two different samples have equal mean values. It can be also interpreted as a test to identify whether the samples belong to the same population.

The ***paired*** two-sample test is conducted on a sample of matched pairs of similar units or one group of units that has been tested twice (a "repeated measures" test) under different conditions. The problem is to find out if those conditions have changed the mean value. For example, the null hypothesis claims that there are no changes of the means caused by those different conditions.

Examples of Unpaired and Paired Tests

- Problem 1: Mobile phone daily usage time

  Comparison of the mean daily usage time of mobile phones conducted for retired seniors and active students is an unpaired test.

  Comparison of the mean daily usage time of *mobile* phones for the same working students when they are at work or at school is a paired test because daily usage is measured on the same elements (students) under different conditions.
- Problem 2: Comparison of car gas mileage

  Comparison of the mean car gas mileage in the far north and in the deserts is an unpaired test.

  Comparison of the mean car gas mileage in the far north and in the deserts is an unpaired test conducted on two different and independent samples.
- Problem 3: Comparison of car gas mileage

  Impact of regular car service on the mean car gas mileage.

  Comparison of the mean car gas mileage conducted on the same cars before and after car service, and therefore it is a paired test.
- Problem 4: Company's profit margin

  Comparison of the monthly profit margin for two branches of the company is an unpaired test.

  Comparison of the company's monthly profit margins conducted on two different and independent population using two samples is an unpaired test.

14.7 Critical Value

14

The ***critical value*** is the value of the random variable, which separates the part of the distribution that contains plausible samples from the extreme samples according to the chosen significance level.

In the two-tailed test, there are two critical values x_{1CR} and x_{2CR} as shown in ◘ Fig. 14.1. For symmetrical distributions like a normal distribution, a binomial distribution with equal probabilities, and other symmetrical distributions, the critical values for a two-tailed test are equidistant from the mean value of the random variable. For this reason, if the mean of the random variable is known, then it is sufficient to find one critical value. The second one will be just symmetric from the mean. For a symmetrical distribution with the zero mean value, like the standard normal distribution, *t*-distribution, or a binomial distribution with the both probabilities equal 1/2, both critical values are numerically the same, but have the opposite signs, i.e., $x_{1CR} = -x_{2CR}$. For the one-tailed test, there is a single critical value.

The critical value can be found by calculating the value of the random variable for which the area under the distribution curve in the tail(s) starting from that value is equal to the significance level. It means that all samples starting from the critical value toward the tail(s) belong to the outliers or the extreme samples. For normal distribution, *z*-distribution, and *t*-distribution, critical values can be calculated by using either the appropriate precalculated distribution tables or computer algorithms.

14.7.1 Calculating Critical Values Using Distribution Tables

To use the standard normal distribution table, the original distribution $X \sim N(\mu,\sigma^2)$ should be first transformed to the standard normal distribution $Z \sim N(0,1)$ by using the transformation in ► Eqs. (11.16) and (14.7) or to the Student's t-distribution using the transformation in ► Eqs. (13.31) and (14.10). Then, the matching *z*- or *t*-value corresponding to the respective significance level alpha can be found by using the appropriate tables (the tables are available in Appendices A and B).

Keep in mind that the null hypotheses claim that there is no difference in the compared parameters. Thus, the mean value for such a claim on the distribution is zero.

14.7.2 Calculating Critical Values Using Software Algorithms

Function NORM.INV in the MS Excel and OpenOffice Calc returns the critical value for a specified significance level in the normal cumulative distribution with the specified mean and variance. There is no need for the transformation of the normal distribution to the standard normal distribution $X \rightarrow Z$ if you use this function because the algorithms return critical value for a normal distribution with any mean and variance.

Function NORM.S.INV in the MS Excel and OpenOffice Calc returns the inverse of the standard normal cumulative distribution. The distribution has a mean of 0 and a standard deviation of 1.

Function T.INV returns the left-tailed inverse of the Student's t-distribution, and function T.INV.2T returns the two-tailed inverse of the Student's *t*-distribution.

14.8 Conducting the *z*-Test

The *p*-value and critical value can be calculated by using the sampling distribution, which is the distribution of the mean values in the variety of all possible samples $\bar{X}$ of a specified size. According to the central limit theorem, if the original population X is distributed normally with the mean μ and variance σ^2, i.e., $X \sim N(\mu, \sigma^2)$, then the sampling distribution $\bar{X}$ is normal too with the mean μ and variance σ^2/n. where n is the sample size, $\bar{X} \sim N\left(\mu,\sigma^2/n\right)$. If the distribution in the original population X is unknown but samples are sufficiently large ($n \geq 30$), then the sam-

Table 14.1 Dependence of sampling distribution on the population distribution and a sample size

		Sample size, n	
		$n < 30$	$n \geq 30$
		Sampling distribution	
Population distribution	Normal	Normal $\bar{X} \sim N\left(\mu, \frac{\sigma^2}{n}\right)$	
	Unknown	Unknown	Normal $\bar{X} \sim N\left(\mu, \frac{\sigma^2}{n}\right)$

pling distribution is approximately normal too, $\bar{X} \sim N\left(\mu, \sigma^2 / n\right)$. This result is summarized in Table 14.1. The sample size $n = 30$ is not a "magic number," but just a reflection of a trend. The larger the samples, the closer the sampling distribution to the normal distribution.

We duplicated this table from the previous chapter because of its importance. Thus, if the original population X is distributed normally or if a sample size equals or exceeds 30, we can use the normal distribution for the sample means $\bar{X}$ with the mean equal the mean of the original population X and the variance equal the variance on the original population X divided by the square root of the sample size.

14.8.1 Calculating *p*-Values Using the Standard Normal Distribution Table

14

Suppose the original population X is distributed normally or the sample size is greater or equal 30; then we can assume a normal distribution in the variety (population) of all possible samples with the same size as our sample. The *p*-value for the normally distributed samples can be calculated by using the cumulative standard normal distribution table (see Appendix A).

To do it, first, we have to apply the transformation from the normal distribution $X \sim N(\mu, \sigma^2)$ to the standard normal distribution $Z \sim N(0,1)$ as defined in ▶ Eq. (11.16),

$$Z = \frac{X - \mu}{\sigma} \tag{14.7}$$

to transfer the mean value on the sample, $\bar{x}$, to the respective $\bar{z}$,

$$\bar{z} = \frac{\bar{x} - \mu}{\sigma} \qquad (14.8)$$

which is referred to as the *z*-score for $\bar{x}$. Then using the z-score, we can find the respective *p*-value using the cumulative standard normal distribution table.

Do not worry about the unknown μ in Eq. (14.8). If the null hypothesis is about matching the mean value of *X* with a specified value μ, then in the null hypothesis, $\bar{x} - \mu = 0$. If the null hypothesis claims that the mean values of two populations are equal, then do not worry too because the difference of these two mean values equals zero and they will cancel each other in Eq. (14.8).

Another parameter in Eq. (14.8) is the standard deviation for variable *X*.

Figure 14.4 illustrates z-scores for different standard deviations for the mean of normally distributed random variable *X*, the percentage portions of the total area under the distribution curve by interval, and the respective cumulative probabilities.

Most likely, we do not know the standard deviation of the original population σ either, but we can estimate it by the standard deviation calculated on the sample *s*.

14.8.2 Calculating *p*-Values Using Software Algorithms

The *p*-value can be calculated directly for the normal distribution with the zero mean value, and any variance $X \sim N(0,\sigma^2)$ by using function Z.TEST in the MS Excel and OpenOffice Calc can be used for hypothesis testing. Function Z.TEST returns the one-tailed *p*-value for a given *z* on the sample. The input parameters are the array that represents a sample; the value of *z*, for which the *p*-value is calculated; and the standard deviation.

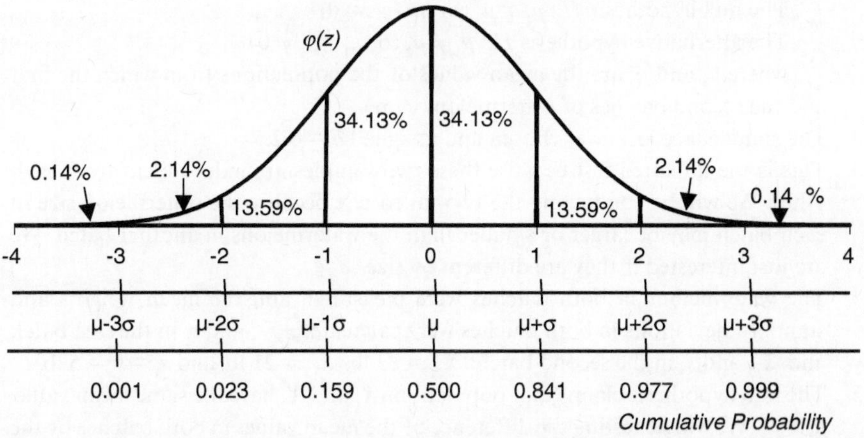

Fig. 14.4 z-score, percent of the total area by interval, and cumulative probability under a normal distribution function

Another function, NORM.DIST, returns the cumulative probability for value x of a normally distributed variable, the mean value, and the standard deviation for the normally distributed variable. With the zero mean value, what is typically occurred in the null hypothesis, the p-value for a negative x is equal to the cumulative probability, returned by the function, while the p-value for a positive x is equal to 1 minus the value returned by the function.

Function NORM.S.DIST returns the cumulative probability for value z for the standard normal distribution similar to NORM.DIST. The p-value for a negative z is equal to the cumulative probability, returned by the function, while the p-value for a positive x is equal to 1 minus the value returned by the function.

Thus, if you have the measurements on a sample as an array, it would be convenient to use Z.TEST. On the other hand, if you have the mean (which is normally equals zero for the null hypotheses) and standard deviation, then it is convenient to use NORM.DIST or NORM.S.DIST.

▶ Example 2: Comparison of Two Large Equal-Size Batches of Watermelons

Two grocery stores received two batches of watermelons from the same supplier. Each store received 100 watermelons. The watermelons received by the first store and the watermelons received by the second store look different in sizes. The supplier says that both batches came from the same farm without any selection by size and the difference in watermelon sizes in two batches is just occasional. The store managers are doubting this.

To solve the problem, two hypotheses were formulated: the null hypothesis and the alternative hypothesis. The null hypothesis claims that both batches came from the same farm, i.e., the mean values of the populations, from where the watermelons came, are the same. The alternative hypothesis says that the mean values of the populations are different. The null hypothesis is tested in the following steps.

1. Formally, the hypothesis are:

   The null hypothesis H_0: $\mu_1 = \mu_2$ (or $\mu_1 - \mu_2 = 0$)

   The alternative hypothesis H_1: $\mu_1 \neq \mu_2$ (or $\mu_1 - \mu_2 \neq 0$)

   where μ_1 and μ_2 are the mean values of the populations from which the first and the second batches of watermelons came.

14

2. The significance level was chosen and assigned $\alpha = 0.2$.
3. This is the unpaired test because these two samples are independent from each other. We will be conducting the two-tailed test because the watermelon size in each batch may be larger or smaller than the watermelons in another batch. We are just interested if they are different by size.
4. The watermelons in both batches were measured, and the mean weights and standard deviations in both batches were calculated, $\overline{x}_1$ and s_1 in the first batch and $\overline{x}_2$ and s_2 in the second batch: $\overline{x}_1 = 23$ lb, $\overline{x}_2 = 21$ lb, and $s_l = s_2 = 5$ lb.
5. The null hypothesis claims that populations X_1 and X_2 have the same mean value, $\mu_1 = \mu_2$. We will be testing the difference of the mean values in both batches by the difference of means in two samples, which is $\overline{x}_1 - \overline{x}_2 = 2$ lb. The null hypothesis claims that the difference of the mean values on the respective populations equals zero, $\mu_1 - \mu_2 = 0$.

6. We assume that the watermelons are normally distributed by size. Also, our samples are large, $n_1 = n_2 = n = 100$. According to ◘ Table 14.1, we believe that the sampling distribution is normal with the standard deviation $\sigma_{\overline{X}} = s_1 / \sqrt{n} = 5/10 = 0.5$ lb.
7. The sample sizes are big, $n = 100 > 30$, so we will conduct the z-test. The z-score for the null hypothesis is $z = (\bar{x}_1 - \bar{x}_2)/\sigma_{\overline{X}} = 2/0.5 = 4$.
8. Using the cumulative standard normal distribution table, we found the *p*-value for the difference of the mean values on two samples. The *p*-value = 0.00003. We may also find the *p*-value by using MS Excel or OO Calc function NORM.DIST as the cumulative probability for the difference of two means on the two samples directly from the collected statistic without transforming it to the *z*-score. We can also use the same function NORM.DIST for the z-score. The result will be the same.
9. As soon as we chose the two-tailed test, each tail of the distribution comprises a half of the assigned significance level, i.e., $\alpha/2 = 0.1$. The comparison of the calculated *p*-value with the significance level for each tail shows that the *p*-value < $\alpha/2$; *hence, the test was significant. Thus, there was enough evidence to reject the null hypothesis, so we reject it. We can conclude with the significance α = 0.02 (or 20%) that the supplier was not truthful claiming that both batches of watermelons came from the same farm. The actual difference in sizes in two batches did not happen occasionally.*

It is important to emphasize one more time that this judgment was made with the significance level 0.02. It means that we still may be wrong in our judgment about the truthfulness of the supplier. ◀

▶ Example 3: Comparison of Two Small Equal-Size Batches of Watermelons

Let's modify the previous problem discussed above in ▶ Example 2. We keep all parameters the same as in ▶ Example 2 except the size of the batches. Each store received ten watermelons, i.e., $n = 10$. The null and alternative hypotheses stay the same as in the previous example; the significance level is the same, $\alpha = 0.2$; and the statistic on the samples is the same, i.e., $\bar{x}_1 = 23$ lb, $\bar{x}_2 = 21$ lb, and $s_1 = s_2 = 5$ lb.

Will the results of the hypothesis testing now be the same as in the previous example?

Steps 1 through 5 are identical to the matching steps in the previous example, so we start with step 6.

1. We assume that the watermelons are normally distributed by size. Our samples are small, $n_1 = n_2 = n = 10$, which is less than 30. According to ◘ Table 14.1, we may still believe that the sampling distribution is normal, though the sample size is less than 30, because we believe that the distribution on the original population is normal with the standard deviation $\sigma_{\overline{X}} = s_1 / \sqrt{n} = 5/\sqrt{10} = 5/3.162 = 1.581$ lb. It is evident that the standard deviation of the sampling distribution in this case, $\sigma_{\overline{X}}$ = 1.581 lb, is much higher than in the previous example, where it was $\sigma_{\overline{X}} = 0.5$ lb.
2. We will conduct the z-test based on the normal distribution in the original population *X*, similar to the previous example. The z-score for the null hypothesis is
   z-score = $(\bar{x}_1 - \bar{x}_2)/\sigma$ = 2 lb/1.581 lb = 1.265.
3. Using the cumulative standard normal distribution table, we found the *p*-value, *p*-value = 0.103.

   As soon as we chose the two-tailed test, each tail of the distribution comprises a half of the assigned significance level, i.e., $\alpha/2 = 0.1$. The comparison of the calculated p-value with the significance level for each tail results in p-value > $\alpha/2$, and the test was insignificant. Thus, there is not enough evidence to reject the null hypothesis, so we accept it. With the significance $\alpha = 0.02$ (or 20%), we can conclude that the supplier was right saying that both batches of the watermelons came from the same farm or at least from the farms with equal average sizes of the watermelons. The actual difference in sizes in two batches has occurred occasionally. ◀

These two examples clearly demonstrate that with the smaller samples, the z-test was statistically insignificant, while with the larger samples, the z-test was statistically significant. What has caused this difference in the test results?

The explanation is in the standard deviation for the sampling distribution. As we discussed earlier in this chapter, sampling distribution is the distribution of the means in the variety of all possible samples. The sampling distribution becomes narrower as the sample size increases. Consequently, the p-values are different for the different sample sizes. The larger the samples, the narrower the sampling distribution, and the higher the p-value for the same statistic.

14.9 The Student's *t*-Test

We are not always sure that the distribution in the population is normal, we not always can have large samples with $n \geq 30$, and we not always can reasonably judge about the standard deviation on the population. How can we test the null hypothesis, if the situation does not look advantageous for assuming the normal distribution for the variety of all possible samples?

14.9.1 *t*-Distribution and *t*-Test

14

The ***Student's t-test*** was named after statistician William Sealy Gosset, who published his paper under the pseudonym "Student." The t-test is a statistical hypothesis test, in which the test statistic follows t-distribution. The ***t-distribution*** is a family of distributions that look almost alike the normal distribution (a little bit broader and lower) with the zero mean. It was developed and is typically used for tests on small samples. For the sample size larger than 20, the t-distribution becomes very close to the normal distribution.

The Student's t-test can be used in any statistical hypothesis tests based on normal distribution with samples of all sizes. However, the most frequent applications of the Student's t-test are:

- On small samples with the unknown distribution on the population when the traditional tests based on the normal distribution are not applicable (◘ Table 14.1)
- In the one-small-sample test to compare the mean on the population with a specified number, when the null hypothesis claims that the mean of a population is equal to that specified number
- In the two-sample test with at least one small sample to compare the means of two random variables on one or two populations, when the null hypothesis claims that the means are equal

14.9.2 Unpaired and Paired Two-Sample *t*-Tests

The ***two-sample t-test*** is one of the most popular statistical tests to compare the mean values on two populations. It can be also interpreted as a test to identify whether the samples belong to the same population.

An ***unpaired*** two-sample *t*-test (also known as ***independent*** two-sample *t*-test) is conducted to test the null hypothesis that the populations represented by these two samples have equal mean values or maybe these two samples belong to the same population.

A ***paired*** two-sample *t*-test is conducted on a sample of matched pairs of similar units or one group of units that has been tested twice (a "repeated measures" *t*-test).

Examples of Unpaired and Paired Tests

- Mobile phone daily usage time

  Comparison of the mean daily usage time of mobile phones conducted for retired seniors and active students is an unpaired test.

  Comparison of the mean daily usage time of mobile phones for the same working students when they are at work or at school is a paired test, because the random variables were measured for the same students in the sample under different conditions.
- Comparison of car gas mileage

  Comparison of the mean car gas mileage in the far north and in the southern deserts is an unpaired test.

  Comparison of the mean car gas mileage before and after car service is a paired test.
- Company's profit margin

  Comparison of the profit margin for two branches of the company is an unpaired test.

  Comparison of the profit margin of the company before and after the employee training is a paired test.

14.10 *t*-Test Technique and Degrees of Freedom

The Student's *t*-test uses a degree of freedom, *df*, for hypothesis testing. Degree of freedom of an estimate is the number of independent pieces of information that are involved in the calculation of the estimate. It is not the same as the number of elements in a sample. Generally speaking, the degree of freedom is by one less than the number of elements in a sample, i.e.,

$$df = n - 1 \tag{14.9}$$

For example, a sample of 12 elements, i.e., $n = 12$, has 11 degrees of freedom, i.e., $df = 12 - 1 = 11$. The degrees of freedom for two samples will be discussed later in the chapter.

The *t*-test technique includes the calculation of the *t*-value and the degrees of freedom, *df*.

Once the t-value and degrees of freedom are calculated, a p-value can be found using the table of values for the Student's t-distribution (see Appendix B) or the appropriate computer algorithms.

When the p-value is found, the judgment about the null hypothesis can be made by following the rule described above in ► Sect. 14.4.

14.10.1 One-Sample *t*-Test

A one-sample t-test is testing the null hypothesis for the mean value on population to be equal to a specified value μ. For a sample of size n that has the mean value $\overline{x}$ and the standard deviation s, the t-value is calculated as

$$t = \frac{\overline{x} - \mu}{s / \sqrt{n}} \tag{14.10}$$

and the degree of freedom for this sample is

$$df = n - 1 \tag{14.11}$$

Example

The null hypothesis states that the mean on the population equals 5, i.e., $\mu = 5$. A sample of size $n = 16$ has the mean $\overline{x} = 6.1$ and the standard deviation $s = 0.9$. Then according to Eqs. (14.10) and (14.11), $t = (6.1 - 5)/(0.9 / 4) = 4.889$, and the degree of freedom $df = 16 - 1 = 15$.

14.10.2 Independent (Unpaired) Two-Sample *t*-Test

A two-sample independent t-test (also referred to as a two-sample unpaired t-test) is conducted on two independent samples to test the null hypothesis claiming that two populations have equal mean values. The test can also be conducted to test the null hypothesis that two samples belong to the same population.

14

Equal Sample Sizes ($n_1 = n_2 = n$)

If two samples have the same size, i.e., $n_1 = n_2 = n$, then the t-value can be calculated as

$$t = \frac{\overline{X}_1 - \overline{X}_2}{s_p \sqrt{\frac{2}{n}}} \tag{14.12}$$

where s_p is the ***pooled standard deviation***

$$s_p = \sqrt{\frac{s_1^2 + s_2^2}{2}} \tag{14.13}$$

and s_1 and s_2 are the standard deviations on the respective samples. The degree of freedom for each sample is $n - 1$, and df for the test is the sum of the degrees

$$df = n_1 + n_2 - 2 = 2n - 2 \tag{14.14}$$

Similar Variances ($1/2 < s_1/s_2 < 2$)

Suppose two samples of different sizes show quite similar standard deviations, i.e., the standard deviations are different not more than in two times ($1/2 < s_1/s_2 < 2$). Then the t-value for the test is

$$t = \frac{\bar{x}_1 - \bar{x}_2}{s_p\sqrt{\frac{1}{n_1} + \frac{1}{n_2}}} \tag{14.15}$$

where the pooled standard deviation is

$$s_p = \sqrt{\frac{(n_1 - 1)s_1^2 + (n_2 - 1)s_2^2}{n_1 + n_2 - 2}} \tag{14.16}$$

The degree of freedom for the test is

$$df = n_1 + n_2 - 2 \tag{14.17}$$

Different Variances ($1/2 > s_1/s_2 > 2$)

If two samples of different sizes show a big difference in the standard deviations, i.e., the standard deviations are different more two times ($1/2 > s_1/s_2 > 2$), then the t-value for the test is

$$t = \frac{\bar{x}_1 - \bar{x}_2}{s_\Delta} \tag{14.18}$$

and $s_\Delta{}^2$, which in this case, is not a pooled variance

$$s_\Delta = \sqrt{\frac{s_1^2}{n_1} + \frac{s_2^2}{n_2}} \tag{14.19}$$

The degree of freedom for this test is

$$df = \frac{\left(\frac{s_1^2}{n_1} + \frac{s_2^2}{n_2}\right)^2}{\frac{\left(s_1^2 / n_1\right)^2}{n_1 - 1} + \frac{\left(s_2^2 / n_2\right)^2}{n_2 - 1}} \tag{14.20}$$

14.10.3 Dependent Two-Sample *t*-Test (Paired)

The *t*-value for a paired test can be calculated as

$$t = \frac{\overline{x}_D - \mu_D}{s_D / \sqrt{n}} \tag{14.21}$$

Here $\overline{x}_D$ is the mean of the differences of the random variables

$$\overline{x}_D = \frac{1}{n}\sum_{k=1}^{n}\left(x_{1k} - x_{2k}\right) = \frac{1}{n}\sum_{k=1}^{n} x_{Dk} \tag{14.22}$$

where two random variables X_1 and X_2 on the sample (or one on each of the two samples) take values $X_1 = \{x_{11}, x_{12}, \dots, x_{1k}, \dots, x_{1n}), X_2 = \{x_{21}, x_{22}, \dots, x_{2k}, \dots, x_{2n})$, and

$$x_{Dk} = x_{1k} - x_{2k} \tag{14.23}$$

and s_D is the standard deviation of these differences of the variables. Please note, it is the standard deviation of the differences rather than the difference of the standard deviations. The degree of freedom *df* is

$$df = n - 1 \tag{14.24}$$

because it is one sample of the pairs.

The comparison of the unpaired and paired tests is given in ◘ Table 14.2.

14.10.4 Calculating *p*-Value for the Student's *t*-Test

The *p*-value for the Student's *t*-test can be calculated by using either the *t*-distribution tables (Appendix B) or the appropriate software functions.

Functions T.TEST or T.DIST or T.DIST.2T return the probability associated with a Student's *t*-test to calculate p-value. Function T.TEST uses the two arrays to represent the samples and can be used for the one-tailed and two-tailed tests. The

14

◘ **Table 14.2** Paired test vs. unpaired *t*-test

	Unpaired *t*-test	**Paired *t*-test**
Definition	A statistical test to test the difference of the means of two independent samples	A statistical test to test the difference of the means of two dependent samples
Relationship between groups	Yes	No
Assumes equal variance of two groups	No	Yes

input for T,DIST and T.DIST.2T consists of the mean and the degree of freedom. T,DIST return the cumulative probability for the one-tailed test and T.DIST.2T for the two-tailed test.

▶ Example 4: Comparison of Two Small Batches of Watermelons of Different Sizes

Let's modify the previous problem discussed above in ▶ Examples 2 and 3. We keep all parameters the same as in ▶ Example 3 except the size of the batches. We also change the standard deviation on sample 2. This time, the first store received 12 watermelons, and the second store received 10 watermelons, i.e., n_1 = 12 and n_2 =10. The null and alternative hypotheses stay the same as in the previous examples; the significance level is the same, $\alpha = 0.2$; the mean values on the samples are the same as previously, i.e., $\overline{x}_1$ = 21 lb and $\overline{x}_2$ = 23 lb; but standard deviations are different s_1 = 5 lb and s_2 = 4 lb. Thus, the situation is as follows:

- n_1 = 12 and n_2 =10
- $\overline{x}_1$ = 23 lb and $\overline{x}_2$ = 21 lb
- s_1 = 5 lb and s_2 = 4 lb

Question: can we consider $\mu_1 = \mu_2$ with significance $\alpha = 0.2$?

The hypothesis test is performed in the following steps.

1. Formally, the hypothesis are:
   The null hypothesis H_0: $\mu_1 = \mu_2$ (or $\mu_1 - \mu_2 = 0$)
   The alternative hypothesis H_1: $\mu_1 \neq \mu_2$ (or $\mu_1 - \mu_2 \neq 0$)
   where μ_1 and μ_2 are the mean values of the populations from which the first and the second batches of watermelons came.
2. The chosen significance level is $\alpha = 0.2$.
3. This is the unpaired test because these two samples are not related to each other. We will be conducting the two-tailed test because we are not interested whether watermelons in one batch came from a farm where the larger or smaller watermelons grow. We are just interested if they are different by size.
4. The watermelons in both batches were measured, and the mean weight and standard deviation in both batches were calculated, $\overline{x}_1$ and s_1 in the first batch and $\overline{x}_2$ and s_2 in the second batch: $\overline{x}_1$ = 23 lb, $\overline{x}_2$ = 21 lb, and s_1 = 5 lb and s_2 = 4 lb.
5. The null hypothesis claims that populations X_1 and X_2 have the same mean value, $\mu_1 = \mu_2$. We will be testing a composite random variable $X_1 - X_2$, which is the difference between two random variables. The values of the means of these random variables in our two samples are $\overline{x}_1 - \overline{x}_2$ = 2 lb. The null hypothesis claims that the difference of the mean values on the respective populations equals zero, $\mu_1 - \mu_2 = 0$.
6. We are not sure about the distribution of the watermelons by weight. Our samples are small, n_1 = 12 and n_2 =10. According to ◘ Table 14.1, we cannot assume that the sampling distribution is normal; hence, we cannot perform the *z*-test for the null hypothesis. We will be using the Student's *t*-test. The standard deviations are different but less than two times, i.e., $s_1/s_2 = 5/4 < 2$, so we will be using Eq. (14.16) to calculate the pooled standard deviation s_p as

$$s_p = \sqrt{\frac{(n_1-1)s_1^2+(n_2-1)s_2^2}{n_1+n_2-2}} = \sqrt{\frac{(12-1)5^2+(10-1)4^2}{12+10-2}} = 4.577$$

The degree of freedom *df* calculated according to Eq. (14.17) is $n_1 + n_2 - 2 = 20$.

7. Thus, we decided to conduct the *t*-test. The *t*-score for the null hypothesis is calculated using Eq. (14.15)

$$t = \frac{\bar{x}_1 - \bar{x}_2}{s_p\sqrt{\frac{1}{n_1} + \frac{1}{n_2}}} = \frac{21 - 23}{4.577\sqrt{\frac{1}{12} + \frac{1}{10}}} = -\frac{2}{4.577 * 0.428} = -1.021$$

Thus, the *t*-score = 1.021.

8. Using the cumulative *t*-distribution distribution table, we found the *p*-value for the difference of the mean values on two samples. The *p*-value = 0.030 for each tail. We may also find the *p*-value by using MS Excel or OO Calc function T.DIST.
9. As soon as we chose the two-tailed test, each tail of the distribution comprises a half of the assigned significance level, i.e., $\alpha/2 = 0.1$. The comparison of the calculated *p*-value with the significance level for each tail shows that the *p*-value < $\alpha/2$; *hence, the test was significant. Thus, there was enough evidence to reject the null hypothesis, so we reject it. We can conclude with the significance* $\alpha = 0.02$ *(or 20%) that the supplier was not truthful claiming that both batches of watermelons came from the same farm. The actual difference in sizes in two batches did not happen occasionally.* ◄

14.11 The Statistical Hypothesis Testing Process

Each hypothesis is a statement regarding specific properties of a population or comparison of different populations. For example:

- The average apartment rent in San Francisco is higher than in Los Angeles.
- The average weight of people in Houston is the same as in Dallas.
- Consumers prefer product A over product B.
- The price of the consumer basket does not exceed a certain amount of dollars.
- The average price of a car model A is the same as of model B.
- and many other ...

14

As we have already learned above, hypothesis testing process includes the following connected logical steps:

- A selected sample is one of the many virtually possible samples, and the statistic on this sample may differ from the parameters on the analyzed population or populations.
- The goal of the hypothesis testing is to make a judgment about the formulated hypothesis proceeding from the statistic collected on a random sample. However, we have no idea how well the selected sample represents the population, because the sample is randomly selected and, thus, can be occasionally chosen from the middle of the distribution of all possible samples or from the far tails of it.
- Two hypotheses are formulated, the null hypothesis and the alternative hypothesis. The null hypothesis H_0 states that the sample does not show any significant difference of the mean value on the population with the specified value or the difference between the mean values of two random variables. Such a null hypothesis is a metaphorical representation of "the presumption of innocence" in the jurisprudence.

- We assign the significance level in a form of probability α (alpha), as the threshold degree to which we allow us being mistaken in our final judgment, if the sample is occasionally selected from the implausible tails of the sampling distribution. The significance factor is chosen and assigned before conducting the test. The significance level is chosen from real-world considerations of consequences and the cost of being mistaken. This is a metaphoric representation of the rule to judge "beyond reasonable doubt" in the jurisprudence.
- The probability is estimated of a randomly selected sample to belong to the category of extreme samples if the null hypothesis is true. This probability is referred to as the *p*-value. This is a very important technical step. The choice of the type of test depends on the sample size and sampling distribution (see ► Table 13.2). It could be *z*-test or *t*-test.
- We compare the calculated *p*-value with the assigned significance level. If the calculated *p*-value is less than the significance level α (chosen by the investigator prior to conducting the test), *p*-value $< \alpha$, this provides us with the enough evidence to reject the null hypothesis, so we reject it and accept the alternative hypothesis. If the *p*-value (calculated) is greater than the significance level, *p*-value $> \alpha$, we consider that there was not enough evidence to reject the null hypothesis and accept it.

The statistical hypothesis testing process described above is schematically illustrated in ◘ Fig. 14.5. Below is the step-by-step description of the hypothesis testing process.

14.11.1 First Comes Research Question

Any research starts with a question. Hypotheses are formulated to answer the research question. A hypothesis could claim a relationship between a parameter on a population with a certain number (equal, greater, lower, not equal) or between two parameters on the same population or on different populations. The relationship may apply to the mean value on the population, say the mean on the population equals or greater, or smaller, or unequal a specified number. The relationship may be a comparison of the means of two variables on the same or on different populations.

It is critical to clearly understand the research question before formulating the hypotheses.

Examples: Research Question

(a) A coin flipped 20 times and resulted in 14 heads and 6 tails. Is it a loaded coin?
(b) A car manufacturer is interested whether the gas mileage of their specific car model meets the country standard.
(c) Do parts supplied by different manufacturers have the same size to be used interchangeably?
(d) Does the employee productivity in our company depend on training?

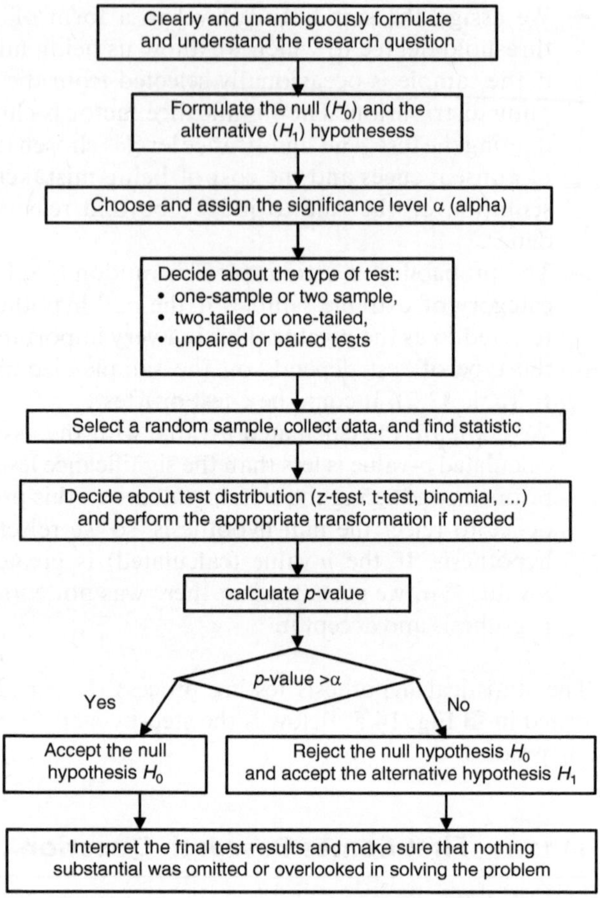

Fig. 14.5 Statistical hypothesis testing process

14.11.2 Formulate the Null Hypothesis (H_0) and the Alternative Hypothesis (H_1)

The null hypothesis H_0, typically, assumes that there is no significant relationship between the analyzed parameter on one population and a specified number or parameters on different populations as claimed in the research question.

The alternative hypothesis H_1 states the difference phrased in the research question. The alternative hypothesis is not the complete negation of the null hypothesis but reflects the sense of the research question. The alternative hypothesis will be accepted if the null hypothesis is rejected in the test.

Examples – The Null and Alternative Hypotheses:

(a) H_0: The coin is fair (a good coin).
H_1: The coin is loaded (have different probabilities for the heads and tails).
(b) H_0: The gas mileage of this car model is matching the country standard.
H_1: The gas mileage of this car model is higher than the country standard.

(c) H_0: The sizes of the parts supplied by both manufacturers are the same.
    H_1: The sizes of the parts supplied by both manufacturers are different.
(d) H_0: The employee productivity in our company does not depend on training.
    H_1: Employee training impacts positively on their productivity.

14.11.3 Choose the Significance Level

Choose the significance level α (alpha) based on the nature of the research problem and the real-world domain. Analyze the consequences; if you are mistaken in your judgment, then make the appropriate choice of the significance level. Remember, the significance level is not a calculatable value but chosen based on your understanding the consequences from being wrong in your final judgment.

Examples – Choosing the significance level:

(a) The confidence in the judgment about the fairness of the coin is quite important for us, so we choose the significance level $\alpha = 0.05$.
(b) The car mileage is an important issue in our market penetration strategy, so we prefer to choose the significance level $\alpha = 0.01$.
(c) Matching the part sizes is an important issue. Thus, $\alpha = 0.05$ would be sufficient significance level for me.
(d) The impact of employee training on productivity is important; however, we understand that many factors are impacting on the training quality and productivity, so we prefer $\alpha = 0.20$.

14.11.4 Decide About Two-Tailed or One-Tailed Test

A decision on the two- or one-tailed test should be made based on the nature and sense of the research question. If the research question relates to "greater than" or "less than," then use the appropriate one-tailed test. On the other hand, if the research question is neutral about the direction, that means that variations on the both tails of the distribution are possible; then use the two-tailed test.

Examples – Choosing One- or Two-tailed Test:

(a) We are concerned about symmetrical properties of the coin, and therefore we will conduct the two-tailed test.
(b) As soon as the problem question is about exceeding the standard, we will conduct the one-tailed test.
(c) The research concerns only whether the sizes are equal to be used interchangeably; therefore, the test will be two-tailed.
(d) The research question implicitly implies that employee training may improve their productivity. Therefore, it will be the one-tailed test.

14.11.5 Select a Random Sample and Collect Data

Selection of a random sample is not an easy task. It may be selected by running a random number generator to pick elements from the population. Sometimes, it is hard or impossible to do. For this reason, researchers are using various methods and techniques for sample generation. We discuss various practical sample generation methods and techniques together with their pros and cons in ► Chap. 15.

Examples – Selecting a Sample (samples) and Collecting Data:

(a) A sample has already been selected, and the measurements have been conducted. There were 14 heads and 6 tails.
(b) We will select a sample using a random number generator to select from the newly manufactured cars, measure the mean gas mileage on the sample, and compare it with the country standard.
(c) For the analysis of the part sizes, we select two independent samples by using systematic sampling (select each k-th part – see the next chapter for details), one from each supplier, and will compare the mean sizes on them.
(d) A sample is built from randomly selected employees, their productivity was measured before and after the appropriate training (paired test), and the difference in the productivity for each employee was measured, and the null hypothesis was test.

14.11.6 Decide About the Test Type

A decision should be made about the test type: z-test or t-test or binomial distribution. If the random variable on the population is normally distributed or the sample size is greater than or equal to 30, we may use the test based on normal distribution. We may use the cumulative standard normal distribution tables or the appropriate computer software for calculating the p-value.

If the sample size is lower than 30 or the distribution on the population is unknown, or two samples have different sizes in the two-sample test, we may use the t-distribution and the Student's t-test.

14

Examples – The Distribution Used in the Test:

(a) Samples are distributed binomially by the number of heads and tail in the sample. So, we can calculate the p-value using binomial distribution and combinatorics.
(b) Cars of the same model are distributed normally by their gas mileage. The sample size exceeds 30, so we can use the z-test. We also can use the Student's t-test. We decide to use the z-test.
(c) Two samples of parts from two suppliers may have different sizes and may have different standard deviations. The Student's t-test is the right choice for this problem.
(d) It is a paired test on two small samples of the same size. We will use the Student's t-test.

14.11.7 Conduct the Test and Calculate *p*-Value for H_0

To conduct the test, we use either the standard tables or computer software.

Examples – Calculating p-value:

(a) To conduct the test on coin tossing, we calculate the *p*-value directly using binomial distribution for probabilities of getting the extreme samples with 14 or more heads or tails in the presumption that the coin is fair.
(b) We use the Excel function NORM.DIST to calculate the *p*-value for the car gas mileage test.
(c) We will calculate the *p*-value for the part size test by using computer function T.DIST.2T for the two-tailed test.
(d) We will be using computer function T.DIST to calculate the *p*-value for employee training test for the one-tailed test.

14.11.8 Reject or Accept H_0 by Comparing the *p*-Value Against the Significance Level

The test was conducted. The *p*-value for the null hypothesis was calculated. Now, the *p*-value should be compared with the chosen significance level alpha. If *p*-value $< \alpha$ (alpha), it means that the test provides enough evidence for rejecting the null hypothesis according to the chosen significance level, so the test is declared significant and, hence, the null hypothesis H_0 is rejected and the alternative hypothesis H_1 is accepted. If *p*-value $> \alpha$, the null hypothesis H_0 is accepted because the test was insignificant and the alternative hypothesis H_1 is rejected.

Examples – Accepting or Rejecting the Null Hypothesis:

(a) The calculated *p*-value $> \alpha$; thus, we do not have enough evidence to reject the null hypothesis, so we accept it. The coin is declared fair with the significance level $\alpha = 0.05$.
(b) The calculated *p*-value $> \alpha$; thus, we do not have enough evidence to reject the null hypothesis and, hence, accept it. The gas mileage of the specified car model meets the country standard with the significance level 0.01.
(c) The calculated *p*-value $< \alpha$; thus, we have enough evidence to reject the null hypothesis. This, we reject the null hypothesis and accept the alternative hypothesis. The parts from different suppliers have different sizes and cannot be used interchangeably.
(d) The calculated *p*-value $< \alpha$; thus, we have enough evidence to reject the null hypothesis. This, we reject the null hypothesis and accept the alternative hypothesis. The training provided to the employees helps to improve the employees' productivity.

14.12 Type I and Type II Errors

14.12.1 False Positive and False Negative Judgments

The notion of statistical error is a fundamental attribute of statistical hypothesis testing. The investigator must choose between two competing statements represented by the null and the alternative hypotheses. The null hypothesis states that there is no effect, while the alternative hypothesis claims that the effect is present. The ***negative*** judgment means that no significant evidence supporting the effect was present and the judgment was made negative to the effect, i.e., to accept the null hypothesis. The ***positive*** judgment means that there was enough evidence supporting the effect and the judgment was made to reject the null hypothesis.

It may occur that we reject the null hypothesis, even if it is true, just because we randomly selected a sample from the extreme outliers that support the effect. Such a judgment is referred to as ***false positive***, just because it made positive to the effect when there is no effect. The false positive judgment is made for the samples on the right from the critical value of the sampling distribution $\overline{x}_{\alpha}$ for the null hypothesis as shown in ◘ Fig. 14.6(a).

On the other hand, it may occur that we accept the null hypothesis, when it is false and the effect is present, also just because of the sample randomly selected from the distribution outliers, which do not support the effect. Such a judgment is referred to as ***false negative***, just because it made negative to the effect when there is no effect. The false negative judgment is made for the samples on the left from the critical value $\overline{x}_{\alpha}$ of the sample means in the sampling distribution for the alternative hypothesis (if the alternative hypothesis is true) as shown in ◘ Fig.14.6(b). Note that the mean value for the alternative hypothesis is different from the mean value for the null hypothesis; therefore, the sampling distributions for the null hypothesis and for the alternative hypothesis in ◘ Fig. 14.6 are shifted against each other.

If a perfect test would be possible, there would be no false positive and no false negative judgments. However, the judgments about the acceptance or rejection of statistical hypothesis are based on probabilities and cannot be done with the hundred percent certainty.

There are two types of error in judging on statistical hypotheses: type I error and type II error. Allegorically, we may illustrate these errors in the following example. There is a poor-quality picture of something, and someone said that it is a picture of a bird. The null hypothesis says that there is no bird on the picture that means "no effect." We may recognize a bird in the picture, when there was no bird there (type I error), or we may fail to recognize a bird, when there is actually a bird in the picture (type II error).

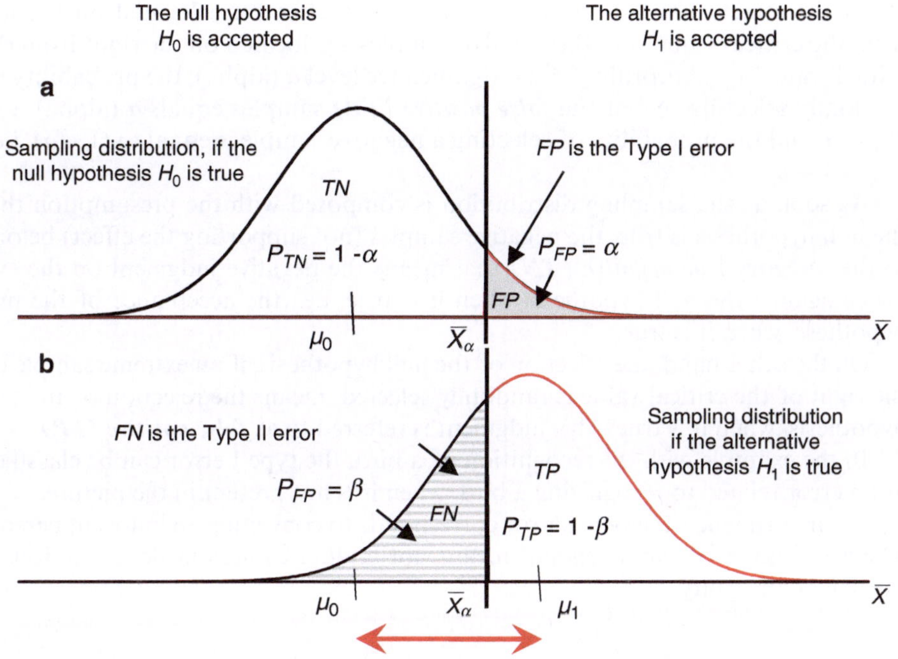

■ **Fig. 14.6** Sampling distribution if **a** the null hypothesis is true, true negative (*TN*) and false positive (*FP*) samples, and **b** if the alternative hypothesis is true, true positive (*TN*) and false negative (*FN*) samples

14.12.2 Type I Error

The type I error is the rejection of a true null hypothesis as the result of a test procedure. This type of error relates to the significance level α (alpha). As was discussed above in this chapter and in the previous chapter, the significance level is the probability chosen and assigned by the investigator to the samples in the sampling distribution for the null hypothesis to be considered extreme outliers. The extreme samples are the samples that provide evidences against the null hypothesis, though all possible samples were composed with the presumption that the mean of the population equals μ_0 as declared in the null hypothesis. Such positive samples belong to the category of ***false positive (FP)*** samples, i.e., the samples, which lead to the rejection of the null hypothesis, though the null hypothesis is true. Those samples, which contain no evidence against the null hypothesis, belong to the category of ***true negative (TN)*** samples.

The type I error is illustrated in ■ Fig. 14.6(a) where the sampling distribution on the left side of the figure composed in the presumption of the null hypothesis is true. The solid vertical line indicates the critical value $\bar{x}_\alpha$ on the population of all possible samples. The critical value divides the samples in the sampling distribution for the null hypothesis according to the significance level as providing negative (no effect) and positive (supporting the effect) evidences about the effect. The true negative samples (no effect) are located on the left from the critical value, and the positive samples are located on the right from the critical value $\bar{x}_\alpha$. According to the significance level α (alpha), the probability of randomly selecting one of the ***false positive (FP)*** samples equals α (alpha), i.e., $P_{FP} = \alpha$, and the probability of selecting a negative sample is equal to $(1 - \alpha)$, i.e., $P_{TN} = 1 - \alpha$.

As soon as the sampling distribution is composed with the presumption that the null hypothesis is true, the negative samples (not supporting the effect) belong to the category ***true negative (TN)*** that means the negative judgment on the evidence against the null hypothesis when it is true, i.e., the acceptance of the null hypothesis when it is true.

On the other hand, the rejection of the null hypothesis, if an extreme sample on the right of the critical value is randomly selected, means the rejection of the null hypothesis, when it is true. This judgment is referred to as ***false positive (FP)***.

In the example with the recognition of a bird, the type I error can be classified as an error related to recognizing a bird, when it is not present in the picture.

In jurisprudence, the type I error corresponds to convicting an innocent person. The acquittance of the defendant means not finding enough evidence to declare the defendant guilty.

14.12.3 Type II Error

The type II error is the failure to reject a false null hypothesis as the result of a test procedure. Suppose we rejected the null hypothesis as false and accepted the alternative hypothesis. The mean value of the population, if the alternative hypothesis is true, μ_1, is different from the mean value of the population, if the null hypothesis is true, μ_0. Thus, the sampling distribution, if the alternative hypothesis is true, is shifted relative to the sampling distribution, if the null hypothesis is true as illustrated in ◘ Fig. 14.6. The samples on the right from the critical value $\bar{x}_\alpha$ in the sampling distribution, if the alternative hypothesis is true (the null hypothesis is false), contain sufficient evidence to support the alternative hypothesis and represent the ***true positive (TP)*** category of samples in the sampling distribution for the alternative hypothesis as shown in ◘ Fig. 14.6(b). However, the left part of the sampling distribution for the alternative hypothesis is on the left from the critical value. This indicates that those samples belong to the extreme outliers for the alternative hypothesis, i.e., they do not have enough evidence to support the effect (to support the alternative hypothesis). Thus, those samples are interpreted in favor of the null hypothesis, though they belong to the sampling distribution for the alternative hypothesis. Those samples belong to the category of ***false negative (FN)*** samples, i.e., the samples that lead to the negative judgment about the effect (acceptance of the null hypothesis), when the alternative hypothesis is true as illustrated in ◘ Fig. 14.6(b).

The probability of selecting a ***false negative (FN)*** sample is measured by parameter β, i.e., $P_{FN} = \beta$. The probability of selecting a ***true positive (TP)*** sample is $P_{TP} = 1- \beta$.

This type of error relates to the situation when a selected sample occasionally belongs to the extreme negative outliers (tails) in the sampling distribution, when the alternative hypothesis is true, thus, occasionally not providing enough evidence to accept the alternative hypothesis. This error is ***false negative (FN)*** error, which means that judgment was made in favor of no effect (the null hypothesis), when the effect is present (the alternative hypothesis was true).

Allegorically, the type II error can be classified as an error of not recognizing a bird, when it is actually present in the picture.

In jurisprudence, a type II error corresponds to acquitting a guilty person.

14.12.4 Relationship Between the Type I and Type II Errors

Type I and type II errors are related. ◘ Figure 14.7 illustrates this relationship by putting side-by-side the distributions presented in ◘ Fig. 14.6. The distribution shown on the left-hand side of ◘ Fig. 14.7 is the sampling distribution in case, when the null hypothesis H_0 is true, and the distribution on the right-hand side of the figure is the sampling distribution in case, when the alternative hypothesis H_1 is true. These distributions have different mean values μ_0 and μ_1 by the nature of the null and the alternative hypotheses.

The part of the left-hand side distribution on the left from the critical value $\overline{x}_\alpha$ represents the ***true negative (TN)*** judgment, i.e., the judgment that those samples do not show significant evidences in favor of the effect (not enough to reject the null hypothesis in favor of the alternative hypothesis H_1), when the null hypothesis H_0 is true. The shaded tail of the left-hand side distribution on the right from the critical value represents the ***false positive (FP)*** category of samples, which provide

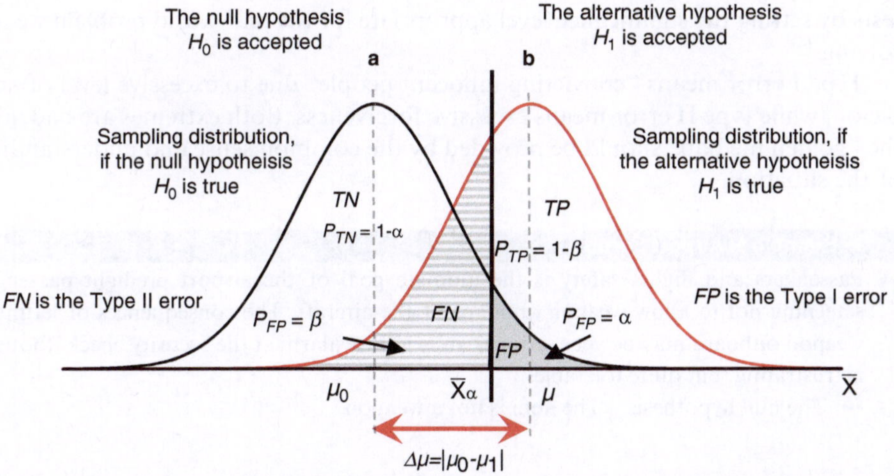

◘ **Fig. 14.7** Comparison of sampling distribution if **a** the null hypothesis is true, true negative (*TN*) and false positive (*FP*) samples, and **b** if the alternative hypothesis is true, true positive (*TN*) and false negative (*FN*) samples

evidences against the null hypothesis H_0, despite the fact that the distribution was composed in the presumption of the null hypothesis H_0 is true. This tail represents the ***type I error***, which is the error of rejecting the null hypothesis H_0, when it is true or detecting the effect when it is not present.

The part of the right-hand side distribution in ◘ Fig. 14.7, which is on the right from the critical value $\overline{x}_\alpha$, represents the ***true positive (TP)*** judgment, i.e., the judgment that the samples show significant evidences in favor of the effect (supporting the alternative hypothesis H_1), when the effect is present, i.e., the alternative hypothesis is true. The textured tail of the right-hand side distribution on the left from the critical value represents the ***false negative (FN)*** category of samples, which do not provide enough evidences of the effect (to support the alternative hypothesis H_1), despite the fact that the distribution was composed in the presumption of the presence of the effect, i.e., alternative hypothesis H_1 to be true. This tail represents the ***type II error***, which is the error of accepting the null hypothesis H_0, when the alternative hypothesis H_1 is true or not detecting the effect when the effect is present.

The probability of false positive (*FP*), P_{FP}, is equal to the significance level α (alpha). The higher the α, the higher the probability of *FP*, and the higher is the type I error associated with *FP*. On the other hand, the higher the β, the higher the false negative (*FN*), and the higher is the type II error. The smaller is the difference between μ_0 and μ_1, the higher are both type I and type II errors.

The judgment threshold (critical value $\overline{x}_\alpha$) is controlled by the significance level. The judgment threshold moves to the left by increasing significance level α (alpha). This leads to the increase of the probability of false positive (*FP*) evidences and reducing the probability of false negative (*FN*). If the judgment threshold moves to the right by reducing the significance level α (alpha), it reduces the probability of false positive (*FP*) and increases the probability of false negative (*FP*) samples. We may control the combination false negative and false positive tests by setting the significance level appropriate for the real-world problem we are solving.[1]

14

Type I error means "convicting innocent people" due to excessive level of suspicion, while type II error means excessive forgiveness. Both extremes are bad, and the "golden median" should be provided by the common sense and understanding of the situation.

▶ Example 5: Airport Security

Passengers and flights safety is the ultimate goal of the airport preflight passenger screening not to allow weapon onboard of the aircraft. The consequences of letting a weapon onboard may be very serious, while a false alarm at the security check, though, is frustrating, but quite tolerable.

- The null hypothesis: "The item is not a weapon."

---

1 The explanation was quite wordy, but it was needed for understanding the concept and avoiding confusion.

- The alternative hypothesis: "The item is a weapon."
- Type I error: "The alarm will sound even when the item is not a weapon."
- Type II error: "The alarm will not sound even when the item is a weapon."

For the reasons discussed above, the threshold is moved in favor of type I error, i.e., false positive tests. It means that we better set up an alarm when there is no weapon or unsafe substance in the baggage than let them squeeze through the security check. ◀

▶ Example 6: Email Spam Protection

We all know how frustrating is receiving spam and wasting time for cleaning our mailboxes. Modern computer security tools provide good spam recognition and filtering. However, nothing can be done with hundred percent certainty. This is applicable to the spam recognition too. It would be more frustrating to lose an important email if it is recognized by the system as a spam.

- The null hypothesis: "The message is not a spam."
- The alternative hypothesis: "The message is a spam."
- Type I error: "The message is classified as a spam even when it is not a spam."
- Type II error: "The message is classified as not a spam even when it is a spam."

For the reasons mentioned above, the spam recognition and filtering computer tools are set up more in favor of the type II error. It means that it better let some spam messages go through than filter out a legitimate email message. Anyway, it is strongly recommended from time to time to check your spam box to make sure that no legitimate emails were filtered out from the mailbox by the recognition error. ◀

14.13 Statistical Power vs. Significance of a Hypothesis Test

14.13.1 Significance vs. Power

Statistical significance of the hypothesis test, which is denoted as α (a Greek character "alpha"), is the probability of rejecting the null hypothesis when it is true. Such a rejecting judgment on the null hypothesis is called ***false positive (FP)*** and illustrated in ◘ Fig. 14.7 as the right part of the sampling distribution for the null hypothesis (the left-hand side distribution) on the right from the critical value $\overline{x}_{\alpha}$. Do not get confused with the term "positive." In a statistical test, the null hypothesis is rejected, if there is enough evidence to reject it. Therefore, the term "positive" is used for the evidences supporting the rejection of the null hypothesis. Note that such a probability is associated with type I error as shown in ◘ Fig. 14.7.

Statistical power of the hypothesis test is the probability of detecting an effect, if such effect is present, ***true positive (TP)***, i.e., the probability of rejecting the null hypothesis if it is false or the probability of accepting the alternative hypothesis if it is true. Such a probability can be increased by increasing the sample size or increasing the significance level as is evident from ◘ Fig. 14.7. Statistical power can be expressed as $(1 - \beta)$, where β (a Greek character "beta") is the probability

Table 14.3 Relationship between true/false judgments about the null hypothesis

		Null hypothesis H_0 is	
		True	*False*
Judgment about null hypothesis	Do not reject (accept)	True negative (probability = $1-\alpha$)	Type II error (false negative) (probability = β)
	Reject	Type I error (false positive) (probability = α) Significance of the test	(True positive) (probability = $1-\beta$) Power of the test

of type II error as shown in Figs. 14.6 and 14.7, i.e., β is the probability of not rejecting (accepting) the null hypothesis when it is false.

The relationship between true/false judgments about the null hypothesis is summarized in the bottom row of Table 14.3.

14.13.2 Calculating the Statistical Power

However, the relationship between α and β is quite complex, though the trend is clear. As is indicated in Fig. 14.7, α and β are represented by the appropriate areas *FP* (false positive) and *FN* (false negative), respectively. As α increases, β decreases, and $(1-\beta)$ increases, and vice versa. Thus, the increase of the significance level α leads to the increase of the power of the test $(1-\beta)$.

14.13.3 The Reasons to Analyze the Test Power

Calculating the power of the statistical test is quite complex, but it is worth the efforts, particularly for the following reasons:

- To find the required sample size to detect an effect. It identifies the minimum required sample size to avoid incorrectly rejecting the null hypothesis.
- To find out if the sample size was sufficient to detect an effect, particularly in the tests with limited budgets.
- To validate the research. Power analysis is an attribute of good science.

Questions for Self-Control for Chap. 14

1. What is a statistical hypothesis?
2. What logical values can a hypothesis have?
3. Can a statistical hypothesis be proven?

4. What does it mean when a statistical hypothesis is accepted?
5. What is the significance level?
6. Can the significance level be calculated?
7. What does "beyond reasonable doubt" mean?
8. What does the central limit theorem state?
9. How are the mean values on all possible samples of the same size distributed?
10. What does a null hypothesis mean?
11. What are the null and the alternative hypotheses?
12. Is the alternative hypothesis the complete negation of the null hypothesis?
13. How is the alternative hypothesis formulated?
14. What is the logic of accepting or rejecting the null hypothesis?
15. What does "not having enough evidence to reject the null hypothesis" mean?
16. What is the *p*-value?
17. How to calculate the *p*-value?
18. What is the critical value and how to calculate it?
19. What are the unpaired and paired tests?
20. What are the one-tailed and two tailed tests?
21. In what cases are the one-tailed and two-tailed tests used?
22. How is the significance level distributed between the sampling distribution tails?
23. What relationship between the p-value and the significance level lead to the rejection of the null hypothesis?
24. What are the *z*-test and *t*-test?
25. What is the Student's *t*-test and why is it needed?
26. At what circumstances is it better to use *z*-test or *t*-test?
27. What is the degree of freedom in statistical hypothesis testing?
28. How to calculate the degree of freedom?
29. What is pooled standard deviation and why is it needed?
30. What is the overall process of testing statistical hypothesis?
31. What are true negative, false positive, true positive, and false negative judgments about a hypothesis?
32. What are the type I and type II errors in statistical hypothesis testing?
33. How are type I and type II errors related?
34. What is the statistical power of the hypothesis test?

? Problems for Chap. 14

1. Using the tables of the cumulative standard probabilities, calculate the probability of $z < 1.42$ for $Z \sim N(0,1)$.
2. A salesman sold apples to 2 individuals, by 40 apples to the first buyer and 40 apples to the second buyer. The salesman chose and packed the apples to both buyers. The statistic on these two purchase are $\bar{x}_1 = 1.2$ lb, $\bar{x}_2 = 1.5$ lb, $s_1 = s_2 = 0.5$ lb, and $n_1 = n_2 = 40$.

   The first buyer suspects that the salesman unfairly gave the larger apples to the second buyer and sold the smaller apples to the first buyer. The salesman claims that he chose the apples randomly. Who is right, the salesman or the first buyer? Does the evidence prove the first buyer's suspicion?

3. We measured the gas mileage of two car models, A and B. Each sample was comprised of ten randomly chosen card of the specified model. The collected statistic is $\bar{x}_A = 30$ m/g, $\bar{x}_B = 35$ m/g, $s_A = 5$ m/g, $s_B = 4$ m/g, and $n_A = n_B = 10$. Is it true with the significance level 0.02 that model B has a better gas mileage than model A?
4. A comparative test was conducted on a group of 25 students before and after the application of the new teaching methodology. The average GPA in this group before the new method was used was $GPA_B = 3.2$ with standard deviation $s_B = 0.4$. The average GPA for the same group of students after the application of the new teaching methodology increased in average by $\Delta GPA = 0.3$ with the marginal standard deviation $s_\Delta = 0.4$. The marginal standard deviation is the standard deviation of the difference in GPA for each student in the group before and after the new methodology was applied. Can we claim with the significance level 0.05 that the GPA increase is the result of the new teaching methodology?
5. The measurement of the car speed on a freeway resulted in the average speed 77 m/h for a group of 35 cars. The standard deviation on this group was 10 m/h. Can we claim with the significance level 0.05 that speed of traffic on this freeway does not exceed the average speed of 75 m/h?

Sampling Experiments

Contents

15.1 Analysis of Samples – 323
15.1.1 Defining the Population of Concern – 323
15.1.2 Choosing the Appropriate Significance (or Confidence) Level – 325
15.1.3 Specifying a Sampling Method to Form a Sample or Samples – 326
15.1.4 Determining the Minimum Sample Size to Meet the Objectives – 326
15.1.5 Forming a Sample or Samples, Collecting Data, and Calculating Relevant Statistic – 326
15.1.6 Making Conclusions About the Population – 327

15.2 Sampling Methods – 327
15.2.1 Random Sampling – 327
15.2.2 Systematic Sampling – 328
15.2.3 Stratified Sampling – 329
15.2.4 Cluster Sampling – 330
15.2.5 Convenience Sampling – 331

15.3 Standard Error, Margin of Error, and Confidence Level – 332

15.4 Margin of Error and Sample Size – 333

15.5 Minimum Required Sample Size – 334
15.5.1 Standard Deviation on the Population Is Known – 334
15.5.2 Standard Deviation on the Population Is Unknown – 334

S. K. Aityan, *Business Research Methodology*, Classroom Companion: Business,
https://doi.org/10.1007/978-3-030-76857-7_15

15.5.3 One Sample for Binomial Distribution – 337
15.5.4 Two Unpaired Samples – 339
15.5.5 Two Paired Samples – 339

15.6 Summary of the Sampling Experiment Process – 340

15.1 Analysis of Samples

Selection and analysis of samples for the purpose of finding parameters on the respective populations is a common method in research, including market research, quality control, sociological studies, clinical trials, political polls, and many other types of research. Sampling experiment is part of a research project. In this chapter, we focus solely on sample selection methods.

In this chapter, we presume that the research problem is already selected, the research design is completed where one of the statistical approaches was chosen, and the type of statistical test is identified – the z-test or t-test. Finding the mean of the population, comparing the means of two populations, and hypothesis testing, including paired or unpaired tests, are among the statistical approaches discussed in this book. In this book, we have discussed two types of statistical tests – the z-test or t-test. Though both types of tests imply normal distribution for the means on the variety (population) of all possible samples of a specified size, the choice of the test type should be made based on the distribution on the original population, the sample size, and knowledge of the standard deviation on the original population. For tests on two samples, the choice of the test type also depends on the comparative sizes of the samples. All these issues have been discussed in the previous chapters. In this chapter, we will solely focus on the sample selection methods including the choice of the sample size.

The sample selection and analysis process comprises several steps:

- Defining the population of concern
- Specifying a random variable or variables and the respective items or events
- Choosing the appropriate significance (or confidence) level
- Specifying a sampling method for selecting items or events to form a sample or samples
- Determining the minimum sample size to meet the objectives
- Forming a sample or samples and collecting data
- Calculating relevant statistic
- Making conclusions about the population

We discuss all these steps one-by-one to make sure that it is clear what to do and how to select a sample or sample and collect viable data.

15.1.1 Defining the Population of Concern

A sample is selected from a respective population, and we must clearly understand what population is of our research concern and what actual population we use. It may occur that we narrow down the population that creates a subpopulation, which parameters may differ from the original population and can be classified as a constraint or limitation of the original population.

▶ Example 1: Checking the Average Potato Size

Mr. Smith grows potato and wants to know when to harvest it. The harvesting time is the time when most potatoes are ready, i.e., reach a specified average size. First of all, he cannot dig out all potato to figure out whether the potato condition is right. For this reason, Mr. Smith decides to conduct a sampling experiment by randomly digging out a certain number of potatoes to identify if they are ready for harvesting.

The potato population for this sampling experiment consists of all potato grown by Mr. Smith – let's call it "Smith's Potato" – and does not include the population of potato grown by others in that area, let's call it "All Potatoes." It is clear that the parameters on the "Smith's Potato" may be different from the similar parameters on the population "All Potatoes" for many reasons. ◀

▶ Example 2: Comparing the Average Height of Men and Women

The research goal is to find the difference of the average height between men and women in San Francisco Bay Area. We identify two populations for the research: men and women in the Bay Area. The difference of heights between men and women in other geographical regions may vary; therefore, the population is limited to the residents of Bay Area. ◀

▶ Example 3: Analysis of the Remote Work Mode

Company ABC plans to move its employees to the online remote mode of work. The employees will work from home rather than from the company office. To analyze the impact of the new work mode on the employee performance, the company conducts a comparative analysis by measuring the employee performance while working in the office versus working from home. The population for the research is comprised of all employees of the company engaged in the regular operations. ◀

The term ***population*** is typically understood as all possible objects, items, or events of our concern.

Specifying a Random Variable or Variables and the Respective Items or Events

15

The term ***population*** is typically understood as all possible objects, items, or events of our concern. On the other hand, mathematically, the term population applies to all possible instances of the random variable. Such a little nuance, if properly managed, creates no confusion. Let's for consistency stay with the understanding of a population as all possible objects, items, or events.

Once the population is identified, we should specify the random variable or the random variables of our concern on the population. It may occur that there is more than one random variable in the population. For example, a human being as an object has many random variables associated with the object. Among them are height, weight, blood pressure, heartbeat rate, and many others. We may specify some variables, say, height and weight, as being the variables of concern for the research and ignore other possible random variables.

We continue the examples given above.

▶ Example 1: Checking the Average Potato Size

The random variable of concern on the population of "Smith's Potato" is the weight of each potato.

This will be single sample analysis. ◀

▶ Example 2: Comparing the Average Height of Men and Women

We define two random variables of concern, one random variable on each population – population of men and population of women. Both random variables measure the height of individual in each population. The variables are unpaired.

This will be a single sample unpaired analysis. ◀

▶ Example 3: Analysis of the Remote Work Mode

Two paired random variables are defined on the population of employees. One random variable measures the employee performance while working from the company's office, and another random variable measures the performance of the same employee while working remotely from home.

This will be a one-sample paired analysis. ◀

15.1.2 Choosing the Appropriate Significance (or Confidence) Level

Significance level (or confidence level) must be chosen before a sample or samples are formed, data are collected, and the statistical analysis is conducted. The significance level depends only in the understanding of the consequences or losses associated with a chance to be wrong in the final judgment about the properties of the population tested on the sample or the samples.

▶ Example 1: Checking the Average Potato Size

The purpose of the analysis is to make a correct decision about potato pricing. The are many other factors influencing the pricing. Thus, it would be sufficient to choose 90% confidence level in this case. ◀

▶ Example 2: Comparing the Average Height of Men and Women

This analysis is related to the healthcare as well as transportation and other application. It would be reasonable to use 95% confidence level. ◀

▶ Example 3: Analysis of the Remote Work Mode

Remote work arrangements are related to employee performance and costs. It is important, but there are many other factors impacting on the performance and costs. The reasonable significance level is chosen 10%, which is the same as 90% confidence level. ◀

15.1.3 Specifying a Sampling Method to Form a Sample or Samples

According to the theoretical foundations of statistics, samples must be selected randomly. However, there are some issues associated with the technique of random selection of a sample. The random selection implies casting of random numbers. Selecting a sample by just pointing a finger introduces a human bias, which may increase the chance of the sample to belong to the category of the extreme outliers. On the other hand, any chance to move a prospective sample closer to the yet unknown mean of the population would be appreciated by the researchers.

There are several practical methods of building samples for statistical analysis. By no means, those methods except random method are theoretically justified, but they offer a reasonable approximation for practical implementation.

These methods are described and discussed in the next section of this chapter. We will continue the above examples as we have the sampling methods discussed.

15.1.4 Determining the Minimum Sample Size to Meet the Objectives

As was discussed in the previous chapters, the sampling distribution for bigger size samples has the narrower standard deviation, inverse of the square root of the sample size. It implies that the means on majority of possible samples are getting closer to the mean of the population. In result, the confidence intervals are getting narrower, and the judgment about hypothesis is getting less fuzzy. If the sample size grows closer to the size of the population, the closer is the statistic on the sample to the parameters on the population, which is a quite expected conclusion. Thus, in any sampling experiment, we have to make a twofold decision about the sample size. On the one hand, the bigger the sample, the closer is the collected statistic to the parameters on the population, but on the other hand, it is technically harder and more expensive to collect bigger samples. Thus, we have to make a certain compromise by limiting the sample size to the minimum size that meets the research and statistical analysis objectives.

We will discuss the determination of the sample size later in this chapter, and then we will continue the above examples.

15.1.5 Forming a Sample or Samples, Collecting Data, and Calculating Relevant Statistic

As the sampling method and the sample size are identified, a sample or samples are formed, and the appropriate data is collected on the sample or samples for the further statistical analysis.

Data collected on the selected sample constitute the basis for calculating the relevant statistic, which will be used for the further statistical analysis.

15.1.6 Making Conclusions About the Population

Statistical testing is conducted on statistic calculated on the collected data. It could be estimating of the mean value on the original population or making judgment about the tested hypotheses according to the chosen significance level.

The conclusions are made about the properties of the population tested on the selected sample or samples. It is critical to make sure that the statistical analysis is relevant to the formulated research question and derived conclusions are viable.

15.2 Sampling Methods

As we already understand, developing the proper sampling technique can greatly affect the quality of results. There are five common types of sampling techniques that can be used subject to the situation and the goal of the sampling:

- ***Random Sampling***: Members of the population are chosen in such a way that all have an equal chance to be measured.
- ***Systematic Sampling***: Every k-th member of the population is sampled.
- ***Stratified Sampling***: The population is divided into two or more strata and each subpopulation is sampled (usually randomly).
- ***Cluster Sampling***: A population is divided into clusters and a few of these (often randomly selected) clusters are exhaustively sampled.
- ***Convenience Sampling***: Sampling is done as convenient, often allowing the element to choose whether or not it is sampled.

15.2.1 Random Sampling

In ***random sampling***, members of the population are chosen in such a way that all have an equal chance to be selected. As you might have already figured out, it is simple random sampling, where each element of the sample is randomly chosen from the population by using a random number generator. An example of random sampling is presented in ◘ Fig. 15.1.

Advantages of Simple Random Sampling

Simple random sampling can be quite efficient and unbiased if there is an equal access to the entire population to ensure equal chances for each member of the population to be chosen and the sampling procedure supports such equal chances and leads to really random unbiased selection.

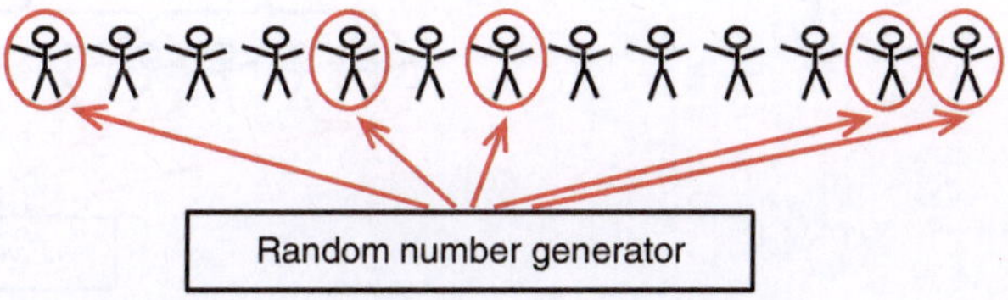

◘ **Fig. 15.1** Example of random sampling

For example, we would like to estimate the percentage of spoiled wine in a collection of bottled wine where all bottles contain the same wine and have been stored in the same conditions. For such estimate, we can select a simple random sample from the collection following the numbers given by a random number generator. Such a sampling may work just fine in this case.

Disadvantages of Simple Random Sampling

The last comment about unbiased random selection is very important. If a formal generator of random numbers is used for the selection procedure and all members of the population are equally available and reachable, then the random sampling could be unbiased. However, such conditions are not always available. Sometimes, we just "point a finger" pretending it is a random choice and forget that such procedure may hide some patterns in the selection method.

Suppose you want to learn the percentage of people who serve in military among all people. For this purpose, you counted on a randomly selected sample on the street those who wear military uniform. Most likely, the result obtained on such sample would be quite off from the actual percentage in the population. There are several reasons for that. First of all, military people are most likely concentrated at the military installations rather than walking on the streets proportional to other people. Secondly, not all military people are wearing uniform while walking on the streets.

15.2.2 Systematic Sampling

In ***systematic sampling***, every k-th element in the population is included in a sample up until the required number of elements is collected in the sample. Choose number k big enough to avoid getting into a structural pattern in the population. It is practical to choose the first element randomly to avoid any biased initiation of the sample. With such a procedure, each element in the population has a known and equal probability to be selected in a sample. An example of a systematic sampling is given in ◘ Fig. 15.2.

Advantages of Systematic Sampling

15

The major advantage of systematic sampling is simplicity. Suppose a company is manufacturing combustion engines for cars. To control production quality, every 50-th engine is given a thorough examination after a test run-up. With the first

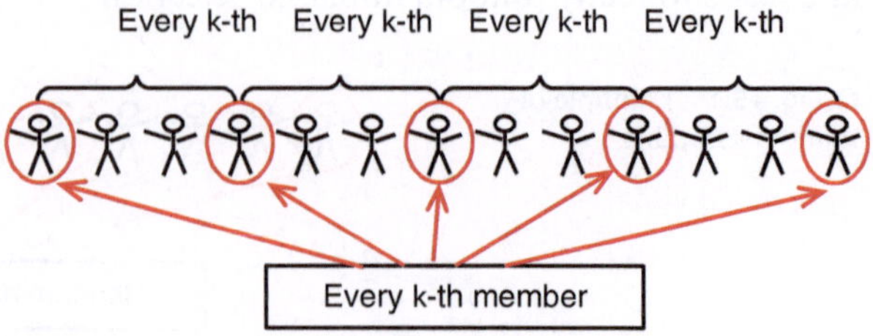

◘ **Fig. 15.2** Example of systematic sampling

engine on the test line randomly selected for examination, the rest of the selection procedure is quite simple.

Disadvantages of Systematic Sampling

We have to be aware that with systematic sampling, there is a chance to capture a structural pattern of the population that would be quite destructing for the concept of sampling. For example, we would like to assess the value of houses in the neighborhood. For this reason, we will include every 5-th house on the street in a sample for evaluation. However, for some reasons, when that neighborhood was built, the builder used five different house designs and built the houses in a pattern by five. Thus with a systematic sampling that selects every 5-th house, we'll collect a wrong sample.

15.2.3 Stratified Sampling

It may occur that a population is not homogeneous but rather divided into two or more subpopulations different by certain specific features important for the purpose of the current analysis. Each such a subpopulation is referred to as ***strata***.

Strata is the plural form of stratum (Latin). Stratum is:

- One of the usually many layers of a substance (such as rock)
- A level of society made up of people of the same rank or position

Stratified sampling is used to make sure that every group is proportionally represented. It would be practical to consider each stratum (or subpopulation) separately and build a sample from subsamples that represent the subpopulations proportionally to their size in the original population. We can use simple random sampling or systematic sampling for each subpopulation. Such a sampling approach is referred to as ***stratified sampling*** that guarantees that all subpopulations are proportionally represented in the final sample for analysis. An example of a stratified sampling is shown in ◘ Fig. 15.3.

Advantages of Stratified Sampling

The major advantage of stratified sampling is that the stratified sampling leads to a balanced sampling. Let's expand the example with quality control at the car

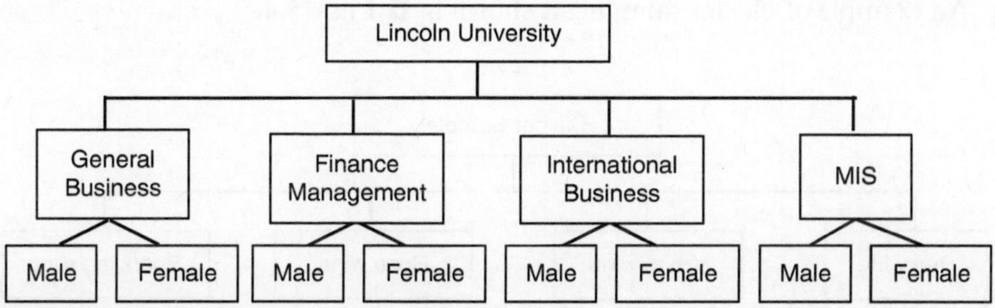

◘ **Fig. 15.3** Example of stratified sampling

engine production plant that we used for systematic sampling. Suppose there are ten different types of engines that are being built on the same assembly line at the same time; 10% of the engines are of type 1, 20% of type 2, 5% of type 3, and so on. Such a situation is quite typical for large engine manufacturing plants. To make sure that all types of engines are given equal to level of quality control, we divide all engines on strata by their types, apply systematic sampling for each stratum, and build a final sample by combining the systematic samples for each engine type proportionally to the production volume of each type of engines.

Disadvantages of Stratified Sampling

Doing stratified sampling requires accurate information about population and the principle of dividing it into subpopulations. It would be inappropriate to divide a population into strata by any parameter which does not have a relationship to the purpose of the current analysis. Such a division would create additional complexity in sampling procedure. However, the most serious problem may arise from a wrong representation of the population by the sample that would lead to wrong conclusions. Suppose we are learning consumer preferences. For some reasons, we divided the population of consumers in two strata by the parameter other than income. The stratified sample has indicated that consumers from one stratum have different preferences that consumer from another stratum.

15.2.4 Cluster Sampling

In ***cluster sampling***, a population is divided into clusters (groups) when natural grouping into cluster is evident. It could be geographical clustering by regions, by counties, or by cities. Then a random sample from that cluster is selected, and the measurements are performed on the clusters included into the sample. The measurements in each cluster included in the sample could be conducted on all elements or on a random subsample selected in each cluster.

Cluster sampling works best when the variations within each cluster are similar to the variations in the population. For example, marketing research has a goal to find out the consumer preferences on iPhone versus other mobile phones. It is assumed that the variation of preferences in the population does not depend on cluster. Then we divide the country into clusters by cities and then randomly select a sample of such clusters to conduct the research in each cluster of the selected sample.

15

An example of cluster sampling is shown in ◘ Fig. 15.4.

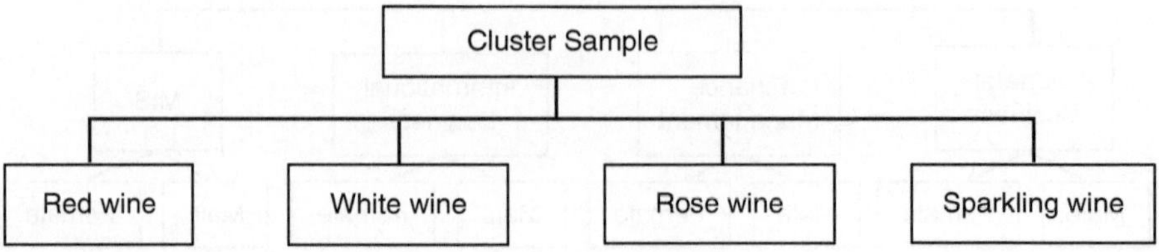

◘ **Fig. 15.4** Example of cluster sampling

Difference Between Cluster Sampling and Stratified Sampling

In cluster sampling, each cluster is treated as an element of the sample. The sample consists of the population of clusters for measurement, and all clusters are presumed to show the same or at least similar variation of the random variable. In stratified sampling, a sample is formed by selecting elements from each stratum.

Cluster sampling is a sampling technique used when "natural" groupings are evident in a statistical population. Cluster can be chosen by geographic area or by some other parameters. It is often used in marketing research. In this technique, the total population is divided into these groups (or clusters), and a sample of the groups is selected. Then the required information is collected from the elements within each selected group. This may be done for every element in these groups, or a subsample of elements may be selected within each of these groups. The technique works best when most of the variation in the population is within the groups, not between them.

Advantages of Cluster Sampling

The major advantage of cluster sampling is in its simplicity. Forming a random sampling throughout the population sometimes would be difficult or even impossible. On the other hand, selecting clusters and conducting measurements on randomly selected clusters is much easier. Let's use the example about iPhone given above. Information about consumer preferences is much easier to collect using the cluster sampling.

Disadvantages of Cluster Sampling

The major disadvantage of cluster sampling is in its relatively low accuracy. Though the clusters are assumed having similar distribution by preferences, such assumption might be quite inaccurate that would lead to inaccuracy of results. Thus, it is advised to use cluster sampling only if it is economically justified.

15.2.5 Convenience Sampling

With ***convenience sampling***, elements of the population are selected based on convenience of picking the elements without forming a random sample or any other samples described above. For example, we want to learn about amount of money people spend annually on travel. For this reason, individuals in a shopping mall were interviewed as they walk by. Some people would be willing to answer to the questions, while some people would not. With the convenience sampling, we limit ourselves with the individuals (or elements of the population) that are easiest to reach rather than best representing the population. Thus, convenience sampling does not correctly represent the population and for this reason is biased.

Another vivid example of convenience sampling is questionnaire about a certain issue randomly sent out by mail. Not all who received the questionnaire will respond. Most likely you will receive the response from those who feel stronger urgency to respond than others. Thus, you got a biased sample.

Advantages of Convenience Sampling

Convenience sampling is much easier to implement than any other sampling method. However, the disadvantages of such sampling significantly offset the convenience of using it.

Disadvantages of Convenience Sampling

In the example of a convenience sampling given above, the results will dramatically vary depending on the location of the shopping mall. Also, most likely, the distribution of people in the shopping mall by their spending on travel might be much off the similar distribution in the entire population. For this reason, we have quite a good chance of selecting an extreme and biased sample. Be careful with convenience sampling.

15.3 Standard Error, Margin of Error, and Confidence Level

The ***standard deviation of the sampling distribution*** indicates the spread of means on different samples on the variety (population) of possible samples. In statistics, it is referred to as the ***standard error of the mean (SEM)*** or just the ***standard error*** or the ***sampling error***. All these terms are synonymous and used interchangeably. Sampling error gives us an understanding of the precision of our statistical estimate of the population mean. A low sampling error implies that we had relatively low variability or a narrower spread in the sampling distribution and, hence, the higher accuracy of the estimate of the population mean within the chosen confidence level *CL*. Just a reminder that there is always a chance, 1 - *CL*, that the estimate is completely wrong.

The ***standard deviation*** on a sample is defined as the standard deviation of the random variable on a single sample.

Thus, let's don't get confused between the standard deviation of the random variable on a single sample and the standard deviation of the sample means on the variety (population) of possible samples:

- The ***standard deviation on a sample*** is defined as the standard deviation of the random variable on a single sample.
- The ***standard deviation of the sampling distribution***, or ***standard error of the mean (SEM)***, or the ***standard error***, and ***sampling error*** all are the synonyms and are defined as the standard deviation of the sample means on the variety (population) of possible samples of a specified size.

In sampling experiments, we can find the confidence interval to estimate how far the mean value on a sample is from the actual mean on the population within the chosen confidence level. We also can test the null hypothesis about the mean value of the population or the mean values on different populations. All these tasks provide the results within the ***margin of error (MOE)*** due to the statistical nature of the problem. The ***margin of error (MOE)*** is expressed as the confidence interval that depends on the confidence level, the sample size, and the standard deviation on the original population. However, the standard deviation on a population is unknown and estimated by the standard deviation on the sample.

It would be very much frustrating to conduct an expensive and time-consuming sampling experiment and then figure out that the margin of error is unacceptably high that makes our efforts meaningless.

As was mentioned above, the margin of error (*MOE*), i.e., the confidence interval, depends on the confidence level, the sample size, and the standard deviation. The confidence level is chosen and assigned according to the nature of the problems and the consequences and cost associated with the possible wrong judgment about the mean on the population. The choice of the confidence level is beyond the sample selection, and this choice is made before conducting a sampling experiment. The standard deviation is attributed to the original population and is also beyond the investigator's control. Thus, the only parameter the investigator may vary is the sample size to meet the required *MOE*, i.e., the required confidence interval. The higher the sample size is, the narrower is the sampling distribution, the smaller is the sampling error, the smaller is the confidence interval, and, hence, the smaller is the margin of error (*MOE*).

A legitimate question arises, how to determine the required minimum sample size to assure the required margin of error in the sampling experiment.

The ***margin of error (MOE)*** in a sampling experiment is defined by the ***confidence interval***, i.e., $MOE = \delta$.

- The ***standard deviation on a sample*** is defined as the standard deviation of the random variable on a single sample.
- The ***standard deviation of the sampling distribution***, or ***standard error of the mean (SEM)***, or the ***standard error***, or ***sampling error*** all are the synonyms and are defined as the standard deviation of the sample means on the variety (population) of possible samples of a specified size.

15.4 Margin of Error and Sample Size

The confidence interval δ for the population mean is the accuracy of the mean estimate under a chosen confidence level. The confidence level *CL* indicates the degree of trust that our judgment is right. If we are right in our judgment, then the estimate of the mean will be with the confidence interval from the mean measured on a sample. However, we may be completely wrong in our judgment with probability $\alpha = 1 - CL$ that would make our estimate no sense at all. The higher is the confidence level, the wider is the confidence interval for the same sample size. On the other hand, confidence intervals get narrow as the sample size grows. Confidence intervals and methods of their calculation were discussed in ▶ Chap. 13.

The confidence interval represents the ***margin of error (MOE)*** for the estimate made to the mean of the population by the mean on a random sample under the chosen confidence level.

The ***required margin of error (RME)*** is the maximum margin of error *MOE* required in the given investigation, i.e., actual *MOE* in the sampling experiment must be lower than or equal to the *RME*

$$MOE \text{ "} RME \tag{15.1}$$

The margin of error *MOE*, also synonymously denoted as δ ($MOE \equiv \delta$), can be calculated according to ▶ Eqs. (13.24) and ▶ (13.34) from ▶ Chap. 13 in the one-sample z-test and *t*-test for a specified confidence level as:

$$\text{(a) } \delta = z_{CR}\frac{\sigma}{\sqrt{n}} \quad \text{using z distribution, if sample is large } (n \geq 30) \text{ or the distribution on the population is normal, and } \sigma \text{ on the population is known}$$

$$\text{(b) } \delta = z_{CR}\frac{s}{\sqrt{n}} \quad \text{using } z \text{ distribution, if sample is large } (n \geq 30) \text{ and } \sigma \text{ on the population is unknown}$$

$$\text{(c) } \delta = t_{CR}\frac{s}{\sqrt{n}} \quad \text{using } t \text{ distribution, typically for small samples } (n < 30) \text{ or if } \sigma \text{ on the population is unknown}$$

$$(15.2)$$

where z_{CR} and t_{CR} are the respective *z*-score and *t*-score; σ and *s* are the standard deviations on the population and on the sample, respectively; and *n* is the sample size. Margin of error $MOE = \delta$ and is synonymous.

The larger the sample size *n*, the smaller is the margin of error δ. In Eq. (15.2), the standard deviations on the population or on the sample come from the composition of the population of the sample and therefore are beyond the investigator's control. The confidence level is reflected is the *z*- and *t*-score.

15.5 Minimum Required Sample Size

15.5.1 Standard Deviation on the Population Is Known

If the standard deviation on the population is known and the population is normally distributed, then the z-distribution can be used to find the margin of error for large samples and the minimum required sample size that can be calculated according to Eq. (15.2a) as

15

$$n = \left(z_{CR} \frac{\sigma}{RME} \right)^2 \tag{15.3}$$

The *z*-score z_{CR} depends only on the chosen significance level α (alpha) and does not depend on the sample size. The confidence level $CL = 1 - \alpha$.

15.5.2 Standard Deviation on the Population Is Unknown

If the standard deviation on the population is unknown, the minimum required sample size can be estimated using *t*-distribution according to Eq. (15.2c) or for large samples using z-distribution according to Eq. (15.2b).

The *t*-score for the *t*-test depends on the chosen significance level α (alpha) and on the degree of freedom, which depends on the sample size. The standard deviation is also unknown before the sample is selected and the statistic is collected. Thus, the direct calculation of the sample size similar to Eq. (15.3) is not formally possible. Thus, it is recommended to conduct preliminary pilot studies to iteratively estimate the standard deviation initially and then to assess the required sample size by matching δ (*MOE*) with the *RME* according to Eq. (15.2c).

The process of estimating the minimum required sample size for the z-test, when the standard deviation on the population is unknown, is as follows:

- Conduct a pilot study with a small sample size to assess the standard deviation on the sample or take it from the previous study.
- Then assess the minimum required sample size using the standard deviation on a small sample.
- Conduct the main sampling experiment using the calculated or a greater minimum sample size.
- Upon completion of the sampling experiment, reassess the minimum required sample size using the standard deviation on the actual sample to make sure that the *MOE* requirements are met. If not, then increase the sample by adding elements from the population.

If similar studies were conducted in the past, then the standard deviation on the sample in the past study could be used instead of conducting a pilot study. However, if the standard deviation on the population is unknown, it is better to conduct the *t*-test based on the Student's *t*-distribution.

If a sample is expected to be large, i.e., $n \geq 30$, then the *t*-distribution becomes very close to *z*-distribution, and then the *z*-distribution and *z*-score can be used for the estimation of the margin of error as in Eq. (15.2b). Thus, the minimum required sample size can be estimated as

$$n = \left(z_{CR} \frac{s}{RME} \right)^2 \tag{15.4}$$

Anyway, it is quite practical to use excessively large samples, if adding more elements to a sample is not related to excessive costs and efforts. As soon as the sample size is estimated, a sample is selected, and the measurements are made, it is necessary to check the actually achieved margin of error according Eq. (15.2). If the achieved *MOE* does not match the *RME* as in Eq. (15.1), then the sample can be increased by randomly adding more elements.

▶ Example 4: Average Height of People in the City

We want to find the average height of adult men in city ABC by measuring the individual height of adult males on a random sample. What should be the sample size to answer the question with the margin of error of 1 inch with the confidence level 95%, i.e., $\alpha = 0.05$? ◀

As soon as people can be taller and shorter than the average height, we will be using two-tailed test and assign $\alpha/2 = 0.025$ for each tail of the sampling distribution. People's height is distributed normally. The z-score or the critical value $z_{CR} = 1.96$ for the two-tailed test with $\alpha = 0.05$. According to the national research, the average height of adult men in the USA is $\mu_{USA} = 70$ inches with the standard deviation $\sigma_{USA} = 3$ inches. We will be using this standard deviation. According to Eq. (15.3), the sample size is

$$n = \left(z_{CR} \frac{\sigma}{RME} \right)^2 = \left(1.96 \frac{3}{1} \right)^2 = 34.6 \approx 35 \tag{15.5}$$

As the sample size was identified, we selected a random sample of size $n = 35$ men. The mean value on the sample was measured $\bar{x}_{City} = 71$ inches with the standard deviation $s_{City} = 4$ inches. The confidence interval provided by such a sample with the confidence of 95% was calculated according Eq. (15.2) as

$$\delta_{City} = z_{CR} \frac{s_{City}}{\sqrt{n}} = 1.96 \frac{4}{\sqrt{35}} = 1.3 \tag{15.6}$$

which is higher than the required margin of error, $RME = 1$. It occurred because the standard deviation on the sample was greater than the standard deviation on the nationwide population, i.e., $s_{City} > \sigma_{USA}$.

In this situation, we may proceed with one of the two scenarios:

Scenario 1 We presume that the standard deviation of men's height in our city matches the nationwide standard deviation, i.e., $\sigma_{City} = \sigma_{USA} = 3$ inches, and the standard deviation measured on the sample $s_{City} = 4$ inches is caused by the specifics of the sample. Thus, we will ignore the result obtain in Eq. (15.5) and declare that the average height of men in our city $\mu_{City} = 71 \pm 1$ inches using the nationwide standard deviation.

Scenario 2 We may assume that the standard deviation measured on the sample better reflects the specifics of our city than the nationwide standard deviation. Recalculate the minimum sample size according to Eq. (15.3) with the standard deviation measured ion the sample, i.e., $s_{City} = 4$ inches, as

$$n = \left(z_{CR} \frac{s_{City}}{RME} \right)^2 = \left(1.96 \frac{4}{1} \right)^2 = 61.5 \approx 62 \tag{15.7}$$

15

Collect a new sample and measure the mean value and the margin of error again. The statistic on the new sample is $\bar{x}_{City} = 71$ inches with the standard deviation $s_{City} = 3$ inches that meets the requirement on the error of margin. Thus, the conclusion is that the average height of men in our city is $\mu_{City} = 71 \pm 1$ inches with the confidence level 95%.

> If the standard deviation on the population is known, then the minimum required sample size for the z-test can be calculated as
>
> $$n = \left(z_{CR} \frac{\sigma}{RME} \right)^2$$
>
> where MOE is the required margin of error.

As soon as the sample size n must be integer, the calculated value size should be rounded up to the integer number.

If the standard deviation on the population is unknown, then the minimum required sample size for the z-test can be found as:
- Conduct a pilot study with a small sample size to assess the standard deviation on the sample or take it from the previous study.
- Then assess the minimum required sample size using the standard deviation on a small sample.
- Conduct the main sampling experiment using the detected or a greater minimum sample size.
- Upon completion of the sampling experiment, reassess the minimum required sample size using the standard deviation on the actual sample to make sure that the *MOE* requirements are met. If not, then increase the sample by adding elements from the population.

15.5.3 One Sample for Binomial Distribution

Binomial distribution describes binary outcomes with probabilities p and $1 - p$, where $0 \le p \le 1$. For example, if we toss a coin, the outcome can be either heads or tails. We can denote the probability of the tails as p and the probability of tails as $1 - p$. If the coin is fair, then $p = 1/2$; otherwise, p may be different from 1/2. The standard deviation on a population with the binomial distribution is

$$\sigma = \sqrt{p(1-p)} \tag{15.8}$$

The main difference between normal distribution and binomial distribution is that binomial distribution is discrete, while the normal distribution can be continuous. You can have 6 heads and 4 tails out of 10 flips of a coin but cannot have 6 ½ heads and 3 ½ tails. Otherwise, the distributions look similar. The critical value z_{CR} can be found using the standard normal distribution tables or the respective computer programs. Thus, the minimum required sample size for a pop can be found by substituting the standard deviation σ in Eq. (15.3) with the one from Eq. (15.7) as

$$n = p(1-p)\left(\frac{z_{CR}}{RME}\right)^2 \tag{15.9}$$

with the rounding it up to the integer number.

The maximum value of the product $p\,(1 - p)$ equals 1/4 at $p = 1/2$. Thus, we can always use $p\,(1 - p) = 1/4$ to be on the safe side, when p on the population is unknown.

▶ Example 5: Percentage of Defective Electronic Chips in the Supply

A large supply of electronic chips was delivered to the company. To assess the percentage of the defective chips, it was decided to collect a sample and calculate the percentage of the defective chips on the sample. What should be the sample size to assess the percentage of the defective parts with the margin of error 3% and the confidence level 95%?

With the confidence level 95%, $\alpha = 0.05$. This is a one-tailed test; hence, the entire α is allocated at the one tail of the sampling distribution. The critical value for one-tailed distribution with $\alpha = 0.05$ is $z_{CR} = 1.645$. ◀

There are two scenarios of solving this problem:

Scenario 1 If testing electronic chips for defects is a relatively cheap procedure and costs and timing of testing are not critical for the company, we will try to reduce the efforts and choose the sample size staying on the safe side. The maximum value of the product p (1 - p) equals 1/4 at p = 1/2. Thus, the sample size is estimated as

$$n = p(1-p)\left(\frac{z_{CR}}{RME}\right)^2 = \frac{1}{2}\left(1-\frac{1}{2}\right)\left(\frac{1.645}{0.02}\right)^2 = 1691.3 \approx 1692 \qquad (15.10)$$

with the sample size n = 1692, and the percentage of the defective parts on the sample was $\bar{x}$ = 12%. We can conclude that the mean percentage of the defective electronic chips in the supply was μ = 12% ± 2% with the confidence level 95%.

It is clear that the sample size was excessively big because we assumed p = 1/2 but it was measured 0.12 on the sample. We can reassess the margin of error by calculating the confidence interval using Eq. (15.2) with the probability p lower than 1/2, but higher than the probability measured on the sample. We may quite safely assume $p = 0.2$. The reassessed confidence interval is

$$\delta = z_{CR}\frac{\sigma}{\sqrt{n}} = z_{CR}\frac{p(1-p)}{\sqrt{n}} = 1.645\frac{0.2(1-0.2)}{\sqrt{1692}} = 0.6\% \qquad (15.11)$$

that exceeds the requirements for the margin for error. Thus, with the chosen sample size, we can conclude that the mean percentage of the defective electronic chips in the supply was μ = 12% ± 0.6% with the confidence level 95%. The actual margin of error exceeds the required margin of error because of the excessively large sample.

15

Scenario 2 If testing electronic chips for defects is an expensive procedure, we will try to find a more accurate minimum sample size to meet the requirements for the margin of error.

We select a preliminary sample of a small size to estimate the probability of defective chips. Suppose a sample of size 30 resulted in the 14% percent of the defective chips. Then the standard deviation on the sample is $s = p\ (1 - p) = 0.14*(1-$

0.14) = 0.1204. We understand that the measurements in a relatively small sample may be quite different from those on the population. To be on a safer side, we double the probability to calculate the minimum sample size, say assume $p = 0.28$. Then the minimum sample size will be calculated as

$$n = p(1-p)\left(\frac{z_{CR}}{RME}\right)^2 = 0.28(1-0.28)\left(\frac{1.645}{0.02}\right)^2 = 1363.8 \approx 1364 \qquad (15.12)$$

A sample of size $n = 1364$ measures the mean $\overline{x} = 11\%$ and the standard deviation $s = 20\%$. Thus, we can conclude that the supply has the mean percentage of defective chips $\mu = 11\% \pm 2\%$.

For the binomial distribution on the population, the minimum required sample size can be calculated as

$$n = p(1-p)\left(\frac{z_{CR}}{RME}\right)^2$$

where *RME* is the required margin of error.

As soon as the sample size *n* must be integer, the calculated value size should be rounded up to the integer number.

15.5.4 Two Unpaired Samples

It is quite complex to accurately estimate the required size of two independent samples for the unpaired test because such an estimation involves too many parameters yet is unknown until the sample is selected and the appropriate measurements are made. It would be easier to make an initial estimate for one-sample test as described above and then do two samples, each not smaller than the estimate for the one-sample test.

15.5.5 Two Paired Samples

The two-sample paired test is actually a one-sample test with measurements conducted on the same sample at different conditions. Thus, the required minimum sample size can be estimated following the rules for the one-sample test to meet *RME* for both conditions.

Some most popular confidence levels and their respective z-scores are shown in ◘ Table 15.1.

Table 15.1 Most popular confidence levels and their respective z-scores

Confidence level	Area between 0 and z-score	Area in one tail (alpha/2)	z-score
80%	0.4000	0.1000	1.282
90%	0.4500	0.0500	1.645
95%	0.4750	0.0250	1.960
98%	0.4900	0.0100	2.326
99%	0.4950	0.0050	2.576

15.6 Summary of the Sampling Experiment Process

- Step 1: Accurately Formulating the Problem for the Sampling Experiment

Accurate and clear formulation of the problem is essential for any research including sampling experiment. Accurately define the population that consists of the random variable *X*, for which we would like to find the population mean, μ.

- Step 2: Choosing the Confidence Level

The confidence level (or the significance level) is chosen according the principles described in ► Chap. 13. The confidence level should be chosen before the experiment is conducted and a sample selected.

- Step 3: Choosing the Sample Size

Choosing a sample size is one of the very important steps in a sampling experiment design. With a larger sample (*n* is high), we can get a higher accuracy of the estimation, while with a smaller sample, the accuracy is going to be lower. It is important to estimate the sample size. It can be done using the methodology described in Sect. 15.5.

- Step 4: Selecting a Sample

Theoretically, a sample must be randomly selected. However, the sample selection techniques discussed in Sect. 15.2 target the minimization of the probability of selecting a sample outside the extreme outliers.

- Step 5: Estimating the Population Mean and Constructing a Confidence Interval

The mean value of the population μ is estimated by the mean measured on the selected sample $\overline{x}$. The confidence interval and, hence, the margin of error are calculated based on the chosen confidence level and the sample size.

- Step 6: Finalizing the Experiment

The achieved margin of error (*MOE*) should be compared with the required margin of error (MRE). If there is a necessity to improve the actual *MOE*, then the sample can be appended by adding random elements and reassessing the mean and *MOE*.

The most important final step in the sampling experiment as in any research is to finally interpret the results and derive conclusions.

Questions for Self-Control for Chapter 15

1. Why are sampling experiments needed?
2. What is the difference between variables on samples and parameters on the population?
3. What are the major challenges of selecting samples?
4. List and describe all types of sampling you know.
5. What is random sampling?
6. What is systematic sampling?
7. What is the difference between stratified and cluster samplings?
8. What are the advantages and disadvantages of convenience sampling?
9. What is standard error on a sample?
10. How to find a needed sample size?
11. How to calculate a confidence interval?
12. What is the percentile for one standard deviation from both sides of the center of normal distribution?
13. What is the percentile for two standard deviations from both sides of the center of normal distribution?
14. What is the percentile for three standard deviations from both sides of the center of normal distribution?
15. What is confidence level?
16. What is the difference between confidence level and significance?
17. What is sampling distribution error alpha?
18. What is the margin of error?
19. What is the required margin of error?
20. How to find the minimum sample size to meet the required margin of error when the standard deviation on the population is known?
21. How to find the minimum sample size to meet the required margin of error when the standard deviation on the population is unknown?
22. How to find the minimum sample size to meet the required margin of error in the two-sample unpaired test?
23. How to find the minimum sample size to meet the required margin of error in the two-sample paired test?

Problems for Chapter 15

1. It is known from previous experiments that the standard deviation of height of men is about 11 cm. How big should be a sample to estimate the mean height of men in the city with the margin of error 3 cm and confidence level 95%?

Survey Method

Contents

16.1 The Purpose of a Survey – 345

16.2 Statistical Nature of Surveys – 345

16.3 Phases of the Survey Method – 346
16.3.1 Preparation for Survey – 346
16.3.2 Conducting the Survey and Collecting Data – 346
16.3.3 Data Processing – 347
16.3.4 Deriving Conclusions and Making Recommendations – 347

16.4 Closed-Ended and Open-Ended Questions – 347
16.4.1 Closed-Ended Questions – 347
16.4.2 Open-Ended Questions – 350

16.5 Constructing a Questionnaire – 350
16.5.1 A Survey Questionnaire as a Story With Variables for Data Acquisition – 350
16.5.2 General Structure of a Questionnaire – 351
16.5.3 The Form, Size, and Format – 351
16.5.4 Anonymity and Confidentiality – 353

16.6 Media for Survey – 353
16.6.1 Verbal Surveys – 353
16.6.2 Printed Paper Surveys – 353
16.6.3 Online Surveys – 354

S. K. Aityan, *Business Research Methodology*, Classroom Companion: Business,
https://doi.org/10.1007/978-3-030-76857-7_16

16.7 Testing the Survey Before Running It – 354
16.7.1 General – 354
16.7.2 Form – 355
16.7.3 Cover and Follow-Up Letters – 355

16.8 Selecting a Sample: Whom to Ask? – 356

16.9 The Sample Size: How Many People to Ask? – 356

16.1 The Purpose of a Survey

A survey is a research method used for collecting data from a group of respondents to collect information and opinions about various topics of interest. Surveys may have multiple purposes, and researchers can conduct it in many ways depending on the chosen methodology and the goals. In the modern time, surveys are an essential tool in social research. Surveys are mostly used to collect subjective information by asking respondent's opinion such as opinion, preference, expectation, intention, health, and other type of information which is hard or impossible to measure objectively. However, surveys may help in collecting some objective information too when the direct access to such information is uneasy or even impossible.

The data is usually obtained by using standardized procedures established for respondents. The process involves asking people for information through a questionnaire, which can be either online or offline. However, with the arrival of new technologies, it is common to distribute questionnaires using digital media such as social networks, email, or URLs.

16.2 Statistical Nature of Surveys

A survey, unless it is conducted on the entire population, is a sample of the answers in filled questionnaire that implies statistical analysis of the statistic collected in the survey:

- To estimate the mean on the respective population
- To make a judgment about the means on two populations

Statistical analysis of the population mean based on statistic collected on a sample was discussed in ► Chap. 13, and statistical hypothesis testing was discussed in ► Chap. 14. Sampling as a combination of methods of selecting the appropriate samples for statistical analysis was described in ► Chap. 15. All those statistical methods are applicable to selecting samples and processing of survey results. Thus, in this chapter, we are focused on the survey design, survey logic, and organizing and conducting the survey.

► Example 1: A Political Poll

A poll conducted with a group of people is used to estimate the opinion of the population about supporting a specified candidate in the election campaign. The result estimates the percentage of supporters together with the margin of error.

► Example 2: Opinion About Customer Satisfaction

A survey conducted on a group of customers to find out customer satisfaction with the company's product or services.

16.3 Phases of the Survey Method

Surveys are self-contained research projects that go through four distinct project phases as any other research projects:
1. Preparation for survey
2. Conducting the survey and collecting responses
3. Data processing
4. Deriving conclusions and making recommendations

The above four phases show specifics related to surveys, which are addressed in this chapter. The logical phase of delivering the results is the same as for any other research project, and for this reason, it is not addressed in this chapter.

16.3.1 Preparation for Survey

The preparation phase is essential for a survey as much as in any other research project. This phase includes the following steps:

1.1. Clearly formulate the main research problem and its purpose. This step includes the formulation of the main question (problem) and subquestions (subproblems) of the survey.
1.2. Develop questionnaire questions for each subproblem.
1.3. Develop the survey questionnaire with sections by subproblems and qualifying questions.
1.4. Decide on the survey media and delivery (paper, Internet, other).
1.5. Decide on the choice of respondents (a sample) for the survey:
   - A sample type
   - A sample selection technique

1.6. Develop the data processing approach and test it on the made-up data.
1.7. Develop a survey conducting plan.

The preparation for a survey should include all other steps relevant to the preparation for research as discussed in detail in ► Chaps. 4, 5, 6, and 7.

16.3.2 Conducting the Survey and Collecting Data

Conducting the survey implies the activities according to the plan developed in the preparation phase. This includes two major activities specific to surveys in addition to all typical activities related to research:

2.1. Establish the survey media as planned.
2.2. Select qualified respondents by meeting qualification parameters.
2.3. Communicate to the respondents as planned.
2.4. Conduct the survey as planned and collect data.

Any deviations from the approved plan must be understood, discussed, and reapproved.

16.3.3 Data Processing

As the survey data is collected, it must be accurately processed and interpreted.

3.1. Data processing should be conducted as planned using methods and tools prepared and tested in advance.
3.2. The results must be interpreted without bias according to the established criteria. Particularly, it relates to the answers provided in a free format.

16.3.4 Deriving Conclusions and Making Recommendations

Deriving final conclusion based on the collected and processed responses is the most important phase of the survey. Conclusions should be derived objectively without bias answering the main question or questions phrased in the survey problem statement.

16.4 Closed-Ended and Open-Ended Questions

Question in the questionnaire can be closed-ended and open-ended.

16.4.1 Closed-Ended Questions

Closed-ended questions are the questions with the preset answers, where the respondents choose one of the answers or multiple answers or none of them. Some closed-ended questions may allow the respondent to choose only one answer, and some may allow choosing multiple answers. Some questions may allow choosing no answer at all, but some may require at least one choice. Examples of closed-ended questions are presented in ◘ Fig. 16.1.

Question 1 in ◘ Fig. 16.1 implies a simple answer "Yes" or "No." Question 2 offers interval choices; question 3 provides qualitative ordinal choices, i.e., qualitative answers, which can be ordered by their strength; and question 4 offers qualitative answers that cannot be placed in any reasonable order except the physical spectrum frequency, which is irrelevant to any business issues.

The initial processing of closed-ended responses consists of counting the number of different responses. The respective histograms can be built according to those counts to analyze the distribution of the opinions in the survey. Some answers like answer 1 in ◘ Fig. 16.1 can be used for qualifying purposes. If the choices for answers can be ordered as in question 3 in ◘ Fig. 16.1, it is advisable to associate the qualitative answers with specified numbers representing a scale for finding the

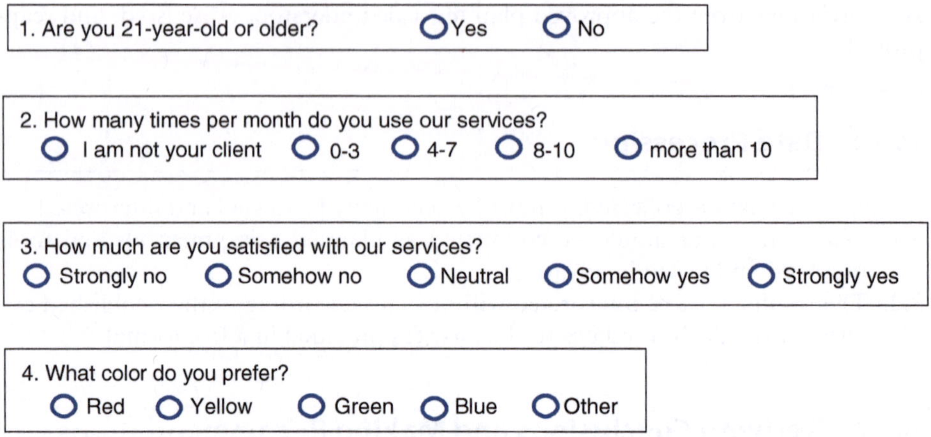

Fig. 16.1 Examples of closed-ended questions

Table 16.1 An example of assigned scale to the ordered answers in a closed-ended question

Choice for answer to a closed-ended question	Assigned numerical values for the answer (Version 1)	Assigned numerical values for the answer (Version 2)
Strongly no	0	-5
Somehow no	1	-2
Neutral	2	0
Somehow yes	3	1
Strongly yes	4	4

overall mean value of all answers to the question or conducting some other quantitative aggregation of the answers. An example of the assigned numerical scale for the different answers in question 3 in Fig. 16.1 is shown in Table 16.1. The assigned numbers represent the degree of the numerical estimate of value adopted by the survey organizer for the answers to the particular question or a group of questions. The numbers may vary and may be not equidistant as shown in the right column (Version 2) in Table 16.1. All depends on the meaning of the assigned values given by the survey designers. However, typically and most frequently, the assigned numbers are equidistant as in the middle column (Version 1) in Table 16.1 stating the uniformity of the chosen scale.

The numerical values of the choices in the closed-ended questions may be or may not be shown in the questionnaire because the respondents are expected to answer qualitatively, but the results are processed quantitatively. However, sometime, it makes sense to show the numerical scale in the questionnaire too to inform the respondents about the relative meaning of the qualitative answers.

The numerical values assigned to the different answers may be used to calculate the mean value of all answers or some other statistic as a score provided by the respondents.

It would be hard and would most of the time make no sense to assign numerical values to the answers, which cannot be ordered like question 4 in ◘ Fig. 16.1 about colors. In this case, the processing may consist only of counting the choice by colors and generating a respective table, a chart, or a histogram.

Taking into account that the respondents in the survey may represent a sample from a much broader population, the observed results may be used to estimate the opinion of the entire population. It can be done using statistical methods of estimating confidence intervals or testing hypotheses as was discussed in ► Chaps. 13 and 14.

The major advantage of closed-ended questions is in the convenience of their initial processing by just counting the answers in each of the multiple choice. The major disadvantage of closed-ended questions is that the respondent may not find the desired answer among the preset choices of answers that prevents the respondent from providing an accurate opinion. This situation may create a confusion that would possibly lead to biased conclusions derived from the survey. Such a situation may occur unknowingly or, possibly, used knowingly to manipulate the results of the survey. Particularly be alert about such situations, when one question includes two related statements. Examples of confusing closed-ended questions are presented in ◘ Fig. 16.2. Question 1 in ◘ Fig. 16.2 has two distinct focus points "should be improved" and "more money." If the respondent answers "Yes," it means that the respondent agrees that education should be improved and adding more money will solve the problem. If the respondent answers "No," it may imply that there is no problem with education. However, there is not preset option to answer, if the respondent believes that education should be improved, but adding money is not the solution. The present answers to question 2 in ◘ Fig. 16.2 implicitly imply that mankind need so much energy as it consumes now. However, if the respondent believes that, we just do not need so much energy. Maybe better to open window in San Francisco than run air conditioner all day long. We are not debating the answers, but just pointing out at a possible confusion.

1. Do you believe that education should be improved and more money allocated to education?
   ○ Yes ○ No

2. What is the best way of reducing consumption of fossil fuel? Choose one answer.
   ○ Switch to solar energy
   ○ Switch to hydro energy
   ○ Switch to nuclear energy
   ○ Switch to wind energy
   ○ Switch to hydrogen energy

◘ **Fig. 16.2** Examples of confusing closed-ended questions

1. What is the most important for you in our services?
   Write your answer here as you feel (limit 100 letters):________________

2. Provide your suggestions for improving your learning experience at our university?
   Write your brief answer here: ________________

Fig. 16.3 Examples of open-ended questions

16.4.2 Open-Ended Questions

An ***open-ended question*** is a question that allows the respondent to provide the answer in a free form. Examples of open-ended questions are shown in Fig. 16.3.

An advantage of open-ended questions is that they allow the respondents to express their opinions exactly as they want. However, the same advantage turns into a significant disadvantage because of the problems associated with the processing of the answers to open-ended questions. To process the answers to the open-ended questions, the answers must be first interpreted and categorized. Interpretation of any free-form statement depends on the subjective opinions of the interpreters, thus introducing a subjective bias of those who are involved in the interpretation of the answers. This makes the open-ended questions very vulnerable to subjective biases of the survey operators. For this reason, it is advisable to avoid open-ended questions unless they are needed to find out something new and unexpected from the respondents.

- *Closed-ended questions* are the questions with the preset answers, where the respondents choose one of the answers or multiple answers or none of them.
- *Open-ended questions* are questions which allow the respondent to provide the answer in a free form.

16.5 Constructing a Questionnaire

16.5.1 A Survey Questionnaire as a Story With Variables for Data Acquisition

A survey is conducted to find out the answer to a research question or questions based on the answers to the questions provided by respondents. By answering the survey questions, respondents fill up the blanks in the "framework story told" by the questionnaire. The questions play the role of variables, and the respondent answers are the values of those variables. Thus, the quality and focus of survey questions, their structure, and the overall logic are crucially important for solving the research problem that led to the survey.

16.5.2 General Structure of a Questionnaire

A survey questionnaire is a structured source of data acquisition, where each respondent provides data according to his/her individual opinion or point of view. A well-designed questionnaire should have separate logical sections related to the respective subquestions for the main research question or questions. Each logical section of the questionnaire consists of the questions, answers to which provide data for answering the subquestion. The structure of a typical questionnaire is shown in ◘ Fig. 16.4.

The first section of the questionnaire is the introductory section that briefly explains the purpose and goal of the survey and provides the appropriate disclaimers. The disclaimer section must state that the questionnaire does not ask to provide the identity of the respondents and will not release their identity in any form. Such explanations and disclaimers are important to make the respondents comfortable and willing to answer the questionnaire.

The verifying and qualifying section follows the introductory section. This section is needed for the questionnaires, for which the demographic information or other aggregate profiling are essential or for the questionnaires for which respondents need to meet specific qualifying requirements.

In the questionnaires, try not to ask unnecessary questions and focus only on the important ones. Most people are not willing to provide personal information, and if the respondents are not comfortable, they will either quit answering or provide false information. Remember, respondents are not obligated to participate in the survey, and they do it on their own will and spend their own time to answering the questions.

16.5.3 The Form, Size, and Format

Participating in the survey is typically voluntary for respondents, and they must be willing and comfortable in providing the answers to the questionnaire. Therefore, the form, format, and size of the questionnaire play an important role in making the respondents willing to participate in the survey.

The size of the questionnaire should be limited to the comfortable number of questions that do not require unreasonably long time to answer. If the number of questions in the questionnaire is too big, the respondents may be unwilling to spend extensive time to it and quit the survey. Thus, it is essential to keep the questionnaire clean of the unnecessary questions and make the questionnaire short enough.

Respondents are normally unwilling to spend their time and participate in a questionnaire if they do not logically understand the questions, their interrelation-

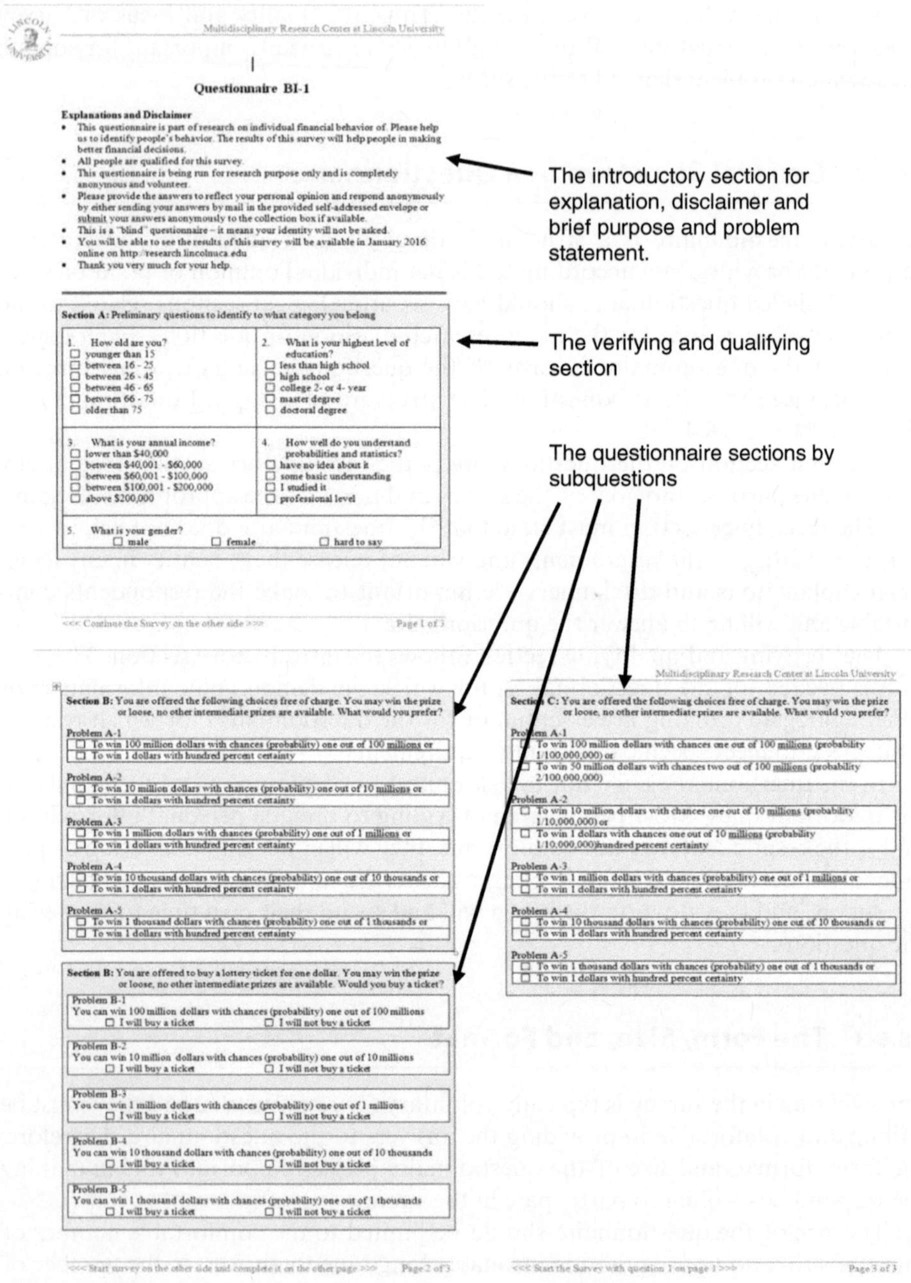
Multidisciplinary Research Center at Lincoln University

Questionnaire BI-1

Explanations and Disclaimer
- This questionnaire is part of research on individual financial behavior of. Please help us to identify people's behavior. The results of this survey will help people in making better financial decisions.
- All people are qualified for this survey.
- This questionnaire is being run for research purpose only and is completely anonymous and volunteer.
- Please provide the answers to reflect your personal opinion and respond anonymously by either sending your answers by mail in the provided self-addressed envelope or submit your answers anonymously to the collection box if available.
- This is a "blind" questionnaire – it means your identity will not be asked.
- You will be able to see the results of this survey will be available in January 2016 online on http://research.lincolnuca.edu
- Thank you very much for your help.

Section A: Preliminary questions to identify to what category you belong

1. How old are you?
☐ younger than 15
☐ between 16 - 25
☐ between 26 - 45
☐ between 46 - 65
☐ between 66 - 75
☐ older than 75

2. What is your highest level of education?
☐ less than high school
☐ high school
☐ college 2- or 4- year
☐ master degree
☐ doctoral degree

3. What is your annual income?
☐ lower than $40,000
☐ between $40,001 - $60,000
☐ between $60,001 - $100,000
☐ between $100,001 - $200,000
☐ above $200,000

4. How well do you understand probabilities and statistics?
☐ have no idea about it
☐ some basic understanding
☐ I studied it
☐ professional level

5. What is your gender?
☐ male ☐ female ☐ hard to say

<<< Continue the Survey on the other side >>> Page 1 of 3

Section B: You are offered the following choices free of charge. You may win the prize or loose, no other intermediate prizes are available. What would you prefer?

Problem A-1
☐ To win 100 million dollars with chances (probability) one out of 100 millions or
☐ To win 1 dollars with hundred percent certainty

Problem A-2
☐ To win 10 million dollars with chances (probability) one out of 10 millions or
☐ To win 1 dollars with hundred percent certainty

Problem A-3
☐ To win 1 million dollars with chances (probability) one out of 1 millions or
☐ To win 1 dollars with hundred percent certainty

Problem A-4
☐ To win 10 thousand dollars with chances (probability) one out of 10 thousands or
☐ To win 1 dollars with hundred percent certainty

Problem A-5
☐ To win 1 thousand dollars with chances (probability) one out of 1 thousands or
☐ To win 1 dollars with hundred percent certainty

Section B: You are offered to buy a lottery ticket for one dollar. You may win the prize or loose, no other intermediate prizes are available. Would you buy a ticket?

Problem B-1
You can win 100 million dollars with chances (probability) one out of 100 millions
☐ I will buy a ticket ☐ I will not buy a ticket

Problem B-2
You can win 10 million dollars with chances (probability) one out of 10 millions
☐ I will buy a ticket ☐ I will not buy a ticket

Problem B-3
You can win 1 million dollars with chances (probability) one out of 1 millions
☐ I will buy a ticket ☐ I will not buy a ticket

Problem B-4
You can win 10 thousand dollars with chances (probability) one out of 10 thousands
☐ I will buy a ticket ☐ I will not buy a ticket

Problem B-5
You can win 1 thousand dollars with chances (probability) one out of 1 thousands
☐ I will buy a ticket ☐ I will not buy a ticket

<<< Start survey on the other side and complete it on the other page >>> Page 2 of 3

Multidisciplinary Research Center at Lincoln University

Section C: You are offered the following choices free of charge. You may win the prize or loose, no other intermediate prizes are available. What would you prefer?

Problem A-1
☐ To win 100 million dollars with chances one out of 100 millions (probability 1/100,000,000) or
☐ To win 50 million dollars with chances two out of 100 millions (probability 2/100,000,000)

Problem A-2
☐ To win 10 million dollars with chances one out of 10 millions (probability 1/10,000,000) or
☐ To win 1 dollars with chances one out of 10 millions (probability 1/10,000,000)hundred percent certainty

Problem A-3
☐ To win 1 million dollars with chances (probability) one out of 1 millions or
☐ To win 1 dollars with hundred percent certainty

Problem A-4
☐ To win 10 thousand dollars with chances (probability) one out of 10 thousands or
☐ To win 1 dollars with hundred percent certainty

Problem A-5
☐ To win 1 thousand dollars with chances (probability) one out of 1 thousands or
☐ To win 1 dollars with hundred percent certainty

<<< Start the Survey with question 1 on page 1 >>> Page 3 of 3

■ **Fig. 16.4** A sample questionnaire with the appropriate sections

ship, and the overall logic of the questionnaire. Remember, a questionnaire is a story with variables. The values of those variables are provided by the respondent's answers. Thus, respondents should be clear about the whole story in the questionnaire to assure the respondents' participation and their reasonable answers.

16.5.4 Anonymity and Confidentiality

Respondents normally do not want their identity to be released and want full confidentiality of their responses. Otherwise, the respondents may not be willing to participate in the survey or will provide made-up information. Therefore, it is crucially important to assure the respondents in their anonymity and confidentiality.

16.6 Media for Survey

Surveys may be conducted in a variety of media. Among possible media are:
- Verbal surveys
- Printed paper surveys
- Online surveys

Sometimes, different types of media are combined in conducting a survey.

16.6.1 Verbal Surveys

Verbal questions and answers compose the simplest media for survey. Typically, such surveys consist of a single or a couple of questions like public opinion polls. The answers are collected and recorded by a survey operator and later combined with the data other operators for further processing.

16.6.2 Printed Paper Surveys

A printed questionnaire is a traditional media for survey. A printed questionnaire is distributed to the selected respondents by:
- Handing manually
- Sending by mail

Typically, such a printed questionnaire is accompanied by a cover letter and a self-addressed and post-stamped envelope for the response. It would be wrong to expect that the respondent has to use his own envelop and buy a post stamp to send the response back to you. The cover letter contains a greeting, a brief explanation of the survey, and the appreciation for participating in the survey. The letter should contain the assurance that the survey will not collect and will not disclose private information. Also, it is always good and encouraging to inform the respondents where they will be able to find the results of the survey, when it is completed.

16.6.3 Online Surveys

Online surveys are conducted using web or email as a medium. In web surveys, the respondents view the questionnaire, the cover letter, and other survey materials, as well as answer the questions online on the respective website. Email surveys deliver the questionnaire by email and offer online responses and submission.

A great advantage of online surveys is in their simplicity for respondents to answer the questions as well as for the survey organizers to collect and organize data automatically without manual processing.

There are many online web-based survey tools available now on the market. Some of them are offered free of charge.

- A *survey questionnaire is a story with variables.* By answering the survey questions, respondents fill up the blanks in the "framework story told" by the questionnaire.
- The *questions play the role of variables*, and the respondent answers are the values of those variables.

16.7 Testing the Survey Before Running It

Once the questionnaire is ready, it should be thoroughly tested to make sure that that it meets the requirements, provides sufficient information to solve the problem, and is not excessively large. It is important to test the following.

16.7.1 General

- Do you have your research problem and the subproblems well formulated?
- Is the questionnaire method the best possible way of getting the desired information?
- Are you asking for information that you could obtain from available records?
- Is the subject worth investigation, and will the respondents consider it worth their time to answer the questionnaire?

- Is the questionnaire of such a length that the recipients may be reasonably expected to give the amount of the time necessary for accurate answers?
- Will be the respondents likely willing or be authorized to supply the answers to your questions?
- Do the questions stimulate supplementary comments and provide a basis for analysis rather than mere fact grubbing?

16.7.2 Form

- Is the questionnaire size proper for handling and filing?
- Do you have enough identifying material and respondents' qualifying questions if necessary at the top of the questionnaire?
- Are the spaces for answers near the right-hand or left-hand margin or in some other place where they will be easy to tabulate?
- Is the general appearance, neatness, and character of the questionnaire designed to encourage complete and accurate answers? Carelessly prepared questionnaires will likely lead to careless answers.
- Have you guaranteed the anonymity of respondents or confidentiality of responses?
- Have you constructed questions so that the answers will be ready for further processing and statistical analysis?
- Have you used headings to identify major divisions of the questionnaire?
- Is the convenient submission of the filled questionnaire provided? Is a self-addressed and post-stamped envelope provided in the case of printed questionnaire, or is a convenient and user-friendly online submission available?
- In the case of printed questionnaire, will the folded conventionally fit the enclosed return envelope? In the case of online survey, make sure that the filled questionnaire is not too big cause submission problem with slow Internet connection.

16.7.3 Cover and Follow-Up Letters

- Are the questionnaires mailed so that they are likely to reach the respondents at a time convenient for them to answer?
- Does a clear, honest, neat cover letter make a courteous appeal to the interest of the addressee?
- Does it have a professional appearance?
- Is a post-stamped, addressed return envelope enclosed if the respondents are communicated by mail?
- Have you planned follow-up letters or phone calls?

16.8 Selecting a Sample: Whom to Ask?

A correctly selected group of respondents is important for any survey by providing a representative sample. Potential respondents can be selected randomly, but quite frequently, respondents need to be qualified for the survey. For example, if a survey is conducted by an airline about passenger satisfaction, the respondents must at least be airline customers. To select such respondents, the questionnaire may contain the qualifying question or questions, or the distribution list for the survey participants may be selected from the airline customers.

If there are different groups of people that fit in your research profile, please make sure that these groups are represented in the right proportion and the respondents are qualified to belong to the proper groups.

If a survey relates to competitive advantages of new type of tennis shows, please be sure that you are asking people who play tennis.

Suppose you are conducting a research on the most demanded color of the necktie for a cloth company. You decide to go door-to-door during your work hours to ask the questions about the preferred color of the necktie. Most likely, the information you collect in the survey will be irrelevant because most people, who wear neckties, are not working from home during the work hours and the people whom you found at home during the work hours are not the people who wear neckties.

Thus, a sample of respondents can be randomly selected from the appropriate clusters or strata as discussed in ► Chap. 15 related to the selection of samples.

Selecting a sample or a group of respondents for a survey has one specific that differentiates this group from samples in other types of research. This differentiation relates to the fact that some or all selected respondents may refuse participating in the survey. The refusal in the participation in the survey may be not random that would change the sample making it biased. For example, a survey is dedicated to customer opinion about the company's services. Randomly selected customers are asked to provide opinions. Psychologically, unsatisfied customers are more willing to participate in such a survey. Thus, the survey results will be biased toward the lower customer satisfaction. An additional research must be conducted to find out the degree of bias and make the appropriate adjustment.

Psychologically, unsatisfied customers are more willing to participate in such a survey. Thus, the survey results will be biased toward the lower customer satisfaction.

16

16.9 The Sample Size: How Many People to Ask?

Assume you have already selected a representative group or groups of people for your study and now you want to know how many people of each group you have to approach with the questionnaire in your research.

Most likely, you would ask questions to a relatively small number of people from the qualified representative groups because you are practically unable to ask questions to the entire population of the groups, which may be thousands or even millions of people.

A choice of the sample size was discussed in the previous chapter in this book.

Questions for Self-Control for Chap. 16

1. What is the purpose of surveys?
2. What are the major phases of the survey method?
3. What are the major steps in the preparation for survey?
4. What activities are involved in conducting survey and collecting survey data?
5. How to plan survey data processing?
6. How to derive the survey conclusions and recommendations?
7. What are closed-ended questions?
8. What are open-ended questions?
9. What are the advantages and disadvantages of closed-ended and open-ended questions?
10. How to process ordinary questionnaire responses?
11. How to process qualitative responses?
12. How to interpret the questionnaire responses?
13. What is the typical questionnaire structure?
14. What content should be presented in the introductory section of a questionnaire?
15. What size is the best for a questionnaire?
16. How important are anonymity and confidentiality for the survey respondents?
17. What types of media can be used for surveys?
18. How important are the cover letter and follow-up for surveys?
19. How to encourage respondents to participate in survey?
20. How to select survey participants?
21. What may cause biased survey results?
22. How does the number of participants impact on the margin of error?

Problems for Chap. 16

1. A company conducts a customer survey to choose the best company's product by the customer feedback. What are, in your opinion, the major biases in such survey?
2. The customer service department analyzed the customer complaints on six products. Product number 4 shows more complains than product number 5. Which product is more popular among customers?

Linear Regression

Contents

17.1 The Purpose of Regression Analysis – 360

17.2 The Principles of Linear Regression – 360

17.3 Definition of the Best-Fit Line – 361

17.4 Finding the Best-Fit Line – 363

17.5 Interpretation of the Regression Line – 366

17.5.1 Variance and Correlation Analysis – 366

17.6 Coefficient of Determination – 367

17.7 Technical Forecasting – 370

17.8 Finding a Relationship Between Variables – 373

17.9 Finding a Trend – 377

17.10 Calculating a Trend Line Using MS Excel or OO Calc Functions – 385

17.11 Confidence Interval for Regression Parameters – 386

17.12 Multiple Regression – 392

S. K. Aityan, *Business Research Methodology*, Classroom Companion: Business,
https://doi.org/10.1007/978-3-030-76857-7_17

17.1 The Purpose of Regression Analysis

Analysis of relationship between variables, trends, and forecasting belongs to the category of most common business research problems. Finding trends in prices and estimating future sales, profit, production, demand, and other business parameters can be done using fundamental and technical analysis. Fundamental analysis relates to the assessment made using actual business fundamentals and financial statements. Technical analysis is based on the analysis of cycles, functional relationship, and time series of variables. A good business trend analysis and forecast should be made from a combination of both perspectives – fundamental and technical.

Linear regression is the appropriate and practically adequate method for technical analysis of trends, relationship between variables, and forecasting. For example, a company's sales forecast can be made based on the past sales using linear regression in the presumption that there are no fundamental changes in the company business. Another example of linear regression can be given by the assessment of a stock price trend. Linear regression is used in the capital asset pricing model. The concept of the regression beta is one of the basics in the analysis of systematic risk of an investment. This originates from the beta coefficient in the linear regression model for the return on the investment as well as the return on all risky assets.

17.2 The Principles of Linear Regression

Linear regression is a linear model that describes the relationship between two variables by a linear equation best fitting the observed data. One variable is referred to as an ***explanatory variable*** or an ***independent variable***, and the other variable is referred to as a ***response variable*** or a ***dependent variable***.

Suppose company Pacific Pelican has recorded their sales for the past 6 years as shown in ◘ Fig. 17.1 and wants to estimate its sales for the next year if no fundamental surprises occur.

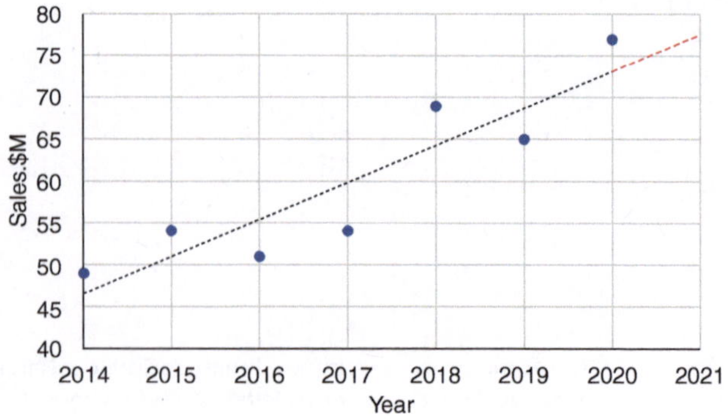

◘ **Fig. 17.1** The observation points and the respective regression line

The dots in ◘ Fig. 17.1 are the annual sales (observed data), and the line is the regression line, i.e., a line that best fits the observed data. The sales forecast can be made by extending the regression line to the next year. The trend line as shown in ◘ Fig. 17.1 is the best-fit line to the observed data. The independent variable in this case is the year, and the dependent variable is the annual sales for each year.

The regression line is the representation of linear relationship with random variations like

$$Y_k = b_0 + b_1 X_k + \varepsilon_k \tag{17.1}$$

where b_0 and b_1 are the estimates of linear relationship between variables Y and X that define the best-fit line and ε is the random variation of Y relative to the linear relationship. Parameter β_0 is referred to as the intercept and b_1 as the regression coefficient.

The example above briefly illustrates the linear regression method. To apply this approach, one has to answer the following questions:

- What is the definition of the best-fit line that fits the observed data?
- How to find the best-fit line?
- What is the forecast and how accurate is it?

Another question relates to the interpretation and meaning of this regression line.

17.3 Definition of the Best-Fit Line

Suppose there are two variables X and Y. X is the independent variable and Y is the dependent variable. The observed data is presented by n observed pairs (x_1, y_1), (x_2, y_2), ... (x_k, y_k), ... (x_n, y_n), as illustrated in ◘ Table 17.1.

The regression line is a line that best fits the observed data. The term "the best" is key that requires its definition. But which line is the best-fitting line? Many lines may look to be a good fit as shown in ◘ Fig. 17.2.

◘ **Table 17.1** Observed values of independent variable X and response variable Y

X	Y
x_1	y_1
x_2	y_2
...	...
x_k	y_k
...	...
x_n	y_n

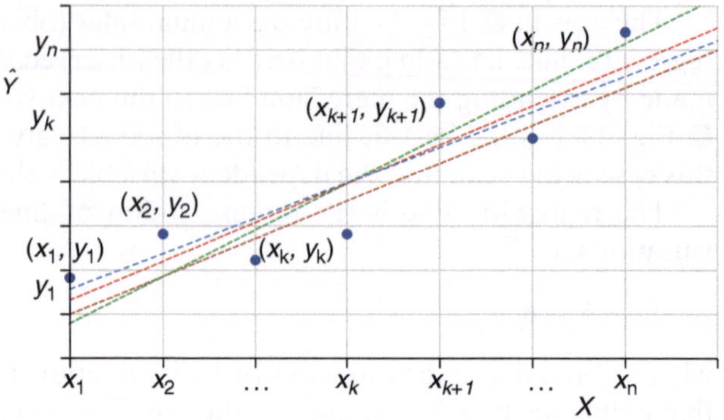

Fig. 17.2 Which line is the best-fitting line?

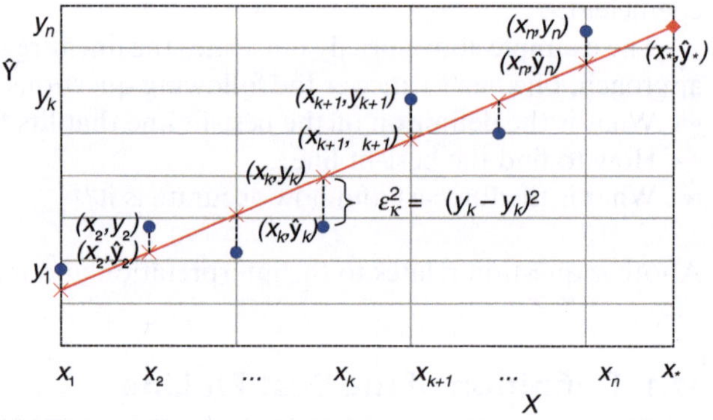

Fig. 17.3 A line and its distance to the observed data

By the best line is understood a line, which is the closest to the observed data. The closest means the line with the minimum distance between the observed points and the line. Suppose there is a line $\hat{Y}(X)$ as shown in Eq. (17.1) and Fig. 17.3

$$\hat{Y} = b_0 + b_1 X \tag{17.2}$$

The distance between observed point (x_k, y_k) as in Table 17.1 and the line as in Eq. (17.1) can be calculated as the distance between point (x_k, y_k) and the point on the line at the matching x_k, i.e., $(x_k, \hat{y}_k)$, as shown in Fig. 17.3. Distances must always be positive. To avoid complications related to possible negative differences between y_k and $\hat{y}_k$, quadratic distance ε_k^2 is calculated as

$$\varepsilon_k^2 = \left(y_k - \hat{y}_k\right)^2 = \left(y_k - b_0 - b_1 x_k\right)^2 \tag{17.3}$$

The total square distance between line $\hat{Y}(X)$ and the observed points $Y(X)$ can be defined as the sum of the square distances from the line to all observed points. Let's call it "residual square error" and denote as $SqErr$,

Table 17.2 Observed values of independent variable *X* and response variable *Y*

X	Y	$\hat{Y}$	ε_k^2
x_1	y_1	$\hat{y}_1 = b_0 + b_1x_1$	$\varepsilon_1^2 = (y_1 - \hat{y}_1)^2 = (y_1 - b_0 - b_1x_1)^2$
x_2	y_2	$\hat{y}_2 = b_0 + b_1x_2$	$\varepsilon_2^2 = (y_2 - \hat{y}_2)^2 = (y_k - b_0 - b_1x_2)^2$
…	…	…	…
x_k	y_k	$\hat{y}_k = b_0 + b_1x_k$	$\varepsilon_k^2 = (y_k - \hat{y}_k)^2 = (y_k - b_0 - b_1x_k)^2$
…	…	…	…
x_n	y_n	$\hat{y}_n = b_0 + b_1x_n$	$\varepsilon_n^2 = (y_n - \hat{y}_n)^2 = (y_n - b_0 - b_1x_n)^2$

$$SqErr = \sum_{k=1}^{n} \varepsilon_k^2 = \sum_{k=1}^{n} (y_k - \hat{y}_k)^2 = \sum_{k=1}^{n} (y_k - b_0 - b_1x_k)^2 \tag{17.4}$$

The observed points, the matching points in line $\hat{Y}(X)$, and the square distance are shown in Table 17.2.

17.4 Finding the Best-Fit Line

The best-fit line for the observed points shown in Table 17.1 is the line that runs closer to the observed points $\{(x_1, y_1) \ldots (x_n, y_n)\}$, i.e., has the lowest possible total square error *SqErr* shown in Eq. (17.4). The observed values of $\{(x_1, y_1) \ldots (x_n, y_n)\}$ are given by the observation and cannot be changed in Eq. (17.3). The only variables in Eq. (17.3) are parameters b_0 and b_1 for line $\hat{Y}(X)$ defined in Eq. (17.2). Thus, total square error is a function of b_0 and b_1, i.e., $SqErr(b_0, b_1)$. To find the best line with the minimum *SqErr*, one has to find such b_0 and b_1 that result in minimum $SqErr(b_0, b_1)$. The necessary condition for minimum of function $SqErr(b_0, b_1)$ is the zero derivatives of $SqErr\,(b_0, b_1)$ by b_0 and b_1, i.e.,

$$\frac{d\left(SqErr\left(b_0,b_1\right)\right)}{db_0} = 0 \quad \text{and} \quad \frac{d\left(SqErr\left(b_0,b_1\right)\right)}{db_0} = 0 \tag{17.5}$$

The expressions for derivatives in Eq. (17.5) can be expanded by using Eq. (17.3) as

$$\frac{d\left(SqErr\left(b_0,b_1\right)\right)}{db_0}=\frac{d\left(\sum_{k=1}^{n}\left(Y_k-b_0-b_1X_k\right)^2\right)}{db_0}=\sum_{k=1}^{n}\frac{d\left(Y_k-b_0-b_1X_k\right)^2}{db_0}=$$
$$=2\sum_{k=1}^{n}\left(Y_k-b_0-b_1X_k\right)\left(-1\right)=0;$$
$$\frac{d\left(SqErr\left(b_0,\beta\right)\right)}{db_1}=\frac{d\left(\sum_{k=1}^{n}\left(Y_k-b_0-b_1x_k\right)^2\right)}{db_1}=\sum_{k=1}^{n}\frac{d\left(Y_k-b_0-b_1X_k\right)^2}{db_1}=$$
$$=2\sum_{k=1}^{n}\left(Y_k-b_0-b_1X_k\right)\left(-X_k\right)=0 \tag{17.6}$$

Equation (17.6) can be simplified and rewritten as

$$\sum_{k=1}^{n}Y_k-\sum_{k=1}^{n}b_0-\sum_{k=1}^{n}b_1X_k=0;$$
$$\sum_{k=1}^{n}X_kY_k-\sum_{k=1}^{n}b_0X_k-\sum_{k=1}^{n}b_1X_k^2=0 \tag{17.7}$$

Taking into account that b_0 and b_1 do not depend on running index k, Eq. (17.7) can be rewritten as

$$\sum_{k=1}^{n}Y_k-nb_0-b_1\sum_{k=1}^{n}X_k=0;$$
$$\sum_{k=1}^{n}X_kY_k-b_0\sum_{k=1}^{n}X_k-b_1\sum_{k=1}^{n}X_k^2=0 \tag{17.8}$$

Thus, there are two linear equations with two variables b_0 and b_1 which are easy to solve and find the respective b_0 and b_1. However, let's conduct some more transformation and simplification of Eq. (17.8) before solving them. The mean values $\overline{X}$ and $\overline{Y}$ of the observed X and Y shown in ◘ Table 17.1 are defined as

$$\overline{X}=\frac{1}{n}\sum_{k=1}^{n}X_k \quad \text{and} \quad \overline{Y}=\frac{1}{n}\sum_{k=1}^{n}Y_k \tag{17.9}$$

Then Eq. (17.8) can be rewritten as

17

$$n\overline{Y}-nb_0-b_1n\overline{X}=0;$$
$$\sum_{k=1}^{n}X_kY_k-b_0n\overline{X}-b_1\sum_{k=1}^{n}X_k^2=0 \tag{17.10}$$

To simplify terms $\sum_{k=1}^{n} X_k Y_k$ and $\sum_{k=1}^{n} X_k^2$ in Eq. (17.10), let's do the following exercises.

Exercise 1 Consider the following expression:

$$\sum_{k=1}^{n}\left(X_k-\bar{X}\right)^2=\sum_{k=1}^{n}X_k^2-2\bar{X}\sum_{k=1}^{n}X_k+\sum_{k=1}^{n}\bar{X}^2=\sum_{k=1}^{n}X_k^2-2n\sum_{k=1}^{n}\bar{x}^2+n\bar{X}^2=\sum_{k=1}^{n}X_k^2-n\bar{X}^2 \quad (17.11)$$

Then from Eq. (17.11), it follows

$$\sum_{k=1}^{n}X_k^2=\sum_{k=1}^{n}\left(X_k-\bar{X}\right)^2+n\bar{X}^2 \quad (17.12)$$

Exercise 2 Consider the following expression:

$$\begin{aligned}\sum_{k=1}^{n}\left(X_k-\bar{X}\right)\left(Y_k-\bar{Y}\right)&=\sum_{k=1}^{n}X_kY_k-\bar{X}\sum_{k=1}^{n}Y_k-\bar{Y}\sum_{k=1}^{n}X_k+n\bar{X}\bar{Y}=\\&=\sum_{k=1}^{n}X_kY_k-n\bar{X}\bar{Y}-n\bar{X}\bar{Y}+n\bar{X}\bar{Y}=\sum_{k=1}^{n}X_kY_k-n\bar{X}\bar{Y}\end{aligned} \quad (17.13)$$

Then Eq. (17.13) transforms into

$$\sum_{k=1}^{n}X_kY_k=\sum_{k=1}^{n}\left(X_k-\bar{X}\right)\left(Y_k-\bar{Y}\right)+n\bar{X}\bar{Y} \quad (17.14)$$

End of Exercises Substituting terms $\sum_{k=1}^{n} X_k Y_k$ and $\sum_{k=1}^{n} X_k^2$ in Eq. (17.10) with the expressions in Eqs. (17.12) and (17.14), Eq. (17.10) transforms into

$$\begin{aligned}&b_0+b_1\bar{X}=\bar{Y};\\&b_0n\bar{X}+b_1\left(\sum_{k=1}^{n}\left(X_k-\bar{X}\right)^2+n\bar{x}^2\right)=\sum_{k=1}^{n}\left(X_k-\bar{X}\right)\left(Y_k-\bar{Y}\right)+n\bar{X}\bar{Y}\end{aligned} \quad (17.15)$$

Two equations in Eq. (17.15) can be solved against variables b_0 and b_1 as

$$b_1=\frac{\sum_{k=1}^{n}\left(X_k-\bar{X}\right)\left(Y_k-\bar{Y}\right)}{\sum_{k=1}^{n}\left(X_k-\bar{X}\right)^2} \quad \text{and} \quad b_0=\bar{y}-\beta\bar{x} \quad (17.16)$$

The origin of the regression line defined in Eq. (17.2) b_0 is the value of $\hat{Y}=b_0+b_1X$ at $X = 0$. This point is referred to as the ***intercept*** and illustrated in ◘ Fig. 17.4. The

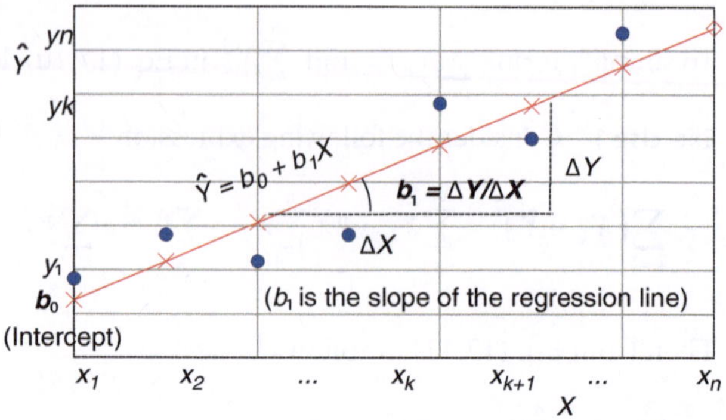

Fig. 17.4 The intercept and the slope of the regression line

intercept represents the value of the dependent variable $\hat{Y}$ with no impact from the independent variable, i.e., at $X = 0$. The coefficient b_1 is the slope of the regression line that represents the marginal rate of impact of independent variable X on the dependent variable $\hat{Y}$ in the linear model.

17.5 Interpretation of the Regression Line

17.5.1 Variance and Correlation Analysis

The expression for the slope of the regression line in Eq. (17.16) can be rewritten using the terms of variance and covariance as

$$b_1 = \frac{\operatorname{cov}(X,Y)}{\operatorname{var}(X)} = \frac{\sum_{k=1}^{n}(X_k - \bar{X})(Y_k - \bar{Y})}{\sum_{k=1}^{n}(X_k - \bar{X})^2} \tag{17.17}$$

Taking into account that the correlation coefficient between two variables X and Y is the covariance normalized by standard deviations of each variable,

$$r_{XY} = \frac{s_{XY}}{s_X s_Y} = \frac{\sum_{k=1}^{n}(X_k - \bar{X})(Y_k - \bar{Y})}{\sqrt{\sum_{k=1}^{n}(X_k - \bar{X})^2}\sqrt{\sum_{k=1}^{n}(Y_k - \bar{Y})^2}} \tag{17.18}$$

the regression slope b_1 in Eq. (17.17) can be rewritten as

$$b_1 = \frac{s_{XY}}{s_X^2} = r_{XY}\frac{\sqrt{\sum_{k=1}^{n}(Y_k - \bar{Y})^2}}{\sqrt{\sum_{k=1}^{n}(X_k - \bar{X})^2}} \tag{17.19}$$

Thus, the slope of the regression line b_1 represents the normalized correlation between variables X and Y. Thus, the slope of the regression line in Eq. (17.2) can be used for finding the correlation coefficient between the dependent and independent variables.

If the regression line pitches up, the correlation between X and Y is positive, i.e., $r_{XY} > 0$, but if the regression line pitches down, the correlation is negative, i.e., $r_{XY} < 0$. If the regression line is horizontal, there is no correlation between X and Y, i.e., $r_{XY} = 0$.

The regression line is defined as a line with the minimum residual sum of square distances between the observed points and the respective points on the line $\hat{Y} = b_0 + b_1 X$

The regression coefficients b_0 and b_1 are

$$b_1 = \frac{\sum_{k=1}^{n} (X_k - \bar{X})(Y_k - \bar{Y})}{\sum_{k=1}^{n} (X_k - \bar{X})^2} \quad \text{and} \quad b_0 = \bar{y} - \beta \bar{x}$$

17.6 Coefficient of Determination

Suppose there are two variables. Variable X is an independent variable and Y is a dependent variable. The set of pairs (X_k, Y_k) are measured in the real-world experiment. The scatter plot of X against Y is shown in ◘ Fig. 17.5 together with the mean values $\bar{X}$ and $\bar{Y}$.

The regression line is the best least square distanced line for actual Ys drawn in the plot. The slope of the line shows the relationship between variables X and Y. For each actual point (X_k, Y_k), the line $\hat{Y}_k$ represents the explained variation of Y against the mean value $\bar{Y}$, and the difference between the actual point Y and the

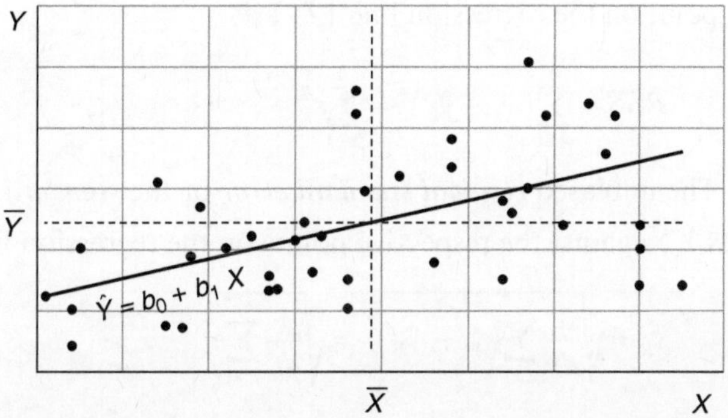

◘ **Fig. 17.5** Scatter plot of (X, Y) relationship and the fitted regression line

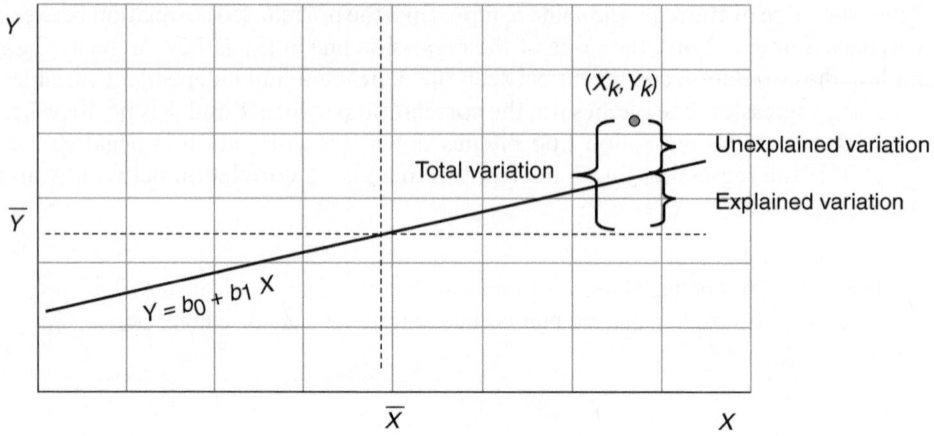

Fig. 17.6 Total, explained, and unexplained variations

point on the line, $|Y_k - \hat{Y}_k|$, represents the unexplained variation caused by random variation from the regression line. The total distance between the actual (X_k, Y_k) and the mean $\overline{Y}$ is referred to as the total variation. These variations are illustrated in Fig. 17.6.

The ***total sum of squares*** of the variation of the observed Y from the mean $\overline{Y}$, TSS, is measured against the mean $\overline{Y}$ as

$$TSS = \sum_{k=1}^{n} (y_k - \overline{y})^2 \tag{17.20}$$

The ***explained sum of squares*** of the variation of the linear model, *ESS*, is measured as the variance of the points in regression line $\hat{Y}$ from the mean $\overline{Y}$ as

$$ESS = \sum_{k=1}^{n} (\hat{y}_k - \overline{y})^2 \tag{17.21}$$

The ***residual or unexplained sum of squares***, *RSS*, of the observed Y is measured as the sum of squared distances between the observed values $\{Y_k\}$ and the respective point on the regression line $\{\hat{Y}_k\}$ as

$$RSS = \sum_{k=1}^{n} (y_k - \hat{y}_k)^2 = \sum_{k=1}^{n} \varepsilon_k^2 \tag{17.22}$$

The unbiased ***residual standard error*** or the ***standard deviation***, s_R, of the observed $\{Y_k\}$ against the respective points on the regression line $\{\hat{Y}_k\}$ can be calculated as

$$s_R = \sqrt{\frac{1}{df}\sum_{k=1}^{n} (y_k - \hat{y}_k)^2} = \sqrt{\frac{1}{df}\sum_{k=1}^{n} \varepsilon_k^2} \tag{17.23}$$

where ε_k is the random error described in Eq. (17.1), the degree of freedom *df* is equal to

$$df = n - k - 1 \tag{17.24}$$

and *k* is the number of predictors, i.e., the number of independent variables in the linear regression. As soon as there is one independent variable *X*, then the number of predictors equals 1, *k* = 1, and the degrees of freedom for dependent variable *Y* according to Eq. (17.24) are

$$df = n - 2 \tag{17.25}$$

The residual variance and the residual standard deviation, s_R, are equal to

$$s_R^2 = \frac{1}{n-2}\sum_{k=1}^{n}(y_k - \hat{y}_k)^2 = \frac{RSS}{n-2} = \frac{1}{n-2}\sum_{k=1}^{n}\varepsilon_k^2$$

and (17.26)

$$s_R = \sqrt{\frac{1}{n-2}\sum_{k=1}^{n}(y_k - \hat{y}_k)^2} = \sqrt{\frac{RSS}{n-2}} = \sqrt{\frac{1}{n-2}\sum_{k=1}^{n}\varepsilon_k^2}$$

On the other hand, the independent variable *X* has no predictors, i.e., *k* = 1, and therefore according to Eq. (17.24) has *n* – 1 degrees of freedom. Thus, the variance and standard deviation of variable X equal

$$s_X^2 = \frac{1}{n-1}\sum_{k=1}^{n}(x_k - \overline{x})^2 \quad \text{and} \quad s_X = \sqrt{\frac{1}{n-1}\sum_{k=1}^{n}(x_k - \overline{x})^2} \tag{17.27}$$

Note that the standard deviation of the independent variable *X* is calculated against the mean value $\overline{X}$, while the residual standard deviation of dependent variable *Y* is calculated against the regression line $\hat{Y}$ that reduces the degree of freedom for *Y* by 1 (Eq. (17.24)).

The ratio of the residual (unexplained) variation *RSS* over the total variation *TSS* may vary in the range

$$0 \le \frac{RSS}{TSS} \le 1 \tag{17.28}$$

If the total variation equals the unexplained variation, *ESS*, the ratio in Eq. (17.28) equals 1. It means that the explained variation equals 0, i.e., the regression line is horizontal and there is no correlation between *X* and *Y*. If the unexplained variation equals 0, the ratio in Eq. (17.28) equals 0. It means that there is no random variation of *Y* and all Y_k lie on the regression line.

The ***coefficient of determination*** R^2 is defined as

$$R^2 = 1 - \frac{RSS}{TSS} \tag{17.29}$$

and describes the closeness of the $\{Y_k\}$ to the regression line. The better the linear regression fits the data in comparison to the simple average $\overline{Y}$, the closer the value of R^2 is to 1.

The ***total sum of squares***, *TSS*, is

$$TSS = \sum_{k=1}^{n} (y_k - \bar{y})^2$$

The ***explained sum of squares*** of the variation of the linear model, *ESS*, is

$$ESS = \sum_{k=1}^{n} (\hat{y}_k - \bar{y})^2$$

The ***residual or unexplained sum of squares***, *RSS*, is

$$RSS = \sum_{k=1}^{n} (y_k - \hat{y}_k)^2 = \sum_{k=1}^{n} \varepsilon_k^2$$

The ***coefficient of determination***, R^2, is defined as

$$R^2 = 1 - \frac{RSS}{TSS}$$

17.7 Technical Forecasting

Forecasting is a complex task that should account for fundamental changes and technical trends. Fundamental changes imply consideration of market, financial, technological, and other changes. Consideration of technical trends is part of technical analysis that accounts for time series and cycle analysis without analysis of the causes. Conceptually, technical analysis presumes that there are no unexpected fundamental changes. A good forecasting should be based on a combination of all former-mentioned forms of analysis. However, technical analysis provides a reasonable forecasting providing that no fundamental changes has occurred for the forecasting period.

Technical forecasting can be done by finding the regression line for the past data and extending it to the future.

▶ Example 1: Sales Forecasting

Suppose a company wants to make a sales forecast for the next year 2021 based in the sales trend from the previous years 2014 to 2020. The company sales by year is shown in the first two columns in ◘ Table 17.3.

Table 17.3 Calculation of the regression line for sales forecast

	k	Year (X_k)	Sales, $M ($Y_k$)	$X_k - \bar{X}$	$Y_k - \bar{Y}$	$(X_k - \bar{X})^2$	$(X_k - \bar{X})(Y_k - \bar{Y})$	$\hat{Y}_k$	$(Y_k - \hat{Y}_k)^2$	$\hat{Y}_k - \sigma$	$\hat{Y}_k + \sigma$
	1	2014	23	–3.00	–10.71	9.00	32.14	21.29	2.94	16.17	26.40
	2	2015	18	–2.00	–15.71	4.00	31.43	25.43	55.18	20.32	30.54
	3	2016	35	–1.00	1.29	1.00	–1.29	29.57	29.47	24.46	34.68
	4	2017	39	0.00	5.29	0.00	0.00	33.71	27.94	28.60	38.83
	5	2018	35	1.00	1.29	1.00	1.29	37.86	8.16	32.74	42.97
	6	2019	37	2.00	3.29	4.00	6.57	42.00	25.00	36.89	47.11
$n =$	7	2020	49	3.00	15.29	9.00	45.86	46.14	8.16	41.03	51.26
		2021						50.29		45.17	55.40
Sum:		14,119	236			28	116		156.86		
Mean:		2017	33.71								

To make a technical forecast, i.e., to make a forecast based on the past trend, one has to:

- Find α and β (Eq. 17.16)) for the regression line $\hat{Y}(X) = b_0 + b_1 X$ (Eq. (17.2)) for the trend formed in 2014–2020
- Extend the regression line $\hat{Y}_{2021} = b_0 + b_1 * 2021$ till $X = 2021$
- The point on the regression line at year 2021, i.e., $\hat{Y}_{2021}$ is the mean forecast for 2021
- The residual standard deviation of the forecast *RSE* is equal to the residual standard error, which is the residual standard deviation according to Eq. (17.26)
  All the above calculations can be conducted either:

- Using a simple calculator, if the amount of data is reasonably small for manual calculations
- Using MS Excel or OO Calc for a significant amount of data
- The data organization for the step-by-step calculations is shown in ◘ Table 17.3. ◄

The columns in ◘ Table 17.3 are designated for the respective components in each row. Column <Year (X_k)> is for years with rows 2014–2020 for the past years and row $X = 2021$ for the forecast year. The column <Sales (Y_k)> shows the past sales by year.

The values in the second row from the bottom "Sum" for columns <Year (X_k)> and < Sales (Y_k)> show the sum of the respective data for the past years, i.e., for all $k = 1, ..., n$. Year 2021 is not included in the sum. The bottom row shows mean (average) values calculated from the appropriate sum divided by n.

Columns < $X_k - \bar{X}$ > and < $Y_k - \bar{Y}$ > are the preparatory columns that show the difference of the respective X_k and Y_k and their means $\bar{X}$ and $\bar{Y}$. Columns < $(X_k - \bar{X})^2$ > and < $(X_k - \bar{X})(Y_k - \bar{Y})$ > show the appropriate value for the respective rows and are used for the calculation of b_0 and b_1 (Eq. 17.16)) for the regression line.

The values of < $(X_k - \bar{X})^2$ > and < $(X_k - \bar{X})(Y_k - \bar{Y})$ > in the row <Sum> show the sums of the values in the respective columns for all $k = 1, ..., n$. Thus, the coefficients α and β can be calculated according to Eq. (17.16) as

$$b_1 = \frac{\sum_{k=1}^{n}(x_k - \bar{x})(y_k - \bar{y})}{\sum_{k=1}^{n}(x_k - \bar{x})^2} = \frac{116}{28} = 4.14 \qquad (17.30)$$

$$b_0 = \bar{Y} - b_1 \bar{X} = 33.71 - 4.14 * 2017 = -8{,}322.43$$

Column < $\hat{Y}_k$ > shows the values on the regression line at the respective X_k including the forecast year 2021. Value of $\hat{Y}_{2021} = b_0 + b_1 * 2021$ is the mean forecast for sales in 2021,

$$\hat{Y}_{2021} = b_0 + b_1 * 2021 = -8{,}322.43 + 4.14 * 2021 = 50.29 \approx 50 \qquad (17.31)$$

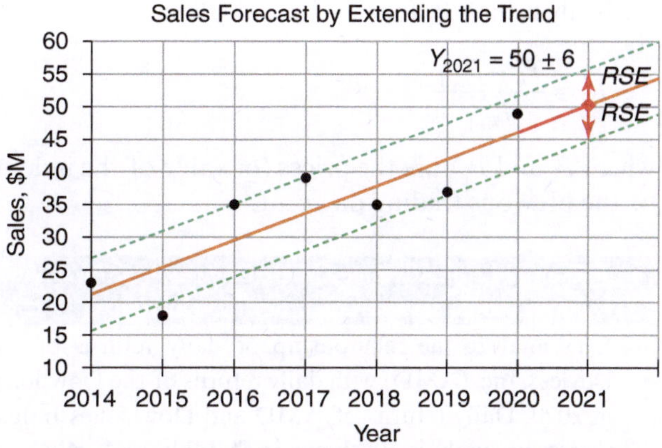

Fig. 17.7 Technical sales forecast by extending the trend from the previous sales data

The residual standard error (or the residual standard deviation) of the forecasted sales from the forecasted value $\hat{Y}_{2021} = 50$ can be expressed in terms of the residual standard error s_R as

$$s_R = \sqrt{\frac{1}{n-2}\sum_{k=1}^{n}\left(Y_k - \hat{Y}_k\right)^2} = \sqrt{\frac{156.86}{5}} = 5.6 \approx 6 \tag{17.32}$$

Thus, the forecasted sale for 2021 is

$$Y_{2021} = 50 \pm 6\$M \tag{17.33}$$

This forecast is illustrated in Fig. 17.7. The chart shows the historical data, the regression line, and the forecasted sales together with the residual standard deviation of the forecast.

17.8 Finding a Relationship Between Variables

The regression line shows the correlation between the explanatory X and response Y variables. If the regression line pitches up, i.e., $b_1 > 0$, the correlation between X and Y is positive, i.e., $r_{XY} > 0$. If the regression line pitches down, i.e., $b_1 < 0$, the correlation is negative, i.e., $r_{XY} < 0$. If the regression line is horizontal, i.e., $b_1 = 0$, there is no correlation between X and Y, i.e., $r_{XY} = 0$.

The following example illustrates the application of linear regression in the stock market.

▶ Example 2: Risk Analysis in Stock Investment

Analysis of daily returns is one of the major analytic approaches in the stock market. Return of some stocks closely follows return of the major indices, say Dow Jones. However, some stocks show higher return or opposite return relative to the Dow Jones index. One of the questions is how a specified stock price follows the overall market conditions. ◀

Daily return R_k for day k is calculated as

$$R_k = \frac{P_k - P_{k-1}}{P_{k-1}} \quad (17.34)$$

where P_k and P_{k-1} are the prices (or value of the index) at close of day k and at close of the previous trading day k - 1.

▶ Example 2(a): Advanced Micro Devices, Inc. (AMD) Against Daily Returns of the Dow Jones Industrial Average Index (DJI) in 2020

Let's analyze the relationship of daily returns of stock prices of Advanced Micro Devices, Inc. (AMD) with daily returns of the Dow Jones Industrial Average index (DJI) in 2020. Daily returns of AMD and Dow Jones Industrial Average and the respective regression analysis are shown in ◘ Table 17.4. ◀

◘ Table 17.4 Regression analysis of daily returns of AMD against DJI in 2020

Trading day of the year	Date	Daily return of DJI (X)	Daily return of AMD (Y)
1	2-Jan-20	1.16%	7.06%
2	3-Jan-20	−0.81%	−1.02%
3	6-Jan-20	0.24%	−0.43%
...			
251	29-Dec-20	−0.35%	−1.11%
252	30-Dec-20	0.24%	1.84%
253	31-Dec-20	0.65%	−0.63%
Mean =		0.05%	0.35%
Min =		−12.93%	−14.64%
Max =		11.37%	16.50%
Stand. deviation:		$s_X = 2.32\%$	$S_R = 3.13\%$
Covariance with DJI =			0.000522
Corr. coeff. with DJI =			0.59
$b_1 =$		Cov(X, Y/Var(X)=	0.9734
$b_0 =$		$\bar{Y} - b_1\bar{X} =$	0.003
$TSS =$			0.373
$ESS =$			0.128
$RSS =$			0.245
$R^2 =$		$1 - RSS/TSS =$	0.343

17

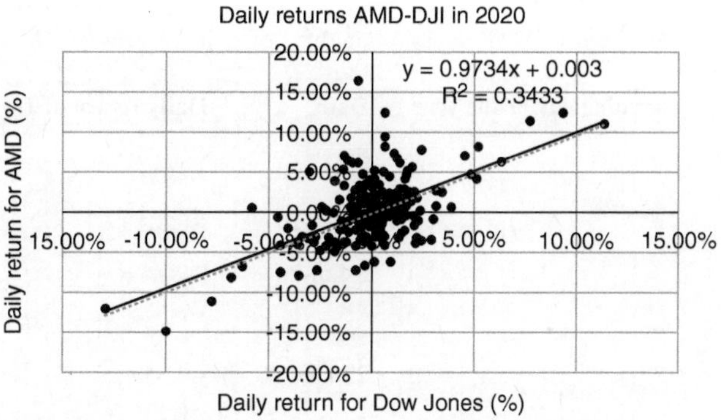

Fig. 17.8 A scatter chart and the regression line for the daily returns for Advanced Micro Devices, Inc. (AMD) against Dow Jones index for 2020

A scatter chart and the regression line for Advanced Micro Devices, Inc. (AMD) against the Dow Jones Industrial Average index (DJI) are shown in Fig. 17.8.

Often, Dow Jones Industrial Average is simply referred to as Dow Jones, though there are many other Dow Jones indices by industries. The expression for the regression line and the coefficient of determination R^2 are also shown in the chart. The regression line can be found by using Eq. (17.16). The covariance of daily returns of AMD and Dow Jones and the variance of Dow Jones for all trading days in 2020 can be calculated using functions COVARIANCE.S and VARA in MS Excel or OO Calc. Note that the covariance and variance are calculated using the respective expressions for a sample rather than for the population, even though we account for all trading days. It is done this way, because the results will be used for the analysis of other periods of time, thus making the base period a sample.

The regression line in Fig. 17.8 shows $b_1 = 0.97$ (rounded) that indicates positive correlation between daily returns of AMD and Dow Jones. This means that AMD stock mostly follows the market trend. Coefficient of determination $R^2 = 0.34$ (rounded), which is closer to 0 than to 1, indicates that the daily returns of AMD are quite scattered against the regression line.

► Example 2(b): Zoom Video Communications, Inc. (ZM) Against Daily Returns of the Dow Jones Industrial Average Index (DJI) in 2020

Now, let's analyze the relationship of daily returns of stock prices of Zoom Video Communications, Inc. (ZM) with daily returns of the Dow Jones Industrial Average index (DJI) in 2020. Daily returns of ZM and Dow Jones Industrial Average and the respective regression analysis are shown in Tables 17.4 and 17.5. ◄

A scatter chart and the regression line for Zoom Video Communications, Inc. (ZM) against the Dow Jones Industrial Average index (DJI) is shown in Fig. 17.9.

The regression line in Fig. 17.9 shows $b_1 = -0.31$ (rounded) that indicates negative correlation between daily returns of ZM and Dow Jones. This means that the daily returns of the ZM stock more often go against the market trend. Coefficient of determination $R^2 = 0.02$ (rounded) which is closer to 0 indicates that the daily returns of ZM are quite scattered against the regression line.

Table 17.5 Regression analysis of daily returns of ZM against DJI in 2020

Trading day of the year	Date	Daily return of DJI (X)	Daily return of ZM (Y)
1	2-Jan-20	1.16%	1.00%
2	3-Jan-20	−0.81%	−2.10%
3	6-Jan-20	0.24%	4.52%
...			
251	29-Dec-20	−0.35%	0.67%
252	30-Dec-20	0.24%	−0.10%
253	31-Dec-20	0.65%	−4.55%
Mean =		0.05%	0.77%
Min =		−12.93%	−17.37%
Max =		11.37%	40.78%
Stand. deviation =		$s_X = 2.32\%$	$S_R = 5.35\%$
Covariance with DJI =			−0.0002
Corr. coeff. with DJI =			−0.133
$b_1 =$		$Cov(X, Y/Var(X)=$	−0.3103
$b_0 =$		$\overline{Y} - b_1\overline{X} =$	0.0079
$TSS =$			0.7327
$ESS =$			0.0130
$RSS =$			0.7196
$R^2 =$		$1 - RSS/TSS =$	0.0178

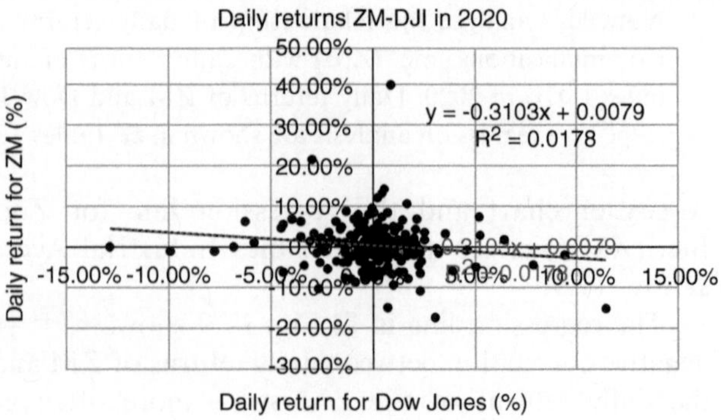

Fig. 17.9 A scatter chart and the regression line for the daily returns for Zoom Video Communications, Inc. (ZM) against Dow Jones index for 2020

▣ **Table 17.6** End of trading week stock prices of Apple Inc. (AAPL) in quarter IV 2020

Date on Fridays in quarter IV 2020	APPL stock price at market close ($)
2-Oct-20	112.83
9-Oct-20	116.77
16-Oct-20	118.82
23-Oct-20	114.84
30-Oct-20	108.67
6-Nov-20	118.69
13-Nov-20	119.26
20-Nov-20	117.34
27-Nov-20	116.59
4-Dec-20	122.25
11-Dec-20	122.41
18-Dec-20	126.66
24-Dec-20	131.97
31-Dec-20	132.69

17.9 Finding a Trend

Trend analysis is an important part of stock market research, market research, business forecasting, and many other types of research in business and economics. Trend for a period can be found as a slope of the regression line in the respective time series.

▶ Example 3: Stock Market Trends

Suppose we want to find a trend of the stock prices of company Apple Inc. (ticker symbol AAPL) in the last quarter of 2020, i.e., for the period of October 1, 2020, through December 31, 2020. Some days, stock prices went up, and some days, they went down. End of trading week historical stock prices of Apple Inc. (AAPL) in quarter IV 2020 are shown in ▣ Table 17.6. The stock price trend for the period is represented by the regression line. ◀

The stock price trend line can be presented in the form of a regression line

$$\hat{Y}(X) = b_0 + b_1 X \quad (17.35)$$

where variable X can be expressed as calendar day, day since the first day of the quarter, or a week number in the quarter. Coefficients b_0 and b_1 can be found using Eq. (17.16).

▶ Variant (a) of Example 1: Stock Trend as Price Against Calendar Days

If variable X is expressed in terms of calendar days, the days must be presented as sequential integer numbers, and the origin must be set as a reference point. Let's set the origin number 1 on date January 1, 1900, according MS Excel; thus, October 2, 2020, is associated with the number 44106. We may choose any other origin date if we wish, because expression for coefficient b_1 uses only difference $X - \bar{X}$. Different origin dates may proportionally impact the value of the intercept α.

Thus, variable X represents last trading days of each week in quarter IV 2020, and variable Y represents the stock price at market close on those days as shown in the second and third columns in ◘ Table 17.7. ◀

Columns 4 through 7 in ◘ Table 17.7 serve as reparatory calculations for coefficients b_0 and b_1 according Eq. (17.16). Two bottom rows in the table present the appropriate sums and means for the respective columns. The regression coefficient b_1 and the intercept b_0 are found using Eq. (17.16)

$$b_1 = \frac{\sum_{k=1}^{n}(x_k - \bar{x})(y_k - \bar{y})}{\sum_{k=1}^{n}(x_k - \bar{x})^2} = 0.19 \qquad \text{and} \qquad b_0 = \bar{y} - b_1\bar{x} = -8,221.60 \qquad (17.36)$$

The stock price trend line calculated according Eq. (17.36) with coefficients α and β from Eq. (17.16) is shown in column 8 < $\hat{Y}_k$ >. Columns 9 through 13 are used for the calculation of the total sum of squares, TSS, explained sum of squares ESS, residual (unexplained) sum of squares RSS, residual (unexplained) standard deviation s_R, and coefficient of determination R^2 according to Eqs. (17.20), 17.21, (17.22), (17.26), and (17.29)

$$\begin{aligned}
TSS &= \sum_{k=1}^{n}(y_k - \bar{y})^2 = 588.03;\\
ESS &= \sum_{k=1}^{n}(\hat{y}_k - \bar{y})^2 = 391.98;\\
RSS &= \sum_{k=1}^{n}(y_k - \hat{y}_k)^2 = 196.05; \qquad (17.37)\\
s_R &= \sqrt{\frac{RSS}{n-2}} = \sqrt{\frac{1}{n-2}\sum_{k=1}^{n}(y_k - \hat{y}_k)^2} = 4.04;\\
R^2 &= 1 - \frac{RSS}{TSS} = 0.67
\end{aligned}$$

17

Table 17.7 Calculating the Apple Inc. (AAPL) weekly stock price trend in quarter IV 2020

	k	End of Week Date (X_k)	Price, $ (Y_k)	$X_k - \bar{X}$	$Y_k - \bar{Y}$	$(X_k - \bar{X})^2$	$(X_k - \bar{X})(Y_k - \bar{Y})$	$\hat{Y}_k$	$(\hat{Y}_k - \bar{Y})^2$	$(Y_k - \hat{Y}_k)^2$	$(Y_k - \bar{Y})^2$	$\hat{Y}_k - S_R$	$\hat{Y}_k + S_R$
	1	2-Oct-20	113.02	–45.36	–7.04	2057.27	319.09	111.49	73.44	2.35	49.49	107.60	115.37
	2	9-Oct-20	116.97	–38.36	–3.09	1471.27	118.33	112.81	52.52	17.32	9.52	108.92	116.69
	3	16-Oct-20	119.02	–31.36	–1.04	983.27	32.45	114.13	35.10	23.91	1.07	110.25	118.01
	4	23-Oct-20	115.04	–24.36	–5.02	593.27	122.15	115.45	21.18	0.17	25.15	111.57	119.34
	5	30-Oct-20	108.86	–17.36	–11.20	301.27	194.31	116.78	10.75	62.66	125.33	112.89	120.66
	6	6-Nov-20	118.69	–10.36	–1.37	107.27	14.14	118.10	3.83	0.35	1.86	114.21	121.98
	7	13-Nov-20	119.26	–3.36	–0.80	11.27	2.67	119.42	0.40	0.03	0.63	115.54	123.30
	8	20-Nov-20	117.34	3.64	–2.72	13.27	–9.89	120.74	0.47	11.58	7.37	116.86	124.63
	9	27-Nov-20	116.59	10.64	–3.47	113.27	–36.88	122.07	4.04	29.98	12.01	118.18	125.95
	10	4-Dec-20	122.25	17.64	2.19	311.27	38.73	123.39	11.11	1.30	4.82	119.50	127.27
	11	11-Dec-20	122.41	24.64	2.35	607.27	58.03	124.71	21.68	5.29	5.55	120.83	128.59
	12	18-Dec-20	126.66	31.64	6.60	1001.27	209.00	126.03	35.74	0.39	43.63	122.15	129.92
	13	24-Dec-20	131.97	37.64	11.92	1416.98	448 51	127.17	50.58	23.07	141.97	123.28	131.05
n =	14	31-Dec-20	132.69	44.64	12.64	1992.98	564.06	128.49	71.14	17.64	159.64	124.61	132.37
Sum:			1,681			10,981	2,075		391.98	196.05	588.03		
Mean:		16-Nov	120.06										

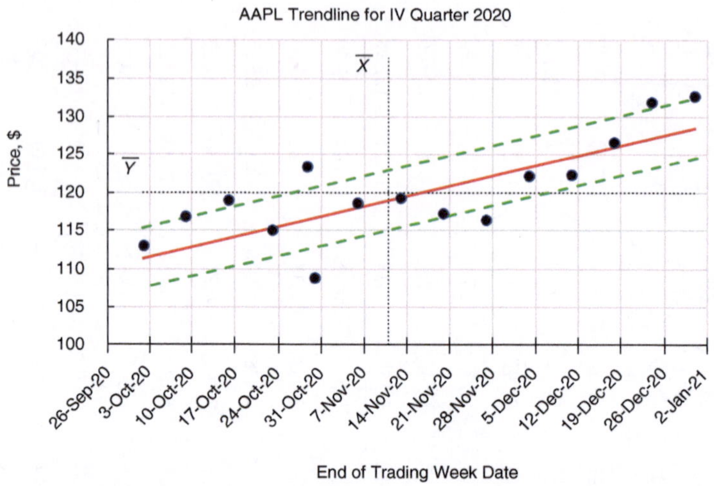

Fig. 17.10 The trend line of the Apple Inc. (AAPL) stock prices in quarter IV 2020 calculated against calendar days

The Apple Inc. (AAPL) actual stock prices at close of the last trading days of each week in quarter IV 2020 and price trend line, $\hat{Y}$, together with residual (unexplained) standard deviation s_R and the mean values of Y and X are shown in Fig. 17.10.

▶ Variant (b) of Example 1: Stock Trend as Price Against Days from the Beginning of the Period

If variable X is expressed in terms of days past from the beginning of the period, it means that in this variant, variable X is the difference between the current day and the first day of the period. ◀

Table 17.8 shows the calculation of the trend line in this case. Column 3 represents variable X as the difference between the current day and the first day of the period. Thus, for the first week of the period, i.e., for October 2, 2020, $X_1 = 0$ as shown in the third column of the table. Variable Y is shown in column 4.

Columns 5 through 8 in Table 17.8 serve as reparatory calculations for coefficients α and β according Eq. (17.16). Two bottom rows in the table present the appropriate sums and means for the respective columns. The regression coefficient b_1 and the intercept b_0 are found using Eq. (17.16)

17

$$b_1 = \frac{\sum_{k=1}^{n}(x_k - \overline{x})(y_k - \overline{y})}{\sum_{k=1}^{n}(x_k - \overline{x})^2} = 0.19 \qquad \text{and} \qquad b_0 = \overline{y} - b_1\overline{x} = 111.49 \qquad (17.38)$$

The stock price trend line calculated according Eq. (17.38) with coefficients b_0 and b_1 from Eq. (17.16) is shown in column 8 < $\hat{Y}_k$ >. Columns 9 through 13 are used

Table 17.8 Calculating the Apple Inc. (AAPL) weekly stock price trend in quarter IV 2020

	k	End of Week Date	Days Since First Week (X_k)	Price, \$ (Y_k)	$X_k - \bar{X}$	$Y_k - \bar{Y}$	$(X_k - \bar{X})^2$	$(X_k - \bar{X})$	$(Y_k - \hat{Y}_k \bar{Y})$	$(\hat{Y}_k - \bar{Y})^2$	$(Y_k - \hat{Y}_k)^2$	$(Y_k - \bar{Y})^2$	$(\hat{Y}_k - S_R$	$\hat{Y}_k + S_R$
	1	2-Oct	0	113.02	−45.36	−7.04	2057.27	319.09	111.49	73.44	2.35	49.49	107.60	115.37
	2	9-Oct	7	116.97	−38.36	−3.09	1471.27	118.33	112.81	52.52	17.32	9.52	108.92	116.69
	3	16-Oct	14	119.02	−31.36	−1.04	983.27	32.45	114.13	35.10	23.91	1.07	110.25	118.01
	4	23-Oct	21	115.04	−24.36	−5.02	593.27	122.15	115.45	21.18	0.17	25.15	111.57	119.34
	5	30-Oct	28	108.86	−17.36	−11.20	301.27	194.31	116.78	10.75	62.66	125.33	112.89	120.66
	6	6-Nov	35	118.69	−10.36	−1.37	107.27	14.14	118.10	3.83	0.35	1.86	114.21	121.98
	7	13-Nov	42	119.26	−3.36	−0.80	11.27	2.67	119.42	0.40	0.03	0.63	115.54	123.30
	8	20-Nov	49	117.34	3.64	−2.72	13.27	-9.89	120.74	0.47	11.58	7.37	116.86	124.63
	9	27-Nov	56	116.59	10.64	−3.47	113.27	-36.88	122.07	4.04	29.98	12.01	118.18	125.95
	10	4-Dec	63	122.25	17.64	2.19	311.27	38.73	123.39	11.11	1.30	4.82	119.50	127.27
	11	11-Dec	70	122.41	24.64	2.35	607.27	58.03	124.71	21.68	5.29	5.55	120.83	128.59
	12	18-Dec	77	126.66	31.64	6.60	1001.27	209.00	126.03	35.74	0.39	43.63	122.15	129.92
	13	24-Dec	83	131.97	37.64	11.92	1416.98	448.51	127.17	50.58	23.07	141.97	123.28	131.05
n =	14	31-Dec	90	132.69	44.64	12.64	1992.98	564.06	128.49	71.14	17.64	159.64	124.61	132.37
Sum:			635	1,681			10,981	2,075		391.98	196.05	588.03		
Mean:		16-Nov	45.36	120.06										

for the calculation of the total sum of squares, *TSS*, explained sum of squares *ESS*, residual (unexplained) sum of squares *RSS*, residual (unexplained) standard deviation s_R, and coefficient of determination R^2 according to Eqs. (17.20), (17.21), (17.22), (17.26), and (17.29)

$$TSS = \sum_{k=1}^{n} (y_k - \bar{y})^2 = 588.03;$$
$$ESS = \sum_{k=1}^{n} (\hat{y}_k - \bar{y})^2 = 391.98;$$
$$RSS = \sum_{k=1}^{n} (y_k - \hat{y}_k)^2 = 196.05; \tag{17.39}$$
$$s_R = \sqrt{\frac{RSS}{n-2}} = \sqrt{\frac{1}{n-2}\sum_{k=1}^{n} (y_k - \hat{y}_k)^2} = 4.04;$$
$$R^2 = 1 - \frac{RSS}{TSS} = 0.67$$

The Apple Inc. (AAPL) actual stock prices at close of the last trading days of each week in quarter IV 2020 and price trend line, $\hat{Y}$, together with residual (unexplained) standard deviation s_R and the mean values of Y and X are shown in ◘ Fig. 17.11.

► Variant (c) of Example 1: Stock Trend as Price Against Weeks of the Period

If variable X is expressed in terms of weeks of the period, it means that in our example, the origin is set on the first week of the period, i.e., on the week of October 2, 2020, as shown in the first column of ◘ Table 17.9. ◄

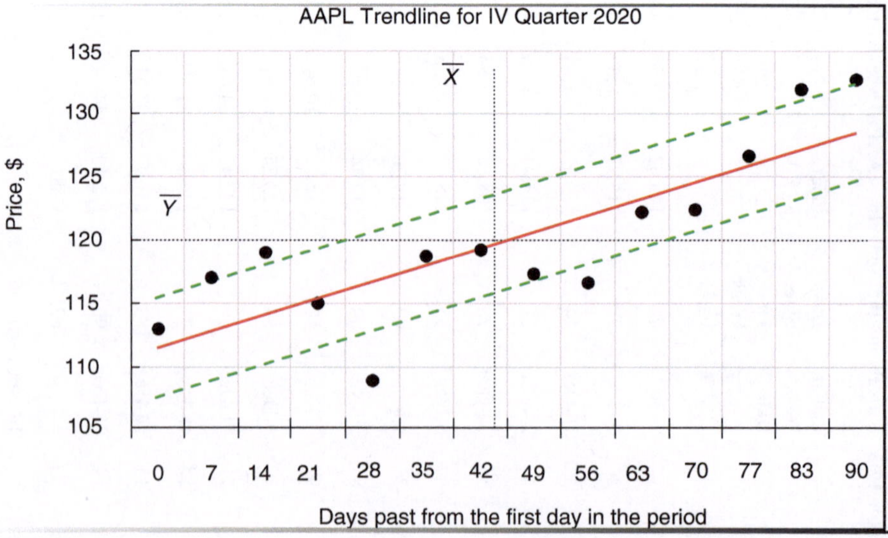

◘ **Fig. 17.11** The trend line of the Apple Inc. (AAPL) stock prices in quarter IV 2020 calculated against days past from the first day in the period

17

Table 17.9 Calculating the Apple Inc. (AAPL) weekly stock price trend in quarter IV 2020

	k (X_k)	Date week	Price, $ (Y_k)	$X_k-\bar{X}$	$Y_k-\bar{Y}$	$(X_k-\bar{X})^2$	$(X_k-\bar{X})(Y_k-\bar{Y})$	$\hat{Y}_k$	$(\hat{Y}_k-\bar{Y})^2$	$(Y_k-\hat{Y}_k)^2$	$(Y_k-\bar{Y})^2$	$\hat{Y}_k-S_R$	$\hat{Y}_k+S_R$
	1	2-Oct	113.02	−6.50	−7.04	42.25	45.73	111.49	73.42	2.35	49.49	107.60	115.37
	2	9-Oct	116.97	−5.50	−3.09	30.25	16.97	112.80	52.57	17.35	9.52	108.92	116.69
	3	16-Oct	119.02	−4.50	−1.04	20.25	4.66	114.12	35.19	23.98	1.07	110.24	118.01
	4	23-Oct	115.04	−3.50	−5.02	12.25	17.55	115.44	21.29	0.16	25.15	111.56	119.32
	5	30-Oct	108.86	−2.50	−11.20	6.25	27.99	116.76	10.86	62.40	125.33	112.88	120.64
	6	6-Nov	118.69	−1.50	−1.37	2.25	2.05	118.08	3.91	0.37	1.86	114.19	121.96
	7	13-Nov	119.26	−0.50	−0.80	0.25	0.40	119.40	0.43	0.02	0.63	115.51	123.28
	8	20-Nov	117.34	0.50	−2.72	0.25	-1.36	120.71	0.43	11.38	7.37	116.83	124.60
	9	27-Nov	116.59	1.50	−3.47	2.25	-5.20	122.03	3.91	29.62	12.01	118.15	125.92
	10	4-Dec	122.25	2.50	2.19	6.25	5.49	123.35	10.86	1.21	4.82	119.47	127.23
	11	11-Dec	122.41	3.50	2.35	12.25	8.24	124.67	21.29	5.10	5.55	120.79	128.55
	12	18-Dec	126.66	4.50	6.60	20.25	29.72	125.99	35.19	0.45	43.63	122.10	129.87
	13	24-Dec	131.97	5.50	11.92	30.25	65.53	127.31	52.57	21.76	141.97	123.42	131.19
$n=$	14	31-Dec	132.69	6.50	12.64	42.25	82.13	128.62	73.42	16.54	159.64	124.74	132.51
Sum:	105		1,681			228	300		395.33	192.70	588.03		
Mean:	7.5	16-Nov	120.06										

Columns 4 through 7 in Table 17.9 serve as reparatory calculations for coefficients b_0 and b_1 according Eq. (17.16). Two bottom rows in the table present the appropriate sums and means for the respective columns. The regression coefficient b_1 and the intercept b_0 are found using Eq. (17.16)

$$b_1 = \frac{\sum_{k=1}^{n}(x_k - \bar{x})(y_k - \bar{y})}{\sum_{k=1}^{n}(x_k - \bar{x})^2} = 1.32 \quad \text{and} \quad b_0 = \bar{y} - b_1\bar{x} = 110.17 \tag{17.40}$$

The stock price trend line calculated according Eq. (17.40) with coefficients b_0 and b_1 from Eq. (17.16) is shown in column 8 < $\hat{Y}_k$ >. Columns 9 through 13 are used for the calculation of the total sum of squares, *TSS*, explained sum of squares *ESS*, residual (unexplained) sum of squares *RSS*, residual (unexplained) standard deviation s_R, and coefficient of determination R^2 according to Eqs. (17.20), (17.21), (17.22), (17.26), and (17.29)

$$\begin{aligned}
TSS &= \sum_{k=1}^{n}(y_k - \bar{y})^2 = 588.03; \\
ESS &= \sum_{k=1}^{n}(\hat{y}_k - \bar{y})^2 = 395.33; \\
RSS &= \sum_{k=1}^{n}(y_k - \hat{y}_k)^2 = 192.78; \\
s_R &= \sqrt{\frac{RSS}{n-2}} = \sqrt{\frac{1}{n-2}\sum_{k=1}^{n}(y_k - \hat{y}_k)^2} = 4.01; \\
R^2 &= 1 - \frac{RSS}{TSS} = 0.67
\end{aligned} \tag{17.41}$$

The Apple Inc. (AAPL) actual stock prices at close of the last trading days of each week in quarter IV 2020 and price trend line, $\hat{Y}$, together with residual (unexplained) standard deviation s_R and the mean values of *Y* and *X* are shown in Fig. 17.12.

Discussion on the Variants of Exercise 3 The trend lines in variants (a) and (b) are identical (Figs. 17.10 and 17.11) as evident from comparing the columns for regression line < $\hat{Y}_k$ > in Tables 17.7 and 17.8. However, the regression coefficients are different (Eqs. (17.36) and (17.38)) because the origins of variable *X* are different. Also, the total sum of squares, *TSS*, explained sum of squares *ESS*, residual (unexplained) sum of squares *RSS*, residual (unexplained) standard deviation s_R, and coefficient of determination R^2 are identical too. This indicates that the regression line does not depend on the choice of variable *X* if the scale of the variable stays unchanged regardless of the variable origin. Both independent variables *X* in variants (a) and (b) have the same scale – number of days.

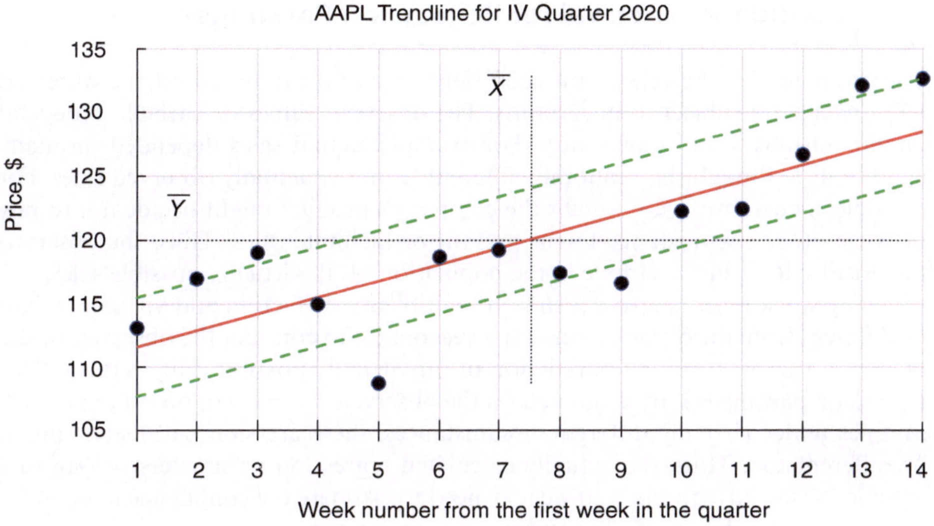

Fig. 17.12 The trend line of the Apple Inc. (AAPL) stock prices in quarter IV 2020 calculated against weeks in the quarter

The trend lines in variants (a) and (c) are practically identical (Figs. 17.10 and 17.12), but with very minor differences in the decimal figures closer to the end of the quarter as evident from comparing the columns for regression line < $\hat{Y}_k$ > in Tables 17.7 and 17.9. These minor variations are caused by variation of scale of variable *X*. A close look at variable *X* in variants (a) and (b) shows that variable *X* has increment of 7 days except the trading week ending on Thursday, December 24, 2020, one day earlier due to the observance of Christmas, when the stock market was closed on Friday, December 25, 2020. Such a little variation of the day increment for variable *X* is the same in both variants (a) and (b), thus, not impacting on the final results.

A close look at variable *X* in variant (c) shows that the week increment is always 1 for all week in the quarter that makes the uniform scale for variable *X*. This little difference caused a slight variation in the regression line and values for *TSS*, *ESS*, and *RSS*. However, all these variations are so minor and can be ignored for any practical purpose.

17.10 Calculating a Trend Line Using MS Excel or OO Calc Functions

The regression line can be found with the direct calculation as shown in Examples 1 and 3 above. However, the same result can be obtained using MS Excel and OO Calc functions such as COVARIANS.S and VARA, TREND, FORECAST.LINEAR, and other functions.

17.11 Confidence Interval for Regression Parameters

The estimates for the regression coefficients α and β are based on the observed $\{Y_k\}$, which are subject to uncertainty. The observed values of variable Y depend on circumstances and might vary. For example, actual sales depended on many conditions and might be randomly different from the actually observed sales. For example, a customer who bought the company's product might decide not to buy or some other circumstance might prevent or facilitate sales. Thus, the observed historical sales is just a sample in the population of all virtually possible sales.

Daily stock returns also depend on multiplicity of factors and virtually might be different from the observed ones. It is reasonable to consider the observed values of Y as a sample from the population of all virtually possible daily returns. The, regression parameters are estimated on the observed sample, but on other possible samples under virtually different circumstances, the regression parameters might be different too. Thus, the actually calculated regression parameters belong to a specific (observed) sample, and we may need to estimate the confidence interval for them in the population of all virtually possible samples.

Imagine a variety of all virtually possible samples $\{\{Y_k\}_m\}$ of the dependent variable Y against the independent variable X. All samples are of size n. The observed values $\{Y_k\}$ for $k = 1, 2, \ldots, n$ belong the observed sample, and the regression line $\hat{Y}(X)$ was found for this sample defined by the regression coefficients b_0 and b_1 calculated on this sample according to Eq. (17.16). However, the regression parameters β_0 and β_1 for the regression line on the population $\hat{Y}(X) = \beta_0 + \beta_1 X$ are unknown. The question is – how close is the estimate for the regression coefficients b_0 and b_1 made on the sample to the parameters β_0 and β_1 on the population? *This question is conceptually similar to the question about the relationship between the mean measured on a sample and the mean of the population discussed* in ► Chap. 13.

To calculate a confidence interval for the slope of the regression line, we need to choose the confidence level, *CL*, estimate the standard error of the sampling distribution of the regression slope, and find the critical value for the variable in the sampling distribution matching the chosen confidence level. Actually, all is very similar to what was described in ► Chap. 13.

According to Eq. (17.24) and for the reason described in Eq. (17.23), the degree of freedom for the linear regression slope with one predictor (independent variable X) equals

$$df = n - 2 \tag{17.42}$$

The residual standard deviation s_R of the dependent variable Y measures square distances between the observed values of Y_k and the respective values of the variable on the regression line $\hat{Y}_k$, with the degree of freedom from Eq. (17.42),

$$s_R = \sqrt{\frac{\sum_{k=1}^{n}(y_k - \hat{y}_k)^2}{n-2}} \tag{17.43}$$

The standard sampling error for the regression slope SE_1 can be expressed as

$$SE_1 = \frac{s_R}{\sqrt{\sum_{k=1}^{n}(x_k - \bar{x}_k)^2}} = \frac{s_R}{s_X\sqrt{n-1}}\sqrt{\frac{\frac{1}{n-2}\sum_{k=1}^{n}(y_k - \hat{y}_k)^2}{\sum_{k=1}^{n}(x_k - \bar{x}_k)^2}} \quad (17.44)$$

The confidence interval for the regression slope β_1 can be estimated based on the estimator on the sample, b_1; the standard sampling error, SE_1; and the critical value in *t*-distribution, t_{CR}, for the matching confidence level, *CL* (or $\alpha = 1 - CL$), and the degree of freedom $df = n - 2$.

The confidence interval for the regression slope β_1 can be constructed as

$$\beta_1 = b_1 \pm t_{CR} SE_1 \quad (17.45)$$

The confidence interval for the regression line intercept β_0 can be constructed from the similar considerations as

$$\beta_0 = b_0 \pm t_{CR} SE_0 \quad (17.46)$$

where:

$$SE_0 = SE_1\sqrt{\frac{1}{n}\sum_{k=1}^{n}x_k^2} \quad (17.47)$$

According to Eq. (17.12), Eq. (17.47) can be rewritten as

$$SE_0 = SE_1\sqrt{\bar{x}^2 + \frac{1}{n}\sum_{k=1}^{n}(x_k - \bar{x})^2} = SE_1\sqrt{\bar{x}^2 + \frac{n-1}{n}s_X^2} \quad (17.48)$$

Taking into account that for large samples with $n > 30$, *t*-distribution becomes quite close to the z-distribution, thus, critical values for *t*-distribution, t_{CR}, can be substituted with critical values, z_{CR}, for z-distribution under the same confidence level, i.e.,

$$\begin{aligned} \beta_1 &= b_1 \pm z_{CR} SE_1 \\ \beta_0 &= b_0 \pm z_{CR} SE_0 \end{aligned} \quad (17.49)$$

The number of degrees of freedom *df* for one dependent variable *Y* is
$df = n - 2$

The confidence interval for the regression slope β_1 can be constructed as
$\beta_1 = b_1 \pm t_{CR} SE_1$

where b_1 is the slope of the regression line on the sample, t_{CR} is the t-critical value for the chosen confidence level CL (or $\alpha = 1 - CL$) and degree of freedom $df = n - 2$, and SE_1 is the sampling standard error for the regression slope,

$$SE_1 = \frac{s_R}{\sqrt{\sum_{k=1}^{n}(x_k - \bar{x}_k)^2}} = \frac{s_R}{s_X\sqrt{n-1}}\sqrt{\frac{\frac{1}{n-2}\sum_{k=1}^{n}(y_k - \hat{y}_k)^2}{\sum_{k=1}^{n}(x_k - \bar{x}_k)^2}}$$

and the residual standard deviation on the observed data s_R is

$$s_R = \sqrt{\frac{\sum_{k=1}^{n}(y_k - \hat{y}_k)^2}{n-2}}$$

The confidence interval for the regression intercept β_0 can be constructed as $\beta_0 = b_0 \pm t_{CR} SE_0$

where b_0 is the intercept of the regression line on the sample, t_{CR} is the t-critical value for the chosen confidence level CL (or $\alpha = 1 - CL$) and degree of freedom $df = n - 2$, and SE_0 is the sampling standard error for the regression intercept,

$$SE_0 = SE_1\sqrt{\bar{x}^2 + \frac{1}{n}\sum_{k=1}^{n}(x_k - \bar{x})^2} = SE_1\sqrt{\bar{x}^2 + \frac{n-1}{n}s_X^2}$$

For large samples with $n > 30$, t-distribution becomes quite close to the z-distribution; thus, critical values for t-distribution, t_{CR}, can be substituted with critical values, z_{CR}, for z-distribution under the same confidence level.

► Example 4: Confidence Interval for Regression Slope for the Price of a Bottle of Beer Subject to the Pack Size

Beer can be sold by bottle or by packs, which contain 6, 12, 18, 24, or 30 bottles. Prices for 10 packs of different sizes were observed in stores and shown in ◘ Table 17.10. ◄

17

The solution to this problem is shown in ◘ Table 17.11. The third column <Price per bottle> shows the price per bottle calculated as the price per pack divided to the number of bottles in the pack.

◘ **Table 17.10** Observed prices for beer for packs of different sizes

Pack size, bottles (X_k)	**1**	**6**	**12**	**18**	**6**	**30**	**12**	**18**	**24**	**1**
Price per unit, \$ (Y_k)	1.72	1.43	1.19	1.08	1.54	0.97	1.28	1.18	1.22	1.9

Table 17.11 Solution table to the problem of prices for beer

	k	Pack size, bottles (X_k)	Price per pack, $	Price per unit, $ (Y_k)	$X_k-\bar{X}$	$Y_k-\bar{Y}$	$(X_k-\bar{X})^2$	$(X_k-\bar{X})(Y_k-\bar{Y})$	$\hat{Y}_k$	$(\hat{Y}_k-\bar{Y})^2$	$(Y_k-\hat{Y}_k)^2$	$(Y_k-\bar{Y};)^2$	$\hat{Y}_k-S_R$	$\hat{Y}_k+S_R$	$\hat{Y}_k$ lower	$\hat{Y}_k$ upper
	1	1	1.72	1.72	–11.80	0.37	139.24	–4.35	1.67	2.78	0.00	0.14	1.53	1.81	1.6569	1.6795
	2	6	8.58	1.43	–6.80	0.08	46.24	–0.54	1.53	2.35	0.01	0.01	1.39	1.68	1.466	1.6016
	3	12	14.28	1.19	–0.80	–0.16	0.64	0.13	1.37	1.88	0.03	0.03	1.23	1.52	1.2369	1.5081
	4	18	19.44	1.08	5.20	-0.27	27.04	–1.41	1.21	1.47	0.02	0.07	1.07	1.35	1.0078	1.4146
	5	6	9.24	1.54	–6.80	0.19	46.24	–1.29	1.53	2.35	0.00	0.04	1.39	1.68	1.466	1.6016
	6	30	29.1	0.97	17.20	-0.38	295.84	–6.55	0.89	0.79	0.01	0.15	0.75	1.03	0.5496	1.2276
	7	12	15.36	1.28	–0.80	–0.07	0.64	0.06	1.37	1.88	0.01	0.01	1.23	1.52	1.2369	1.5081
	8	18	21.24	1.18	5.20	–0.17	27.04	–0.89	1.21	1.47	0.00	0.03	1.07	1.35	1.0078	1.4146
	9	24	29.28	1.22	11.20	–0.13	125.44	–1.47	1.05	1.10	0.03	0.02	0.91	1.19	0.7787	1.3211
$n =$	10	1	1.9	1.9	-11.80	0.55	139.24	–6.48	1.67	2.78	0.05	0.30	1.53	1.81	1.6569	1.6795
										ESS	RSS	TSS				
Sum:		128.0		13.5			847.6	–22.788		18.86	0.16283	0.7755				
Mean:		12.8		1.4												

The regression line $\hat{Y}(X)$ for this data is found using Eq. (17.16) and has the following b_0 and b_1:

$$b_1 = \frac{\sum_{k=1}^{n}(x_k - \bar{x})(y_k - \bar{y})}{\sum_{k=1}^{n}(x_k - \bar{x})^2} = -0.03 \quad \text{and} \quad b_0 = \bar{y} - b_1\bar{x} = 1.70 \tag{17.50}$$

Thus, the regression line is estimated on the given sample as

$$\hat{Y} = 1.70 - 0.03X \tag{17.51}$$

The confidence interval for slope of the regression line can be found using Eq. (17.45).

$$\beta_1 = b_1 \pm t_{CR} SE_1 \tag{17.52}$$

The standard error for the regression slope

$$SE_1 = \frac{s_R}{s_X\sqrt{n-1}} = \frac{0.14}{9.71 * 3} = 0.0049 \tag{17.53}$$

where residual standard deviation s_R (Eq. (17.26)) for the dependent variable Y and the standard deviation s_X (Eq. (17.27)) for the independent variable X are

$$s_R = \sqrt{\frac{1}{n-2}\sum_{k=1}^{n}(y_k - \hat{y}_k)^2} = 0.14 \text{ and } s_X = \sqrt{\frac{1}{n-1}\sum_{k=1}^{n}(x_k - \bar{x})^2} = 9.70 \tag{17.54}$$

Suppose we chose the confidence level $CL = 95\%$ ($\alpha = 1 - CL = 5\%$). The degree of freedom $df = n - 2 = 8$. As soon as the sample is small ($n = 10$), we are using the t-distribution. The critical value t_{CR} can be found from the t-distribution tables for the chosen confidence level and given degree of freedom, and it is $t_{CR} = 2.31$. Thus, the confidence interval for the regression slope is

$$\beta_1 = b_1 \pm t_{CR} SE_1 = 1.70 \pm 0.01 \tag{17.55}$$

The two right columns in Table 17.11 show the regression lines for the lower and upper estimates for the regression slope on the population. The scatter plot for the prices per bottle of beer for different pack sizes and the regression line on the sample and the lower and upper estimates for the regression slope on the population are shown in Fig. 17.13.

17

► Example 5: Confidence Interval for Regression Parameter of Daily Returns of Stock Against Market Index

Let's revisit Example 2 about the relationship between daily returns of a stock against daily returns of the market index Dow Jones Industrial Average index (DJI) in ► Sect. 17.8. The daily returns for Advanced Micro Devices, Inc. (AMD) presented in Table 17.4 constitute a sample, one of all virtually possible set of daily returns. The return on each day depends on many factors and could possibly be quite different.

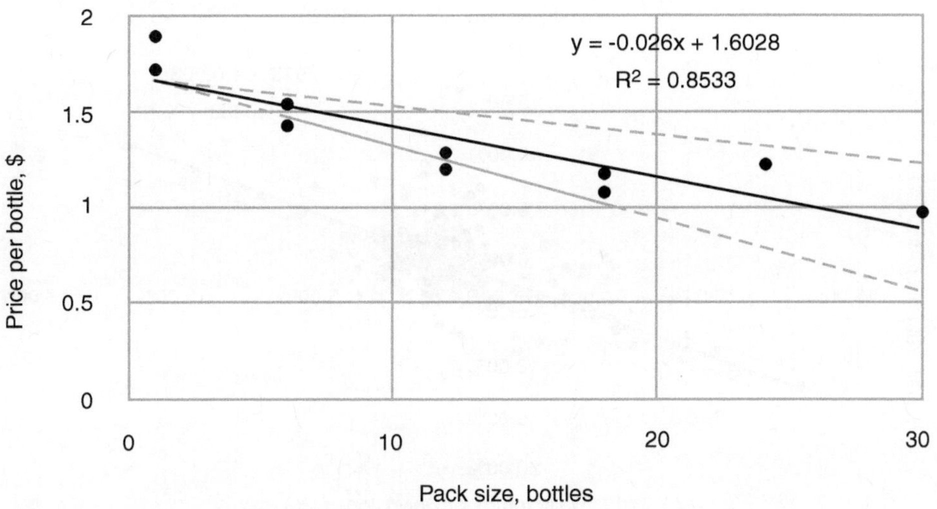

Fig. 17.13 The scatter plot for prices per bottle of beer together, the regression line on the sample, and the upper and lower estimates for the regression slope on the population

As we already know, estimates of the regression coefficients b_0 and b_1 are subject to sampling uncertainty; see ► Chap. 13. Therefore, we will never exactly know the true value of these parameters from the data on a sample data. However, we may construct confidence intervals for the intercept and the slope parameter.

Let's revisit Table 17.4 and estimate the confidence interval for the regression parameters β_0 and β_1 with the confidence level 95%. The number of trading days $n = 253$; thus, we can use a critical value for z-distribution. The critical value for a two-sided test with confidence level $CL = 95\%$ in z-distribution is $z_{CR} = 1.96$.

According to Eq. (17.41), the degree of freedom for the regression slope $df = 253–2 = 251$. The residual standard deviation for the dependent variable Y is $s_R = 0.031$; the standard deviation of the independent variable X is $s_X = 2.32\%$; then the standard sampling error for the regression slope, SE_1, is

$$SE_1 = \frac{s_R}{s_X\sqrt{n-1}} = \frac{3.13}{2.32*15.9} = 0.085 \tag{17.56}$$

and the standard sampling error for the regression intercept, SE_0, is

$$SE_0 = SE_1\sqrt{\bar{x}^2 + \frac{n-1}{n}s_X^2} = 0.085*\sqrt{0.005^2 + \frac{252}{253}0.023^2} = 0.002 \tag{17.57}$$

Thus, with the confidence level 95%, the regression parameters for the daily returns of Advanced Micro Devices, Inc. (AMD) against Dow Jones Industrial Average index (DJI) are

$$\begin{aligned}\beta_1 &= b_1 \pm z_{CR}SE_1 = 0.973 \pm 1.96*0.085 = 0.973 \pm 0.167\\ \beta_0 &= b_0 \pm z_{CR}SE_0 = 0.003 \pm 1.96*0.002 = 0.003 \pm 0.004\end{aligned} \tag{17.58}$$

and the regression line on the population can be estimated as

$$\hat{Y} = (0.003 \pm 0.004) + (0.973 \pm 0.167)X \tag{17.59}$$

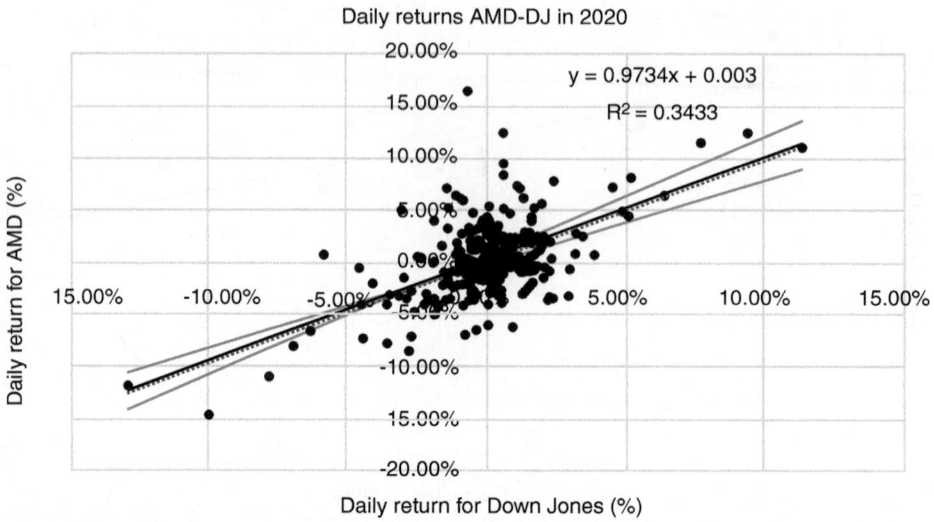

Fig. 17.14 A scatter chart and the regression line with the low-band and the upper-band estimates for the daily returns for Advanced Micro Devices, Inc. (AMD) against Dow Jones index for 2020

The scatter chart of the daily return of Advanced Micro Devices, Inc. (AMD) against Dow Jones Industrial Average index (DJI) shown in Fig. 17.8 together with the confidence interval low-band and upper-band regression lines according to Eq. (17.52) are shown in Fig. 17.14. ◀

17.12 Multiple Regression

The multiple regression model extends the concept of the simple regression model to more than one independent variable (predictor). Suppose we want to analyze the dependence of income on years in school (1–12 in elementary, middle, and high school and 13–20 in college or university) and on person's age. The dependent variable Y represents the income of the individual, the independent variable X_1 represents the number of years in school, and X_2 represents the person's age. Please do not get confused with the names of the variables. X_1 and X_2 are the names of the variables rather than their values. Suppose the appropriate data is collected as shown in Table 17.12.

17

The dependence of Y on X_1 and X_2 for this data can be defined as

$$Y_k = b_0 + b_1 X_{1k} + b_2 X_{2k} + \varepsilon_k \tag{17.60}$$

where b_0, b_1, and b_2 are the regression coefficients and the respective regression plane can be defined as

$$\hat{Y}(X) = b_0 + b_1 X_1 + b_2 X_2 \tag{17.61}$$

Table 17.12 Observed dependent and independent variables

X_1 (years in school)	x_{11}	x_{12}	x_{13}	x_{1n}
X_2 (age)	x_{21}	x_{22}	x_{23}	x_{2n}
Y (income)	y_1	y_2	y_3	Y_n

It was not a type in the previous sentence. With two independent variables (predictors) X_1 and X_2, the set of $\{Y_k, (X_1, X_2)\}$ and $\hat{Y}(X_1,X_2)$ are extended to the three-dimensional space, and the regression $\hat{Y}(X_1,X_2)$ represents a plane in a three-dimensional space rather than a line as it was with one independent variable.

A multiple regression model is used for the estimation of the effect of the independent variables (predictors) X_1 and X_2 on Y. Finding the regression plane implies the same concept as finding the regression line in a simple linear regression with one independent variable discussed above in this chapter. The regression coefficients, the intercept b_0 and two regression slopes b_1 and b_2, which form a regression plane can be found under minimum condition of residual sum of squares RSS such as

$$RSS = \sum_{k=1}^{n}(y_k - \hat{y}_k)^2 = \sum_{k=1}^{n}(y_k - b_0 - b_1 x_{1k} - b_2 x_{1k})^2 = \sum_{k=1}^{n}\varepsilon_k^2 \tag{17.62}$$

where ε_k^2 is the square distance between the observed point Y_k and the respective point on the regression plane $\hat{Y}_k$ at (X_{1k}, X_{2k})

$$\varepsilon_k^2 = (y_k - \hat{y}_k)^2 = (y_k - b_0 - b_1 x_k)^2 \tag{17.63}$$

For more independent variables, the dimensions of the regression space grow as $m + 1$, where m is the number of the independent variables (predictors).

Questions for Self-Control for Chap. 17

1. What is the purpose of regression analysis?
2. What are the principles of linear regression?
3. What is the regression line?
4. How to estimate the regression coefficients?
5. What are the slope and the intercept of the regression line?
6. What is the total sum of squares and what is its meaning?
7. What is the explained sum of squares and what is its meaning?
8. What is the residual sum of squares and what is its meaning?
9. What is coefficient of determination and what is its meaning?
10. What is the relationship between the slope of the regression line and correlation coefficient between dependent and independent variables?
11. What is the degree of freedom?
12. How many degrees of freedom does the dependent variable have?

13. What is daily rate of return in the stock market?
14. What is a scatter plot?
15. How to find a trend?
16. How to do technical forecasting using linear regression?
17. What are the confidence intervals for the regression parameters and what does it mean?
18. How to estimate the confidence intervals for the regression parameters?
19. What is multiple linear regression?

Problems for Chap. 17

1. A retailer has the historical sales for the last 6 years as shown in the tables below.

Year	2016	2017	2018	2019	2020	2021
Sales ($M)	106	104	110	114	115	120

Make the technical forecast for the retailer sales in 2022.

2. The height and weight in a group of ten people are shown in the table below.

Height (cm)	180	175	182	168	178	165	180	185	172	173
Weight (kg)	92	76	85	64	80	64	79	81	68	67

Find the regression line to estimate how the weight depends on height of these persons.

3. Calculate the correlation coefficient between the height and the weight in the group shown in the table in problem 1.
4. Estimate the confidence intervals for the regression parameters for the population of people represented by the sample in the table in problem 1 with the confidence level 95%.
5. Take a stock of your choice and estimate the daily return of this stock against the daily return of the market index for the chosen stock. Find the regression line and estimate the confidence intervals for the regression line.

Comparative Analysis

Contents

18.1 Purpose and Specifics of Comparative Analysis – 396

18.2 The Process of a Comparative Analysis – 398

18.3 Data Organization and Information Structure for Comparative Analysis – 399

18.4 Qualitative Comparative Analysis and Harvey Balls – 401

18.5 Models for Industry and Business Analysis – 403

18.5.1 SWOT Model – 403

18.5.2 PEST Model – 405

18.5.3 Porter's Five Forces Model – 408

S. K. Aityan, *Business Research Methodology*, Classroom Companion: Business,
https://doi.org/10.1007/978-3-030-76857-7_18

18.1 Purpose and Specifics of Comparative Analysis

Comparative research is essential for making right decisions in business. Decisions are always associated with the comparison and analysis of choices. Each choice, typically, presents multiple features for comparison and analysis depending on the goals, purpose, scope, priorities, resources, capabilities, constraints, available information, and many other factors and conditions.

Two or more objects, processes, products, phenomena, opportunities, ideas, theories, or any other entities can be subjected to the comparative analysis. Comparison may be done for:

- Companies
- Competitors
- Markets
- Business models
- Products
- Services
- Countries
- Economies
- And many other things

Many questions related to select may lead to a comparative analysis. For example:

- What TV set does better fit my requirements?
- How competitive are our company products in the market?
- What business models would be optimal for our enterprise?
- What is the most optimal option of investment for our business?
- Which country political and economic situation is the most suitable for investment?
- What stock to select for the maximal return?

In business research, comparative analysis could be conducted to identify:

- The best product for the given purpose
- The best business model for the established goal
- The most optimal supplier
- The best location for a business
- The best candidates for a given position
- The best investment opportunity
- The most adequate marketing approach
- And many other

A comparative analysis of the same entities can be conducted in many different ways subject to the goal and objectives. Thus, first the goal and objectives of the analysis must first be clearly formulated. For example, a comparative analysis for choosing a car may have different goals:

- A car for occasional driving
- A car for commuting to work

- A car for taxi or rideshare
- A car for limousine service
- Or some other goals

The objectives for the car selection problem for the goals mentioned above could be as follows:
- A nice car meeting the aesthetical taste of the driver for occasional driving
- A comfortable car with reasonably good gas mileage for commuting to work
- A fuel-efficient car to increase profitability of taxi or rideshare services
- A representative car for limousine service
- Or some other objectives for other objectives

The objectives above are shown as illustrations for the clarification of the role of objectives. Definitely, the objectives for the real-world problems can be more complex.

Another example of the goal and objective for a comparative analysis is the choice of a supplier or suppliers. Such research may be conducted with a number of different objectives, such as:
- To find a supplier with the cheapest product
- To find a supplier with the highest product quality
- To find the most reliable supplier
- To find a supplier with the shortest delivery time
- And so on

The constraints for such a goal and objectives could be formulated as follows:
- A supplier that does not supply to the competitors
- A supplier that holds patents on its products
- A supplier that has sufficient resources to increase the supplied quantity of needed
- And so on

To meet the goals and objectives in the comparative analysis, the appropriate data must be collected, properly structured, and processed. The most important thing is to derive the appropriate conclusions form the analysis. This chapter is dedicated to the methodology and methods most frequently used in the comparative research in business.

It would be a big mistake to understand a comparative research just as a comparison of the related data. Any comparative analysis is a research that must answer a question or questions asked.

> The key element in a comparative analysis is data analysis and analytic conclusions that lead to the selection of the right choice or making an appropriate business decision meeting the established goal, objectives, and constraints.

Comparative analysis of different entities requires different methods, which are readily available. There is a variety of methods available for comparative research in business and economics.

18.2 The Process of a Comparative Analysis

Goals and objectives for comparative analysis may significantly vary, and different goods and services have different features. A comparative analysis as any other research is initiated with a question, the answer to which is unknown. Each such a question includes the goal, objectives, and constraints and is asked under certain underlying conditions. The underlying conditions represent the actual external conditions, which are very important because they may crucially impact on the results of the analysis.

The question for the comparative analysis should include the objectives and constraints such as the purpose of an umbrella and, possibly, the price constraints. The underlying conditions may include the frequency of rains in the area or a season. All this must be clearly stated.

Remember a comparative analysis is a research, and the research problem must be clearly stated. Clearly formulate all underlying conditions. It is very important to have the conditions stated as a part of your problem statement.

The general process of a comparative research is illustrated in ◘ Fig. 18.1.

Clearly state the question, objectives, and constraints for the comparative analysis. This comes from your intentions of the goal of the analysis. Second, clearly formulate the underlying conditions. The underlying conditions come from the external conditions and will impact on your decision about the analysis results.

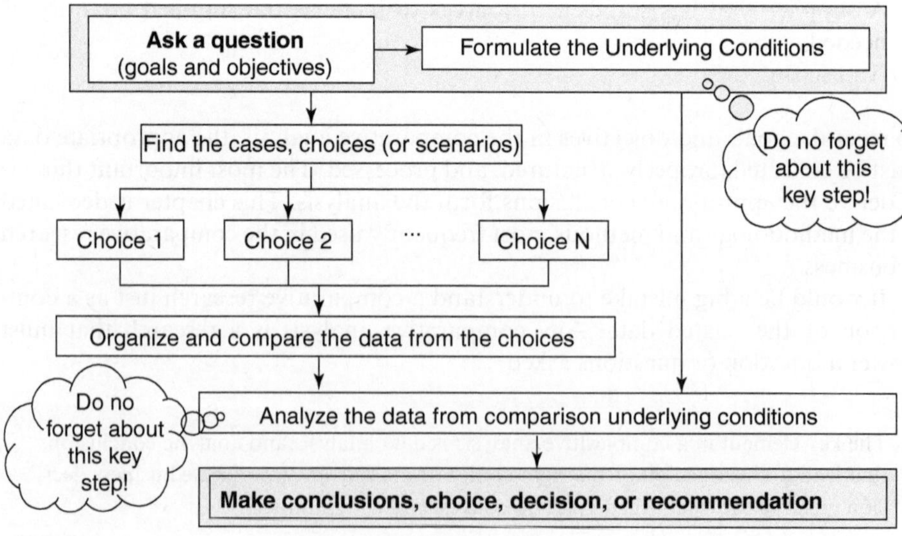

◘ **Fig. 18.1** The process of comparative analysis

18

Then identify the cases, choices, or scenarios, which you will be analyzing and from which you will be making your choice or choices. Data for the comparative analysis for all choice should be thoroughly collected and organized by categories. The data are compared by categories meeting the underlying conditions. The results of the analysis lead to the conclusions related to the choices, decisions, and recommendation answering the initial question that initiated the comparative analysis.

▶ Example 1

Ms. Smith wants to buy an umbrella, and before making a buying decision, she wants to compare available choices. The objective is to find an umbrella for the occasional usage. The underlying conditions are that there are quite rare rains in the area. Among the choices are:

- Classic umbrellas
- Compact umbrellas
- Pocket umbrellas
- Golf umbrellas
- High wind umbrellas

Analyzing the choices and matching them with the underlying conditions leads to a decision to buy a pocket umbrella. The other choices are less convenient for the occasional usage with rare rains. ◀

18.3 Data Organization and Information Structure for Comparative Analysis

Not all problems for a comparative analysis are so simple and straightforward as in the problem presented in Example 1 above. Some comparative studies involve significant and diverse information, which is not easy to comprehend at one glance. In such studies, the information for the comparative analysis should be organized by categories of data. It is also helpful to assign scores to each type of data to be used for numerical assessment. Data organized by categories allows better perception of the comparative data, while randomly organized data obscure the perception. Remember, the goal of comparative analysis is the conclusion, choice, decision, or recommendation rather than just data collection.

▶ Example 2: Comparative Analysis of Cars

Suppose the task is to conduct a comparative analysis on different models of cars. The distinctive information for the analysis is categorized as shown in ◘ Table 18.1. ◀

A score is assigned for each feature that will be used for deriving the conclusions of the analysis. The scores may represent the priorities of certain features, their importance, or some other factors impacting on the conclusions. The scores in ◘ Table 18.1 are left blank because they depend on the underlying conditions. The

Table 18.1 A structured data table for comparative analysis of different modifications of Toyota Camry

		Camry LE		Camry LE Hybrid		Camry XSE	
		Feature	Score	Feature	Score	Feature	Score
Financial							
1	Basic MSRP price	$24,970		@27,270		$35,545	
2	Rebates	$1000		None		$2500	
3	Financing interest (%)	0.9		1.9		0.9	
4	Down payment	None		$1500		None	
5	Warranty (basic)	3 yr. / 36,000 mi		3 yr. / 36,000 mi		3 yr. / 36,000 mi	
6	Warranty (powertrain)	5 yr. / 60,000 mi		5 yr. / 60,000 mi		5 yr. / 60,000 mi	
Body style and convenience							
1	Number of door	4		4		4	
2	Number of seats	5		5		5	
3	Cargo space	14.1		15.1		15.1	
4	Navigation	Yes		Yes		Yes	
5	Tire pressure monitor	Yes		Yes		Yes	
6	Back up camera	Yes		Yes		Front & Rear	
7	Basic wheel rim size	16”		16”		18”	
8	Basic tire size	295/65R16		295/65R16		235/45R18	
Powertrain							
1	Horse power	202		208		301	
2	Number of cylinders	4		4		6	
3	Engine (liters)	2.5		2.5		3.5 liter	
4	Gas mileage MPG	28/39		51/53		22/32	
5	Fuel trunk capacity (gal)	14.4		13.2		15.8	
6	Drivetrain	FWD		FWD		FWD	

underlying conditions in this case may include gas prices and some other external factors, which impact on the scores and hence on the derived conclusions.

Data for a comparative analysis should be organized by categories for clear interpretation.

Scores are added to the comparative analysis to enable quantitative factors to derive conclusions.

18.4 Qualitative Comparative Analysis and Harvey Balls

Sometimes, it is hard to assign quantitative scores to different features, particularly, when there is no scale for measurement. In such a case, qualitative ordinal scores become more appropriate. The ordinal scores present qualitative order of quality assigned to the features in comparison to each other. It could be "better" or "worse" in the simplest case. It could be "excellent," "good," "average," "below average," "poor," or some other qualitative scores.

In the comparative analysis of product features from competing vendors, the qualitative ordinal scores such as "leadership status," "meets majority of requirements," "missing some requirements," "meets few expectations," and "not present" are frequently used.

Harvey balls are a quite convenient approach that provides a quite illustrative tool for qualitative comparative analysis. Harvey balls are named after their inventor – Harvey Poppel. The meaning of Harvey balls is illustrated in ◘ Table 18.2.

A score with the Harvey balls is represented in the form of circles differently filled with a color. The higher degree of filled color in the circle indicates the better quality of the feature. When the Harvey balls are used as the scores, the intensity of colors in all features of a certain choice presents the overall quality of that choice. However, keep I mind that this method presumes equal contribution of each feature to the assessment of quality of the product.

▶ Example 3: Harvey Balls for Comparative Analysis of Competing Products

This example illustrates the application of Harvey balls for the comparative analysis of competing products by different vendors. ◘ Table 18.3 presents the comparison of CRM software products by five vendors. Not to invoke any bias or advertisement to the currently active CRM vendors, this example provides comparison of the products by the vendors from the first decade of the twenty-first century. ◀

Table 18.2 Harvey balls definition for qualitative comparative analysis

Icon	Description
●	Leadership Status
◕	Meets majority of requirements
◑	Missing some requirements
◔	Meets few expections
○	Not present

Table 18.3 A comparative analysis of CRM vendors with Harvey balls

Product Features	Vendor				
	Idiom	Kana	eGain	RightNow	Paramon
General					
Usability	●	◑	◕	◔	●
Customer Valuation	○	●	○	◔	○
Escalation Path	◑	◑	●	●	●
Chat	●	●	●	●	●
Technology					
Web-based Technology	●	●	●	●	●
Integration Capabilities	●	◑	●		
Knowledge Base					
Content Evolution	◕	◕	◕	◑	◕
Self Learning Knowledge Base	◑	◕	◑	◕	◕
Multilingual Capabilities					
Cross-Lingual Knowledge Base	○	○	◑	○	●

Visual perception of the colored circles in each row provides the qualitative assessment of different features in the products by vendor. On the other hand, visual perception of the colored circles in each column provides qualitative assessment of the overall quality of the products by vendor. The higher the color density in the column, the higher the overall quality of the product. This is true if all features are equally representing the product quality.

18

> Harvey balls are a convenient tool for visual interpretation in the comparative analysis.

18.5 Models for Industry and Business Analysis

Data collected for the comparative analysis are just facts. However, the interpretation and meaning of the data are key for deriving the conclusions. Good data structure and data organization help in understanding the overall picture of the object or objects under consideration. More data is engaged in the description of an object, and better structured and organized data and information about the object should be for the description and analysis of the object. Thus, having and using a well-representative and adequate model is very important for the description, analysis, and comparison of complex objects.

There is a variety of models available for the analysis of different situations in business. Among them are the most frequently used models such as SWOT (Strengths, Weaknesses, Opportunities, and Threats), PEST (Political, Economic, Social, and Technological), and other models.

18.5.1 SWOT Model

SWOT model combines four microeconomic categories, such as strengths, weaknesses, opportunities, and threats, and is typically used in the competitive analysis (◘ Fig. 18.2). Strengths and weaknesses describe the company's resources and capabilities uses in business that indicate relative strengths or weaknesses of the company in comparison with the competition. Each category should be filled in with the specific information relevant to the category. Though strengths and weaknesses are internal characteristics of a company, each strength of the company indicates a weakness of its competitors and vice versa. Strengths could include patents, new products, new technologies used by the company, special resources, specially trained employees, and other factors. Opportunities and threats are external characteristics that indicate the effect of the market on the company. Opportunities may include growing market, special demand, competitors' problems, and many other external factors impacting the company's business from the outside world. Weaknesses are the opposite from the strengths, and threats are the opposite from the opportunities.

Typical factors included in the SWOT analysis categories are presented in ◘ Table 18.4.

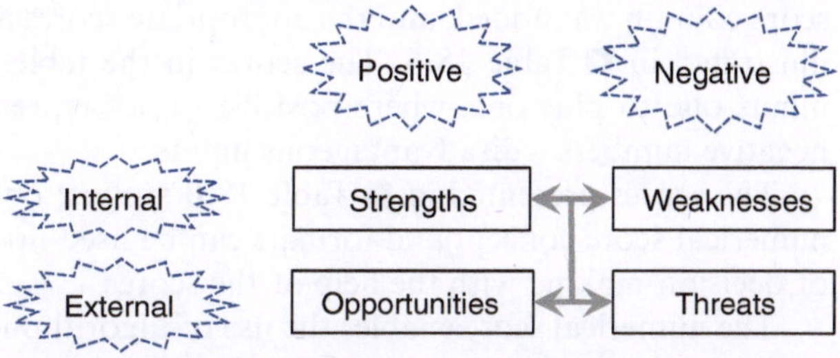

◘ **Fig. 18.2** SWOT analysis

Table 18.4 Possible factors in the SWOT analysis categories

SWOT analysis			
Internal		External	
Strengths	**Weaknesses**	**Opportunities**	**Threats**
Strong and recognized brand names Patents, trade secrets, and know-how Good equipment and new technology Cost and quality advantages Well-established reputation among customers Exclusive access to limited natural resources High-efficiency distribution networks Good customer service Other	No recognized brand names Lack of patents, trade secrets, and know-how Old equipment and outdated technology High cost and low quality Poor reputation among customers No access to limited natural resources Poor distribution networks Poor customer service Other	Unsatisfied customer need and demand Favorable changes in regulation New technology Loosening of trade barriers and tariffs Competitor's problems Other	New substitute products by competitors Changes in consumer tastes non-favorite to the company's products and services New regulations not favorite for the company Increased tariffs, trade barriers, and taxation Other

SWOT analysis by its foundation is a qualitative method. To enable quantitative approach, a column with scores against each factor in the categories can be added as shown in Table 18.1.

▶ Example 4: SWOT Analysis of an Internet Service Provider

An Internet service provider conducts a SWOT analysis for its competitive positioning in the market, which is presented in Table 18.5. ◀

The information in Table 18.5 provides a qualitative basis for the conclusions in the SWOT analysis. To enable quantitative approach for the SWOT analysis, the score column was added, and the appropriate scores are assigned for each factor as illustrated in Table 18.6. The scores in the table are based on the scale from minus one to plus one, where positive values represent advantageous input and negative numbers – disadvantageous inputs.

The scores presented in Table 18.6 are just one of the types of scores. The numerical score concept and formats can be used upon the goals and convenience of decision-making with the help of the scores.

The numerical score enables the use of algorithmic approaches in finalizing the results of the analysis.

Table 18.5 SWOT analysis of an Internet service provider

Strengths
1. New modern equipment
2. Well-trained technicians
Weaknesses
1. Poor customer service
Opportunities
1. Growing customer base in the area
Threats
1. A larger competitor plans to enter this area
2. Mobile service providers offer Internet connection to the customers

Table 18.6 Quantitative SWOT analysis of an Internet service provider with the numerical scores

Strengths	*Score*
1. New modern equipment	0.8
2. Well-trained technicians	0.9
Weaknesses	
1. Poor customer service	−0.7
Opportunities	
1. Growing customer base in the area	0.6
Threats	
1. A larger competitor plans to enter this area	−0.7
2. Mobile service providers offer Internet connection to the customers	−0.8

18.5.2 PEST Model

PEST model consists of four categories of macroeconomic conditions such as political, economic, social, and technological as shown in Fig. 18.3. These conditions represent the macroeconomic environment for the company. Each category should be filled in with the specific information relevant to the category.

Political factors include regulations, legal issues, restrictions and limitations, and other rules of doing business under which the company must operate.

Table 18.7 Typical content of PEST analysis categories

PEST analysis			
Political	**Economic**	**Social**	**Technological**
• Government nondiscrimination policy • Employment laws • Tax regulation • Export/import restrictions and limitations • Environmental protection regulations • Political stability • Many other factors	• Local life standard • Average wages • Economic growth • Inflation rate • Interest rates • Currency exchange rates • Many other factors	• Population and its growth • Life expectancy and age distribution • Level of consumer education • Healthcare • Employment and career attitudes • Religion • Many other factors	• Market modernization and rate of technological change • R&D activity and technology transfer • Automation and integration • Production quality • Technology incentives

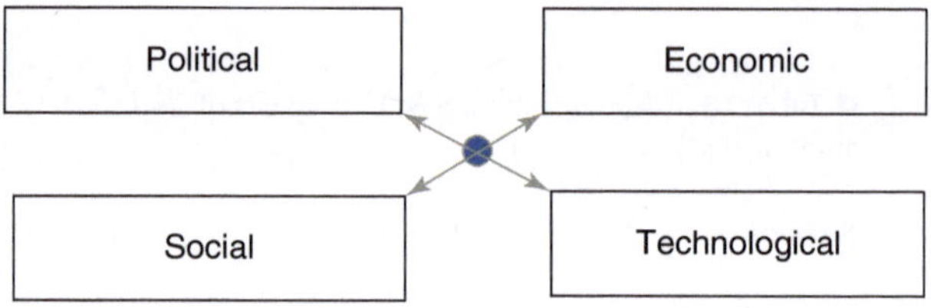

Fig. 18.3 PEST analysis

Economic factors should reflect macroeconomic aspects of the market situation including purchasing power of potential and existing customers, investment rules and policies, monetary situation, cost of capital, and other economic factors.

Social factors include cultural, demographic, national specifics, and aspects of the market which impact on the company operations and growth.

Technological factors can significantly impact on the company strategy by impacting on production, quality, lower or increase barriers to entry, and creating competitive advantage.

Competitors that operate in different geographic areas may have different macroeconomic environments that may create competitive advantage or disadvantage. Typical factors in the PEST analysis categories are presented in Table 18.7.

To enable quantitative approach, a column with scores against each factor in the categories can be added as shown in Table 18.1.

▶ Example 5: PEST Analysis of an Internet Service Provider

The information in Table 18.8 provides a qualitative basis for the conclusions in the SWOT analysis. To enable quantitative approach in the PEST analysis, the score column was added, and the appropriate scores are assigned for each factor similar to the SWOT analysis and as illustrated in Table 18.9. ◀

18

Table 18.8 PEST analysis of an Internet service provider

Political
1. Political situation in the country of business is unstable
2. Government tries to ration Internet access
Economic
1. Economy is growing
2. Consumer income is relatively low
Social
1. Consumers are socially active and enthusiastic about usage of the Internet
Technological
1. The network infrastructure is relatively weak
2. Only modern technology is used for building the Internet infrastructure

Table 18.9 Quantitative PEST analysis of an Internet service provider with the numerical scores

Political	***Score***
1. Political situation in the country of business is unstable	0.8
2. Government tries to ration Internet access	0.9
Economic	
1. Economy is growing	0.7
2. Consumer income is relatively low	−0.4
Social	
1. Consumers are socially active and enthusiastic about usage of the Internet	0.6
Technological	
1. The network infrastructure is relatively weak	−0.7
2. Only modern technology is used for building the Internet infrastructure	0.8

Typically, SWOT and PEST analyses are complementary parts of a more comprehensive business analysis that examines together microeconomic internal and external factors as well as the external macroeconomic factors as illustrated in Fig. 18.4.

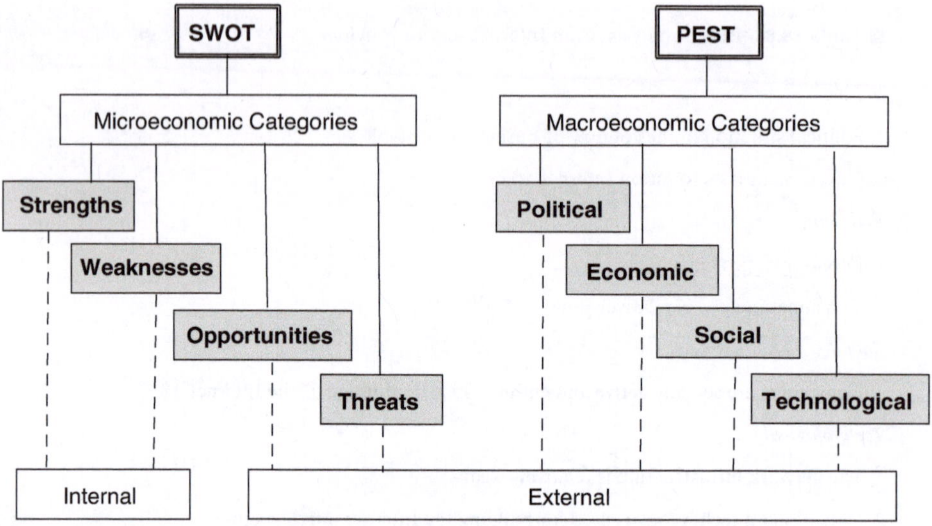

Fig. 18.4 Porter's Five Forces model for industry competition

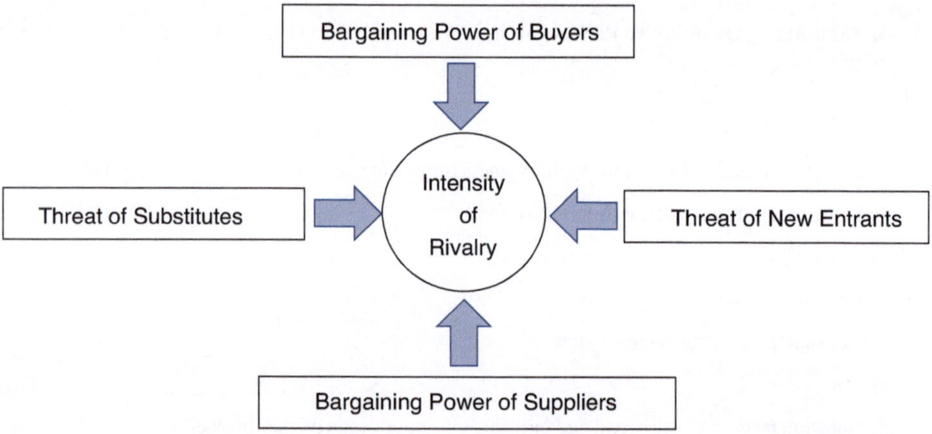

Fig. 18.5 Porter's Five Forces model for industry competition

18.5.3 Porter's Five Forces Model

Porter's Five Forces is another model for competitive analysis. According to this model, competition is driven by five forces presented in Fig. 18.5. Each force represents a category of relevant factors. These factors should be entered into each
18 category. Competition in the modern economy has reached high degree and, therefore, is referred to as rivalry. It is the first force. The other four forces are bargaining power of buyers, bargaining power of suppliers, threat of substitutes, and threat of new entrance. By new entrants we understand new rivals entering the market. All these forces together drive the competition. Porter's model can be applied to strat-

Table 18.10 Typical factors defining the forces in Porter's Five Forces model

Porter's Five Forces model for competitive analysis				
Bargaining power of buyers	**Bargaining power of suppliers**	**Threat of substitutes**	**Threat of new entrants**	**Intensity of rivalry**
• This force represents the consumer power in their effect on pricing and quality • The fewer consumers have more power if there are many sellers • Consumers have lower powers if they are buying fewer products or if there are few sellers or the product is unique	• This force examines the power of supplier to increase the price • The supplier power is high if there are few suppliers The maximum supplier power takes place if the supply is unique • The supplier's power is low, if there is lower demand on the supply or the supplied product, service, or commodity is readily available	• This force shows how easy can the competitors offer a substitute product, including services or commodity, and how easy can the consumers switch to the competitive products • The threat is high if the product can be easily copied or emulated by the competitors • The threat is low, if the product is hard to copy or emulate • The threat is high if consumers can easily switch to the substitute products • The threat is low if switching to the substitute product is impossible or hard	• This force analyzes how easy new potential competitors can enter the market • The threat is high, when the entrance barriers are low and potential competitors can easily penetrate the marketplace • The threat is low, when there are significant barriers such as legal, techno logical, business, or other barrier that prevent newcomers from entering the industry	• How intense is the competition • The number of existing competitors and their impact • Intensity of competi-tion is high when only few businesses are competing in the market and when the industry is growing • Intensity of competition is typically low when many businesses are present in the market and the industry is not growing

egy analysis in any segment of the economy to analyze the level of competition within the industry.

Typical factors defining the forces in Porter's model are presented in Table 18.10.

▶ Example 6: Five Forces Analysis of Tesla, Inc.

Tesla, Inc. is a publicly traded company (NASDAQ: TSLA) engaged in the manufacturing of electric cars and headquartered in Palo Alto, CA, which is located in Silicon Valley. The first manufacturing plant is located in Fremont, just across the San Francisco Bay from Palo Alto over the Dumbarton Bridge. Currently, Tesla operates several plants involved in the production of their electrical cars. ◀

Table 18.11 Five Forces analysis of Tesla, Inc.

Intensity of rivalry
• The market of electric cars is rapidly growing that is very attractive for other car manufacturers. This creates intensive competition from other electric car manufacturers • Total world sales of electric cars grew to 2.3 vehicles in 2020 despite the COVID-19 pandemic with 1.3 million cars sold in China and 500 thousand cars in Europe. Tesla built over 509 thousand cars in 2020 • Practically all major car manufacturers currently joined the race in the competition for the market of electric cars. The major competitors are BMW (Germany), Nissan (Japan), Chevrolet (GM, USA), Ford (USA), Kia (South Korea), NIO (China), and many others • Tesla has significant resources and capabilities, but the competition is extremely active in the real fight for markets, particularly in American, Chinese, and European markets • Tesla cars have a distinctive advantage with the higher mileage driven without recharging the battery. However, the competitors are catching up • A well-developed network of supercharging stations across the USA, specifically serving Tesla cars, provides a distinctive advantage for Tesla cars particularly in the USA
Bargaining power of buyers
• Buying power in the market of electric cars is sufficient to support the growing sales • The rapidly expanding market attracts more customers beyond the category of expensive luxury cars and has launched a price war for reducing manufacturing costs to reduce current price level and keep up with the growing sales volume for successful competition
Bargaining power of suppliers
• Supply of modern high-efficiency batteries is a critical factor for maintaining competitive advantage • Initially, Tesla used batteries produced by Panasonic, but now Tesla built its own Giga plants for manufacturing the batteries for its cars that create a significant competitive advantage
Threat of substitutes
• A rapidly growing supply of electric cars by competitors creates a visible market pressure and threat, particularly in China, with growing number of local manufacturers • European manufacturers of electric cars offer a variety of electric cars too • All these create a significant competitive pressure
Threat of new entrants
• New competitors are joining the market of electric cars that create serious pressure and threat • Tesla maintains its leadership position but has to closely watch the entrants and quickly react on changes in technology. Manufacturing and production cost to maintain its leadership

The conclusions derived from the Five Forces analysis shown in Table 18.11 analysis are as follows:

18 Tesla has its world leadership position in the manufacturing electric cars and has sufficient resources and capabilities to maintain it in the future. However, the increasing intensity competitive rivalry and growing resources put in this market by the competitors requires close attention.

SWOT, PEST, and Porter's Five Forces are the most usable models for competitive analysis.

Questions for Self-Control for Chap. 18

1. Why is comparative analysis needed?
2. What can be compared?
3. What is the key element of a comparative analysis?
4. What are the important underlying conditions for comparative analysis?
5. Why are the underlying conditions for comparative analysis important?
6. What is the process of a comparative analysis?
7. How to organize data in a comparative analysis?
8. What are the Harvey balls and why are they convenient in a comparative analysis?
9. What are the major models for comparative analysis in business?
10. What is the SWOT analysis?
11. What is the PEST analysis?
12. How are SWOT and PEST analysis related?
13. What is Porter's Five Forces model for business analysis?

Problems for Chap. 18

1. Choose two products or companies and conduct a comparative analysis.
2. Choose a company, collect information about it, and conduct SWOT analysis.
3. Choose a company, collect information about it, and use scores to quantify the conclusion on the company SWOT analysis.
4. Choose a company, collect information about it, and conduct PEST analysis.
5. Choose a company, collect information about it, and use scores to quantify the conclusion on the company PEST analysis.
6. Choose a company, collect information about it, and conduct Five Forces analysis.
7. Choose three companies and provide comparison analysis in these companies.

Conducting Research

Contents

Chapter 19 Theories, Experiments, Data Collection, and Analysis – 415

Chapter 20 Deriving Conclusions – 441

Chapter 21 Ethical and Legal Issues of Research – 449

Theories, Experiments, Data Collection, and Analysis

Contents

19.1 Developing Theories – 417

19.2 Business Experiment – 418

19.3 Computer Simulation – 418

19.4 Data Collection – 419

19.5 Cyber Intelligence – 419

19.6 Measurements – 420
19.6.1 Sense of Data – 420
19.6.2 Accuracy of Measurements – 420
19.6.3 Number Rounding Rules – 421
19.6.4 Significant Figures and Decimal Places – 422
19.6.5 Scientific Notation for Numbers – 424
19.6.6 Operations with Numbers of Specific Accuracy – 425

19.7 Accuracy and Rounded Numbers – 427

19.8 Units of Measurement – 429
19.8.1 Time – 429

S. K. Aityan, *Business Research Methodology*, Classroom Companion: Business,
https://doi.org/10.1007/978-3-030-76857-7_19

19.8.2 Metric System – 430
19.8.3 English System – 434
19.8.4 Conversion Between the Metric and English Systems – 436

19.9 Qualitative Data Collection and Analysis – 438

19.1 Developing Theories

A ***theory*** is a logically proven and self-consistent explanation or prediction that is derived from facts, hypotheses, or other theories. Every theory begins with the facts or phenomena and incorporates hypotheses and logical rules and constructs as precepts that lead to expanded and self-consistent logical constructs.

Business and economics are complex systems, which aggregate behavior, and behavior of their components and separate players is not easy to understand and explain. Multiple theories have been developed in the attempt to explain facts, processes, and different aspects in economic systems, markets, and business environment.

Research in business and economics belongs to the category of applied research and, therefore, should be based on real-world data, pursues real-world practical purpose, and aims real-world goals.

A theory is originated with a purpose of explaining unexplained facts or for the purpose of making predictions about the course of processes or activities. A hypothesis or hypotheses or existing theories are taking as the starting point of a new theory. Then the initial hypotheses and theories undertake logical transformation using formal rules that lead to a new set of formally proven or justified statements forming the body of a new theory or an expansion of the existing theory. Any theory should be logically justified and self-consistent.

As soon as research in business and economics belongs to the category of applied research, the newly developed theory should have a clear practical purpose and, hence, be tested and validated on the real-world data.

▶ Example 1: The Theory of General Value

The concept of value is the major cornerstone of business. The primary strategic goal of any business is maximization of its net present value. The tradition concept of value is directly related to money. Such an approach creates some confusion. If money and value are identical, then companies should not spend money on charity because it reduces net present value in terms of money. There are many other unexplained facts associated with such an understanding of value.

A recently introduced theory of general value[1] interprets value as having two components: monetary and nonmonetary. Companies have the primary strategic goal of maximizing its general value. This new theory explains this fact and many other real-world facts associated with companies' goals, operations, and competitive strategies. The theory of general value also explains and predicts behavior of businesses and individuals in decision-making. ◀

1 Aityan S.K. (2013). The Notion of General Value in Economics, International Journal of Economics and Finance, Vol. 5, No.5, pp. 1–14

19.2 Business Experiment

Real-world data are collected from observation under specific conditions. However, the required specific conditions may not be available when needed or may hardly occur without other side effects that disturb the observation. For this reason, researchers may artificially create conditions needed for the observation and data collections. Observation and data collection under artificially established conditions is referred to as an ***experiment***.

Experiments in business research are a quite common way of conducting specific observations and collecting data for research, for example, market experiments, experiments on new manufacturing processes, experiments in business process, and many other.

► Example 2: Experiment on Market Demand

Knowledge of market demand is very important for setting proper pricing. The demand curve is defined as the quantity demanded as a function of the price. In a reasonable price range, the demand is well approximated by a linear function. The current price and current sales quantity define one point on the demand curve. To find another point, the seller may conduct an experiment by temporarily setting a discounted price to find the new demand with the new price. Thus, the demand line can be found by these two points. This knowledge is then used for setting the optimal price. ◄

19.3 Computer Simulation

Not all experiments are easy or even feasible to set. Some types of experiments need unfeasible efforts, substantial expenditures, or unreasonably long time. In some predictive experiments, the results will be known only in the future. A ***computer simulation***, which is also referred to as a ***computer experiment***, is frequently conducted to resolve such challenges.

In a computer simulation, all variables, dependencies, conditions, and rules required for the experiments are virtually implemented on a computer, and the results of the simulation are computed and recorded. Usage of computer simulation in research including business research has significantly grown over the last couple decades as the computer power significantly evolved.

► Example 3: Computer Simulation of Stock Trading Strategies

Success of stock trading significantly depends on the chosen strategy. Different strategies include different principle and rules. However, how to figure out which strategy works better for a specific stock or a portfolio under given circumstances? It would take a long time and may unreasonably burn and waste too much money to test each strategy and choose the best one in the real-world environment under given circumstances.

19

In the computer simulation, the suggested trading strategies are tested on the past trading data or on a forward-looking randomly generated data to examine and compare the profitability from the trading strategies. ◄

19.4 Data Collection

Data collection is one of the most important steps in research. Depending on the quality of data, the research may end up successfully or fail or produce unreliable conclusion.

Data for research may be collected by the research team who conducted the research or taken from other research group or groups or taken from publications. By its natures, data sources could be primary and secondary. The definition and description of primary and secondary sources were discussed in ► Chap. 5. Accuracy and reliability of data depend on the nature of the data, measurement methods, and procedures.

► Example 4: Data Collection for Stock Research

The researcher plans to analyze the correlation of returns of two different stocks. The most reliable data for this research can be obtained directly from the appropriate stock exchange or from other sources providing primary information from the exchanges. It could be ► finance.yahoo.com or some other financial websites. ◄

19.5 Cyber Intelligence

The Internet is a good source of information including information on business and economy. Some information is provided free of charge, but the access to some information requires payment.

Search is the major mechanism of finding information on the Internet. However, the Internet is overwhelmed with information that creates a challenge of finding the needed information. Despite the readily available Internet search engines, information search has become a quite sophisticated procedure, which not always brings desired results. Search results typically bring a lot of irrelevant information that creates a challenge of filtering that information in the attempt to find the relevant information within the information brought by the search engine. Such a filtering is not an easy task at all. Sometimes, the relevant information is not present in the search results too, and additional efforts are needed to find it.

The term ***cyber intelligence*** is referred to as advanced search approaches and strategies used on the Internet for finding the relevant information by applying multiple and sophisticated search techniques for finding information which is not directly available in the straightforward search. Sometimes, such information can be found as an auxiliary information or even information leaks in apparently irrelevant searches. Such searches should not imply breaking in the protected sources or search with the violation of legal or ethical constraints.

► Example 5: Search for Customers of the Competing Companies

Some companies are trying not to reveal their customers in the attempt of protecting their customer base from the competing rivals. A direct search will not return any results. However, search on specific product features may result in finding the companies that use the products of your interest.

Please note that it is a legally correct search. ◄

19.6 Measurements

19.6.1 Sense of Data

Data can be quantitative and qualitative. Collection of qualitative data implies categorical judgment which is subjective and, possibly, biased. Collection of quantitative data implies numeric measurements which is more objective, if the appropriate measurement, processing rules, and procedures are followed.

▶ Example 6: The Dinosaur Age (a Joke)

Once, a group of students came to a paleontological museum to see dinosaur's fossils. A museum guide showed them a dinosaur's skeleton and told that this dinosaur is 65 million and 4 years old. This sounded exciting, and one student asked a question:

"How did you learn that this dinosaur is sixty-five million and four years old?"

The guide responded:

"Oh. It is easy. I've been working at the museum already for four years, but when I just joined the museum four years ago, my advisor told me that this dinosaur was sixty-five years old."

You might have noticed that something sounded strange in the explanation of the dinosaur's age. ◀

▶ Example 7: The Revenue Forecast

It is quite typical to hear how a startup CEO present the company's business plan and makes a forward-looking statement about the expected company's revenue in 4 years that sound something like the following:

"We will start with just 1000 customers in the first quarter of the first year and sell our products for $999.95 per unit. We will increase the customer base by 15% each quarter, and in the fourth year, we expect our annual revenue as $26,714,469.33."

I always ask a question:

"Are you sure that it will be $26,714,469.33 with exactly 33 cents?"

The presenter calmly responds with a strongly asserting expression on his face:

"Sure, it easy to prove by simple calculation. Take 1000 customers as the initial base and increase it by 15% each quarter, then multiply the total number of customers in the fourth year by the product price and you will get exactly $26,714,469.33. By the way, I did not even mention that we may increase the price on the annual basis. However, I want to stay on the conservative estimate."

All sounds correct and very asserting. What do you think about this? Does such a number make sense? ◀

19.6.2 Accuracy of Measurements

19

Measurement is a comparison of the measured object with another object accepted as the unit measurement. If a desk is 4 feet long, it means that a 1'foot unit object fits four times along the desk. Is it exactly four times? Maybe the desk is 1/16 of inch shy from fitting 1 foot unit four times? Maybe just opposite? All depends on the accuracy of the measurement.

We cannot measure things with the unlimited accuracy. The accuracy of measurement depends on many factors such as accuracy of the measuring device and nature of the measured object. For example,

- A car odometer can measure a distance with the accuracy of miles but cannot measure within accuracy of inches.
- When measuring a human body height, do not even try to do it with the accuracy better than 1 centimeter (half inch) because a human body height varies within 1–2 centimeters during each day. In the morning, humans are normally higher than in the evening because of the body pressure on the spine during our vertical walking at the daytime.
- Heisenberg's principle of uncertainty in quantum mechanics states that the momentum and the position of a quantum object cannot be accurately measured both at the same time – either momentum or position. Business research is far from quantum mechanics, but this example was given for the sake of completeness of the picture.

Thus, measurements are made within the accuracy allowed by the measuring devices and the nature of the measured object.

Coming back to the examples given above, when the distance between two cities measured by a car odometer is 63 miles, it means that the actual distance rounded to an integer number is 63 miles. The actual distance could be 62.6 miles or 63.3 miles or any other distance which equals 63 if rounded to the nearest integer number.

A human height of 180 cm means that the actual height at the time of measurement was rounded to the nearest integer. It could be 180.4 cm or 179.7 cm or any other actual height rounded to integer 180 cm.

> Measurements are made within the accuracy allowed by the measuring devices and nature of the measured object.

19.6.3 Number Rounding Rules

Rounding reduces the accuracy of a number as a measurement by adjusting the number to the closest value of the original number. Before rounding a number, first decide to what accuracy the number should be rounded.

The number rounding rule is quite simple – a number can be rounded to the reduced accuracy by adjusting the number to the nearest value of the original number. The rule can be decomposed as following:

- If the rightmost kept digit in the number is followed by 5, 6, 7, 8, or 9, round the number up, i.e., increase the rightmost kept digit by 1.
- If the rightmost kept digit in the number is followed by 0, 1, 2, 3, or 4, round the number down, i.e., keep the rightmost kept digit as is.

▶ Example 8: Number Rounding

- Rounding number 834,235 to thousands results in 834,000 or $834*10^3$.
  - If you use notation 834,000, you have to mention that the number is rounded to thousands or just say 834 thousand.
  - Notation $834*10^3$ automatically means that there is 834 thousand.
- Rounding number 1956 to hundreds results in 2000 or $20*10^2$.
  - If you use notation 2000, you have to mention that the number is rounded to hundreds or just say 20 hundred.
  - Notation $20*10^2$ automatically means that there is 20 hundred. It is not $2*10^3$ because zero followed 2 in number 20 is a significant figure the same as it could be any other number.
- Rounding number 13.6746 to hundredth results in 13.67. ◀

- If the rightmost kept digit in the number is followed by 5, 6, 7, 8, or 9, round the number up, i.e., increase the rightmost kept digit by 1.
- If the rightmost kept digit in the number is followed by 0, 1, 2, 3, or 4, round the number down, i.e., keep the rightmost kept digit as is.

19.6.4 Significant Figures and Decimal Places

Significant figures are the number of digits in a numerical value, often, that contribute to the degree of accuracy of the value obtained as a measurement or as the result of processing of the measured data. Significant figures are counted as the number of digits after the first non-zero digit in the original number. Zeros on the right from the first non-zero digit are also meaningful digits and must be counted too. The digits after decimal point are contributing to the significant figures too.

▶ Example 9: Examples of Significant Figures

- All three numbers 123, 12.3, and 1.23 have three significant numbers.
- Number 000500 has three significant figures, which are 500.
- Number 0034010.20 has seven significant figures, i.e., all digits after left non-zero digit 3 and including the digits after the decimal point. The sign does not impact on the significant figures.

- Leading zeros are not significant to the left of non-zero digits. For example, 32, 3.2, and 00.0000032 have two significant figures.
- Zeros are significant if positioned between two non-zero digits ("captive"). For example, 40.05, 4005, and 0.4005 all have four significant figures.

The number of ***decimal places*** in a decimal fraction is the number of digits after the period in a decimal fraction. It identifies the decimal accuracy in a decimal fraction. ◀

▶ Example 10: Examples of Significant Figures and Decimal Places

- 123.45 has five significant figures and two decimal places.
- 10.304 has five significant figures and three decimal places.
- 001.500 has four significant figures and three decimal places. ◀

▶ Example 11: Significant Figures and Degree of Accuracy

◘ Tables 19.1 and 19.2 show examples of number 35.034 rounded to a specific number of significant figures and decimal places. ◀

▶ Example 12: Decimal Places and Degree of Accuracy

An example of number 0.035147 rounded to a specific significant figures and decimal places is shown in ◘ Tables 19.3 and 19.4. ◀

Rounding to the significant figures or decimal places exceeding the significant figures or decimal places in the original number is formally possible but does not make sense because such a rounding does not increase the actual accuracy but creates a confusing illusion of it.

Rounded numbers represent the accuracy of measurement.

◘ **Table 19.1** An example of rounding number 35.074 to significant figures

Accuracy (number of significant figures)	Rounded to significant figures	
0	N/A	
1	4*10	
2	35	
3	35.1	
4	35.07	
5	35.074	
6	35.0740	Formally possible but does not make sense

Table 19.2 An example of rounding number 35.074 to decimal places

Accuracy (number of decimal places)	Rounded to decimal places	
0	35	
1	35.1	
2	35.07	
3	35.074	
4	35.0740	Formally possible but does not make sense
5	35.07400	Formally possible but does not make sense
6	35.074000	Formally possible but does not make sense

Table 19.3 An example of rounding number 0.035147 to significant figures

Accuracy (number of significant figures)	Rounded to significant figures	
0	N/A	
1	0.04	
2	0.035	
3	0.0351	
4	0.03515	
5	0.035147	
6	0.0351470	Formally possible but does not make sense
7	0.03514700	Formally possible but does not make sense
8	0.035147000	Formally possible but does not make sense

19.6.5 Scientific Notation for Numbers

19

Scientific notation is a format for expressing numbers that are too large or too small to be conveniently written in decimal form. In scientific notation, numbers are written in the form $m*10^n$, where n is an integer, positive or negative, referred to as the exponent and m is typically a number between 1 and 10 referred to as the mantissa. The mantissa consists of the significant figures of the original number.

■ **Table 19.4** An example of rounding number 0.035147 to decimal places

Accuracy (number of decimal places)	Rounded to decimal places	
0	0.0	
1	0.0	
2	0.04	
3	0.035	
4	0.0351	
5	0.03515	
6	0.035147	
7	0.0351470	Formally possible but does not make sense
8	0.03514700	Formally possible but does not make sense

■ **Table 19.5** Examples of scientific notation for numbers

Decimal notation	Scientific notation
0.000000354	$3.54*10^{-7}$
0.025	$2.5*10^{-2}$
−0.17	$-1.7*10^{-1}$
5	$5*10^{0}$
47.281	$4.7281*10^{1}$
571,24	$5.7124*10^{2}$
300,000	$3*10^{5}$

► **Example 13: Scientific Notation of Numbers**

■ Table 19.5 shows examples of scientific notation for numbers vs. decimal notation. ◄

19.6.6 Operations with Numbers of Specific Accuracy

The major principle behind basic mathematical operations with numbers, such as multiplication, division, summation, or subtraction, states such operations cannot result with a higher accuracy than the original numbers involved in the operations. This principle is defined as the following:

- The result of multiplication or division cannot have more significant figures than the lowest number of significant figures of the numbers involved in the operation.
- The result of summation and subtraction cannot have more decimal places than the lowest number of decimal places in the numbers involved in the operation.

First, perform mathematical operations with the given numbers and then round the result according to the rules above.

▶ Example 14: Summation and Subtraction of Rounded Numbers

Let's perform the following operations as shown in ◘ Table 19.6. ◀

▶ Example 15: Multiplication and Division of Rounded Numbers

Let's perform the following operations as shown in ◘ Table 19.7. ◀

- The result of multiplication or division cannot have more significant figures than the lowest number of significant figures of the numbers involved in the operation.
- The result of summation and subtraction cannot have more decimal places than the lowest number of decimal places in the numbers involved in the operation.

◘ **Table 19.6** An example of summation and subtraction of rounded numbers

	Operation	Explanation
(a)	$6.38 + 0.00123 = 6.38123 \approx 6.38$	The first number has two decimal places, and the second number has five decimal places. The result is rounded to the lowest decimal places which is 2
(b)	$6.38 + 0.\ 0123 = 6.3923 \approx 6.38$	The first number has two decimal places, and the second number has four decimal places. The result is rounded to the lowest decimal places which is 2
(c)	$6.38 + 0.0173 = 6.3973 \approx 6.40$	The first number has two decimal places, and the second number has five decimal places. The result is rounded to the lowest decimal places which is 2
(d)	$6.3821–1.\ 01 = 5.3721 \approx 5.37$	The first number has four decimal places, and the second number has two decimal places. The result is rounded to the lowest decimal places which is 2
(e)	$6.3821–1.1 = 5.2821 \approx 5.3$	The first number has four decimal places, and the second number has one decimal place. The result is rounded to the lowest decimal places which is 1

Table 19.7 An example of multiplication and division of rounded numbers

	Operation	Explanation
(a)	6.38 * 2.1 = 13.398 ≈13	The first number has 3 significant figures and the second number has 2 significant figures. The result is rounded to the lowest significant figures which is 2
(b)	6.38 * 0. 0123 / 2.0 = 0.039237 ≈0.039	The first number has 3 significant figures, the second number has 3 significant figures, and the third number has 2 significant figures. The result is rounded to the lowest significant figures which is 2
(c)	6.38 * 0.01754 = 0.0111905 ≈ 0.112	The first number has 3 significant figures and the second number has 4 significant figures. The result is rounded to the lowest significant figures which is 3

19.7 Accuracy and Rounded Numbers

Rounded numbers and their notation represent the accuracy of measurements and, hence, the accuracy of the results obtained from mathematical operations performed on those numbers.

Mathematically, all the following numbers
5000,000.00
5000,000
$5000*10^3$
$5.00*10^6$
$5.0*10^6$
$5*10^6$
are equal and mean five million. However, those numbers have different meaning as measurements or processed results originated from measurements.

- Number 5000.000.00 means five million with the accuracy to two digits after the decimal point. It is a number rounded to two decimal places with all zeros as meaningful numbers. Actually, it is a number from interval (4,999,999.50; 5000,000.49). Zeros in this number are meaningful numbers rather than an indication of an order of magnitude.
- Number 5000,000 means five million with the accuracy to one. This number represents any value form interval (4,999,995.00; 5000,004.99). Any number from this interval can be rounded to 5000,000 ignoring decimal places. Zeros in this number are meaningful numbers rather than an indication of an order of magnitude. It means that any variation within 1 stays beyond the accuracy. The accu-

racy of this number is lower than in the previous bullet, because digits after the decimal point are removed and can have any value that is rounded to 5000,000.

- Number $5000*10^3$ means five million with the accuracy to thousand. This number represents any value form interval ($4995*10^3$; $5004*10^3$) or (4995,000.00; 5004,999.99), i.e., any number that has four significant figures. It means that any variation within 1000 stays beyond the accuracy. The accuracy of this number is lower than in the previous bullet.
- Number $5.00*10^6$ means five million with the accuracy to ten thousand. This number represents any value form interval ($4.995*10^6$; $5.004*10^6$) or (4995,000.00; 5004,999.99), i.e., any value that has three significant figures. It means that any variation within 10000 stays beyond the accuracy. The accuracy of this number is lower than in the previous bullet.
- Number $5*10^6$ means five million with the accuracy to million. This number represents a value form interval ($4.5*10^6$; $5.4*10^6$) or (4,500,000.00; 5,499,999.99), i.e., any value that has one significant figure. It means that any variation within 1 million stays beyond the accuracy. The accuracy of this number is lower than in the previous bullet.

▶ Example 16: Accuracy of the Revenue Projection

The forward-looking estimate for the company revenue in the fourth year of operations made in Example 7 was presented as $26,714,469.33. That estimate was made by accurate calculations with the sale of 1000 units in the first quarter at price $999.95 per unit and subsequent growth of sales by 15% each quarter.

Let's analyze the accuracy of the initial numbers and the result. The initial sales of 1000 units is a guess. Even if such a guess is correct, the actual sales may vary, for example, 987 units or 1123 units. Nothing can be forecasted with the full certainty. Let's estimate the accuracy of the sales as 10%, i.e., the expected initial sales is $10*10^2$ units. It means that the initial sales is expected in the interval from $9.5*10^2$ to $10.4*10^2$ of the chosen units. Such a notation means that the sales will be around 1000 with no expectation about the second significant figure. The quarterly sales growth is estimated as 15%. Is it an exact growth percentage? Maybe, it will be 14%, maybe 13%, or maybe 16% growth. Let's accept that the quarterly growth is expected in the interval from 13% to 17%.

According to the low-end estimate with the initial sales 9500 units and quarterly growth 13%, the sales in the fourth year is $20,494,993.40 $\approx 2*10^7$. According to the upper-end estimate with the initial sales 10,499 units and quarterly growth 18%, the sales in the fourth year is $38,956,194.47 $\approx 4*10^7$. Thus, the exact calculation of the revenue with ten significant figure, as it was done in Example 7, makes no sense because of possible variations within the error of the initial sales and the growth rate estimates.

Thus, the fourth year revenue estimate is within interval ($\$2*10^7$; $\$4*10^7$). Such an estimate can be presented with only one significant figure as $\$3 \pm 1*10^7$. This makes sense and does not present the digits beyond the accuracy, which carry no meaningful information. ◀

19

Significant figures and decimal places should not exceed the accuracy of the respective measurements and the accuracy of the processed results.

19.8 Units of Measurement

Measurements should be performed using commonly acceptable specified quantities referred to as units of measurement.

A unit of measurement is a formally defined reference quantity adopted and used as a standard for measurements by convention or by law. Measurement is a process of determining how large or small an actual examined quantity is as compared to a basic reference quantity of the same kind. In the other words, measurement is a comparison of a quantity associated with measured object with the appropriate unit quantity.

There are many fundamental measures used in science. However, we will not discuss the full scope of all possible scientific measures and units and limit the discussion by some the most popular measures and units in common life and business research. If the reader is interested in learning the complete system of units, the information is commonly available in many sources including the Internet. The most frequently used measures and units in common life and business research are:

- Length
- Volume
- Mass
- Weight
- Time
- Temperature

There are many different systems of units. Among the most usable in common life and business are two systems:

- Metric system
- English system

The metric system is the most used and commonly adopted system of units in the world. All countries except three – the USA, Liberia, and Myanmar (former Burma) – and partially UK have adopted and use the metric system. The United States Congress passed the Metric Conversion Act in 1975, which declared metric system as the preferred system of the USA, and the US Metric Board was created to implement the conversion from English to the metric system. However, the attempt mostly failed, and the English system is still in common use in the USA. Science and most engineering activities such as airspace and automotive are slowly converting to the metric system in the USA. In the UK, some units are used from the metric (temperature) but some (length, weigh, volume) from the English system.

19.8.1 Time

In both metric and English systems, time for the common purpose is measured in seconds (s), minute (min), hour (h), day (d), and year (y). These units and the relationships between them are shown in ◘ Table 19.8.

Table 19.8 Most frequently used fundamental units of metric system

Unit	Symbol	Relationship
Second	s	
Minute	min	1 min = 60 s
Hour	h	1 h = 60 min
Day	d	1 d = 24 h
Year	y	1 y = 365(6) d

(Comment: A normal year has 365 days. Each fourth year is called a leap year and has 366 days)

The definition of the second as the unit of time was formally redefined by the atomic radiation frequency as 1 s = 9,192,631,770 oscillations of the Cesium^{133} (Cs^{133}) atom.

19.8.2 Metric System

In metric system, length is measured in meters (m), volume is measured in liters (l), and mass and weight are measured in grams (g). The names and symbols for decimal multiples and submultiples of the units in the metric system and their relationship are shown in Tables 19.9a and 19.9b.

Length

The unit of ***length*** in metric system is the ***meter***. The meter was originally defined in 1793 as one ten-millionth of the distance from the equator to the North Pole. The definition of the meter was changed several times, and since 1983, the meter is redefined as the length of the path travelled by light in vacuum during a time interval of 1/299792458 of a second. The derived units of length for different multiples and submultiples of 10, such as kilometer, centimeter, millimeter, and other can be expressed simply by the appropriate repositioning of the decimal point and does not require any additional calculation.

The names and symbols for major decimal multiples and submultiples of the units of length in the metric system and their relationship are shown in Table 19.10.

Area

Area in English system is measured in squares of the appropriate units of length. There are some other less frequently used units of liquid volume in English system. The names and symbols for major units of volume in English system and their relationship are shown in Table 19.11.

Table 19.9a Names and symbols for major decimal multiples of the units of length in the metric system

Factor (multiples)	Name	Symbol
10^1	Deca	da
10^2	Hecto	h
10^3	Kilo	k
10^6	Mega	M
10^9	Giga	G
10^{12}	Tera	T
10^{15}	Peta	P
10^{18}	Exa	E
10^{21}	Zetta	Z
10^{24}	Yotta	Y

Table 19.9b Names and symbols for major decimal submultiples of the units of length in the metric system

Factor (submultiples)	Name	Symbol
10^{-1}	Deci	d
10^{-2}	Centi	c
10^{-3}	Milli	m
10^{-6}	Micro	μ
10^{-9}	Nano	n
10^{-12}	Pico	p
10^{-15}	Femto	f
10^{-18}	Atto	a
10^{-21}	Zepto	z
10^{-24}	Yocto	y

Volume

The unit of ***volume*** in the metric system is the ***liter.*** One liter is the volume of one cubic ***deciliter***. One cubic deciliter is a cube with each side equal to 10 cm. The names and symbols for major decimal multiples and submultiples of the units of length in the metric system are shown in Table 19.12.

Mass and Weight

Terminologically, the base unit for mass and weight in the metric system is gram.

Table 19.10 Names and symbols for major decimal multiples and submultiples of the units of length in the metric system

Factor	Name	Symbol	Relationship
Base	Meter	m	
10^3	Kilometer	km	I km = 10^3 m
10^{-1}	Decimeter	dm	1 dm = 10^{-1} m
10^{-2}	Centimeter	cm	1 cm = 10^{-2} m
10^{-3}	Millimeter	mm	1 mm = 10^{-1} cm = 10^{-3} m
10^{-9}	Nanometer	nm	1 nm = 10^{-9} m

Table 19.11 Major units of area in the metric system

Name	Symbol	Relationship
Square centimeter	sq cm, cm^2	
Square meter	sq m, m^2	1 m^2 = 10^4 cm^2
Square kilometer	sq km, km^2	1 km^2 = 10^6 m^2
Hectare	ha	1 ha = 10^4 m^2 = 1/100 km^2

The gram was initially defined as the mass and weight of one milliliter (one cubic centimeter) of pure water at the temperature of melting ice, but later the temperature was changed to 4 °C that is the temperature of maximum density of water. For all practical purposes, we can use this definition. However, the official base unit for mass and weight in the metric system is one kilogram, which equals 1000 grams, but it is more formally correct to say that one gram is one thousandth of a kilogram. In 2019, the kilogram was redefined more accurately in terms of the Planck constant h.

Scientifically, the term "kilogram" is applicable to measuring mass. Weight is measured in Newtons (system SI, 1 N = 1 kg*m/s^2), but for common purposes, weight in kilograms is commonly used and acceptable.

Thus, terminologically, the name of the unit of mass or weight is based on the term "gram" with possible prefixes as in Table 19.8, and the base value is defined for one kilogram. Please do not get confused with this fact.

The names and symbols for major decimal multiples and submultiples of the units of weight in the metric system and their relationship are shown in Table 19.13.

Table 19.12 Names and symbols for major decimal multiples and submultiples of the units of volume in the metric system

Factor	Name	Symbol	Relationship
Base	Liter	l (L)	1 L = 10^{-3} m^3 = 10^3 cm^3
10^1	Decaliter	dal	1 dal = 10 L
10^2	Hectoliter	hl	1 hl = 10^2 L =
10^3	Kiloliter	kl	I kl = 10^3 m
10^6	Megaliter	Ml	1 ml = 10^3 kl = 10^6 L
10^{-1}	Deciliter	dl	1 dl = 10^{-1} L = 100 cm^3
10^{-2}	Centiliter	cl	I cl = 10^{-2} L = 10 cm^3
10^{-3}	Milliliter	ml	1 ml = 10^{-3} L = 1 cm^3
10^{-6}	Microliter	µl	1 µl = 10^{-3} cm^3

Table 19.13 Names and symbols for major decimal multiples and submultiples of the units of mass and weight in the metric system

Factor	Name	Symbol	Relationship
Formal base	Kilogram	kg	1 kg = 10^3 g
Terminological base	Gram	g	1 g = 10^{-3} kg
10^{-3}	Milligram	mg	1 mg = 10^{-3} g
10^{-6}	Microgram	µg	1 µg = 10^{-6} g
10^{-9}	Nanogram	ng	1 ng = 10^{-9} g
10^6	Ton (metric)	t	1 t = 10^3 kg = 10^6 g

Temperature

The ***degree of Celsius*** is the official unit for measuring temperature in the metric system denoted as ^{0}C and named after Anders Celsius (1701–1744), who introduced a similar scale. The ***Celsius scale*** is also known as the ***centigrade scale***. The Celsius scale has two reference points of temperature:

- 0 °C is the freezing point of pure water at 1 atm pressure (a typical pressure at sea level).
- 100 °C is the boiling point of pure water at 1 atm pressure (a typical pressure at sea level).

- The temperature interval between 0 °C and 100 °C is divided into 100 equal intervals, each representing one degree of Celsius.

The lowest possible temperature is –273.15 °C. At this temperature, all molecular motion stops, and only quantum motion continues. This temperature is referred to as ***absolute zero***. Temperatures below the absolute zero are fundamentally impossible. In 2014, Italian scientists were able to cool a one cubic meter copper vessel to –273.144 °C, which was extremely close to the absolute zero.

In physics, chemistry, and other natural sciences, temperature is measured in the Kelvin scale. The Kelvin scale is identical to the Celsius scale with the only difference that 0 K equals the absolutes zero, i.e., -273.15 °C. One degree in Celsius scale is equal to one degree in Kelvin. The notation for temperature in the Kelvin scale is "K" without the degree sign "^{0}." For example,

0 K = –273.15 °C

273.15 K = 0 ° C

373.15 K = 100 ° C

General conversion between the Celsius and Kelvin scales can be expressed as shown in Eq. (19.1)

T K = T°C – 273.15 and T°C = T K + 273.15 (19.1)where T K is temperature in Kelvin degrees and T ^{0}C is temperature in Celsius.

19.8.3 English System

English (or Imperial or British) system of measures has the following units.

Length

Length in English system is measured in ***inches***, ***feet***, ***yards***, and ***miles***. Historically, one foot was defined as the typical length of a human foot. In the past, such a unit was used in many local systems such as Greek, Roman, Chinese, French, English, and American. Local feet were varying.

There are some other units of length, but they are used less frequently.

The names and symbols for major units of length in English system and their relationship are shown in ◘ Table 19.14.

The inch can be equally denoted as "in" or as a double prime ". The foot can be equally denoted as "ft" or as a single prime '. Thus, 4" and 4 in equally mean the length of four inches, and 7' and 7 ft equally mean the length of 7 feet.

A nautical mile is equal to one minute of latitude. It is slightly more than a statute (land measured) mile (1 nautical mile = 1.1508 statute miles). Distance in aviation, navy, and sea shipping is measured in nmi.

Area

Area in English system is measured in squares of the appropriate units of length. There are some other less frequently used units of liquid volume in English system. The names and symbols for major units of volume in English system and their relationship are shown in ◘ Table 19.15.

19

Table 19.14 Major units of length in English system

Name	Symbol	Relationship
Foot (plural feet)	ft or ‘	
Inch	in or “	12 in = 1 ft
Yard	yd	1 yd. = 3 ft. = 36 in
Mile (statute mile)	mi	1 mi = 1760 yd. = 5280 ft. = 63,360 in
Nautical mile	nmi	1 nmi = 1.151 mi

Table 19.15 Major units of length in English system

Name	Symbol	Relationship
Square inch	sq in, in^2	
Square foot	sq ft, ft^2	$1\ ft^2 = 144\ in^2$
Square mile	sq mi, mi^2	$1\ mi^2 = 5280^2\ ft^2$
Acre	ac	$1\ ac = 4840\ yd^2 = 1/640\ mi^2$

Volume

Volume in English system is measured in ***gallons***, ***fluid ounces***, ***pints***, ***quarts***, and ***barrels***. There are some other less frequently used units of liquid volume in English system. The names and symbols for major units of volume in English system and their relationship are shown in Table 19.16.

Mass and Weight

Mass and weight are measured in English system in ***ounces***, ***pounds***, ***short tons***, and ***long tons.*** The short ton is typical for the USA, while the long term is used in the UK. The names and symbols for major units of volume in English system and their relationship are shown in Table 19.17.

Temperature

Fahrenheit scale for measuring temperature does not formally belong to English system. It is named after Dutch scientist Daniel Gabriel Fahrenheit (1686–1736). Only a few countries including the USA, Belize, Palau, the Bahamas, and the Cayman Islands use Fahrenheit as their official temperature scale.

The Fahrenheit scale is defined by two reference points: The zero point 0 °F is the freezing temperature of a solution of brine made from a mixture of water, ice, and ammonium chloride. The other reference point was his best estimate of the

Table 19.16 Major units of length in English system

Name	Symbol	Relationship
Gallon	gal	1 gal = 4 qt = 8 pt
Fluid ounce	oz	1 oz. = 1/16 pt. = 1/32 qt
Quart	qt	1 qt = 1/4 gal
Pint	pt	1 pt. = 1/2 qt = 1/8 gal
Barrel	bbl	1 bbl = 42 gal

Table 19.17 Most frequently used fundamental units of metric system

Name	Symbol	Relationship
Once	oz	1 oz. = 1/16 lb
Pound	lb	1 lb = 16 oz
Short ton	sh.tn	1 sh.tn = 2000 lb
Long ton	lton	1 lton = 2,40 lb

average human body temperature, which was set at 96 °F. The human body temperature was later adjusted by about 2.6 °F up.

In comparison to the Celsius scale, the freezing temperature of pure water is 32 °F = 0 °C, and the temperature of boiling water is 212 °F = 100 °C.

19.8.4 Conversion Between the Metric and English Systems

It is important to know how to convert the units of measurement in the metric and in English systems. Some most important conversions are shown in Tables 19.18 and 19.19.

Conversion from Fahrenheit to Celsius scales and from Celsius to Fahrenheit are shown below in Eq. (19.2)

$$T^{\circ}\mathrm{C} = \left(T^{\circ}\mathrm{F} - 32\right) * \frac{5}{9} \quad \text{and} \quad T^{\circ}\mathrm{F} = T^{\circ}\mathrm{C} * \frac{5}{9} + 32 \qquad (19.2)$$

Feet to centimeters	Centimeters to feet
1 ft. = 30.48 cm	1 m = 3.281 ft

19

Miles to kilometers	Kilometers to miles
1 mi = 1.609 km	1 km = 0.6215 mi

Pounds to kilograms	Kilograms to pounds
1 lb = 0.454 kg = 454 g	1 kg = 2.20 lb

Fahrenheit to Celsius	Celsius to Fahrenheit
$T^{\circ}\text{C} = \left(T^{\circ}\text{F} - 32\right) * \frac{5}{9}$	$T^{\circ}\text{F} = T^{\circ}\text{C} * \frac{5}{9} + 32$

Table 19.18 Conversion of the units of length between the metric and English systems

English		Metric		Conversion	
Name	**Symbol**	**Name**	**Symbol**	**English → metric**	**Metric → English**
Inch	in	Centimeter	cm	1 in = 2.54 cm	1 cm = 0.394 in
Foot	ft	Centimeter	cm	1 ft. = 30.48 cm	1 cm = 0.03281 cm
Foot	ft	Meter	m	1 ft. = 0.3048 m	1 m = 3.281 ft
Yard	yd	Meter	m	1 yd. = 0.9144 m	1 m = 1.094 yd
Mile	mi	Kilometer	km	1 mi = 1.609 km	1 km = 0.6215 mi
Nautical mile	nmi	Kilometer	km	1 nmi = 1.852 km	1 km = 0.5400 nmi

Table 19.19 Conversion of the units of area between the metric and English systems

English		Metric		Conversion	
Name	**Symbol**	**Name**	**Symbol**	**English → metric**	**Metric → English**
Acre	ac	Hectare	ha	1 ac = 0.405 ha	1 ha = 2.47 ac
Sq foot	ft^2	Sq meter	m^2	1 ft^2 = 0.093 m^2	1 m^2 = 10.8 ft^2
Sq yard	yd^2	Sq meter	m^2	1 yd^2 = 0.836 m^2	1 m^2 = 1.20 yd^2
Sq mile	mi^2	Sq kilometer	km^2	1 mi^2 = 2.590 km^2	1 km^2 = 0.3891 mi^2

Table 19.20 Conversion of the units of weight between the metric and English systems

English		Metric		Conversion	
Name	Symbol	Name	Symbol	English → Metric	Metric → English
Ounce	oz	Gram	g	1 oz. = 28.350 g	1 g = 0.0353 oz
Pound	lb	Kilogram	kg	1 lb = 0.454 kg = 454 g	1 kg = 2.20 lb
Short ton	sh.tn	Metric ton	t	1 sh.tn = 0.907 t	1 t = 1.103 sh.tn
Long ton	lton	Metric ton	t	1 lton = 1.016 t	1 t = 0.984 lton

19.9 Qualitative Data Collection and Analysis

Qualitative data cannot be formally measured. Colors, taste, attitude, satisfaction, and many other entities are good examples of qualitative data. Qualitative data can be structured by subjective categories defined by the researchers or commonly understood in the society. As soon as qualitative data cannot be formally measured, the judgment on the belongingness to different categories is subjective and can easily present subjective bias.

However, there are no ground general rules applied for the analysis of qualitative data. Analysis of qualitative data should typically begin with the understanding and interpretation of that data. Two major approaches could be used in qualitative data analysis: deductive and inductive.

Qualitative data is not easy to analyze because such data cannot be measured and, hence, compared. Nobody can say what difference is greater: red vs. green or blue vs. orange. However, colors may be described in the RGB format. The abbreviation RGB stands for red, green, and blue. In RGB format, each color is represented by three integer numbers in the interval (0, 255). For instance, in the RGB format, color (255,0,0) is pure bright red, color (0,255,0) is pure bright green, and color (0,0,255) is bright pure blue. Color (255,255,255) is white, and color (0,0,0) is black. Other combinations of numbers describe the appropriate mixture of colors. If colors are represented in the RGB format, the appropriate metrics can be developed and used for numerical measurements, comparison, and analysis. However, creating a good metrics matching subjective description of colors is a challenging task. What could be RGB numbers for colors qualitatively described as "cold green" and "warm green." Professionals with extensive experience in working with color may take this challenge and develop numerical metrics matching the qualitative description of colors.

The RGB format is mostly used in computer technologies. Another color format mostly used in printing industry is CMYK. This abbreviation stands for cyan, magenta, yellow, and black. Professionals in printing industry believe that CMYK better represents printed colors than RGB, but let's leave this discussion to color professionals.

▶ Example 17: Comparison of Color Shades

Colors are represented in the RGB format are described as (R,G,B), where R, G, and B are integer numbers in the interval (0, 255). Then qualitative comparative categories "brighter" and "dimmer" can be quantified as $(\alpha R,\ \alpha G,\ \alpha B)$, where α is a fraction $0 \le \alpha \le 1$ and $\alpha R,\ \alpha G,\ and\ \alpha B$ are rounded to the closest integer. The higher the α, the brighter the color, and the lower the α, the dimmer the color.

Different levels of satisfaction, quality assessment, and other categories, which can be ordered by their strength, can be quantified by assigning the appropriate numbers. For instance, the levels in questionnaires maybe quantifies as matching the qualitative judgments the assigned numbers. ◀

▶ Example 18: Quantification of Qualitative Data

Suppose we should collect data on customer satisfaction with the company's customer service. The qualitative data are categorized as "excellent," "good," "average," "fair," and "poor." We might collect all feedbacks and calculate how many customers assessed the quality of customer service as "excellent," "good," "average," "fair," and "poor." We can plot a distribution function for the categories, but we have no metrics for a more detailed description and analysis: "excellent," "good," "average," "fair," and "poor."

The most common approach to such a problem is to assign a numerical value to each category: "excellent," 4; "good," 3; "average," 2; "fair," 1; and "poor," 0. The assigned numbers should carry semantics, and under some circumstances, the numerical differences between the categories can be ununiform. If we want to emphasize poor and excellent services, the assigned numbers may look as 6, 4, 3, 2, and 0 with a greater gap for the largest and lowest categories.

Quantification of most qualitative data is still subjective, and therefore it would be inappropriate to discuss precision of that data. ◀

? Questions for Self-Control for Chap. 19

1. What is a theory?
2. What is business experiment?
3. What is computer simulation?
4. What is cyber intelligence?
5. What is involved on the act of measurement?
6. What are the number rounding rules?
7. What is the difference between significant figures and decimal places?
8. What is the rounding rule for summation and subtraction of rounded numbers?
9. What is the rounding rule for multiplication or division of rounded numbers?
10. What is the scientific notation for numbers?
11. What is the accuracy of a rounded number?
12. What does the term "unit of measurement" mean?
13. What major units of measurement do you know?
14. What systems of measurement do you know?
15. What system of measurements is adopted in the USA?
16. What system of measurements is adopted in Europe?
17. What is the conversion of temperature from Celsius to Fahrenheit scale?
18. What is the conversion of temperature from Fahrenheit to Celsius scale?

19. How many meters in one kilometer?
20. How many feet in one mile?
21. How to collect qualitative data?
22. What is the framework for qualitative data?
23. How to quantify qualitative data?

Problems for Chap. 19

1. What is the value of 45.987 rounded to three significant figures?
2. What is the value of 45.987 rounded to two decimal places?
3. The length of the room is measured as 5.3 m, and the width of the same room is measured as 3.12 m. What is the area of the room?
4. The height of a building is reported as 25 m. The TV antenna installed on the roof is 2.53 meters tall according to the manufacturer specification. What is the total height of the building together with the antenna?
5. An airplane has flown 2150 nmi. What is this distance in km?
6. A person's height is 6′1″. How tall is the person if measured in cm?
7. Mr. Smith wants to buy 3 kg of apples. How many pound (lb) is it?

Deriving Conclusions

Contents

20.1 The Role of Conclusions in Research – 442

20.2 Research Result Evaluation – 442

20.2.1 Research Problem and Subproblem Assessment – 442

20.2.2 Research Design Assessment – 443

20.2.3 Data Quality Assessment – 443

20.3 Research Result Interpretation – 444

20.4 First Answer Subquestions and Then the Main Question – 445

20.5 Cause and Effect Rather Than Value Judgment – 446

20.6 Make Recommendations and Predictions if Applicable – 446

20.7 New Questions Arise From Research Conclusions – 447

S. K. Aityan, *Business Research Methodology*, Classroom Companion: Business,
https://doi.org/10.1007/978-3-030-76857-7_20

20.1 The Role of Conclusions in Research

For any research project in any scientific discipline, deriving conclusions is the final, and most important, step in the research process. Conclusions are the answers to the research problem stated in the beginning of the research. Conclusions should address all questions and subquestions formulated in the problem statement. The answers in the conclusions are not always expected to be positively final or completely closing the research questions. Sometimes, conclusions could be negative saying that no answer could be found using the chosen research methods, procedures, or data, or it could not be found at all, or it needs some additional study. Research is a journey to land of unknown, and we cannot always expect to find the answers. Thus, negative answers are answers too. In any case, conclusions must be logically derived from the results of the research and justified.

20.2 Research Result Evaluation

Once the research results are obtained, they should be evaluated and interpreted before answering the problem question. The research evaluation consists of a retrospective review of the research purpose, methods and methodology of the problem-solving and data collection, processing, and interpretation to achieve research objectives. All this is analyzed from the perspective of the ability to derive the conclusions to answer the research questions.

The research evaluation is a flexible process based on the researcher experience, knowledge, and familiarity with the research domain. In the twenty-first century, the research evaluation process should be conducted on the multidisciplinary bases to avoid biased or incomplete picture obtained with a view from one or limited angles of view.

20.2.1 Research Problem and Subproblem Assessment

It may sound strange that evaluation of the research problem (question) and subproblems (subquestions) should be done in this step of the research. A comprehensive assessment of the research problem including the subproblems must be conducted in the step of research problem formulation. There is no doubt about it. Without in-depth problem assessment in the early stage of the research project, the research project becomes meaningless. It is true. However, it is important to come back and retrospectively reevaluate the problem statement at this stage when the results have been already obtained. Such a retrospective analysis is needed to make sure that with the collected and processed data and evidence, the problem statement is still valid, and the logic of subproblems is complete and sufficient for deriving the conclusions to answer the main question or questions of the research.

▶ Example 1: Research Problem Assessment

Company XYZ initiated market research for the purpose of expanding its retail business to a new territory in Oakland, California. The research problem is "Feasibility of retail expansion to Oakland, California." The subproblems are "Analysis of market demand in Oakland," "Analysis of competition," "Cost analysis of the expansion," "Supply chain analysis and forecast," and "Sales forecast."

The reevaluation of the problem statement with the new evidence obtained upon the completion of the research activities before drawing the conclusions revealed that the COVID-19 pandemic has crucially changed the retail business in the area and the company has to find a new business model matching the changed conditions before concluding on the research results. Thus, the research statement should be appended, and research results should be updated. ◀

20.2.2 Research Design Assessment

A research design is a research plan that includes research methods, procedures, data collection, and processing plan. However, any research is a journey to the land of unknown, and it would be no surprise if new evidence shows that some preliminary planned methods, procedures, or data collection or processing plans do not work or are not applied under the specific conditions of the research, which could not be predicted before the actual data was collected. In this case, the research design should be reevaluated and appended to meet the new circumstances.

▶ Example 2: Research Design Assessment

In 1985, Coca-Cola has introduced a new formula for its drink. The comprehensive market research conducted in a form of testing revealed that consumers liked the new coke. However, when the new coke was released, consumers did not want to buy it, and company took losses and returned to the old formula. To assure consumers that they are buying the old drink, the labels on the bottles showed "Classic Coca Cola." Such a label was used for a couple of decades. "New Coke" remained available on the market for some time under name "Coke II" but never became successful and was discontinued in 1992.

It is easy to say now, but nevertheless, if the Coca Cola research team assessed their research design before drawing the conclusions and changing the drink production formula, the company may avoid troubles with the new coke.

According to the research design, consumers were asked what drink they liked better. However, a better question would relate to the consumers' desire to buy the new coke rather than just like it. ◀

20.2.3 Data Quality Assessment

Collected data constitute the foundation of the research results. Methods and procedures for collecting and processing data were identified and chosen in the research design. The appropriate evaluation of those methods and procedures was also performed in that step. However, the actual data collection and processing may introduce specific variations and adjustments to the original plan developed in the research design. The data sources described in the research design may undertake some changes, or data quality and accuracy may not be as good as expected, or data validation might be compromised for any reason. This may result in the overall lower data quality that may compromise the overall research results. Also, some new data sources may appear during the research that should be taken into consideration too.

For this reason, retrospective evaluation of the collected data and data sources is an important activity to ensure quality of the research results.

Data quality should be evaluated in the following dimensions:

- Completeness
- Internal consistency
- External consistency

Violation of any of these factors might lead to incorrect research results.

▶ Example 3: Data Quality Assessment

A research on employee loyalty was analyzing the current status and the problems associated with the issue.[1] The data was collected in the San Francisco Bay Area using the survey method. The survey questionnaire was distributed randomly on streets, in retail centers, and at bus and BART (subway) stations. Such a distribution may introduce a bias due to uneven probabilities of people of different professions to be found at those questionnaire distribution points. Once the respondent answers were collected, the data quality assessment was conducted by comparing the obtained distribution of the respondents by industry and their belongingness to the categories of managers or regular employees. The obtained distributions were compared with the similar distributions obtained from other independent sources such as official state information or other third-party research. The comparison confirmed the similarity of the distributions that confirms data quality that the respondents proportionally represented the California work force. ◀

20.3 Research Result Interpretation

Research results consist of research findings and new facts obtained in the research. Therefore, research results are often synonymously called research findings. The results are used for deriving the research conclusions, which are the answers to the research questions. To be used for deriving the conclusion, research results must be interpreted to provide semantics of the results for the purpose of the research.

1 Aityan, S.K. and T.K. Gupta (2012). Challenges of Employee Loyalty in Corporate America, Business and Economics Journal, vol. 2012, BEJ-55, pp.1–13

Wrongly interpreted results may lead to wrong or irrelevant conclusions. The interpretation should provide semantical connection of the results with the research question or questions for the purpose of derived answers.

► Example 4: Interpretation of Research Results

A research project is conducted to compare production quality at two commercial food delivering companies A and B. Random samples of food were collected from each company for the examination. The results showed that food from company A arrives stale more frequently than food from company B. It is hard to derive relevant conclusions from the examination results. There could be many various possibilities for the results: (a) company A is less cautious about the freshness of their food, (b) suppliers of kitchen A provide stale food, or (c) food transportation from company A to their clients takes longer time. These three possible interpretations would lead to three different conclusions and recommendations of the research. ◄

20.4 First Answer Subquestions and Then the Main Question

Problem questions are typically big enough and hence are decomposed into logically related subquestions. The answer to each subquestion is derived from the related research findings. The subquestions are formulated in such a way that the answers to them constitute a logical basis for answering the main research questions phrased in the problem statement.

► Example 5: Using Gym During Work Hours

The company management discusses establishing a free of charge gym for the company employees and allows the employees to use the gym up to 30 minutes every day during work hours and unlimitedly before or after work hours. It is no doubt that such an arrangement has positive social impact. The company wants to find out if such an arrangement increases total production outcome.

The main research question:

- What would be the impact from arranging a gym and allowing employees to use it during work hours as well as off-work hours?

Subquestions:

- What would be the impact of using gym during work hours on the employee's productivity?
- What would be the optimal time for the use of gym during work hours to increase total daily production outcome?
- How would physical exercises impact on the number of the employee's sick days per year?
- How do employee attitude and stress level impact on the production output?
- How would physical exercise impact on the employee attitude and stress relief? ◄

Once the subquestions are answered, the answer to the main research question can be derived from the answers to the subquestions.

20.5 Cause and Effect Rather Than Value Judgment

Conclusions are answers to the research question or questions. However, such answers should reveal cause-and-effect relationships found in the research if such relationship exists. Research conclusions should not present the researchers' value judgment or bias.

Humans have their own judgments and biases. Researchers are also humans and may have their own personal perception, judgments, and biases related to the area of research. However, research conclusions must be free of such subjective influence. Sometimes, it is not easy to do but ultimately necessary and important.

Introduction of personal bias or value judgment to research conclusions may significantly or completely impair the scientific value of the research project.

20.6 Make Recommendations and Predictions if Applicable

Applied research always has practical purpose. Recommendations are suggested practical actions drawn from research results and conclusions. Recommendation should be constructive and feasible aiming improvement of the existing situation. Any recommendation in business or economic research should analyze and address the priority of the recommended improvement, its feasibility, and potential benefits from the implementation of the suggested recommendation.

Research conclusions that reveal new dependencies or relationships may lead to predictions of new results in the future under certain conditions. Good research often makes predictions, which can be verified in the future research. Such predictions build a logical bridge between the current research and its extension in the future.

► Example 6: Interpretation of Research Results

A research project is conducted to analyze the impact of employee training on their productivity. Two groups were randomly formed from the company employees, and their productivity was measured using the company's established productivity metrics. One group of employees underwent specialized professional training, while another group did not receive this training. Once the first group of employees completed the training, the productivity of the employees in these two groups was measured again. The difference of the productivity of each employee was registered and processed.

The productivity difference is compared with the time and resources spent for the training that result in practical recommendations on the optimal level of training and resources dedicated to the training for the best outcome for the company. ◄

20.7 New Questions Arise From Research Conclusions

The pyramid of knowledge is endless, and every new portion of knowledge added to the pyramid of knowledge may bring up new questions. The more we learn, the more questions arise. These new questions constitute the basis for new research. Such a process is continuously going on feeding up the never-ending progress in research.

▶ Example 7: Automation of Customer Service Versus Individual Touch

Customer service is a very important and costly business activity. Every call to the customer service incurs dozens of dollars of expenses to the company. Thus, minimization of the number and duration of physical calls and replacing them with automated services have great potential for companies. Many research projects have been conducted in this area to find out the best level of automation.

Research showed significant potential of reduction of expenses by call avoidance strategies, i.e., the replacement of live agents with the automated online answers to frequently asked questions (FAQs) with the automated navigation. Such an approach resulted in dramatic service cost cuts.

However, customer satisfaction with the automated FAQ may drop that may lead to the reduction of the customer base. This issue brought up a new research in the replacing of the flat FAQ with the multilevel knowledge base together with the advanced navigation.

The advanced knowledge base brought up the issue of multiple languages for serving global customers, which led to the next level research.

Customer with non-standard questions may spend extensive time navigating to the answer in fully automated customer services without finding the answer. Such customers need a human agent who helps in finding the answer and resolving the issue. This leads to the next level research addressing the optimal combination of the automated services and human agents in the modern CRM (customer relationship management) system.

This example showed a chain of questions coming from the answers to the previous questions that led to a chain of research projects. ◀

Questions for Self-Control for Chap. 20

1. What is the role of conclusions in research?
2. Why is research result evaluation needed?
3. What is the sense of research problem and subproblem assessment?
4. Why is a research design assessment needed?
5. How to do a research design assessment?
6. What is the role of data quality assessment?
7. How can data quality impact on the research results?
8. What does research result interpretation mean?

9. What is the rationale for research result interpretation?
10. How to derive conclusions in a research with many subquestions?
11. How important is finding cause-and-effect relationship in research results?
12. Why should researchers avoid value judgment and bias when deriving the conclusions of a research?
13. What is the rationale for making recommendations from the applied research?
14. How to make recommendations from research conclusions?
15. How can predictions be made from the research results and conclusions?
16. How do research results and conclusions initiate new research projects?

Ethical and Legal Issues of Research

Contents

21.1 Difference Between Law and Ethics – 450

21.2 Ethical Aspects of Research – 450

21.3 Ethics in Business Research – 451

21.4 Data Collection Ethics – 451

21.5 Ethics of Research Topic – 451

21.6 Information Privacy – 453

21.7 Plagiarism – 453
21.7.1 Can Words and Ideas Really Be Stolen? – 454
21.7.2 Forms of Plagiarism – 454
21.7.3 Preventing Plagiarism – 455

21.8 Legal Aspect of Research – 456

21.9 A Research Ethics Board – 456

S. K. Aityan, *Business Research Methodology*, Classroom Companion: Business,
https://doi.org/10.1007/978-3-030-76857-7_21

21.1 Difference Between Law and Ethics

Law is a system of rules and guidelines which are enforced through social institutions to govern behavior, wherever possible.

Ethics, also known as moral philosophy, is a branch of philosophy that involves systematizing, defending, and recommending concepts of right and wrong behavior.

Ancient Greek philosophers Aristotle (384–322 BC), Plato (429–347 BC), and Socrates (470–399 BC) considered the virtues to be central to a well-lived life. They regarded the ethical virtues (justice, courage, temperance, and so on) as complex rational, emotional, and social skills.

Ethics covers imperfections of law caused by its conceptual and systemic limitations and particularly concerns about the concept of "right" and "wrong" from the general human perspectives rather than from the formal word of law.

21.2 Ethical Aspects of Research

Ethics is a moral norm comprised of specific rules of behavior and conduct that guide people's lives and personal and business relationships and activities. Research that involves human subjects or participants raises unique and complex ethical, legal, social, and political issues.

There are four objectives in research ethics:

- Be honest in all scientific activities and communications. Honestly report data, results, methods and procedures, and publication status. Do not fabricate, falsify, or misrepresent data. Do not deceive colleagues, sponsors, or the public.
- Protect human participants.
- Ensure that research is conducted in a way that serves interests of individuals, groups, and/or society as a whole.
- Examine specific research activities and projects for their ethical soundness, looking at issues such as the management of risk, protection of confidentiality, and the process of informed consent.

Term ***fabrication*** or ***falsification*** refers to making up data or research results. Sometimes, researchers are so much believing in their hypotheses or expected results that they start unintentionally emphasizing the data and results supporting their expectations and sifting out or paying less attention to the data and results opposing their expectations. Sometimes, such temptations are hard to resist, but remember that research is the quest for truth rather than a tool for promoting our personal belief and expectations.

Violation of ethical conduct may include actions, which may not be punishable by law but inconsistent with the moral foundation and ethical values.

> Research in the quest for truth rather than a tool for promoting out personal beliefs and expectations.

21.3 Ethics in Business Research

Ethical conduct in research is needed to ensure that no one is harmed or suffers from the research and its consequences. Violation of ethical conduct may include actions, which may not be punishable by law but inconsistent with the moral foundation and ethical values:

- Attempts to go around the nondisclosure agreement using legal loopholes
- Breaking participants' confidentiality
- Misrepresenting research results
- Exposing people or respondent names without their permission
- Avoiding legal liability
- Making false or deceiving promises unenforced by law
- Manipulating people's behavior using undisclosed information or special knowledge or experience
- Plagiarism explicit or even implicit

Ethical conduct in research requires personal integrity from the researchers, project manager, research sponsors, and other participants of the research project.

All the participants of research must be ethically and fairly treated by the research team. The following guidelines may help researchers in this:

- Explain the purpose and potential benefits of the study.
- Assure participants that their privacy and their rights will not be violated.
- Obtain informed consent from the participants. In serious cases, the consent must be obtained in the written form.

21.4 Data Collection Ethics

Most research projects imply data collection. The data collection process and data itself should be within ethical boundaries and comply with ethical principles and rules. Collected data, though is very important for the research, may violate the participant's right to privacy.

People may be uncomfortable disclosing their private relationship, income/debt level, or other information, particularly if it is not related to specific purpose of the research. Asking such questions may violate fundamental ethical principles and lead to the collection of false data.

Sometimes, the collected data may be used against the people who provided the data or used to manipulate people's behavior. First, collecting such information, if not given knowingly and voluntarily, is unethical and manipulative. Also, research participant will be unwilling to provide such information.

21.5 Ethics of Research Topic

Research finds truth, but not all truth is ethical. Some research topics imply unjustified unethical treatment of or experimentation on human or any other living creatures. However, the key focus here is on words "unethical" and "unjustified."

Testing a new vaccine or a new medication is an experimentation. However, it is justified and ethical if all ethical requirements are met and ethical rules are followed. Even under these conditions, the judgmental decision must be made by a group of appointed individuals or a committee. Medical and biological experiments on animals help saving many human lives in the future. However, cruelty is not justifiable even for very noble purposes. Any experimentation that has a potential to reprogram the human mind or negatively impact on the future lives is unethical.

Some black and white examples of unethical research are clear for majority of people. However, there are many "gray area" cases, where judgment is not crispy clear. Many things depend on an individual and on a culture. This is a big field for discussions and judgments.

Nevertheless, there are certain commonly accepted principles and rules, which must be mandatorily followed regardless of the individual feeling and beliefs and cultural diversity.

► Example 1: Stanford Prison Experiment

The Stanford prison experiment is a very strong example of unethical experiments. The experiment took place in August of 1971. To avoid any misrepresentation or interpretation inaccuracy, the comment on this experiment is given literally by quote.

"The purpose of the experiment was to study the causes of conflict between prisoners and those who guard them. Twenty-four male students were randomly assigned the role of either guard or prisoner, and then set up according to their role in a specifically designed model prison located in the basement of the psychology building on Stanford's campus. It soon became apparent that those who had been given the role of guard were taking their job very seriously. They began to enforce harsh measures and subjected their "prisoners" to various degrees of psychological torture. If that's surprising, perhaps it is even more surprising that many of the prisoners in the experiment simply accepted the abuses. The authoritarian measures adopted by the guards became so extreme that the experiment was abruptly stopped after just six days."[1]

Dr. Philip George Zimbardo a professor emeritus at Stanford University was known for his Stanford prison experiment. Below is his quote about the experiment:

"How we went about testing these questions and what we found may astound you. Our planned two-week investigation into the psychology of prison life had to be ended after only six days because of what the situation was doing to the college students who participated. In only a few days, our guards became sadistic and our prisoners became depressed and showed signs of extreme stress. Please read the story of what happened and what it tells us about the nature of human nature."[2]

---

1 Retrieved on February 12, 2021, from ► https://www.onlinepsychologydegree.info/unethical-experiements-psychology/

2 Retrieved on February 12, 2021, from ► https://www.prisonexp.org/

Does it mean that Prof. Zimbardo and his team were unethical people? Not at all! Prof. Zimbardo is a well-known psychologist with high-level ethical and moral standards. The topic of Stanford experiment is quite interesting too from the research point of view. However, the experiment turned in the unexpected directions and revealed unexpected psychological consequences, which were categorized as unethical, and the experiment was shut down. ◄

21.6 Information Privacy

The term ***information privacy*** can be understood as the right of individuals or private organizations to keep their private information protected from unauthorized collection and dissemination. It is also known as ***privacy of information***, ***data privacy***, or ***data protection***. Information privacy comprises a broad spectrum of levels and issues associated with it. Some aspects of information privacy are protected by law, but some are only on ethical level.

Different countries established different levels of information privacy protection by law. Laws and regulations related to information privacy are evolving over time, particularly now, when the rapid progress in information technology and the Internet provides technological possibility of collection of information and its rapid dissemination.

Ethical aspects of information privacy protect those parts of information which is not formally covered by law or regulation. Norms of ethics significantly depend on social norms, understanding of good and bad that constitutes moral principles of each society and even local communities.

21.7 Plagiarism

According to the Merriam-Webster Online Dictionary, to "plagiarize" means:

- To steal and pass off (the ideas or words of another) as one's own
- To use (another's production) without crediting the source
- To commit literary theft
- To present as new and original an idea or product derived from an existing source

In other words, plagiarism is an act of fraud that involves both stealing someone else's work and lying about it afterward. Not only explicit copying is qualified as plagiarism. All of the following are considered plagiarism:

- Turning in someone else's work as your own copying words or ideas from someone else without giving credit
- Failing to put a quotation in quotation marks
- Giving incorrect information about the source of a quotation or citation
- Changing words but copying the sentence structure of a source without giving credit to the original authors and the source
- Copying so many words or ideas from a source that it makes up majority of your work, whether you give credit or not (see our section on "fair use" rules)

21.7.1 Can Words and Ideas Really Be Stolen?

According to US law, the answer is yes. The expression of original ideas is considered intellectual property and is protected by copyright laws, just like original inventions. Almost all forms of expression fall under copyright protection as long as they are recorded in some way (such as a book or a computer file).

The penalties for plagiarism can be surprisingly severe, ranging from failure of classes and expulsion from academic institutions to heavy fines and jail time!

Changing the words of an original source is not sufficient to prevent plagiarism. If one has retained the essential idea of an original source, but did not cite it, then no matter how drastically the text, context, or presentation may have altered, that individual has still plagiarized.

21.7.2 Forms of Plagiarism

Plagiarism may be done in many different forms, which can be classified by the following categories:

Complete Plagiarism

A person submits someone's work, written or verbal, as his/her own work under his/her own name. It could be an idea, a book, a paper, a thesis, an assignment, a home task, or any other documents, speech, or presentation.

Missing Reference

A person copies ideas, text, or phrases without referencing the source.

Misleading Citation

A person provides a reference to the source of the information, but the reference does not point to the source. It may be a sincere typographical error, but if such references persist or frequently occur, this is a vivid indication on intentional plagiarism.

Potluck Paper

A person tries to disguise plagiarism by copying from different sources and mixing up phrases and sentences, making them sound like his/her original text or speech. Such form of plagiarism is uneasy to catch but possible, particularly with the use of modern tools in information technology.

Self-Plagiarism

A person intensively copies from his/her own previous work presenting this as a new work, which is mostly a variation of the previous work. There is no doubt that knowledge continuously evolves from the existing knowledge and copying some minor parts of your own or someone else's previous works for continuity of the presentation of material is perfectly fine. However, forming a new work mostly of your previous work with minor variations constitutes plagiarism.

I would like to make an accent on this form of plagiarism because many young researchers try to publish many papers in the race for growing their number of publications and use this form of plagiarism as an option to grow their publication list. This is a logical consequence from the policies of some universities and other research institutions of judging researchers by the number of their publications.

21.7.3 Preventing Plagiarism

Plagiarism is almost always a symptom of educational problems. Plagiarism is quickly becoming part of our educational culture. More and more students are turning to the Internet for quick "shortcuts" around the rewarding but time-consuming work of writing research papers. A large part of the problem is unawareness of the issues. Often, students do not even know that they are plagiarizing, and those who do know are often unaware of the seriousness of the offense and its possible consequences.

Another part of the problem lies in the factors that make students likely to plagiarize:

- Poor research skills
- Attitudes toward grades and schoolwork
- Poor time management skills
- The perception that peers are cheating and skewed risk-reward assessments
- A desire to meet administrative requirements for number of publications per period

Modern information technology provides good tools for testing and catching plagiarism. One of the software tools, which is used at our university, is TurnItIn (► turnItIn.com) that checks submitted papers on copying and duplication of material and returns a comprehensive status report. There might be many other similar tools available now or coming soon. I've mentioned this tool only because our university uses it rather than for any other reason.

Thus, plagiarism is a systemic problem that can be solved by individual integrity of researchers, appropriate level of education, promoting honesty, and improving administrative standards and rules.

> Plagiarism is almost always a symptom of educational problems and poor administrative policies.

21.8 Legal Aspect of Research

Legal aspects of research are associated with the compliance of research with existing law and regulations. Legal compliance generally refers to acting in accordance with international, national, state, and/or local laws of the group of countries, state, or local municipality.

Some ethical issues discussed above are regulated by law; thus, they fall into the category of legal compliance.

Activities of conducting research belong either to the category of for-profit or not-for-profit business activities. First of all research organizations should comply with the taxation and financial regulations as well as the labor and other business-related regulations applied to the territory, where the research institution is registered and where it is conducting research.

► Example 2: Research Compliance

An Internet company conducts a research by collecting customer information and customer activities without authorization from customers or forceful authorization as part of the service contract. Legal issues may arise in the countries or localities where unauthorized customer data collection is illegal or restricted. Unethical aspect of such research is that profiling customers by processing their data and activities, particularly using methods of artificial intelligence, reveals features of the customer character, of which the customer is unaware himself. This allows the company to manipulate customer behavior and activities for the company benefits. ◄

21.9 A Research Ethics Board

Compliance with the ethical rules is the responsibility of the researchers, managers, and project sponsors and should be led, managed, and controlled by the research organizations involved in such research by forming special committees or boards for this purpose.

A Research Ethics Board (REB), Ethical Review Board (ERB), Independent Ethics Committee (IEC), an Institutional Review Board (IRB), or any other similar committee or board is a type of committee that controls the application of fundamental rules of research ethics by reviewing the methods proposed for research to ensure that they are ethical and do not violate the established rules and procedures. Such committees or boards may have different names but all are engaged in the very important activity – enforcing ethical conduct in research.

It is important not to turn the activities and power of such committees and boards into excessive bureaucracy and unnecessary obstacles in research. However, sufficient control is needed to ensure ethical conduct and prevent possible violation, possibly, only by unawareness.

▶ Example 3: Unethical Consumer Manipulation

To avoid any legal problems, this example does not reveal any names and identities. A pharmaceutical company conducted comparative research on its product versus the competitive products. The company contracted a specialist in neuro-linguistic programming (NLP) to edit the research report in such a way that it legally includes the complete results of the comparative research but emphasizes the strongest features of the company's product versus the competition and makes the weaknesses of the product legally reported but practically barely visible on the report.

Such a conduct is legally unpunishable but ethically wrong because it deceives the consumers and manipulates their opinions on the choice of the product. ◀

Questions for Self-Control for Chap. 21

1. What is the difference between law and ethics?
2. What does constitute ethical aspects of business research?
3. Is it ethical to tweak data to support the researcher's point of view or expectation?
4. To what degree human participants in research must be protected?
5. What is data fabrication or data falsification?
6. What is understood by ethical conduct in business research?
7. What could be ethical issues of data collection?
8. Is any research ethical?
9. Can be research topic unethical?
10. What are ethical issues related to information privacy?
11. What is plagiarism?
12. What are the forms of plagiarism?
13. What are legal aspects of research?
14. What does term research compliance mean?
15. What are legal requirements of international research?
16. What is a research ethics board?
17. What are the responsibilities of research ethics board?

Problems for Chap. 21

1. What is the value of 45.987 rounded to 3 significant figures?

Delivering the Results

Contents

Chapter 22 Writing Research Report – 461

Chapter 23 Making Presentations – 481

Writing Research Report

Contents

22.1 Delivery of Research Results – 463

22.2 Developing Report Outline – 463

22.3 Typographical Gradations – 464

22.4 Types of Outline Numbering Systems – 465

22.5 Suggested Generic Structure of the Research Report – 467

22.6 The Report Title Page – 468

22.7 Providing Chapter Transition – 468

22.8 Formatting the Research Report – 469

22.9 Writing the Introduction Part – 471
22.9.1 The Introduction Part of the Report – 471
22.9.2 The Purpose of the Research – 471
22.9.3 Definition of Terms – 471

22.10 Review of Literature – 472

22.11 Problem Statement – 472

22.12 Research Objectives – 473

S. K. Aityan, *Business Research Methodology*, Classroom Companion: Business,
https://doi.org/10.1007/978-3-030-76857-7_22

22.13 Research Methods, Tools, Techniques, and Procedures – 473

22.14 Data Collection and Analysis – 473
22.14.1 Data Collection – 473
22.14.2 Data Analysis – 474
22.14.3 The Interpretation Process – 474

22.15 Research Findings and Analysis – 476

22.16 Conclusions, Recommendations, and Predictions – 476

22.17 Bibliography and Citation – 477

22.18 Appendices – 477

22.19 Structuring the Summary Section – 478

22.20 Acknowledgment – 478

22.1 Delivery of Research Results

You have completed your research. Now you should deliver the results. If your research results, including all your findings, conclusions, recommendations, and predictions, are not properly delivered, nobody would be aware of it and nobody would be able to use it. Then, most likely, all your efforts in conducting the research would get wasted.

In other words, if you do not tell people about the answers you have found to the research question or questions, nobody will know the answers.

There are many different ways of delivering research results. Among them are writing a research report, publishing a paper and a book, making a presentation, or delivering the results in any other appropriate way.

In this chapter, we will focus on writing research reports. However, writing research papers and books basically follows a similar process and similar rules.

Writing a research report begins with developing its logical structure. A report or any other document must be well structured, complete, logical, clear, and illustrative. If the research report or other document is written in such a way, then the reader can easily get the information out; follow the research logic; understand the research conclusions, recommendations, and possible predictions; and clearly see the relevance of the conclusions to the research problem statement, as well as the methods of finding the answers to the research questions. If the research report, paper, book, or the presentations are not well structured, the research efforts may become hidden or even wasted.

Thus, a good research needs a good and clear delivery. However, even an exceptional research delivery cannot help in acceptance of a poorly conducted research.

Remember, the major consideration is not how you can put all the information in your report but how easy it will be for your reader to get the information out and understand it. The reports, papers, books, and presentations are done for the readers. Your readers expect to find the information presented in a logical and clear order.

22.2 Developing Report Outline

The report structure is set in the report outline. A report outline is a list of the report headings including their hierarchy. The term heading means the title of a report section or a subsection. The complete list of the report sections and subsections constitutes the report structure. Such a structure plays a role of the report skeleton that holds together the entire report.

A research report is a complete story about the research project. To develop a report outline, logically break the entire story into a sequence of logically consistent sections. Each section can be further divided into a sequence of logically consistent subsections as the second level of the structure, possibly, the third level. Do not make the structure too deep without special need for it.

Type the initial version of the report outline and save it as a computer file. Doing it on a computer is not compulsory, but it will help in the outline development by reducing the volume of multiple writing-rewriting by hand.

Thus, the initial version of the outline is created and saved. Once it is done, leave the outline alone and switch your activities to something else. Come back to the outline next morning. You will definitely notice that something in the outline is not as logical or good as you want. It occurs because you subconsciously kept working on the outline even when you switched your activity to doing something else. Fix the inconsistencies in the outline, save it, and switch to doing something else. Keep up with such a routine until, one morning, you open the outline and find it logical and good, not needing any changes. It means that the outline is ready. Now you have to write the content in each section and subsection of the outline to complete the report.

Do not worry if during the report writing process, you decide to modify the report outline. It is normal and may occur because as you are writing the report, you are still assessing its structure.

When the report is ready, the outline with the page numbers of the headings becomes the report table of contents.

An outline is the skeleton of the document – report, paper, book, or presentation.

The outline development process:

- Write the outline and switch your activity to something else.
- Next morning come back and review the outline. Fix the outline as you feel appropriate.
- Keep following the routine until one morning you do not find any inconsistency in the outline. Thus, the outline is ready.
- Start writing the report text.

Outline + heading page numbers = table of contents

22.3 Typographical Gradations

Visual perception of a text depends on upper- (capital) or lowercase; regular bold, italic, or underscored characters; centered, left aligned, or justified text; and Arabic or Roman numbering. Using visual perception helps emphasize the document structure without additional explanations or special comments. Upon these premises, a conventional system of typographical gradation has been established for constructing headings in the reports. The gradation system is based upon common sense and includes the following rules:

- A text written with capital letters is more important than a text written with lowercase letters.
- A free-standing (above the line of writing) heading is more important than a run-in (in-line) heading.
- An underlined heading is more important than one not underlined.
- A centered heading is more important than a side heading. This is not a strong feature.

A conventional system of typographical gradation has been established upon these premises for constructing headings in the reports. Such a system is not formally rigid and may vary at different publishers. However, most people intuitively understand and follow it.

▶ Example 1 – Examples of typographical gradation

It is visually clear, by the typographical gradation, which of the three headings shown in ◘ Fig. 22.1 below have different importance. ◀

22.4 Types of Outline Numbering Systems

Most publishers and organizations require the document body headings to be numbered. There are two outline numbering systems in general use:
- Numeric (or decimal)
- Alphanumeric

A numeric system may use Roman and/or Arabic numbers or their mix for different levels of headings. In a mix of Roman and Arabic numbers, Roman numbers are typically used for the higher-level headings.

The alphanumeric system uses letters and numbers for different levels of headings: Roman and/or Arabic numbers combined with upper- and lowercase letters.

The most popular numbering system is the numeric (decimal) system with Arabic numbers used on all major levels of headings as shown in the example in ◘ Fig. 22.2. As is evident from the example, the report summary and bibliography often are not numbered headings because they do not belong to the report body. Appendices are typically numbered differently from the heading number-

INTRODUCTION
Industry Status
Common environment

◘ **Fig. 22.1** Example of a typographical gradation

ing in the report body. The appendices in the example illustrated in ◘ Fig. 22.2 are numbered with capital letters as Appendix A, Appendix B, and so on.

◘ Figure 22.3 presents an example of an alphanumeric numbering with a mix of Roman and Arabic numbers and letters on different levels of the heading hierarchy.

Summary
1 Introduction
  1.1 History of the problem
  1.2 Recent progress
    1.2.1 Customer oriented approach
    1.2.2 Business oriented approach
  1.3 Problem statement
  1.4 Purpose of the research
2 Review of Literature
3 Methods
  3.1 Survey methods
  3.2 Data processing methods
…
Bibliography
Appendix A. Standard Normal Distribution Table
Appendix B. Case Studies

Numeric outline numbering with Arabic numbers used on major levels of headings

◘ **Fig. 22.2** An example of the numerical numbering of the report headings

◘ **Fig. 22.3** An example of the alphanumeric numbering of the report headings

Summary
I Introduction
  a) History of the problem
  b) Recent progress
    1. Customer oriented approach
    2. Business oriented approach
  c) Problem statement
  d) Purpose of the research
II Review of Literature
III Methods
  a) Survey methods
  b) Data processing methods
…
Bibliography
Appendix A. Standard Normal Distribution Table
Appendix B. Case Studies

22.5 Suggested Generic Structure of the Research Report

The report structure represents the research type, the research methods, data used in the research, and the researcher's preferences in delivering the research results. Experienced researchers already learned how to structure the research report to deliver the result in the best way. Organizations and publishers may have their own requirements for the report structure. ◘ Fig. 22.4 presents a generic framework, which can be used with some modifications for the development of the research report structure.

The outline in ◘ Fig. 22.4 shows only the first level of headings leaving the internal structure of the second- and the lower-level headings up to the report author. The order of the items in the outline in ◘ Fig. 22.4 may vary to better represent the report specifics and logical flow. Some sections (headings) may be combined or split if needed.

Summary, acknowledgments, and bibliography are typically not numbered sections of the report. An appendix or appendices, if they are present in the report, typically have the numbering different from the other sections of the report. However, it depends on the standards adopted at your organization or required by the publisher. Check first with them before deciding on the numbering standard.

The content and structure of the research report may vary subject to the type of research and other circumstances. The structure shown in ◘ Fig. 22.4 is a suggested structure of a typical report, but the authors may use their own understanding and opinion as well as the formal requirements for their reports.

◘ **Fig. 22.4** A suggested generic structure of a research proposal

The title page that includes the research title
Summary
Acknowledgements.
1. Introduction
2. The purpose of the research and the research goal(s)
3. Definition of terms. In this section, list and define all terms which need clarification.
4. Review of literature
5. Problem statement. In this section the author(s) should provide and explain the research problem statement including subproblems, hypotheses (if applicable), scope,and limitations.
6. Research objectives
7. Research design that includes methods and procedures. data sources and data collection techniques and methods, data processing and data analysis techniques and methods
8. Data collection,
9. Data processing, findings, and analysis
10. Research findings
11. Conclusions, recommendations, and predictions

Bibliography
Appendices (if applicable)

22.6 The Report Title Page

The report title must be clearly stated without ambiguity to adequately reflect the research topic. The report title is not the problem statement but the short descriptive name of the research project.

Typically, the research title is placed on a separate page, which is referred to as the report title page. The same page also shows the author(s), organization, purpose of the report (if applicable), and the date of the report submission.

Please do not get confused with the purpose of the research and purpose of the report. For example, the purpose of a research is to analyze the impact of globalization on the international investment, while the purpose of the report is fulfillment of the requirements for the master's degree as shown on the title page.

A typical sample title page for the graduate research report is presented in ◘ Fig. 22.5. The format of the title page may vary. Different organizations, agencies, and schools may have specific requirements for the report title page or may have it flexible.

22.7 Providing Chapter Transition

Chapter transition skillfully constructed can smoothly lead the reader from chapter to chapter, particularly in the content chapters related to the research project activities and findings. Chapter transition implies a logically uninterrupted flow of information delivery from chapter to chapter. This can be achieved either by well-constructed sequential report outline, where the information flow is linearly straight and smooth without logical side branches.

◘ Fig. 22.5 A sample title page of the proposal

Lincoln University, Oakland, CA

Correlation Analysis for Managing International Investment Portfolios

Research Proposal
for
Master Thesis
(BA399, MBA Research Project)

Presented to
Graduate Committee of Lincoln University

by
John Smith
Advisor: Prof. Sam Adams

December 2021

Chapter transition can be also achieved by a quick recap of the previous chapter in the beginning of the current chapter and a quick summary of the major elements of the chapter at the end of that chapter. This helps provide a logical bridge between chapters in the report.

▶ Example 2 – Chapter transition

A content chapter in the report may start with the following phrase:

- "This chapter describes the results obtained using the data collected according to the plan and methods described in the previous chapter."

The same chapter may conclude at the end with a brief summary of the results obtained in the chapter with a logical bridge to the next chapter:

5 "The results obtained in this chapter will be used in the research conclusions derived in the next chapter." ◀

22.8 Formatting the Research Report

Report formatting includes the paper size; font face and size; line spacing; page numbering; formats for figure and table captions and cross-references, bibliography, and references; layout of the title page; one side or double-side printing; and many other possible formatting details.

Report formatting guidelines and rules can be set up by a related publisher or an organization. Some publishers and organizations establish strict formatting rules, some publishers and organizations provide flexible guidelines as a desired framework, and some organizations establish no formatting rules leaving the formatting decision upon the authors' common sense, taste, and understanding.

All three variants have cons and pros. Strict formatting rules lead to the standardized look and feel of all reports released by the publisher or the organization. On the other hand, strict rules may be inconvenient to the authors and their vision of the document. Flexible formatting guidelines make all documents look more or less alike but leave room for the authors to use the formatting details they find better reflecting their vision of the document. Establishing no formatting rules at all gives more formatting freedom to the authors but has two major drawbacks – all documents in the organization may look absolutely differently that does not provide a perception of solid organization, and it also forces the authors to choose some formatting rules, even though they may have no preference that may create more pressure and unnecessary confusion.

▶ Example 3 – Flexible formatting guidelines

Lincoln University has established flexible formatting guidelines. The guidelines suggest formatting rules but allow the students to use their own modification if they find them more appropriate for their report. However, most students are just learning how to write reports and use the guidelines as they are.

The Lincoln University formatting guidelines are the following:

The section headings should have numbering with Arabic numerals as shown in ◘ Fig. 22.6. The content structure shown in ◘ Fig. 22.6 is flexible and depends on the research topic and domain.

The Lincoln University report formatting guidelines suggest the following:

- 1.5 space typing.
- All fonts must be "Times New Roman."
- The content: font size 12.
- The title: font size 20.
- Main sections: size 14 bold.
- Subsections: font size 12 bold.
- Sub-subsections: font size 12 bold.
- Table titles, figure capture: font size 12.
- Double-side printing preference.

The rationale behind such formatting recommendations is as follows. The recommended font size is most comfortable for reading for the majority of people. The 1.5 line space typing provides sufficient space to put comments in the report text using computerized comments or by hands. A double-side printing saves paper and library storage space. Most printers support a double-side printing feature. ◄

◘ Fig. 22.6 Numeric numbering of document headings with Arabic numerals

Title page
Acknowledgement
Summary
1 Introduction
  1.1 The Area of Research
  1.2 The Research Purpose
  1.3 Definition of Terms
2 Review of Literature
3 The Problem Statement
  3.1 The Main Problem
  3.2 Subproblems
  3.3 Research Objectives
4 Research Methodology
  4.1 Logic
  4.2 Methodology
  4.3 Experiment Design
  4.4 Data Collection Sources and Methods
5 Data Collection and Analysis
  5.1 Data Collection
  5.2 Data Processing and Analysis
6 Research Findings and Analysis
  6.1 Research Findings
  6.2 Analysis and Interpretation of the Research Findings
7 Conclusions and Recommendations
  7.1 Conclusions
  7.2 Recommendations
  7.3 Predictions (if available)
Bibliography
Appendices

22.9 Writing the Introduction Part

22.9.1 The Introduction Part of the Report

This section of the report provides a comprehensive background review, description, and analysis of the current situation in the research area.

A good "Introduction" should lay out a clear understanding of the area of the research and provide a background for the research problem as well as justify timeliness and necessity of the research problem. Thus, the research problem that is going to be formulated later in the report should be viewed as logically justified and natural.

The content in the introduction should provide the background and set the stage for the research problem, so your reader will logically see a problem evolving. The introduction should provide an easy transition to the problem statement itself.

Restrict the introduction information to few pages, perhaps not more than three or four pages at the most for the graduate research reports. For larger-scale reports, the introduction may be longer, appropriate to the research scale. Do not make the background material a full-scale history of your topic.

Close this section with a transition statement that leads naturally to the problem statement in the problem statement section.

22.9.2 The Purpose of the Research

The purpose of the research must be clearly and accurately formulated:
- A research problem is a question raised for inquiry, consideration, or solution.
- A purpose, however, is the reason for which the research is conducted.

The purpose of the research answers the main question WHY of the research:
- Why is the research needed?

The purpose of the research should answer some other questions too:
- How will the research results improve the current situation?
- Who will benefit from the research results?

Without clearly and accurately formulated purpose, applied research, is not justified to spend time and efforts.

22.9.3 Definition of Terms

The primary purpose of the "Definition of Terms" section is to specify the precise meaning intended for words or terms which may be unclear or subject to different interpretations for the readers.

All special terms used in the report, which could be misinterpreted by the reader, must be clearly defined in this section of the report before the terms are used.

Definition of terms is an important part of the report because without clearly defined terms, different people might understand the terms used in the report differently that would lead to confusion, misunderstanding, or misinterpretation of the research problem, methods, findings, or conclusions.

Definition of terms should be placed in the report before the terms are used. There are three options for placing the definitions of terms in the report:

- Insert as a subsection in the "Introduction" chapter.
- Define in apposition, the first time the term is used in any place of the report.
- Include as a glossary of terms in the "Appendix."

22.10 Review of Literature

Section "Review of Literature" or "Literature Review" provides a comprehensive description and analysis of the current situation in the area of research based on the data and other relevant information available in related literature and other reliable sources.

The main purpose of the literature review is to identify a void in the existing knowledge. This void, when identified, will show how the research presented in the report helped to add new knowledge to the void in the pyramid of knowledge. The research presented in the report most likely fits into a framework of a broader research.

Other purposes of the literature review are:

- To contribute ideas for the research design
- To furnish evaluative techniques or criteria
- To provide opinions or perspective about your problem area
- To identify findings that support or contrast findings of the current research

22.11 Problem Statement

The problem statement represents the research question and may be formulated as:

- A single question
- A general question with two or more specific subquestions

The problem statement can be phrased in the question or in the form of an affirmative statement.

The research scope and limitations define the boundaries and constraints applied to the research.

Formulation of the problem statement was discussed in ► Chap. 4 of this book.

22.12 Research Objectives

Research objectives describe what the research is planned to accomplish in answering the research question. This formulates the framework and criteria for the completeness of the research results according to the problem statement.

22.13 Research Methods, Tools, Techniques, and Procedures

This section of the report is known as research design and was described in ► Chap. 6. This section of the report is normally named "Methods," "Methods and Procedures," or "Research Design."

This section should include the following items whichever is applicable to your research:

- The research design
- Methods, tools, techniques, and procedures whatever is applicable to the research
- Tests, scales, and criteria
- If survey is used, then questionnaire construction, testing, media, implementation, and follow-up
- If sampling techniques are used, then sampling methods, target error margin, and criteria
- Statistical techniques and confidence level
- Hypotheses, testing procedures, and acceptance criteria
- Mathematical approaches, methods, algorithms, and techniques
- Experiment design, procedures, variables, and controls
- Data collection sources and methods

Do not overload this section of your report with the unnecessary details of methods and procedures. If a detailed description of any method, tool, technique, or procedure is too lengthy, fully placing it in this section of the report may break the logical flow of the report. In this case, this section must contain only an overview and main features, of the method, while the detailed description should be provided in the appropriate appendix.

22.14 Data Collection and Analysis

22.14.1 Data Collection

Data collection is an important step in the research process. The quality of data plays a decisive role in the outcomes of the research. This section describes data sources, data collection techniques and procedures, data verification methods, and data accuracy and data completeness according to the research design. Also, it is necessary to explain whether the data is primary or secondary.

Different types of data need different techniques, procedures, and methods. This section must be written with the sufficient details that would allow third-party readers to collect similar data, if needed to verify the research results.

22.14.2 Data Analysis

The collected data must be organized, processed, interpreted, and analyzed according to the methods and techniques described in the research design. The analyzed and interpreted data constitute the factual bases for the research results and conclusions.

Data analysis includes revealing by reasoning the meaning of the collected facts and interpreting the data for deriving conclusions about data. The research report should contain an impartial presentation of the facts based on a critical, exhaustive, and studious inquiry. The person making an analysis should:

- Have a knowledge of the field
- Have good judgment
- Be honest in evaluating
- Be free from bias and prejudice

Ask yourself questions about the data:

- How do these findings compare with related research or literature mentioned previously?
- Why is this feature significant?
- What benefits are involved?
- Who will benefit?
- What trends are evident?
- What effects might these trends have?
- How are these facts, events, or features related?
- What correlations exist between or among these features?
- What values can be identified – economic, social, political, or any other?
- What generalization can be made about the statistical spectrum other than the central tendency, the average?
- What is the effect of accepting or rejecting the hypothesis?
- What is the relationship to the study objective?

22.14.3 The Interpretation Process

The data interpretation process has two distinct steps:

- The first step is that of recognizing the researcher's attitude toward the problem that leads to the solution.
- The second step in interpretation is reasoning about the facts. Reasoning is simply a process of arriving at sound conclusions through using inferences and deductions.

Interpretation by Reasoning

Several techniques are used in reasoning that contribute to the reader's acceptance of the conclusions:

- **Logic** – Connection of the various facts and events, developed during research, into a logical order that can lead to the conclusions along a rational reasoning path
- **Inference** – Making statements about the unknown based on the known using formal logic and inference rules
- **Analogy** – Making statements about the unknown based on the known by its resemblance with the known by essential aspects
- **Correlation** – Making statements about the unknown by comparison of the timelines of unknown and known

Precision and depth in showing how the facts relate to the problem are important in research. Facts should be true and verifiable; they are not open to questions. An assumption, an inference, or an opinion might be questioned because it is not reasonable under the circumstances; a fact may not.

Without analysis and reasoning, real research is impossible. Research is dependent upon the elements with which reasoning is concerned. It reveals the meaning of facts through a refined technique of thinking.

In addition to using the factors involved in the reasoning process, you can give meaning to facts by:

- Pointing out effects or consequences
- Giving implications
- Determining relationships
- Noting similarities and differences

In addition to using the factors involved in the reasoning process, you can give meaning to facts by:

- Pointing out effects or consequences
- Giving implications
- Determining relationships
- Nothing similarities and differences
- Identifying trends
- Determining merits or faults
- Making generalizations
- Noting causes and effect
- Determining functions
- Pointing out the significance of facts
- Noting recurrences or the lack of them
- Evolving descriptive concepts
- Proposing theories

> Facts may be easily misinterpreted and set to a biased interpretation by mistake or even on purpose. Never do it!

22.15 Research Findings and Analysis

Research findings, also referred to as research results, are new facts, relationships, or processes discovered in the research.

Research results in a theoretical research are presented in the form of a theory derived from the initial statements by using rules of inference. Results of a simulation research come from the computer algorithms acting as logical inference on the initial conditions of the simulations. Results of the experimental research or research-based or live observations depend on the collected data and processing methods.

The research findings should meet the research objectives and constitute the foundation for deriving conclusions. The interpreted research findings lead to the research conclusions.

22.16 Conclusions, Recommendations, and Predictions

The research findings constitute the basis for deriving conclusions. The findings represent new facts, relationships, or processes found in the research. Conclusions are the answers to the research questions phrased in the problem statement, which are logically derived from the results of the research.

Each subquestion in the problem statement needs its own answer or answers, and the answer to the main research question is logically constructed from the answers to the subquestions.

Research conclusions should be written clearly, logically, and unambiguously to provide clear and concise answers to the research questions.

Recommendations are practical actions recommended for implementation based on the research results and conclusions. Any recommendations made in the research report should refer to a specific part of the report, where the appropriate situation is described, and also to the respective research findings and conclusions, where the related conclusions are made. A recommendation is a suggested action to improve the existing situation based on the findings and conclusions made in the report. Any recommendation in business or economic research should analyze and address the priority of the recommended improvement, its feasibility, and potential benefits from the implementation of the suggested recommendation.

Predictions may be also made as an additional outcome from the conclusions and recommendations. Predictions represent logically justified expectations of new facts, relationships, and processes, which may be found or occur in the future based on the conclusion and recommendations made in the research.

▶ Example 4 – Conclusions, recommendations, and prediction of the research on the company's competitive positioning

Sales of a medical device company showed decline, and the company conducted a research project to find the reasons of the decline and find the best competitive positioning for the purpose of increasing its revenue.

The comparative research findings (results) showed that the competitors introduced new important features, which were missing in the company's product.

The conclusion derived from the research findings states that the missing features made the company's product substandard that resulted in the sales decline.

The recommendations based on the conclusions and the research findings suggest adding the missing features to make the products competitive. The recommended improvements have high priority and would cost the company $30M to implement. However, the product's quarterly sales are expected to grow by $50M.

The prediction states that with the improved product, the company becomes the market leader and will expand its market share, which is expected to result in additional $35M quarterly sales. ◀

22.17 Bibliography and Citation

Bibliography is a list of sources of the information used in the research and cited (referenced) in the report. There are a variety of standards, often referred to as styles, for the presentation of bibliography. Publishers and organizations may adopt specific styles for bibliography. The major bibliography and citation styles are:

- APA (American Psychological Association) is used by Education, Psychology, and Sciences.
- MLA (Modern Language Association) style is used by the Humanities.
- Chicago/Turabian style is generally used by Business, History, and the Fine Arts.
- IEEE's (Institute of Electrical and Electronics Engineers) publication on citation standards covers books, conference technical articles, online sources, periodicals, theses, and more.

Each bibliography and citation style may have different variations. To learn more about styles, please refer to specialized sources.

Some commonly used styles used for bibliography and citations with multiple examples are presented in ▶ Chap. 5.

22.18 Appendices

Appendices were first discussed in this book in ▶ Chap. 7 "Research Proposal." An appendix (singular) and appendices (plural) are special section or sections in the report that contain auxiliary information, which is mentioned in the document, but do not fit into the balanced logical flow of the document.

▶ Example 5 – An appendix with the standard normal distribution table

A good example of an appendix could be given using the content of this book. ▶ Chapter 11 introduces the method of finding cumulative probability using standard normal distribution table with the illustration on its fragment presented in ▶ Fig. 11.13. However, presenting the full-scale table would disturb the smooth flow of the chapter. For this reason, the full standard normal distribution table is presented in Appendix A. A fragment of the table shown in ▶ Fig. 11.13 is sufficient to understand how to work with the table, but if the reader wants to use the table for any numbers, the full table in Appendix A is available for this purpose. ◀

22.19 Structuring the Summary Section

The summary is a brief recitation of the major points made in the document – in this case, in the report. Though the summary is placed in the beginning of the document as shown in ◘ Figs. 22.6 and ▶ 7.1, it should be written the last, when the entire document is ready. The summary helps the readers to find out if the document is of interest for them. The readers first read the summary and then the documents itself, if they found it interesting. Thus, the summary is a very important part of a document.

In research reports, this section is typically called "Summary"; in business plans, the summary is called "Executive Summary," in journal papers "Abstract."

22.20 Acknowledgment

The section "Acknowledgment" is used for expressing gratitude and giving credits to individuals and organizations for help and assistance in the research. This is not compulsory to do so, but it is considered a good manner to say thanks to all who helped you.

? Questions for Self-Control for Chapter 22

1. How to deliver research results?
2. What is report outline?
3. How to develop a report outline?
4. What is the relationship between the report outline and the table of contents?
5. Describe the typographical gradation of characters and numbers.
6. What is the best structure of a research report?
7. What is a generic structure of a research report?
8. What is the report title page?
9. What information should be placed on the research report title page?
10. How to organize the report title page?
11. What is understood by smooth chapter transition?
12. How to provide chapter transition?
13. How to format your research report?
14. Who establishes the formatting requirements and rules for a research report?
15. How should section headings of the report be numbered?
16. How to write the introduction part of the research report?
17. What should be included in the introductory part of the research report?

18. What is the difference between the purpose of the research and the purpose of the report?
19. Why is definition of terms important in the research report?
20. Where should be the definition of terms placed in the research report?
21. What is the role of the review of literature in a research report?
22. What are the role and place of the problem statement in the research report?
23. What is understood by research objectives?
24. What is the role of description of research methods, tools, techniques, and procedures in the research report?
25. How important is to report data collection and data analysis?
26. What is understood by research findings?
27. What is the difference between research findings and research results?
28. What is the role of research conclusions and how to write this section?
29. How to form and write recommendations?
30. What is understood by research predictions and how are they made?
31. What is the role of bibliography in the research report?
32. What standards (or styles) for bibliography formatting do you know?
33. How to provide citation (cross-referencing) in the research report?
34. What is the role of appendices in the research report?
35. What is the role of summary in the research report?
36. When should report summary be written?
37. What is the role of acknowledgment section in the research report?

Making Presentations

Contents

23.1 Specifics of Presentations – 482

23.2 Developing Presentation Outline and Timeline – 483

23.3 Developing Presentation Slides – 484

23.4 Slide Design and Animation – 485

23.5 Get Prepared for the Presentation and Questions – 486

23.6 Making Presentations – 487

23.7 Answering Questions – 490

S. K. Aityan, *Business Research Methodology*, Classroom Companion: Business,
https://doi.org/10.1007/978-3-030-76857-7_23

23.1 Specifics of Presentations

Thesis defense, business, conference, public, and university lectures and presentations are very different by their structure, timing, and the audience. However, all of them have a lot in common as of their conceptual framework, preparation technique, and presentation strategy and tactics.

23

Making a good research presentation requires good presentation skills, a thorough preparation, and proper delivery. You may easily recall the presentations which were very interesting and exciting for you, while you might also recall the presentations which were quite boring and difficult to understand and follow even the topic was quite exciting. In this chapter, we will discuss how to make a good presentation. Definitely, the topic must be of interest for the audience, and the delivered material must bring good value to the audience; otherwise neither a good content nor good presentation skills would help.

Preparing and making a presentation is an art principally different from writing a paper. When you make a presentation for live audience, you have a luxury of communicating to the audience with an instant feedback which you do not have with writing a paper. Communication with the audience goes far beyond just verbal dialog but also includes various channels of information such as eye contact, spontaneous questions and comments, and nonverbal feedback in the form of poses, gestures, and other behavioral patterns.

A good presenter must be able to use all kinds of the feedback to control the presentation flow, quality, and perception.

Presentation timing is one of the most important constraints of any presentation. Different types of presentations are limited to a specific time. Presentations at master thesis defense are typically constrained to 15 minute and presentations at conferences are limited to 15 or 30 minutes subject to the conference schedule, keynote speeches to 1 or 2 hours, and university lectures to 2 or 3 academic hours. An academic hour lasts 45 or 50 minutes.

Using less time for your presentation than scheduled reduces the volume and depth of the information you could deliver to the audience. It is presumed that the scope and depth of your knowledge in the field are much greater than the time limitations of your presentation and you would appreciate any minute for your presentation to share your knowledge and present new information.

A quite more typical situation is when the presenter breaks the given time constraints and extends the presentation time because he or she has not yet delivered the planned information by the end of the given time. This creates a number of problems. At conferences, you take the time from the presenters who were scheduled to present after you. Such a cascade of delays of the next presentations will end up with cancelation of the presentations scheduled for the end of the session. Neither presenters nor audience would appreciate it. The audience also has their plans for the planned presentations, and abusing their patience is not good too.

Thus, the best is to use exactly as much time for your presentation as scheduled. In this chapter, we discuss how to plan, develop, and make presentations that last as long as scheduled and cover the planned material.

Control the timing of your presentation and make its duration exactly as scheduled.

23.2 Developing Presentation Outline and Timeline

First, you should develop the presentation outline. The presentation outline is the structure of the presentation similarly to one developed for a report. It is the presentation skeleton. Assign timing to each section (item) in the presentation outline as shown in ◘ Table 23.1. The timing for each section defines the time needed, in your opinion, to cover the material in that section of the presentation. The outline plus timing is the *presentation timeline*, similarly as the outline plus page numbers is the document table of contents.

The sum of times for each section in the presentations is the total time planned for the presentation. This sum is shown in the bottom of the timelines in ◘ Table 23.1. The calculated timing for the presentation – as the sum of timing for each section – should match the time assigned for your presentation by the organizers or by yourself. If the calculated total time does not match the time scheduled by the organizers or allocated by yourself, then adjust the timing for each section in the timeline to have the total timing exactly equal the scheduled timing. It may take several iterations to converge the process. Finally, when the total time in the timelines matches the allocated time, your presentation timelines are ready.

Presentation outline + timing for each section = presentation timelines.

Do not make the sections in the outline too detailed as in case of a report outline. Any presentation to a live audience may imply timing uncertainty caused by the reaction of the audience to your presentation, unexpected questions, or even your

◘ **Table 23.1** Example of a presentation timeline

#	Description	Timing
1	Introduction	2
2	Problem statement and purpose	3
3	Methods and procedures	2
4	Data collection	1
5	Results and findings	3
6	Conclusions and recommendations	3
7	Acknowledgment	1
Total minutes		**15**

own assessment of the presentation flow. For example, if you are given 15 minutes for the presentation, break the presentation time into approximately five or seven sections as illustrated in ◘ Table 23.1. The table shows just a sample, and the real content and number of sections may vary for different presentations.

The most critical parts of a research presentation are:

- Problem statement and purpose
- Research design including hypotheses, methods, and procedures.
- Data collection and processing
- Research findings
- Conclusions, recommendations, and predictions

23.3 Developing Presentation Slides

MS PowerPoint or OpenOffice Impress are very convenient and commonly used media for presentations.

Once the timelines for your presentation are ready, develop the MS PowerPoint or OpenOffice Impress presentation slides. The following guidelines will help in the development of good presentation slides:

- Presentation slides are not intended for a long text but mostly should contain bulleted information to guide the presentation.
- One informative slide should take no less than 2 minutes of the presentation time. The illustrative slides may take much shorter time.
- All slides in the presentation must be similarly designed to provide a solid impression.
- The text on the slides should have:
  - For slide format 4:3 – font size no lower than Times New Roman 24 or similar by the apparent size for text and size 20 for header and footer
  - For slide format 16:9 – font size 24 no lower than Times New Roman 24 or similar by the apparent size for text and size 20 for header and footer

  The smaller font sizes may be poorly visible or not visible for the audience. Not everybody in the audience has perfect vision.
- Each slide except the title slide must show the slide number and the total number of slides shown as slide 11 of totally 28 slides in the right-bottom corner of a sample slide in ◘ Fig. 23.1. The slide number is needed for references in possible discussion and questions. The total number of slides helps the audience to comfortably manage their level of focus and interest in the presentation.

Once the presentation slides are ready, you may add a column to the presentation timelines with the slide numbers matching the respective sections of the presentation as illustrated in ◘ Table 23.2.

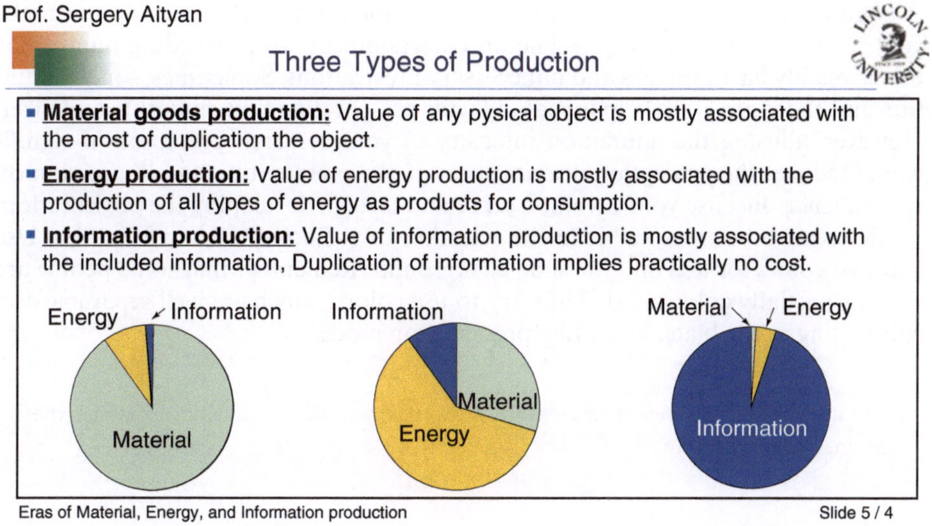

Fig. 23.1 A sample presentation slide

Table 23.2 A sample presentation timeline with timing and respective slide numbers

#	Description	Slide #	Timing
1	Introduction	1	2
2	Problem statement and purpose	2	3
3	Methods and procedures	3–5	2
4	Data collection	6,7	1
5	Results and findings	8–10	3
6	Conclusions and recommendations	11–13	3
7	Acknowledgment	14	1
Total minutes			15

23.4 Slide Design and Animation

Your presentation would look better if the slides were nicely designed. MS PowerPoint or OpenOffice Impress provide tools for designing slides. Also, these applications offer a variety of ready-to-use slide designs. Technically, you can make a flashy design for your slides with fancy slide transitions and extensive animation.

A good design always makes you presentation look better. However, do not make you research presentation look line an entertainment with exceeding number of unreasonably flashy images and unnecessary illustrations. Sometimes, some animation and slide transition help in making your presentation flow smoothly and nicer. However, abusing the animation intensity in your research presentation significantly reduces the perceptional seriousness of the presentation and impression on the audience. Just use your common sense and taste in developing the presentation.

Be creative but reasonable in the selection of the color scheme for slides. Use contrast colors for text and the slide background. Remember that some people are fully or partially color blind. Thus, try to use colors, which are well separable and contrasting in the black and white presentation mode.

> Do not make you research presentation too flashy in design and do not abuse the animation intensity in it.

> Use colors, which are well separable and contrasting in the black and white presentation mode to help color blind people.

23.5 Get Prepared for the Presentation and Questions

Once the timeline and the presentation slides are ready, it is a good time to prepare yourself for the presentations.

- Think about your presentation style, explanations, and examples.
- Make sure that you are in possession of all auxiliary materials for the presentation. You must have sufficient reserve in width and depth of the presented material to answer questions and provide additional information if needed.
- Practice your presentation using timeline and slides.

Do not memorize the entire text of your presentation. Better think what you will say in each section. You may practice some special phrases if you feel it is necessary. You know the material you are presenting.

However, prepare and memorize the first and the last phrases of the presentation for a smooth rolling in and rolling out of the presentation.

You may practice your presentation with your friends and ask them to comment on your presenting manner and style.

The audience may ask questions during and after presentations. Be prepared for them. Some questions may be uneasy, and it would be better if you are prepared for them. Think about the most possible questions and try to come up with the most difficult questions. Such questions may vary subject to the research domain and topic.

There is no generic set of questions. The following are some of the most frequent questions you better to be prepared to answer in business research presentations:

- What is the main problem you wanted to solve?
- Why is this research important?
- Who is going to use the result of your research?
- How can the results of your research be used for practical purposes?
- What is the most important result of your research?
- What is the most important discovery you made in this research?
- What are the most important conclusions, recommendations, or predictions you made in your research?
- How important and how feasible are the recommendations you made?
- What benefit you expect the company will have if your recommendations are implemented?
- What was the most important contribution to the knowledge pool you made by this research?
- What was the most important contribution you personally made to this research?
- What did you personally learn during this research?

There could be many other questions. Please think of them in advance. Prepare clear and accurate answers to these questions and other potential questions you might be asked in the presentation.

23.6 Making Presentations

Your presentation begins soon. Do not get anxious or nervous. Relax and concentrate on the upcoming presentation. This couple of minutes before the presentation would not help you to get better prepared but may make you more nervous and psychologically unbalanced. Just relax. It is the best you can do.

The presentation started. If the chairman or the moderator introduces you to the audience, then do not introduce yourself again. However, if you want to say something important about yourself, do it but briefly. If you were not introduced to the audience, then introduce yourself, but be very brief, particularly in short presentation, where every minute counts.

Start the presentation with the first phrase you prepared and memorized by heart as it was advised in the previous section dedicated to the preparation for the presentation. This gives you a nice and smooth rolling in the presentation.

Make your presentation as it flows using the slides and the timeline as the guiding milestones. It is perfectly fine to have your timeline and watch handy to track the time flow of the presentation.

You know well your material, so just deliver it using normal language speaking like you are speaking to your friends. Control your language but do not worry; the audience forgives you for some possible little bumpiness in phrasing as long as your presentation delivers valuable information and the audience is engaged.

Behave naturally, speak with the normal pace, and do not rush; otherwise your audience may lose track and psychologically disconnect from your presentation.

Establish rapport with the audience and engage it by finding their focus of interest. Sense the feedback. The audience always provides immediate real-time feedback if you know how to read it – expressed attention to the presentation, gestures, and many other little signs.

Establish and maintain eye contact with the audience. Randomly choose a person from the audience and establish a brief eye contact. Do not keep it for any extended time. Randomly switch to another person and keep doing it most of the time during the presentation. Do it randomly not following any specific regular pattern like you are scanning the audience.

Remember, do not switch slides more frequently than one informative slide in 2 minutes of presentation; otherwise your audience will have no chance to read it, understand the slide, and follow your speech. In short presentations, you may switch slides little faster, but not much faster. Give the audience the chance to read and comprehend it. Illustration slides with simple pictures can be switched much faster.

Do not read all what is written on the slides. Presentation is not reading the information from slides. Slides provide bullet-wise headings for your speech. Also remember that people read faster than you speak. Thus, if you keep reading all written on the slides, the audience gets bored and loses interest because they are always ahead of you. You may read some special things from the slides to emphasize the statement on the slide, if it is worth it. Remember, your major task is presenting the material. Use the information on the slides as the structural guidelines that provide a skeleton for your presentation and tell the audience your story. Relax and speak as it naturally goes, try to describe what you wanted to describe, and explain what you wanted to explain.

Follow the timelines of your presentation. You may have a list with the timelines and watch handy for the better control of time. The presentation slides guide you through the presentation. Your audience consists of people who watch you and listen to your presentation. Their questions, if allowed during the presentation, behavior, gestures, body language, and eyes provide a priceless feedback that allows you to adjust your presentation on-the-fly by slowing down or speeding up or providing more explanations.

If, at any moment during your presentation, you think that you are running out of the time allocated in the timeline for this section, but still have undelivered material, and need more time for the current section of your presentation, you must make an immediate decision:

- Either wrap it up or just cut this section and move to the next section to stay on the timeline track.
- Extend the time by borrowing it from the next section in the timeline.

This is a very important decision, which you must make on-the-fly to control your presentation.

If the undelivered material in the current section is not crucial for understanding the presentation, just cut it. Your audience may fill up the gap by interpolating what you have already said. Similarly, as it is done in movies. If you want to show a person entering the room, coming to the chair at the fireplace, and taking a seat in the chair, you can show the person entering the room and then just showing him taking a seat in the chair. The rest is interpolated in the minds of the audience.

If you believe that the undelivered part of the information is crucial for understanding your presentation, then borrow the time from the next section of the presentation. Yes! Borrow! It means that the next section of the presentation will become shorter exactly by the time you borrowed from it to extend the timing of the current section. Go for it if you believe that the undelivered information in the current section deserves it.

Keep up with the presentation timing:

- Taking less time for the presentation than given is bad for you because you have not used the time for better explanation of your work.
- Taking more time for the presentation than given is even worse because everybody has time limits and has many other things to do. Most likely, you are also using time allocated for other speakers. Be considerate.

Some presenters try to write down the presentation text and memorize it in advance. It is not a good practice. Your presentation to a live audience is not a monologue given by radio. Your audience consists of live people who watch, listen, and react on your presentation. Your interaction with the audience may need some dynamic adjustments during the presentation. Also, presenting a memorized text most likely does not allow you to establish rapport and connect psychologically with the audience. Speak like you speak to friends and use the slides and the timeline as the presentation milestones.

Do not memorize the presentation text. Speak as it flows using your timelines and slides as the guide in the presentation.

A memorized presentation text makes you a prisoner of your own presentation text and you get pre-engaged with the task not to forget a phrase rather than communicating to the audience.

Behave naturally, make eye contact with the audience, randomly one person at a time, but don't stare

- If in any section of your timelines, you feel that it is taking longer than planned, wrap it up and cut this section and move to the next one. You better miss some minor part of the information you planned to deliver than run out of the total time in your presentation.
- If the undelivered information is crucial for understanding your material, then borrow time for it from the time allocated in the timeline for the next section of

your presentation. Yes! Borrow! It means that the next section of the presentation will become shorter exactly by the time you borrowed from it to extend the timing of the current section. Go for it if you believe that the undelivered information in the current section deserves it.

23.7 Answering Questions

Research presentations are normally followed by discussion, questions, and answers. Sometimes, questions are allowed during the presentation too. There are no bad questions. Any question is good because it gives the presenter an opportunity to tell more than was told in the presentation. Even hard questions should be appreciated by the presenter because they are giving a very good chance to demonstrate in-depth knowledge and ability to conduct logical analysis.

Always thank the person who asked you a question. Do it briefly without excessive excitement but show your appreciation.

Never say that the question is easy or stupid, and do not make any negative or disrespectful comments about the question itself or the person who asked the question. Answer respectfully to all questions.

Provide a brief but focused and accurate answer to the question. Do not be lengthy and fuzzy in your answers. Once you answered the question, it is a good manner to ask if the person, who asked the question, is satisfied with the answer. It may occur that you misunderstood or misinterpreted the question.

Always remember that answering questions gives you a chance to tell more about your research, the related challenges, and the outcomes that you did not tell in the presentation due to the time limits.

There are no bad questions. Any question is good because it gives the presenter an opportunity to tell more than was told in the presentation.

Provide a brief but focused and accurate answer to the question.

Questions for Self-Control for Chapter 23

1. What is the presentation outline?
2. What is the presentation timeline?
3. How important is to control the presentation timing?
4. How to prepare the presentation slides?
5. Why slide numbering is important?
6. Why showing the total number of slides is helpful?
7. What font size is good for presentation slides?
8. What are the most critical parts of a research presentation?

9. How to control presentation timing during the presentation?
10. How to establish rapport with the audience?
11. Why establishing eye contact with the audience is important?
12. How to establish eye contact with the audience?
13. Does the presenter need to develop and memorize the presentation text in advance?
14. How fancy should research presentation slides be?
15. How much animation is better to use in the presentation slides?
16. What should be the types of color scheme for the presentation slides?
17. How to answer to the questions from the audience?
18. Are there bad questions?
19. How long and detailed must be the answer to a question?

Supplementary Information

Appendix A – 494

Appendix B – 501

Appendix C – 504

S. K. Aityan, *Business Research Methodology*, Classroom Companion: Business,
https://doi.org/10.1007/978-3-030-76857-7

Appendix A: The Standard Normal Distribution Tables

A1. The Standard Normal Cumulative Probability Table

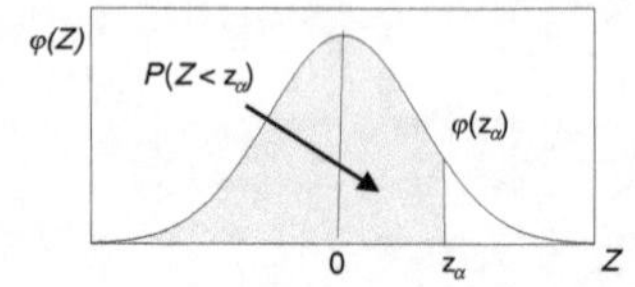

To find the cumulative standard normal probability $P(z_\alpha) = P(Z < z_\alpha)$ for a given positive value of $Z = z_\alpha$ ($z_\alpha > 0$) using the standard normal cumulative probability table (■ Table A.1 in Appendix A), select the row matching the value of z_α trimmed to the first decimal figure of number a and then select the column matching the second decimal addition of a. The respective cumulative probability $P(z_\alpha) = P(Z < z_\alpha)$ is found in the intersection of the selected row and the selected column. Just a reminder, $P(z_\alpha)$ and $P(Z < z_\alpha)$ are the synonymous notations that mean the probability of all $Z < z_\alpha$.

For example, if $z_\alpha = 1.27$, then z_α trimmed to the first decimal figure is 1.2, and the second decimal addition is 0.07. The overall z_α is $1.2 + 0.07 = 1.27$. The method of finding the cumulative standard normal probability using the standard table $P(1.27) = P(z_\alpha < 1.27)$ is shown in ■ Fig. A.1. $P(1.27) = P(Z < 1.27) = 0.8980$.

The cumulative standard normal probabilities for negative values of Z can be found from the same table utilizing the symmetry of the standard normal distribution around $Z = 0$, i.e.:

$$P(-Z) = 1 - P(Z) \tag{A.1}$$

For example, $P(Z = -1.27) = 1 - P(Z = 1.27) = 1 - 0.8980 = 0.1020$.

The standard normal cumulative probability for any $Z > 4$ equals 1.0000 with the accuracy of four decimal figures and, thus, is not shown in ■ Table A.1.

Table A.1 The standard normal cumulative probability table

z_α	0	0.01	0.02	0.03	0.04	0.05	0.06	0.07	0.08	0.09
0.0	0.5000	0.5040	0.5080	0.5120	0.5160	0.5199	0.5239	0.5279	0.5319	0.5359
0.1	0.5398	0.5438	0.5478	0.5517	0.5557	0.5596	0.5636	0.5675	0.5714	0.5753
0.2	0.5793	0.5832	0.5871	0.5910	0.5948	0.5987	0.6026	0.6064	0.6103	0.6141
0.3	0.6179	0.6217	0.6255	0.6293	0.6331	0.6368	0.6406	0.6443	0.6480	0.6517
0.4	0.6554	0.6591	0.6628	0.6664	0.6700	0.6736	0.6772	0.6808	0.6844	0.6879
0.5	0.6915	0.6950	0.6985	0.7019	0.7054	0.7088	0.7123	0.7157	0.7190	0.7224
0.6	0.7257	0.7291	0.7324	0.7357	0.7389	0.7422	0.7454	0.7486	0.7517	0.7549
0.7	0.7580	0.7611	0.7642	0.7673	0.7704	0.7734	0.7764	0.7794	0.7823	0.7852
0.8	0.7881	0.7910	0.7939	0.7967	0.7995	0.8023	0.8051	0.8078	0.8106	0.8133
0.9	0.8159	0.8186	0.8212	0.8238	0.8264	0.8289	0.8315	0.8340	0.8365	0.8389
1.0	0.8413	0.8438	0.8461	0.8485	0.8508	0.8531	0.8554	0.8577	0.8599	0.8621
1.1	0.8643	0.8665	0.8686	0.8708	0.8729	0.8749	0.8770	0.8790	0.8810	0.8830
1.2	0.8849	0.8869	0.8888	0.8907	0.8925	0.8944	0.8962	0.8980	0.8997	0.9015
1.3	0.9032	0.9049	0.9066	0.9082	0.9099	0.9115	0.9131	0.9147	0.9162	0.9177
1.4	0.9192	0.9207	0.9222	0.9236	0.9251	0.9265	0.9279	0.9292	0.9306	0.9319
1.5	0.9332	0.9345	0.9357	0.9370	0.9382	0.9394	0.9406	0.9418	0.9429	0.9441
1.6	0.9452	0.9463	0.9474	0.9484	0.9495	0.9505	0.9515	0.9525	0.9535	0.9545
1.7	0.9554	0.9564	0.9573	0.9582	0.9591	0.9599	0.9608	0.9616	0.9625	0.9633
1.8	0.9641	0.9649	0.9656	0.9664	0.9671	0.9678	0.9686	0.9693	0.9699	0.9706
1.9	0.9713	0.9719	0.9726	0.9732	0.9738	0.9744	0.9750	0.9756	0.9761	0.9767
2.0	0.9772	0.9778	0.9783	0.9788	0.9793	0.9798	0.9803	0.9808	0.9812	0.9817
2.1	0.9821	0.9826	0.9830	0.9834	0.9838	0.9842	0.9846	0.9850	0.9854	0.9857
2.2	0.9861	0.9864	0.9868	0.9871	0.9875	0.9878	0.9881	0.9884	0.9887	0.9890
2.3	0.9893	0.9896	0.9898	0.9901	0.9904	0.9906	0.9909	0.9911	0.9913	0.9916
2.4	0.9918	0.9920	0.9922	0.9925	0.9927	0.9929	0.9931	0.9932	0.9934	0.9936
2.5	0.9938	0.9940	0.9941	0.9943	0.9945	0.9946	0.9948	0.9949	0.9951	0.9952
2.6	0.9953	0.9955	0.9956	0.9957	0.9959	0.9960	0.9961	0.9962	0.9963	0.9964
2.7	0.9965	0.9966	0.9967	0.9968	0.9969	0.9970	0.9971	0.9972	0.9973	0.9974
2.8	0.9974	0.9975	0.9976	0.9977	0.9977	0.9978	0.9979	0.9979	0.9980	0.9981
2.9	0.9981	0.9982	0.9982	0.9983	0.9984	0.9984	0.9985	0.9985	0.9986	0.9986
3.0	0.9987	0.9987	0.9987	0.9988	0.9988	0.9989	0.9989	0.9989	0.9990	0.9990

(continued)

Table A.1 (continued)

z_α	0	0.01	0.02	0.03	0.04	0.05	0.06	0.07	0.08	0.09
3.1	0.9990	0.9991	0.9991	0.9991	0.9992	0.9992	0.9992	0.9992	0.9993	0.9993
3.2	0.9993	0.9993	0.9994	0.9994	0.9994	0.9994	0.9994	0.9995	0.9995	0.9995
3.3	0.9995	0.9995	0.9995	0.9996	0.9996	0.9996	0.9996	0.9996	0.9996	0.9997
3.4	0.9997	0.9997	0.9997	0.9997	0.9997	0.9997	0.9997	0.9997	0.9997	0.9998
3.5	0.9998	0.9998	0.9998	0.9998	0.9998	0.9998	0.9998	0.9998	0.9998	0.9998
3.6	0.9998	0.9998	0.9999	0.9999	0.9999	0.9999	0.9999	0.9999	0.9999	0.9999
3.7	0.9999	0.9999	0.9999	0.9999	0.9999	0.9999	0.9999	0.9999	0.9999	0.9999
3.8	0.9999	0.9999	0.9999	0.9999	0.9999	0.9999	0.9999	0.9999	0.9999	0.9999
3.9	1.0000	1.0000	1.0000	1.0000	1.0000	1.0000	1.0000	1.0000	1.0000	1.0000
4.0	1.0000	1.0000	1.0000	1.0000	1.0000	1.0000	1.0000	1.0000	1.0000	1.0000

zα	0	0.01	0.02	0.03	0.04	0.05	0.06	0.07	0.08	0.09
0.0	0.5000	0.5040	0.5080	0.5120	0.5160	0.5199	0.5239	0.5279	0.5319	0.5359
0.1	0.5398	0.5438	0.5478	0.5517	0.5557	0.5596	0.5636	0.5675	0.5714	0.5753
0.2	0.5793	0.5832	0.5871	0.5910	0.5948	0.5987	0.6026	0.6064	0.6103	0.6141
0.3	0.6179	0.6217	0.6255	0.6293	0.6331	0.6368	0.6406	0.6443	0.6480	0.6517
0.4	0.6554	0.6591	0.6628	0.6664	0.6700	0.6736	0.6772	0.6808	0.6844	0.6879
0.5	0.6915	0.6950	0.6985	0.7019	0.7054	0.7088	0.7123	0.7157	0.7190	0.7224
0.6	0.7257	0.7291	0.7324	0.7357	0.7389	0.7422	0.7454	0.7486	0.7517	0.7549
0.7	0.7580	0.7611	0.7642	0.7673	0.7704	0.7734	0.7764	0.7794	0.7823	0.7852
0.8	0.7881	0.7910	0.7939	0.7967	0.7995	0.8023	0.8051	0.8078	0.8106	0.8133
0.9	0.8159	0.8186	0.8212	0.8238	0.8264	0.8289	0.8315	0.8340	0.8365	0.8389
1.0	0.8413	0.8438	0.8461	0.8485	0.8508	0.8531	0.8554	0.8577	0.8599	0.8621
1.1	0.8643	0.8665	0.8686	0.8708	0.8729	0.8749	0.8770	0.8790	0.8810	0.8830
1.2	0.8849	0.8869	0.8888	0.8907	0.8925	0.8944	0.8962	0.8980	0.8997	0.9015
1.3	0.9032	0.9049	0.9066	0.9082	0.9099	0.9115	0.9131	0.9147	0.9162	0.9177
1.4	0.9192	0.9207	0.9222	0.9236	0.9251	0.9265	0.9279	0.9292	0.9306	0.9319

Fig. A.1 Finding the cumulative standard normal probability for $Z = 1.27$ using the cumulative standard normal probabilities table (Table A.1)

A2. The Centered Standard Normal Cumulative Probability Table

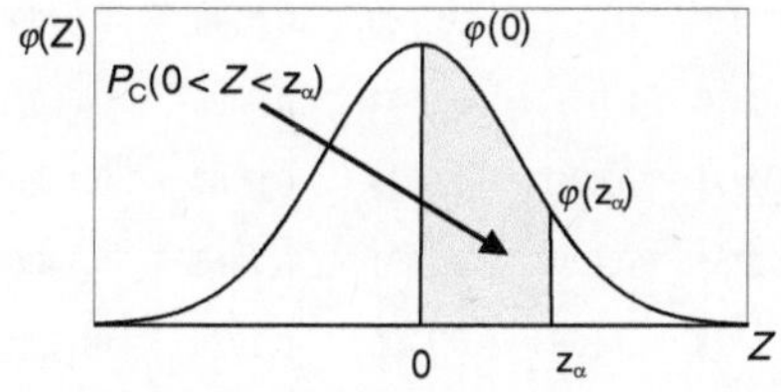

The standard normal distribution $\varphi(Z)$ is a symmetric function with the symmetry around $Z = 0$, i.e., $\varphi(-Z) = \varphi(Z)$. For this reason, the $P(Z < 0) = 0.5$, because the area under $\varphi(Z)$ in the interval $Z < 0$ equals exactly the area under $\varphi(Z)$ in the interval $Z > 0$. Thus, the standard normal probability calculated for the interval $P_C(Z < z_\alpha) = P(0 < Z < z_\alpha)$ is exactly by 0.5 less than the cumulative standard normal probability $P(Z < z_\alpha)$.

$$\mathrm{PC}(Z < z_\alpha) = P(0 < Z < z_\alpha) = P(Z < z_\alpha) - 0.5 \tag{A.2}$$

Such a probability is referred to as the ***centered standard normal cumulative probability*** and shown in ◘ Table A.2. As evident from comparing ◘ Tables A.1 and A.2, all probabilities in ◘ Table A.2 are by 0.5 less than the respective probabilities in ◘ Table A.1. Centered cumulative standard normal probabilities can be found from ◘ Table A.2 using the same method as for ◘ Table A.1 described above as shown in ◘ Fig. A.2.

For example, if $Z = 1.27$, then Z trimmed to the first decimal figure is 1.2, and the second decimal addition is 0.07. The overall $Z = 1.2 + 0.07 = 1.27$. The method of finding the centered cumulative standard normal probability $P_C(Z = 1.27)$ is shown in ◘ Fig. A.2. $P_C(Z = 1.27) = 0.3980$.

The standard normal cumulative probabilities $P(Z)$ can be found for positive Z from the centered standard normal cumulative probabilities as $P(Z) = P_C(Z) + 0.5$. For example, $P(Z = 1.27) = P_C(Z = 1.27) + 0.5 = 0.3980 + 0.5000 = 0.8980$.

Table A.2 The centered standard normal cumulative probability table

z_α	0	0.01	0.02	0.03	0.04	0.05	0.06	0.07	0.08	0.09
0.0	0.0000	0.0040	0.0080	0.0120	0.0160	0.0199	0.0239	0.0279	0.0319	0.0359
0.1	0.0398	0.0438	0.0478	0.0517	0.0557	0.0596	0.0636	0.0675	0.0714	0.0753
0.2	0.0793	0.0832	0.0871	0.0910	0.0948	0.0987	0.1026	0.1064	0.1103	0.1141
0.3	0.1179	0.1217	0.1255	0.1293	0.1331	0.1368	0.1406	0.1443	0.1480	0.1517
0.4	0.1554	0.1591	0.1628	0.1664	0.1700	0.1736	0.1772	0.1808	0.1844	0.1879
0.5	0.1915	0.1950	0.1985	0.2019	0.2054	0.2088	0.2123	0.2157	0.2190	0.2224
0.6	0.2257	0.2291	0.2324	0.2357	0.2389	0.2422	0.2454	0.2486	0.2517	0.2549
0.7	0.2580	0.2611	0.2642	0.2673	0.2704	0.2734	0.2764	0.2794	0.2823	0.2852
0.8	0.2881	0.2910	0.2939	0.2967	0.2995	0.3023	0.3051	0.3078	0.3106	0.3133
0.9	0.3159	0.3186	0.3212	0.3238	0.3264	0.3289	0.3315	0.3340	0.3365	0.3389
1.0	0.3413	0.3438	0.3461	0.3485	0.3508	0.3531	0.3554	0.3577	0.3599	0.3621
1.1	0.3643	0.3665	0.3686	0.3708	0.3729	0.3749	0.3770	0.3790	0.3810	0.3830
1.2	0.3849	0.3869	0.3888	0.3907	0.3925	0.3944	0.3962	0.3980	0.3997	0.4015
1.3	0.4032	0.4049	0.4066	0.4082	0.4099	0.4115	0.4131	0.4147	0.4162	0.4177
1.4	0.4192	0.4207	0.4222	0.4236	0.4251	0.4265	0.4279	0.4292	0.4306	0.4319
1.5	0.4332	0.4345	0.4357	0.4370	0.4382	0.4394	0.4406	0.4418	0.4429	0.4441
1.6	0.4452	0.4463	0.4474	0.4484	0.4495	0.4505	0.4515	0.4525	0.4535	0.4545
1.7	0.4554	0.4564	0.4573	0.4582	0.4591	0.4599	0.4608	0.4616	0.4625	0.4633
1.8	0.4641	0.4649	0.4656	0.4664	0.4671	0.4678	0.4686	0.4693	0.4699	0.4706
1.9	0.4713	0.4719	0.4726	0.4732	0.4738	0.4744	0.4750	0.4756	0.4761	0.4767
2.0	0.4772	0.4778	0.4783	0.4788	0.4793	0.4798	0.4803	0.4808	0.4812	0.4817
2.1	0.4821	0.4826	0.4830	0.4834	0.4838	0.4842	0.4846	0.4850	0.4854	0.4857
2.2	0.4861	0.4864	0.4868	0.4871	0.4875	0.4878	0.4881	0.4884	0.4887	0.4890
2.3	0.4893	0.4896	0.4898	0.4901	0.4904	0.4906	0.4909	0.4911	0.4913	0.4916
2.4	0.4918	0.4920	0.4922	0.4925	0.4927	0.4929	0.4931	0.4932	0.4934	0.4936
2.5	0.4938	0.4940	0.4941	0.4943	0.4945	0.4946	0.4948	0.4949	0.4951	0.4952
2.6	0.4953	0.4955	0.4956	0.4957	0.4959	0.4960	0.4961	0.4962	0.4963	0.4964
2.7	0.4965	0.4966	0.4967	0.4968	0.4969	0.4970	0.4971	0.4972	0.4973	0.4974
2.8	0.4974	0.4975	0.4976	0.4977	0.4977	0.4978	0.4979	0.4979	0.4980	0.4981
2.9	0.4981	0.4982	0.4982	0.4983	0.4984	0.4984	0.4985	0.4985	0.4986	0.4986
3.0	0.4987	0.4987	0.4987	0.4988	0.4988	0.4989	0.4989	0.4989	0.4990	0.4990
3.1	0.4990	0.4991	0.4991	0.4991	0.4992	0.4992	0.4992	0.4992	0.4993	0.4993
3.2	0.4993	0.4993	0.4994	0.4994	0.4994	0.4994	0.4994	0.4995	0.4995	0.4995

Table A.2 (continued)

z_α	0	0.01	0.02	0.03	0.04	0.05	0.06	0.07	0.08	0.09
3.3	0.4995	0.4995	0.4995	0.4996	0.4996	0.4996	0.4996	0.4996	0.4996	0.4997
3.4	0.4997	0.4997	0.4997	0.4997	0.4997	0.4997	0.4997	0.4997	0.4997	0.4998
3.5	0.4998	0.4998	0.4998	0.4998	0.4998	0.4998	0.4998	0.4998	0.4998	0.4998
3.6	0.4998	0.4998	0.4999	0.4999	0.4999	0.4999	0.4999	0.4999	0.4999	0.4999
3.7	0.4999	0.4999	0.4999	0.4999	0.4999	0.4999	0.4999	0.4999	0.4999	0.4999
3.8	0.4999	0.4999	0.4999	0.4999	0.4999	0.4999	0.4999	0.4999	0.4999	0.4999
3.9	0.5000	0.5000	0.5000	0.5000	0.5000	0.5000	0.5000	0.5000	0.5000	0.5000
4.0	0.5000	0.5000	0.5000	0.5000	0.5000	0.5000	0.5000	0.5000	0.5000	0.5000

zα	0	0.01	0.02	0.03	0.04	0.05	0.06	0.07	0.08	0.09
0.0	0.0000	0.0040	0.0080	0.0120	0.0160	0.0199	0.0239	0.0279	0.0319	0.0359
0.1	0.0398	0.0438	0.0478	0.0517	0.0557	0.0596	0.0636	0.0675	0.0714	0.0753
0.2	0.0793	0.0832	0.0871	0.0910	0.0948	0.0987	0.1026	0.1064	0.1103	0.1141
0.3	0.1179	0.1217	0.1255	0.1293	0.1331	0.1368	0.1406	0.1443	0.1480	0.1517
0.4	0.1554	0.1591	0.1628	0.1664	0.1700	0.1736	0.1772	0.1808	0.1844	0.1879
0.5	0.1915	0.1950	0.1985	0.2019	0.2054	0.2088	0.2123	0.2157	0.2190	0.2224
0.6	0.2257	0.2291	0.2324	0.2357	0.2389	0.2422	0.2454	0.2486	0.2517	0.2549
0.7	0.2580	0.2611	0.2642	0.2673	0.2704	0.2734	0.2764	0.2794	0.2823	0.2852
0.8	0.2881	0.2910	0.2939	0.2967	0.2995	0.3023	0.3051	0.3078	0.3106	0.3133
0.9	0.3159	0.3186	0.3212	0.3238	0.3264	0.3289	0.3315	0.3340	0.3365	0.3389
1.0	0.3413	0.3438	0.3461	0.3485	0.3508	0.3531	0.3554	0.3577	0.3599	0.3621
1.1	0.3643	0.3665	0.3686	0.3708	0.3729	0.3749	0.3770	0.3790	0.3810	0.3830
1.2	0.3849	0.3869	0.3888	0.3907	0.3925	0.3944	0.3962	0.3980	0.3997	0.4015
1.3	0.4032	0.4049	0.4066	0.4082	0.4099	0.4115	0.4131	0.4147	0.4162	0.4177
1.4	0.4192	0.4207	0.4222	0.4236	0.4251	0.4265	0.4279	0.4292	0.4306	0.4319

Fig. A.2 Finding the centered standard normal cumulative probability for $Z = 1.27$ using the centered standard normal cumulative probability table (Table A.2)

A3. The Table of Critical Values for Significance and Confidence Levels

Critical values of *z*-scores z_α for significance level α or matching confidence levels $CL = 1 - \alpha$ can be found from Tables A.1 and A.2 by finding the probability matching CL and then tracking the row and the column to find the respective z_α. However, the respective *z*-scores can be found for some most frequently used significance α or matching confidence CL levels directly from Table A.3 for two-tailed distribution and from Table A.4 for one-tailed distribution

Table A.3 Two-tailed critical values (z-score) for significance and confidence levels

$\alpha =$	0.001	0.01	0.05	0.025	0.1	0.2
$\alpha/2$ (each tail) =	0.0005	0.005	0.025	0.0125	0.05	0.1
Confidence level = $1 - \alpha =$	0.999	0.99	0.95	0.975	0.9	0.8
Confidence level (%) =	99.9%	99%	95%	98%	90%	80%
z-score for two tails: $z_\alpha =$	**3.291**	**2.576**	**1.960**	**2.241**	**1.645**	**1.282**

Table A.4 One-tailed critical values (z-score) for significance and confidence levels

$\alpha =$	0.001	0.01	0.05	0.025	0.1	0.2
Confidence level = $1 - \alpha =$	0.999	0.99	0.95	0.975	0.9	0.8
Confidence level (%) =	99.9%	99.0%	95.0%	97.5%	90.0%	80.0%
z-score for right tail: $z_\alpha =$	**3.090**	**2.326**	**1.645**	**1.960**	**1.282**	**0.842**
z-score for left tail: $z_\alpha =$	**−3.090**	**−2.326**	**−1.645**	**−1.960**	**−1.282**	**−0.842**

Appendix B: Student's *t*-Distribution Tables

B1. Finding Critical Value for a Given Significance and Degree of Freedom

The table of critical values t_{CR} for student's t-distribution for different significance levels α (or the confidence levels CL = 1 − α) and different degrees of freedom *df* is presented in ◘ Table B.1.

To find the critical value t_{CR} for a given significance level α (or the confidence level CL = 1 − α) and a given number of degrees of freedom *df*, select the appropriate row in the table according to the degree of freedom and the appropriate column according to the chosen significance level. Please take into account that two-sided and one-sided distributions have different portions of significance α per each tail. For the one-sided distribution, the entire area of the single extreme side equals α (◘ Fig. B.1a), but for the two-sided distribution, each tail of the distribution has $\alpha/2$ area (◘ Fig. B.1b).

For example, if the significance level is chosen $\alpha = 0.05$, the test is two-sided, and a selected sample has $df = 7$, then as shown in ◘ Fig. B.2, we select the appropriate column that matches the significance level $\alpha = 0.025$ for a two-sided test and the appropriate row that matches $df = 7$. Then the resulted critical value t_{CR} is located in the intersection of the row and the columns ◘ Fig. B.2.

◘ **Table B.1** Table of critical values t_{CR} for student's *t*-distribution

Two-sided: α =	0.2	0.1	0.05	0.025	0.01	0.001
One-sided: α =	0.1	0.05	0.025	0.0125	0.005	0.0005
Confidence level =	80%	90%	95%	97.5%	99%	99.9%
df			***Critical value*** (t_{CR})			
1	3.078	6.314	12.706	25.452	63.657	636.619
2	1.886	2.920	4.303	6.205	9.925	31.599
3	1.638	2.353	3.182	4.177	5.841	12.924
4	1.533	2.132	2.776	3.495	4.604	8.610
5	1.476	2.015	2.571	3.163	4.032	6.869
6	1.440	1.943	2.447	2.969	3.707	5.959
7	1.415	1.895	2.365	2.841	3.499	5.408
8	1.397	1.860	2.306	2.752	3.355	5.041
9	1.383	1.833	2.262	2.685	3.250	4.781
10	1.372	1.812	2.228	2.634	3.169	4.587

(continued)

Table B.1 (continued)

11	1.363	1.796	2.201	2.593	3.106	4.437
12	1.356	1.782	2.179	2.560	3.055	4.318
13	1.350	1.771	2.160	2.533	3.012	4.221
14	1.345	1.761	2.145	2.510	2.977	4.140
15	1.341	1.753	2.131	2.490	2.947	4.073
16	1.337	1.746	2.120	2.473	2.921	4.015
17	1.333	1.740	2.110	2.458	2.898	3.965
18	1.330	1.734	2.101	2.445	2.878	3.922
19	1.328	1.729	2.093	2.433	2.861	3.883
20	1.325	1.725	2.086	2.423	2.845	3.850
21	1.323	1.721	2.080	2.414	2.831	3.819
22	1.321	1.717	2.074	2.405	2.819	3.792
23	1.319	1.714	2.069	2.398	2.807	3.768
24	1.318	1.711	2.064	2.391	2.797	3.745
25	1.316	1.708	2.060	2.385	2.787	3.725
26	1.315	1.706	2.056	2.379	2.779	3.707
27	1.314	1.703	2.052	2.373	2.771	3.690
28	1.313	1.701	2.048	2.368	2.763	3.674
29	1.311	1.699	2.045	2.364	2.756	3.659
30	1.310	1.697	2.042	2.360	2.750	3.646
40	1.303	1.684	2.021	2.329	2.704	3.551
50	1.299	1.676	2.009	2.311	2.678	3.496
60	1.296	1.671	2.000	2.299	2.660	3.460
70	1.294	1.667	1.994	2.291	2.648	3.435
80	1.292	1.664	1.990	2.284	2.639	3.416
90	1.291	1.662	1.987	2.280	2.632	3.402
100	1.290	1.660	1.984	2.276	2.626	3.390

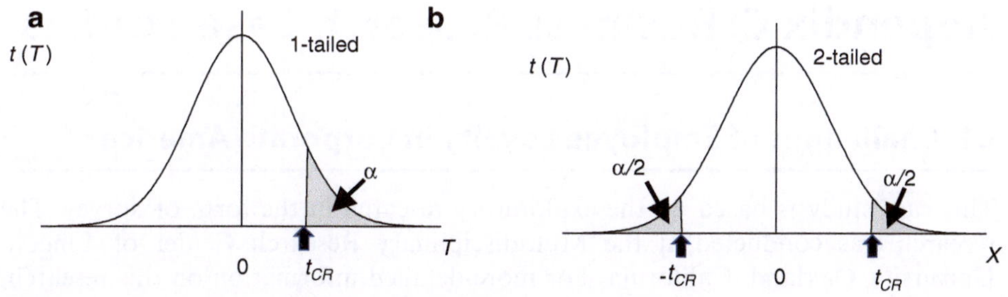

Fig. B.1 **a** One-sided and **b** two-sided distributions

Two-sided: per each side α/2 =	0.2	0.1	0.05	0.025	0.01	0.001
One-sided: α =	0.1	0.05	0.025	[illegible]0125	0.005	0.0005
Confidence level =	80%	90%	95%	[illegible]	99%	99.9%
df			*t-score (tCR)*			
1	3.078	6.314	12.706	[illegible]	[illegible]	[illegible]
2	1.886	2.920	4.303	[illegible]	[illegible]	[illegible]
3	1.638	2.353	3.182	4.177	5.841	12.924
4	1.533	2.132	2.776	3.495	4.604	8.610
5	1.476	2.015	2.571	3.163	4.032	6.869
6	1.440	1.943	2.447	2.969	3.707	5.959
7	1.415	1.895	2.365	2.841	[illegible]	[illegible]408
8	1.397	1.860	2.306	2.752	[illegible]	[illegible]
9	1.383	1.833	2.262	2.685	[illegible]	[illegible]

α = 0.05 two-sided: per each side α = 0.025

df = 7

Critical Value

Fig. B.2 An example of finding the critical value t_{CR} for a sample with $df = 7$ under chosen significance level $\alpha = 0.05$ for a two-sided test

Appendix C: Business Research Case Studies

C1. Challenges of Employee Loyalty in Corporate America

This case study is based on the exploratory research in the form of survey. The research was conducted at the Multidisciplinary Research Center of Lincoln University, Oakland, California. For more detailed information on this research, please refer to the following paper:

Aityan, Sergey K. and Gupta, Tripti K. Pandey (2012). Challenges of Employee Loyalty in Corporate America, *Business and Economics Journal*, vol. 2012, BEJ-55, pp.1–13. (URL: ▸ https://astonjournals.com/manuscripts/Vol2012/BEJ-55_Vol2012.pdf)

This research was dedicated to the analysis of issues and challenges of developing employee loyalty. The research was conducted in the form of a survey in Oakland, California. The survey revealed a serious disconnect between the opinions of managers, including executives, and nonmanagement employees on issues of employee loyalty, trust in management, mutual respect between management and nonmanagement employees, and other related questions. The survey showed that the majority of employees do not feel loyalty from their employer, do not believe that companies take their interests into account, and do not trust or respect their managers, while most managers positively assessed the situation. This disparity needs to be thoroughly addressed by companies in order to improve employee loyalty.

Companies with loyal employees have a significant competitive advantage and a higher rate of survival compared to companies with less loyal employees. Loyal employees are assets to a company, and their retention is key to its success. Given their importance, employers need to be able to identify and retain loyal employees. The fact that an employee has been working for a company for 20 years doesn't automatically guarantee his or her loyalty. For example, an employee might have difficulty finding a better job opportunity due to a lack of marketable skills.

Although the growth of hi-tech industries has resulted in a stronger dependence of companies on employee loyalty, the loyalty situation in corporate America is not improving. Analysis conducted in recent years showed a decrease in employee loyalty. Its declining trend may spell potential problems for companies. In order to find ways to improve the situation, we have to first identify major problems that cause the decline of employee loyalty. The goal of this research was to identify most serious problems with employee loyalty in corporate America today which have to be addressed in order to improve the situation.

Research purpose

The purpose of this research was clearly phrased in the previous paragraph.

Problem statement

The problem statement (the research question) was formulated as follows:

- What level of mutual understanding and respect is established between management and regular employees?

The research question had three subquestions:

- How do managers show loyalty to their employees?
- How do regular employees feel loyalty from their managers?
- What is the motivation for regular employee to show loyalty to their managers?

The scope and limitations of this research constrained the research to the San Francisco Bay Area.

Research design

The research design contained the following items:

- The research planned in the form of survey.
- The questionnaires distributed randomly on the streets and in public places.
- Self-addressed stamped envelopes distributed together with the questionnaires.
- The questionnaires contained questions for verification of the demographic and business proportions in the area.
- The responses to be statistically processed.

Data collection and processing

The survey was conducted as planned. Two hundred fifty questionnaires were distributed on the streets and in public places together with the self-addresses and stamped envelopes. No information was asked or tracked about the respondents' identity. Typically, the response rate in such surveys with the questionnaires distributed on streets is very low. In this case, the response rate was 60% that indicated a high level of interest of the respondents to the problem.

Results

The results of the survey revealed a significant disconnect between the managers' and regular employee' points of view.

The distribution of the respondents by industry and job categories according to the survey is shown in ◘ Figs. C1.1 and C1.2 that indicated that the respondents adequately represent the workforce.

◘ Figures C1.3 and C1.7 show the opinions of management and nonmanagement employees about the relationship between company management and employees (◘ Figs. C1.4, C1.5, C1.6, and C1.7).

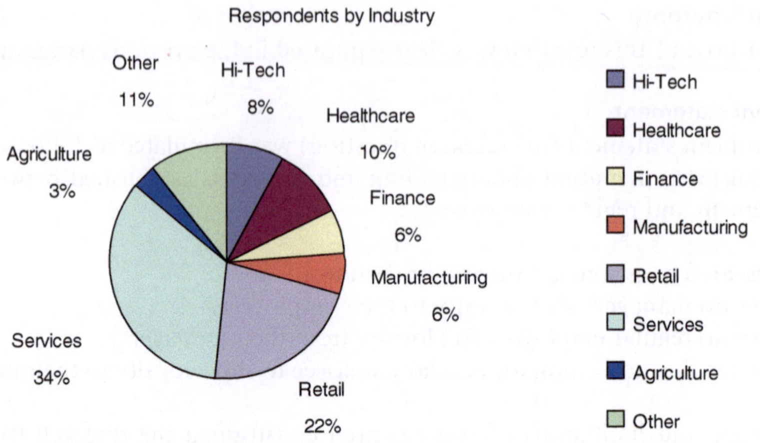

Fig. C1.1 Distribution of respondents by industry

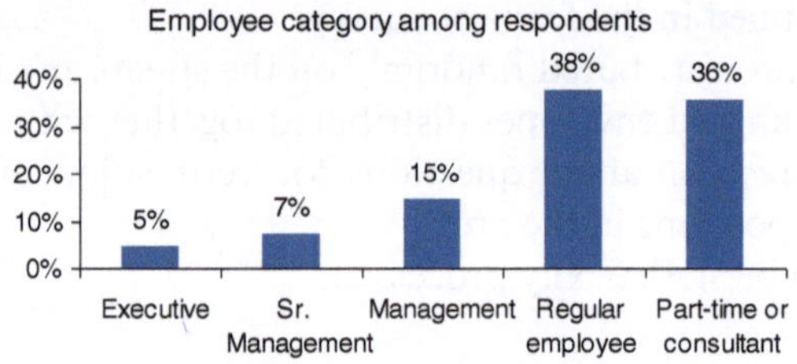

Fig. C1.2 Distribution of respondents by job category

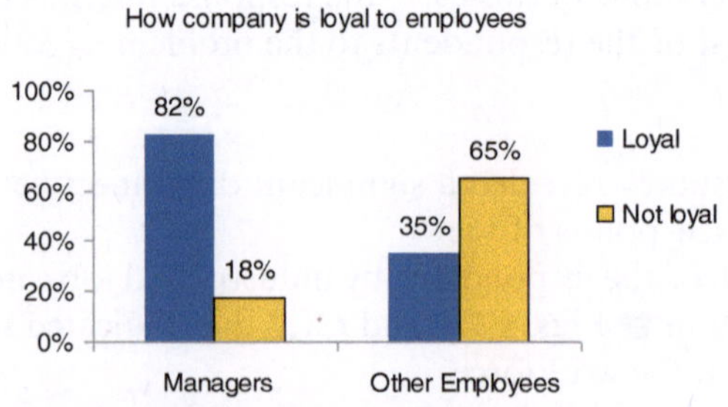

Fig. C1.3 Respondents' opinion on how companies are loyal to their employees by the point of view of managers and nonmanagement employees

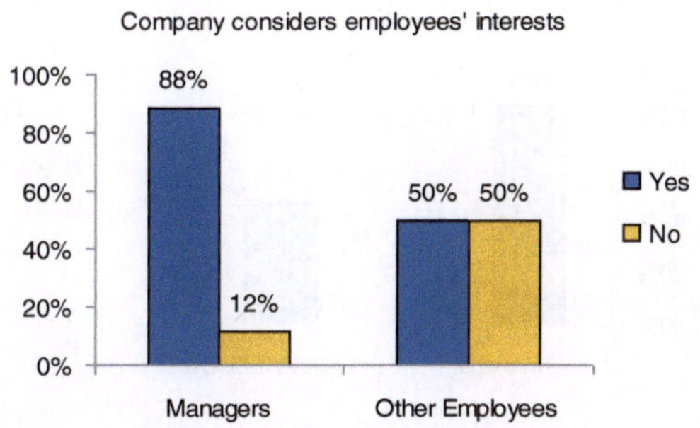

Fig. C1.4 Opinion on how companies consider employees' interests in their decisions by view of managers and nonmanagement employees

Fig. C1.5 Opinion on trusting company's management by view of managers and nonmanagement employees

Fig. C1.6 Opinion on whether companies respect their employees and their contribution by view of managers and nonmanagement employees

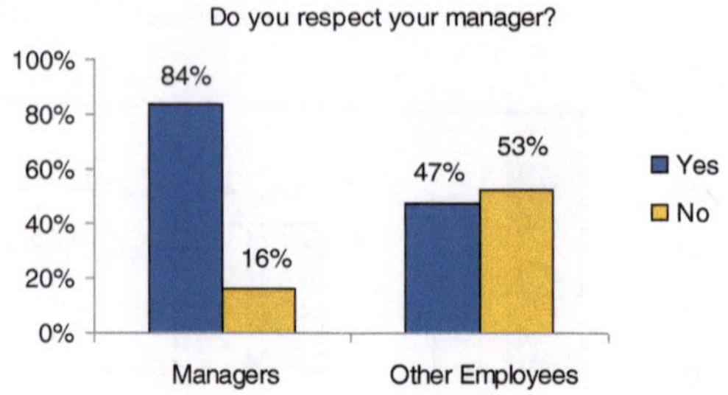

Fig. C1.7 Opinion on whether employees of both categories, managers and employees, respect their managers (to whom they report) by view of managers and nonmanagement employees

Conclusions

Analysis of the research results led to the conclusions that there was a significant perceptual gap between management and nonmanagement employees about the relationship between the management and other employees in the companies in the San Francisco Bay Area. Managers and nonmanagement employees differently view the situation that creates misunderstanding and lack of trust and synergy between these categories of employees. Such a situation is destructive and cannot help in building employee loyalty. Loyalty is not a one-sided coin and must be built from both sides.

Recommendations

This research made first steps in understanding and analyzing the problems of employee loyalty in the industry. More research is needed to identify specific reasons and causes of such disconnect and suggest the ways of resolving the problem.

Post-publication comments

The comments on this publications and references to it in other publications indicated that this problem is common for the industry around the world rather than being a specific of the companies in the San Francisco Bay Area.

C2. Time-Shift Asymmetric Correlation Analysis of Global Stock Markets

This case study is based on the research using descriptive statistics. The research was conducted at the Multidisciplinary Research Center of Lincoln University, Oakland, California. For more detailed information on this research, please refer to the following paper:

Aityan, Sergey K.; Ivanov-Schitz, Alexey K.; and Izotov, Sergey S. (2010). Time-shift asymmetric correlation analysis of global stock markets, *Journal of International Financial Markets, Institutions and Money*, vol. 20, issue 5, pp. 590–605

This research was dedicated to the analysis of the global stock market. The goal of the research was to find a reliable metrics for identifying the involvement of national stock markets in the global economy and their leadership positions as of their impact on other stock markets.

Correlation analysis is used for finding a degree of "synchronicity" of random variables. Returns on stock or stock market indices can be considered a random variable for the stock market analysis. Conventional correlation analysis is fundamentally unable to find out any cause-and-effect relationships between random variables. Also, the application of the conventional correlation analysis for studying international stock markets operating at different hours was criticized for a possible bias caused by one market on another due to different trading hours.

This research introduced a new method of the time-shift asymmetric correlation analysis for the analysis of the mutual impact of stock exchanges with different but nonoverlapping trading hours. This method allowed for the analysis of the degree of global integration between stock markets of different countries and their influence on each other. Next-day correlation (NDC) and same-day correlation (SDC) coefficients are introduced. Correlations between major US and Asia-Pacific stock market indices are analyzed. Most NDCs are statistically significant, while most SDCs are insignificant. NDCs grow over time, and the US stock market plays a pacemaking role for the Asia-Pacific region. The correlation coefficients can be used as a measure of the degree of globalization for the corresponding countries.

Research purpose

The purpose of this research was to develop a convenient and robust approach for measuring mutual influence of global stock markets. That influence could be used for measuring the degree of involvement of those markets in the globalization process.

Problem statement

The problem statement (research questions) was formulated as follows:

- How could correlation analysis be modified to measure influence of international stock markets?

The research question had three subquestions:

- How to solve the bias problem of the application of the conventional correlation analysis to random processes with time difference?
- How to measure cause-and-effect influence on random processes occurred at different times?

The scope and limitations of this research constrained the research to the analysis of mutual influence of the US and Asia-Pacific stock market indices in the first decade of the twenty-first century. The time period for this research was extended till 2015 in the book on *Stock Market Investment* (Sergey K. Aityan, 2016, Section 8.2.3 Time-Shift Correlation Analysis for International Markets, pp.179–182, *Stock Market Investment*, ISBN:978-1536817904).

Research design

The research design contained the following items:

- The research modifies the conventional correlation analysis in descriptive statistics.
- Data collected form the primary sources from the respective stock exchanges.

Development of the theory

The time-shift asymmetric correlation analysis, when applied to international markets, is based on the fact that different markets operate at different times and, therefore, one of them will operate with more recent information than another market. For example, on any trading day, US stock exchanges operate using the results of Japanese stock exchanges for the same *calendar* trading day. On the other hand, on the next trading day, Japanese stock exchanges operate with information available about the results of US stock exchanges from the previous calendar trading day as shown in ◘ Fig. C2.1.

To proceed with the time-shift correlation analysis, we need to introduce the following terms:

- Same-day correlation (SDC) is the correlation coefficient between two indices (or individual stock prices) at market close on the same calendar day.
- Next-day correlation (NDC) is the correlation coefficient between two indices (or individual stock prices) at market close on two adjacent trading days: for the first component on the earlier calendar trading day and, for the other one, on the following trading day.

The meaning of SDC and NDC as defined and described above is illustrated in ◘ Fig. C2.1.

According to the definition above, the trailing SDC and NDC for two stocks or indices *A* and *B* trading on two stock exchanges, which operate at different hours, can be calculated as follows:

$$\rho_{AB,t,n}^{SD} = \frac{\sigma_{AB,t,n}^{SD}}{\sigma_{A,t,n}^{SD}\sigma_{B,t,n}^{SD}} \quad \text{and} \quad \rho_{AB,t,n}^{ND} = \frac{\sigma_{AB,t,n}^{ND}}{\sigma_{A,t,n}^{SD}\sigma_{B,t,n}^{ND}} \tag{C.1}$$

where $\rho_{AB,t,n}^{SD}$ is the trailing SDC and $\rho_{AB,t,n}^{ND}$ is the trailing NDC. The same-day trailing standard deviations $\sigma_{A,\,t,\,n}$ and $\sigma_{B,\,t,\,n}$ are calculated as traditional trailing standard deviations, while the next-day standard deviation, $\sigma_{B,t,n}^{ND}$, is time-shifted 1 day ahead (for the next day) as

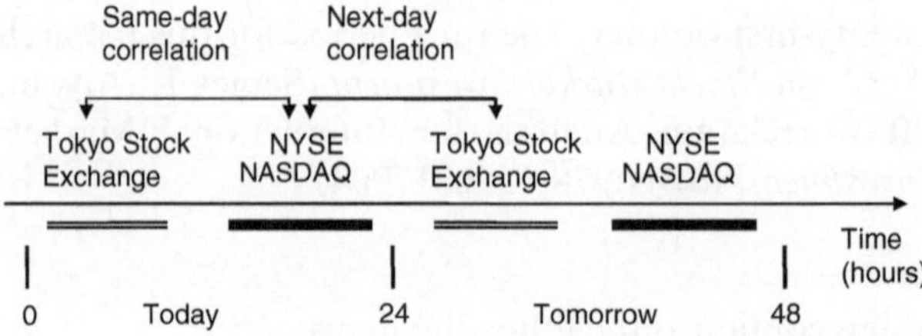

◘ **Fig. C2.1** SDC and NDC for Dow Jones Industrial Average (USA) and Nikkei 225 (Japan) indices

$$\sigma^{\text{SD}}_{A,t,n} = \sqrt{\frac{1}{n-1}\sum_{k=0}^{n-1}\left(\text{LR}_{A,t-k} - \overline{\text{LR}_{A,t,n}}\right)^2}$$

$$\sigma^{\text{SD}}_{B,t,n} = \sqrt{\frac{1}{n-1}\sum_{k=0}^{n-1}\left(\text{LR}_{B,t-k} - \overline{\text{LR}_{B,t,n}}\right)^2} \tag{C.2}$$

$$\sigma^{\text{ND}}_{B,t,n} = \sqrt{\frac{1}{n-1}\sum_{k=0}^{n-1}\left(\text{LR}_{B,t+1-k} - \overline{\text{LR}_{B,t+1,n}}\right)^2}$$

Thus,

$$\sigma^{\text{ND}}_{B,t,n} = \sigma^{\text{SD}}_{B,t+1,n} \tag{C.3}$$

The same-day covariance $\sigma^{\text{SD}}_{AB,t,n}$ is calculated as the conventional trailing variance as in Eq. C.2, while the next-day covariance $\sigma^{\text{ND}}_{AB,t,n}$ is calculated with the shift of $\left(\text{LR}_{B,t-k} - \overline{\text{LR}_{B,t-k}}\right)$ by 1 day ahead (for the next day), similarly to $\sigma^{\text{ND}}_{B,t,n}$ as

$$\sigma^{\text{SD}}_{AB,t,n} = \frac{1}{n-1}\sum_{k=0}^{n-1}\left(\text{LR}_{A,t-k} - \overline{\text{LR}_{A,t,n}}\right)\left(\text{LR}_{B,t-k} - \overline{\text{LR}_{B,t,n}}\right)$$

$$\sigma^{\text{ND}}_{AB,t,n} = \frac{1}{n-1}\sum_{k=0}^{n-1}\left(\text{LR}_{A,t-k} - \overline{\text{LR}_{A,t,n}}\right)\left(\text{LR}_{B,t+1-k} - \overline{\text{LR}_{B,t+1,n}}\right) \tag{C.4}$$

Then Eq. C.1 for the SDC, $\rho^{\text{SD}}_{AB,\,t,\,n}$, and NDC, $\rho^{\text{ND}}_{AB,\,t,\,n}$, can be rewritten as follows:

$$\rho^{\text{SD}}_{AB,\,t,\,n} = \frac{\sum_{k=0}^{n-1}\left(\text{LR}_{A,t-k} - \overline{\text{LR}_{A,t-k}}\right)\left(\text{LR}_{B,t-k,n} - \overline{\text{LR}_{B,t-k,n}}\right)}{\sqrt{\sum_{k=0}^{n-1}\left(\text{LR}_{A,t-k} - \overline{\text{LR}_{A,t-k,n}}\right)}\sqrt{\sum_{k=0}^{n-1}\left(\text{LR}_{B,t-k,n} - \overline{\text{LR}_{B,t-k,n}}\right)}}$$

$$\rho^{\text{ND}}_{AB,\,t,\,n} = \frac{\sum_{k=0}^{n-1}\left(\text{LR}_{A,t-k} - \overline{\text{LR}_{A,t-k,n}}\right)\left(\text{LR}_{B,t-k+1,n} - \overline{\text{LR}_{B,t-k+1,n}}\right)}{\sqrt{\sum_{k=0}^{n-1}\left(\text{LR}_{A,t-k} - \overline{\text{LR}_{A,t-k,n}}\right)}\sqrt{\sum_{k=0}^{n-1}\left(\text{LR}_{B,t-k+1,n} - \overline{\text{LR}_{B,t-k+1,n}}\right)}} \tag{C.5}$$

Please note that the terms related to asset B in Eqs. C.1–C.5 for $\sigma^{\text{ND}}_{B,\,t,\,n}$, $\sigma^{\text{ND}}_{AB,\,t,\,n}$, and $\rho^{\text{ND}}_{AB,\,t,\,n}$ are shifted by 1 day ahead.

Table C2.1 An example of a date matching algorithm for same-day and next-day correlations

Date	Daily rate of return on market A	Daily rate of return on market B	Pair for same-day correlation	Pair for next-day correlation
D_1	$LR_A(D_1)$	Market closed	–	$LR_A(D_1)*LR_B(D_5)$
D_2	Market closed	Market closed	–	–
D_3	Market closed	Market closed	–	–
D_5	$LR_A(D_5)$	$LR_B(D_5)$	$LR_A(D_5)*LR_B(D_5)$	$LR_A(D_5)*LR_B(D_6)$
D_6	$LR_A(D_6)$	$LR_B(D_6)$	$LR_A(D_6)*LR_B(D_6)$	–
D_7	$LR_A(D_7)$	Market Closed	–	–
D_8	$LR_A(D_8)$	Market Closed	–	$LR_A(D_8)*LR_B(D_9)$
D_9	$LR_A(D_9)$	$LR_B(D_9)$	$LR_A(D_9)*LR_B(D_9)$	$LR_A(D_9)*LR_B(D_{12})$
D_{10}	Market closed	Market closed	–	–
D_{11}	Market closed	Market closed	–	–
D_{12}	Market closed	$LR_B(D_{12})$	–	–
D_{13}	$LR_A(D_{13})$	$LR_B(D_{13})$	$LR_A(D_{13})*LR_B(D_{13})$	Subj. to future date

When the data points of return on assets A and B in Eq. C.5, for the time-shift asymmetric analysis, are shifted by 1 day, a problem with the date matching arises because the trading days and market holidays in different countries may be different. The date matching algorithm is illustrated in Table C2.1, where $LR_X(D_k)$ means the logarithmic return of asset X on date D_k.

Data collection and processing

The primary data on the major stock market indices was collected from the respective US and Asia-Pacific stock exchanges, and the time-shift correlation analysis was conducted according to the developed theory.

Results

The calculated 180-day trailing NDC $\left(\rho_{AB,\,t,\,n}^{ND}\right)$ and SDC $\left(\rho_{AB,\,t,\,n}^{SD}\right)$ for DJI-N225 and IXIC-N225 (DJI, Dow Jones Industrial Average (USA); IXIC, Nasdaq Composite (USA); and Nikkei 225 (Japan) Indices) are shown in Fig. C2.2 for the 2013–2015 time period.

It is evident from Fig. C2.2 that the NDC is greater than SDC for both pairs, DGI-N225 and IXIC-N225. Both NDCs are in the moderate to relatively high range, while both SDCs are in the low to negligibly low range. This fact clearly points out that the Japanese stock market mostly follows the US stock market, but the performance of the US stock market is mostly independent of the Japanese stock market.

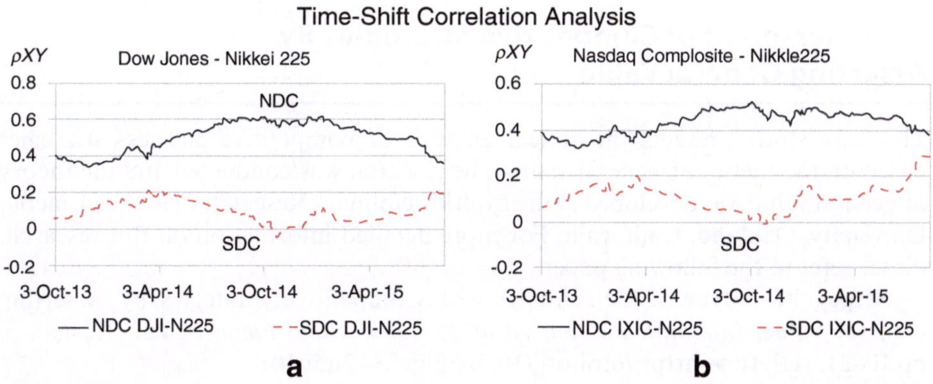

Fig. C2.2 NDC and SDC for **a** DJI-N225 and **b** IXIC-N225 (DJI, Dow Jones Industrial Average (USA); IXIC, Nasdaq Composite (USA); and Nikkei 225 (Japan) Indices)

Similar results were obtained for other Asia-Pacific versus major *US stock market indices. The US stock market indices were* Dow Jones Industrial Average (DJI) and Nasdaq Composite (IXIC). The Asia-Pacific stock market included:

- Japan – Nikkei (N225)
- South Korea – KOSPI Composite Index (KS11)
- Singapore – Straits Times Index (STI)
- Hong Kong (China) – Hang Seng Index (HSI)
- Taiwan – Taiwan Weighted Index (TWII)
- China – Shanghai Composite (SSEC)
- Malaysia – FTSE Bursa Malaysia KLCI (KLSE)
- Indonesia – Jakarta Composite Index (JKSE)

Conclusions

The time-shift correlation method provides a robust approach for a comparative analysis of global stock markets, particularly, for the stock exchanges with non-overlapping trading hours. This method turned the weakness of the conventional correlation analysis into strength by revealing the stock markets that set the pace and the markets that follow the trend.

The time-shift correlations can be used as a measure of the degree, to which different stock markets are integrated into global economy.

Recommendations

Due to the asymmetry indicated by the same-day and next-day correlations coefficients, it is recommended to use it in the international trading strategies.

Predictions

It is expected that the correlations between stock market will increase as the globalization process progresses in the world.

C3. Assessment of Competitive Strategies By Asserting General Value

This case study presents theoretical analysis of competitive business strategies based on the theory of general value. The research was conducted and the theory of general value was developed at the Multidisciplinary Research Center of Lincoln University, Oakland, California. For more detailed information on this research, please refer to the following paper:

Sergey K. Aityan (2020). Analysis of Competitive Strategies by Asserting General Value, *International Journal of Economics and Finance*, Vol. 12, No. 5, pp.10–21. (URL: ► https://doi.org/10.5539/ijef.v12n5p10)

Please also refer to the following publications for the foundations of the theory of general value:

Sergey K. Aityan, Alexey K Ivanov-Schitz, and Eugenia Logunova (2017). Measuring the Nonmonetary Component of General Value for Goods and Services, *International Journal of Economics and Financial Issues*, vol. 7, No. 3, pp. 69–81

Sergey K. Aityan, Alexey K Ivanov-Schitz, and Shakar Thapa (2016). Measuring the Nonmonetary Component of General Value of Jobs, *Advances in Social Sciences Research Journal*, Vol.3, No.12, pp.1–33. (DoI:► https://doi.org/10.14738/assrj.312.2414, URL: ► http://scholarpublishing.org/index.php/ASSRJ/article/view/2414/1516)

Sergey K. Aityan (2013). The Notion of General Value in Economics, *International Journal of Economics and Finance*, vol. 5, No. 5, pp. 1–14. (URL: ► http://www.ccsenet.org/journal/index.php/ijef/article/view/26698)

Companies use the approach of cost or differentiation advantage in the analysis of competitive strategies for goods or services. If a firm is the cost leader, then it pursues the cost leadership strategy, and if a company offers the best differentiation, then the firm uses the differentiation strategy. However, majority of companies are not cost or differentiation leaders and compete in the market with the mix of cost and differentiation advantages. How can such companies assess their competitive positioning? Can a firm pursue both cost and differentiation leadership? What will occur in the market in this case?

Competitive strategies are utilizing value proposed to the customers. However, considering value only as equivalent of money would not provide a full picture of value proposition. According to the theory of general value (Aityan, 2013), value is presented as a linear composition of the monetary and nonmonetary components of value, i.e.:

$$V = V^M + V^N \tag{C.6}$$

where V is general value and V^M and V^N are the monetary and nonmonetary components of value, respectively. The monetary component represents the respective amount of money or, more accurately, the perception of that amount of money, i.e., utility of money. The nonmonetary component of value represents the level of satisfaction not directly related to the money. The level of satisfaction as well as the utility of money strongly depends on the subjective perception of an individual or a group of people, which also reflects cultural aspects and specific circumstances.

Nonmonetary value represents the level of satisfaction that may include a variety of factors such as satisfaction of using the product, brand name, fashion, convenience, ease of use, social perception, lifestyle, habits, hobbies, acceptance by the group of people, and many other factors, which are not directly related to the cost or price. The methodology of measuring nonmonetary value is based on the indifference principle, when two products offer equal general values but different monetary and nonmonetary values. Then the difference in the nonmonetary values can be found by the difference of the respective monetary values (Aityan et al., 2026, 2017).

Research purpose

The purpose of this research was to develop a balanced approach for assessing the competitive strategies.

Problem statement

The problem statement (the research question) was formulated as follows:

- How to assess competitive advantage of a company from the perspective of general value?

The research question had three subquestions:

- How do consumers make their buying decision by asserting value of goods or services?
- How do competing companies assess general value of their goods or services?
- What is the major objective in competitive strategies?

Research design

The research design contained the following items:

- It is a theoretical research.
- The research is based on the theory of general value.

Results

The major principle formulated and adopted in this research stated that all decisions and actions should lead to the increase of the net present general values.

◘ Figure C3.1 shows two products, *A* and *B*, which offer the same general value, while their monetary and nonmonetary components are different. The higher price for product *B* is compensated by a higher nonmonetary value (satisfaction, differentiation, or need) of product *B* relative to product *A*, resulting in the equal general values for both products.

Two products, which offer the same general value for the consumer as shown in ◘ Fig. C3.1, are equally competitive in the market, if there are no additional constraints influencing the consumers' buying decisions such as price constraints or differentiation constraints (quality, specific features, etc.). For example, product *B* in ◘ Fig. C3.1 offers higher differentiation (nonmonetary value) than product *A*,

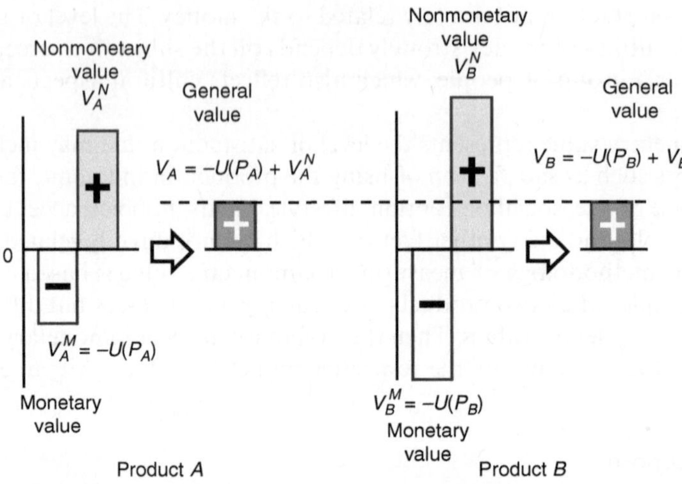

Fig. C3.1 An example of the equal general values of products *A* and *B* for a specific consumer

but on the other hand, product *B* is more expensive than product *A*. However, in result, both products offer the same general values. Thus, the consumer should be indifferent about buying either product unless the consumers have certain constraints in their buying decision-making.

An example of competition on the market of computer monitors

Currently outdated CRT computer monitors were the primary computer monitors on the market up to the end of the twentieth century. Later, they were replaced by the flat panel monitors. Let's use this case for the competitive analysis based on the assessment of general value as illustrated in Fig. C3.2.

It is obvious that flat panel monitors offer the higher nonmonetary value than CRT monitors due their convenience and, in the present time, quality of picture. The monetary value of goods for the consumers is represented by the perception of their price, maintenance, and, possibly, final utilization costs. For the sake of simplicity, let's use the price itself as the product monetary value as it was discussed above in this paper.

Up to the late 1990s, flat panel monitors were extremely expensive compared to the matching CRTs. For this reason, consumers were not interested in the flat panels, and the CRTs dominated the market. Flat panel monitors were not present in the consumer market at all because of their negative general value caused by the high price (Fig. C3.2a). In the late 1990s, production costs and, hence, the price for the flat panel monitors were reduced, and their general value turned positive, though it was still much lower than the general value of the CRTs (Fig. C3.2b). During this period, flat panel monitors appeared in the consumers' market but had quite low market share.

At the turn of the century, the production costs and, hence, prices for the flat panel monitors were significantly reduced to the degree that general values of flat

	CRT Monitors / Flat Panel Monitors	
Mid 1990s (a)	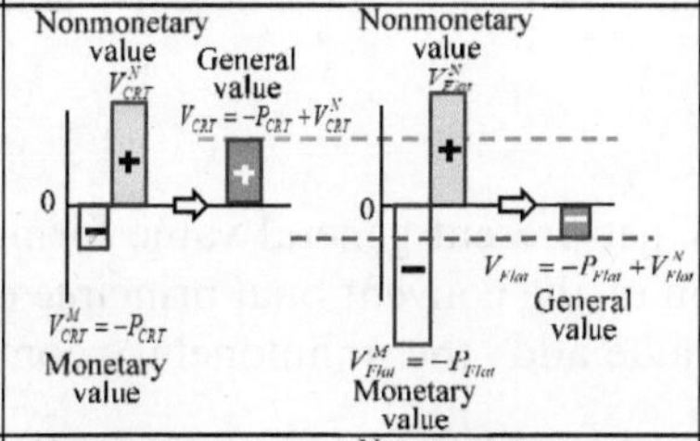	• General value of CRTs was positive • General value of Flat panel monitors was negative. • Flat panel monitors were not present in the consumer market.
Late 1990s (b)	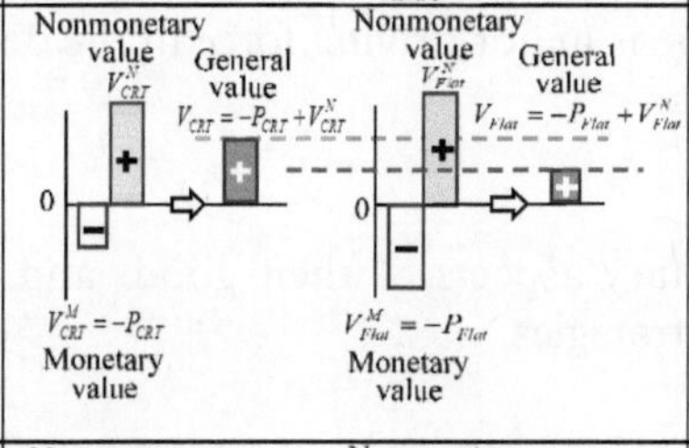	• General value of CRTs was positive • Cost of flat panel monitors and price reduced (monetary value) and quality improved (nonmonetary value) that made general value of flat monitors positive but stll lower, thanthe general value of CRT monitors. • Flat panelmonitors appeared in the consumer market but weak in their competition with the CRT monitors.
Early first decade of 2000s (c)	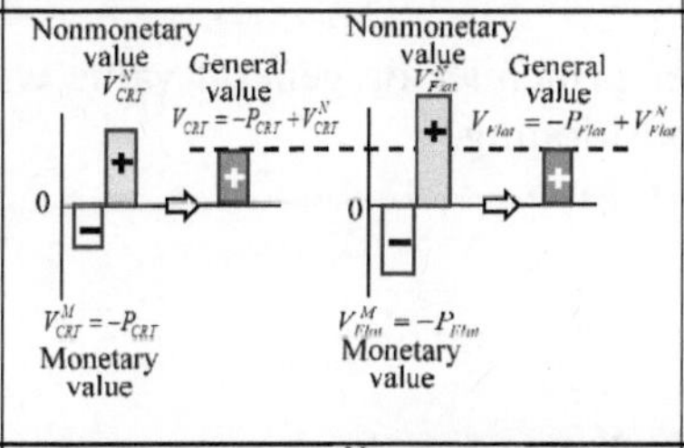	• General value of CRTs stayed positive though their nonmonetary value declined. • Cost of flat panel monitors and price reduced (monetary value), quality improved (nonmonetary value) that made general value of flat monitors positive and matching general value of CRT monitors. • Both, flat panel and the CRTs equally competed in the consumer market.
Late first decade of 2000s (d)	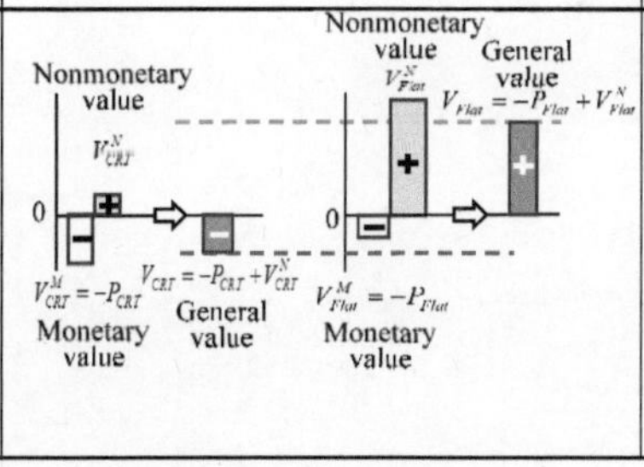	• Nonmonetary value of CRTs significantly dropped making their genral value negative. • Cost of flat panel monitors and price significantly dropped (monetary value) and quality improved (nonmonetary value) thatbroughtgeneral value of flat monitor much higherrelative to the CRTs. • CRTs lost inthe competition and washed out from the market.

Fig. C3.2 Competition between CRT and flat panel monitors from the perspective of general value

monitors and the CRTs equalized; thus, both types of monitors had almost the same general value (Fig. C3.2c). In result, both types of monitors were equally competitive in the market in the early 2000s. The progress in the flat panel monitor technology has led to a significant drop in the production cost and significant improvement in the quality of flat panel monitors. Thus, by the end of the first decade of the twenty-first century, the general value of flat panel monitors significantly increased, while general value of the CRTs had dropped as shown in Fig. C3.2d. As a result, CRT monitors had been washed out from the market.

The schematic analysis above has clearly and explicitly demonstrated a constructive approach applying the concept of general value in competitive analysis.

Among competing products, i.e., goods or services, the products with the higher general value succeed in the competition. Products with the negative general values are forced to leave the market.

Conclusions

The new principle of maximization of net present general value formulated and adopted in this research is the extension of the conventional principle of maximization of net present value. General value adds the nonmonetary component of satisfaction to decision-making criteria.

Thus, maximization of general value is major driving force in the development of competitive strategies.

Recommendations

Companies should consider nonmonetary aspects of their goods and services in the development of their competitive strategies.

Predictions

Competitive strategies developed under principles of general value will result in more robust and realistic competitive positioning.